APOLLOS OLD TESTAMENT
COMMENTARY

9

1 & 2 KINGS

TITLES IN THIS SERIES

APOLLOS OLD TESTAMENT
COMMENTARY

9

1 & 2 KINGS

Series Editors
David W. Baker and Gordon J. Wenham

LISSA M. WRAY BEAL

Apollos
Nottingham, England

InterVarsity Press
Downers Grove, Illinois 60515

InterVarsity Press, USA
P.O. Box 1400
Downers Grove, IL 60515-1426, USA
World Wide Web: www.ivpress.com
Email: email@ivpress.com

APOLLOS (an imprint of Inter-Varsity Press, England)
Norton Street
Nottingham NG7 3HR, England
Website: www.ivpbooks.com
Email: ivp@ivpbooks.com

InterVarsity Press®, USA, is the book-publishing division of InterVarsity Christian Fellowship/USA® www.intervarsity.org and a member movement of the International Fellowship of Evangelical Students.

Inter-Varsity Press, England, is closely linked with the Universities and Colleges Christian Fellowship, a student movement connecting Christian Unions throughout Great Britain, and a member movement of the International Fellowship of Evangelical Students. Website: www.uccf.org.uk

USA ISBN 978-0-8308-2509-7 (print)
USA ISBN 978-0-8308-9622-6 (digital)
UK ISBN 978-1-78359-031-5

Set in Sabon 10/12pt

Typeset in Great Britain by CRB Associates, Potterhanworth, Lincolnshire

Library of Congress Cataloging-in-Publication Data
A catalog record for this book is available from the Library of Congress.

British Library Cataloguing in Publication Data
A catalogue record for this book is available from the British Library.

P	20	19	18	17	16	15	14	13	12	11	10	9	8	7	6	5	4	3	2	1
Y	31	30	29	28	27	26	25	24	23	22	21	20	19	18	17	16	15	14			

CONTENTS

To my parents,
Douglas Kenmure Wray and
Virginia May Wray,
with love and gratitude.

For the LORD is good and his covenant love endures for ever;
His faithfulness continues from generation to generation.
(Ps. 100:5)

EDITORS' PREFACE

The Apollos Old Testament Commentary takes its name from the Alexandrian Jewish Christian who was able to impart his great learning fervently and powerfully through his teaching (Acts 18:24–25). He ably applied his understanding of past events to his contemporary society. This series seeks to do the same, keeping one foot firmly planted in the universe of the original text and the other in that of the target audience, which is preachers, teachers and students of the Bible. The series editors have selected scholars who are adept in both areas, exhibiting scholarly excellence along with practical insight for application.

Translators need to be at home with the linguistic practices and semantic nuances of both the original and target languages in order to be able to transfer the full impact of the one into the other. Commentators, however, serve as interpreters of the text rather than simply its translators. They also need to adopt a dual stance, though theirs needs to be even more solid and diversely anchored than that of translators. While they also must have the linguistic competence to produce their own excellent translations, they must moreover be fully conversant with the literary conventions, sociological and cultural practices, historical background and understanding, and theological perspectives of those who produced the text as well as those whom it concerned. On the other side, they must also understand their own times and culture, able to see where relevance for the original audience is transferable to that of current readers. For this to be accomplished, it is not only necessary to interpret the text, but one must also interpret the audience.

Traditionally, commentators have been content to highlight and expound the ancient text. More recently, the need for an anchor in the present day has also become more evident, and this series self-consciously adopts this approach, combining both the traditional and the modern. Each author analyses the original text through a new translation, textual notes, a discussion of the literary form, structure and background of the passage, as well as commenting on elements of its exegesis. A study of the passage's interpretational development in Scripture and the church concludes each section, serving to bring the passage home to the modern reader. What we intend, therefore, is to provide not only tools of excellence for the academy, but also tools of function for the pulpit.

David W. Baker
Gordon J. Wenham

AUTHOR'S PREFACE

In 1986 as I prepared to attend Northwest Bible College in Edmonton, Alberta, my parents gave me my first study Bible. It was big, and its weight signalled the serious task about to be undertaken. I still have that Bible, filled with notes and jottings, prayer requests and answers. I can flip to the back and find there a chart of the kings of Israel and Judah. My old notations make clear my discovery: more kings were failures than successes.

The fates of these leaders captured my imagination and I always suspected I'd be spending more time with them in study. It delightfully came in the form of a commentary project that has undergirded my ministry for several years.

I started this commentary project not quite knowing the journey ahead. But I knew intuitively that I would need companions on the way. As I prepare to send the manuscript to Inter-Varsity Press, I have fully experienced the truth of that intuition. So, although it seems a pitifully insufficient acknowledgment, I give my thanks to many. This commentary is my work, but your lives and prayers have lifted me up and held me to the task.

Thank you to the many prayer partners through these six years: Cheryl Shea, Stephanie Douglas Bowman, my family, my home group, and colleagues past and present. You never once said you were tired of hearing my excitement or woes as I worked through a text that variously felt impossible, challenged my heart, informed my classes or brought me to worship. May your faithfulness be repaid.

Thank you to Stan Hamm, my dean at Providence Theological Seminary who enabled my sabbatical year and helped me guard precious time for writing. Thanks must also go to my colleagues who during that year graciously excused my participation in preparing an Association of Theological Schools in the United States and Canada visitation report. My students at Providence Theological Seminary voiced their interest and encouragement, and their reflections on the insights I brought to class helped shaped my conclusions. Special thanks are given to Martha Loeppky, whose tireless efforts at tracking down inter-library loan materials saved countless hours and made my task immensely lighter.

Regarding the editing process, I wish to thank the series editors Dr David W. Baker and Dr Gordon J. Wenham. Their wise and judicious comments on the manuscript have immeasurably improved it. Grateful thanks are given to Mr Eldo Barkhuizen for his careful work during the copy-editing phase, and to Dr Philip Duce, Senior Commissioning Editor at Inter-Varsity Press, who shepherded the whole project with grace and skill.

Finally, for my husband Steven. You never doubted that God would reveal his word and prayed to that end. You asked the most difficult questions, got the humour of the narratives, and sustained me through all the seasons of writing. Your love was always there: sure, kind and strong. For these blessings I give thanks.

I dedicate this volume to my parents, Douglas Kenmure Wray and Virginia May Wray. They taught me the responsibilities and joys of worship. They were the first to believe his call for me, and their support through the years has never failed.

From him, and through him and to him are all things. May the King receive all glory!

Lissa M. Wray Beal

ABBREVIATIONS

TEXTUAL

Ed.	Editions of the Hebrew text according to Kennicott
LXX	Septuagint
LXX*	LXX Old Greek
LXX^{82}	LXX miniscule manuscript 82
LXX^{127}	LXX miniscule manuscript 127
LXX^A	LXX Codex Alexandrinus
LXX^{AL}	LXX Codex Alexandrinus and Lucianic Recension
LXX^B	LXX Codex Vaticanus
LXX^{-BA}	LXX excepting Codices Vaticanus and Alexandrinus
LXX^{BO}	LXX Codex Vaticanus and Origen's Hexaplaric Recension
LXX^{-BO}	LXX excepting Codex Vaticanus and Origen's Hexaplaric Recension
LXX^{-BO56}	LXX excepting Codex Vaticanus and Origen's Hexaplaric Recension 56
LXX^L	LXX Lucianic Recension
LXX^{-L}	LXX excepting Lucianic Recension
LXX^{min}	LXX in medieval miniscule manuscripts
LXX^O	LXX Origen's Hexaplaric Recension
MS(s)	Manuscript(s)
MT	Masoretic Text
Par	Paralipomenon (Greek Chronicles)
Syr	Syriac
Tg(s)	Targum(s)
Tg^f	Targum Jonathan
Vg	Vulgate
V^{MSS}	Vulgate Codex Manuscripts
Vrs	All or most of the Versions

HEBREW GRAMMAR

abs.	absolute
act.	active
adv.	adverb
appos.	apposition, appositional

art.	article
coh.	cohortative
com.	common
conj.	conjunction
cons.	consecutive
const.	construct
cop.	copulative
DDO	definite direct object marker
dittog.	dittography
f.	feminine
gen.	genitive
hiph.	hiphil
hith.	hithpael
imp.	imperative
impf.	imperfect
inf.	infinitive
interr.	interrogative
juss.	jussive
K	Kethibh (the written Hebrew text)
m.	masculine
Mp.	*Masora parva*
ni.	niphal
nom.	nominative
ptp.	participle
pass.	passive
pf.	perfect
pi.	piel
pl.	plural
pr.	pronominal, pronoun
prep.	preposition
pu.	pual
Q	Qere (the Hebrew text to be read out)
Q[Occ]	Qere of the western tradition
sg.	singular
subst.	substantive, substantivally
suff.	suffix

MISCELLANEOUS

ANE	Ancient Near East(ern)
Arab.	Arabic
Aram.	Aramaic
AV	Authorized (King James) Version
DH	Deuteronomistic History

ed(s).	editor(s)
Dtr	the Deuteronomist
esp.	especially
ET	English translation
ft	foot/feet
Hebr.	Hebrew
kg	kilogram(s)
l	litre(s)
lb	pound(s)
lit.	literally
m	metre(s)
NASB	New American Standard Bible
NET	New English Translation
NIV	New International Version
NJB	New Jerusalem Bible
NKJV	New King James Version
n.p.	no page given
NRSV	New Revised Standard Version
NT	New Testament
OT	Old Testament
RSV	Revised Standard Version
trans.	translation, translated by
v(v).	verse(s)

JOURNALS, REFERENCE WORKS, SERIES

AB	Anchor Bible
ABD	D. N. Freedman (ed.), *Anchor Bible Dictionary*, 6 vols., New York: Doubleday, 1992
ABR	*Australian Biblical Review*
AbrN	*Abr-Nahrain*
AJET	*African Journal of Evangelical Theology*
AJSLL	*American Journal of Semitic Languages and Literature*
ANEP	J. B. Pritchard (ed.), *The Ancient Near East in Pictures Relating to the Old Testament*, 2nd ed., with Supplement, Princeton: Princeton University Press, 1969
ANES	*Ancient Near Eastern Studies*
ANET	J. B. Pritchard (ed.), *Ancient Near Eastern Texts Relating to the Old Testament*, 3rd ed., with Supplement, Princeton: Princeton University Press, 1969
AOAT	Alter Orient und Altes Testament

ARAB	D. Luckenbill (ed.), *Ancient Records of Assyria and Babylonia*, 2 vols., Chicago: University of Chicago Press, 1926–7
ARI	A. Grayson (ed.), *Assyrian Royal Inscriptions*, 2 vols., Wiesbaden: Harrassowitz, 1972, 1976
AUSS	*Andrews University Seminary Studies*
BA	*The Biblical Archaeologist*
BAR	*Biblical Archaeology Review*
BASOR	*Bulletin of the American Schools of Oriental Research*
BBR	*Bulletin for Biblical Research*
BCOT	Baker Commentary on the Old Testament
BDB	F. Brown, S. R. Driver and C. A. Briggs (eds.), *The Brown-Driver-Briggs Hebrew and English Lexicon*, Peabody: Hendrickson, 1996; repr., Boston: Houghton, Mifflin, 1906
BHS	K. Elliger and W. Rudolph (eds.), *Biblia Hebraica Stuttgartensia*, 2nd ed., Stuttgart: Deutsche Bibelstiftung, 1977
BI	*Biblical Illustrator*
Bib	*Biblica*
BibInt	*Biblical Interpretation*
BJRL	*Bulletin of the John Rylands Library*
BKAT	Biblischer Kommentar, Altes Testament
BN	*Biblische Notizen*
BR	*Bible Review*
BSac	*Bibliotheca sacra*
BT	*The Bible Translator*
BTB	*Biblical Theology Bulletin*
BWANT	Beiträge zur Wissenschaft vom Alten und Neuen Testament
BZAW	Beihefte zur Zeitschrift für die alttestamentliche Wissenschaft
CBQ	*Catholic Biblical Quarterly*
CBQMS	Catholic Biblical Quarterly Monograph Series
ConBOT	Coniectanea biblica: Old Testament Series
DDD	K. van der Toorn, B. Becking and P. W. van der Horst (eds.), *Dictionary of Deities and Demons in the Bible*, 2nd ed., Leiden: Brill; Grand Rapids: Eerdmans, 1999
Did	*Didaskalia*
DOTP	T. D. Alexander and D. W. Baker (eds.), *Dictionary of the Old Testament: Pentateuch*, Downers Grove: InterVarsity Press
EA	J. A. Knudtzon (ed.), *Die El-Amarna-Tafeln mit Einleitung und Erläuterungen*, Aalen: Ott Zeller, 1964
EI	*Eretz Israel*

ExAud	*Ex Auditu*
ExpTim	*Expository Times*
FOTL	Forms of the Old Testament Literature
GKC	E. Kautzsch (ed.), *Gesenius' Hebrew Grammar*, rev. and trans. A. E. Cowley, Oxford: Clarendon, 1910
HALOT	L. Koehler and W. Baumgartner (eds.), *Hebrew and Aramaic Lexicon of the Old Testament*, 5 vols., Leiden: Brill, 1994–2000
HOTTP	D. Barthélemy (ed.), *Preliminary and Interim Report on the Hebrew Old Testament Text Project*, vol. 1, New York: United Bible Societies, 1979
HS	*Hebrew Studies*
HTR	*Harvard Theological Review*
HUCA	*Hebrew Union College Annual*
IBD	J. D. Douglas et al. (eds.), *Illustrated Bible Dictionary*, 3 vols., Leicester: Inter-Varsity Press, 1980
IDB	G. A. Buttrick et al. (eds.), *Interpreter's Dictionary of the Bible*, 4 vols., Nashville: Abingdon, 1962
IDBSup	C. Krim (ed.), *Interpreter's Dictionary of the Bible: Supplementary Volume*, Nashville: Abingdon, 1976
IEJ	*Israel Exploration Journal*
Int	*Interpretation*
JANES	*Journal of the Ancient Near Eastern Society*
JAOS	*Journal of the American Oriental Society*
JBL	*Journal of Biblical Literature*
JBQ	*Jewish Biblical Quarterly*
JCS	*Journal of Cuneiform Studies*
JESOT	*Journal for the Evangelical Study of the Old Testament*
JETS	*Journal of the Evangelical Theological Society*
JFSR	*Journal of Feminist Studies in Religion*
JHS	*Journal of Hebrew Scriptures*
JITC	*Journal of the Interdenominational Theological Center*
JM	P. Joüon, T. Muraoka, *A Grammar of Biblical Hebrew*, Rome: Editrice Pontificio Istituto Biblico, 2005
JNES	*Journal of Near Eastern Studies*
JNSL	*Journal of Northwest Semitic Languages*
JQR	*Jewish Quarterly Review*
JSOT	*Journal for the Study of the Old Testament*
JSOTSup	Journal for the Study of the Old Testament, Supplement Series
JSS	*Journal of Semitic Studies*
JTS	*Journal of Theological Studies*
JTSA	*Journal of Theology for Southern Africa*

KAI	*Kanaanäische und aramäische Inschriften*
KTU	M. Dietrich, O. Loretz and J. Sanmartin (eds.), *Die Keilalphabetischen Texte aus Ugarit*, AOAT 24.1, Neukirchen-Vluyn: Neukirchener Verlag, 1976
LHBOTS	Library of Hebrew Bible / Old Testament Studies
LJRC	*Listening: Journal of Religion and Culture*
NAC	New American Commentary
NCBC	New Century Bible Commentary
NEAEHL	E. Stern (ed.), *The New Encyclopedia of Archaeological Excavations in the Holy Land*, 4 vols., Jerusalem: Carta, 1993
NEAEHLSup	*Supplementary Volume* of *NEAEHL*, ed. E. Stern, Jerusalem: Carta, 2008
NIB	L. E. Keck (ed.), *The New Interpreter's Bible*, 12 vols., Nashville: Abingdon, 1993–2002
NIBCOT	New International Biblical Commentary on the Old Testament
NICOT	New International Commentary on the Old Testament
NIDB	K. Doob Sakenfeld (ed.), *The New Interpreter's Dictionary of the Bible*, 5 vols. Nashville: Abingdon
NIDOTTE	W. A. VanGemeren (ed.), *New International Dictionary of Old Testament Theology and Exegesis*, Carlisle: Paternoster; Grand Rapids: Zondervan, 1996
NIVAC	New International Version Application Commentary
NRTh	*La nouvelle revue théologique*
OBO	Orbis biblicus et orientalis
OTL	Old Testament Library
OtSt	*Oudtestamentische Studiën*
PEQ	*Palestine Exploration Quarterly*
Presb	*Presbyterion*
PRSt	*Perspectives in Religious Studies*
QR	*Quarterly Review*
RB	*Revue biblique*
RefR	*Reformed Review*
ResQ	*Restoration Quarterly*
RevExp	*Review and Expositor*
SBL	Society of Biblical Literature
SBT	Studies in Biblical Theology
SJOT	*Scandinavian Journal of the Old Testament*
SLJT	*Saint Luke's Journal of Theology*
SR	*Studies in Religion*
ST	*Studia theologica*
STRev	*Sewanee Theological Review*
SwJT	*Southwestern Journal of Theology*

TDNT	G. Kittel and G. Friedrich (eds.), *Theological Dictionary of the New Testament*, trans. G. W. Bromiley, 10 vols., Grand Rapids: Eerdmans, 1964–76
TDOT	G. J. Botterweck, H. Ringgren and H.-J. Fabry (eds.), *Theological Dictionary of the Old Testament*, 15 vols., Grand Rapids: Eerdmans, 1974–2006
TGUOS	*Transactions of the Glasgow University Oriental Society*
ThTo	*Theology Today*
TMSJ	*The Master's Seminary Journal*
TWOT	R. L. Harris and G. L. Archer, Jr., and B. K. Waltke (eds.), *Theological Wordbook of the Old Testament*, Chicago: Moody, 1980
TynB	*Tyndale Bulletin*
UF	*Ugarit-Forschungen*
VoxEv	*Vox Evangelica*
VT	*Vetus Testamentum*
VTSup	Supplements to Vetus Testamentum
WBC	Word Biblical Commentary
WO'C	Bruce K. Waltke, M. O'Connor, *An Introduction to Biblical Hebrew*, Winona Lake: Eisenbrauns, 1990
WTJ	*Westminster Theological Journal*
ZAW	*Zeitschrift für die alttestamentliche Wissenschaft*

INTRODUCTION

1. THE STORY OF 1 – 2 KINGS

As the name implies, the corpus of 1 – 2 Kings covers the era of Israel's monarchic rulers. Beginning with the transition of power from David to his son Solomon, the narrative pursues its course until the exile of both the northern and southern kingdoms, and the effective end of the monarchy in Israel.

Taking up the preceding promise to David of an ongoing dynasty (2 Sam. 7), 1 – 2 Kings begins with a lengthy narrative of Solomon and the establishment of the dynasty in his time. Dynastic establishment is effected by David's fiat of succession and the concomitant anointing and acclamation of the successor. The attainment of peace and prosperity in Solomon's reign (1 Kgs 4 – 5) enables Solomon to build the temple (1 Kgs 6 – 8). The temple is not only a place for worship of YHWH according to Deuteronomistic norms, but also stands as a testament to the consolidation of Solomon's rule and YHWH's approval of the dynasty. Sadly, despite the several warnings given Solomon to walk in YHWH's laws, statutes and commandments, Solomon's reign at several points reveals his failure to do so and the outcome is the establishment of foreign worship in Jerusalem and its environs (1 Kgs 11).

The promise granted David is not without the possibility of chastisement should his descendants disregard YHWH's torah (2 Sam. 7:14). Solomon's reign concludes with adversaries threatening Israel's peace, and a new promise that much of the kingdom will be torn from the Davidic line. The establishment of Jeroboam's rule over the northern tribes in the time of Solomon's son sets in motion the trajectory for the remainder of the corpus as kings of north and south rise and fall.

From 1 Kgs 12 to 2 Kgs 17 the narrative alternates between the northern and southern kingdoms, with vignettes and more extended narratives exploring selected events from the lives of the monarchs. The rule of each monarch is measured by particular criteria, foremost of which is their obedience to the deuteronomic law regarding worship practices. In the south the presence of the temple as the dwelling place of YHWH ensures some measure of cultic faithfulness, although not all cultic practices fall under the aegis of the Deuteronomistic norm. In the north kings are uniformly disobedient, and in 2 Kgs 17 the northern kingdom falls to the advancing Assyrian Empire. The chapter details the theological reasons for the fall and exile of the northern kingdom: primary are the cultic disobedience of both king and people.

The remaining chapters of 2 Kings turn to the fate of the southern kingdom. Despite the warning example of the northern kingdom's demise and the reforming efforts of Hezekiah (2 Kgs 18) and Josiah (2 Kgs 22 – 23), Judah's cultic life continues to deteriorate. This decline reaches its nadir in the apostasy of Manasseh, who, as a southern Ahab, walks in the ways of the nations. For his apostasy, final judgment is pronounced upon Judah. Despite the reforming efforts of Manasseh's grandson Josiah, final judgment falls upon Judah at the hands of the Babylonian Empire; they are carried into exile, their king is deposed and imprisoned in the Babylonian court, and their temple and city are destroyed as YHWH's wrath is outpoured.

Yet the final verses of 2 Kings leave the future open: the promises granted David, and more – the covenant commitment of YHWH to his people is yet operative. Though disobedient to the point of the ultimate chastisement of exile, God's people may yet again experience his covenant grace.

The corpus of Kings attends to monarchic rulers and the effects of their rule upon the nation. It attends to issues of the nation and those in power. Yet the book is not a cold accounting of events without the colouration of individual lives. Many kings are developed characters whose personal lives as much as their executive powers shape the theology that clearly underlies the books. Kings marry, sicken, pray, build residences and give gifts, and the selective recounting of such events enlivens the kings as much as speaks to theological emphases.

Other individuals rise to prominence as the history unfolds. Prophets play a prominent role: Elijah and Elisha, for instance, are key figures from 1 Kgs 17 to 2 Kgs 13. Royal family members and nobility (such as Bathsheba [1 Kgs 1 – 2] and Naboth [1 Kgs 21]) precipitate great events. Palace functionaries (such as Obadiah [1 Kgs 18]) represent kings, and otherwise unknown and ordinary folk (such as the besieged women [2 Kgs 6:26–30] or Hiel of Bethel [1 Kgs 16:34]) provide crucial plot turns or commentary within the ongoing story.

But it is the kings around whom the story revolves. These figures are, however, indicators of two other important characters in 1 – 2 Kings. The first character is YHWH. Kings serve at YHWH's behest and the monarchy is his allowance given his people when they rejected his own kingship (1 Sam. 8 – 12; Deut. 17:14–20). The monarchy is given in the hope of wise and godly leadership and the kings are intended as pointers to the one they represent as co-regent.

The kings also point to a second character: the covenant people of God. For good or ill, the people follow the king as they followed pre-monarchic leaders. With the leadership of Moses and Joshua, YHWH's people escaped servitude and in hope entered the Promised Land. Both Moses and Joshua led the people in covenant making and renewal before YHWH (Exod. 19 – 24; Deut. 29; Josh. 24). Under the judges Israel was repeatedly called to repentance and covenant faithfulness. Kings were to lead the people to follow YHWH, to worship him truly and enjoy the life of promise. The tragedy is that the life of promise too quickly degenerated to servitudes: syncretized and aberrant worship, corvée labour for monumental building projects, and the ongoing encroachment of foreign armies with the ultimate loss of national life and servitude in Babylon – a new Egypt.

1 – 2 Kings tells this tragedy, but because it tells the story of YHWH's involvement with his people, it is never a story without hope and the possibility of new life.

2. 1 – 2 KINGS IN THE CANON

Although the present formation of Kings divides the narrative into two books, that division is artificial and practical. Originally reproduced on ancient scrolls, the narrative's length could not easily be accommodated on even the longest scroll. The present division of 1 – 2 Kings provides for two blocks of fairly equal length, each reproducible on a single scroll. The connection between the two books is apparent as, in its present form, the reign of Ahaziah begins in 1 Kgs 22 but ends in 2 Kgs 1.

It is helpful to examine the different places in which the books appear in both the Hebrew and the English canons of Scripture. Early witnesses to the Hebrew canon (for instance, Josephus [*Against Apion* 1.37–43], the Prologue to Sirach, and even the NT [Luke 24:44]) reveal its division into three main sections: the writings of Moses (the Pentateuch), the Prophets (including the Former and Latter Prophets) and the Writings. Kings is placed in the Former Prophets, with Joshua,

Judges and Samuel; the Latter Prophets include Isaiah, Jeremiah, Ezekiel and the Twelve.

The English canon (the one reflected in most English translations today) was shaped in response to the concerns and understandings of the early church. No longer placed in a discrete section of Former Prophets, Kings is now in a large section known as the Historical Books that includes books from Joshua to Nehemiah.

Before discussing the import of the placement of Kings in the English Bible, a discussion of its placement in the Former Prophets illuminates many of the themes and theological concerns of Kings. This discussion is especially important as often the prophetic outlook of Kings is overlooked. Given modern discourse concerning historical chronology and verifiability, the classification of Kings as one of the Historical Books can foreground those questions, overshadowing the important consideration of Kings's prophetic character. This brief discussion serves as an introduction only; many of the items surfaced here are examined in greater detail later in this introduction.

2.1. The prophetic character of 1 – 2 Kings

One obvious indication of the prophetic outlook of Kings is the many prophets in its chapters. These prophets include major characters whose words and action strongly shape the narratives (Nathan, Elijah, Elisha, Micaiah, Huldah), as well as those mentioned in passing (Jehu [1 Kgs 16:1]; Jonah [2 Kgs 14:25]), and even prophets who remain unnamed (1 Kgs 20:13, 22, 35; 2 Kgs 9:1; 17:13). Wherever prophets appear, they are not simply incidental characters but forward the narrative and its themes. By their actions, confrontations with power and prophecies, they communicate YHWH's will for king and people.

The prophetic character of Kings is also apparent in the emphasis on the fulfilment of the prophetic word. The prophets as YHWH's covenant mediators speak his word, and that word is fulfilled with an inevitability that speaks to its power. Gerhard von Rad (1953: 74–92) provides the classic exploration of this phenomenon. He rightly argues that the fulfilment of the prophetic word is repeatedly noted in Kings (1953: 74–92; see 7.3 below). The fulfilment of this word is a primary theological theme undergirding the corpus.

Finally, the placement of Kings within the Former Prophets reveals a conviction that the events recorded therein are interpreted from the divine perspective. Not simply a neutral listing of historical occurrences, the presentation is shaped to reveal YHWH's activity and his purposes in the life of his covenant people. Within that prophetic record the prophets serve as reliable guides to understand this divine perspective.

2.2. The historical character of 1 – 2 Kings

In the English canon Kings is included in the section of Historical Books. This placement indicates the early church understood the book plays a unique role in the historical unfolding of YHWH's plan. For the church that plan culminates in Jesus the Messiah. This recognition does not preclude the prophetic character of the book but reflects an additional appropriation of its message.

The canonical placement in the Historical Books reveals the conviction that the book has a historiographic intent. The exploration of the meaning and implications of this intent is addressed later in this introduction (5.2). This is an important discussion in a modern age concerned with questions of history and chronology, but these modern questions must not displace a more lasting theological pursuit, which is the focus of the present discussion.

The placement of Kings within the Historical Books reveals a theological understanding that reaches deeper than concerns about historical verifiability. The church understood it was part of, because a continuance of, the long history of YHWH's unfolding will that culminates in the person of Jesus Christ. Not only is what YHWH did in the nation of Israel pertinent to that nation in its own time, not only is what YHWH did in the nation of Israel pertinent to that nation's own reflection upon its history, but YHWH's action in Israel's history is a historical preparation for Jesus the Christ. Likewise, the church that arose out of his life was grafted in to that same history (Rom. 11:17).

The English canon, then, makes plain that Jesus Christ and his church cannot be wholly understood on the basis of the NT alone. His character, words, actions, and especially his death and resurrection, take up the covenants traced through Israel's history and expressed in Kings. And in the study of Kings can be found words, actions and types that illuminate Jesus' life, and the necessities that called forth that life.

2.3. 1 – 2 Kings in relation to the larger canon of Scripture

1 – 2 Kings is indelibly connected to the larger canon of Scripture. It draws upon, and informs other books within the canon and, although the nature of the dependence or influence is not always without dispute (e.g. the relationship of Kings to Jeremiah or Isaiah), the book is clearly part of a larger whole, connected by overarching plot, language and themes.

The connection to the Pentateuch has already been alluded to. Kings is aware of the promises made to Abraham and posits the Abrahamic Covenant as instrumental to the relationship between YHWH and Israel. It is to the Abrahamic Covenant that YHWH's persistent commitment to Israel is credited (1 Kgs 18:36; 2 Kgs 13:23). To the role of the priests and the sacrificial system recorded in Exodus and Leviticus Kings pays little attention. However, Kings is not without cultic concern. That concern is reflected in the centrality of the temple to the life of the nation. Deuteronomy provides the call to worship YHWH at the place he will choose as a dwelling for his name (Deut. 12:5; 16:5–6). This call finds its fulfilment in the Jerusalem temple (1 Kgs 8:13–20), where the ark is housed. Worship in that temple is prescribed according to the norms of Deuteronomy, and Israel and their king are repeatedly called to live by the statutes and laws of Deuteronomy. The temple is a symbol of YHWH's favour upon king and nation, but even more a symbol of YHWH's living presence in the midst of his people and their ability to call upon him in prayer (1 Kgs 8).

The importance of Deuteronomy to Kings is part of a larger phenomenon. Deuteronomy can be viewed as an introduction to the large block of literature (Joshua–Kings) that records Israel's entry into, life in and exile from the land. The influence of Deuteronomy upon Joshua–Kings has long been recognized and raises questions regarding the authorial relationship of Deuteronomy to these books (see further at 'Critical issues of authorship and date', below).

The canonical relationship of the books extending from Deuteronomy to Kings is one of narrative arc: Deuteronomy prepares Israel by providing the torah for successful life in the land. Joshua narrates the entry into the land and, what is left uncompleted in Joshua is taken up in Judges 1. The remainder of Judges speaks of the ongoing failure of Israel to live according to the deuteronomic code and YHWH's chastisement of a wayward people. It is the two books of Samuel that move the nation from the charismatic leadership of judges to dynastic monarchy, narrating the lives of the first two kings, Saul and David. David's life ends and the succession passes to Solomon in 1 Kgs 1 – 2. Kings takes Israel and Judah through five hundred years that end in exile, fulfilling the curses outlined in Deuteronomy.

Kings also has a particular canonical connection to the chronicler's history. The chronicler retells what is contained in Kings, addressing the theological concerns of the post-exilic era. Much of the chronicler's work is a verbatim account of material from Kings, and specific citations (2 Chr. 16:11; 20:34; 25:26) suggest the chronicler often used Kings as source material (Williamson 1982: 17–23).

The prophetic nature of Kings connects it with the prophetic corpus of the so-called Writing Prophets. These prophets, like the prophets within Kings, similarly stand as covenant mediators between YHWH and the people. Thus, for instance, Jeremiah can be cited as calling Israel back to covenant life. Within the prophetic corpus Jeremiah also has a more specific connection to Kings. He prophesied in Jerusalem during the final years of the southern kingdom and his work addresses many of the same historical events with substantial verbatim repetition (for instance, the fall of Jerusalem [Jer. 39]; the governorship of Gedaliah [Jer. 40 – 41]).

Finally, a consideration of canonical connections must move to the canon of the Christian tradition. Beyond viewing the NT story as a continuance of the history unfolded in Kings (as above), there are more specific connections, the most pertinent being the presentation of Christ as the king of Israel. He is born of the Davidic line (Matt. 1:1–17; Luke 1:69; Rom. 1:3) and at his birth is sought as Israel's king, the anointed one (Matt. 2:2; Luke 2:11). His trial and crucifixion are as Israel's king (Matt. 27:29, 37, 42; Mark 15:2, 26; Luke 22:67; 23:3, 38) and his commission to his followers is with sovereign authority (Matt. 28:18–20). There is no doubt that in the NT, YHWH the king of Israel (Exod. 15:18; 19:6; 1 Sam. 8:7; 12:12; Pss 93:1; 95:3; 96:10) is embodied in Jesus of the line of David. That which every king in 1 – 2 Kings does with greater or lesser degrees of failure, Jesus the Christ does with perfect success.

3. DISTINCTIVE FEATURES OF 1 – 2 KINGS

Several elements of structure and content distinctively mark 1 – 2 Kings. An overview of some major distinctions prepares a reader to enter the book.

3.1. Continuity with 1 – 2 Samuel

The first distinctive is immediately apparent, for the story continues without preamble the narrative of 1–2 Samuel. Knowledge of 1 – 2 Samuel is necessary to contextualize the story. The story's continuity is apparent in the Greek versions (LXX) where the four books are called 1 – 4 Kingdoms, or Reigns. Further, not all Greek texts divided Samuel from Kings at the same point; the Lucianic edition of the LXX continues 1 – 2 Reigns through to 1 Kgs 2:11 (a division similarly made in Josephus' *Antiquities*).

In 1 Kgs 1 – 2 there is a strong sense of engaging a story already in motion. Many of the characters (such as Bathsheba, Nathan, Zadok, Joab, Abiathar and Solomon) enter the narrative as if the audience already knows their history. Even the reasons for the factional alliances with Adonijah and Solomon find possible explanations in Samuel. Further, King David – presented as a frail and impotent man – is only a reminder of who he *was* in Samuel: a strong, virile king. And Adonijah's accoutrements of royalty – chariots, horsemen, runner – echo the similar actions of Absalom (2 Sam. 15:1) and raise the narrative question 'Will Adonijah succeed where Absalom failed?'

Because of the continuity with 1 – 2 Samuel, 1 Kgs 1 – 2 easily transitions the account to trace the line of David in Solomon. Once the succession is decided in Solomon's favour and the dynasty promised David in 2 Sam. 7 is set in motion, it is the second promise of 2 Sam. 7 that must be answered:

Is Solomon the son who will build the house for YHWH? Thus the opening chapters again broach issues raised in 1 – 2 Samuel and anticipate the answer as Kings unfolds.

3.2. Northern and southern kingdoms as the people of YHWH

A second distinctive is an alternating reportage of northern and southern monarchs that begins with the reign of Jeroboam and continues until the fall of the northern kingdom. The whole of Kings can be structured as follows:

Southern kingdom		Northern kingdom	
	1 Kgs 1:1 – 11:43 Solomon		
	1 Kgs 12:1–19 United kingdom lost		
		1 Kgs 12:20 – 14:20	Jeroboam I
1 Kgs 14:21–31	Rehoboam		
1 Kgs 15:1–8	Abijam		
1 Kgs 15:9–24	Asa		
		1 Kgs 15:25–31	Nadab
		1 Kgs 15:33 – 16:7	Baasha
		1 Kgs 16:8–14	Elah
		1 Kgs 16:15–20	Zimri
		1 Kgs 16:21–28	Omri
		1 Kgs 16:29 – 22:40	Ahab
1 Kgs 22:41–50	Jehoshaphat		
		1 Kgs 22:51 – 2 Kgs 1:18	Ahaziah
		(2 Kgs 2 Interlude: succession of Elisha)	
		2 Kgs 3:1 – 9:26	Jehoram
2 Kgs 8:16–24	Jehoram		
		2 Kgs 9:1 – 10:35	Jehu
2 Kgs 8:25 – 9:29	Ahaziah		
(2 Kgs 11:1–16 False reign of Athaliah)			
2 Kgs 11:1 – 12:21	Joash		
		2 Kgs 13:1–9	Jehoahaz
		2 Kgs 13:10–13	Jehoash
		(2 Kgs 13:14–25 Interlude: death of Elisha)	
2 Kgs 14:1–22	Amaziah		
		2 Kgs 14:23–29	Jeroboam II
		2 Kgs 15:1–7	Azariah
		2 Kgs 15:8–12	Zechariah
		2 Kgs 15:13–16	Shallum

Southern kingdom		Northern kingdom	
		2 Kgs 15:17–22	Menahem
		2 Kgs 15:23–26	Pekahiah
		2 Kgs 15:27–31	Pekah
2 Kgs 15:32–38	Jotham		
2 Kgs 16:1–20	Ahaz		
		2 Kgs 17:1–6	Hoshea
		(2 Kgs 17:7–37 Peroration on the northern kingdom)	
2 Kgs 18:1 – 20:21	Hezekiah		
2 Kgs 21:1–18	Manasseh		
2 Kgs 21:19–26	Amon		
2 Kgs 22:1 – 23:30	Josiah		
2 Kgs 23:31–35	Jehoahaz		
2 Kgs 23:36 – 24:7	Jehoiakim		
2 Kgs 23:8 – 25:29	Jehoiachin		
2 Kgs 24:18 – 25:7	Zedekiah (elevated during Jehoiachin's exile)		

Although the coverage alternates between northern and southern kingdoms, the alternation is not evenly spaced. For example, kings from Nadab to Jehu are all northern, with only a brief intrusion by two southern kings; a similar block of northern kings moves from Zechariah to Pekah. The alternation makes an attempt at synchronicity; thus, for example, Rehoboam, Abijam and Asa all rule during Jeroboam's reign; Nadab through to Ahab all rule during Asa's lengthy forty-one year reign; Jehoshaphat ascends the throne during Ahab's rule; southern Jehoram during northern Jehoram's, and so on. The final run of southern monarchs occurs because the northern kingdom ended with Hoshea.

There are also places in the history where a king comes to power before the reign of the previous monarch ends. For instance, Solomon comes to power while David still rules; Jehu usurps power from the ruling Jehoram; Zedekiah is appointed in place of the deposed and exiled Jehoiachin. In these cases the movement from one monarch to another is not tied to the death of the preceding monarch. In addition, although the above schema does not indicate such, there are several places where the accumulated years of the king's reign exceeds the limits of time between fixed historical points (see further below under 'The problem of chronology'). In these instances periods of co-regency are posited as a solution. In these co-regencies the transition from one monarch to another is less than clear.

The alternating reportage works at a purpose greater than attempting to synchronize the kingdoms. It communicates that though a divided kingdom, and though the northern kingdom immediately takes the path of apostasy, both Israel and Judah together are YHWH's people; both are covenanted to him under Abraham and Sinai.

Finally, the narrative is selective in the material presented for each king. In some cases a notation of only a few verses is provided (e.g. for the kings from Zechariah to Pekah). That much more could be said of these kings is brought out by the consistent refrain of the 'other deeds' a king accomplishes (e.g. 2 Kgs 15:11, 15, 21, 26, 31). Nor does the length of a king's reign comport with the amount of reportage: Asa's forty-one-year reign has fifteen verses while Solomon's forty-year reign has eleven chapters; Azariah's fifty-two-year reign has only seven verses while Manasseh's fifty-five-year reign has eighteen verses. This attests not only to the selective nature of the accounting but suggests a reason for such selectivity: the events of some reigns are simply more important to the book's message and receive more extensive coverage.

3.3. Regnal summaries as structuring device

A third distinctive within Kings is the regnal summaries that open and close each monarch's reign, almost without exception. This envelope device opens a reign with a summative introduction, then pertinent events are reported, and then the closing summary concludes a reign. Reportage on each king always has the companion kingdom in view as the opening summary notes that 'X [southern king] began to reign in the nth year of Y [northern king]'. In this way the relationship to one another of YHWH's people in northern and southern kingdoms is maintained. Other pertinent information, such as length and place of reign, as well as an evaluation of the king's reign, is also included in introductory summaries of northern and southern kings. Each closing summary includes a reference to source material(s), other events of the king's reign, a named successor, and (often) a notice of death and burial (see 'Form and structure', 1 Kgs 14).

A few monarchs have one or both of the summaries missing. Solomon and Jeroboam have no opening summary, as each monarch ascends the throne in the midst of unusual events in the previous monarch's rule. Jehu, who usurps the throne in Jehoram's reign (2 Kgs 9 – 10), also has no opening regnal summary. Yet, as each establishes his rule over the respective kingdom, a closing summary appears as a sign of monarchic legitimacy. Several monarchs have no closing regnal summary. Ahaziah of Judah and Jehoram of Israel both die in the progress of Jehu's coup and, although a brief notation of Ahaziah's accession appears to mark his death (2 Kgs 9:29), the onrushing nature of the coup allows no pause for closing summaries. Hoshea, the last king of the north, is imprisoned by Assyria. Once removed from the land the story passes over him and no closing summary is provided. Similarly, Jehoahaz ends his life in Egypt (2 Kgs 23:24), and Jehoiachin and Zedekiah are both exiled to Babylon (2 Kgs 24:12, 15; 25:7) and no closing summary is provided. The absence of closing summaries at the point the northern and southern kingdoms ends rhetorically demonstrates the upheaval of the era. Finally, one ruler has neither an opening nor a closing summary: Athaliah (2 Kgs 11). As an Omride, a usurper and a woman in a nation where male rule is prescribed, she is an illegitimate monarch. The lack of regnal summary communicates this illegitimacy.

3.4. 1 – 2 Kings as paradigms

A fourth distinctive is the use of two kings as paradigms against which subsequent kings are evaluated. David is the paradigm for his southern successors, while Jeroboam is the northern paradigm. David serves as a positive paradigm of kingship and this is presented in several ways in 1 – 2 Kings. He urges Solomon to follow the torah of Moses (1 Kgs 2:2–4) and it is for David's sake that YHWH maintains a 'lamp' in Jerusalem (see 'Comment', 1 Kgs 11:36). This is because David is one who has 'done right in YHWH's eyes' and kept YHWH's statutes and commandments (1 Kgs 11:33). David's paradigmatic value also stems from the Davidic Covenant (2 Sam. 7) in which YHWH commits himself to David and his descendants. This, together with David's adherence to deuteronomic law and his desire to build YHWH's temple, mark him as a true Deuteronomistic king. Southern kings are measured by the Davidic example of compliance with Deuteronomistic criteria: observance of YHWH's torah, and commitment to worship in the Jerusalem temple according to Deuteronomistic norms.

All subsequent Davidic kings are compared to David either explicitly (1 Kgs 15:3, 9; 2 Kgs 14:3; 16:2; 18:3; 22:2) or implicitly by comparison to a father who is himself compared to David (1 Kgs 22:43; 2 Kgs 15:3, 34; 23:32, 37; 24:9, 19). Southern kings can also occasionally miss the Davidic mark completely; their actions are then compared to Israelite or foreign ways (2 Kgs 8:18, 27; 2 Kgs 21:2).

Jeroboam's negative paradigm arises out of his promulgation of the alternative cult (1 Kgs 12:26–33). Subsequent kings walk in the 'sin of Jeroboam which he caused Israel to sin' (1 Kgs 15:26, 34; 16:26, 31; 22:52; 2 Kgs 3:3; 13:2, 11; 14:24; 15:9, 18, 24, 28). This sin is represented by the golden calves (2 Kgs 10:29). Whereas southern kings adhere to the Davidic paradigm to greater or lesser degrees, all northern kings follow the paradigm of Jeroboam without exception. Even those who reign briefly and would have no actual time to reveal their attitude towards Jeroboam's sins are measured negatively (e.g. Zimri; 1 Kgs 16:19). Ahab's introduction of the destructive Baal cult does not alter the paradigm: it is the sin of the

founder that sets the direction for northern monarchs. The peroration on
Israel's fall does cite other sins, but Jeroboam's cult remains the central
mark of Israel's apostasy (2 Kgs 17:16, 22; cf. vv. 12, 15).

3.5. The deuteronomic code

The evaluative criteria for each paradigm centres on the king's adherence
to the torah of Moses, particularly although not exclusively as that torah
touches on issues of worship. It is the centrality of the torah as indicative
of Israel's covenant life that is the next distinctive of 1 – 2 Kings.

David's death-bed charge to Solomon (1 Kgs 2:2–4) urges him to torah
obedience using terms common to the book of Deuteronomy. Solomon is
to 'keep the charge of YHWH' (Deut. 11:1), 'to walk in his ways' (Deut.
8:6; 10:12; cf. Josh. 1:7) and to follow his 'statutes, commandments and
judgments' (Deut 4:40; 8:11; 26:17; 30:16), as written in the 'torah of
Moses'. This last reference to the torah of Moses takes up the words of
the charge given Joshua to keep 'the torah my servant Moses gave' (Josh.
1:7–8). In that context the torah of Moses is also referred to as 'this book
of the torah', a term used of the laws found in Deuteronomy (Deut 28:61;
29:20; 30:10; 31:26). David charges Solomon and his descendants to align
with the covenant, particularly as given in Deuteronomy.

The covenant life outlined in Deuteronomy prepares the people for life
in the land (Deut. 4:1, 40) and disobedience to the deuteronomic code will
lead to expulsion from the land (Deut. 28:36–68). Thus both people and
king are repeatedly urged to walk in the torah (1 Kgs 2:2–4; 6:11–13; 9:6–9).
Their failure to do so does not result in immediate expulsion, however.
YHWH's commitment to the Davidic Covenant forestalls judgment (1 Kgs
11:31–32, 34–46; 15:4; 2 Kgs 8:19), as does YHWH's commitment to
the earlier Abrahamic Covenant (2 Kgs 13:23). Yet when exile comes
as the covenant's ultimate judgment, anticipated return is also couched in
the terminology of Deuteronomy (Deut. 4:20; 1 Kgs 8:51).

The reference to the torah as contained in Deuteronomy is part of a
larger phenomenon by which the theological emphases of Deuteronomy
remain influential throughout Joshua–Kings. These deuteronomic
emphases are taken up in the Former Prophets, both in their content and
in a mode of language unique to Deuteronomy. A classic study of the
emphases and language of Deuteronomy in Joshua–Kings is found in
Moshe Weinfeld (1972). He argues that, using specific deuteronomic
linguistic style (which he collates in an extensive appendix), several theological tenets unite Joshua–Kings to Deuteronomy. Those tenets include
the observance of the law and loyalty to the covenant noted here, but also
include the struggle against idolatry; the centralization of the cult; exodus,
covenant and election; exclusive worship of YHWH; inheritance of the
land; retribution and material motivation; fulfilment of prophecy; and

the election of the Davidic dynasty (Weinfeld 1972: 1). Each of these shapes 1 – 2 Kings.

Although the reference to the 'book of the torah of Moses/this book of the torah' may not encapsulate all the present book of Deuteronomy (see section 4 below, 'Critical issues of authorship and date'), the deuteronomic law is a standard for kings and people throughout 1 – 2 Kings. Further exploration of the deuteronomic underpinnings in 1 – 2 Kings is explored below (7.1).

3.6. Reform of worship

A final distinctive in 1 – 2 Kings is the repeated presence of reforming monarchs. The building and dedication of the temple by Solomon is a high point in Israel's religious life. YHWH's cloud of glory inhabits the temple (1 Kgs 8:10) as it earlier inhabited the tabernacle (Exod. 40:34–38). It is this indwelling presence that alone consecrates the temple. The temple also serves as a place of sacrifice, and also particularly as a place of prayer (1 Kgs 8:27–53).

Worship falls very quickly from the ideal of this dedication. Solomon himself compromises the sanctuary's central role as YHWH's exclusive place and this sets a trajectory of apostasy that continues and worsens. In the north Jeroboam institutes an alternative cult with its primary shrine at Bethel. Over time the northern kingdom not only continues to worship YHWH in this unauthorized cult, but becomes entangled with Baal worship introduced by Ahab (1 Kgs 16:29–33). The nadir of Judah's history is Manasseh's reign, as worship of YHWH is forsworn and becomes that of the surrounding nations (2 Kgs 21).

Countering these negative tendencies are several reforms. In the south those of Asa (1 Kgs 15:11–15), Jehoshaphat (1 Kgs 22:46), Jehoash (2 Kgs 12:4–16) and Hezekiah (2 Kgs 18:1–4) restore some elements of the cult, but are neither extensive nor long lasting. In the apostate north reform is a rarer phenomenon. Jehoram rejects the sins of Ahab, but not those of Jeroboam (2 Kgs 3:2–3). Jehu's reform effectively eradicates Baal worship, but he too continues in the sins of Jeroboam (2 Kgs 10:28–29).

The incomplete nature of these reforms stands in contrast to that of Josiah (2 Kgs 22 – 23). This king, lauded far beyond any previous king (2 Kgs 22:2; 23:25), reforms both southern and northern cults. He exceeds the efforts of all previous reforms and wholly restores the Jerusalem cult to its initial state. He also removes all trace of the Baal and Jeroboam cults in the north. In this, Josiah's reform is the culminating point of the whole narrative, fulfilling and extending all reforming zeal before him. Yet, though extensive, his reform does not last. On his death the cult quickly returns to apostasy (2 Kgs 23:32, 37; 24:9, 19) and the sins of

Manasseh (2 Kgs 21:1–9), for which the nation is judged (2 Kgs 21:9–16; 23:26–27).

4. CRITICAL ISSUES OF AUTHORSHIP AND DATE

The books of Kings make no overt claims for authorship. Authorship is traditionally ascribed to an individual in the exilic period who recorded the monarchic history to his own day. In this task he drew upon written sources including the Book of the Acts of Solomon (1 Kgs 11:41), the Book of the Chronicles of the Kings of Judah (1 Kgs 14:29 *et passim*), and the Book of the Chronicles of the Kings of Israel (1 Kgs 15:31 *et passim*). The Babylonian Talmud tractate *Baba Bathra* 15a cites Jeremiah as this author. The claim probably arises from recognition that Jer. 52 replicates 2 Kgs 24:18 – 25:30.

The work of Julius Wellhausen (1883, 1889) sets the tone for critical biblical studies for the next century, positing multiple sources throughout the Pentateuch and into the Historical Books. For instance, he argued that previously edited prophetic material was taken up into a primary edition of Kings during the monarchic period. Later an exilic editor made slight revisions from a deuteronomic perspective.

Martin Noth's work *Überlieferungsgeschichtliche Studien* (translated as *The Deuteronomistic History*) appeared first in 1943. It challenged prevailing notions of compositional history and set a new agenda for the discussion of the corpus Deuteronomy–Kings. He argued that a single exilic author composed a unified narrative of Israel's history in the land, which comprised the books Deuteronomy–Kings. This work was composed in the exilic period in an attempt to explain the tragedy of exile. Its view of Israel's history was wholly negative: a long slide from the goodness of the deuteronomic law to the reality of exile with no visible hope of return or redemption.

This Deuteronomistic author/redactor had numerous available sources that included the original book of Deuteronomy, and these he wove into the narrative. As an author he provided unity to the corpus by inserting his own comments and theological reflections in his own unique style. These theological reflections retrospectively and prospectively assessed the history and included speeches in the mouths of key characters (Josh. 1, 23; 1 Sam. 12; 1 Kgs 8) and summarizing reflections in the narrator's voice (Josh. 12; Judg. 2:11–19; 2 Kgs 17:7–23). A chronological framework that included the lengths for kings' rules as well as the eras of the judges provided further unity to the work.

The book of Deuteronomy stands as the work's prologue and is itself a work of the Deuteronomistic author. Taking an existing deuteronomic law (Deut. 4:44 – 30:20) the author appended his own introduction and conclusion (Deut. 1:1 – 4:43; 31:1 – 32:44 [Deut. 33:1 – 34:12 as a later addition]).

Incorporated as the prologue to the Deuteronomistic History ('DH': Deuteronomy to 2 Kings), the deuteronomic law provided the standards and ideals that govern the whole of the Deuteronomistic author's work.

A frequent criticism of Noth's work is its consistently pessimistic outlook. In a programmatic essay entitled 'The Themes of the Book of Kings and the Structure of the Deuteronomistic History', in the volume *Canaanite Myth and Hebrew Epic* (1973), Frank Moore Cross argued that an original edition by a Deuteronomistic author (Dtr1) appeared in the reign of Josiah, while further redactional work by an exilic Deuteronomist (Dtr2) brought the history up to date and minimally expanded the work in the light of the exile.

The first edition carried two primary themes: the sins of Jeroboam by which the northern kingdom fell, and the promises made to David that at several points brought reprieve and hope to the southern kingdom. It is this latter theme that Cross found countered Noth's pessimistic reading of the history. The promise to David provided consistent hope throughout and at the history's close (2 Kgs 25:27–30). In the juxtaposition of the themes of threat and promise Cross found a propagandistic work of the Josianic era that supported the king's reform.

Cross posited a second edition that added a subtheme to 1 – 2 Kings, that is, the exile of the southern kingdom due to the sins of Manasseh. Found primarily in 2 Kgs 21 and 23:25b–27, short glosses were inserted throughout the history to forward this theme (e.g. Deut. 28:36–37, 63–68; Josh. 23:11–13, 15–16; 1 Sam. 12:25; 1 Kgs 2:4; 6:11–13; 8:25b, 46–53; 9:4–9; 2 Kgs 17:19; 20:17–18). It is this theme that provided a theological reading of history in order to explain the reality of exile.

The two main theses of Noth and Cross provide a basis for further refinements that reflect scholars' understandings of the various emphases (credited to redactional layers) and the historical point at which such emphases entered the history. For instance, subsequent work revised Noth's single exilic author, positing three redactional layers. To the work of an exilic author were added redactions by first a priestly editor, and then a nomistic editor (i.e. one whose concern is with issues of law), working in the exilic period (see Smend 1971; Dietrich 1972; and Veijola 1975, 1977). Compositional activity is also posited in later eras of Persian and Greek dominance.

In the above approaches phenomena such as perceived disjunctions in the narrative's flow or grammatical structure, repetitions or differing emphases are taken as indicators of redactional layers and editorial activity. Unfortunately, no agreement exists regarding the presence of redactional activity, the era to which such activity is attributed and the process by which the redacted text came together. Both on a large scale and in the minutiae of chapter, paragraph and verse, scholars can offer widely differing accounts of compositional activity. The subjective nature of the exercise is apparent, for one person's narrative disjunction is another's example of narrative art; repetitions are credited to redactional layering or authorial intent; different emphases are credited to redactional schools (e.g. prophetic, nomic, Josianic, etc.) or to the complex theological workings of one author.

The compositional history of the text is impossible to ascertain with certainty. Further, none of these 'pre-texts' is available to the reader. Even if such pre-texts existed, they have been taken up into a new work – the present text – and thus their intents and meanings have similarly been reset into something larger. Given that, this commentary takes an approach that reckons the literary work of 1 – 2 Kings to be a composition that draws upon many traditions and indeed cites source materials (The Book of the Chronicles of the Kings of Judah/Israel for instance). Other sources such as prophetic traditions, annalistic accounts and court records may also underlie the present text. Some of the theories of such composition are noted in this commentary. But tracing the history of the text's composition remains peripheral to this commentary's approach.

This work takes as a given the canonical form of the text and focuses on the narrative held within that form. Ultimately, however many redactional hands the text passed through (if any), the final set of hands understood the narrative in its present form – with whatever disjunctions, repetitions or variations of emphasis – to express the theological, historiographical and narrative purposes of that final hand, directed to a particular initial audience.

Finally, as the narrative ends with Israel in exile and given the emphases of 1 – 2 Kings, it does seem that it is an exilic editor/author who formulated the present text. There is an apologetic urgency to the emphases that signals a desire to explain the reality of the covenant curse of exile now visited upon the people. Thus it is that historical and social location that this commentary understands as the place in which Kings was finally formulated. The narrative does, of course, speak to all subsequent generations, but it speaks first to that generation to whom it is addressed: those in exile. To those in exile it provides an apologia for the reality of exile. But it does so not without hope: the Davidic Covenant and the covenants forged with Israel at Sinai and with Abraham each echo through its pages, pointing to the continuing faithfulness of YHWH. Those in exile can still hope, on the basis of the covenants, that YHWH's gracious hand will be extended once more.

5. 1 – 2 KINGS AS HISTORIOGRAPHY

5.1. Defining historiography

As noted above (see 2.2), 1 – 2 Kings is here considered as historiographic literature that intends a representation of events that occurred in the past.

The nature and purpose of historiographical literature are conceived in various ways, many of which undermine or dismiss any connection the biblical text might have to actual events in history (see the discussions in V. Long 2002). The following comments surface some of the pertinent issues in the discussion and how they are understood within this commentary.

An initial question is the definition of historiography. John Van Seters in *In Search of History* (1983: 1) presents as a starting point the definition coined by historian Johan Huizinga. Thus history is the 'intellectual form in which a civilization renders account to itself of its past'. Van Seters explores the implications of the definition and nuances it by considering the 'intellectual form' to be history writing.

A more expansive definition is provided by Iain Provan, V. Philips Long and Tremper Longman III in *A Biblical History of Israel* (2003: 49). Its usefulness to this discussion justifies a lengthy quotation:

> Testimony – 'storytelling' – is central to our quest to know the past. In fact, all historiography is story, whether ancient, medieval, or modern. Historiography is ideological narrative about the past that involves, among other things, the selection of material and its interpretation by authors who are intent on persuading themselves or their readership of certain truths about the past. This selection and interpretation is always made by people with a particular perspective on the world – a particular set of presuppositions and beliefs that do not derive from the facts of history with which they are working, but are already in existence before the narration begins. . . . All knowledge of the past is in fact more accurately described as faith in the interpretations of the past offered by others, through which we make these interpretations (in part or as a whole) our own.

The definition provided by Provan et al. is a clear reminder that no historiographical account is neutral; every historian writes from an interpretative position and in order to communicate and persuade others of that position. For the biblical text that position is decidedly theological: it wishes to teach something of God and of his ways in the world (Provan 1995: 10–15). It understands events of Israel's history to be intimately involved with YHWH and that proper understanding of the events of Israel's past cannot be arrived at without recognizing that theological reality. Thus 1 – 2 Kings, while relating events of Israel's past, does so not simply to record those past events but to present and interpret those events through a theological lens: YHWH is the only God, and commits himself to Israel by covenant towards the blessing of the whole world.

The recognition in the definition by Provan et al. of the positioned historiography of 1 – 2 Kings is similar to Van Seters' explication of

Huizinga's definition. Among other items, Van Seters notes that historiography in ancient Israel is 'not primarily the accurate reporting of past
event. It also considers the reason for recalling the past and the significance
given to past events.' More, that ancient Israelite historiography 'examines
the causes of present conditions and circumstances . . . [as] . . . primarily
moral' (Van Seters 1983: 4–5).

5.2. Historiographical considerations

5.2.1. The biblical text and historiography

The definition above also points to another consideration adopted by this
commentary. That is that 1 – 2 Kings (and the biblical text in general) is
a primary text for information about ancient Israel's past. Thus it is not
a text that can be secondarily interpreted only through more neutral or
objective artefacts, such as extra-biblical writings or archaeological dis-
coveries. Each of these comes with its own inherent ideology, and each,
like the biblical text, must be interpreted. They cannot provide a more
neutral or so-called objective window into the ancient past, and thus
cannot provide an authoritative 'control' on the biblical text's presentation. Nor does the decidedly ideological or theological nature of the
biblical text disqualify it as a reliable source of information about the past.
Its theological outlook is part and parcel of ANE reportage: all ancient
historiography has such a world view. Given the parameters of a theological world view, one need not disqualify such reportage as historically
suspect a priori (Provan et al. 2003: 3–50). Further, such dismissal would
be irrational in an attempt to discover Israel's past, for the biblical account
provides the one continuous narrative of Israel's ancient past that is
available to us (Provan et al. 2003: 98).

5.2.2. Reading with literary competency

Affirming the value of the biblical text as a primary witness to Israel's
ancient past requires careful attention to the norms of ancient historiographical presentation. One must read with literary competency that
asks after the nature, purpose and scope of the ancient biblical account.
First, it bears repeating that ancient historiography is not concerned with
a bald reportage of the 'facts' or mere antiquarian interest. Biblical
reportage seeks the theological meaning inherent in the facts. Of course,
modern historiography is equally governed by guiding principles: ideologies likewise direct its nature, purpose and scope, as noted by Provan
et al. above. Unfortunately, however, modern scientific sensibilities can
fallaciously conclude that modern historiography is a neutral reportage

of 'just the facts'. More, that modern historiography in its (supposed) neutrality, chronological presentation and accuracy of detail is the standard by which all historiography should be measured.

Secondly, the application of such notions of modern historiography to the biblical text ends up discounting not only its manner of reportage (for it is decidedly not neutral), but its method of reportage. The biblical account (and ancient historiography in general) does not adhere to modern notions of the import to historiography of chronological presentation and comprehensiveness. This is the second area in which careful attention must be given to the norms of ancient historiography.

If chronological reporting marks a modern standard for historiography, such is not the case in ancient historiography. This is more than apparent in 1 – 2 Kings by the simple recognition of the alternating reportage of northern and southern kingdoms. Thus the narrative advances events in one kingdom and then moves backwards in time to take up events in the other kingdom's storyline. Nor is the narrative unduly concerned to present individual vignettes and stories in chronological order. For instance, the accounts of Elisha's' ministry in 2 Kgs 4 may easily be collected together for thematic purposes; no indication necessitates that the vignettes are chronologically ordered. Similarly, the account of Hezekiah's interaction with the Babylonians (2 Kgs 20) stands chronologically before the events of 2 Kgs 18 – 19 (see 'Comment'); the ordering principle is not chronology but theological and thematic. It simply goes against the nature and scope of ancient historiography if one holds 1 – 2 Kings to a strict standard of chronology because it is historiography. To do so applies a modern standard to an ancient genre.

In the same way that 1 – 2 Kings does not operate within a strict chronological framework, it also does not operate under strict parameters of comprehensiveness. The biblical accounting of the monarchic period is extremely selective. One need only consult the closing regnal summary for each reign to know that much more was known and could be reported about a king's reign. While much more *could* be said, what *is* said supports the theological purposes of the authors. Often, the matters that might concern modern historiographers such as financial exigencies, military endeavours or political wranglings are the very things 1 – 2 Kings is pointedly unconcerned about. Its pursuit is directed towards Deuteronomistic concerns of cult and covenant; military, political or financial matters when presented generally illustrate the king's or nation's alignment with these concerns.

The third area of literary competency considered in this commentary is one that understands the nature and purpose of 1 – 2 Kings to be representational historiography. It is true that the accounts in 1 – 2 Kings are not themselves the actual event – the historical events are no longer directly accessible to experience. All that remains is the testimony of the narrative accounts in 1 – 2 Kings as noted in the definition by Provan et al. above.

As representational historiography, the accounts are referential and not merely fictional or aesthetic. The difference between referentiality and fictionality is the degree to which the author is constrained by the actualities of the subject matter. At times, material remains (such as archaeology or epigraphy) give support to the biblical account as representational and not simply fictive; these, together with the account's apparent purpose within its broader literary context, suggest its referential nature (V. Long 1994: 58–68).

Finally, a corollary to the representational nature of the accounts is that they represent past events in narrative form. As narrative historiography, the accounts of the past are artistically drawn. Not only are they selective in their reportage, but they also contain elements of good storytelling, relating the past through narrative means. Thus plot becomes a crucial element of the individual narratives and the whole monarchic history. Plot includes elements such as narrative introduction, plot complication and development, crisis and resolution. Characterization is equally important in Israelite historiography. Characters can be fully developed, stereotypically drawn or simply agential to plot development. The narrator serves as a character within the accounts and shapes the narrative in many ways. The narrator might advise concerning 'off stage' elements that are not played out before a reader's eyes, foreshadow upcoming events or comment on a character's actions or thoughts. Space and time play a crucial role in Israelite historiography. Time moves quickly or slowly according to the import of events narrated, and gaps in time or events invite the audience into the account. Spatial attention can highlight a crucial intimate conversation or a broad field of battle. Dialogue demonstrates both selectivity and artistic crafting in the pursuit of the point the author wishes to communicate. Throughout, motifs and repetitions, hyperbole and irony are utilized to affect the readers, drawing them into the historiographical drama and moving them to concurrence with the author's purposes. All of these techniques are found in Israelite historiography and are crucial elements that artistically shape the account's representation of events (Alter 1981; V. Long 1994: 68–87; Amit 2001a; Walsh 2010a). This commentary takes these elements of representational historiography seriously, understanding that the artistry of the narrative form is a crucial part of narrative meaning. Because of this assumption, many of these elements are noted in the 'Form and structure' and 'Comment' sections.

5.3. Israelite historiography and external witnesses

The consideration of Israelite historiography as representational acknowledges that the biblical narrative relates real-world events and persons. That real world has also produced other witnesses to it such as artefacts of epigraphy and archaeology. These artefacts are seriously considered in this commentary. For instance, the Babylonian Chronicles that speak to the events during Judah's last years (see 'Comment', 2 Kgs 24 – 25), or the ANE concepts of the cosmic mountain that underlie the biblical presentation of the temple (see 'Explanation', 1 Kgs 6 – 7), are considered helpful in unfolding the biblical text.

As noted above (5.2.1), these accounts are not neutral. They demonstrate their own ideologies, as does the biblical text. Because the extra-biblical materials are not neutral or objective, they do not function as an authoritative arbiter of the historical value of statements and events depicted in the biblical text. But by the same token they should not unnecessarily be dismissed as having nothing to add to the portraiture drawn by the biblical accounts. Both attest to an ancient past; the inspired nature of the biblical text does not insinuate that no other attestations to that past have value in uncovering it.

The external witnesses to the ancient past prove helpful in three primary ways. First, by providing examples of ancient historiography from the world Israel inhabits they give further examples of the genre. These can be compared and contrasted to the genre found in the biblical text and lead to an increased literary competency necessary to hear the Bible's ancient historiography rightly. Secondly, they often speak to events and people that touch the life of ancient Israel. Where and how that testimony aligns with or diverges from the biblical account is a helpful aid in a consideration of the past and how each witness has shaped it (Provan et al. 2003: 99–100). Finally, extra-biblical witnesses paint a vibrant context of the ANE world, producing a probable background within which one can situate the biblical account.

6. THE PROBLEM OF CHRONOLOGY

One historical issue in Kings is that of its chronology. A wealth of chronological data appears in Kings. These include the pervasive notations in the regnal formulae of the length of kings' reigns and synchronization to the reigns of the sister nation, occasional synchronization to the reigns of foreign kings (2 Kgs 25:8) and even the regnal year in which certain events occur (1 Kgs 14:25; 2 Kgs 12:6; 18:9). It appears, then, that part of the books' historiographical intent includes careful consideration of chronological markers. In the introduction to Edwin Thiele's comprehensive work on this topic William Irwin remarks that 'chronology is the one sure basis of accurate historical knowledge' (Thiele 1983: 25). One might conclude then that Kings's chronological data would easily lead to 'accurate historical knowledge'. One need only compare the length and dates of kings' reigns to internal and external data to chart a clear monarchic chronology.

Unfortunately, the chronology of Kings is far from clear. When compared to verifiable external dates and to fixed points provided internally, it is often confused and frequently appears contradictory. A few examples will suffice to prove the point:

- Two monarchic epochs in the north and south fall within the same fixed points. The first is bounded by the accession of Rehoboam and Jeroboam I in the same year (1 Kgs 12) and the deaths of Jehoram and Ahaziah in the same year (2 Kgs 9). Between these two fixed points, one would assume a total of the regnal years provided for kings of north and south would add up to the same number – but they do not. In the south, 98 years 7 days pass; in the north the same period is measured by only 95 years. The second epoch is bounded by the accession of Jehu and Athaliah in the same year Jehoram and Ahaziah are murdered (1 Kgs 9 – 11) and the fall of Samaria in Hoshea's ninth year, which is Hezekiah's sixth year (2 Kgs 18:10). Again one would assume a tally of the regnal years for both kingdoms would be the same. But the discrepancy is even more marked: 143 years 7 months for the north, and 166 years for the south.
- The monarchic chronology can be equally difficult to comport with known extra-biblical dates. For instance, the biblical chronology from Jehu to the fall of Samaria counts 143 years 7 months. Yet Assyrian records set the year of Jehu's accession in 841 BC and depict him in the Black Obelisk doing obeisance to Shalmaneser III (*ANET* 281) in that year. That allows only 120 years to the fixed point of Samaria's fall in 722/721 BC.
- A similar difficulty ensues when one attempts to align Hezekiah's fourteenth year (2 Kgs 18:13) with any known invasion of Sennacherib. Hezekiah comes to the throne in Hoshea's third year (2 Kgs 18:1), that is, 729 BC. Hezekiah's fourteenth year is thus calculated as 715 BC. Yet no campaign by Sennacherib aligns with that date; his invasion is rightly placed in 701 BC, leaving a discrepancy of 14 years.
- Throughout the chronology in kings, comparison of the length of reign with the synchronism to the sister kingdom is discrepant. Just one example of this prevalent discrepancy shows the problem: Jeroboam II rules 41 years (2 Kgs 14:23). Since Azariah of Judah's accession occurred in Jeroboam's twenty-seventh year (2 Kgs 15:1), Jeroboam's death occurred 14 years after Azariah's ascension. Jeroboam's successor, Zechariah, would, one assumes, come to the throne in Azariah's fourteenth year. But the text notes Zechariah's ascension in Azariah's thirty-eighth year (2 Kgs 15:8). How to account for the missing years?

- Repeatedly, chronologies show absolute discrepancy in the details. Thus does Azariah of Judah ascend his throne in Jehoram's eleventh year (2 Kgs 9:29) or his twelfth (2 Kgs 8:25)? Or Asa rules 41 years (1 Kgs 15:10) and Omri rules for 12 years from the thirty-first year of Asa (i.e. ruling until after Asa's death). How is it that Omri's son begins his rule in Asa's thirty-eighth year (1 Kgs 16:29)? Such examples are numerous.

One might simply conclude that the numbers are confused either in the original source material or in the work of subsequent scribes and forgo any attempt at reconciliation. But this impedes at several points one's ability to understand the confusing chronological progress of the narratives and the relation of events and monarchs one to another. Other responses to the chronological difficulty include attempts to change the numbers, perhaps in reliance upon other textual traditions (such as the LXX). But what fixed points can guide such a process so that it does not devolve into guesswork or fabrication? One might also conclude that the biblical chronology should be synchronized to known external dates (such as Jehu's accession and the fall of Samaria). But again, how does one then ensure one 'fits' the kings accurately into this framework?

Rather than despairing of the MT dating system, it is possible to accept it virtually without revision as representing a consistent chronological schema. This schema comports at almost every point with external dating records from Assyria and Babylon as well as provides internal consistency within the biblical chronology. Work towards this schema, which takes into account knowledge of ANE dating practices and considers the scribal practices used throughout Kings, is best represented by the work of Edwin Thiele (see Thiele 1983; see also DeVries, *IDB* 1:580–599).

Thiele argues for consistency in the MT dating system if several presuppositions are considered. First, two different systems were in place in the ANE for counting regnal years. The first is the non-accession (or antedating) system. In this system a king counts as his first year the year of his accession, regardless of whether that accession occurred early or late in the year. For example, if a king's reign was counted as ten years under the non-accession system, the king actually reigned for nine years plus some portion of the accession year. Problematically, accession years are actually double-counted in this system: as the last official year of the preceding king, and the first year of the successive king. In each reign, one extra year is counted and the tally of regnal years is overblown by this double count. The second system is the accession-year (or postdating) system. It gives an accurate tally of regnal years over time because double-counting did not occur; a king's reign was not counted until the first year after the accession year.

Examination of the regnal data in the biblical text would be simplified if Israel and Judah each used the same system consistently. But the evidence suggests that during the first years of the divided monarchy (from Rehoboam to the death of Omri) the southern kingdom employed the accession (postdating) system, while the northern kingdom employed the non-accession (antedating) system. With the death of Omri the southern kingdom switched to the non-accession (antedating) system, perhaps spurred by the joining of the southern royal house to the more powerful Omride dynasty through marriage (2 Kgs 8:18). Thus from the death of Omri both kingdoms followed the non-accession (antedating) system – but only until the reign of Jehoash of Israel (2 Kgs 13:10). In his reign the record for both kingdoms adopts the accession (postdating) system, possibly under the growing Assyrian influence which used that means of calculation. Further investigation of the chronological data introduces yet another anomaly in calculating regnal years. It appears that when synchronizing a king's reign to that of the opposing kingdom, scribes applied to the opposing king the system of calculation current in the scribe's own kingdom.

A second major presupposition employed in Thiele's system considers the evidence for whether the two kingdoms mark the New Year in the spring (Nisan, i.e. Mar.–Apr.) or the autumn (Tishri, i.e. Sept.–Oct.). If the two kingdoms used different New Year dates, the synchronization statements could vary as much as one to three years, depending on whether the accession/non-accession systems were in place in one or both of the nations, and whether their New Year calculations vary by half a year or fall in the same month (Thiele 1983: 45–46).

It is clear from the biblical text and the archaeological evidence of the Gezer Calendar (DeVries, *IDB* 1:485) that Judah's New Year began in Tishri (1 Kgs 6:1, 37–38; 2 Kgs 22:3; 23:23). The evidence for Israel is not so clear, however. Jeroboam is known as an innovator concerning the calendar (see 'Comment', 1 Kgs 12:32–33) and the adoption of the Nisan New Year, celebrated in Babylon, Assyria and during this time also in Egypt (coinciding with Jeroboam's exile there) may be an innovation that Jeroboam adopted. The presupposition that Jeroboam directed such an innovation allows for an accounting of some of the chronological discrepancies in Kings (DeVries, *IDB* 1:586).

A final presupposition of co-regencies and rival reigns is presented by Thiele. One example of co-regency begins the whole corpus: Solomon is elevated to the throne while David remains king; it is some time after Solomon's coronation that King David dies, and for that period they share a co-regency.

The presupposition of co-regencies especially enables an accounting of the widely divergent regnal years from Jehu's accession to the fall of Samaria. As noted above, against this 120-year era is a tally of regnal years for the north of 143 years 7 months and for the south of 166 years. Examining the biblical record, Thiele (1983: 61–65; cf. DeVries, *IDB* 1:587–596) proposes several co-regencies and rival monarchies. Only one co-regency is specifically mentioned (Jotham and Azariah in 2 Kgs 15:5); others are proposed as a solution to the chronological conundrum when they might be implied from accounts of monarchic sickness, captivity or the threat of war. Yet others are implied from clues in the regnal data. For instance, Jehoram of Israel comes to the throne both in the eighteenth year of Jehoshaphat (2 Kgs 3:1) and in the second year of Jehoram, Jehoshaphat's son (2 Kgs 1:17). If Jehoram of Judah was appointed co-regent during Jehoshaphat's sixteenth year, the 'discrepant' regnal synchronizations make perfect sense: Jehoshaphat's eighteenth year was also the second year of his son Jehoram's co-regency. Such a co-regency could be warranted at the time of Jehoshaphat's battle alliance with Israel against Aram (1 Kgs 22) to ensure monarchic oversight in Jehoshaphat's absence and unchallenged succession should Jehoshaphat die in battle.

In the south a total of six co-regencies are proposed (Jehoshaphat and Asa, Jehoram and Jehoshaphat [noted above], Amaziah and Azariah, Jotham and Azariah, Ahaz and Jotham, and Manasseh and Hezekiah). In the north one co-regency is proposed (Jehoash and Jeroboam II). Additionally, two periods of rival concurrent monarchies are proposed in the north (Omri and Tibni, and Menahem and Pekah). Counting the rival monarch's regnal years successively rather than concurrently would inflate the total number of years counted.

Thiele's work has received good acceptance and further clarification and support, although it is not without its detractors (see recently Tetley 2005). Yet it provides a coherent system against which the apparent chronological discrepancies dissipate. It allows the MT to stand largely unchallenged, and suggests solutions that are consonant with the historical practices of the eras in question. This commentary works with Thiele's chronological system; those places where other solutions are adopted are clearly indicated.

7. THEOLOGY OF 1 – 2 KINGS

As discussed above, 1 – 2 Kings is a historiographic representation of Israel's history that is theologically motivated. It traces several theological themes and these are explored in this commentary in each chapter in sections entitled 'Form and structure', 'Comment' and 'Explanation'. But preparatory to that exploration it is helpful to take a moment to provide a broader and more comprehensive overview of some of the most prominent theological themes found in 1 – 2 Kings.

The author(s) of 1 – 2 Kings directed their theologically motivated account to an exilic audience in Babylon. But, as it is the conviction of this commentary that the Bible is an inspired text intended to shape the life of the church and its members, the theological presentation in 1 – 2 Kings speaks not only to an exilic audience. As inspired Scripture, 1 – 2 Kings speaks theologically into the context and to the concerns of the church today. For each of the theological themes outlined below, suggestions are forwarded as to the application of these themes within the church.

7.1. The normative influence of the deuteronomic law

Section 3.5 above notes the defining influence of the deuteronomic law in the charge David gives his son (1 Kgs 2:2–4) and how that charge calls all successive kings and indeed the people of Israel to covenant keeping. The influence of the deuteronomic law on the course of the narrative and its theology cannot be overestimated.

Of particular importance in 1 – 2 Kings is the deuteronomic pre-scriptions regarding correct worship under the covenant. Deuteronomy 12:5, 16:5–6 centralize worship 'at the place YHWH should choose to place his name there'. As the history unfolds, the 'place' is revealed as Jerusalem. It is in the temple where YHWH's name dwells (1 Kgs 8:29, 48) that Israel is to worship, eschewing other sites. Once the temple is completed, worship at the high places is discounted. Failure to remove the high places is a negative evaluation against kings (1 Kgs 16:14; 22:43; 2 Kgs 12:3; 14:4; 15:4, 35; 16:4); only those who remove them are fully approved (2 Kgs 18:4; 23:4–25).

In Solomon's dedicatory prayer for the temple he emphasizes YHWH's exclusive claim to Israel's worship. In this he takes up another thematic found in Deuteronomy. Solomon addresses YHWH, noting there is 'no God like you in the heavens . . . or the earth' (1 Kgs 8:23; Deut. 4:39), a reality he later returns to by stating that 'YHWH, he is God; there is no other' (v. 60; Deut. 4:35, 39). In that same prayer Solomon petitions YHWH to answer the prayers directed to the temple, so that 'all the peoples of the earth may know that YHWH is God' (v. 60; Deut. 4:35, 39; 7:9).

Concomitant with the pursuit of exclusive worship of YHWH in the Jerusalem temple, Kings has an abhorrence of idolatry that is communi-cated in deuteronomic terms. Much of Kings (1 Kgs 17 – 2 Kgs 10) follows the ministry of Elijah and Elisha against the Baalism of the Omrides. This apostasy, as well as other expressions, such as Solomon's false worship (1 Kgs 11) and Manasseh's worship (2 Kgs 21), violates the deuteronomic code against foreign gods. Israel is not to 'go after' them (Deut. 6:14; 8:19; 11:28; 13:3; 28:14; 1 Kgs 11:10; 21:26; 2 Kgs 17:15) or 'serve' them (Deut. 7:4; 11:16; 13:7, 14; 17:3; 28:36, 64; 29:25; 1 Kgs 9:6; 2 Kgs 21:21). Even specific practices such as worshipping 'on every high hill and under every green tree' (Deut. 12:2; 1 Kgs 14:23; 2 Kgs 16:4; 17:10) and 'passing [children] through the fire' (Deut. 18:10; 2 Kgs 16:3; 17:17; 21:6) are pro-hibited in deuteronomic terms. To worship idols is variously described as 'an abomination' (Deut. 7:5, 26; 13:15; 17:4; 18:9; 20:18; 1 Kgs 14:24; 2 Kgs 16:3; 21:2, 11), 'detestable' (Deut. 29:16; 1 Kgs 11:5, 7; 2 Kgs 23:24), and such idols are called *gĕlûllîm*, a word that shares the root (*gll*) of the word 'dung'.

The election of Israel, their deliverance out of Egypt to Sinai (Horeb) and the covenant forged there are referenced in Kings in the language of Deuteronomy. YHWH rescues Israel with a strong hand, great might and outstretched arm (Deut. 4:34; 5:15; 7:19; 11:2; 26:8; 1 Kgs 8:42 and Deut. 9:29; 2 Kgs 17:36). The covenant is a demonstration of YHWH's eternal love (Deut. 4:37; 4:7–8, 13; 10:15; 23:6; 1 Kgs 10:9) by which he chose Israel (Deut. 4:37; 7:6–7; 10:15; 14:2; 1 Kgs 3:8), making them his own people (Deut. 21:8; 26:15; 1 Kgs 8:33–34, 38, 43, 52). As king and people walk in the torah, they prove their identity as covenant people. But when they walk outside the deuteronomic norms of the covenant, they face discipline and ultimately exile from their land.

The normativity of the deuteronomic code found in the 'book of the torah' (Deut 28:61; 29:20; 30:10; 31:26) shows its authoritative influence upon the theology of the authors of 1 – 2 Kings. For these authors, Deuteronomy and the covenant life defined by its law code held an inherent authority that directed their thinking, their actions and their reflections upon their own history. The authors at this point may self-consciously have styled the writings of Deuteronomy as Scripture. If not, that they upheld the authority of the corpus was a Spirit-directed step towards such recognition. Certainly now, read within the canon of Scripture, the attitude of the authors of Kings towards Deuteronomy is understood as submission before Scripture.

The deuteronomic submission to the authority of a written text is a model for the church's own stance before the authoritative text of Scripture. While the life of the church rightly also attends to the lessons of tradition and reason, it is to Scripture that it owes its first allegiance. Scripture is the clearest voice of YHWH and the right stance before that voice is to listen. Hezekiah, and Josiah after him, demonstrates such a stance; it involves openness to the words of Scripture, willingness to come under its convicting power, attention to its right interpretation within one's context, and action that arises out of that interpretation.

Ideally, Israelite kings were to develop such a listening heart by their own reading of and meditation upon the deuteronomic covenant (Deut. 17:18–19). The church, too, is called upon to hide the word of God in its heart. Means to develop this listening heart are personal devotion and study of both the Old and New Testaments, the regular corporate reading of Scripture before the gathered people, faithful exposition of Scripture, and attention to where and how the Spirit calls the church to action. It is work that requires commitment, but it is work that is borne out of love for the church's Lord and is sustained and directed by the Spirit. Jesus' words are this: 'If you love me, you will keep my commandments' (John 14:15). To do so, one must know those commandments and apply them in each new generation of the church's life.

It is apparent from the deuteronomic code that it is exclusive worship of YHWH that is its defining element. Israel is to love YHWH with heart, soul, mind and strength (Deut. 6:5). In a context of competing claims for Israel's allegiance they are to focus their devotion on YHWH alone, meditating upon him, speaking and teaching of him, and marking their world in such ways that he could not be overwritten, especially when life brought material abundance (Deut. 6:10–12). In our own culture of loudly competing claims for attentive devotion, this deuteronomic admonition similarly calls the church to abandonment. It is an abandonment to love and relationship that supersedes all other claims: material wealth, consumerism, political and religious smugness – all these must fall under the umbrella of Christ's call. It is then that these secondary claims are purified and rightly ordered into the holistic fabric of a life claimed by him.

7.2. The covenant made with David

The culminating sin of the era of the judges is Israel's rejection of YHWH's rule and the call for a human king (1 Sam. 8:7–8; 12:12–17). Yet YHWH chooses the institution of monarchy to work out his purposes for Israel and through Israel to the world. The choice of David in the face of Saul's failure (1 Sam. 16:1–13) becomes the locus for YHWH's purposes in the monarchic history. David's kingship is ratified by YHWH's covenant in 2 Sam. 7, and the temple and dynasty attest not only to YHWH's approval of David but of the monarchic role exercised by his descendants.

The covenant instituted on David's behalf is itself subject to the Mosaic Covenant and the kingly line is disciplined by its laws (2 Sam. 7:14), particularly as they are formulated in the deuteronomic code (see 7.1 above). David's charge to Solomon makes clear the standard to which his dynasty must adhere (1 Kgs 2:2–4). The Mosaic Covenant under which the Davidic Covenant is positioned is itself a further outworking of the Abrahamic Covenant. The Abrahamic Covenant is the catalyst for the exodus (Exod. 2:23–25), and in the exodus and Sinai YHWH calls to himself a kingdom of priests (Exod. 19:6). It is through this kingdom that the Abrahamic promise of blessing for all nations is to spring.

The book of Kings opens with this background assumed and simply continues a story already in motion. The succession of Solomon continues YHWH's purposes begun in Abraham, and furthered in the Sinaitic and Davidic Covenants. The succession of Solomon also confirms the dynastic promise granted David. The temple's completion fulfils the second promise of the Davidic Covenant – that David's son will build YHWH's house.

The temple's importance is not only its role as witness to the Davidic Covenant and YHWH's approval of that line. It also serves as an end point of Israel's deliverance from Egypt and of her wilderness journeys (1 Kgs 6:1). As Moses prepared Israel for entry to the land, he called them to worship YHWH in the place approved by him. When they enter the land and find rest, they are to worship at the place YHWH puts his name (Deut. 12:5, 10–14; 16:5–6). As the history unfolds, this place of rest is revealed as Jerusalem and it is there the temple is built (2 Sam. 7:1–2; 1 Kgs 5:4–5). It houses the ark as witness to the Mosaic Covenant, it attests to the Davidic Covenant, and by the manifestation of YHWH's glory it affirms YHWH's promise to dwell in his people's midst (1 Kgs 8:1–21).

For the remainder of the history the covenant with David is bound up with the temple. When Solomon is punished for covenant disobedience, the whole kingdom is not wrest from his hands because of YHWH's choice of David and the city (1 Kgs 11:32, 34, 36). This same reason repeatedly forestalls YHWH's judgment (1 Kgs 15:4; 2 Kgs 8:19), and temple and dynasty endure. In the end, when it is no longer possible to forestall judgment, the destruction of the temple occurs in hand with the end of Davidide rule (2 Kgs 24:10 – 25:21).

The final verses of 2 Kings leave open the possibility that a king may return to the throne of David in Jerusalem. Jehoiachin is granted slight reprieve in his captivity, and his changed fortunes – to say nothing of the fact he remains alive – leaves the future open to hope. The Davidic Covenant rests upon YHWH's choice and not upon human ability. As always, YHWH is faithful to what he promises. Though the dynasty's scions could be disciplined, their failure does not entail the end of YHWH's promise of an everlasting dynasty.

The prophetic books recount the enduring nature of that hope as they look ahead to a restored Davidic monarch (Isa. 9:2–7; 11:1–9; Jer. 23:1–8; 30:9; Ezek. 34:23–24; 37:24; Hos. 3:5; Mic. 5:1–5). It is the Christian tradition that recognizes the fulfilment of these hopes in Jesus of the royal line of David (Matt. 1:1–17; Rom. 1:3). He is the King of all kings, and the Lord of all lords (Rev. 19:16), the royal son of YHWH appointed to rule over all (Ps. 2:7–9; Acts 13:33; Heb. 1:5; 5:5).

How might the Davidic Covenant speak to the church today? First, it is helpful to remember that the Davidic Covenant is indelibly tied to history. It is an event that draws from YHWH's past dealing with Israel and itself becomes part of YHWH's future dealings with Israel. YHWH is unfolding a long plan, and each new step has echoes of the past and reverberates into the future. Though fresh, the Davidic Covenant is seamlessly tied into Israel's story.

The same is true of what God does in Jesus Christ in forming the church. Cross, resurrection, Pentecost – all are part of a long history that stretches back to the garden. Though there is radical newness in the events of Christ, the church cannot understand itself apart from its history. It comes from Israel and is going towards a future formed by that past.

Similarly, each generation of the church extends that history further still. To understand itself the church must look not only to the long history of the OT, but to the NT and church history. Each of these is under

YHWH's control and each continues the one story. The church's self-identity cannot be accurate if it unheedingly throws off those past voices. Therefore, its interpretative traditions, its hymnody and liturgy, its past and current polity and dissensions are needful voices as the church today seeks to find its path.

A second way the Davidic Covenant might speak to the church lies in its advent hopes. It is a church that waits the return of the king in his full and recognized glory. Its task in the waiting time is twofold. First, it must faithfully attend to its king. It attends to his voice, looking to the pages of Scripture as its primary listening post. It also attends to the king by recounting to upcoming generations the truth of his kingship. In the same way post-exilic Israel, awaiting the return of a Davidic king, attended to Scripture and communicated its hopes to a new generation. Secondly, as an advent people the church not only attends to its king. It must also wait as Israel waited. It is a task that at times seems too long for continued hope and faithful living. But it is in the place of yearning hope that it finds joy and energy to continue faithfully in the tasks appointed it. It is in its desire to be found doing his will when he comes that it presses on in its journey. It awaits his coming (with lamps lit), so that, on his arrival, it might be found awake and working.

Finally, the Davidic Covenant also speaks to that time of waiting. While the Covenant gave certainty of its enduring nature, each generation under that Covenant was called to live by the deuteronomic law. In the same way, each generation – and each individual in the church – is called to live under the righteous rule of her king. By the demonstration of his justice, peace and righteousness it is to make his fame known that others might come to see the 'wisdom of Solomon' in the life of the church.

7.3. The power of the prophetic word

YHWH's will communicated through the prophets is always an expression of the covenants that exist between Israel and YHWH. Each of the covenants instituted by YHWH is present in 1 – 2 Kings. Thus the ancient covenant with Abraham can be cited as the basis for YHWH's work (1 Kgs 18:36; 2 Kgs 13:23). The covenant made with David, with its emphasis on the dynastic house and the temple, is a key component of Solomon's reign. The promises granted David are also the reason YHWH consistently delays judgment against the southern kingdom (1 Kgs 15:4; 2 Kgs 8:19). Finally, the Sinaitic Covenant is everywhere present in 1 – 2 Kings. It is especially the formulation and language of that covenant in Deuteronomy that influences 1 – 2 Kings. The 'laws, statutes, and judgments' of Deuteronomy are the standard of covenant life.

As the prophets hold Israel to covenantal standard, they themselves take on the prophetic mantle of Moses; they are the 'prophets like unto Moses'

(Deut. 18:15), continually challenging Israel to live life by covenant norms. The scope of their ministries operates in two spheres in Kings: that of the monarch, and that of the people.

In the realm of the monarch, prophets are instrumental in appointing and deposing kings. This is clearly illustrated as the corpus begins. It is Nathan who is instrumental in Solomon's progress to the throne. In the northern kingdom dynastic rule is not so stable as in the southern kingdom, and many dynasties rise and fall. Again prophets feature largely in these events, as it is by their word that kings and dynasties are appointed (1 Kgs 11:29–39; 2 Kgs 9:6–10) and deposed (1 Kgs 11:9–13; 14:7–11, 14; 16:1–4; 21:19–24).

The prophets also challenge and encourage kings while they rule. Under the covenant, kings are to meditate upon and live out faithful covenant life (Deut. 17:18–20). Through their example and leadership true worship is instituted or subverted (1 Kgs 11:1–8; 12:25–33; 16:30–33; 2 Kgs 18:3–4; 21:2–9; 23:1–24) and covenant life protected. The king's influence over his people often led YHWH to use prophetic ministry to overturn evil dynasties. For instance, it is a prophet who confronts Jeroboam at the consecration of the Bethel altar (1 Kgs 13:1–5) and it is a prophet (Elijah) who repeatedly confronts Ahab over covenantal failures. Elijah charges Ahab as a troubler of Israel (1 Kgs 18:18) and has the power to summon him to a showdown between Baal and YHWH (1 Kgs 18). When Ahab sins over Naboth's vineyard against covenant norms, it is the prophet who calls him to task. And when Ahab sins under the covenantal proscription on warfare (1 Kgs 20), it is a prophet who condemns him.

Throughout the history of Israel and Judah many unnamed prophets warn of covenant failures (2 Kgs 17:13; 21:10). But the prophetic ministry was not always confrontational. Prophets stood by kings as encouragers towards covenant life (1 Kgs 20:13, 22; 2 Kgs 5:8; 6:9–10; 19:5–7, 20–34; 22:18–20). Again, because the kings were YHWH's appointed leaders and prophets his appointed messengers, it is unsurprising that they interact so frequently – it is the people's life under covenant that is at stake.

The prophets' ministry is also operative in the people's sphere. In a dramatic example, Elijah addresses the people at Carmel, urging them back to covenant life (1 Kgs 18:21–40). Elisha's prophetic ministry functions before the people in more intimate settings (2 Kgs 4). For both prophets the issues at stake are those of covenant life. Once again YHWH's prophets serve as his covenant mediators.

At all times and in both spheres the prophetic word proves sure and ineluctable. What the prophets say by the word of YHWH comes to pass. It is the same power exhibited in Gen. 1 in which YHWH speaks and it is done, now demonstrated in the realm of human history. The fulfilment of the prophetic word is so crucial to the theology of 1 – 2 Kings that the books frequently provide specific notice of such fulfilment. This has been carefully demonstrated by Gerhard von Rad in his programmatic essay that traces the phenomenon of prophecy and fulfilment (1953: 74–92). Building on his work, one notes many places where the prophetic word is noted as fulfilled; for instance, see the table below.

Prophetic Word	Fulfilment
1 Sam. 2:30–36	1 Kgs 2:27 (Eli's priestly house supplanted)
2 Sam. 7:13	1 Kgs 8:20 (Solomon builds temple)
1 Kgs 11:29–39	1 Kgs 12:15b (secession of kingdom to Jeroboam)
1 Kgs 13:3	1 Kgs 13:5 (altar split apart)
1 Kgs 14:6–16	1 Kgs 15:29 (Jeroboam's house destroyed)
1 Kgs 16:1–7	1 Kgs 16:12 (Baasha's house destroyed)
Josh. 6:26	1 Kgs 16:34 (Jericho rebuilt with loss)
1 Kgs 22:17	1 Kgs 22:35–38 (Ahab killed)
1 Kgs 21:21–26	1 Kgs 21:27–29; 2 Kgs 9 – 10 (Ahab's house destroyed)
2 Kgs 1:6	2 Kgs 1:17 (Ahaziah dies)
2 Kgs 2:21	2 Kgs 2:22 (Water healed)
2 Kgs 4:16	2 Kgs 4:17 (Shunammite births a son)
2 Kgs 10:30	2 Kgs 15:12 (Jehu's dynasty to fourth generation)
1 Kgs 13:2	2 Kgs 23:16 (Josiah defiles Bethel altar)
2 Kgs 21:10–15	2 Kgs 24:2 (Judah destroyed by raiders)

Additionally, there are many places where a prophetic pronouncement is fulfilled without any specific notice of fulfilment – it is left to the reader to correlate the two events (e.g. the word of rain [1 Kgs 17:1; 18:1] comes without a specific fulfilment notice).

The fulfilment of prophetic words communicates the sovereign power of YHWH. He is able to fulfil what he proclaims. This suggests that he knows the ends to which history runs: he is no pawn in history's course – he is its author (as explored further below).

It is this power of YHWH's word that is the sole mark of his prophets: they are called to speak his word ('Thus says YHWH') and it is its fulfilment that proves their calling. Thus, before Elijah embarks on the great covenant challenge (1 Kgs 18), his prophetic mantle is proven. And it is proven by events transpiring according to his word (1 Kgs 17; see 'Comment'). One need not question the ability of Elijah to fulfil his prophetic role as covenant mediator in 1 Kgs 18: his prophetic credentials have already been revealed and affirmed.

The power of YHWH to fulfil his word is not limited to Kings. As noted above, it finds expression in the first verses of Genesis and this same power is attested throughout the OT. Isaiah rightly declares that it goes forth from YHWH's mouth and does not return empty but accomplishes YHWH's desires and purposes (Isa. 55:10–11).

YHWH's faithfulness to his word and his power to effect it are given final expression in Jesus Christ. Against the backdrop of YHWH's powerful word in the OT, John's appellation of Jesus as 'The Word' (John 1:1) is apt. As the full expression of the glory of God (John 1:14), Jesus' life and ministry is the true 'Thus says YHWH'; as YHWH, he is YHWH's word. He effects that completely (John 5:19–30), both in its judgment upon sin and in its grace to his creatures.

In the life of the individual believer, as in the life of the church, the prophecy–fulfilment schema of the monarchic era – now expressed in Christ the King – brings a comfort and certainty within the uncertainties of individual and corporate life. The church has been brought into Christ: that is certain. It lives in Christ: that is granted by the Spirit. And it looks towards the yet-future fulfilment of the word of Christ's return. These are certain because they are YHWH's word – made true in The Word. And, as the monarchic history also shows, the Word's fulfilment is safeguarded by YHWH's power. The church's walk – faithful or unfaithful – cannot set these certainties aside.

7.4. The sovereignty of YHWH over history

Much that has already been said of the theological themes in 1 – 2 Kings shows those themes intricately connected to the theme of YHWH's sovereign rule over history. This theme is apparent in Kings in several ways. First, the obvious fact must be noted that YHWH works in the realm of human history. He calls the nation of Israel, gifts them with covenant law, establishes them in a land in which they are ruled over by monarchs. All this happens in the material, embodied world of time and space. There is no supramundane world in which YHWH works in Kings. It is confined within the bounds of human history. In this world of history his great purposes under the Abrahamic, Mosaic and Davidic Covenants are fulfilled.

However, while it is one thing to say that YHWH's plans are worked out in the realm of history, it is another to say that he works in sovereign power over that history. He does so by shaping that history to his will while all the time allowing Israel to think, respond and act as they will.

One area in which this is evident in Kings is in the existence of the monarchy. As noted above (7.2) Israel's request for a king was a sinful rejection of YHWH's kingship. But in granting this request YHWH does not subvert his will. Rather, the institution of monarchy has already been determined as part of that will. Thus in the canonical presentation the law of the king (Deut. 17:14–20) precedes and anticipates the request itself. And when the request is made (1 Sam. 8), YHWH acknowledges the sinfulness of it, but insists that Samuel grant what the people ask. There is full knowledge on YHWH's part of the people's future under the monarchy, but also how that future furthers YHWH's purposes.

It is also apparent that YHWH rules over history in the matter of succession. First, that the Davidic line continues virtually uninterrupted (the exception is the coup of Athaliah; 2 Kgs 11) stands in distinct contrast to the multiple dynasties of the north. The Davidic Covenant anticipates continued Davidic rule, and thus it happens; only at the word of YHWH is the Davidic rule interrupted (first by secession; 1 Kgs 11 – 12; and secondly by exile; 2 Kgs 25). In the north, dynastic change is frequently at the behest of YHWH's word (1 Kgs 14, 16, 21; 2 Kgs 9) and subsequent events occur in the mundane realm of history to fulfil what YHWH has already spoken. A similar power is also exercised over foreign rule. In 2 Kgs 8 (cf. 1 Kgs 19:15) the prophetic word proclaims a change of dynasty in Aram, and subsequent human actions bring that word's fulfilment.

YHWH's rule over history is particularly apparent as the nations interact with Israel. As in the book of Judges, it is the nations that serve YHWH's purpose of disciplining wayward Judah and Israel. Egypt (1 Kgs 14:25), Aram (1 Kgs 20, 22; 2 Kgs 9, 13), Moab (2 Kgs 3), Assyria (2 Kgs 15 – 20) and Babylon (2 Kgs 20 – 25) all serve this purpose. That these nations act in response to YHWH's sovereign control is the focus of Isaiah's oracle to Hezekiah (2 Kgs 19:25–34). Assyria's action against Judah was ordained from the 'days of old' and was planned by YHWH (vv. 25–26); it was by YHWH's will that Assyria gained power and used that power against YHWH's people. However, while Assyria's action against Jerusalem was planned by YHWH, the nation has freedom in how it comports itself within that plan. They are able to overstep the power granted them and bring undue action against Jerusalem (vv. 22–24, 27–28). Yet even here YHWH exercises control and chastises Assyria (vv. 28, 32–37).

The nations are not only part of YHWH's disciplinary action against his people; they also work for the benefit of YHWH's people. Thus Hiram of Tyre stands ready and equipped at the precise time of Solomon's temple's construction. A previous treaty with David paves the way for continued and beneficiary negotiations for workers and materials. And in the midst of these preparations it is Hiram who acknowledges YHWH's hand in the events of history: YHWH has brought the wise Solomon to the throne (1 Kgs 5).

Finally, YHWH's power over history is particularly evident in the ministries of his prophets in 1 – 2 Kings (see 7.3 above). He repeatedly fulfils the prophetic word in many areas: judgment (1 Kgs 11, 21), dynastic change (1 Kgs 14, 16, 21), the role of foreign nations vis-à-vis Israel (2 Kgs 19), victory or defeat in battle (1 Kgs 20, 22; 2 Kgs 18 – 19).

Even the prophets themselves are commissioned by YHWH to effect change in history. In 1 Kgs 19:15–18 Elijah is commissioned to three tasks: he is to anoint Hazael king of Aram, Jehu king of Israel, and Elisha as the prophet's successor. As the history unfolds, each of these events transpires (see 2 Kgs 8 – 10; 1 Kgs 19) – but not all at the hand of Elijah. He effects only the anointing of Elisha; Elisha anoints Hazael, and an unnamed disciple of Elisha anoints Jehu. Thus, while a prophet can proclaim

YHWH's will and be commissioned to accomplish it, that will is not dependent on any one prophet to fulfil it. Its execution is at the hand of YHWH, who moves people and events to his desired ends.

For the church, no less than ancient Israel, there is a great sense of surety in YHWH's sovereign will enacted in history. Having created the cosmos and his people, he does not abandon them to the vicissitudes of chance. Nor (even more comforting) does he abandon his people – or his church – to their own devices, plans and purposes. There is a wise, good and loving God who directs the sweep of history. Equally reassuring, that history is directed to a known end. We are not bound endlessly to repeat the failures of history: there is coming an end in which the plans and purposes of God will be wrapped up. Because of YHWH's sovereign control of history, there is coming a time in which all will be well and very well.

Of course, this does not leave the church free to abandon the world. It is called to discern the movement of God in history and to work for the good of all peoples in that history. If YHWH's plan concludes with the end of sin, death, poverty, oppression and inequity, then the church's true vocation is to proclaim and act out those realities as part of its identity in Christ.

YHWH's sovereignty over history is equally pertinent as the church stands at a time of great paradigm shift. Its common bonds are often under threat. It struggles to speak with credibility to a society that has little use for organized religion. Theological education (both in the academy and the parish) is being forcefully reshaped – when it is counted needful at all – by forces (financial, demographic and technological) beyond its control. If ever there was a time for the church to be reminded that YHWH knows the way through these realities to a perceived (and good) future, it is now.

He is a God who acts in the arena of history. In it he is sovereign. Thanks be to God.

7.5. The twin realities of judgment and grace

The book of Deuteronomy undergirds the theology in 1 – 2 Kings. The deuteronomic covenant makes very clear the judgment that will come upon covenant disobedience (Deut. 28:15–68). Included are varied judgments that affect areas such as crops, livestock, health and military endeavours – all treaty curses common in the ANE milieu. These judgments climax in the dispossession and foreign exile.

Immediately as Solomon's rule begins there are clues that, great though it is, it is not perfect. From his succession through to his death there is both wisdom and covenant failure (as explored in the commentary on Solomon's reign in 1 Kgs 1 – 11). The secession of the northern kingdom is immediately followed by the institution of Jeroboam's false cult, and in his footsteps all subsequent northern kings follow. To the sins of Jeroboam

are added the sins of Ahab (1 Kgs 16:29–33) and these dual threats call
forth the ministries of both Elijah and Elisha. No northern king is free of
covenant violations.

The south fares marginally better. The presence of the temple and the
stabilizing influence of the Davidic dynasty appear to forestall, but not to
prevent, the encroachment of cultic violations. All kings are guilty of
letting the high places continue; only Hezekiah and Josiah are credited
with their removal (2 Kgs 18:4; 23:8, 13, 15, 19). Judah does not worship
YHWH by strict Deuteronomistic norms, and in the reign of Manasseh
(2 Kgs 21) Judah's sins become as heinous as those of Israel and the nations
(2 Kgs 21:2–3).

In the light of the plethora of covenant violations it is not surprising
that both Judah and Israel are summoned to covenant faithfulness, and
with that, either implicitly or explicitly, warned of coming judgment.
Solomon's reign begins with David's charge that he carefully adhere to
the covenant (1 Kgs 2:2–4). YHWH also warns of the consequences of
covenant violations (1 Kgs 6:11–13; 9:2–9; 11) and Solomon is judged when
these violations turn his heart (1 Kgs 11:9–13). Much later in the Davidic
line judgment is pronounced upon Judah (2 Kgs 21:10–15). In the northern
kingdom judgment comes rapidly on the heels of Jeroboam's sins (1 Kgs
14:7–16) and finds full expression in 2 Kgs 17.

Two observations are pertinent in the light of the extensive and specific
words of judgment against northern and southern kings. First, YHWH's
concern for his people's adherence to covenant norms is for the maintenance of covenant relationship. He is jealous over that relationship (Deut.
6:13–15), warning against other gods who will lead Israel astray from him.
He desires that his people walk in the way of the covenant, choosing
YHWH as their God, and returning his merciful love with all their hearts,
souls, minds and strength (Deut. 6:4–5). In this way the bounty and
goodness of covenant life in the land is open to them.

Secondly, God's grace remains despite persistent covenant disregard. The
covenant offences committed early in the monarchy are such that YHWH
could have brought exile upon them immediately. Instead, YHWH extends
patience and grace to his wayward people. Foreign nations are sent to
discipline his people. Drought, siege and famine are likewise utilized as
covenant warnings, urging Israel back to the goodness of covenant commitment. YHWH sends prophets, particularly in Israel's dark hours under
the Omrides (1 Kgs 17 – 2 Kgs 9), whose purpose is to show YHWH as the
true Lord of life. YHWH does not remove his presence from the temple,
nor fail to listen to his people's prayers. Instead, he remains a covenant
presence in their midst, and only when his mercy is exhausted by the
people's persistent rejection does he turn his face from them (2 Kgs 23:27).

Throughout the book of Kings, then, is the dual reality: YHWH's
judgment against covenant sinfulness, and YHWH's grace that forestalls judgment as long as possible. There is always the hope that the

extension of grace will lead to the people's repentance – indeed, it does happen in response to Elijah's ministry, if only temporarily (1 Kgs 18:39). YHWH is a God 'compassionate and gracious, slow to anger and over-flowing in love and faithfulness, extending love to thousands and forgiving wickedness, rebellion and sin'. But he is also a God 'who does not leave the guilty unpunished' (Exod. 34:6–7). These two realities are traced through all of 1 – 2 Kings, and, even in the judgment of exile, the hope is that Israel might yet repent and return to their faithful covenant partner (Deut. 30:1–10). It is, then, YHWH's grace that is the last word, offering the promise of repentance and return, even from exile.

The NT church is no stranger to the loving discipline of God. Discipline is an exercise of judgment, for it marks off those areas of life that must change so that the believer may walk fully in New Covenant life. Such judgment may even be severe for those who resist or turn from God. There is great grace in the exercise of this discipline. It anticipates our cooperation, is aware of our weakness and believes the work of the Spirit to perfect the image of Christ within us. All of this is for the church, as for Israel, a work of God's love towards us, for God 'disciplines all that he loves, chastening all he accepts as his children' (Heb. 12:6). By it he transforms the church's members from glory to glory into the image of their King.

7.6. Kingship as a tutor that leads to Christ

At several points in this introduction (3.4, 3.5, 7.1) the normative influence of the deuteronomic code is noted as a means by which northern and southern kings are evaluated. By these criteria, only Hezekiah and Josiah are fully approved kings. Yet even Hezekiah does not receive full commendation when he foolishly welcomes Babylon (2 Kgs 20:16–18).

For an exilic audience the history explains the exile. Part of that explanation is the kings' consistent covenant failure. By their example the people are likewise led astray, and both king and people face judgment. In the consistent failure of the kings there is an additional theological theme when 1 – 2 Kings is considered from the perspective of the NT. This can be illustrated in a brief look at the reign of three prominent kings: Solomon, Jeroboam and Josiah.

Solomon's rule is glorious in many ways. Wisdom and fame attend him as YHWH's gifts (1 Kgs 3). Both his wisdom and wealth are evident in the temple project and it rightly serves as the pinnacle of his monarchy. Yet for all the glories of the temple, and for all his wisdom, his rule is continually shadowed. He is a wise and great king, but even as he assumes the throne his heart turns from fully honouring the covenant. By marrying Pharaoh's daughter, by setting the people to hard labour, by numerous cult infractions, he shows his wisdom does not extend far enough. His heart is ultimately untouched, and it turns from YHWH. A king in which so much hope is placed, and by whom much is accomplished, fails. Will any king come who can be fully wise, fully great, and whose heart fully follows after YHWH?

Jeroboam is raised to the throne by the word of YHWH. He is promised an enduring kingdom as was granted David. The only requirement to receive this enduring dynasty is covenant obedience. When he gains his throne, however, he seems to forget that it is guaranteed by YHWH and he himself attempts to secure it. He quickly turns from the covenant in pursuit of this goal and institutes an alternative cult. This cult not only negates the possibility of an enduring dynasty, but because of it he and all successive Israelite kings are judged. It is the sins of Jeroboam that lead the north astray. Will any king come who, when given great promises, believes YHWH's word and walks according to covenant? Will he trust YHWH's promise and walk in obedience?

Josiah is the one king who is wholly approved by the Deuteronomistic standard. Loving YHWH with all his heart, soul, mind and strength he reforms the cult. But even though he returns worship to pure forms, his righteousness is not enough to forestall the judgment proclaimed under Manasseh's reign. Will any king come whose righteousness is enough to forestall or divert judgment from YHWH's people?

Sadly, within 1 – 2 Kings the answer to each of these questions is 'no'. No king comes whose heart is fully true to YHWH's ways, trusts that attention to YHWH's covenant enables his promises, or whose righteousness removes judgment. One reads 1 – 2 Kings with an increasing sense of the futility of human kingship. By its end, kingly failure has whetted the appetite for at least one king who could meet such criteria.

The NT proclamation is that such a king has come. In Jesus, YHWH the divine king is incarnated. He alone of the Davidic line has a heart that loves YHWH completely and without change. He follows the deuteronomic norms, and it is indeed the book of Deuteronomy he quotes when Satan tempts him to serve another god (Matt. 4:4, 7, 10). He is also the king who trusts that by his obedience God's promises will be fully realized and his kingdom secured (Matt. 26:39, 42–44). And he is the only king whose righteousness averts judgment – not because YHWH once again forestalls it to a later date, but because it is poured out in full upon the Righteous One.

The apostle Paul talks of the OT law as a guide or guardian that leads to Christ (Gal. 2:23–25), a tutor by whom we are trained to long for and recognize the fullness of truth revealed in Christ. The book of 1 – 2 Kings is such a tutor. It shows the failure of human kingship. It creates a longing and hope that there might be one king whose heart is right and turned in loving obedience to YHWH. When Jesus comes as God, the divine king, he is that longed-for king. In him is the king of God's own choosing. He fulfils his office with heart, soul, mind and strength, even unto death.

8. THE APPROACH OF THIS COMMENTARY

Like the other volumes within the Apollos series, this commentary engages the text of 1 – 2 Kings through specific investigative lenses. For the most part, one chapter of biblical text is treated in each commentary chapter. Where a narrative clearly crosses chapter boundaries, the commentary treats this larger portion of Scripture in one commentary unit. For instance, the accession of Solomon in 1 Kgs 1 – 2 is joined in one commentary chapter, and the rule of Zedekiah in 2 Kgs 24:18 – 25:7 is joined as one unit in the commentary discussion.

Each commentary chapter first provides a fresh translation of the biblical text, and a brief selection of philological and text-critical notes. For those conversant with the biblical languages, these notes provide direction to translational decisions made by the author and provide sources for further study.

A following section considers elements of form and structure. Included in this section might be a discussion of source, form or redaction-critical issues. As often the scholarly community draws disparate conclusions from such study, and because this commentary takes the final form of the text as its locus of study, such comments are brief and direct the interested reader to further resources in the discussion. Closer attention to structure, motifs and narrative themes is included in this section and arises from a commitment to consider the canonical text now before us.

The comments proper work through the text in detail in a paragraph-by-paragraph rather than a verse-by-verse approach. The purpose of the comments is to hold before the reader issues of narrative concern, and historical and lexical import. Canonical considerations are also an important part of this section, as texts and verses that illuminate the passage are engaged.

Finally, an explanation examines the meaning of the chapter in the context of biblical theology. Explanations might trace a prominent theme through the OT and, as this commentary understands biblical theology to encompass both Old and New Testaments, often the explanation extends to touch points in the NT and the life of the church.

TEXT AND COMMENTARY

1 KINGS 1:1 – 2:46

Translation

[1:1]Now King David was old, advanced in years, and though they covered him with blankets he could not keep warm[a]. [2]So his servants said to him, 'Let them seek for my lord[a] the king a young virgin woman and let her serve the king and be his attendant. She will lie in your bosom to warm my lord[a] the king.' [3]So they sought for a beautiful young woman throughout all the territory of Israel and found Abishag the Shunammite and brought her to the king. [4]The young woman was very beautiful. She became the king's attendant and served him, but the king did not have sex with her.

[5]Adonijah[a] son of Haggith exalted himself, saying, 'I will be king!' He prepared chariots[b] for himself, and horsemen, and fifty men who ran before him. [6](His father had never challenged him, saying, 'Why do you act this way?' He was also very good looking, and she had borne[a] him after Absalom.) [7]He conferred with Joab son of Zeruiah and with Abiathar the priest, and they supported Adonijah. [8]But Zadok the priest, and Benaiah son of Jehoiada, and Nathan the prophet and Shimei and Rei[a] and David's own guard were not for Adonijah. [9]Then Adonijah sacrificed sheep, oxen and fattened cattle by the Stone of Zoheleth, which is near En-rogel. He invited all his brothers, the king's sons, and all the men of Judah who[a] were the king's servants. [10]But he did not invite Nathan the prophet or Benaiah or the guard or his brother Solomon.

¹¹Then Nathan said to Bathsheba, Solomon's mother, 'Haven't you heard that Adonijah Haggith's son has become king – but our lord David doesn't know? ¹²Soᵃ come, let me advise you so that you may save your life and the life of your son Solomon. ¹³You must go in to King David and say to him, "Haven't you sworn, my lord the king, to your maidservant, saying, 'Your son Solomon will be king after me and he will sit upon my throne?' Why then is Adonijah king?" ¹⁴While you are there speaking with the king, I will come in after you and confirm your words.'

¹⁵So Bathsheba went to the king in the inner chamber (the king was very old; Abishag the Shunammite was serving the king). ¹⁶Bathsheba bowed and did obeisance to the king. The king said, 'What do you want?ᵃ' ¹⁷She answeredᵃ, 'My lord, you have sworn by YHWH your God to your maidservant, saying, "Solomon your son will be king after me, and he will sit upon my throne." ¹⁸And now Adonijah has become king, yet you, my lord the kingᵃ, are unaware of it! ¹⁹He has sacrificed many oxen, fattened cattle and sheep, and invited all the king's sons, Abiathar the priest and Joab the commander of the army. But your servant Solomon he has not invited. ²⁰And you, my lord the king: the eyes of all Israel are upon you to declare to them who shall sit upon the throne of my lord the king after him. ²¹Otherwise, when my lord the king dies, I will be – I and my son Solomon – considered offenders!'

²²While she was speaking with the king, Nathan the prophet arrived. ²³They announced to the king, 'Nathan the prophet!' When he came before the king, he did obeisance to the king with his face to the ground. ²⁴Nathan said, 'My lord the king, have you said, "Adonijah will be king after me and he will sit upon my throne?" ²⁵For he has gone down today and sacrificed many oxen, fattened cattle and sheep. He has invited all the king's sons, the leaders of the armyᵃ and Abiathar the priest. They are eating and drinking before him and are saying, "Long live King Adonijah!" ²⁶But me – even me your servant, Zadok the priest, Benaiah son of Jehoiada, and your servant Solomon he has not invited. ²⁷Was this done by my lord the king, but you have not advised your servantᵃ who will sit upon the throne of my lord the king after him?ᵇ'

²⁸Then King David answered and he said, 'Summon Bathsheba to me!' She came into the king's presence and stood before the king. ²⁹Then the king swore, 'As YHWH lives, who has redeemed my life from all distress, ³⁰surely as I swore to you by YHWH the God of Israel, saying, "Solomon your son will be king after me; he will sit upon my throne in my place." Thus I will do this day.' ³¹Bathsheba bowed her face to the ground and did obeisance to the king. She said, 'May my lord King David live for ever!' ³²Then King David said, 'Summon to me Zadok the priest, Nathan the prophet and Benaiah the son of Jehoiada.' They came before the king. ³³The king said to them, 'Take your lords' servants with you and have my son Solomon ride on my mule, and bring him down to Gihon. ³⁴Zadok the priest, with Nathan the prophet, shall anointᵃ him there as king over Israel. You shall blow the shofar and say, "Long live King Solomon!" ³⁵Then you shall come up after him and he shall enter and sit upon my throne and he shall rule in my place, for him I have appointed to be ruler over Israel and Judah.' ³⁶Benaiah the son of Jehoiada answered the king, 'Amen! Thus may YHWH the God of my lord the king declare! ³⁷Just as

YHWH was with my lord the king, thus may he be[a] with Solomon and make his throne greater than the throne of my lord, King David.'

[38]So Zadok the priest went down, with Nathan the prophet, Benaiah the son of Jehoiada, and the Cherethites and Pelethites, and they set Solomon upon King David's mule and brought him to Gihon. [39]Zadok the priest took the horn of oil from the tent and anointed Solomon. They blew the shofar and all the people said, 'Long live King Solomon!' [40]All the people went up after him [a]playing flutes and greatly rejoicing so that the earth was split with their noise.

[41]Now Adonijah, along with all his guests, heard this as they finished eating. When Joab heard the noise of the shofar he said, 'Why is the city in an uproar?' [42]While he was speaking, Jonathan the son of Abiathar the priest entered. Adonijah said, 'Come in, for a worthy man like you brings good news!' [43]Jonathan answered Adonijah, 'No; our lord King David has made Solomon king! [44]The king has sent with him Zadok the priest, Nathan the prophet, Benaiah son of Jehoiada, and the Cherethites and Pelethites. They have made him ride upon the king's mule, [45]and Zadok the priest and Nathan the prophet have anointed him as king at Gihon. Now they have gone up from there rejoicing and the city is in an uproar – that is the noise that you have heard. [46a]Even now Solomon sits upon the throne of the kingdom. [47]Moreover, the king's servants have come to bless our lord King David, saying, "May God[a] make the name of Solomon better than your name, and may his throne be greater than your throne." And the king has bowed himself upon the bed; [48]moreover, the king has said, "Blessed be YHWH the God of Israel who has today appointed one to sit upon my throne while my eyes see it."' [49]Then all the guests of Adonijah were terrified and arose and went, each his own way. [50]But Adonijah was afraid of Solomon and arose and went and seized the horns of the altar.

[51]It was reported to Solomon, 'Adonijah is afraid of King Solomon and has taken hold of the horns of the altar, saying, "Let King Solomon swear to me today that he will not kill his servant with the sword."' [52]Solomon answered, 'If he will act worthily, not one of his hairs will fall to the ground. But if wickedness is found in him, then he will die.' [53]Then King Solomon sent and they brought him down from the altar. He came and did obeisance to King Solomon. And Solomon said to him, 'Go to your house.'

[2:1]When David's death drew near, he charged Solomon his son, [2]'I am going the way of all the earth, so be strong and act a man. [3]Keep the charge of YHWH your God, to walk in his ways, keep his statutes, his commandments, his judgments and his testimonies as written in the torah of Moses so that you will have success in all that you do and wherever you go[a]. [4]Then YHWH will effect his word that he spoke concerning me, saying, "If your sons guard their way to walk before me in truth with all their heart and with all their soul, then you shall not lack a man upon the throne of Israel."

[5]'Moreover, you know what Joab the son of Zeruiah did to me – what he did to the two leaders of the armies of Israel, to Abner the son of Ner, and to Amasa son of Jether. He killed them and imposed the blood of war in a time of peace, and put the blood of war on my belt[a] that was about my loins[a], and on my shoes[a]

that were on my feet[a]. [6]Now act according to your wisdom and do not let his grey head go down to Sheol in peace.

[7]'But to the sons of Barzillai the Gileadite show kindness; let them be with those who eat at your table, for thus they assisted me when I fled from your brother Absalom.

[8]'And behold! Shimei the son of Gera the Benjaminite from Bahurim is with you. He cursed me with a terrible curse on the day I went to Mahanaim. He came down to meet me at the Jordan and I swore to him by YHWH, saying, "I will not put you to death with the sword." [9]But now do not leave him unpunished, for you are a wise man and you know what you should do to him: bring down his grey head in blood to Sheol.'

[10]Then David slept with his fathers and he was buried in the city of David. [11]The time that David ruled over Israel was forty years; in Hebron he ruled seven years, and in Jerusalem he ruled thirty-three years. [12]So Solomon sat upon the throne of David his father and his dominion was firmly established.

[13]Then Adonijah son of Haggith came to Bathsheba, Solomon's mother. She said, 'Do you come peacefully?', and he said, 'Peacefully.' [14]He said, 'May I have a word with you?' And she said, 'Speak!' [15]He said, 'You know that the kingdom was mine, and that all Israel expected me to rule. But the kingdom has turned and become my brother's – for it was his from YHWH. [16]Now, I request one thing from you[a]; do not refuse me!' And she said to him, 'Speak!' [17]So he said, 'Please speak to Solomon the king (for he will not refuse you) that he would give to me Abishag the Shunammite for a wife. [18]Then Bathsheba said, 'All right; I will speak on your behalf to the king.'

[19]So Bathsheba went to King Solomon to speak to him on behalf of Adonijah. The king rose to greet her and did obeisance to her. Then he sat upon his throne and set a throne for the king's mother and she sat at his right hand. [20]She said, 'I request one small thing from you; do not refuse me.' The king said to her, 'Ask, my mother, for I will not refuse you.' [21]She said, 'Let Abishag the Shunammite be given to Adonijah your brother as a wife.' [22]But King Solomon answered and said to his mother, 'Why do you request Abishag the Shunammite for Adonijah? Ask for him the kingdom, for he is my older brother – even for him, and for Abiathar the priest and for Joab son of Zeruiah!' [23]Then King Solomon swore by YHWH, saying, 'Thus may God do to me, and even more, for against his life Adonijah has spoken this word! [24]Now, as YHWH lives who established me and placed me upon the throne of David my father, and who has made a house for me just as he promised, today Adonijah will be put to death.' [25]Then King Solomon sent by the hand of Benaiah son of Jehoiada, and he fell upon him and he died.

[26]To Abiathar the priest the king said, 'Go to Anathoth! – to your fields[a] – for you are a dead man. I will not kill you today for you carried the ark of the Lord YHWH before David my father, and you were afflicted in everything in which my father was afflicted.' [27]So Solomon removed Abiathar as priest to YHWH in order to fulfil the word of YHWH that he had spoken concerning the house of Eli in Shiloh.

[28]When the news reached Joab (now Joab had supported Adonijah, but had not supported Absalom[a]), Joab fled to the tent of YHWH and seized the horns of the

altar. [29]It was reported to King Solomon that Joab had fled to the tent of YHWH and was beside the altar. Solomon sent Benaiah son of Jehoiada, saying, 'Go! Fall upon him!' [30]When Benaiah came to the tent of YHWH, he said to him, 'Thus says the king, "Come out!"' He said, 'No; for here I will die.' Benaiah brought the king word, saying, 'Thus Joab spoke, and thus he answered me.' [31]Then the king said to him, 'Do just as he said; fall upon him and bury him. So you shall remove from me and my father's house the undeserved blood that Joab shed. [32]For YHWH has brought back his blood upon his head because he fell upon two men more righteous and better than himself. He killed them with the sword, and my father David did not know: Abner son of Ner, the commander of the army of Israel, and Amasa son of Jether, the commander of the army of Judah. [33]So may their blood come back upon the head of Joab and the head of his seed for ever. But to David and to his seed, and his house, and his throne, may there be peace from YHWH for ever.' [34]So Benaiah son of Jehoiada went up and fell upon him and killed him and he was buried at his house in the wilderness. [35a]Then the king appointed Benaiah son of Jehoiada over the army in his place, and Zadok the priest the king appointed in place of Abiathar.

[36]Then the king sent and summoned Shimei and said to him, 'Build for yourself a house in Jerusalem, and dwell there. You shall not go out anywhere from there. [37]In the day that you go out and cross the Kidron River, know without doubt that you will surely die. Your blood will be on your own head.' [38]Shimei replied to the king, 'The decision is fair. Just as my lord the king has spoken, thus will your servant do.' So Shimei dwelt in Jerusalem many days. [39]After three years, two of Shimei's servants fled to Achish son of Maacah, king of Gath. It was told Shimei, 'Your servants are in Gath.' [40]So Shimei arose and saddled his donkey and went to Gath to Achish to search for his servants. Thus Shimei went and brought his servants from Gath.

[41]It was reported to Solomon that Shimei had gone from Jerusalem to Gath and had returned. [42]Solomon sent and summoned Shimei and said to him, 'Did I not have you swear by YHWH? I solemnly warned you, saying, "On the day you go out and go anywhere, know without doubt that you will surely die." And you said to me, "The decision is fair; I will obey." [43]Why then have you not kept the oath to YHWH, and the commandment that I commanded you?' [44]The king said to Shimei, 'You know – that is, your heart knows – all the evil that you did to my father. May YHWH return your evil on your head. [45]But King Solomon shall be blessed, and the throne of David established before YHWH for ever.' [46a]And the king commanded Benaiah son of Jehoiada, and he went out and fell upon him and he died. Thus the kingdom was established by the hand of Solomon.

Notes on the text

1:1.a. 'keep warm': qal from the root *ḥmm*, 'be or become warm' (BDB 328). A possible alternative root, *yḥm*, suggests sexual activity, although there is no clear evidence of this root in qal.

2.a. LXX[B], Vg have 'our lord' (twice), matching the pronoun to the plural noun 'servants'.

5.a. *'ădōnîyāh* in 1:5, 7, 18; 2:28; *ădōnîyāhû* elsewhere in the chapters.

5.b. *rekeb* here as a collective; commonly paired with pl. *pārāšîm* (WO'C 282, n. 22).

6.a. *yālĕdāh*, 'she had borne', is qal pf. 3 f. sg. and refers back to Haggith (v. 5; so Devries 2003: 2). Gray (1970: 78, n. g) argues that 'his mother' (*'immô*) has dropped out after the verb and so reads 'his mother [i.e. Bathsheba] bore him'. MT emphasizes which child is eldest.

8.a. *wĕrē'î*, 'and Rei', is a proper name. LXX[L] reads, *wĕšim'î wĕrē'ayw*, 'Shimei and his friends'.

9.a. Some Syr MSS have a waw cop., 'all the men of Judah and the servants of the king', identifying an additional group of invitees. MT reads as an explanatory apposition, limiting the guest list due to needs of secrecy.

12.a. *wĕ'attāh*, 'so', signals action that should follow previous information. Nathan considers his advice to Bathsheba a necessary response to Adonijah's actions.

16.a. *mah-lāk*, literally, 'what to/for thee?' (see BDB 552 and examples at Gen. 21:17; Josh. 15:18; 2 Sam. 14:5; 2 Kgs 6:28).

17.a. *lô* is left untranslated, as the context makes it extraneous.

18.a. Reading with multiple versions (LXX, Tg, Syr) for contrastive emphasis, *wĕ'attâ 'ădōnî hammelek*, 'yet *you*, my lord, the king', rather than MT *wĕ'attâ 'ădōnî hammelek*, 'and *now*, my lord, the king'. MT has the same contrast in v. 20.

25.a. LXX[L] reads *ûlĕ šar yō'āb* , 'and General Joab', for MT 'the leaders of the army' (*ûlĕśārê haṣṣābā'*). The MT implies the inclusion of Joab.

27.a. Reading with Q, 'your servant', for MT 'your servants'. Nathan positions himself as primary advisor.

27.b. A simple question introduced by *'im* rather than *hă* in cases where what is really a double question suppresses the 'first member of [that] double question' (GKC §150f).

34.a. MT has 3 m. sg. *māšaḥ* noting the priest's primary role in anointing to kingship (as v. 39 indicates). LXX[BL] and Syr's 3 m. pl. include Nathan, perhaps consulting v. 45.

37.a. MT K expresses Benaiah's wish with the jussive 'may he be'; Q ensures YHWH's participation with the indicative, 'he will be'.

40.a. The second *hā'ām* untranslated as extraneous.

46.a. Each of vv. 46–48 begins with the adv. *wĕgam*. Hardly indicative of successive redactional work (contra Jones 1984a: 51, 104), it narratively confirms the enactment and acceptance of David's oath.

47.a. Reading 'God' with Q and with multiple MSS, LXX[L], Vg. K reads, 'your God'.

2:3.a. 'and wherever you go' (*wĕ'ēt kol-'ăšer šām*) reads in LXX* as 'according to all that I have commanded you' (*kĕkol-'ăšer 'aṣawwekā*). The MT reading echoes Josh. 1:7, 'to have success wherever you go' (*taskîl* *běkōl 'ăšer talak*), and likewise deals with success following from obser-vance of the *tôrâ* of Moses.

5.a. MT reads, 'his belt', 'his loins', 'his shoes' and 'his feet'. The 1 com. sg. pr. suff. 'my' (LXX^L, Vg) is read here, so that David makes clear the guilt is upon his house.

16.a. *mě'ittāk* uses the 2 m. sg. suff. to address Bathsheba. The usage is not infrequent (GKC §135o).

26.a. *'al* read as *'el*, and *śādêkā* is the older, sg. form (GKC §93ss), yet translated here for sense as 'fields'.

28.a. The parenthetical statement of Joab's allegiances in LXX^{-BO} reads Adonijah and Solomon. The more difficult MT is retained.

35.a. LXX adds after this verse verses 35a–o, summarizing Solomon's wisdom, marriage to Pharaoh's daughter, building projects, temple offerings, officials, and concludes with substantially the content of 1 Kgs 2:8–9.

46.a. Following the report of Shimei's execution, LXX includes twelve extra verses, indicated as vv. 46a–l, a summary of the extent, peace and wealth of Solomon's kingdom. The final verse (46l) reads differently from MT v. 46b, which it replaces: 'Solomon, David's son, ruled over Israel and Judah in Jerusalem.' A close parallel to MT's 'Thus the kingdom was estab-lished by the hand of Solomon' appears in LXX v. 35 following the note of Benaiah's appointment over the army, and reads, 'thus the kingdom was established in Jerusalem'.

Form and structure

1 Kgs 1 and 2 conclude David's narrative and begin Solomon's. The chapters assume knowledge of 1 – 2 Samuel and simply continue the story. Even King David – presented as a frail and impotent man – is only a reminder of who he *was* in Samuel: a strong, virile king.

1 Kgs 1 is a tight narrative unit structured into two thematic panels (1 Kgs 1:5–27, 28–50) bracketed by a prologue (1:1–4) and epilogue (1:51–53). Each panel has an instigating event or command, with consequent execution or reportage:

Prologue	David's frailty (vv. 1–4)
Panel 1	Event: Adonijah's bid for power (vv. 5–10)
	Reportage A: Nathan to Bathsheba (vv. 11–14)
	Reportage B: Bathsheba to David (vv. 15–21)
	Reportage C: Nathan to David (vv. 22–27)
Panel 2	Command: Acclamation of Solomon (vv. 28–37)
	Execution: Solomon is made king (vv. 38–40)
	Reportage: Jonathan to Adonijah (vv. 41–50)
Epilogue	Solomon's first act as king (vv. 51–53)

Two verbal motifs characterize the panels. The first panel focalizes around knowledge (note the verb 'to know' [*yd'*] in vv. 11, 18, 27, and in v. 4 of sexual knowledge). After Adonijah's bid for the throne, three reports reveal different levels of knowledge of the plan. Throughout, David's knowledge is consistently deficient. In the second panel the motif is of blessing (vv. 31, 36–37, 47–48), and as the panel closes, the two themes are ironically blended. Adonijah is filled with fear when he knows Solomon is blessed (vv. 49–50).

The central issue of the chapter is the succession, and the phrase 'he/who will sit upon the/my throne' is used repeatedly (vv. 13, 17, 20, 24, 27, 30, 35, 46, 48; cf. 1 Kgs 2:19). All Israel wonders 'who shall sit upon the throne . . . after him' (v. 20). More, David is 'King David' (eight times), 'my/our lord the king' (fifteen times), 'the king' (thirty-two times) and 'O king' (once). David's power to determine the succession is proven, as a fourfold reference to 'King Solomon' (vv. 51, 53) concludes the narrative.

1 Kgs 2 takes up Adonijah's fate after the first eleven verses conclude David's reign. Vv. 2b–4 contain Dtr phraseology and nomic concern found in passages such as Josh. 1:6–9, while vv. 5–9 begin with disjunctive *wĕgam* and have no apparent thematic connection to vv. 1–4; indeed, the *wĕgam* could be read as continuing a list of directives from a source different from vv. 2b–4. The text's possible complex prehistory is also suggested by the dual summative statements on Solomon's reign (2:12 and 2:46), particularly as the intervening material makes the first summary seem premature. Further, 2:10–11 could readily be placed following 1:53 or 2:4 with no loss of narrative flow and may be displaced to accommodate inserted materials. Positing variant sources and a lengthy compositional history can explain the narrative disjunctions (see Devries 2003; Noth 1968), but they also work as part of the present coherent and connected narrative, and it is to this final, narrative shape that this discussion now turns.

A frame structure (2:1, 10–12, 46b) focuses on succession – the thematic concern of 1 Kgs 1. The frame structure recalls David's imminent death (1 Kgs 1:1), the dynastic transition from David to Solomon, and anticipates a narrative of the fate of those considered a threat to Solomon's rule. The first frame (2:1, 10–12) encloses David's two charges. The second frame (2:10–12, 46b) encloses Solomon's response to the second of those charges.

2:1	Frame: death of David and charge to Solomon	
	2:2–4	First charge: Deuteronomistic obedience to ensure success
	2:5–9	Second charge: disposition of David's enemies and friends (Joab, Barzillai, Shimei)

2:10–12   Retrospective/prospective frame: death of David and
establishment of Solomon's kingdom

    2:13–35   Disposition of the Adonijah party (Adonijah,
Abiathar, Joab)
    2:36–46a   Disposition of Shimei

2:46b   Narrative frame: the kingdom is established to Solomon

David's second charge gives a negative command against each of Joab
and Shimei. These two commands encircle a positive command concerning
Barzillai. Solomon's actions also move from negative (against Adonijah)
to (relatively) positive (against Abiathar) to negative (against Joab). Once
Joab is executed, Solomon turns to Shimei, the remaining member named
for reprisal on David's list.

Comment

1:1–4

David's age and ANE norms of dynastic succession (Ishida 1977; Thornton
1962–3) make succession the key question of the chapter.
    Abishag is from Shunem, a town in the Jezreel hills in Issachar's
allotment (Josh. 19:18). 'Shunammite' has been at times erroneously identified with the 'Shulammite' (Song 7:1). Even if one assumes Solomon is
the lover in Song, there is no evidence Abishag is his partner, nor does
Song identify Abishag with the Shulammite (Hess 2005: 209, n. 15 for a
summation of possibilities). She is described as a 'young virgin woman'
(*naʿărâ bĕtûlâ*; cf. Deut. 22:23, 28; Judg. 21:12; Esth. 2:2–3). *bĕtûlâ* can
refer to a virgin, or simply to a young woman of marriageable age (Wenham
1972). It is unlikely a king would take a female servant who did not evidence
societal norms of female sexuality (DeVries 2003: 12), and Abishag should
indeed be considered a virgin.
    She 'lies in his bosom' possibly only to warm the king as a 'medical
prescription' (Jones 1984a: 89), or to arouse him sexually (as the term can
imply; see 2 Sam. 12:3; Mic. 7:5). The narrative statement that David did
not have sex with Abishag suggests his present impotency in contrast to
past virility. His frailty shows the need for a succession plan.

1:5–10

Adonijah is David's fourth male child, borne to him in Hebron after
Amnon, Chileab and Absalom (2 Sam. 3:2–5). As the eldest surviving child

(2 Sam. 13:28–29; 2 Sam. 18:14–15), dynastic succession should accord him the throne; and this is Adonijah's conclusion, indicated by his emphatic '*I* will be king!' The ostentatious chariotry, horsemen and heralds mark him as the crown prince, as they marked Absalom (2 Sam.15:1).

The parenthetical comment (v. 6) grounds the son's action in the father's inaction. Additionally his 'very good looks' compare him to Absalom (2 Sam. 14:25), and, to date, each narrative of Israel's kingly contenders has noted a striking physical presence (1 Sam. 10:23–24; 16:12; 2 Sam. 14:25; 1 Kgs 1:6). Finally, mention of his birth order (v. 6) again places him in the anticipated line of succession. Yet the echoes of Absalom (the chariotry, etc.; his good looks) raise the following question: 'Will he suffer Absalom's fate?'

Adonijah gathers key supporters. Joab was David's military leader, appointed after Jerusalem's capture (1 Chr. 11:6). A successful army leader (2 Sam. 10; 12:26–28; 23:8–29; 1 Chr. 11:10–47; 18:15), he is loyal to David (2 Sam. 3:27; 11:14–16; 14:1–22; 2 Sam. 20:9–10), although David publicly disavows and curses Joab (2 Sam. 3:29, 39).

Abiathar is custodian of the ephod by which David enquires of YHWH (1 Sam. 23:6–12; 30:7–8). Possibly early in David's consolidated rule (2 Sam. 8:17), and certainly from the time of Absalom's rebellion, Abiathar and Zadok are priests to David, sharing custody of the ark, working for David during Absalom's rule (2 Sam. 15:24–29, 35–36) and facilitating David's return after the rebellion (2 Sam. 19:11–12).

Solomon's supporters are also drawn from military and religious spheres. This group claims YHWH's support and Zadok the priest is listed first. Nathan the prophet has ministered to David on questions of dynasty (2 Sam. 7) and challenged him regarding Bathsheba (2 Sam. 12 – a narrative that culminates in the birth of Solomon, the one 'loved by YHWH' [Jedidiah; 2 Sam. 12:24–25]).

One of David's mighty men (2 Sam. 23:20–23), Benaiah first appears as the leader of the Cherethites and Pelethites (2 Sam. 8:18; 20:23), foreign mercenaries who are David's own guard (2 Sam. 15:18; 20:7). Benaiah is Solomon's hatchet man in the disposal of Solomon's challengers (1 Kgs 2) and replaces Joab as leader of the army (1 Kgs 2:35).

Rei is a name nowhere else noted, but perhaps known to the original audience. His connection to David is now obscure. Shimei may be the son of Ela (1 Kgs 4:18), but he is most likely the son of Gera who opposed David (2 Sam. 16:5–12) but sued for and received pardon (2 Sam. 19:18–20), a pardon that is subverted when Solomon gains the throne.

The factions may align along personal rivalries among the military, religious or familial groups. Alternatively, two rival cultic groups – an older Nob priesthood represented by Abiathar, and a Jebusite cult represented by Zadok – may vie for power, although the existence of such parties is difficult to prove (Olyan 1982). The real divide may lie between the old guard of David's Hebron years (Joab, Abiathar, Haggith) and a new faction of David's Jerusalem years (Nathan, Zadok, Benaiah), each with divergent ideologies regarding monarchic rule over a united kingdom, and the capital's location (Jones 1984a: 91; Provan 1995: 24–25).

As did Absalom (2 Sam. 15:7–12), Adonijah gives a meal at En-rogel. Just 546 yd (0.5 km) from Gihon and outside the city walls it is a perfect place for clandestine meetings (e.g. in 2 Sam. 17:17). The Stone of Zoheleth translates 'Sliding Stone' or 'Rock Slide', giving a characteristic of its terrain. At the feast Adonijah's supporters would commit publicly to Adonijah, perhaps even by covenant, and both Bathsheba (1 Kgs 1:19) and Nathan (1 Kgs 1:25) recognize the gathering support as a threat to Solomon (K. Roberts 2000: 642; Mettinger 1976). Adonijah includes 'all the men of Judah' (and not Israel), which supports the possibility that Adonijah's faction comprised David's Hebron-based leaders: those whose vision of kingship centred on Judah and excluded Israel.

The invitation list (vv. 9–10) contrasts the two factions, and Solomon as Adonijah's contender is dramatically named last.

Invited:
A   all his brothers the king's sons
    B   all the men of Judah who were the king's servants
Not invited:
    B'   Nathan the prophet, Benaiah the guard
A'   his brother Solomon

1:11–27

Three reports comprise these verses (see 'Form and structure'). Primarily dialogic, the reportage reveals the concerns and characters of Nathan and Bathsheba, but also creates ambiguity around the validity of Solomon's claim and the purported succession oath.

11–14. Nathan asserts Adonijah has already 'become king', hoping to spur Bathsheba to action. He unnecessarily names Adonijah's mother, possibly to fuel (or initiate) a rivalry between the women. The king's mother would be honoured and hold power (perhaps as a *gĕbîrâ*, 'great lady'; so Ishida 1977: 156–158; C. Smith 1998: 144–147; Bowen 2001; see further 'Comment' at 1 Kgs 15:13).

So intertwined are the coup and her fate that Nathan instructs her to save her own life (v. 12). Nathan's speech to Bathsheba follows a chiastic pattern in which the outer shell (vv. 11, 13d) focuses on kingship ('Adonijah has become king'; 'Why then is Adonijah king?') and the inner core focuses on Bathsheba's personal concerns (vv. 12–13); it is the inner core by which he seeks to appeal to her.

The oath he claims is nowhere recorded in 2 Samuel, but may be connected to recognition of the uniqueness of Solomon (2 Sam. 12:24–25).

The oath, of course, may *not* exist; Nathan may hope to incite Bathsheba's compliance in a *coup d'état*, however personally or piously motivated it might be on Nathan's part. That the narrative ambiguity supports either reading is attested to by the varied opinions of commentators. Indeed, 'we are *meant* to wonder . . . [the narrative] raises uncomfortable questions not only about their [Nathan and Bathsheba's] honesty but about the whole process by which Solomon becomes king' (Walsh 1996: 12 [his italics]; cf. Provan 1995: 25–26). One may assume (as does this commentary) that such an oath *did* exist, but the textual ambiguity requires this interpretative decision be held lightly. Certainly, the narrative ambiguity contributes to the text's theological message.

15–21. The king's wife has ready access into the king's private chambers. Bathsheba's submissive posture ('bowed and did obeisance') and address (v. 17, 'my lord'; vv. 18, 20 [twice], 21, 'my lord the king'; v. 17, 'your maidservant'; and v. 19, 'king') are not those limited to royalty; they are commonplace greetings. They do, however, frame her petition in favourable terms.

Bathsheba reverses the chiasm of personal concerns and kingship (see vv. 11–13 above). She begins and ends with personal concerns (the oath made to her, and her threatened life; vv. 17, 21) and places the kingship at the centre of the chiasm (vv. 18–20). She also declares that 'Adonijah has become king', urging David to declare the succession. As Bathsheba was moved to action by personal concerns, she now hopes to move David to action by dynastic concerns.

Bathsheba notes the oath was sworn 'by YHWH your God' (v. 17), cleverly reminding David of the key player in his whole life, who promised to found his dynasty (2 Sam. 7:8–12). Moreover, Bathsheba cleverly re-arranges the recitation of the guest list so that 'all the king's sons' stand in first position. This must astonish David – can *all* his sons be for Adonijah? Do none of them serve David? Then, when of all those not invited, Bathsheba names only 'your servant Solomon', David must be filled with relief: only his son beloved by YHWH and cited by oath stands as David's servant.

Finally, after casting Solomon so favourably, she broaches the succession. She insists that 'all Israel' awaits David's declaration – this, when Adonijah's actions must still be broadly unknown. She warns David of the inevitable outcome to herself and her son should no such declaration be made. They will be considered 'offenders' (*ḥaṭṭā'îm*). If indeed there were no oath, the offence would lie in their collusion for the throne. In the face of an oath, their offence would lie in their person: while Solomon and his mother live, Adonijah's crown is not assured.

22–27. Nathan is announced by his prophetic role. His puzzled query ('have you said . . . was this done') and chiding ('you have not advised your servant') pretend ignorance but Nathan knows the real events. He confirms several of Bathsheba's statements: the oath, the sacrifice and invited guests

– but he, too, adroitly alters the guest list. No mention is made of Joab but only of the 'leaders of the army', thus communicating Adonijah's military support. David must act before this solidifies. By avoiding Joab's name Nathan ensures David's attention is not misdirected to personal revenge against his relative and long-term associate.

Hoping to move David to action, Nathan indicates the acclamation of royal investiture, 'Long live King "X"' (1 Sam. 10:24; 2 Kgs 11:12; 2 Chr. 23:11; cf. 2 Sam. 16:16) has gone up. He reminds David of ongoing loyalty (v. 26), placing himself and Solomon at the beginning and end of the list as 'servants'. Nathan's own loyalty is three times emphasized, 'But *me*, *even me*, *your servant*.' Such support should urge David to act on the question of who will sit upon the throne after him (v. 27).

1:28–37

Nathan's words have their intended effect. To ensure dynastic stability and the nation's future, David swears by 'YHWH the God of Israel' (v. 30). The oath attests to two sworn facts (each introduced by *kî*, v. 30): David will enact a previously sworn oath, and that oath named Solomon his successor. David affirms his commitment to enact the oath 'this day', instituting a co-regency. Solomon is appointed ruler or king-designate (*nāgîd*; v. 35, cf. 1 Sam. 9:16; 10:1; 2 Sam. 7:8), and acclaimed as 'king' (*melek*; vv. 30, 34). Satisfied, Bathsheba politely calls for long life for King David.

David communicates in imperatival verbs (vv. 33–35) that seal the fate of Solomon and Adonijah. He outlines the installation in three steps. First, Solomon must be conducted to sacred Gihon (Ps. 110:7), riding a mule as a sign of royal favour. Secondly, Zadok, together with Nathan (vv. 34, 45), is to perform the cultic rite of anointing to signify YHWH's choice and the king's induction into office (1 Sam. 10:1; 16:1, 12–13; 2 Sam. 12:7; 2 Kgs 9:3; 11:12). Nathan may deliver a prophetic oracle (1 Sam. 9:27 – 10:7; 2 Kgs 9:7–10; cf. Pss 2 and 110, which may contain such an oracle) and Solomon is anointed king over the cultic people ('*am*), Israel. The shofar (trumpet), and acclamation 'Long live King Solomon!' attest to the event (2 Sam. 15:10; 2 Kgs 9:13). Thirdly, Solomon takes the throne as co-regent with David, and sole regent after his death.

Benaiah's 'Amen' ('let it be so') and blessing loyally affirm David's decision and petitions for YHWH's confirmation of David's choice. Beyond the anointing, the confirmation is YHWH's continued presence.

1:38–50

Solomon is strangely passive throughout the two scenes (vv. 38–40; 41–50) that enact David's commands. In this way, the narrative communicates that this installation is the will of YHWH towards Solomon, and (contra Adonijah) not his own grasping after the throne.

David's command is honoured immediately. Zadok's role is primary, as he takes the oil from the sacred tent or tabernacle that housed the ark (2 Sam. 6:17; 1 Kgs 3:15; 8:1–6) and anoints Solomon. Witnessing the ceremony are 'all the people' – surely hyperbolic, for certainly Adonijah's party is not in attendance, nor was there time for an official gathering of peoples from Jerusalem and the country. Once the shofar is blown and the acclamatory cry is given, loud rejoicing metaphorically splits the earth, showing the people recognize YHWH's favour upon Solomon.

A short distance away Adonijah's party hears the jubilant shouts. Their total ignorance of the cause marks the scene as ironic. Adonijah's party began with knowledge of his plan for kingship; now they are ignorant of YHWH's plan. Joab speculates and Adonijah anticipates 'good news'.

Jonathan twice refers to David as 'our lord King David', affirming his loyalty (vv. 43, 46). He has witnessed the succession events and refutes Adonijah's expectation of good news: the succession is complete, congratulations have been given and David has given his blessing. Each is more damning to Adonijah's hopes, and brings new knowledge: the throne is, for now, beyond his grasp.

Given this new knowledge the guests depart with alacrity, leaving Adonijah alone as at the narrative's commencement. He hopes now not for a throne, but for clemency. He signals this by the ancient practice of grasping the horns of the altar (Exod. 21:12–14; Burnside 2010).

1:51–53

Now titled 'King', Solomon answers Adonijah's fears with justice. Conversely, his actions in the next chapter will justify others' fear of him, and raise doubts about his commitment to justice.

Solomon shrewdly commits to pardon Adonijah if he 'acts worthily' – that is, relinquishes any claim to the throne. To challenge the throne is 'wickedness' worthy of death. The *rapprochement* between the brothers is tentative. Adonijah only 'returns to his house' but the threat of future coups remains.

2:1–12

1–4. Near death, David twice charges Solomon. The first resembles that given Joshua (Josh. 1:6–9) and echoes Deuteronomistic phrasing. Solomon is to be 'strong' (Josh. 1:6–7, 9), 'keep the charge of YHWH' (Deut. 11:1), 'walk in his ways' (Josh. 1:7; Deut. 8:6; 10:12) and follow his 'statutes,

commandments and judgments' (Deut. 4:40; 8:11; 26:17; 30:16), as written
in the 'torah of Moses' (Josh. 1:7–8; cf. Deut. 28:61; 29:20; 30:10; 31:26).
The first outcome will be 'success in all that you do' (Deut. 29:8 [ET 9];
cf. Josh. 1:7) and the second that 'YHWH will effect his word' (Deut. 9:4
[ET 5]), that is, the word of dynastic rule for the Davidides. While that
dynasty is confirmed, it is also now conditionalized. Each generation must
do as David has just charged Solomon (2:3); they must 'guard their way'
(2:4) with all their heart and soul (Deut. 4:29; 6:5; 26:16; 30:2, 6). This
conditionalization does not discharge the Davidic covenant, but emphasizes the obligations of its recipients (cf. 6:12–13; 8:25; 9:4, 6–7).

5–9. David's second charge seems at odds with the tenor of the first, for
how can the dispatch of David's enemies comport with torah obedience?

Joab's murder of Abner and Amasa were acts of personal vengeance
performed at crucial points in David's consolidation of the kingdom
(2 Sam. 3:21–39; 20:1–13). For neither murder does David take immediate
punitive action against Joab, and it is unlikely David's present command
reflects a delayed sense of justice. David uses the old grievance to cover
the political exigency of Joab's death. Aligned with the pro-Judahite
Adonijah party, Joab is a threat to Solomon and a united Israel; his removal
is crucial to their consolidation.

David also seeks dynastic stability by removing bloodguilt from David's
house (2 Sam. 3:28–29). Solomon is to discover by his 'wisdom' how to
bring this about (v. 6). It is a chilling first appearance of the word 'wisdom'
(ḥokmâ) in the narrative, for it is a wisdom that contextualizes politically
expedient murder in torah obedience (vv. 2–4).

David charges Solomon to demonstrate kindness (ḥesed) towards
Barzillai's descendants. Barzillai had supported David during Absalom's
revolt (2 Sam. 17:27–29; 19:31–32). Because Barzillai's actions do not
threaten the continuance of the dynasty, Solomon's compliance is passed
over in the ensuing narrative.

The action towards Shimei connects (as in the action against Joab)
political and dynastic motivations but adds the motivation of personal
vengeance. Shimei had earlier cursed David (2 Sam. 16:5–14) but David
acknowledged it as from YHWH (2 Sam. 16:10–12). He swore that Shimei
would not die (2 Sam. 19:23), although his reference to a limitation of
bloodshed 'today' (v. 22) leaves future retribution a possibility. David's
charge to Solomon represents the event quite differently. He labels Shimei's
curse as 'terrible', and neglects his own assessment that it was 'from
YHWH'. David also alters the oath given Shimei from 'You shall not die'
to 'I will not put you to death with the sword', thus enabling another to
accomplish the deed. Given Shimei's support of Solomon (1 Kgs 1:8), there
can be little political gain in killing Shimei. Personal vengeance seems a
more likely motivation. Yet, by couching Shimei's words as a 'terrible
curse', David supplies a dynastic reason to remove him: his death will
break the power of the curse upon the house of David.

10–12. David is buried in the City of David and a summative report of his rule repeats information from 2 Sam. 5:4–5, the point at which David becomes king over all Israel. The repetition thus brackets David's rule over the United Kingdom, which kingdom Solomon now receives. That Solomon 'sat upon the throne of David' (v. 12) is retrospective of the theme of 1 Kgs 1:13, 17, 20, 27, 30, 35, 46, 48. But it is also prospective, for Adonijah may at any time threaten that throne. Until Adonijah is disposed of, the throne's establishment is in jeopardy.

2:13–35

13–25. Adonijah instigates the action by approaching Bathsheba. The common greeting (lit. 'Is it peace?'; *hăšālôm*) has ironic overtones: the queen is on her guard (Wray Beal 2007:162–163; cf. Garsiel 1991: 385).

Adonijah initiates the dialogue, which she allows through her imperative 'Speak!' (vv. 14, 16). He attempts to justify his eventual request for Abishag in several ways. First, he presents himself as the injured party by noting that the kingdom was his – a return to his insistent 'I will be king' of 1 Kgs 1:5. Secondly, in a return to the theme of knowledge (Garsiel 1991: 383–384), his emphatic '*You* know' shows he believes Bathsheba undermined his succession. Thirdly, he claims that 'all Israel' expected him to rule – a claim belied by the events of ch. 1. Fourthly, he assures Bathsheba he accepts Solomon as YHWH's choice.

Despite his attempt to downplay his request, it cannot be construed as anything other than a claim to the throne. Abishag's non-sexual relationship with David was unlikely to be believed by all the court (see comments at 1 Kgs 1:2–4; Garsiel 1991: 382–383) and to claim a member of the king's harem would be viewed as an overt claim on the throne (2 Sam. 3:6–7; 12:8; 16:21; see Cushman 2006: 339). Adonijah's request, then, is difficult to comprehend. Perhaps he felt his assertion that he no longer sought the crown would ease the king's suspicions; perhaps his sense of right to the throne was strong enough that he willingly assumed the risk of the request. Regardless, 'If Adonijah did in fact behave as claimed, he deserved to be executed – for stupidity' (Cross 1973: 237)!

Bathsheba's complicity can be construed as naive, vindictive or opportunistic against the Adonijah party, which included Joab, her first husband's murderer (Berlin 1982: 75; Wesselius 1990: 345–348). It is most likely that Bathsheba as queen mother shrewdly works to eliminate the rival son (Cushman 2006: 339–340). She omits all Adonijah's attempted justifications from the request, stripping it of any neutrality. She also adds that Adonijah is Solomon's brother – as a brother, and therefore a claimant to the throne, the request is not 'small' as Bathsheba suggests (v. 20).

Solomon draws the obvious conclusion (v. 22) and implicates the main conspirators besides Adonijah. His oath before YHWH carefully blames

Adonijah for his own death (v. 23), publicly absolving the king from bloodguilt and enabling him to claim adherence to torah, as David had charged. Adonijah's words have threatened the dynastic security and so 'today Adonijah will be put to death'.

Faithful Benaiah is reintroduced and his hand enacts the king's will (v. 46b). His action throughout the chapter is to 'fall upon' Solomon's enemies (vv. 25, 29, 31, 34, 46), and his ready compliance comports with his support of Solomon's enthronement (1:36–37).

26–27. Out of respect for past service the king stays Abiathar's death. Banishing him to Anathoth, Solomon's awkward 'Anathoth! Go!' reveals his rage against Adonijah also falls on Abiathar (vv. 22–23). The narrator's fulfilment notice of the word against Eli (1 Sam. 2:30–36) is the first such notation in Kings. It demonstrates the role of the narrator to pronounce such words (see Wray Beal 2007: 177–189) and introduces an important theological emphasis within Kings: YHWH's word will come to fulfilment.

28–35. Joab seeks asylum in the sanctuary according to ancient legal practice (Exod. 21:12–14; Burnside 2010). Benaiah is reluctant to break asylum – he wants Joab to 'come out'. The standoff becomes an opportunity for Solomon to justify the execution. He claims his actions are for the purpose of preventing further bloodguilt against himself and his dynasty (vv. 31, 33) and that Joab's execution is at YHWH's will (v. 32). On both accounts Solomon can claim his own innocence from wrongdoing towards Joab. The narrator, however, has already indicated that it is the realpolitik of Joab's part in Adonijah's bid for the throne that is the driving force behind the execution (v. 28).

Benaiah falls upon Joab, kills and buries him. Thus the coalition of Adonijah, Abiathar and Joab is removed. Their replacement is noted: Solomon as king, Benaiah as military leader and Zadok as priest.

2:36–46

Only the negative action David charged against Shimei remains to be completed. Solomon appears reluctant simply to execute Shimei, perhaps hesitant to alienate Benjaminite supporters by unjustly murdering one of their own (see Halpern 2001: 400). Instead, he sets an arbitrary condition likely to be broken. Then Solomon can act and claim Shimei's blood rests upon his own head rather than upon Solomon's house. Shimei has little choice but to acquiesce to the condition.

After three years, the condition is broken. Shimei's pursuit to extradite his servants, while not technically taking him across the Kidron, does violate the spirit of Solomon's command, and thus Solomon interprets it (Gray 1970: 111).

Solomon acts swiftly against Shimei. Whereas his initial interaction with Shimei was a dialogue (vv. 36–38), now Solomon engages in monologue

– the narrative technique hastens the outcome and vests that outcome solely in Solomon's interpretation and command (vv. 42–45). Solomon significantly enhances the condition set in the dialogue. First, he asserts the condition prohibited Shimei to 'go out and go anywhere'. More significantly, Solomon twice recalls the commitment was made under oath to YHWH – a detail nowhere in the initial dialogue. By such an oath, Solomon claims Shimei has brought his own blood upon his head. Further, Solomon's final conclusion is 'May YHWH return your evil on your head.' The execution by Solomon's hand cannot be held to his account.

But Solomon is not untainted. His final words to Shimei (v. 44) reveal the real reason for Shimei's execution: the evil Shimei perpetrated against David. Dynastic motivations mix readily with personal vengeance, but Solomon is fixed upon dynastic concerns. He explains that the execution of Shimei neutralizes the oath against David, blesses Solomon and establishes the Davidic throne before YHWH (v. 45). Benaiah once again falls upon his victim, and, as a final comment on the whole chapter, the kingdom rests established by the hand of Solomon. Whoever else has been involved in the executions, they remain the work of Solomon, the king.

Explanation

The succession to the throne is the crux of these chapters. How that succession transpires raises crucial questions regarding Solomon's reign, particularly whether it is ordained by YHWH, or whether it is contrived by the political machinations of Nathan and Bathsheba to further their own chosen candidate for the throne; how one answers that question cannot but colour one's further assessment of Solomon's rule. The narrative is not susceptible to an easy determination of the question, and the answer is perhaps that the two options are both true. Solomon is both the God-ordained successor to David and he achieves the throne by flawed human instrumentality. The two are held in tension through the chapters, and are never definitively resolved.

The single greatest evidence that Solomon's accession is merely the outworking of wholly human connivance is that the oath cited by Nathan and Bathsheba (1:13–17) and affirmed by David (1:30) is nowhere recorded. Solomon's birth is given particular narrative attention as part of the larger complex of David and Bathsheba (2 Sam. 11 – 12). Solomon is also specially named by YHWH, indicating his 'beloved' status (2 Sam. 12:24–25). Such attention suggests a special role for Solomon but does not include any oath regarding Solomon's accession.

Added to the absence of an oath in the narrative of 2 Samuel, several other elements suggest the possibility that Solomon's succession is achieved without the express approval of YHWH. Strangely, while 1 Kgs 1 proceeds largely by dialogue, YHWH is markedly absent from the speeches. Never does he affirm by oath or oracle that the events fulfil his desires. The silence is suggestive and may be construed as revealing his non-sponsorship of the events. Further, Nathan's approach to Bathsheba and later her approach to David can be construed as cool manipulation of an aged king to further personal agendas of political power or personal gain. Finally, if the oath regarding Solomon is non-existent, and given ANE practices of succession by primogeniture, Solomon's succession is questionable.

It is the question of primogeniture that opens several reasons for reading the narrative as affirming YHWH's selection of Solomon as the dynastic successor. The narrative continues the biblical theme of the ascendency of the younger over the older. Thus Isaac is elevated over Ishmael, Jacob over Esau, Joseph over his eleven brothers, and David himself over his brothers. The elevation is not predicated upon any particular characteristic discernible in the individual (for instance, Jacob is a trickster and Joseph is boastful before his brothers). Rather, the selection is revealed as wholly dependent upon YHWH's sovereign choice. Regarding David, God's choice is made on criteria not obvious to the human eye (1 Sam. 16:7), and that do not guarantee David's righteousness (with Bathsheba a case in point). Regarding Isaac, the decision rests on YHWH's prior determination that the promises given Abraham would reside in Sarah's offspring and not those of Hagar (Gen. 17:19–21). Jacob and Esau are both sons in the line of promise, but YHWH reveals his selection of Jacob prior to his birth (Gen. 25:23).

Each case of sibling elevation takes place through YHWH's will and works towards sustaining and furthering covenantal promises given Abraham. These promises find new expression in the Mosaic covenant, and the monarchic ruler is to uphold the covenant in national life (Deut. 17:18–20). Anomalies against primogeniture throughout the covenantal history alert one to the unique work of YHWH, signalling his sovereign will in the progress of the covenant made with Abraham. Solomon's elevation over his older brother suggests a similar moment in the covenant story. While YHWH is silent in the chapters, the pattern against primogeniture suggests his presence and sovereign direction.

Further elements in the narrative add to the construal of Solomon as YHWH's choice. The introduction of Solomon within the context of the long David and Bathsheba narrative and the naming of Solomon as beloved in YHWH's sight is mentioned above. These anticipate some particular role for Solomon in the narrative; the accession provides that role. Additionally, Solomon's passivity in the accession, by which others bring him to the throne (e.g. Nathan, Bathsheba, David and Zadok), is of a piece with the divine selection of key monarchs before (Saul, David) and after him (Jeroboam) in which unfolding events and actions of others (such as prophets) are instrumental to gain the throne. Along with Solomon's passivity, Adonijah's portrayal as a new Absalom (see 'Comment') can only be taken as a negative assessment of Adonijah's bid for the throne apart from YHWH's will, and is intended to contrast with Solomon's successful (because ordained?) bid.

Finally, while no narrative account is given of the proclamation of the oath cited by Nathan, Bathsheba and David, its absence does not require its non-existence. Whether or not it at one time existed in a source available to Dtr, its absence may be a narrative lacuna withheld to this moment for dramatic effect. Yet, assuming that such an oath does indeed exist does not expunge Nathan's and Bathsheba's actions and words of their shrewdness, or even their calculation to manipulate the king to immediate action. YHWH may indeed have ordained Solomon to the throne, but that is achieved in the very real world.

As in all the progress of covenant history, YHWH's sovereign will cannot be applied to human subjects in some ethereal realm divorced from the material, and fallen, world. Having created the world, YHWH commits himself to action within that world. In these chapters it takes place in the midst of realpolitik, the division of support among the religious and military leaders between one candidate and the other. It is the subscription of Bathsheba by Nathan, and their shrewd presentation to David of the state of events that seeks to move him to immediate action on behalf of their candidate. It is the involvement of YHWH's prophet in the presentation of an oath that may possibly not ever have been sworn. And, once Solomon takes the throne, it is the establishment of that throne through a 'wisdom' that undermines torah prescriptions while casting those attempts as righteously upholding those same torah prescriptions.

Who can say how YHWH may accomplish his purposes? Given his incarnational commitments by which his work takes place in the material world, he repeatedly accomplishes his will through frail and questionably righteous people and systems. So Abraham and Sarah precipitately resort to concubinage. A trickster is forced to flee, is himself tricked and twelve tribes ensue. Monarchic rule, flawed as it necessarily will be (1 Sam. 8), is a vehicle by which YHWH works towards the fulfilment of promises to the blessing of the whole world. Solomon ascends the throne by YHWH's will and through human instrumentality with all its shadowed motivations and actions. Solomon's establishment of his throne also uses such human instrumentality – and a kind of wisdom that hardly comports with any collection of quaint proverbial sayings.

Solomon's accession and reign is often seen only through a lens of aggrandized glory. This is faithful to much of what is presented of Solomon in the biblical text. His reign is greater than any other and is presented in hyperbolic fashion (see chs. 3, 4, 10). However, his reign is also grounded in the material world and these chapters evidence that reality and fore-shadow trends throughout Solomon's rule. Solomon's rule may be glorious, but it is also flawed in fundamental ways. 1 Kgs 3 – 11 reveal both the glory and the shadow. To allow only Solomon's aggrandizement is, perhaps, to succumb to the gnostic temptation of divorcing the exercise of YHWH's will from the arena of the mundane (Reno 2010: 26–27).

This is perhaps the whole point of Solomon's narrative in the context of the Christian canon. His rule is the Christian precedent of the tale of Camelot in which a glorious kingdom has feet of clay. The rot within Solomon's kingdom is the rot of the mundane world – flawed in the very midst of hopeful greatness. Whatever hopes one held that David's son would attain heights of greatness untainted by sin are immediately dashed in these opening chapters. The progress of Solomon's narrative similarly presents him as flawed in the midst of greatness: one is presented with a wise, blessed and lauded king who nevertheless falls short. And that failure is replicated in myriad ways through the lives of every subsequent king in the northern and southern kingdoms.

In this, the book of Kings within the Christian canon is a tutor that leads to Christ (Gal. 3:24). The ambiguities that surround Solomon's accession and dog his reign continually remind that he is not perfect. He cannot provide the righteous rule that reflects Deuteronomistic ideals of kingship, nor do any kings after him. One reaches the end of 1 – 2 Kings with a pressing question: 'Will any king come who does fulfil the righteous requirements of kingship?' The question may have been pressing for the exilic community. Their own king was held at the hands of Babylonian realpolitik. As the community reflected upon its history, it was apparent that human kingship was flawed – even beyond its moments of greatness. While there was some comfort in the reminder that YHWH's purposes were not hindered by realpolitik but were able to work even there, the question must have remained: 'Will any king come who fulfils the righteous requirements of kingship?'

Within the Christian canon that king is shown to be David's greater son, the Christ. All the dashed hopes engendered by the long years of kingship are fully met in him, the righteous King. Allowing the tension within the Solomon narrative of mundane and sinful humanity and God-ordained glorious kingship anticipates a canonical and Christological resolution.

1 KINGS 3:1–28

Translation

[1a]Solomon allied himself by marriage to Pharaoh, king of Egypt. He took Pharaoh's daughter and brought her to the City of David until he had finished building his house and the house of YHWH and the wall around Jerusalem. [2]Until that time[a], however, the people were sacrificing at the high places, for the house for YHWH's name had not been built. [3]Solomon loved YHWH, walking in the statutes of David his father; however, he sacrificed and burned incense at the high places.

⁴The king went to Gibeon to sacrifice there, for it was the great high place. Solomon offered a thousand burnt offerings upon that altar. ⁵In Gibeon YHWH appeared to Solomon in a night dream, and God said, 'Ask what I should give you.'ᵃ ⁶Solomon said, 'You have done great kindness to your servant David my father, just as he walked before you in truth and in righteousness and with an upright heart towards you. You have kept this great kindness towards him and have appointed for him a son to sit upon his throne, as it is today. ⁷So now, O YHWH, my God, you have made your servant reign after David my father although I am a small boy; I do not know how to go out or come in. ⁸And your servant is in the midst of your people whom you have chosen – a great people that cannot be numbered, and so numerous, they cannot be countedᵃ. ⁹So, giveᵃ your servant a listening heart to govern your people, discerning between good and evil. For who is able to govern this your great people?'

¹⁰It was pleasing in the eyes of the Lord that Solomon had requested this thing, ¹¹so God said to him, 'Because you have requested this thing and have not requested for yourself long life, nor have requested for yourself riches, nor have requested the life of your enemies, but have requested for yourself the ability to understand in order to perceive justiceᵃ, ¹²behold, I have acted according to your words. I have given to you a wise and discerning heart. No one like you has been before you, nor will any arise like you after you. ¹³Evenᵃ what you have not asked I have given you – evenᵃ riches and honour – so that there will not be any like you among the kings all your days. ¹⁴Now, ᵃif you will walk in my ways, to keep my statutes and my commandments just as David your father walked, then I will lengthenᵃ your days.' ¹⁵Then Solomon awoke and realized it was a dream. He came to Jerusalem and stood before the ark of the covenant of the Lord and offered up burnt offerings and made peace offerings and gave a feast for all his servants.

¹⁶Then two women, prostitutes, came to the king and stood before him. ¹⁷One woman said, 'Oᵃ, my lord, this woman and I dwell in one house, and I gave birth with her in the house. ¹⁸On the third day after I gave birth, this woman also gave birth. Now, we were together – no stranger was with us in the house – only the two of us were in the house. ¹⁹Then the son of this woman died in the night because she lay upon him. ²⁰She arose in the middle of the night and took my son from beside me (now your handmaid was sleepingᵃ). She lay him in her bosom, and her dead son she lay in my bosom. ²¹When I arose in the morning to nurse my son – he was dead! I examined him closelyᵃ in the morning, but he was not my son whom I had borne!' ²²Then the other woman said, 'No, for my son is the living one and your son is the dead one!' But this one said, 'No, for your son is the dead one and my son is the living one!' Thus they argued before the king.

²³Then the king said, 'The one says, "This my son is the living one, and your son is the dead one!" but the other says, "No, for your son is the dead one while my son is the living one!"' ²⁴The king said, 'Bring me a sword!' So they brought the sword to the king. ²⁵The king said, 'Cut the living child in two. Give half to the one woman, and half to the other woman.' ²⁶Then the woman, whose son was living, said to the king (for her compassion was aroused concerning her son), 'Please, my lord! Let them give her the living childᵃ; surely don't kill him!' But the

other said, 'He will be neither yours nor mine; divide him!'[b] [27]Then the king answered and said, 'Give to her the living child[a] and do not kill him. She is his mother.' [28]All Israel heard the judgment that the king rendered and they were in awe before the king for they saw that the wisdom of God was in him to accomplish justice.

Notes on the text

1.a. MT 3:1 appears in LXX as 5:14a (after 4:34 ET). 'Solomon allied . . . king of Egypt' does not appear at 5:14a in LXX. MT 9:16–17a appears in LXX as 5:14b. The transpositions attest to the composite nature of the text. Further, LXX 5:14a piously asserts Solomon built YHWH's house before his own. LXX 2:35c, almost identical to 5:14a, makes the same assertion by stating that Solomon built 'his house and the house of the LORD first'. MT affords no such pious protection for the order of Solomon's building projects.

2.a. 'Until that time' is literally 'until those days' (*hayyāmîm hāhēm*), that is, the days when the temple project was completed.

5.a. *šĕ'al māh 'etten-lāk*, 'ask what I should give to you', taking the impf. 'I should give' modally, as an obligation (WO'C 508; Chisholm 1998: 93) arising out of YHWH's own covenant commitments towards the Davidic dynasty and Solomon.

8.a. *wĕlō' yissāpēr mērōb*, 'so numerous, they cannot be counted', does not appear in LXX*. MT should stand as repetitive emphasis.

9.a. *wĕnātattā*, 'so give', translating the pf. as a command (Chisholm 1998: 101) that echoes YHWH's demand that Solomon 'ask' (v. 5).

11.a. *lišmōa' mišpāṭ*, 'in order to perceive justice'. gives a judicial context of judging difficult cases (cf. 2 Sam. 14:17), as demonstrated in the following narrative.

13.a. YHWH's gracious gift is triply emphasized with the adv.: 'even what you have not asked . . . even riches . . . even honour' (*wĕgam . . . gam . . . gam*).

14.a–a. A personal conditional promise is granted here for length of life to Solomon, expressed by the *'im* plus waw cons. (WO'C 526–527).

17.a. *bî* as a particle of entreaty by which a social inferior addresses a superior. Always followed by 'my lord' (BDB 106); cf. v. 26.

20.a. LXX deletes the aside that the woman was sleeping, strengthening her testimony by avoiding the troublesome question of her ability to know these events while asleep.

21.a. *wā'etbōnēn 'ēlāyw*. Here the hith. of *byn* followed by the prep. *'el* as 'to consider or examine something carefully'.

26.a. Reading the qal pass. part. *yālûd* as the noun *yeled*, 'child', with some MSS.

26.b. 'divide him!': the object is unexpressed but understood in MT.

27.a. See n. 26.a above.

Form and structure

A brief introduction to Solomon's established kingship consists of three separate notations concerning Solomon's marriage, building plans and worship at the high places (vv. 1–3), which provide crucial information for evaluating Solomon (see 'Comment'). The introduction, together with further statements regarding Pharaoh's daughter and Solomon's worship practices found at 9:24–25, act as a bracket around Solomon's rule over Israel. The following section (9:26 – 10:29) deals with Solomon's reign in its international perspective.

Following the introduction, the first section of the paragraph is enclosed with a double bracket. In 3:4–5 Solomon offers sacrifice at Gibeon and YHWH first appears to him in a dream. Following the content of the dream, 3:15 reverses the bracket: Solomon wakens from the dream and returns to Jerusalem to sacrifice. The closing bracket shifts the locus of worship from Gibeon to Jerusalem, and Solomon's worship in Jerusalem in v. 15 anticipates his great temple project of 1 Kgs 5 – 8, which (theoretically) will exclude the continuance of worship at the high places.

The dream sequence finds parallels in other Syro-Palestinian texts (Husser 1999; Seow 1984). Other Egyptian parallels (Herrmann 1953–4; Görg 1975), although geographically more distant, suggest common forms. In the Ugaritic *Aqhat* and *Kirta* legends, incubation practices result in night visions, while the *Kirta* legend has a king who like Solomon rejects certain items (riches and power) in favour of others (progeny). YHWH's grant of riches, honour and long life reflects similar bequests in the Syro-Palestinian texts and reflects an established ideology of blessings bestowed upon kings by the patron god. The conformity to accepted sequences experienced by legendary kings becomes an 'integral element[s] in the legitimation of Solomonic kingship' (Seow 1984: 152; cf. Porten 1967: 114–115).

The dream sequence is linked to the narrative of the prostitutes by the temporal marker 'then' (*'āz*). The linkage may attest to an originally independent narrative, or simply a narrative transition employed by one author. The narrative stands as proof Solomon's request for wisdom was granted, as the epilogue makes clear (3:28). The story is structured simply, with the statement of the dispute (vv. 16–23) followed by the king's wise resolution (vv. 24–27). The story shares elements common to folkloristic tales of similar situations, although none is contemporaneous or identical to the biblical account (Gressmann 1907: 212–228; Montgomery 1951: 108–109). Ancient Mesopotamian examples of kings recording difficult judgments as proof of exemplary kingship may explain the widespread nature of such tales (Wiseman 1973). The narrative evidences one of the areas in which Solomon exercises his wise governance; further examples are found in 1 Kgs 4 – 5.

Comment

3:1–3

The kingdom established (2:46), Solomon brokers a politically significant alliance with Pharaoh, possibly Siamun of the Twenty-First Dynasty, 978–960 BC (Malamat 1963a: 11; Horn 1967: 12–13). Pharaoh's secession of Gezer to Solomon upon his wedding (9:16) contributes to Solomon's expanding empire (4:24[5:4]).

Alliances through marriage (hith. of *ḥtn*; see Gen. 34:9; Deut. 7:3; Josh. 23:12; 1 Sam. 18:21–27; 1 Kgs 3:1; 2 Chr. 18:1; Ezra 9:14) are negatively evaluated, for, except for David's alliance to Saul through Michal (1 Sam. 18:21–27), all are alliances by marriage to foreign or wicked kings. The action is a breach of covenant (Deut. 7:3) and thus of David's charge (2:3–4). Pharaoh's daughter remains lodged in the citadel on the south-eastern hill until temple and palace are completed (7:8). Mention of her compromises Solomon's reign at the outset and ultimately brings it under judgment (11:9–11).

The order of Solomon's building projects (3:1) likewise censures Solomon (Provan 1995: 44–45). The palace is built before the temple and although the temple project is related before that of the palace (1 Kgs 6 – 7), the disproportionate length of time spent building the king's house (thirteen years; 6:38) compared to building the temple (seven years; 7:1), and the fact that the palace project interrupts and thus delays full completion of the temple, suggests misplaced priorities on Solomon's part. The two exceptive clauses ('however'; vv. 2–3) do not mitigate Solomon's misplaced priorities. Worship at the high places and not in the Deuteronomistically sanctioned temple occurs precisely because Solomon attends first to his palace project.

'High places' (sg. *bāmâ*; pl. *bāmôt*) appear over 100 times in the OT as regular features of Israelite religion, whether legitimate or illegitimate. Textual, archaeological and sociological studies reveal much about the high places (Henton Davies, *IDB* 2:602–604; Nakhai 1994; Zevit 2001; King and Stager 2001). Often within or adjacent to settlements, they were found on high hills but also in valleys. As open-air sites or roofed sanctuaries or houses (1 Kgs 12:31; 13:32; 2 Kgs 17:29, 32), cult objects such as sacred pillars (*maṣṣēbôt*), wooden poles (*'ăšērâ*), altars and ceramic stands were placed in them. They were legitimate places for Yahwistic worship during the tribal and early monarchic periods (1 Sam. 9:11–25; 10:5), but were considered unorthodox once the temple was completed (Deut. 12:5). The sites continued, however, in both kingdoms (1 Kgs 12:31; 2 Kgs 18:17–37; 23:15, 18) as part of a two-tiered system of royal cult and traditional, local sites. Kings are measured by their attitude towards them, with full approval granted only to those who removed them (2 Kgs 18:4; 23:8).

The exceptive clause in v. 3 is in tension with the glowing summation that Solomon 'loved YHWH, walking in the statutes of David his father'. Here the love refers not primarily to an expression of emotion (although emotion was not excluded), but to covenant loyalty (Deut. 5:10; 7:9; Josh. 22:5; 23:11). The 'love' credited to Solomon is predicated of him only here, and 11:1–2, where his love is given to 'many foreign women' to whom he 'held fast in love'. In retrospect, the summative statement of Solomon's love given to foreign women and their idols, together with the aspersions cast on Solomon in 3:1–3 reveal that even at the start of his reign his love of YHWH cannot be wholehearted.

3:4–15

Gibeon, 4 miles (7 km) north-west of Jerusalem, is identified with the excavation site of el-Jib. Located in Benjamin, the tribe of Saul, it had witnessed rancorous encounters between Davidide and Saulide supporters and perhaps existed as a prior military venue (2 Sam. 2:12–17; 20:8; cf. Ahlström 1993: 504). As the prominent cult location in Benjaminite territory, Solomon's sacrifice there asserted his role as legitimate king in a common ANE fashion (Seow 1984: 144–145). It also suggests an attempt at rapprochement between Davidide and Saulide political interests.

The liberality of Solomon's sacrifice at Gibeon emphasizes his piety. With those in 3:15, it narratively frames Solomon's dream. YHWH's appearance signals the deity's acceptance of the Gibeon sacrifice; his revelation to Solomon confirms his role as king. Yahweh's question to Solomon 'Ask what I should give you' introduces the core dialogue between Solomon and Yahweh.

There are three parts to Solomon's request. First, he carefully positions himself as the inheritor of YHWH's promise to David, twice referencing YHWH's 'great kindness' (ḥesed gādôl), or covenant loyalty, towards David (2 Sam. 7:15), fulfilled in his elevation to the throne.

Secondly, Solomon depicts himself as a humble supplicant. He emphasizes the enthronement is by YHWH's instrumentality ('*you* have done . . . *you* have kept'). Strangely, he makes no mention of the very human instrumentality in procuring and establishing the throne. He also depicts himself as a 'small boy', but his reference to his youth cannot be taken at face value as he has by now fathered children (he rules forty years [1 Kgs 11:42] and is succeeded by a forty-one-year-old son [1 Kgs 14:21]). Rather, reference to youthful inexperience is polite deference, such as in Jeremiah's encounter (Jer. 1:6). Evidence of his youth is that he does not know 'how to go out or come in', a reference primarily to his lack of military leadership (Deut. 28:6; 31:2; Josh. 14:11; 1 Sam. 18:13; 29:6; 2 Sam. 5:2; 1 Kgs 15:17; see van der Lingen 1992). Further, he voices consternation at his inability to lead Israel (v. 9).

Finally, Solomon's request is the ability to govern (*lišpōṭ*), which would encompass all the activities (judicial, military, political and cultic) expected of a Deuteronomistic king. Such governance includes discernment between good and evil and flows from a 'listening heart', the seat of both thought and emotion. Listening is the required stance before the deuteronomic law (Deut. 4:1; 6:4; cf. 17:18), which law David has charged Solomon to keep. Additionally, Solomon's request for a listening *heart* hearkens back to David's own heart before YHWH (1 Sam. 13:14; 1 Kgs 3:6; 14:8; 9:4 *et passim*), which David advised Solomon is crucial to sustained Davidic kingship (2:4).

YHWH is pleased Solomon does not supplicate for personal advantage (v. 11) and grants both what Solomon requests and what he does not. First (v. 12), YHWH's enthusiasm to grant Solomon's request is indicated in his double statements 'I have acted according to your word' and 'I have given to you a wise and discerning heart'. Such a grant results in Solomon's incomparability. Secondly (v. 13), YHWH begins to address what Solomon has *not* requested. 'Riches and honour' (v. 13) is tangible evidence of YHWH's blessing upon Solomon's governance. This grant, too, results in Solomon's incomparability. Only the grant of long life is not given outright. Rather, YHWH attaches long life to Solomon's commitment to observe the law – as Solomon boasted David did (v. 6), and with which David charged Solomon.

An important addition to YHWH's grant to Solomon is that, while Solomon requested a 'listening heart' (v. 9), YHWH now grants a heart characterized as 'wise and discerning' (v. 12). The accreditation of wisdom to Solomon is the third instance of this word in 1 Kings (2:6, 9). To this point, Solomon's wisdom is the shrewdness of realpolitik. In the subsequent narrative Solomon does demonstrate wisdom from YHWH (3:16–28); however, he continues his involvement in realpolitik both nationally and internationally. It is facile to bifurcate Solomon's reign and suggest that the wisdom before this dream is the human wisdom of realpolitik, and the wisdom after this dream is divine wisdom. Both parts of Solomon's life show a complex character who acts wisely and obeys torah, and who acts expediently for realpolitik and breaks torah. That YHWH conditions the promise of long life suggests that he knows Solomon will (as he has already done) choose the latter course more often than the former.

The dream concludes and Solomon offers sacrifices in Jerusalem, shifting the cultic centre to the Deuteronomistic site, the place of YHWH's choice. The move is one preparation towards temple building. For the first time, the narrative states the location of YHWH's ark in the Jerusalem tent, making explicit what has only been implicit (1:39, 49; 2:28–34). Providing a celebratory feast for those who assist his government, he acknowledges YHWH's hand upon his throne.

3:16–28

A complainant and respondent appear before Solomon, both unnamed prostitutes and recent mothers. The complainant presents a case to Solomon, resting her case primarily upon the assertion of events that have transpired while she herself slept, and upon her close observation of the dead child. Her motherly familiarity with her own, slightly older, child is the basis of her claim. As first to speak, her testimony seems valid (Prov. 18:17), and Solomon's decision clear.

The second prostitute gives testimony that makes the case a seemingly insoluble riddle – both for Solomon, and for the reader. She questions the complainant's assertion, offering no alternative account of the events, but asserting her claim as the rightful mother of the living child. The continued argument of the complainant and respondent, and Solomon's summation of the problem, show the difficulty of the case: it is one woman's word against another's. There are no outside witnesses, as the complainant's testimony indicates (v. 18). No character references are called for because the women are liminal women – prostitutes on the edges of social respectability. Perhaps Solomon should consider the complainant's testimony true: as the respondent makes no counterclaim yet, how could the complainant assert what occurred while she slept? Perhaps, then, Solomon should consider the complainant a false accuser who presents a bold lie. Or does the respondent's terse response indicate her guilt? How is Solomon to judge?

Solomon's proposed solution successfully arouses the compassion of the mother of the living child. Her compassion is a deeply felt emotion (the same phrase appears in Gen. 43:30; Hos. 11:8). Here the phrase is particularly appropriate, for 'compassion' (*raḥămîm*) shares the same root as 'womb' (*reḥem*), thus emphasizing her compassion arises out of her mother-love. Whether or not Solomon would actually divide the child is beside the point. Rather, he alone is able by his wisdom to solve the riddle, thus providing true justice.

For the reader, however, the riddle remains. Solomon indicates the true mother by stating, 'Give to her the living child . . . she is his mother,' which in no way indicates *which* of the two women he means. Unfortunately, several English versions (e.g. NRSV, NIV) attempt to solve the riddle by reading 'give . . . to the first woman', thus making the claimant the real mother. The Hebrew does not specify which woman Solomon indicates when he makes his pronouncement, nor how he reaches his judgment. But that it is acknowledged as 'justice' by all is the whole point. Textually, the riddle remains unsolvable for the reader, and there are several studies that explore this phenomenon (Lasine 1989; Rendsburg 1998; van Wolde 1995). The reader cannot resolve the dilemma; Solomon does so only by divine wisdom.

Like a refrain, the conclusion (v. 28) returns to Solomon's request that would enable him to 'govern' (from the root *špṭ*) the people (v. 9), and

YHWH's grant of wisdom (*ḥokmâ*). Israel stands in awe of the judgment (from the root *špṭ*; cf. 3:11) of the king that he renders *špṭ* (cf. 3:9 [twice]) as evidence of God's wisdom (*ḥokmâ*; cf. 3:12). Whatever ambiguity surrounds Solomon's rule to this point, the solved riddle demonstrates YHWH's acceptance of King Solomon by granting him ability to govern. The ambiguity surrounding Solomon's character will continue throughout chs. 4–11, and out of that ambiguity will arise the final judgment passed upon him. But for now, the narrative lauds the king as YHWH's choice over Israel.

Explanation

The granting of divine wisdom (*ḥokmâ*) is a mark of YHWH's approval and affirmation of Solomon's reign. Wisdom is a predominant theme in Solomon's narrative, first appearing as human shrewdness and skill (2:6, 9) and, following the impartation of divine wisdom in this chapter, cited as evidence of YHWH's hand upon Solomon's reign (4:29–34; 10:4, 6–9). At the end of Solomon's reign, not even his many sins fully expunge the remembrance and wonder of Solomon's wisdom (11:41). God's grant is ongoing divine guidance, which, if heeded, enables wise governance (3:28; see Fretheim 1999: 33).

The solution of the riddle demonstrates Solomon's wise (*ḥkm*) and discerning (*bîn*) heart granted by YHWH (v. 12), which enables him to govern (*špṭ*) with discernment (*bîn*; v. 9). The pericope sets Solomon's wisdom in an ideal light but it stands in tension with the misplaced priorities of vv. 1–3 and Solomon's false worship practices (11:4-6). Why does the grant of wisdom not lead Solomon to redirect those priorities, and prevent his descent into false worship?

The issue turns on Solomon's ability to listen, and how that relates to YHWH's gift of wisdom. The relationship of listening to wisdom is a theme elsewhere in Scripture. It appears in Moses' exhortation on wisdom in Deut. 4:1–9. There Israel is urged to hear (*šmʻ*; v. 1) YHWH's statutes (*ḥuqqîm*) and judgments (*mišpāṭîm*). Careful observance of torah will enable successful entry to the land; more, it demonstrates Israel's wisdom (*ḥkm*) and understanding (*bîn*; v. 6). So crucial is the stance of listening (*šmʻ*) that it is again enjoined on Israel in its central text, the Shema (Deut. 6:4; cf. v. 3).

Israel is gifted greatly but it is their response of listening to YHWH's torah that proves their wisdom. Solomon, too, is greatly gifted by YHWH. But the deuteronomic law already enjoins upon Solomon what his attitude should be in the face of YHWH's gift: he is to listen to torah as Israel should listen. In effect, Solomon's request for a listening heart (v. 9) asks for what should already be his stance towards YHWH. When YHWH grants him a wise and discerning heart (v. 12), the grant understands listening to be requisite to the gift. When Solomon fails to listen to torah, his heart of wisdom and discernment is compromised and fails.

The themes of the Deuteronomy text resonate in the book of Proverbs, and the association of Solomon with Proverbs (Prov. 1:1; 10:1; cf. 1 Kgs 4:32) brings the understanding of wisdom gained in Solomon's narrative to Proverbs. The connections are highlighted by key words found in Proverbs that echo both Deuteronomy and Solomon's narrative. For instance, the introduction (Prov. 1:1–7; 2:1–9) reveals that reading Proverbs is a means to wisdom (*ḥkm*), understanding (*bîn*), words of insight (*bînâ*) and exercising justice (*mišpaṭ*). Further, the introduction reveals that the wise man (*ḥkm*) who listens (*šm'*) will gain understanding (*bîn*) of (among other things) riddles (*ḥîdôt*; such as the women, and later the Queen of Sheba present to Solomon; 10:1; cf. Judg. 14:12; Ezek. 17:2; Ps. 49:4). Solomon has been granted YHWH's wisdom in order to govern with justice, and in 1 Kgs 3:16–28 he exhibits the marks of the wise man noted in Proverbs.

In both Proverbs and Deuteronomy wisdom arises out of listening. In Deuteronomy Israel is to listen to torah. In Proverbs the term 'torah' at times may have the law in view (e.g. 28:4, 7, 9; 29:18), but is most often used of parental instruction (e.g. 1:8; 3:1; 4:2; 6:20, 23; 13:14). That instruction, however, arising in an Israelite context and canonized in their scriptures, is gathered within the purview of the Mosaic law. As Proverbs cites YHWH as the source of wisdom (1:7), its utilization of the divine name is a reminder of the covenant in which torah is revealed (Exod. 3; cf. Longman 2006:101). By this reminder, the wisdom of Proverbs is connected with the torah of covenant. Listening in Deuteronomy and Proverbs is therefore either explicitly or implicitly to the law, the torah of Moses. This aligns with the charge given Solomon. He, too, is to attend to the law so that he will have success (2:2–4). YHWH's grant of divine wisdom does not negate this earlier charge that is itself a repetition of the deuteronomic charge to hear and obey. The gift of divine wisdom given Solomon does not function independently of Solomon's own attitude to torah (Fretheim 1999: 33).

Additionally, Proverbs predicates knowledge upon the foundation of the 'fear of YHWH' (Prov. 1:7; 2:1–6). Using 'knowledge' (*da'at*) as a synonym for 'wisdom' (*ḥokmâ*), the verse sets the pursuit of knowledge/wisdom into a context of dependence and subservience to YHWH (Longman 2006: 100–103). It is this response that teaches wisdom (Prov. 15:33), which gives kings the ability to govern justly (Prov. 8:12–21). As in the case of listening as a starting point for wisdom, the fear of YHWH also arises inwardly but is expressed outwardly through righteous living.

Like all Israelites, Solomon is called to hear and obey YHWH's law; in this is expressed the fear of YHWH. The deuteronomic charge urges Israel to love YHWH (Deut. 6:5) and 1 Kgs 3:3 notes that Solomon does love YHWH, but this is set in a context that queries the depth of this love. The measurement applied to Solomon's wisdom will not change. If he listens, he will be wise and YHWH's divine gift will operate unimpeded. If he does not listen – if his heart loves falsely or incompletely – he will not listen as he should and, regardless of any divine grant of wisdom, he will not act according to torah or out of fear of YHWH. His wisdom will be shadowed at best and this is indeed what occurs. There are moments and events of great wisdom in Solomon's reign, but it is the state of his heart – whether he listens or not – that determines the extent of wisdom's display in his reign. Ultimately, it is the state of his heart that directs his reign and sets the direction for the remainder of the book of Kings (1Kgs 11:1–13; 26–40).

Interestingly, Moses' call to Israel to listen to torah so as to display their wisdom (Deut. 4:5–6) is followed by a warning as to what will occur should they not listen. Failure to listen (and thus failure at wisdom) leads to idolatry (Deut. 4:15–31). This is indeed what happens during Israel's time in the land. Their failure to listen to YHWH and his commands eventuates in idolatry, and for this they are cast from the land (2 Kgs 17:7–23 [vv. 14–15]; 21:9–16 [v. 9]). The same failure and eventuality is demonstrated in Solomon's rule. No longer fearing YHWH, he ceases to listen. He turns his heart towards other gods, breaching the first two commandments.

The NT reveals the same pattern. God addresses, and his people listen as their identifying characteristic. The Christ came as the *logos*, the word that addresses. It is that address that calls forth the church. In its ongoing life, its attentive ear to YHWH's address in Christ reveals its love for God, and that love is demonstrated in obedience to the commandments of Christ (John 14:15, 21). And thus is its wisdom demonstrated.

In the midst of the great grace gifts given by God for the building up of the church (Rom. 12:6–8; 1 Cor. 12:7–11; Eph. 4:7–13), the call to listen is never negated. The exercise of such gifts without listening follows the same pattern as Solomon. There may be moments and works of greatness to the glory of God, but in and through those same works will be the same shadow of Solomon's rule, whose end is apostasy and idolatry.

1 KINGS 4:1–34 [MT 4:1 – 5:14]

Translation

[1]Now King Solomon was king over all Israel. [2a]These were his leaders: Azariah the son of Zadok the priest[b]. [3]Elihoreph[a] and Ahijah the sons of Shisha[b], scribes.

Jehoshaphat son of Ahilud, the recorder. [4]Benaiah the son of Jehoiada, over the army.

Zadok and Abiathar, priests. ⁵Azariah the son of Nathan, over the governors. Zabud the son of Nathan, priest and king's advisor. ⁶Ahishar[a] was the steward, and Adoniram the son of Abda, over the forced labour.

⁷Solomon had twelve governors[a] over all Israel, and they provisioned the king and his house. They each provided food for one month in the year. ⁸ᵃThese were their names: Ben-hur, in the hill country of Ephraim. ⁹Ben-deker in Makaz and in Shaalbim, Beth-shemesh, and Elon-beth-hanan. ¹⁰Ben-hesed in Arubboth (Socoh was his, and all the land of Hepher). ¹¹Ben-abinadab in all Naphath-dor (Taphath the daughter of Solomon was his wife). ¹²Baana son of Ahilud in Taanach, Megiddo and all of Beth-shean, which was beside Zarethan below Jezreel from Beth-shean until Abel-meholah as far as the other side of Jokmeam. ¹³Ben-geber in Ramoth-gilead. He had the villages of Jair the son of Manasseh, which are in Gilead. He also had the region of Argob, which is in Bashan; sixty great cities with walls and bronze bars. ¹⁴Ahinadab son of Iddo, in Mahanaim. ¹⁵Ahimaaz in Naphtali (he had taken Basemath the daughter of Solomon for a wife). ¹⁶Baana son of Hushai, in Asher and Aloth. ¹⁷Jehoshaphat son of Paruah, in Issachar. ¹⁸Shimei son of Ela, in Benjamin. ¹⁹Geber son of Uri, in the land of Gilead, the land of Sihon king of the Amorites, and of Og king of Bashan. And there was one governor who was over the land of Judah[a]. ²⁰ᵃJudah and Israel were as numerous as the sand that is upon the seashore in abundance. They ate and drank, and were happy.

²¹[5:1]ᵃSolomon ruled over all the kingdoms from the River to the land of the Philistines, even to the border of Egypt. Tribute was brought and they served Solomon all the days of his life. ²²[5:2]Solomon's food for one day was thirty measures of fine flour and sixty measures of meal, ²³[5:3]ten fat oxen and twenty pasture-fed oxen, one hundred sheep, besides deer, gazelle, roebuck and fattened geese. ²⁴[5:4]For he had dominion in every region across the River from Tiphsah to Gaza and over all the kings of the region across the River. He had peace in all his regions on every side. ²⁵[5:5]And Judah and Israel dwelt securely; every man under his vine and his fig tree, from Dan to Beer-sheba, all the days of Solomon.

²⁶[5:6]Solomon had forty thousand[a] stalls of horses for his chariots, and twelve thousand horsemen. ²⁷[5:7]And these governors provided King Solomon and all who came to King Solomon's table, each in his month; they left nothing lacking. ²⁸[5:8] They brought to the designated place barley and straw for the horses[a] and steeds[b], each according to his measure.

²⁹[5:9]God gave wisdom to Solomon, and very great discernment, and breadth of mind as the sand upon the seashore. ³⁰[5:10]The wisdom of Solomon was greater than the wisdom of all the sons of the east and than all the wisdom of Egypt. ³¹[5:11]He was wiser than any man – wiser than Ethan the Ezrahite, Heman, Calcol and Darda the sons of Mahol. His name was known in all the surrounding nations. ³²[5:12]He spoke three thousand proverbs, and his songs were one thousand and five. ³³[5:13]He spoke concerning trees – from the cedar that is in Lebanon to the hyssop that grows on the wall. He spoke also concerning animals, birds, creeping things and fish. ³⁴[5:14]Men came from all the peoples to hear the wisdom of Solomon, *sent* from all the kings of the earth who had heard of his wisdom.

Notes on the text

2–6.a. This list appears here in LXX; a different list of officials appears at (LXX) 2:46h.

2.b. The article on *hakkōhēn* indicates the high priest is intended (JM 137h; GKC §126d).

3.a. Elihoreph is a Hebraized derogation of an Egyptian name (Mettinger 1971: 29–30).

3.b. The father of Elihoreph and Ahijah is Seraiah, here listed as 'Shisha', a mistaken reading of a borrowed Egyptian scribal title, *sš*. For the confusion of the father's name, and textual variants (2 Sam. 8:17; 20:25; 1 Chr. 18:16) see Mettinger 1971: 25–30, 45–49.

6.a. Ahishar is unique in the list as there is no patronymic. Reading as 'his brother, leader of' (*'ăḥî šār*; Montgomery 1951: 119; Mettinger 1971: 10–11) is not convincing.

7.a. Reading MT ni. part. m. pl. of root *nṣb* in vv. 5, 7, 27 [5:7]; nominal form in v. 19. Some MSS have m. pl. nominal in vv. 7, 27.

8.a–19.a. The names in vv. 8–11, 13 are patronymics only. No textual witnesses support the theory early MSS were damaged and proper names lost (Montgomery 1951: 120; Gray 1970: 134).

19.a. Following LXX, which reads 'over the land of Judah', perhaps dropped in MT due to haplography with v. 20.

20.a. The verse appears in LXX, 1 Kgs 2:46 ab.

21.a.–25[5:1–5].a. Similar to LXX 1 Kgs 2:46 k, e–g.

26[5:6].a. LXX and 2 Chr. 9:25 cite four thousand stalls and chariots. The number in Kings may be a scribal error, or an ideological rendering.

28[5:8].a. *sûsîm* as chariot horses (see v. 26).

28[5:8].b. *rākeš*, 'steeds', possibly messenger horses (Esth. 8:10) or chariot horses (Mic. 1:13).

Form and structure

A variety of source materials occur in this chapter. The annalistic administrative lists in vv. 2–6, 8–19 appear contemporaneous to Solomon, perhaps being the 'annals of Solomon' (11:41; DeVries 2003: 66). They provide details of the national administrative apparatus. The varied materials in vv. 21–25 (rulership: vv. 21, 24; provision: vv. 22–23; peace and safety for Israel: vv. 24–25) focalize around the theme of Solomon's international influence. Even the provisioning of Solomon's table (vv. 22–23), which could easily be appended to the earlier notation of the governor's monthly provision (v. 7), is set within an international context to suggest Solomon's tributary wealth provisioned his table (v. 21).

Regardless of the text's date and compositional history, its present structure appears to laud Solomon's reign. 1 Kgs 4:1, 21 each begin a section with a statement regarding Solomon's rule, first over 'all Israel' and secondly over 'all the kingdoms'. Each section details Solomon's rule within that context (2–20; 22–28), and ends with hyperbolic statements regarding Solomon's wise governance.

Verses 29–34 eulogize Solomon's great wisdom in modes familiar to wisdom literature: proverbial, poetic and encyclopedic. The wisdom mode could date the material to either an early (Solomonic) or late (post-exilic) era (Scott 1955; DeVries 2003). A Solomonic context is supported as ANE royal inscriptions similarly contain hyperbole of monarchic power, wealth and peace (Weinfeld 1983; B. Long 1984: 75–77).

The encomium is bipartite in structure. Each section notes Solomon's wisdom in general terms (vv. 29, 32), provides specific examples (vv. 30–31a, 33) and concludes with consequent international fame (vv. 31b, 34; Walsh 1995: 480). The concluding note of Solomon's international fame is a fitting conclusion to chs. 3–4, where Solomon's wisdom is acknowledged and celebrated in Israel and Judah (3:28; 4:20, 25) and then spills out to the surrounding nations (vv. 29–34).

Tempering the praise of vv. 29–34 is the notation (vv. 26–28) of Solomon's stables and the governors who provision them. Deut. 17:14 indicates kings are not to multiply horses. Instead, their military needs are to be met by YHWH the divine warrior. The placement of this notation (which might easily have accompanied earlier references to the governors [vv. 5, 7]) cautions against a naive reading of the encomium.

Comment

4:1–6

The passage details Solomon's administrative governance over 'all Israel' (v. 1), a phrase that throughout 1 Kgs 1 – 11 designates the united kingdom (1:20; 2:15; 3:28; 8:62, 65 [cf. vv. 1–2]; 11:16, 42; only in 5:13 [5:27] does 'all Israel' refer solely to the north). Both north and south benefit from Solomon's governance (vv. 20, 25) as he exerts his dynastic claim over the whole land, thus creating a sense of national unity.

Solomon's governing officials serve in the primary cultic, administrative and military roles, and a degree of continuity exists with David's government. Jehoshaphat serves as recorder (*mazkîr*) in David's court (2 Sam. 8:16) and retains his post as chief protocol officer, attending to state and household ceremony and royal communications (Mettinger 1971). Likewise, Adoniram retains his post over the forced labour (2 Sam. 20:24). Azariah is high priest, replacing Zadok and Abiathar, who served under David (2 Sam. 20:25) until early in Solomon's reign (1 Kgs 2:27). The royal scribes (*sōpĕrîm*) Elihoreph and Ahijah inherit their office from their father Shisha, who was David's scribe (see 'Notes on the text', 3.b) and are responsible for domestic and international royal correspondence as well as royal annalistic records. Benaiah's office over the army assumes the narrative in 2:28–35. His prior leadership over the Cherethites and Pelethites (2 Sam. 8:18) is not reassigned and perhaps is conjoined to his new role.

Three new roles appear and speak to necessary bureaucratic growth as the kingdom expands. Azariah is governor (*něṣîb*) over the land (cf. v. 19), supervising Solomon's district governors (*niṣṣābîm*) in the collection and distribution of provisions. Together with Zabud, Azariah is assumedly son to Nathan the prophet; their appointments may recognize Nathan's instrumentality in Solomon's accession. Zabud's role is that of 'king's advisor', literally 'friend of the king' (*rē'eh hammelek*). Mentioned only during the reigns of David (2 Sam. 15:37; 16:16; 2 Chr. 27:33) and Solomon (1 Kgs 4:5), the role was possibly originally an honorary one that over time gained the status of official counsellor (Mettinger 1971: 63–69; *HALOT* 1264). Ahishar serves as steward (lit. 'over the house'), responsible for royal estates, trade and mining. This new role continues through the monarchic period in both kingdoms (18:3; 2 Kgs 10:5; 15:5; 18:18, 37; 19:2; Isa. 22:15; 36:3, 22; 37:2).

4:7–20

7–19. Twelve district governors provision Solomon's court and stables on a monthly rotation (vv. 22–23, 27). Military and priestly personnel may have been included in this civic largesse (Redford 1972). Given such demands, the amounts indicated (v. 22) are reasonable. Two governors are the king's sons-in-law and the list may reflect a later era of Solomon's rule when his daughters were of marriageable age.

The taxation system consolidated political and economic authority to Solomon's capital (Heaton 1974: 53). The reason behind the district boundaries is unclear. Given the disparate agricultural abilities of each region, equalization of agricultural and economic potential cannot be the main reason. Nor, given Solomon's need for creating a unified state, can it be an attempt to inflict economic hardship upon certain areas. Rather, following traditional tribal units where possible, and possibly in the light of political and ethnic considerations, the king divided the country into homogeneous geographical units (see Aharoni 1979).

The list highlights the names of the governors (v. 8), rather than the district boundaries. Many governors are introduced with a patronymic (vv. 12, 16–19; six governors), although anomalies exist. Ahimaaz in Naphtali has no patronymic, an oddity for the king's son-in-law. The familiarity may be explained if he is the well-known son of Zadok, who played a key role during Absalom's rebellion (2 Sam. 15:27; 17:17–21; 18:19–29), and the brother of Azariah the priest (v. 1).

The greater anomaly is the listing by patronymic only (vv. 8–11, 13; five governors). The proper name need not be lost due to damage to the list (see 'Notes on the text', 8.a.–19.a.), nor need be non-Israelite (Heaton 1974: 54; Alt 1959: 198–213). The names are Semitic, and the list with its mixture of patronymic only (possibly evidential of an identifying nickname) and given name with patronymic conforms to similar lists in Ugaritic and Akkadian epigraphy from the period in question (Hess 1997; Naveh 1990).

Despite the vagaries of the territories' delineation, a clockwise progression of districts two to seven surround the first district, Ephraim. These districts are identified primarily by names of villages and cities and have some affinity to tribal boundaries. Following these seven districts, districts eight to ten are clustered together in the north, and districts eleven and twelve are located contiguous to one another in the south (see Beitzel 1985: 125; for cross-referencing of place names to modern Arab and Hebrew names, together with locations on the Israel-Survey grid, see Aharoni 1979: 429–443). Of the last five districts, all but district twelve are designated according to tribal names and generally follow the location of the ancient tribal areas. Thus there is a pattern to the list: an inner ring maintaining some approximation to tribal boundaries, and an outer north–south cluster with greater approximation to tribal boundaries and maintaining appropriate tribal names. In the light of this, the suggestion of some scholars (G. Wright 1967: 58–68) that Solomon has undertaken a massive reorientation of tribal allotments seems untenable (so Aharoni 1979: 316; DeVries 2003: 71–72; Gray 1970: 135–136; Mettinger 1971: 118–119).

The twelfth district is situated in the 'land of Gilead, the land of Sihon king of the Amorites, and of Og king of Bashan'. The identification is problematic in that it overlaps with the description of the sixth and seventh districts. There is also an overlap in the names of the district governors of districts six (Ben-geber) and twelve (Geber). Considering the overlaps between these three districts, v. 19a should be considered a duplication or variant of v. 13. Serving as a 'historical footnote' (Jones 1984a: 144; Mettinger 1971: 122), it describes a pre-Solomonic condition in the Transjordan of only one administrative area supervised by Geber son of Uri. Solomon realigned the territory into two districts (six and seven).

Eleven districts are thus far represented. The twelfth is found in v. 19b, 'there was one governor over the land of Judah'. Over this twelfth district of Judah is one governor who may be Ahishar (v. 6), who oversees the royal estates. Alternatively, Azariah (v. 5) may be the governor of this district as well as the supervisor of the eleven governors.

20. Solomon's wise administration fulfils Abrahamic promises regarding the people's greatness (Gen. 22:17; 32:12; Josh. 11:4; 2 Sam. 17:11). The needs of all the people are abundantly met and celebrated in idyllic terms not uncommon in ANE literature (KAI 215, line 9, cited in Seow 1984: 143; B. Long 1984: 76). The idyllic and hyperbolic nature of the summary

is evident given subsequent assessments of Solomon's rule as harsh and exploitative (e.g. 5:13[27]; 9:15; 12:4).

4:21–34

21–25. Solomon's administration extends beyond the borders of Judah and Israel from the Euphrates to Philistia to the wadi el-'Arish (v. 21). His kingdom approximates that of David's (2 Sam. 8:1–14; 10; 11:1; cf. 1 Chr. 18–20; Myers, *IDB* 1:776–778) and of the boundaries promised Abraham (Gen. 15:18). A later addition from a perspective east of the Euphrates (v. 24; cf. Ezra 8:36; Neh. 2:7, 9; 3:7) refines the boundaries by citing Tiphsah (on the northern reaches of the Euphrates near its northward turn, east of Aleppo) as the extent of the kingdom.

So completely does Solomon fulfil Abrahamic promises and Davidic aspirations that the complete subjugation of 'all the kingdoms' (vv. 21, 24 [twice]) on 'all sides' (v. 24) for 'all the days' (vv. 21, 25) is noted. Regardless of the extent of historical reality in this picture (Provan et al. 2003: 251–254), its hyperbolic terms emphasize Solomon's wondrous administrative wisdom. Solomon's rule (*mšl*; v. 21), like his proverbial sayings (*mšl*; v. 32), evidences his wisdom.

Solomon's ideal kingdom is indicated by the overflowing tribute of numerous subjugated kings that, all the days of Solomon's life, make his court a wonder. The depiction of the peace and wealth of Solomon's reign, and the lavishness of his court, are not dissimilar to the depiction of other royal administrations found in ANE royal inscriptions (Weinfeld 1983: 93–104). Solomon's idyllic administration provides a context of peace, well-being and wholeness (*šālôm*) that enables security of life for Judah and Israel from Dan to Beersheba. This security is depicted in terms that anticipate the messianic era envisioned by Micah (Mic. 4:4) in which the full covenant life is experienced in the blessing of secure rest, in food and drink (v. 25; cf. v. 20).

26–28. Practically, the maintenance of Solomon's dominion (vv. 21, 24) would necessitate the military might and swift-riding messengers suggested in v. 27. However, this practicality sounds an ominous note, particularly as it comes immediately before the encomium. Whom will Solomon trust for the greatness of his rule? His many horses and military might, or YHWH? In the light of Deut. 17:16 Solomon's horses reveal his disobedience to deuteronomic law and this must colour how one reads the encomium. Solomon is good and wise, yes, but as each chapter thus far has raised questions about the glory and wisdom of Solomon's reign, the same occurs here.

The textual traditions are varied on the number of stalls for Solomon's horses (see 'Notes on the text', 26[5:6].a). The MT tradition of forty thousand continues the hyperbole of Solomon's greatness – here undercut by the deuteronomic warning. Comparing the statements elsewhere of Philistine chariots numbering three thousand with six thousand chariot-eers (1 Sam. 13:5), and Ahab's muster of two thousand chariots (The Monolith Inscription in *ARAB* 1: §§595–596, 601, 610–611, cited in Miller and Hayes 1986: 258–259), a count of four thousand seems historically viable. Twelve thousand *pārāšîm* (here translated as 'horsemen'; the term can refer either to horses or to horsemen) attests to the common practice of charioteers mounted three to a chariot (Exod. 14:7; 2 Kgs 9:25).

29–34. The encomium rounds out the narratives of 1 Kgs 3 – 4 with linguistic connections that hold these chapters together as evidence of Solomon's wisdom from God.

The passage begins, 'God gave (*ntn*) wisdom (*ḥkm*) to Solomon', and stands as a reminder that God requests, 'Ask what I will give (*ntn*) to you,' (3:5) and in which YHWH confirms that 'I will give (*ntn*) . . . a wise (*ḥkm*) heart. It is also reminiscent of the people's acknowledgment of the given wisdom (*ḥkm*) of God in 3:28. The 'very great discernment' (*tĕbûnâ*) connects the summary to 3:9, 11–12, where verbal forms related to 'dis-cernment' are employed. In a similar way, the 'breadth of mind [lit. 'heart']' of 4:29 recalls crucial references to Solomon's heart regarding the wisdom of God (3:9, 12).

Another significant linguistic connection is found in the usage of the word 'hear' (*šm'*; 4:34), where twice it is told that Solomon's wisdom is heard by all peoples and kings of the earth. The international 'hearing' mirrors the prior 'hearing' of the people Israel (3:28). Even more, it mirrors the earlier 'hearing' of Solomon's own heart (3:9, 11). Because Solomon hears, God's wisdom is heard throughout Israel and beyond. Unfortunately, it will also be the state of Solomon's heart (11:4) that causes Israel's later misfortune.

Solomon's wisdom, in typical ANE fashion, is expressed in grand terms. It is greater than the shared wisdom traditions of Israel's neighbours to the east (see Matt. 2:1) and west (4:30), and superlative in comparison to individual men known within the wisdom tradition (Ethan and Heman; see Pss 88 – 89; Calcol and Darda, 1 Chr. 2:6). Finally, so great is Solomon's wisdom that his name is known internationally. Its international scope ties the epilogue thematically to 1 Kgs 3:13 and YHWH's promise to Solomon of both fame and honour. 1 Kgs 4:31 fulfils the promise of honour, and as the kings come to Solomon they bring tribute (4:21), thus fulfilling the promise of riches.

Beyond administration and governance, the epilogue extends Solomon's wisdom into areas of proverbial wisdom, song and observations from nature. Compiling observations from nature was a common motif in the wisdom tradition, demonstrating the compiler's wisdom (Job 38 – 41; Prov. 30:15–31). The prolific nature of Solomon's observations is apparent from the large, round numbers taken to mean 'a great many'. Probably a later addition to the encomium, the comments associate Solomon with the larger biblical wisdom tradition. In the context of the epilogue, the nations and kings travel to hear both this proverbial wisdom and his wisdom in justice and governance. In all these ways Solomon is presented in ANE terms as the ideal, wise king. None other can compare with him, and all this is evidence of YHWH's hand upon his rule.

Explanation

Continuing the hyperbolic exposition of Solomon's great wisdom that eventuates in wealth, peace, tribute and honour, this chapter is a commentary on YHWH's faithfulness to his promises. It also provides a commentary on the longing of God's people for his just rule on earth.

The chapter's primary narrative goal is to demonstrate YHWH's blessing upon Israel. As Solomon operates out of YHWH's wisdom, promises made long ago to Abraham, and also to David, are fulfilled. The people as 'numerous as the sand that is upon the seashore' fulfils the ancient promise to Abraham (Gen. 22:17). His extensive kingdom, inherited from the conquests of David, fulfils the promise given to Abraham (Gen. 15:18–19; cf. Deut. 1:7). David was promised 'rest' (*nûaḥ*) from his enemies, and Solomon's people have 'peace' (*šālôm*; vv. 25[5:5]). Solomon will later, while speaking of YHWH's promise to David, refer to this peace as 'rest' (5:4[18]).

The record of Solomon's great reign is not free of trouble, however. The mention of the forced labour (v. 6), the administrative network that will take from the people as per Samuel's prediction (1 Sam. 8:11–18), and the horses and wealth that contravene the law of the king (Deut. 17:16–17) alert the reader that not all is well in Camelot. Like the negative notes in Joshua that are later taken up in Judges, the negative elements are mentioned here, but taken up and highlighted in chs. 5, 10–11. Thus there is an awareness that that greatness is undercut and ultimately fails.

For an exilic people framing the final edition of Kings, the retention of these hyperbolic expressions of Solomon's greatness does much more than provide a narrative of what Israel once hoped for, but lost. Certainly, the passage does add to the polemic that seeks to explain Israel's exile. But with no ruling king, and with any return to such governance only a dim hope, the recall of Solomon's greatness is more than polemic.

First, it affirms a conviction that YHWH remains true to what he has promised both Abraham and David. The record of the fulfilment of YHWH's promises in Solomon's rule is a testimony that YHWH will remain faithful to his covenants in the present generation of exile. The ending of the Kings corpus leaves open the possibility of the king's return, and the rebuilding of nation and temple. Particularly as the promises to David are kept alive in the 'lamp' passages (1 Kgs 15:4; 2 Kgs 8:19), there remains a hope for those in exile that God will once again bless Israel and its king. A similar testimony to God's faithfulness to his covenant appears in exilic prophets such as Jeremiah (23:5–6; 31:31–37; 33:14–16) and Ezekiel (37:15–28). The glory of Solomon's rule is part of the exilic hope in YHWH's covenant faithfulness: what he has done in Solomon's reign is a reminder of his commitment to ancient promises, even in the place of exile.

For a people in exile there is, secondly, a great hope in looking back to a king who was both so great and so flawed. Despite the divine wisdom granted Solomon, his rule fails. Yet, even in the midst of that failure, God's purposes are not thwarted, for he appoints Jeroboam to kingship until a time when the Davidic dynasty has been disciplined (11:29–39). The failure of Solomon was foreseen in YHWH's plan, and taken up by the divided kingdom that furthered the purposes of YHWH. If, then, God is able to incorporate such failure into his sovereign designs for his people, would he not be able, similarly, from the great failure of the exile, to raise up new directions for his purposes? This hope may account in part for the chronicler's post-exilic presentation of Solomon as a great hero. As Israel in exile pondered their own failure, and as they ventured back to the land, a valorized Solomon became a paradigm of hope. The chronicler chose to emphasize that God's purposes are achieved through great heroes, even flawed ones, precisely because YHWH works through his power graciously manifested in his covenant with Israel (Konkel 2006: 105).

The record of Solomon as the great, wise king provided a third avenue for Israel's theological reflection. Knowing that Solomon's rule failed, the inclusion of the hyperbolic expression of its greatness voices a desire for the reality of such a kingdom on earth. Perhaps the great tragedy of 1 Kgs 4 is that Solomon appears close to providing such a utopian kingdom, but could never do so because as a fallible human he ruled fallibly. What was hoped for and presented as a near possibility in Solomon would serve as a reminder that the earthly king was a regent. He was a substitute – and a poor one, however great the king – for Israel's true king, YHWH.

The concept of YHWH as Israel's king is an early one (Exod. 15:18; Deut. 33:5), and Israel's request for a visible king was understood as a rejection of YHWH's rule (1 Sam. 8:7; 12:12). As king, YHWH had rescued his people out of Egypt and entered into royal covenant with them at Sinai. The psalter includes Israel's prayers and praises and several of the psalms proclaim that God ('ĕlōhîm) or YHWH is king (47:8; 93:1; 96:10; 97:1; 99:1; cf. 95:3; 29:10). Recent research suggests that the metaphor of YHWH's kingship may be a governing metaphor for the whole psalter (G. Wilson 1985; McCann 1993: 27; Mays 1994: 6–7). As divine king, YHWH is a perfect template of Solomon's idyllic rule. As king, YHWH delivers and rescues his people from enemies, rules them justly and righteously, and provides for all their needs – and all of this without any failure or shadow.

In the light of Solomon's failed rule, and in the exilic and post-exilic eras in the light of the inability to place another Davidide upon the throne,

Israel's reflections regarding kingship appear to be instrumental in the shaping of the psalter. The first three of the psalter's five books focus on the Davidic monarchy. In them David's rule is first lauded and then lamented. The third book of the psalter ends with the apparent failure of the Davidic monarchy, and the end of the Davidic Covenant (Ps. 89:38–51). The exilic and post-exilic reflection on these events led Israel to recall the premonarchic era in which YHWH himself was king. This emphasis is apparent in the fourth and fifth books of the psalter as Israel's exodus and wilderness sojourn and YHWH's kingly care of the people during that time are recalled. Israel is thus directed back to YHWH as king, rejoicing in his reign. The psalter's shape directs post-exilic Israel to look to YHWH as their saving king. In complete reliance upon him they wait in eschatological hope for his earthly rule instituted once again (de Claissé-Walford 1997; McCann 1993).

It seems impossible, knowing the canonical story of Solomon in Kings not to read 1 Kgs 4 without acknowledging the sad ending of the story. But it is the failure of this king that serves as a reminder that no earthly king can rule with perfect wisdom, justice and power. These kings are imperfect regents, but their failure and all the pain it engenders for God's people is a reminder that only God can rule the kingdom for which we long.

The NT proclaims that this King has indeed come – humbly, and without any of the grandeur of Solomon's court. But, hidden as his royalty was, it did save, reveal wisdom and speak justice. His future return will inaugurate the kingdom hoped for in Solomon, longed for in the psalter and awaited through the chequered years of history.

1 KINGS 5:1–18[MT 5:15–32]

Translation

[1][15]Hiram king of Tyre sent his servants to Solomon[a], for he had heard that they had anointed him as king after his father (for Hiram had always been a friend to David). [2][16]Solomon sent to Hiram, saying, [3][17]'You know that David my father was not able to build a house for the name of YHWH his God[a] because of the wars that surrounded him, until YHWH put them under the soles of his feet[b]. [4][18] But now YHWH my God has given me rest all around; there is neither adversary nor misfortune. [5][19]Therefore, I intend to build a house for the name of YHWH my God just as YHWH spoke to David my father, saying, "Your son, whom I will put on your throne after you, he will build the house for my name." [6][20]And now[a] command that they may cut for me cedars[b] of Lebanon. My servants will work with your servants. I will give you whatever you say for your servant's wages for you know there is among us no one who knows how to cut timber[b] like the Sidonians.'

⁷⁽²¹⁾When Hiram heard the words of Solomon, he was very pleased and said, 'Blessed be YHWHᵃ this day, for he has given David a wise son over this great people.' ⁸⁽²²⁾Hiram sent to Solomon saying, 'I have received the message you sent to me. I will meet all your need with cedar and fir trees. ⁹⁽²³⁾My servants will bring themᵃ down from Lebanon to the sea, and I will make them into rafts *to travel* by seaᵇ to the place that you shall specify to me, and I will dismantle them there and you shall carry themᶜ away. Then you shall meet my need by giving provision for my household.' ¹⁰⁽²⁴⁾So Hiram provided all Solomon needed of cedar and fir trees. ¹¹⁽²⁵⁾And Solomon gave Hiram 20,000 measures of wheat as foodᵃ for his household, and 20 measuresᵇ of fine oil. Thus Solomon would give to Hiram yearly. ¹²⁽²⁶⁾YHWH had given wisdom to Solomon just as he promised him. There was peace between Hiram and Solomon and the two of them made a covenant.

¹³⁽²⁷⁾King Solomon levied forced labour from all Israel, and the levy was thirty thousand men. ¹⁴⁽²⁸⁾He sent them to Lebanon, ten thousand a month by shifts; they were in Lebanon one month and then two months at home. Adoniram was over the forced labour. ¹⁵⁽²⁹⁾Solomon had seventy thousand burden-bearersᵃ and eighty thousand stonecutters in the mountains, ¹⁶⁽³⁰⁾besides Solomon's three thousand three hundred ᵃ supervisors who were over the work – the ones who ruled over the people who were doing the work. ¹⁷⁽³¹⁾ᵃSo the king commanded and they quarried great and valuable stones to lay the foundation of the house with dressed stone. ¹⁸⁽³²⁾The builders of Solomon and Hiram and the Gebalitesᵃ cut and prepared the timbers and the stones to build the house.

Notes on the text

1[15].a. LXX* 'and Hiram sent his servants to anoint Solomon' seeks to honour Solomon by one king's anointing another. Syr reads as LXX and adds further honour: 'and Hiram sent a blessing to Solomon'.

3[17].a. LXX reads, 'YHWH my God' for MT 'YHWH his God', whereby Solomon references David's relationship to YHWH.

3[17].b. 'his feet' in many MSS, LXX, Vg, Tg. Q 'my feet' is an effort to account for David's having peace, without building the temple.

6[20].a. 'And now' (*wĕ'attâ*) is the common transition in a letter to its core request (Pardee 1982: 173; see 2 Kgs 5:6; 10:2).

6[20].b. MT reads, 'cedars . . . timber'. 'Timber' acknowledges the various woods of vv. 8, 10.

7[21].a. Hiram names YHWH (denoting the God of Israel). LXXᴸ makes the specification explicit with 'YHWH, the God of Israel'.

9[23].a. MT omits the 3 m. pl. pr. suff. by haplography. Following LXX, it is here provided (*yōridûm*, 'and they will bring them down').

9[23].b. MT 'I will make them rafts on the sea', glossed for sense.

9[23].c. The 3 m. pl. pr. suff. is provided: 'you shall carry *them*'.

11[25].a. *makkōlet* is a hapax legomenon and may be a misreading of *ma'ăkāl* ('food'; so LXXᴬᴼ).

11[25].b. The measure of oil is confused here. LXX reads 20,000 baths (cf. 2 Chr. 2:9), which grossly exaggerates the provision.

15[29].a. The qal act. part. *nōśē'* is omitted from translation as an interpretative gloss for *sabbāl*, 'burden bearer'.

16[30].a. The number of supervisors varies in the translations from three thousand five hundred to three thousand seven hundred (LXX[BLO]; cf. 9:23).

17[31].a. In LXX* vv. 17–18[31–32], together with 6:37–38a, follow the atnach in 6:1. See further at 'Form and structure'.

18[32].a. The Gebalites are known from Josh. 13:5. Emendation is unnecessary.

Form and structure

Solomon exercises his wisdom on the international stage by establishing, on his own terms, a covenant with Hiram. Treaty terms are the focus of vv. 1–12, and a brief additional note presents Solomon's system of forced labour. The treaty negotiates provisions for the temple, which is the pinnacle of Solomon's career. A treaty for the glorious temple is juxtaposed to the forced labour that represents the nadir of Solomon's career and later fuels rebellion against the dynasty (1 Kgs 12). By this juxtaposition the temple project cannot be construed in wholly positive terms. Once again Solomon's wise rule is overshadowed by negative actions.

The passage has several thoroughly integrated Deuteronomistic phrases (vv. 3–5[17–19]; see 'Comment'), making clear discernment of underlying source material impossible. Original records of the correspondence between the kings is a possible source for the 'and now' (v. 6) used in ANE letters to signal the core request after the preliminaries. The details of the levy and builders (vv. 13–18) may arise from archival records recording the number, type and disposition of the workers (vv. 13–14a, 15), their supervision (vv. 14b, 16) and the loci of work: timber and stone (v. 18). The MT text places the records as the final preparation for temple building against the LXX, which places vv. 17–18 after 1 Kgs 6:1a as part of the actual construction account.

The correspondence (vv. 7–12) is stylized around key words that emphasize the relationship of Solomon's wisdom to the drafting of the covenant, and that reveal Hiram's covenanted subordination to Solomon. The section could be diagrammed in this way:

A   Hiram praises YHWH for 'giving a wise son' to David (v. 7)

    B   The needs of Hiram and Solomon are contrasted: Solomon is promised 'all your need'; Hiram requests only 'my need' (vv. 8–9)

B'   The provisions to Hiram and Solomon are contrasted:
     Hiram 'gives' Solomon 'all his need'; Hiram is 'given'
     only provision (vv. 10–11)
A' YHWH is credited with 'giving wisdom' to Solomon
     (v. 12)

The negotiations (B, B') are couched in the context of Solomon's
'wisdom', which both Hiram (v. 7) and the narrator (v. 12) recognize
as given by YHWH. That wisdom brokers a favourable treaty for Solomon.
Hiram promises and supplies 'all' the needs of Solomon; by contrast, Hiram's needs are stated and supplied without superlatives. The
simple narrative technique effectively places Hiram in an inferior position
within the treaty covenant – evidential of Solomon's wisdom!
     The wise treaty negotiations result in peace (v. 12) and building materials
for the temple. By this point Solomon's wisdom is apparent in his pursuit
of YHWH (ch. 3), in his justice (ch. 3), and in his national and international administration (ch. 4). Now, by couching temple preparations in
the context of wisdom, the temple is likewise subsumed under the rubric
of wisdom. Indeed, the temple becomes the greatest expression of that
wisdom.

Comment

5:1–12

Hiram of Tyre is known primarily through the biblical text, although
Josephus refers to his reign in excerpts from the non-extant Hellenic
historians Menander and Dius (*Apion* 1.17–18, lines 106–127). Tyre was
a coastal city founded during the early third millennium BC on an island
near the shore. A dominant Phoenician city and trading hub, it exercised
colonial power in Cyprus and eventually as far as Carthage. Only its defeat
by Alexander the Great retired its international and commercial dominance
(Katzenstein 1973: 74–95). Primary exports included timber from the
Lebanon mountains (Fritz 2003: 61), a commodity previously supplied to
David by Hiram (2 Sam. 5:11–12).
     Hiram is labelled the 'friend' of David (*'ōhēb*, lit. 'one who loves'). This
is a term of international relations common to the ANE that characterized
the loyalty and friendship forged under covenant between independent
kings (as here), a sovereign and vassal, or a king and his subject. By it, one
treaty partner acknowledges the relationship of covenant commitment
owed its partner (Moran 1963: 78–81). David and Hiram appear to have
forged such a relationship. The early tenth century and David's war against
the Philistines was a probable setting for a covenant forged against a
common enemy, Philistia. Philistia's defeat would increase Tyre's coastal

dominance, and an alliance with Israel would ensure protected access to inland trading routes.

Hiram's delegation, sent either when Solomon became co-regent with his father or sole ruler after his death, was dispatched according to international protocol to honour a monarch's accession (see Amarna letters Nos. 33–34, in Moran 1992; cf. 2 Sam. 10:1–2) and sought continuance of the relationship established with David. The negotiations that follow this greeting are not to 'mutual advantage' (contra Gray 1970: 151). Solomon is wholly in charge and Hiram responds as a vassal to his overlord (DeVries 2003: 84; Provan 1995: 63–64; Sweeney 2007: 102). In this way the rhetoric furthers the hyperbolic presentation of Solomon's greatness (1 Kgs 4:21, 24).

Solomon begins negotiations and 'sends' to Hiram, and a response is 'sent' in return (v. 7). Solomon's words are filled with Deuteronomistic phrasing and particularly evoke 2 Sam. 7 (e.g. 'house for the name of YHWH his/my God', and 'house for my name' [v. 5; cf. 2 Sam. 7:13; 1 Kgs 8:18–19]; 'YHWH has given rest all around' [v. 4; cf. 2 Sam. 7:1, 11; Deut. 12:10; 25:19; Josh. 21:42; 23:1]). The phrases focus on political as well as theological concerns: Davidic dynasty and temple building.

Solomon's negotiations with Hiram begin with three preliminary steps. He first rationalizes the delay in temple building (v. 3), asserting Hiram's knowledge that David's wars prevented him from building the temple. (The chronicler theologizes the rationale [1 Chr. 22:7–10; 28:2–6].) The emphatic address ('*you* know') rhetorically places Hiram in a position of knowledge as an equal partner to David – an equality the chapter as a whole will undermine. Hiram knows the reason for the project's delay and thus of the project in which David purposed to build YHWH's house (2 Sam. 7).

Solomon next asserts the removal of the hindrance, as YHWH has 'given me rest all around' (v. 4). So complete is this rest in Solomon's rule that neither 'adversary' nor 'misfortune' can be found (v. 4; cf. 4:20–25), two nouns that evoke other aspects of Solomon's reign. 'Misfortune' (*pega'*) has the same root as in 2:25, 29, 31–32, 34, 46, where Solomon's enemies are 'struck' (*pg'*). There Solomon's 'wisdom' (2:6, 9) is displayed in real-politik. Now Solomon's wisdom is displayed in the temple project (vv. 7, 12; cf. 'Form and structure' above), enabled by the lack of 'misfortune'. The second nominal resonance is that the lack of 'adversary' (*śāṭān*) is short-lived: Hadad and Rezon appear as adversaries against Solomon in 11:14, 23, 25. The wise temple builder turns his heart from YHWH (11:4) and YHWH sends adversaries to discipline the king.

Solomon concludes by asserting he will build the temple for YHWH's name. It is the place of YHWH's choice (Deut. 12:5, 11; 14:23–24; 16:2, 6, 11; 26:2), where his power resides while he remains transcendent (see 'Comment', 1 Kgs 8). Solomon's conclusion leads to the core negotiation, which is the request for building materials. The phrase 'and now' is typical in ANE letters and signals the end of preliminaries and transition to a letter's core (see 'Notes on the text'). Solomon's request is really an imperative 'command' (*ṣwh*; v. 6). Later, Solomon will command his own workers (v. 17, using the same root), suggesting that he places Hiram in the same category as his servants. The peremptory command to Hiram is tempered, however, by Solomon's offer that Hiram set the wages for the Sidonian workers. Solomon does offer the appearance of equality and (even) magnanimity in the treaty he negotiates. Solomon requests cedars cut by Hiram's Sidonian lumbermen, skilled in logging (v. 6). Solomon's corvée force will work alongside the Sidonians, cutting timber.

The core of Hiram's response is details of provision and payment. He will send two types of trees (vv. 8, 10): cedar (*ʾărāzîm*) and fir (*bĕrōšîm*, variously translated as 'cypress' or 'juniper'; 'fir' is a broad term encompassing several conifer types; Trevor 1962; Zohary 1982: 106–107). Native to Phoenicia, both trees were by size and durability suitable for temple construction. Cedar was used in several places inside and outside the temple as beams, pillars, panelling and decorative work (1 Kgs 6:10, 15–18; 36; 7:2, 12). Fir was used in non-structural details such as flooring, panelling and doors (1 Kgs 6:15, 34; cf. 2 Chr. 3:5). Most of the transport was by sea (2 Chr. 2:15 indicates Joppa as the arrival port), and in the arduous journey up to Jerusalem the materials were transported by wagon over prepared roadbeds (Fritz 2003: 61). The expense and effort reveal the temple's importance in Solomon's kingdom.

Hiram's wage is food for his royal household – a desirable commodity for a nation whose narrow coastal strip affords little arable land. Approximately 800 tons of wheat ([800,000 kg] 20,000 cors; a measure of dry or liquid materials) and 1,760 gallons ([8,000 l] 20 cors) of oil annually compares to Solomon's annual household provision of 32,000 cors of meal (4:22). Similar payment probably continued for the twenty-year period of temple building (1 Kgs 9:10). In addition to payment in foodstuffs, Solomon also deeds cities to Hiram (9:11–14; see 'Comment' there).

Hiram begins his response with an expression of great pleasure (v. 7). The pleasure reflects the historical reality of the renewed Israelite–Phoenician relationship. Hiram also, like the foreigner Jethro (Exod. 18:10), and like Kings David and Solomon (1 Sam. 25:32, 39; 1 Kgs 1:48; 8:15, 56), blesses YHWH (*bārûk YHWH*), acknowledging David's wise (*ḥākām*) son (v. 8). Contextually, the praise responds to Solomon's proposal for the temple project and the acknowledgment of his right as chosen descendant of David (v. 5). Hiram's praise and his generous provision thus affirm Solomon's dynastic claim and his decision to build the temple as YHWH's will.

The praise also connects Solomon's wisdom to the temple project, a quality later tied to the treaty relationship by which temple materials are supplied (v. 12). The dual notation of Solomon's wisdom given by YHWH

(vv. 7, 12) encloses the preparatory plans, setting even the beginnings of temple building in the context of YHWH's wisdom. The temple will be the finest expression of Solomon's wisdom, although the project already lies under a pall (see 'Comment' on 3:1–3). Solomon's wisdom, while God-given, is neither complete nor perfect. In this passage, however, such reservation recedes from view.

Within the envelope structure (vv. 7, 12), several contrasts characterize Solomon as great (cf. 4:21, 24, 34). The first contrast involves who 'hears' (*šm'*) whom. Hiram is the one who 'hears' in this passage. He hears of Solomon's anointing and responds by sending messengers (v. 1); he hears Solomon's request and responds with praise and counterproposal (v. 7). Solomon, on the other hand, nowhere 'hears' Hiram, and, to demonstrate this attitude, no narrative response is provided to Hiram's proposal in vv. 7–9. Solomon's actions are not precipitated by 'hearing' but arise out of his role as a great and wise king.

A second contrast involves Hiram's counterproposal (vv. 8–10) to Solomon's initial work plans (v. 6) and emphatically stresses the division of labour. Hiram begins by emphasizing that '*I* will meet all your need' and that his servants (the original proposal included Solomon's servants) will transport the timber. He continues with the emphatic '*I* will make them into rafts,' while Solomon provides the shipping destination. Then, by contrast, Hiram affirms '*I* will dismantle them' while '*You* [emphatic] shall carry them away.' Finally, to round out the contrastive emphasis, '*You* shall meet my need.'

The counterproposal clearly adds to and clarifies Solomon's original proposal. Curiously, Solomon sends no response. Instead, a summary statement suggests Solomon found the details acceptable and the agreement functions year by year (vv. 10–11). Vv. 13–18, however, reveal that Solomon works according to his original proposal: his workers join Hiram's in Lebanon. Thus Solomon's initial word is the final word. Whatever give and take occurred in the actual historical reality of the treaty, the narrative presentation of it highlights Solomon's dominance over Hiram. Hiram is characterized as a vassal king subservient to the greater king, Solomon.

A third contrast also emphasizes Solomon's superiority. Three times the word 'need' (*ḥēpeṣ*) is used (vv. 8–10). Hiram's message to Solomon is that he will provide 'all your need', and this promise is realized in v. 10 as Hiram supplies 'all Solomon needed'. Hiram's request is only that Solomon provide 'my need' – the superlative 'all' is missing. While Solomon's provision to Hiram is extremely lavish, no summative statement indicates all the need of Hiram's household is met (v. 11).

Finally, the summary statement (v. 12) couches the terms of the treaty in the context of YHWH's wisdom. By treaty, the two kings 'give' to one another (*ntn*; vv. 10, 'provided', 11 [twice], 12). Hiram gives to Solomon cedar and fir trees. Solomon gives to Hiram on a yearly basis wheat and oil for his household. This human giving arises because YHWH has first given Solomon wisdom (1 Kgs 3), and the gift is acknowledged by Hiram in his praise of YHWH (v. 7). All the parties are aware of the gift given by YHWH. It has enabled the present agreement, and peaceful relationship continues in expanding economic ventures that contribute to the temple project (9:26–28; 10:11–12).

5:13–18

To build the temple and palace Solomon sets in place a conscripted labour force, or corvée, from 'all Israel', that is, both Judah and Israel (1 Kgs 1:20; 3:28; 4:1, 7; 11:42). The force was forced labour, not slave labour (used in 1 Kgs 9:15–23). Such labour is not uncommon in the ANE, being conscripted for occasional building projects and other state works (Mendelsohn 1962; Mettinger 1971: 128–139). Under the supervision of Adoniram (1 Kgs 4:6), thirty thousand men in each three-month period (a hundred and twenty thousand each year), worked in shifts of ten thousand men, one month in Lebanon and two months 'at his home', that is, working on Solomon's projects in Jerusalem. The corvée was levied from 'all Israel', but, given the proportional size of northern Israel to Judah, northern Israel supplied a greater number of workers. Over time, this disproportion, and the helplessness of the people against such forced labour, fuelled already-existing tensions between the house of David and the northern tribes, resulting in the revolt and succession of the northern tribes (1 Kgs 12). Solomon's labour force worked alongside Hiram's men in the logging, transport and building operations.

In addition to conscripts for timber work, Solomon's labour force includes stonecutters and burden bearers (a hundred and fifty thousand in total). These worked at ashlar quarries in the Israelite hill country, cutting stones up to 7 feet (2 m) in size (Shiloh and Horowitz 1975). Cutting and transporting the ashlar blocks was difficult and expensive work, so the stones are noted as 'valuable' (v. 17). The difficulty and expense of the work is emphasized in that the supervisory team is specifically noted: three thousand three hundred supervisors worked with the men. Assisting the workers of Hiram and Solomon in the preparation of the wood and stone were men of Gebal (Byblos), a city north of Tyre and Sidon that Joshua had not been able to take (Josh. 13:5), and known for its timber works. Despite human and material costs the work proceeds at the king's command (v. 17), a further reminder of the king's power.

Explanation

Building preparations precede the culminating event of Solomon's reign – the temple project. The importance of the temple is signalled in that it is the structural centre of Solomon's narrative (chs. 6–8; see Walsh 1996: 373).

The project is precipitated because YHWH has given 'rest' (*hēnîaḥ*, from the root *nwḥ*; 5:4[18]). The same state is described as 'peace on every side' (*šālôm*, from the root *šlm*; 4:24[5:4]). Thus the man of peace, Solomon (*šĕlōmô*), who has rest/peace on every side, undertakes to build the temple; 1 Chr. 22:9). Solomon's preparations at a time of 'rest' evoke two other passages regarding Israel's life in the land. First, it clearly evokes the Davidic promise, a passage in which it is twice noted YHWH has 'given rest' (*hēnîaḥ*; 2 Sam. 7:1, 11). David's response to YHWH's rest is a desire to build a temple, which, of course, YHWH declines until David's son is enthroned (vv. 12–13). It is the similar conditions of peace that trigger Solomon's own desire for temple building.

Secondly, temple building and the state of rest or peace connect to Moses' last words in Deuteronomy. Moses describes the people's entry into the land and the 'resting place' (*mĕnûḥâ*, from the root *nwḥ*; Deut. 12:9) of their inheritance. There YHWH will 'give rest' (*hēnîaḥ*; v. 10) from their enemies. It is in this context that the call to worship at the place YHWH chooses (vv. 11, 14) is issued and, while Israel worships at various national sanctuaries (e.g. Gilgal, Bethel, Shechem, Gibeon, Shiloh), within the DH it is ultimately Jerusalem and its temple that become the chosen place at which YHWH's name dwells (1 Kgs 8:10–13, 18–20). Solomon's preparations, then, are intimately tied to YHWH's purposes for Israel's well-being, and their covenant relationship with YHWH expressed in their worship.

Solomon's preparations, undertaken under the rubrics of 'rest' and 'peace', also evoke a further-reaching (indeed cosmic) narrative that underlies the canon. After God's work of creation, Gen. 2:2–3 reveals that YHWH 'rested' (*šbt*) from his work. The day of rest, of Sabbath, is set apart from the six creation days, for no work is accomplished in it; rather, YHWH blesses and sanctifies the day, signalling the fullness of what he has created, and the ongoing enjoyment of it. In the garden YHWH and his human creation enjoy intimate fellowship and presence one with the other. All this is the experience of the Sabbath day of rest. The day is also unique in that only this day, apart from the days of creation, has a beginning but no ending. No refrain 'there was evening and there was morning' closes the Sabbath day. 'The seventh day, it seems, stretches forward and beyond the counting of days. . . . It extends to the ends of the ages . . . [and contains] within itself the fullness of time' (Reno 2010: 60).

The creation account reveals that in the setting of the perfect garden YHWH enjoys perfect fellowship with Adam and Eve. But, of course, that fellowship is marked by the fragility of humanity, the 'best and worst that the human partner brings to God's designs' (Balentine 1999: 81). Because of the breaking of human fellowship with YHWH in Gen. 3, the Sabbath rest, blessing and sanctification are imperfectly experienced by humans. But the breaking of human fellowship does not inhibit YHWH's own rest, and the day-without-ending continues as YHWH rests. In the remainder of the Scriptures is revealed how YHWH works to restore humanity once again to the Edenic experience of Sabbath rest in the presence of YHWH.

The temple, as the tabernacle before it, stands as a symbolic restoration of the Edenic Sabbath (Childs 1974: 541–542; Sailhamer 1992: 298; Balentine 1999: 64–65). It is the place where, as in YHWH's day of Sabbath rest, the potential for restoration of God's people into his presence exists. Because YHWH remains in the unending day of his Sabbath rest, he is present to his people and, should they by the means he has prescribed (i.e. in faith) enter the temple, they too will experience his Sabbath rest. It is not surprising, then, that both temple and tabernacle exhibit symbols of an Edenic garden: plants, trees, waters (1 Kgs 6:18, 32, 35; 7:18–20, 23–24, 36; see further in 'Comment' at 1 Kgs 6 – 7).

However, because of humanity's fragility, sinfulness inevitably intrudes upon YHWH's provision for the restoration of Sabbath rest. It is the sin of the first couple that breaks the original Sabbath rest; the sin of the golden calf breaks the Sabbath rest promised in the tabernacle – even as that tabernacle is revealed to Moses; the sin of Israel breaks the Sabbath rest of the temple. The exposition of Solomon's rule in this commentary has explored the darker aspects of his rule and wisdom. In this chapter the use of forced labour casts a shadow upon the temple project. Once the temple is completed, Solomon's rule worsens, threatening the continued restoration of Sabbath rest the temple symbolizes (1 Kgs 9:6–9).

The ongoing hope for restoration of Sabbath rest seems, on these bases, impossible of recovery. But such is not the case, because the temple, echoing the Sabbath rest of the creation, is only a shadow of a deeper cosmic reality. The temple stands as a patterned replica of YHWH's own dwelling or temple in the heavens, as the epistle to the Hebrews reveals (Heb. 8:1–6). Into that true tabernacle Jesus the Christ has entered as a true high priest. There, without any shadow of sin such as marred the original creation, the tabernacle and the temple, he has enacted the sacrifice that finally restores and offers to humanity the Sabbath rest of God's eternal Sabbath day. That 'Today', says the epistle writer, is still proffered to those who would enter by faith into what YHWH has provided (Heb. 4:1–11).

Solomon's preparations, undertaken in rest and peace, are preparatory for the earthly temple, a representative of Edenic creation in which YHWH hallows a day of rest, and a copy of the true temple in heaven. The rest associated with Solomon's temple preparations relates intertextually to images of YHWH's own Sabbath rest, so that the message of the canon proclaims the true temple stands open, for ever without shadow because of the one who – for all – has entered.

1 KINGS 6:1 – 7:51

Translation

⁶:¹In the four hundred and eightieth yearᵃ after the sons of Israel came out from the land of Egypt, in the fourth year of Solomon's reign over Israel, in the month of Ziv, which is the second month, he began to build the house for YHWH. ²The house that King Solomon built for YHWH was 60 cubits long and 20 *cubits* wide and 30 cubits highᵃ. ³The porch at the front of the house's nave was 20 cubits wide across the house's width and 10 cubits deep along the house's front. ⁴He made framed latticed windows for the house. ⁵He built a structure against the house's wall, surrounding the house's wall all around, encompassing both the nave and the inner sanctuary and he made side rooms all around. ⁶The structure's lower storey was 5 cubits wide, its middle storey was 6 cubits wide and its third was 7 cubits wide, for he set offsets around the outside of the house so that nothing was fastened to the walls of the house.

⁷Now the house was built with stone dressed at the quarry so that no hammers, adzes or any iron tool were to be heard in the house while it was being built.

⁸The entry to the lower storeyᵃ was on the south side of the house. One went up by stairsᵇ to the middle storey and from the middle storey to the thirdᶜ. ⁹So he built the house and finished it: he roofed the house with cedar rafters and planks. ¹⁰He built the structure against the whole house 5 cubits high. It was joined to the house by cedar timbers.

¹¹The word of YHWH came to Solomon, ¹²'This house that you are building – if you will walk in my statutes and carry out my judgments, and keep all my commandments to walk in them, then I will establish my word with you that I promised to David your father. ¹³I will dwell in the midst of the sons of Israel and will not forsake my people Israel.'

¹⁴So Solomon built the house and finished it.

¹⁵He constructed the walls of the house inside with cedar boards, from the floor of the house to the ceiling. He covered *them* on the inside with wood and he covered the floor of the house with cypress boards. ¹⁶He built 20 cubits of the rear of the house with cedar planks from the floor to the ceiling; he built this as an inner sanctuary, a holy of holies. ¹⁷And the house, that is the naveᵃ, was 40 cubits long in front of *the inner sanctuary*.

¹⁸The cedar within the house had carvings of gourds and open blossoms. All was cedar; no stone was to be seen. ¹⁹*He built* an inner sanctuary in the midst of the house past the naveᵃ, to set there the ark of the covenant of YHWH. ²⁰The inner sanctuary was 20 cubits long, and 20 cubits wide, and 20 cubits high and he overlaid it with fine gold. Then he madeᵃ a cedar wood altar. ²¹Solomon overlaid the inside of the house with fine gold. He drew gold chains across the front of the inner sanctuary, and overlaid it with gold. ²²He overlaid the whole house with gold until the entire house was completed. And also he overlaid the whole altar of the inner sanctuary with gold.

²³In the inner sanctuary he made two cherubim, each 10 cubits high out of olive

wood. ²⁴The length of the cherub's one wing was 5 cubits, and the second 5 cubits; 10 cubits from wingtip to wingtip. ²⁵The second cherub was also 10 cubits; both cherubim had the same measure and shape. ²⁶The height of the one cherub was 10 cubits, as was the second cherub. ²⁷He placed the cherubim in the midst of the inner house. They spread the wings of the cherubim and the wing of one touched the wall, and the wing of the second cherub was touching the other wall, and in the centre of the house their wings touched one another. ²⁸He overlaid the cherubim with gold.

²⁹He carved all the walls of the house roundabout, in the inner^a and outer *rooms*, with carved engravings of cherubim, palm trees and open blossoms. ³⁰He overlaid the floor of the house with gold, both the inner and outer rooms. ³¹And for the doorway of the inner sanctuary he made olive-wood doors, the frames and doorposts five-sided. ³²He made two doors of olive wood and carved on them carvings of cherubim, palm trees and open blossoms, and he overlaid them with gold and spread gold on the cherubim and palm trees. ³³Likewise, he also made for the doorway of the nave four-sided doorposts of olive wood. ³⁴The two doors were cypress wood. The two leaves of the one door pivoted and the two leaves^a of the second door pivoted. ³⁵He carved cherubim and palm trees and open blossoms and overlaid them with gold evenly applied on the carved work.

³⁶And he built the inner court with three courses of hewn stone and a course of cedar beams.

³⁷In the fourth year in the month of Ziv the house of YHWH was founded. ³⁸And in the eleventh year in the month of Bul (the eighth month) he finished the house in all its parts and according to all its plans. Thus he was seven years in building it.

⁷:¹ᵃHis own house Solomon took thirteen years to build, and he finished all his house. ²He built the House of the Forest of Lebanon 100 cubits long and 50 cubits wide and 30 cubits high^a upon four rows^b of cedar pillars, and cedar beams upon the pillars. ³It was panelled in cedar above the side chambers that were upon the forty-five pillars, fifteen in each row. ⁴There were windows in three rows, with window facing window in three groups. ⁵And all the doorways and doorposts had squared frames, opposite one another in three groups.

⁶He made the Hall of Pillars^a 50 cubits long and 30 cubits wide, with a porch in front of it and pillars and a canopy^b in front of that. ⁷He made the Hall of the Throne where he gave judgment (i.e. the Hall of Judgment). It was panelled with cedar from floor to ceiling^a. ⁸His own house where he dwelt, in the other court outside the hall, was this same workmanship. And he made a house like this hall for the daughter of Pharaoh, whom Solomon had married.

⁹All these were of costly stones, cut according to measure, dressed with the saw inside and out, even from the foundation to the coping and from the outside to the great courtyard. ¹⁰It was founded with large costly stones; stones of 10 and 8 cubits, ¹¹and there were costly stones above dressed to measure, and cedar. ¹²The great court all around had three rows of dressed stones, with a row of cedar beams, as had also the inner court of the House of YHWH and the porch of the house.

[13]King Solomon sent and brought Hiram from Tyre. [14]He was a widow's son from the tribe of Naphtali, but his father was Tyrian, an artisan in bronze. He was filled with skill, cleverness and knowledge for crafting any type of bronze work and he came to King Solomon and did all his work.

[15]He cast[a] two pillars of bronze. The height of the first was 18 cubits and its circumference was 12 cubits and the second was the same. [16]He made two cast bronze capitals to top the pillars. The height of the first capital was 5 cubits and the height of the second was 5 cubits. [17]An interwoven lattice work with festooned chain work adorned the capitals that were atop the pillars; seven for the first capital and seven for the second capital. [18]So he made the pillars, with two rows surrounding each lattice work made to cover the capitals that were above the pomegranates; so he did for the second capital. [19]The capitals that were on top of the pillars in the porch were lily work, 4 cubits. [20]And there were capitals on the two pillars; moreover, close above the rounded projection beside the lattice work there were two hundred pomegranates in rows all around both capitals. [21]He erected the pillars at the porch of the nave; he erected the right pillar and named it Jachin, and the left pillar and named it Boaz. [22]Lily work was on top of the pillars. So the work of the pillars was finished.

[23]Then he made the cast sea. It was round, 10 cubits from brim to brim and 5 cubits high. Its circumference was 30 cubits. [24]There were ornamental gourds under its brim all around, ten to a cubit, encircling the sea completely. There were two rows of ornamental gourds, cast when it was cast. [25]It stood on twelve oxen, three facing north, three west, three south, and three east; the sea *was set* on top of them and their hindquarters faced inwards. [26]It was a handbreadth thick and its brim fashioned like the brim of a cup, like a lily blossom. It held two thousand baths.

[27]He made the stands, ten, of bronze, each stand was 4 cubits long and 4 cubits wide and 3 cubits high[a]. [28]This was the construction of the stands[a]: they had frames, and the frames were between the crossbars. [29]On the frames between the crossbars were lions, oxen and cherubim. And upon the crossbars, both above and below the lions and oxen, were wreaths of hammered work[a]. [30]And each stand had four bronze wheels with bronze axles and its four corners had supports. Beneath the basin were cast supports with wreaths beside each. [31]And its opening[a] was inside the crown, extending upwards 1 cubit. Its opening was round, in the form of a pedestal, a cubit and a half *wide*. Also on its opening were carvings, but their frames were squared, not round. [32]The four wheels were under the frames and the axle-trees of the wheels attached to the stand. And the height of each wheel was one and a half cubits. [33]The work of the wheels was like a chariot wheel: their axle-trees, rims, spokes and hubs were all cast.

[34]There were four supports at the four corners of each stand. The supports were part of the stand itself. [35]On the top of the stand was a round band half a cubit high. Also on top of the stand were its handles[a]; its frames were a part of it. [36]He engraved on the panels of its handles and upon its frames cherubim, lions and palm trees, as each had space, and there were wreaths all around. [37]He made ten stands this way. All of them had the same casting, measure and shape.

[38]Then he made ten bronze basins. Each held 40 baths; each basin measured 4 cubits and each basin stood upon one stand of the ten stands. [39]He placed the stands, five on the right and five on the left side of the house and the sea he placed on the right side of the house, eastwards towards the south.

[40]Then Hiram made the pots[a], shovels and bowls.

So Hiram finished all the work that he did for King Solomon on the house of YHWH: [41]two pillars, two bowls for the capitals that were on the top of the pillars, and two interwoven lattice works to cover the two bowls for the capitals that were on the top of the pillars; [42]four hundred pomegranates for the two interwoven lattice works (two rows of pomegranates for each interwoven lattice work to cover the two bowls of the capitals that were on the two[a] pillars); [43]ten stands and the ten basins on the stands; [44]one sea, and the twelve oxen beneath the sea.

[45]The pots, the shovels and the bowls, even all these utensils that Hiram made for King Solomon for the House of YHWH out of polished bronze, [46]he cast[a] them in the plain of the Jordan, in clay moulds[b], between Succoth and Zarethan. [47]Solomon left all the utensils *unweighed*[a] because there were so very many; the weight of the bronze could not be determined.

[48]And Solomon made all the objects that were in the house of YHWH: the golden altar; the table that had the bread of presence upon it, of gold; [49]the lamp-stands (five on the right and five on the left before the inner sanctuary), of pure gold; and the flowers, lamps, tongs, of gold; [50]the cups, snuffers, bowls, pans, firepans, of pure gold; and the façades[a] for the doors of the inner house (the holy of holies), and the doors of the house (i.e. the nave), of gold.

[51]Thus all the work that King Solomon did on the house of YHWH was finished. Solomon brought in the consecrated items of David his father – the silver, the gold and the utensils – and put them in the treasuries of the house of YHWH.

Notes on the text

6:1.a. LXX reads, 'four hundred and fortieth year'; MT and LXX[L] follow Dtr's schematic chronology.

2.a. Length and height vary in LXX*. The architectural terms and construction details throughout the chapters are often uncertain and the Versions' variants and alterations suggest attempts to clarify. MT is followed whenever possible and the multiple variants are rarely discussed; see DeVries 2003 for such engagement.

8.a. Reading with LXX and Tg *hattaḥtōnâ* , 'lower storey', for MT *hattîkōnâ*, 'middle storey'.

8.b. LXX, Tg, Vg suggest a winding staircase (Montgomery 1951: 148).

8.c. Reading MT *haššĕlišîm* with some MSS, Syr, Vg as *haššĕlišît*, 'third'.

17.a. As is, MT 'the house, that is the nave' wrongly identifies the house with the nave. LXX* omits 'the house'; LXX further clarifies with a final addition, 'before the inner sanctuary'. This is the reading followed here.

19.a. 'in the midst of the house, past [lit. 'inside'] the nave' suggests the most inner, secure part of the complex, past all preliminary approaches.

20.a. Following LXX, Solomon 'made' the altar. MT 'overlaid the altar' anticipates v. 22.

29.a. MT *millipnîm* as *lipnîmâ* with v. 30; cf. Syr, Tg.

34.a. MT *qĕlāʿîm*, 'curtains', is read with Vrs as *ṣĕlāʿîm*, 'leaves', following the first occurrence in the verse.

7:1.a.–12. LXX* transposes these verses after MT v. 51, recognizing the disruptive nature of the palace-building section.

2a.–3. The height is omitted in LXX*.

2.b. LXX designates three rows of pillars (MT has four). LXX assumes forty-five pillars in three ranks of fifteen (v. 3). However, the 'fifteen in each row' (v. 3) refers not to the pillars, but to the side chambers (Montgomery 1951: 164).

6.a. Whether the Hall of Pillars is an anteroom to the House of the Forest of Lebanon or a room situated elsewhere in the palace complex, and whether the porch structure of v. 6b is that of the Hall of Pillars or an additional antechamber to the House of the Forest of Lebanon, is uncertain (Montgomery 1951: 164–165; Gray 1970: 179–180).

6.b. The *ʾāb* with the pillars is an unknown architectural term translated as 'canopy' (NRSV, NKJV), 'overhanging roof' (NIV), 'threshold' (NASB), 'cornice' (NJB).

7.a. MT 'from floor to floor' is read with Syr, Vg as 'from floor to ceiling' [*haqqôrôt*; cf. 6:15–16]).

15.a. Reading with LXX καί ἐχώνευσεν (Hebr. *wayyiṣṣōq*, 'he cast') for MT *wayyāṣar*, 'he fashioned'.

27.a. The stands are larger in LXX: 5 cubits (8 ft [2 m]) by 4 (7 ft [2 m]) by 6 (10 ft [3 m]).

28.a. Against MT sg. 'stand', reading pl. with Vrs and in agreement with the following pr. suff.

29.a. 'hammered work' (*maʿăśê môrād*) assumes the root of the abs. noun to be *rdd* (see Montgomery 1951: 180).

31.a. 'its opening' refers to the stand. The pr. suff. is rightly read as f. sg. (with Syr) and not as m. sg. as in MT. The repeated references in the MT verse are f. sg. (Montgomery 1951: 180).

35.a. 'handles' (so DeVries 2003: 105), from *yĕdôt*, rather than 'axle-trees' (vv. 32–33), which would not be found on top of the stand.

40.a. With LXX, Vg and 2 Chr. 4:11 emending *hakkiyyôrôt* ('basins' – which have already been completed) to *hassîrôt* (a 'cooking pot' for meat; cf. v. 45).

42.a. With LXX, reading 'two pillars' (*šĕnê*) for MT 'in front of' (*pĕnê*).

46.a. 'he cast' with LXX*; MT is explicative.

46.b. 'in clay moulds' (lit. 'in the thickness of the soil') refers to deep clay deposits suitable for making large moulds (Gray 1970: 199).

47.a. *unweighed* follows LXX (so NRSV, NASB, NIV). MT hiph. *nwḥ* can translate 'Solomon let lie [ie. did not weigh?]' (so Devries 2003: 106) or 'Solomon deposited [in the temple?]' (so Gray 1970: 197); each translation may assume the vessels were not weighed, as specified in the second half of the verse.

50.a. The hapax *pōtôt* is translated as 'hinges' (NASB) or 'sockets' (NRSV), but the malleability of gold makes it impractical for stress-bearing structures. 'Façades' follows G. Driver (1937: 38; so Gray [1970: 202]), who aligns the Hebr. word to an Akkadian cognate meaning 'forehead'; thus 'front', 'outside'.

Form and structure

Solomon's 'wise' preparations (see 'Form and structure', 1 Kgs 5) enable the building project of 1 Kgs 6 – 7. The chapters are bound together thematically and by a structural envelope (6:1; 7:51), which indicates both concern temple construction. An embedded account of palace building interrupts the temple project (see n. 7:1.a.–12). Its positioning is intentional and provides yet another subtle shadowing of Solomon's reign (see 'Comment', 7:1).

Despite that shadowing, the temple is the high point of Solomon's career, fulfilling the promises given in 2 Sam. 7 and standing as a visible reminder of YHWH's commitment to the Davidic dynasty. As such, it glorifies Solomon as the one appointed to build YHWH's house and whose wisdom enables both its preparation and execution. The greater glory, however, goes to YHWH. He gave David the promise of a 'house' (*bayit*), that is, a temple and dynasty, and he provided the requisite wisdom for the project (1 Kgs 3:10–13; 5:3–12). Ultimately, YHWH is glorified in that the project is the visible locus of YHWH's dwelling 'in the midst of the sons of Israel' (v. 13). In this he continues his gracious covenantal presence with his people.

The passage is the centre of a narrative block (3:1 – 9:25) that examines Solomon's reign first from a national perspective before turning to its international scope (9:26 – 10:29). The section is bracketed by verses that highlight the competing interests of a house for Pharaoh's daughter and a house for YHWH (see 'Form and structure', 1 Kgs 9), and can be broadly set out as below (see further examples in Porten 1967; Walsh 1996: 151; Olley 2003).

> A   3:1–2 Opening bracket: houses for YHWH and Pharaoh's
> daughter
> > B   3:3 – 4:34[5:14] Focus on Solomon's national affairs
> > > C   5:1–18[5:15–32] Preparation for temple building
> > > > D   6:1 – 7:51 Temple (and palace) building

D' 8:1–66 Temple dedication
   C' 9:1–23 Response to Solomon's temple
A' 9:24–25 Closing bracket: houses for YHWH and Pharaoh's
daughter
[B' 9:26 – 10:29 Focus on Solomon's international affairs]

Within 1 Kgs 6 – 7, elements speak of possible redactional shaping and layers, although no consensus exists regarding the extent or evidence for such work (see DeVries 2003: 89–93 for one example). The insertion regarding the palace work has already been mentioned and its placement may show a redactor's hand. Additionally, notations of work completed bracket the text (6:1; 7:51) and are found interspersed throughout, including at the transition to the palace-complex narrative (6:37–38; 7:1). These notations suggest places at which redactional layers have been pieced together. Further redactional work may be apparent in the placement of the prophetic word (6:11–13), which, together with a resumptive repetition (v. 9a, 14a), awkwardly interrupts the narrative flow. Despite these and other possible indicators of redactional composition, the narrative does now stand as a coherent whole, whose interruptions could as easily evidence narrative intention as awkward redactional work. It is the final form of the narrative that is the subject of study in this commentary, and that final form can be outlined as below.

   I. Introduction; chronological notice of completion (6:1)
  II. Record of building work (6:2 – 7:50)
    a. Temple building (6:2–38)
    b. Palace buildings (7:1–12)
    c. Temple furnishings (7:13–50)
      i. Work in bronze by Hiram, detailed and summarized
       (vv. 13–47)
      ii. Work in gold by Solomon, summarized (vv. 48–50)
 III. Conclusion; notice of completion (7:51)

Whatever the passage's compositional history, identifiable literary forms are present within it, such as the common prophetic form 'the word of YHWH came to X'. Little by way of narrative characterizes the passage, but apparent archival items abound. They detail construction materials, measurements and architectural design. Such records were probably maintained within palace scribal guilds, or the temple priesthood. The presentation of these archival excerpts is in a style similar to ANE accounts and inscriptions of temple building activities (B. Long 1984: 83; Hurowitz 1992). By this measure, Solomon's building projects accord with ANE norms, and also align with the ideology present in such documents. That ideology asserts that a king whose reign has gained peace and prosperity for the people should undertake a temple-building project. It is the temple's completion that attests to the god's approval and support of the monarch.

Finally, a word should be said about key difficulties the passage presents. First, many of the architectural terms within the passage are otherwise unknown and cannot be certainly translated, nor their descriptions wholly understood. Here recent archaeological exploration of Levantine temples sheds light on previously opaque architectural features. The 'Ain Dara temple in northern Syria is a particularly close contemporary to Solomon's temple, with striking similarities of architectural detail and style (Monson 2000; see also Stinespring, *IDB* 4:534–547). Secondly, the passage is not intended as an architectural blueprint and, while imaginative reconstructions are attempted, the text does not provide enough detail for certainty regarding several features (see examples in Keel 1978: 155–156). Finally, despite the use of archival sources, there is evidence the passage was written or reworked much later (1 Kgs 8:8) and it may be that some of the details reflect later developments to the Solomonic plan.

Despite real challenges to configuring the temple, they do not inhibit the passage's clear message. Solomon's greatest achievement is the grand temple that stands as a reminder of YHWH's covenant presence in the midst of his people, and that calls them to appropriate expressions of worship sanctioned by their God. Ultimately, however grand the building, and however much the people look to it as an assurance of YHWH's favour (Jer. 7 is the extreme example), only if they are a people committed to covenant life, walking in YHWH's statutes, judgments and commandments (6:12), will YHWH dwell with them. Once again, it is an issue of the heart and of the will.

Comment

6:1–38

1–14. Solomon's fourth year is 967 BC (DeVries, *IDB* 1:587). The second month, Ziv (equivalent to Apr.–May), is one of three pre-exilic Canaanite names for the months. These Canaanite names are always used in reference to the temple or its dedication (Ziv, Ethanim and Bul; 6:1, 37–38; 8:2). The Canaanite names were in the monarchic period replaced by a numbering system (thus Ziv is the second month). Later still, during the exile, a third system came into use, which utilized Babylonian names (DeVries, *IDB* 1:485–486).

A more revealing date is that of the 'four-hundred and eightieth year'. The number is probably symbolic, denoting twelve generations of 40 years. This symbolically references all the twelve tribes rescued out of Egypt. The number could also be calculated as a schematic of the years presented in the history itself. Thus 40 years for Moses in the wilderness + 296 years for the judges (calculated from the years presented in Judges) + 40 years for Eli (1 Sam. 4:18) + 40 years for David (1 Kgs 2:11) + 4 years of Solomon's reign to date (1 Kgs 6:1) + 20 years of the ark's residence at Kiriath Jearim (1 Sam. 7:2) + 40 years presumed for Joshua's leadership after Moses death = 480 years (Sweeney 2007: 108; for a different calculation, particularly of the era of the judges, see Noth 1991: 34–44). The point of either calculation is its *terminus a quo* that indelibly links the temple to Moses and the great saving events of exodus and Sinai. In it YHWH displays his sovereignty over the cosmos and over nations and covenants with a delivered people to be his own possession. The temple is built in the light of these realities and reflects them in its symbolism and use.

Verses 2–14 summarize the external features of the temple. The length 98 feet (30 m), the width 33 feet (10 m) and the height 49 feet (15 m), it is a long-house temple common in the ANE, particularly the Levant (Stinespring, *IDB* 4:540; Keel 1978: 154; Monson 2000). Long-house temples typically divide into three areas. Solomon's temple thus has a porch as wide as the house (the adjoined side rooms extend beyond the porch), whose roof is supported by the large pillars (7:15), a main room or nave and a cube-shaped inner sanctuary at the far end of the building from the porch. Like other temple structures, the whole may have been set upon a platform of rubble or stone.

Two other features are mentioned in the overview. First are the 'framed latticed windows', a phrase whose difficulty of translation has led to various conceptions: recessed windows and/or frames, latticed windows of varying configurations, clerestory windows – even 'enclosed observation windows' (Sweeney 2007: 104). The excavation of the 'Ain Dara temple now suggests a solution, for it contains several faux windows carved into the stone work with carved recessed frames, and a lattice-design 'covering' a portion of the false opening (Monson 2000: 34). As the faux windows admit no light or escape of smoke, there may have been small windows for this purpose high up in the walls, although they are not mentioned in the description. At any rate, the nave is a dark, mysterious room. The second feature is the side chambers built around three sides of the temple. Each of the three levels is successively wider, and a system of offsets prevents the chambers leaning against the holy building and protects its sanctity. The chambers are accessed by a ladder or stairway structure. Once again, the 'Ain Dara temple incorporates similar side chambers, although their usage is uncertain.

The building is fashioned of stone dressed at the quarry, but not further finished with iron tools on site. The whole is then roofed in cedar. Preventing stone dressing on site appears to be a pious extension of the rule that only unhewn stones be used for altars of worship (Exod. 20:25; Deut. 27:5–6). But there is also the unexpressed marvel of the perfection of the initial quarrying so that the large stones articulated without further tooling.

A notation (v. 9a) concludes the exterior features built of stone (vv. 2–8), and the passage briefly enumerates the exterior wooden features (vv. 9b–10); further references to woodwork concern interior features (vv. 15–34). Before turning to those interior features, however, a prophetic word serves as a reminder of the house's essential character. Though made of costly materials and beautifully adorned, it is not itself a surety of YHWH's continued habitation in the midst of his people (Solomon later affirms YHWH cannot be contained in a building; 8:27). The one necessity for YHWH's continued presence is the covenant upheld by torah observance by king and people. The temple is YHWH's gracious choice to dwell in a visible structure, but, as always, he looks to his people's commitment under the covenant as the basis of his presence. Asserting this essential reality, the account returns, by a resumptive repetition (vv. 9:1, 14), to the details of the temple structure.

15–38. In contrast to the previous section's emphasis on exterior stonework, these verses explore the interior stonework. It is wholly covered with costly wooden boards of cedar and cypress. They are obtained via the contract forged with Hiram (5:7–10[21–24]) and so complete that 'no stone was to be seen' (v. 18). The panelling is richly carved in garden motifs and cherubs (vv. 18, 29, 32), and similar motifs appear in contemporaneous Levantine temples (Monson 2000: 33). The fecundity of YHWH's natural world is suggested, but the garden motifs also evoke the earlier Edenic garden as the place in which YHWH initially dwelt with his people. The garden was the point at which the heavenly and earthly realms intersected and was considered the centre of the cosmos and the very gate of heaven. Now that place is represented in the temple (see 'Explanation', 1 Kgs 5; and below).

The back third of the main room is the inner sanctuary. A perfect (33 ft [10 m]) cube, its height is 16 feet (5 m) less than the nave's. A short flight of steps from the nave's floor to the sanctuary's entrance can account for the difference, and the aspect of ascending to YHWH's place attests to the ANE association of the god with high mountains and the heavens (cf. the stairway of Jacob's vision; Gen. 28:12; Keel 1978: 171). The windowless room may reflect the idea that YHWH dwells in darkness (Ps. 18:9–11[10–12]; 1 Kgs 8:12); certainly it enhances the *mysterium tremendum*.

Fine gold is used in copious quantities within such holy precincts. The 'overlay' in both rooms may be gold plating, gilding or even inlay (Konkel, *NIDOTTE* 3:832–833). An altar of cedar placed proximate to the inner sanctuary in the nave is for burning incense (Exod. 30:1–10; 1 Chr. 28:18). It is likewise overlaid with gold. Gold chain work, while not elsewhere mentioned in the temple, somehow divides the two chambers; perhaps the chain holds together a curtain at the inner sanctuary's doorway (Exod. 26:33).

The holiest place within the temple, the inner sanctuary, houses YHWH's most holy relic, the ark. To signify its holiness the ark is also overlaid with gold. It contains the Ten Commandments (Deut. 10:2, 5; 1 Kgs 8:9) and atop it is the mercy seat where YHWH 'meets' with the high priest (v. 19;

Exod. 25:10–22). Towering over this small chest (one and a quarter by three-quarters of a metre) stand two wooden cherubs overlaid with gold. They face forwards, towards the entry, and each is approximately 16 feet (5 m) high with a 16-foot wingspan. The open wings span the room's width and meet in its centre, arching over the chest.

Cherubs are typical ANE figures, usually with the body of a lion, eagle's wings and a human head. They are often engraved on thrones as supporting figures and the strength, speed and wisdom of each component creature acts to guard the power of the deity's appointed monarch (Keel 1978: 171). However, no human monarch but only YHWH's sovereign lordship is honoured in this holy place. No actual throne is placed in the small room, for YHWH is 'enthroned upon the cherubs' (1 Sam. 4:4; 2 Sam. 6:2; 2 Kgs 19:15; Isa. 37:16; Pss 80:1[2]; 99:1). The cherub statues represent YHWH's heavenly throne, for which the ark is a footstool (Pss 99:5; 132:7; 1 Chr. 28:2).

Having moved from the stone exterior through the temple's interior to its most holy place, the survey of the temple turns outwards again. The rooms' striking carving and overlay is noted once again before attention turns to the doors of the inner sanctuary (vv. 31–32) and the nave (vv. 33–35). Both doors and frames are of costly wood, carved with cherubs and garden images, and overlaid with gold. The nave's doors are specifically noted as bifold. The doorposts are five sided in the inner sanctuary, and four sided in the nave, a configuration that has long posed difficulties for interpreters. Suggestions such as 'the portal consisting of pentagonal posts' (DeVries 2003: 86) or 'the pilaster of the doorposts was five sided' (Sweeney 2007: 105) imagine a doorway with faceted doorposts. Monson suggests the 'Ain Dara temple windows and doorways, in the Mediterranean and Mesopotamian world, provide a solution (Monson 2000: 35). The description may be of the architectural feature of rebating (fitting several recessed frames together in a 'nested' configuration), which could be produced in stone, as in the 'Ain Dara windows, or in wood. On this analogy, the doorframes of the inner sanctuary and the nave have five and four recesses, respectively.

Leaving the temple proper, the survey passes through the inner courtyard's three courses of hewn stone topped by cedar. The survey complete, a closing chronological notation is provided; the work of the temple took seven years. As in 6:1, an old Canaanite name is given for the month (see 'Comment', 6:1). More work remains to be done (as 7:13–50 reveals), and until YHWH's presence fills the temple (8:10–11) it remains a lifeless shell, however grand.

7:1–51

1–12. Juxtaposing the record of the palace complex to the completion of the temple complex at this point returns us again to the ambiguity and shadowing surrounding Solomon's reign. Whether in reality the temple is built concurrently with the palace, vv. 1–12 are placed here to suggest Solomon delays work on the temple furnishing (vv. 13–50) until his own home is complete. That delay means that the people continue to worship on the high places rather than at the Deuteronomistically sanctioned temple (see 'Comment', 1 Kgs 3:1–3). A further negative mark against Solomon is the contrasting years for each project: thirteen for the palace, but only seven for the temple. Nor is the contrast simply a reflection on the size of each project. Instead, the grammar shows it is a negative contrast by placing the object ('his own house') before the subject-verb. Thus while he is 'seven years in building [the temple], *his own house* Solomon took thirteen years to build'. Even more, while he finishes the temple (and, by this passage's placement, the completion is only partial), he finished 'all' his house. Grand though his project is, Solomon is once again presented in an ambiguous light.

Five buildings or sections of the palace are noted and, as in the temple, costly cedar panelling is prominent. The House of the Forest of Lebanon is the largest of the palace buildings and larger than the temple complex. Its many cedar pillars make it seem like a Lebanese forest – thus its name. Its size marks it as an assembly hall, although it also serves as an armoury and possibly a treasury (1 Kgs 10:17, 21; Isa. 22:8). Along the sides of the room are three storeys, each with fifteen rooms, possibly for armoury or treasury storage. Architecturally featured windows in each storey face one another across the room.

A second building, the Hall of Pillars, may abut the great assembly hall, perhaps serving as its porch (the width of the Hall of the Forest is the same as the length of this second hall; Sweeney 2007: 117). Almost half the size of the assembly hall, it has its own porch and a canopy supported by pillars. The final building named is the Hall of the Throne, or the Hall of Judgment. Its size is not given and it may also be adjoined to, or found within, the other two buildings. Here the king pronounces judgments. Finally, the king's personal house adjoins a courtyard contiguous to the Hall of Judgment, and his wife's house stands close by. Both are the same style as the Hall and house not only the royals but their retinue and servants.

The palace complex, like the temple complex, is built of costly hewn stones topped by cedar planking. The palace stones are 11 feet (3.5 m) by 11 feet and, unlike the temple stones, are dressed on site. The complex has a large outer courtyard whose construction is similar to the temple's inner court (6:36). The courses of stone and cedar serve as a wall for the palace complex's privacy and protection.

13–47. Solomon now arranges for the bronze items needed in the temple. He hires Hiram (not the king of 1 Kgs 5) of the tribe of Naphtali. He is described in terms reminiscent of Bezalel, for he is filled with 'skill, cleverness and knowledge' (v. 14; Exod. 31:3–4; 35:31). Bezalel was a full Israelite and his work was in silver and gold as well as bronze. By contrast, Hiram is a half-Israelite and his work is limited to bronze work. The passage emphasizes this: there are nine references to 'bronze' and eight to 'cast/casting'. By comparison, King Solomon prepares all the items of fine gold (vv. 48–50).

Four major items are described: the pillars (vv. 15–22), the sea (vv. 23–26, 39b), the stands (vv. 27–37) and their associated basins (vv. 38–39a). In each case the item is introduced, its dimensions provided along with details of its design, construction or ornamentation, and its placement described.

The two bronze pillars, together with their intricate capitals decorated with common ANE motifs of pomegranates and lilies or lotus flowers (Keel 1978: 164–165) stand 33–36 feet (10–11 m) high against the temple's 49 foot (15 m) façade. Placed on the porch of the nave, they flank its doorways and support a canopy (1 Chr. 3:15). Jachin is erected on the door's right (assumedly the north side as one approaches the entry from the east), and Boaz on the left. The origin of the names is debated, but 'Boaz' (*bō'az*) is best read as derived from 'in/with strength' (*bĕ 'ōz*). 'Jachin' (*yākîn*) is the hiph. impf. form of the root *kwn*. Thus 'he establishes'. The meaning of the names could be read in two different ways. If read separately, Boaz is a reference to YHWH's strength in the midst of his people, for which he is exalted, and in which the king rejoices (Ps. 21:1, 13[2, 14]), while Jachin affirms that YHWH has established either the temple or the Davidic dynasty with which the temple is intertwined. If the Davidic dynasty is in view, it is a desire that has achieved reality in Solomon (1 Kgs 2:12, 24, 45–46). Alternatively, the names might be read (from right to left) as a phrase, 'he establishes in strength'. The pillars thus represent the foundations of the earth and the stability of creation due to YHWH's sovereignty (Ps. 82:5; Prov. 8:29; Isa. 24:18; Jer. 31:37; Mic. 6:2; Sweeney 2007: 122). Either reading is an impressive proclamation to those who enter the temple.

The massive sea, approximately 16 feet (5 m) across and 3 feet (1 m) high, holds upwards of 9,898 gallons (45,000 l). It is shaped and decorated in the consistent floral theme, evoking the Edenic garden. The strong oxen upholding it represent strength, and the four directions, the four quadrants of the earth – another expression of YHWH's power over the cosmos. The sea stands in the temple courtyard before the nave's entrance (v. 39b) and serves the priest's needs for ritual washing during sacrificial offerings (2 Chr. 4:6). Its size is more than adequate for such use and points to its symbolic representation. In the enclosed sea is symbolized the chaotic waters of the world, now tamed by YHWH's power. Such mythic imagery of a god's power over the waters is common in the ANE. In the biblical text YHWH's power over the waters is expressed in both the cosmic realm (Gen. 1:9–10; Pss 18:14–16[15–17]; 29:10; 74:12–15; Isa. 27:1; Nah. 1:4) and the historical realm (Exod. 15:4–10; Pss 77:16–20[17–21]; 89:9–10[11–12]).

The ten stands are large water stands, each approximately 7 feet (2 m) square and slightly more than 3 feet (1 m) high. Each stand has a square frame with supportive panels set upon a complex axle system with wheels about 2 feet (0.6 m) high. Decoration includes palm trees (v. 36), wreaths (vv. 29–30, 36) and animals depictive of strength, speed and wisdom (vv. 29–30, 36; Keel 1978: 171). The size and weight of the stands and the capacity of their basins for 21 gallons (96 l) would make them difficult to manoeuvre, and thus they are set in place, five on either side of the courtyard (v. 39a). Each square stand opens into a round crown supported by its own square frame. The crown securely receives the basin of water in which the burnt offerings are washed (2 Chr. 4:6).

Besides these large items manufactured by Hiram, he also made sets of pots, shovels and bowls, and other implements needed for temple service. The bowls are perhaps used for the sprinkling of blood (Lev. 1:5) and are mentioned together with the pots, shovels and other implements for serving at the altar of burnt offering (Exod. 27:1–3). The altar of burnt offering is not included in the list of manufactured items but it is certain an altar is located in the courtyard and used during the temple's dedication (8:64; see also 2 Kgs 16:14). This altar may be a previously manufactured one (perhaps for tabernacle worship) incorporated into the temple service (1 Kgs 1:50; 2:28).

Hiram's work is on behalf of Solomon, as a concluding notice indicates (v. 40b). A summative list of the manufactured items includes details of the foundry's location east of the Jordan, where ample materials necessary for the process are close to hand. As a final note of the grandness of the enterprise, Solomon does not attempt to weigh the utensils crafted: their weight is beyond measure.

48–50. In a fitting tribute, the most costly items are 'made' by Solomon. In reality he does not personally craft them but only directs their work. Precious gold items are prepared for the nave, as well as the façade work for the doors of the nave and inner sanctuary. The golden altar of incense (6:20, 22; Exod. 30:1–10) is placed before the entry to the inner sanctuary, and to the side of the nave is the golden table (Exod. 25:23–30). Rather than the single lampstand of the tabernacle (Exod. 25:31–40), ten seven-branched stands provide light. Their flowers (*peraḥ*; Exod. 25:31), lamps (*nērôt*; Exod. 25:37) and tongs for snuffing (*melqaḥayim*; Exod. 25:38) are singled out for notice. Cups (*sippôt*) are used in the cult (Exod. 12:22; 2 Kgs 12:13), and snuffers (*mĕzammĕrôt*) – a word that derives from 'knife' (*mazmērâ*) – for trimming the wicks. The 'bowls' (*mizrāqôt*) is the same word found in v. 45, where *mizrāqôt* are used in the nave, not at the courtyard's altar. The 'pans' (*kappôt*) are set on the table for incense (Exod. 25:29; Num. 7:14), and the 'firepans' (*maḥtôt*) hold the coals for burning incense (Lev. 10:1; 16:12).

51. The summative list ends the account of temple building and a final notation of its completion is given, noting that 'all' the work is finished.

Earlier such notations of completion used the root *klh* for 'finish' (6:9, 14, 38; 7:1, 40); now the root *šlm* is used. The change signals finality: the work truly is completed. It also plays on the name of King Solomon (*šĕlōmô*) who directs the work.

The king brings in David's consecrated treasures – an action that looks backwards, and forwards. It acknowledges that David received the promise of a dynastic house (*bayit*) but was denied the right to build YHWH's house (*bayit*). Despite this denial, he amassed treasures for YHWH's house in preparation for his son's work (2 Sam. 8:10–12). Solomon's action also looks forwards, for he will bring the treasures up as part of the consecration ceremonies that follow (8:4). It is consecration that enables the treasures David gathered finally to be put to their holy use.

Explanation

The lengthy and detailed account of the temple's construction is not only the focal point of Solomon's reign, but is the high point of Israel's covenant history. The chapter places the temple's construction in temporal relationship to the events of the exodus (v. 1), a deliverance that arises out of YHWH's covenant with Abraham (Exod. 2:23–25; 3:6–10). At Sinai the Mosaic Covenant expands upon the Abrahamic Covenant, drawing the nation into covenantal relationship with YHWH. The tablets of the covenant are housed in the ark in the temple's most holy place (1 Kgs 6:19; 8:9), and thus the structure serves as a visual reminder of the defining Mosaic Covenant. Additionally, the temple attests to YHWH's covenant with the Davidic House (2 Sam. 7). The temple, built by the promised son, shows YHWH's approval and support of the Davidic House, and the dynastic commitment to worship YHWH in the temple.

The temple's place as a witness to the nation's covenant history only partially explains the length and detail of the present account. Of far greater importance is the temple's connection to YHWH, the God of the covenant history. The temple is built for YHWH (vv. 1–2) so that he might dwell in the midst of his people (vv. 11–13). Preparation of a building suited to Israel's holy, divine king and redeemer requires careful attention. The present narrative's length and attention to detail acknowledges the magnitude of the building's purpose. All other reasons for which the building is constructed find meaning only in the building's foremost purpose: the temporal locus of YHWH's holy presence.

The temple serves as the locus of YHWH's presence among his people. But in no way is YHWH confined to or housed in the temple, as Solomon later makes clear (1 Kgs 8:27, 30, 32, 34, 36, 39, 43, 45, 49). YHWH is utterly transcendent (Isa. 66:1–2) and the temple serves only as the footstool of his heavenly throne (Ps. 132:7). Israel had before encountered this transcendent God at Sinai. In Moses' remembrance of the event he stresses that no form of any sort was visible to the people (Deut. 4:15), and for this reason he prohibits the making of any representational image, for such would be idolatry (Deut. 4:15–18). All that is rightly included in the inner sanctuary is the record of YHWH's covenant-making words to Israel. It is through words that YHWH confronted Israel at Sinai: Israel assembled to hear them, YHWH spoke them, the Ten Words were written and were to be followed (Deut. 4:9–14) – all this in the absence of any form for God (Deut. 4:12).

Further comparison to Sinai reveals another crucial aspect of the temple's role in Israel's covenant life. Extending that comparison to the tabernacle makes the comparison more pointed. Each serves as a place at which YHWH's presence is manifested (Exod. 19:9, 11, 18–20; 40:34; 1 Kgs 8:10–11). In each, YHWH's manifestation is by his will alone; no human compulsion can command YHWH's presence, for he remains utterly free. Each manifestation is preceded by careful preparation: Sinai requires boundaries be set around the holy place (Exod. 19:12, 21–22), and personal consecration is required of people and priests (Exod. 19:14–15, 22). The tabernacle also delineates holy space and includes areas of increasing holiness from a courtyard to an inner sanctuary. It is built to specifications of material and structure and also specifies its furnishings, priestly garments and cultic items (Exod. 25 – 31). Similarly, the temple structure specifies areas of increasing holiness from the courtyard to the inner sanctuary. Costly gold is used in the places of greater holiness and entrance into the holy places is strictly proscribed (1 Kgs 8:6).

The mountains of Sinai and Zion serve as stationary locales at which YHWH chooses to presence himself with his people. Between these two stands the tabernacle, serving as a 'portable Sinai'. It enables YHWH's holy presence (manifested at a prepared mountain) to travel in the midst of the people in a similarly prepared but portable holy place. Only when another stationary locale on another mountain is carefully prepared is the portable tabernacle rendered unnecessary.

The sacred, prepared space, represented by Sinai, the tabernacle and the temple is richly undergirded by ANE mythic ideas. These ideas further reveal the meaning inherent in Solomon's temple. The first is that in the ANE the temple was considered the earthly embodiment of the cosmic mountain. This mythic mountain was the home of the god and the primeval hill from which flowed the beginning of all creation. Ziggurats in Assyria, pyramids in Egypt, the temple Esagila in Babylon all depict this cosmic mountain on which the god resides (Keele 1978: 113–118). A similar idea attaches to the Jerusalem temple. One 'goes up' to Jerusalem (Ps. 122:4) and also ascends steps to the inner sanctuary (see 'Comment', 6:20); it is the 'mount of YHWH' (Ps. 24:3; Isa. 2:2), 'his holy mount' (Pss 2:6; 3:4[5]; 43:3; 48:1[2]; 99:9) and 'Mount Zion' (Pss 74:2; 78:68; 125:1; 133:3). Even though the temple mount is geographically lower than several surrounding hills (Keele 1978: 115), by virtue of the sacred temple, it is considered the highest, and the mythic, mountain: the place of YHWH, holy because of his presence.

Associated with the idea of the cosmic mountain, a second ANE idea connects the mythic mountain with the creation of the cosmos. The hill emerges from the waters of chaos when they are tamed by the god. From his holy mountain abode the god founds the earth, creates all that is, sends out life-giving waters and sustains creation in fruitfulness and order. The Edenic echoes in the temple are intentional (see 'Comment'; see also 'Explanation', 1 Kgs 5). The temple, as the holy mountain is the place of creation – the original garden. The mythic associations are depicted in the iconographic temple decorations and are a testimony to all visitors of YHWH's creative and sustaining power (Keele 1978: 113; Bloch-Smith 1994: 27). That power extends not only to the nation of Israel, but to all the earth.

Finally, as the earthly embodiment of the cosmic mountain, one rightly enters the temple precinct through 'gates of eternity' (Ps. 24:7, 9). Because the temple building is not itself eternal, the reference refers not at all to the duration of the physical temple gates; rather, it acknowledges that as one enters the temple, one passes into an eternal realm: the numinous place of YHWH the eternal God. The temple is the link between earthly and heavenly realms, as were the tabernacle and Sinai before it. Although YHWH is not contained by these structures, and remains always free to dwell or depart, by his gracious presence in them he makes them 'identical to heaven' (Keele 1978: 172). It is for this reason that protections and cautions must be observed when building and entering the temple. It is an awesome privilege that cannot be taken lightly.

The privilege of coming 'before YHWH' in these holy places (Deut. 4:10; 1 Kgs 8:62) cannot be taken as a given. As stated, YHWH's presence can never be coerced but always remains his free and gracious gift. He gives it freely under the covenant and YHWH's people are called to embrace covenant life fully (1 Kgs 6:11–13). By obedience to covenant statutes they signal their ongoing desire for such life. Obedience crafts them as a holy people (Lev. 11:44–45), a prerequisite for YHWH's continued covenant presence.

However, the hope that the temple project would enable YHWH's continued presence in his people's midst failed. Both at Sinai and during the long years of the tabernacle Israel did not live out covenant obedience. Prophets warn Israel (and later, Judah) that YHWH will abandon temple and people if they persist in their sin. The history of 1 – 2 Kings reveals that YHWH's people do not heed his prophets or the warning signs in their own history. The temple project ultimately fails and, abandoned by YHWH, it is destroyed and his people exiled by foreign armies brought by his hand.

YHWH's repeated means by which he dwelt with his people were not exhausted, however. In the NT the fullest and most unexpected 'temple' is erected in the incarnation of Jesus the Christ. Fully human and fully divine he joins these two realms – a new cosmic mountain linking heaven and earth. The mythic ideas of the ANE that attach to the cosmic mountain also appear in Jesus: in the human man all the fullness of deity dwells (Phil. 2:8; Col. 1:19). He creates and sustains the cosmos and all creatures (John 1:3–4; Col. 1:15–18), and only through his own self is entry found into the eternal realm of God (John 14:6; Phil. 2:6–11).

In Jesus the Christ the *place* of holiness (Sinai, tabernacle, temple) now becomes a *person* of holiness who moves freely in Israel. As YHWH he tabernacles among sinful people (John 1:14; 2:19–22), but no barriers protect his holy glory. It is seen and handled by disciples (1 John 1:1), religious leaders (John 3:1–15), the sick and demon-possessed (Mark 3:1–5; 5:1–20; Luke 4:31–35; 5:12–13) and sinners and outcasts alike (Luke 4:1–26; 5:27–31; 7:36–50).

The NT extends the metaphor of Jesus as God's new temple. He is not only the temple, but also stands as its high priest and great sacrifice. As high priest, he alone is able to effect entry into the holy place – the true inner sanctuary of heaven and God's presence (Heb. 9 – 10). By this new and living way a new covenant is forged that depends solely on Christ. In him as new tabernacle, priest and sacrifice all the hopes of the Solomonic temple are for ever realized.

1 KINGS 8:1-66

Translation

[1]Then[a] Solomon assembled the elders of Israel with all the heads of the tribes, the leaders of the father's households of the sons of Israel to King Solomon in Jerusalem to bring up the ark of the covenant of YHWH from the City of David, that is, Zion. [2]So every Israelite man was assembled to King Solomon at the festival in the month Ethanim, which is the seventh month. [3]All the elders of Israel came and the priests carried the ark. [4]They brought up the ark of YHWH, and the tent of meeting, and all the holy utensils that were in the tent; the priests and Levites brought them up. [5]King Solomon and all the congregation of Israel who had assembled before him were with him before the ark, sacrificing so many sheep and oxen they could not be counted or numbered. [6]The priests brought the ark of the covenant of YHWH to its place in the house's inner sanctuary, the holy of holies, beneath the wings of the cherubim. [7]For the cherubim spread their wings over the place of the ark so that the cherubim covered the ark and its poles above. [8]The poles were so long that the ends of the poles were visible from the holy place before the inner sanctuary, but were not visible from the outside. They are there to this day. [9]There was nothing in the ark except the two stone tablets that Moses had placed there at Horeb when YHWH made a covenant with the sons of Israel when they came out from the land of Egypt. [10]And when the priests came out

from the holy place, the cloud filled the house of YHWH [11]so that the priests were not able to stand to minister because of the cloud, for YHWH's glory filled the house of YHWH.

[12a]Then Solomon said,

[b]'YHWH has said that he would dwell in thick darkness.
[13]I have surely built a lofty house for you;
  a place for your dwelling for ever.'

[14]Then the king turned about and blessed all the assembly of Israel, while all the assembly of Israel was standing. [15]He said, 'Blessed be YHWH the God of Israel who spoke by his mouth with my father David and by his power fulfilled it, saying, [16]"From the day I brought my people Israel out from Egypt I did not choose a city from all the tribes of Israel to build there a house for my name, but I chose David to be over my people Israel." [17]Now it was in my father David's heart to build a house for the name of YHWH the God of Israel, [18]but YHWH said to my father, David, "Because it was in your heart to build a house for my name – you did well that it was in your heart – [19]however, you shall not build the house but your son who shall issue from your loins, he shall build the house for my name." [20]Now YHWH has upheld his promise that he spoke, and I have arisen[a] after my father, David. I sit upon Israel's throne[a], just as YHWH promised, and I have built the house for the name of YHWH the God of Israel. [21]I have provided there a place for the ark in which is the covenant of YHWH, which he made with our fathers when he brought them out from the land of Egypt.'

[22]Then Solomon stood before the altar of YHWH in front of the whole assembly of Israel. He spread his hands to the heavens [23]and said, 'O YHWH, the God of Israel! There is no god like you in the heavens above or on the earth below who keeps covenant and steadfast love towards your servants who walk before you with all their[a] heart, [24]who has kept with your servant, David my father, that which you promised him. With your mouth you promised and by your power you have fulfilled *it*, as it is this day. [25]And now, O YHWH, the God of Israel, keep for your servant, David my father, that which you have promised him, saying, "There shall never fail *to be* your descendant sitting before me upon the throne of Israel, if only your sons will guard their ways, to walk before me just as you have walked before me." [26]So now, O God of Israel, let your word be confirmed, which you promised to your servant David my father.

[27]'But will God really dwell on the earth? Behold, the heavens and the highest heavens cannot contain you – how much less this house, which I have built! [28]But attend to the prayer of your servant and his supplication, O YHWH my God, to listen to the cry and the prayer that your servant prays before you today. [29]May your eyes be open towards this house night and day, to the place of which you said, "My name will be there" to listen to the prayer that your servant prays towards this place. [30]Hear the supplication of your servant and your people Israel when they pray towards this place; may you hear from[a] your dwelling place, even heaven, so to hear and forgive.

[31]'If[a] a man sins against his neighbour and places an oath upon him causing him to swear, and the oath comes before your altar in this house, [32]then hear in heaven, act and judge your servants to condemn the wicked by bringing his actions upon his head, and to vindicate the righteous by giving to him according to his righteousness.

[33]'When your people Israel are struck by an enemy because they have sinned against you, and they return to you and praise your name, and pray and plead with you in this house, [34]then hear in heaven and forgive the sins of your people Israel and bring them back to the land that you gave their fathers.

[35]'When the heavens are shut and there is no rain because they have sinned against you, and they pray towards this place and praise your name and turn from their sin when you afflict them, [36]then hear in heaven and forgive the sin of your servants and your people Israel. Indeed, teach them the good way that they might walk in it, and give rain upon your land that you have given to your people for an inheritance.

[37]'When famine is in the land, or pestilence, blight, rust, locust swarm or grasshopper, if their enemy distresses them in one of their cities[a], whatever plague or sickness *comes*, [38]whatever prayer, whatever plea is made by any individual[a] (who knows the affliction of his own heart and spreads his hands to this house), [39]then hear in heaven your dwelling place and forgive, act and render to each according to all his ways, whose heart you know (for you alone know the heart of all people) [40]so that they may fear you as long as they live on the earth that you have given to our fathers.

[41]'And also to the foreigner who is not of your people Israel, when he comes from a far land on account of your name – [42]for they will hear of your great name, strong hand and outstretched arm – and if he shall come and pray towards this house, [43]then[a] hear in heaven your dwelling place and act according to all that the foreigner asks of you so that all the peoples of the earth may know your name to fear you like your people Israel, and to know that your name is invoked over the house that I have built.

[44]'When your people go out to battle their enemy on the path you send them, and they pray to YHWH towards the city that you have chosen and the house that I have built for your name, [45]then hear in heaven their prayer and their plea and uphold their cause.

[46]'When they sin against you (for there is none who does not sin) and you are angry with them and give them to an enemy and their captors take them captive to the enemy's land, far or near, [47]if they come to their senses in the land to which they have been taken captive, and they repent and make supplication to you in the land of their captors saying, "We have sinned and done wrong; we have acted wickedly," [48]and they return to you with all their heart and all their soul in the land of their enemies who have captured them and they pray to you towards their land that you have given their fathers, *and towards* the city that you have chosen, and the house that I have built for your name, [49]then hear their prayer and supplication in heaven your dwelling place and uphold their cause [50]and forgive your people who have sinned against you, and all their transgressions that

they have committed against you. Grant them compassion in the eyes of their captors that they may have compassion on them – [51]for they are your people and your inheritance whom you brought out from Egypt, from the midst of the iron furnace.

[52]'May your eyes be open to the supplication of your servant and your people Israel, listening to them in their every cry to you. [53]For you have set them apart for yourself as an inheritance from all the peoples of the earth, just as you promised through your servant Moses when you brought our fathers out of Egypt, O Lord YHWH.'

[54]When Solomon finished praying to YHWH all this prayer and supplication, he arose from before the altar of YHWH, from kneeling with his hands outstretched to heaven. [55]He stood and blessed all the assembly of Israel with a loud voice, saying, [56]'Blessed be YHWH who has given rest to his people Israel according to all he promised. Not one word has failed from all his good promise that he spoke through Moses his servant. [57]May YHWH our God be with us just as he was with our fathers. May he not abandon us or forsake us, [58]but incline our hearts[a] towards him, to walk in all his ways and keep his commandments, statutes and judgments that he commanded our fathers. [59]May these my words by which I have made supplication before YHWH be near to YHWH our God day and night to uphold the cause of his servant and his people Israel in each day's affairs [60]so that all the peoples of the earth may know that YHWH is God; there is no other. [61]Now, let your heart be wholly with YHWH our God, to walk in his statutes, and to keep his commandments as it is this day.'

[62]The king and all Israel with him were making sacrifice before YHWH. [63]Solomon sacrificed peace offerings, which he offered to YHWH: twenty-two thousand oxen and one hundred and twenty thousand sheep. Thus the king and all the sons of Israel dedicated the house of YHWH.

[64]In that day the king consecrated the centre of the court before the house of YHWH, for there he made the burnt offering, grain offering and the fat of the peace offerings because the bronze altar that was before YHWH was too small to contain the burnt offering, grain offering and the fat of the peace offerings. [65]At that time Solomon observed the festival and all Israel was with him, a great assembly, from Lebo Hamath to the wadi of Egypt. They celebrated before YHWH our God[a] two weeks[b]: fourteen days in total. [66]On the eighth day he sent the people away. They blessed the king and went to their tents rejoicing and glad of heart on account of all the good that YHWH had done for David his servant and for Israel his people.

Notes on the text

1.a. '*az* plus impf., which begins the chapter, can express logical sequence but can also link events temporally (often concurrently) but not necessarily sequentially to the preceding events (Rabinowitz 1984). Narratively, Solomon dedicates the structure after its completion; historically, he may have done so at some point during the work, perhaps after the structure's completion but before the bronze and gold work (7:13–50).

12.a.–13. Appears in LXX* after v. 53, with explicative 'then Solomon said *concerning the house that he had built*'.

12.b. LXX* begins the poem, 'YHWH has made the sun known [LXX^L 'set'] in the heavens', which makes explicit the contrast to the inner sanctuary as the 'dark place' (DeVries 2003: 113, 117; Sweeney 2007: 132). LXX* concludes the poem, 'Is it not written in the Book of the Song [in Hebr. *šyr*]?'; possibly a corruption of the Book of Jashar (in Hebr. *yšr*; Josh. 10:13; 2 Sam. 1:18); see Montgomery 1951: 191.

20.a. LXX^L emphasizes YHWH's role: 'he has raised me'; 'he has set me upon the throne'.

23.a. LXX is sg. 'your servant who walks . . . his heart', referring to David.

30.a. MT *'el* is read with Syr and 2 Chr. 6:21 as *min*, 'from'.

31.a. MT *'ēt 'ăšer* is read with 2 Chr. 6:22 (cf. Syr, Vg) as conditional *'im*.

37.a. MT 'in the land of their [lit. 'his'] cities [lit. 'gates']' is a probable corruption. Reading with LXX 'one of their [lit. 'his'] cities'.

38.a. With LXX^BL, the MT phrase 'of all your people Israel' is omitted as a 'late ideology of particularism' (DeVries 2003: 118; cf. Montgomery 1951: 203).

43.a. Beginning the verse with cop., as in 2 Chr. 6:33, many MSS, LXX, Syr.

58.a. 'hearts' with many MSS, LXX, Vg.

65.a. After 'YHWH our God', LXX^BL adds 'in the house that he had built, eating and drinking and rejoicing in the presence of YHWH our God'. MT's omission may be by haplography.

65.b. In LXX* the festival is only one week. It is explicitly two weeks in MT, and implicitly two weeks in 2 Chr. 7:8–9: a dedicatory festival followed by Tabernacles. The eighth day of v. 66 follows the second festival.

Form and structure

Together with 1 Kgs 6 – 7, this chapter is the core of 1 Kgs 1 – 11 and the high point of Solomon's rule (see 'Form and structure', 1 Kgs 6 – 7). The report of Solomon's prayer and the dedicatory rituals surrounding it draw upon long-standing traditions. The account sets forth theologies that are key to an understanding of 1 – 2 Kings and to which the subsequent history frequently returns.

The chapter is structured with Solomon's dedicatory prayer and petitions at its centre. In its opening narrative (A; see below) Solomon assembles the people to bring the ark to its resting place and dedicate the temple (v. 1). In its closing narrative (A') the dedicatory rites take place and Solomon dismisses the people (v. 66). Both narratives note the seventh-month feast (vv. 2, 65; see 'Comment') and preparation and dedication are accompanied by many sacrifices (vv. 5, 62–64). The narrative accounts enclose a word of blessing pronounced by Solomon upon the people (B, B'), which in turn encloses Solomon's prayer (C). The start of sections B, C and B' are marked by Solomon's changed posture: turning to bless the people (v. 14), standing before the altar with hands raised to heaven (v. 22) and rising again to bless the people (vv. 54–55):

A   Bringing the ark to the temple (vv. 1–13)
    B   Solomon blesses the assembly: focus on Davidic traditions
       (vv. 14–21)
       C   Solomon's prayer (vv. 22–53)
          1. Prayer for the Davidic promise (vv. 22–26)
          2. General preamble to petitions (vv. 27–30)
          3. Seven petitions (vv. 31–51)
          4. General epilogue to petitions (vv. 52–53)
    B' Solomon blesses the assembly: focus on Mosaic traditions
       (vv. 54–61)
A' Dedicating the temple (vv. 62–66)

The core of the chapter is Solomon's dedicatory prayer. It begins with a plea for YHWH's continued promises to David (vv. 22–26) and takes up the one element of the Davidic promise omitted in vv. 14–21. Solomon next begins a long supplication to YHWH (vv. 27–53), urging that he 'hear and forgive' his people. A preamble and epilogue cite reasons for such attention (vv. 27–30, 52–53), reasons that are deeply embedded in the history of the people. Solomon's seven petitions suppose specific occasions of prayer; in each he asks that YHWH hear in heaven and respond with forgiveness and action. The final petition is the longest (vv. 46–51) and, although it envisions the people repenting and petitioning YHWH in their captivity, it offers no word of release from exile. It envisions instead compassion from their captors and the reminder that YHWH remains their God even in exile. The seriousness of the message (vv. 46–51) is heightened by the use of the similar-sounding *šwb* (repent, return) and *šābâ* (captor, captive, capture).

Throughout the chapter Solomon is the main actor but not the only character. David and Moses, and the traditions of Davidic Covenant and exodus, abound, joining the temple to YHWH's earlier interactions (see 'Comment'). YHWH, too, is a prominent character throughout, and his covenant faithfulness is evident in the use of his covenant name 'YHWH' (*et passim*), and 'YHWH the God of Israel' (vv. 15, 17, 20, 23, 25–26). The ark, too, is evoked as the 'ark of the covenant of YHWH' (vv. 1, 6; cf. v. 3). The present reality of God with his people is served through the appellation 'YHWH our God' in the mouth of Solomon (vv. 57, 59, 61) and the narrator (v. 65). Even the terms used of the people ('congregation of Israel', 'assembly of Israel', 'my people Israel') are reminders of a people identified as YHWH's own at Sinai. Although the dedication of the temple marks a new era in Israel's covenant life, it is not an era *sui generis*, but one indelibly tied to Israel's history.

The chapter combines different genres, including narrative (vv. 1–6, 62–66) and reportage of prayer (vv. 22–53). A poetic fragment appears in the form of a prayer of dedication (vv. 12–13) that reflects a common ANE dedicatory inscription form. The form includes an address to a particular deity, a dedicatory declaration of what the builder has accomplished and a statement of intention for the dedicated building (B. Long 1984: 97–98).

The combination of various genres, perceived expansions (for instance, the repeated references to the assembled parties in vv. 1–3), and the perception of traditions held by interested groups (for instance, the perceived priestly traditions of vv. 1–11, the Deuteronomistic traditions of vv. 27–30 [and a later Deuteronomist in places such as vv. 44–53]) has led to theories of redactional composition. As usual, little consensus is apparent. Often assumptions regarding the interests of different groups within Israel (such as priestly concerns by a priestly writer), and the dates at which such groups were active, colour the results in a circular manner (thus Jones 1984a places all so-called priestly concerns with a late priestly writer). However the present text came together, it does now stand as a powerfully articulate and nuanced piece of theological literature, and it is this whole that is the subject of this discussion.

Comment

8:1–13

The temple is completed in the eighth month of the eleventh year (6:38) but is dedicated in the seventh month, Ethanim (equivalent to Sept.–Oct.). Whether the dedication pre-empted the completion (perhaps of the bronze and gold work) by one month or was delayed eleven months is uncertain; both are possible given the opening temporal marker ('*āz*; see 'Notes on the text'). At any rate, the alignment of the dedication to the Feast of Tabernacles (Lev. 23:35–44; Deut. 16:13–17) provides several evocative associations. First, the feast commemorates the wilderness years of Israel's tent-dwelling when YHWH's portable tabernacle facilitated his continual guiding presence. Now the ark rests in a permanent dwelling signifying YHWH's abiding presence. YHWH, however, remains utterly free, for he abides only by his gracious will. Secondly, the festival marks the incoming harvest of year end and anticipates the end-time fullness of all nations turning to YHWH (Zech. 14:16; Isa. 2:2–4; 56:6–8). Thus the chapter's references to the nations (the Canaanite month Ethanim [see 'Comment', 1 Kgs 6:1], the foreigner [v. 41] whom YHWH answers so that 'all peoples of the earth may know your name' [v. 43]) points to the festival's eschatological fulfilment. Thirdly, the feast may be the great seventh-year Feast of Tabernacles at which the torah was read (Deut. 31:9–13). If this particular festival year is in view, references to the ark, which held the tablets, and Solomon's urgings to 'walk in YHWH's statutes, and keep his commandments' (v. 61) are particularly apropos. Finally, the Feast of Tabernacles was characterized by great joy (Deut. 16:14). The dedication of the temple during this feast has this effect upon Israel (v. 66).

Solomon assembles 'all the congregation of Israel' (v. 5). The group is inclusive and enumerates tribal and family leaders, and priests so that 'every Israelite man' (v. 2) gathers. The inclusive group marks it as an auspicious occasion and the whole covenant people gather to bring the ark into the inner sanctuary; it is for this purpose the building is prepared (1 Kgs 6:19).

Israel's history reminds the gathering of the inherent danger in handling the ark (2 Sam. 6:1–15). Stipulations outlined in Num. 4 ensure its safe transport while the innumerable sacrifices Solomon offers serve to sanctify and honour its passage. The ark is successfully transported, and its arrival to 'its place', the 'house's inner sanctuary', the 'holy of holies' and beneath 'the wings of the cherubim' (v. 6) emphasizes this point by using the terminology of 1 Kgs 6. With the ark are transported the wilderness tabernacle (Exod. 27:21; 40:1) and its utensils. Because the tabernacle's ongoing use is not required, no further attention is given it; even its disposition is not related.

The ark's transport is without mishap, but it remains unseen whether YHWH will accept the new building. Before this is revealed, a digression recalls two items that tie this narrative to the exodus narrative – thus revealing the ark is the same item over which YHWH earlier presenced himself (Exod. 25:22). The first item mentioned is the poles. They are a reminder of the ark's portability: no building can prevent its removal nor contain the God associated with it. Mention of the poles is a warning and foreshadowing of this real possibility. The second item is Moses' stone tablets of the covenant. They are all that is in the ark (Deut. 10:1–5); there 'was nothing in the ark' except these tablets: no rod (Num. 17:25), no manna (Exod. 16:33) and certainly no God. It is absolutely clear that YHWH is not somehow housed in the ark; it houses only the testament to the Sinai covenant. This, too, is a warning lest Israel mistake the ark and temple as substitutes for or guarantors of YHWH's presence, or engage in idolatry directed to the holy relics. This danger is realized, as Jeremiah charges Israel with trusting the temple as the guarantor of their safety and covenant life (Jer. 7).

Besides powerful warnings, the digression builds suspense. Will the temple be acceptable to YHWH? The tension resolves as YHWH's glory chases the priests from the temple. The miracle of the exodus tabernacle is repeated (Exod. 40:34–35) in the astounding visible proof of YHWH's presence in his people's midst. The temple is accepted.

Solomon marks the event with a fragment of poetry (see 'Notes on the text'). He states that YHWH dwells in thick darkness or cloud ('ărāpel), a covering that is noted at Sinai (Exod. 20:21; Deut. 4:11; 5:22) and elsewhere (2 Sam. 22:10; Ps. 97:2; Job 22:13) and evokes the existence of YHWH in darkness (ḥōšek) before there was light (Gen. 1:1–3). The connection of this darkness to the 'lofty house' is, however, not at first self-evident. The LXX texts attempt to make an explicit connection, contrasting the darkness of the inner sanctuary to YHWH's first creative act of light (see 'Notes on the text'). The explication is not necessary, however, when one imagines the dimness of the inner sanctuary. YHWH has long been associated with dark cloud and now that association continues in this grand house where he might dwell for ever (Ps. 132:13–14). Later Solomon will nuance what it means for YHWH to dwell in the house (vv. 16–20, 27–30). For now he is content to proclaim that he has built such a dwelling – a fact he strongly emphasizes as he speaks to the people in the next verses.

8:14–21

Solomon directs the poem to YHWH while facing the altar. He now turns to address the people standing in the temple court. His blessing is not so much a blessing of the people (although they do reap the benefits of what Solomon relates) as it is a historical recitation of events precipitating the temple project. While Solomon focuses on the Davidic Covenant, he begins and ends (vv. 16, 21) with the earlier exodus event. Thus the traditions of Moses and exodus/Sinai that underlie vv. 1–11 are not entirely lost in this retrospective of David. Throughout Solomon refers to David as 'my father David' (vv. 15, 17–18, 20), an appellation that notes his own close association with the chosen king.

Solomon loosely quotes elements of the Davidic Covenant found in 2 Sam. 7 (vv. 16, 18–19), and interprets their fulfilment (vv. 17, 20–21). He notes that historically YHWH has not chosen a city in which to raise a temple. Instead, he has chosen David to be over 'my people Israel'. Solomon affirms the choice has indeed been fulfilled in history by YHWH's power (vv. 15–16). He next notes that YHWH, while lauding David's heart's desire to build the temple, remits that privilege to David's 'son' (vv. 17–19). Solomon then interprets that son to be himself, although, interestingly, with no comment about his own heart – a lacuna that will become more pointed as the chapter progresses. The identification of Solomon as the chosen son is emphasized by noting that while YHWH 'upheld' (from *qwm*) his promise, Solomon has 'arisen' (from *qwm*) to fulfil it; he is the 'son' of 'my father David' (vv. 15, 17–18, 20). Also Solomon emphasizes what he has done: 'I have arisen . . . I sit upon the throne . . . I have built . . . I have provided a place for the ark.' There is a return of the old ambiguity surrounding Solomon's actions, as what began as a blessing for the people becomes an apologetic for Solomon's role as the fulfilment of YHWH's promises.

8:22–53

Blessing flows into petition as Solomon turns again to the altar and stretches his hands in a typical prayer posture (Exod. 9:29; Ezra 9:5; Job 11:13). He reaches towards heaven, where YHWH dwells (v. 30), and invokes 'YHWH the God of Israel' (v. 22). The prayer will end as it began, with YHWH's name on Solomon's lips (v. 53).

22–26. Solomon bases his first petition on two of YHWH's characteristics, which he now proclaims. YHWH's incomparability is lauded (Exod. 15:11; Deut. 4:39; Ps. 86:8, 10), and his covenant faithfulness is proclaimed (Exod. 15:13; Deut. 7:9, 12; Ps. 86:13; 1 Kgs 3:6). Solomon has just noted the state of David's heart (vv. 17–18), and the reference to YHWH's covenant faithfulness kept with those who 'walk before you with all their hearts' may be a further reference to David.

Solomon explicates this covenant faithfulness by noting that what YHWH promised with his mouth he fulfilled by his power (v. 24), recalling his earlier affirmation of YHWH's covenant faithfulness (v. 15). YHWH fulfilled this covenant in the past (by placing David upon the throne) and the present (by accepting the temple built by Solomon). Now Solomon asks YHWH also to fulfil 'that which you have promised' (vv. 25–26) under the Davidic Covenant: continuous dynastic succession, which Solomon describes in the conditional terms communicated by David (1 Kgs 2:4).

Solomon refers to David not just as 'my father David' (as in vv. 15, 17–18, 20), but as 'your servant, my father David' (vv. 24–26). As the prayer progresses, Solomon attributes that servant role to himself; he becomes 'your servant' (vv. 28 [twice], 29–30, 52; also 'his servant' in v. 59) who has built the temple and now prays on behalf of the people.

27–30. Solomon built a 'place for your dwelling for ever' (v. 13). Now, he rhetorically exposes the impossibility of an incomparably powerful God's dwelling in any tangible way on earth, much less any temple built by human hands (v. 27). Later, Isaiah will make the same affirmation (Isa. 66:1). Solomon had nuanced his original claim of building a dwelling place for YHWH with the repeated reference to the house as a place for the 'name of YHWH' (five times in vv. 16–21). He now further clarifies the distinction here. YHWH's dwelling is in heaven (v. 30; see also vv. 32, 34, 36, 39, 43, 45, 49); his presence in the temple might be conceived as a hypostatic presence, a real extension of his power but not the full essence of his being.

YHWH's presence makes the structure a conduit so that any petition offered in or towards the temple is heard in heaven. On this basis Solomon three times urges YHWH to hear (*šm'*) prayers offered towards the place (vv. 28–30). YHWH's attentiveness is likened to having eyes opened to the temple. The urging is twice made on behalf of 'your servant' as Solomon prays on behalf of the people. Then the urging is made on behalf of 'your servant' *and* 'your people Israel'. From his heavenly dwelling place YHWH is called upon to hear and forgive. Solomon's plea recognizes that the temple is a visible assurance of YHWH's attention to Israel's 'prayers' (nominal form of the root *pll* in vv. 28 [twice], 29, 38, 45, 49; hith. verbal form in vv. 29–30, 33, 35, 42, 44, 48) and 'supplications' (nominal form of the root *ḥnn* in vv. 28, 30, 38, 45, 49, 52; hith. verbal form in vv. 33).

31–51. The basis for petitionary prayer laid out, Solomon gives seven specific examples. These petitions may be offered in the temple itself (vv. 31, 33), towards it (vv. 35, 42, 38), towards YHWH's chosen city (v. 44) and even from exile towards the 'promised land, the chosen city and the house' (v. 48). The prayers may be offered by an individual (v. 31), but most are offered by 'your people Israel' (vv. 33, 36, 44, 46), and even may be offered by a foreigner (v. 41), proving that YHWH's house is indeed a house of prayer for all nations (Isa. 56:7). Each petition affirms the stance of the preamble (vv. 27–30), that YHWH dwells in heaven but hears prayer offered in (or towards) the temple. As in the preamble, YHWH is repeatedly asked to 'hear and forgive' (vv. 34, 36, 39, 49–50), but is also petitioned to act and render justice (vv. 32, 39, 43) and uphold the cause of YHWH's people (vv. 45, 49). Often YHWH's answer serves a didactic function, teaching Israel to walk in YHWH's ways or fear him (v. 36, 40) and, in the case of the foreigner, that all the earth would know YHWH's name and fear him as Israel does (v. 43; here one thinks of the example of Naaman [2 Kgs 5]).

Of the individual petitions, the first (vv. 31–32) has as its background legal texts concerning the unfair application of an oath (Exod. 22:7–12; Num. 5:11–31). The petition is for YHWH's justice according to the parties' actions.

Several of the petitions concern various calamities listed as curses for Israel's covenant unfaithfulness in Deuteronomy 28:

Petition 2 (vv. 33–34)	Deut. 28:25, 48	Defeat, exile
Petition 3 (vv. 35–36)	Deut. 28:24	Rain
Petition 4 (vv. 37–40)	Deut. 28:21–22, 38, 59	Famine, blights, siege
Petition 7 (vv. 46–50)	Deut. 28:53–63	Exile

These petitions, in particular, are audacious. They ask for YHWH's forgiveness when, in the covenant ceremony that seals the covenant curses, it is specifically stated that YHWH will not forgive but will fully execute the covenant curses (Deut. 29:18–29).

The fifth petition, made by the foreigner (vv. 41–43), arises from knowledge of YHWH's saving name, strong hand and outstretched arm (Deut. 4:34;

5:15). Individuals do come to Israel on account of Solomon's fame (1 Kgs 4:34[5:14]; 10:1), but now they come on account of Solomon's God.

Three of the petitions concern military conflict, siege or exile (vv. 33–34, 37, 44) and the last (and longest) petition turns to exile, which, in the light of human sin, Solomon considers inevitable. An extended wordplay between similar-sounding roots (*šbh*, 'captors, captive'; and *šwb*, 'turn, return, repent'; see 'Form and structure') alternates between the reality of captivity and the possibility of repentance. Thus

> when 'their captors take them captive' (*wěšābûm šōbêhem*) (v. 46)
> 'if they come to their senses' (*wěhēšîbû*) (v. 47)
> '[where] they have been taken captive' (*nišbû-šām*) (v. 47)
> 'and they repent' (*wěšābû*) (v. 47)
> in the land of their captors' (*bě'ereṣ šōbêhem*) (v. 47)
> 'and they return to you' (*wěšābû*) (v. 48)
> in the land of those 'who have captured them' (*'ăšer šābû*) (v. 48)

Solomon repeatedly holds out the hope that the people will repent and turn. However, the verses ultimately conclude with the people in captivity. There is no statement of 'return' (*šwb*) to the land. Yet even in captivity Solomon asks that YHWH 'hear and forgive' (vv. 49–50). He petitions too that their captors (*šōbêhem*) will show compassion, a petition based on the strength of YHWH's past saving acts and his ongoing covenant faithfulness to his inheritance, Israel (vv. 50–51; cf. Deut. 4:20). In the mention of deliverance from Egypt (v. 51) there yet lies a glimmer of hope that YHWH (incomparable, powerful, faithful) will effect deliverance so that the people return to the land once again.

52–53. The epilogue revisits the preamble, calling again for YHWH's attentive eyes and listening ears (v. 29). The call is couched in the past: YHWH has saved his people as his unique inheritance by delivering them from Egypt, just as promised to Moses. He is the God who listens to his people, who will 'hear and forgive'.

8:54–61

Blessing the people once more, Solomon speaks twice of YHWH's faithfulness. First, he recalls the fulfilment of promises made to Moses – specifically, the rest granted Israel, a reference to their establishment in the land, and to which the temple attests (Deut. 12:9; 25:19; Josh. 21:43–45; 23:1; 2 Sam. 7:1–2; 1 Kgs 5:4–5[18–19]). Secondly, he speaks of YHWH's past presence with the fathers. On the basis of past faithfulness, Solomon asks for three things. He desires that YHWH continue his faithful presence, neither abandoning nor forsaking Israel (even in the inevitable exile, vv. 50–51). He asks that his petitions continually stand before YHWH on behalf of himself and the people. As YHWH acts on their behalf it will demonstrate to all peoples what Israel has experienced: that YHWH is God, and there is none other. Finally, he calls the people to covenant obedience (vv. 58, 61). In this call he initially identifies himself with the people as he expresses the hope YHWH will 'incline our hearts towards him' (v. 58). But when he urges the people to the necessity of letting 'your hearts be wholly with YHWH' (v. 61), no such identification is made. Despite his admonition, and similar admonitions he himself receives (1 Kgs 2:4; 3:14; 6:11–13; 9:1–9), he abandons the torah and his heart turns elsewhere (1 Kgs 11:1–9). It is a tragic background note to his petitions.

8:62–66

'All Israel' from Lebo Hamath in northern Syria (Josh. 13:5; 2 Kgs 14:25) to the wadi el-'Arish includes northern and southern reaches of Solomon's kingdom. The large number of people, plus the significance of the dedication, calls for sacrifices so abundant that the bronze altar is insufficient to accommodate them all. The consecrated temple courtyard serves as an altar upon which burnt and grain offerings are offered (Lev. 1 – 2, 6). The fat portions of the peace offerings are likewise consumed, and the balance provides a joyous meal (Lev. 3:1–7; 7:11–21).

Seven days of dedicatory rituals are followed by another seven for the Feast of Tabernacles (Deut. 16:13; 2 Chr. 7:9). The people, filled with festal joy (Deut. 16:14), are dismissed to their homes. They are mindful of YHWH's goodness to David and to the people, probably seeing the temple's completion as tangible evidence of these realities. For the king's blessings and prayers the people bless him in return.

One expects the idyllic conclusion (v. 66) and it is along the lines that Israel 'ate and drank, and was happy' (4:20) and 'dwelt securely, every man under his vine and his fig tree, from Dan to Beer-sheba, all the days of Solomon' (4:25[5:5]). But the idyllic moment is short lived. The chapter is immediately followed by a grave warning against covenant unfaithfulness and apostasy (9:1–9). It will go unheeded. In a few years Israel will again return 'to their tents' (8:66) – not in peaceful celebration, but in open rebellion (12:16). Apostasy will already exist in Jerusalem (11:1–13) and will be soon coming in the north (12:25–33). The joyous celebration of this chapter will be only a sad memory.

Explanation

The high point of Israel's history in the land is the completion of the temple. At its dedication, although YHWH remains transcendent, his glory fills the temple, attesting to his presence with his covenant people.

The chapter acknowledges YHWH's covenants with Israel several ways. The tablets of the covenant are noted as the temple's most holy relic, a continual reminder of the relationship forged on Sinai. That no image of Israel's god resides in the inner sanctuary recalls the transcendence of the God with whom they are covenanted. His words remain with them to call them continually to covenant life (Deut. 4:9–20). The deliverance out of Egypt serves as a reminder of the saving actions of their covenant partner (vv. 16, 21, 51, 53, 56–61). Their entry into the Promised Land is likewise noted (v. 48) – a promise that extends back to Abraham and precipitates YHWH's answer to the cry of the Israelite slaves (Exod. 2:23–25). The chapter similarly recalls the temple's connection to the Davidic Covenant (vv. 15–20, 24–26, 48). It is the temple that affirms YHWH's commitments made to David and his descendants.

By emphasizing YHWH's presence and recalling both the Sinaitic and Davidic Covenants, the chapter recognizes that the temple's value rests upon these realities. It is not the temple that keeps the covenants in place; it is only a witness to them. Even more, it is the underlying reality of YHWH's presence and his commitment to the covenants that is the foremost factor in the covenants' continuance. Additionally, the chapter's emphasis on YHWH's presence and the covenants points to the people's responsibilities for the ongoing covenant. As they faithfully recollect covenant history (via David and Moses) and faithfully obey covenant statutes (represented by the tablets), they acknowledge the God of the covenant. Only in this way are they able to continue in covenant life. Finally, while the sacrificial system is highlighted, neither in this chapter nor throughout Kings, it must be said that this means of realignment to covenant life is not denied. Solomon offers sacrifices (vv. 5, 62–64) and subsequent kings and prophets show regard for this element of covenant life (1 Kgs 13:2–3; 2 Kgs 16:10–16; 18:4; 23:4–20).

It is not surprising that in a chapter which emphasizes these underlying covenant realities by which covenant is sustained, its introduction of prayer is wholly couched in covenant concerns. Solomon's prayer recognizes covenant realities and points to prayer as another means by which Israel faithfully remains in covenant.

Solomon is not the only individual to offer prayer in the OT. Abraham intercedes on behalf of Sodom and Gomorrah (Gen. 18:23–33), and Moses on behalf of Israel (Exod. 32:31–32; Num. 14:13–19). David prays in thanksgiving and for the fulfilment of YHWH's promise (2 Sam. 7:18–29). Jeremiah prays for the wicked and for himself (Jer. 10:23–25; 12:1–4; 20:7–18), while Daniel's prayer of repentance pleads for mercy (Dan. 9:4–19). Even the psalter – that great book of praises – acknowledges its character as a book of prayers (Ps. 72:20; see also the superscriptions of Pss 17, 86, 90, 92, 142).

While Solomon joins many others in the OT who pray, his prayer as the temple is dedicated is wholly characterized by covenant concerns. It is intricately tied to the Mosaic and Davidic Covenants and YHWH's presence. The seven petitions Solomon forwards (vv. 31–51) arise from these covenantal realities: from remembering them (vv. 14–30) Solomon boldly makes his petitions. In this he lives out the admonition of Deut. 4:5–14. There Israel is called to remember continually the covenant YHWH has made, and to remember the nearness of YHWH to them. It is in the context of such memory that prayer arises (v. 7).

Another striking covenantal characteristic in Solomon's prayer is how closely the seven petitions align with the covenant as expressed in its legal texts and covenant curses (see 'Comment', vv. 31–51). In making his petitions Solomon assumes YHWH's willingness to hear and forgive beyond what is expressed in the curses themselves. But he does not go beyond the reach of the covenant in petitioning for YHWH's mercy. The covenant continually calls for Israel to turn towards YHWH that they might experience covenantal blessings. Solomon takes this to heart in his prayers, and for each petition he presents the petitioner's actions. These actions are either a conscious acknowledgment of sin and repentance or an acknowledgment of YHWH's lordship: oath-making before YHWH (v. 31), repentance and return (vv. 33, 35, 47–48), acknowledgment of need and subsequent petition (v. 38, 44), or movement towards the God of Israel (v. 42) (see further in Boda 2009: 166–171). Audacious though Solomon's petitions for mercy might be when compared to the covenant curses that inform them, they are not so audacious in the light of the covenant's openness to Israel's repentance and right actions towards YHWH. Nor are they audacious given YHWH's demonstrable intention through history to draw near to his covenant people despite their sinfulness.

Finally, Solomon's prayer shows a crucial covenant characteristic. Upon finishing his prayer he urges Israel to incline their hearts towards YHWH so that they might keep his covenant statutes (vv. 58, 61). This attitude is juxtaposed with YHWH's favourable response to his people's petitions on a daily basis so that all peoples might know that YHWH is God (v. 59). Here is the crux of the covenant: it calls Israel to love YHWH with heart, soul, mind and strength so that they might walk rightly in the covenant (Deut. 6:4–9). Only in this way can Israel live out their calling to be a kingdom of priests to the nations (Exod. 19:6). The centre of the covenant is a relationship of love that results in wholehearted devotion and obedience. Such a heart rejoices at the covenant nearness of YHWH in the temple, and turns with expectancy to him in prayer.

For an exilic audience, and for later generations who likewise experience covenant discipline, these verses have particular resonance. Though exiled, Israel are deprived of the temple, they come to understand that YHWH does not abandon his people. He presences himself in their midst, even in a foreign land (Ezek. 1, 8–10). The invitation to repentance under the covenant remains open for Israel to take up. Should they act to acknowledge YHWH's sovereignty and covenant love, they have the assurance that their prayers and supplications will be heard, and that YHWH will act to uphold his people's cause in each day's affairs (v. 59).

The exilic understanding of YHWH's commitment to, and presence with, his people takes an unexpected turn in the NT. There Jesus is presented as the temple of God (see 'Explanation', 1 Kgs 6 – 7). Yet, unlike the Jerusalem temple, Jesus comes as the incarnation of God who now *does* dwell in the temple while also dwelling in heaven. Now prayers addressed to God through the 'temple' of the God-Man are heard in the very throne room of God, for Jesus has ascended there as Lord and Christ. God's ear remains attentive towards the cries of his people throughout the world. No place is too distant that God does not hear every prayer lifted up in the name of Jesus.

1 KINGS 9:1–25

Translation

[1]Now when Solomon had finished building YHWH's temple, and the king's palace, and all that he desired to do[a], [2]YHWH appeared to Solomon a second time, just as he had appeared to him in Gibeon. [3]YHWH said to him, 'I have heard your prayer and your supplication that you made before me. I have consecrated this house that you have built by putting my name there[a] for ever. My eyes and my heart will be there always.

[4]'As for you, if you will walk before me just as your father David walked, with integrity of heart and with uprightness, doing[a] all that I have commanded you, and you keep my statutes[b] and judgments, [5]then I will establish the throne of your kingdom over Israel for ever, just as I promised your father David, "You shall not lack a man upon the throne[a] of Israel."

[6]'But if[a] you and your sons ever turn aside from following me and do not keep my commandments and my statutes[b] that I gave you, but go and serve other gods and bow down to them, [7]then I will cut off Israel from the land that I have given them, and the house that I have consecrated for my name I will cast from me. Israel will become a proverb and a byword[a] among all peoples. [8]And this house will become a heap of ruins[a]. Everyone who passes it will be appalled and hiss. They will say, "For what reason has YHWH done this to this land and to this house?" [9]They will answer, "Because they abandoned YHWH their God who brought out their fathers from the land of Egypt. They embraced other gods, bowed down[a] to them and served them. Therefore, YHWH has brought all this calamity upon them."'[b]

[10a]At the end of twenty years, during which time Solomon built the two houses – YHWH's temple and the king's palace [11](Hiram king of Tyre had supplied Solomon with trees of cedar and pine, and as much gold as he desired) – then King Solomon gave to Hiram twenty cities in the land of Galilee. [12]Hiram went

out from Tyre to see the cities that Solomon had given to him but they did not please him. [13]So he said, 'What are these cities that you have given me, my brother?' and he called them 'the land of Cabul[a]', as they are called to this day. [14]Now Hiram had sent 120 talents of gold to the king.

[15a]This is the account of the corvée that King Solomon levied to build YHWH's house, his own house, the Millo, the wall of Jerusalem and Hazor, Megiddo and Gezer. [16](Pharaoh king of Egypt had gone up, and captured Gezer, and burned it with fire, and killed the Canaanites who dwelt in the city. He gave it as a dowry to his daughter the wife of Solomon. [17]So Solomon rebuilt Gezer.) And he built lower Beth-horon, [18]and Baalath, and Tamar[a] in the wilderness in the land of Judah, [19]and all Solomon's storage cities, and the cites for chariots and horses, and whatever Solomon desired to build in Jerusalem, Lebanon and all the land of his dominion.

[20]All the people who remained of the Amorites, the Hittites, the Perizzites, the Hivites and the Jebusites who were not from the sons of Israel, [21]their sons who remained after them in the land (whom the sons of Israel were not able to destroy), Solomon levied them as enslaved labour, as it is to this day. [22]But Solomon did not make slaves[a] of the sons of Israel. They were his soldiers[b], servants, leaders, officers, chariot commanders and horsemen. [23a]There were five hundred and fifty men as supervisors over Solomon's work, having charge over the labourers.

[24]Then[a] Pharaoh's daughter went up from David's city to her house that he had built for her. Then he built the Millo.

[25]Three times in a year Solomon would offer up burnt offerings and peace offerings upon the altar that he had built to YHWH, offering incense[a] with them[b] *on the altar*[c] before YHWH. Thus he finished the house.

Notes on the text

1.a. For MT *ḥāpēṣ la'ăśôt* , 'he desired to do', BHS proposes changing the finite verb to read, *ḥāšaq la'ăśôt*. The root *ḥšq* is found in the similar phrase in v. 19 (*ḥāšaq libnôt*, 'he desired to build') and Syr, Tg. The expression in vv. 1, 19 is similar, but the inf. differs (v. 1, 'to do'; v. 19, 'to build').

3.a. *lāśûm-šĕmî šām*, 'by putting my name there'. The lamed plus inf. gives more detail about, and explains the preceding action of, consecration (*hiqdaštî*) (JM §124o).

4.a. The inf. 'doing' (*la'ăśôt*) further defines the finite verb, 'walk . . . with integrity . . . and uprightness' (GKC §114o).

4.b. *ḥuqqâ*, 'my statutes', is read with a cop. as in 2 Chr. 7:17.

5.a. *mē'al kissē'* takes up the language of 2:4 and 8:25 (slightly modified) and should remain, contra LXX 'ruling over' (*môšēl bĕ*).

6.a. *'im*, 'if', is read with an adversative cop. as in LXX, Syr, Vg, 2 Chr. 7:19.

6.b. *ḥuqqōtay* with cop., according to several MSS and Vrs.

7.a. *lĕmāšāl wĕlišnînâ* ('a proverb and a byword'; Deut. 28:37; 2 Chr. 7:20; Jer 24:9). LXX's 'a destruction and a byword' abbreviates a fuller phrase (Deut. 28:37; *lĕšammâ . . . wĕlišnînâ*).

8.a. MT's puzzling *'elyôn*, 'high, exalted', read here with Vrs, *lĕ'iyyîn* ('a heap of ruins'; cf. Job 30:24; Ps. 79:1; Jer. 26:18; Mic. 1:6; 3:12).

9.a. *wayyištaḥăwû* with Q as 3 m. pl.

9.b. In LXX, MT v. 24 follows v. 9, noting Pharaoh's daughter's influence upon Solomon to abandon YHWH.

10.a.–11. Both these verses serve as background to the main action signalled in v. 12 by the cons. plus impf. 'Hiram went out'. V. 10 is the temporal background ('at the end of twenty years'). All of v. 11 is subject to the temporal clause. The adv. *'āz*, 'then', plus impf. *yittēn*, 'he gave', is explained as a 'yiqtol with no iterative or durative aspect, and thus having the value of qatal', which 'with the adverb *'āz* this use of yiqtol is common in prose' (JM §113h, i) and speaks of the one-time payment by Solomon of the cities.

13.a. *kābûl* may comprise *kĕ*, 'as', and *bûl* ('nothing' – although elsewhere unattested in Hebr.). LXX exchanges kaph with gimel, reading *gĕbûl* and translating as *ὅριον*, 'boundary'. Both are derogatory.

15.a. MT vv. 15–25 are dispersed in LXX (see at 2:35f–k, 46d; 5:14b; 9:9a; 10:22a–c in LXX*; detail in DeVries 2003: 130).

18.a. Reading *tāmār* with K as a southern city guarding the route to Elath (cf. Ezek. 47:19; 48:28). The Q reading (*tadmōr*), together with many MSS., LXX^L, Syr, Tg, Vg and 2 Chr. 8:4 identify the later city of Tadmor in Syria.

22.a. The sg. noun 'slave' read as a collective.

22.b. 'his soldiers' glosses MT 'the men of battle'.

23.a. *'ēlleh*, 'these', is glossed for sense as 'there were'.

24.a. Reading the difficult *'ak* (surely) as *'āz*, 'then'. The verse is found in substantially this form in LXX at 9:9, with 'then' (*τότε*).

25.a. *wĕhaqṭêr*, 'offering incense'. The inf. abs. continues the frequentative of the preceding finite verb (*wĕhe'ĕlâ*, 'and he would offer up burnt offerings'; GKC §113z).

25.b. Glossing the collective sg. 'with it' to 'them'.

25.c. 'on the altar' is glossed for sense.

Form and structure

Three sections (vv. 1–9, 10–14, 15–23), together with a concluding notation (vv. 24–25), provide a narrative response to the temple dedication. Verse 1 contextualizes the chapter into all of Solomon's building projects, and his work (vv. 2–9, 10–14) and the corvée labour necessary to it (vv. 15–23) feature large in the chapter. Thematically, the chapter ends at 9:25 and vv. 26–28 are included with Solomon's international affairs (10:1–29).

The dream (vv. 1–9) is YHWH's response to Solomon's 'prayer and supplication' (v. 3) at the temple dedication (8:28, 54 *et passim*, where the nouns 'prayer' and 'supplication' as well as the related verbal forms are repeatedly used; see 'Comment', 8:28). The dream also stands with the dream report in ch. 3, bracketing material primarily concerned with Solomon's national affairs. The two dreams are connected in several ways. In each a ni. verb notes that YHWH appeared (*r'h*) to Solomon at Gibeon and the citation of a second appearance (9:2) heightens the connection. In both, YHWH's positive response employs the language of the request (see the commentary on 1 Kgs 3:10–14 and below) and goes beyond what was requested: in 3:13 riches and honour are granted beyond Solomon's request; in 9:3 the temple endures 'for ever' and 'always' although not specifically requested by Solomon (8:25–30). Finally, each dream report includes a conditional promise of long life (3:14) and an everlasting dynasty (9:5).

The second section (vv. 10–14), an etiological fragment perhaps from annals collected under Solomon's administration (10:41), notes the twenty years of construction (6:38 and 7:1). The etiology includes background information (vv. 10–11), the main action (vv. 12–13) and a final notation of payment (v. 14). The narrative location after the completion of the building projects sets it temporally with the dream report, connecting the two sections.

The final section of this chapter on the corvée (vv. 15–23) may also represent an annalistic source. Although no temporal marker is present, the building projects have necessitated the corvée levy and the account flows logically from the preceding material. Temple and palace, and several other projects, are included: the Millo, wall and several cities. The cities and the digression regarding the dowry (vv. 15–19) are background to the main thought: Solomon's enslavement of non-Israelites.

The narrative conclusion (vv. 24–25) revisits the chapter's topics of Pharaoh's daughter (v. 16), the Millo (v. 15) and temple practices (vv. 1, 2–10). Solomon's role in the temple project is similarly revisited through wordplay: on the altar in the new temple Solomon (*šĕlōmōh*) would continually offer peace offerings (*šĕlāmîm*) and such sacrifices signal the temple's completion (*šillam*). The narrative has earlier signalled the completion (*šlm*) of the temple (7:51). Solomon's established practice of sacrifices, following on from the approval of the temple (vv. 1–9), signal all is in order, and the narrative thus proceeds to other aspects of Solomon's rule.

The conclusion also provides a satisfying and intentional conclusion to 1 Kgs 3:1 – 9:25. When viewed in parallel fashion, 3:1–3 and 9:24–25 show obvious similarities. In the same order, each deals with the following:

Pharaoh's daughter	3:1–2	9:24
Her residence in the city of David	3:2 (its commencement) and 3:1 (other building, which precedes her residency)	9:24 (her residency signals the temple's completion [cf. 7:8])
Sacrifices of people/king	3:2–3	9:25
Temple	3:2 (not yet built)	9:25 (the house is finished)

The mirror effect brackets a narrative centred on national affairs, with the temple project its central focus. The narrative includes references to foreign marriage (3:1–2; 7:8; 9:24) and non-Deuteronomistic worship (3:2–3). The concluding verses (9:24–25) link the two topics. Although the temple's completion aligns worship to Deuteronomistic norms (9:25), such orthodoxy is shortlived. By 1 Kgs 11:1–10, worship once again degenerates, linked to Pharaoh's daughter, whom Solomon loved alongside many other foreign women (11:1–2).

Comment

9:1–9

1–3. YHWH's words echo Solomon's dedicatory prayer, and the temporal location places them after Solomon's building projects and the achievement of 'all that he desired (*ḥašaq*; also at v. 19; 2 Chr. 8:6; Isa. 21:4) to do'. The passion behind Solomon's achievements is suggested by the root (*ḥšq*) of the word 'desired'. The root is used variously of YHWH's love for Israel (Deut. 7:17; 10:15), Israel's love for YHWH (Ps. 91:14) and a man's love for a woman (Gen. 34:8; Deut 21:11).

YHWH appears to Solomon as he appeared at Gibeon, presumably during a night dream at Jerusalem or during dedicatory cultic practices (8:62–66). YHWH affirms he has 'heard' Solomon, as he has 'heard' his people in times past. In most instances YHWH hears and responds to relieve his people's distress (e.g. Exod. 3:7; 6:5; Deut. 5:28; 2 Kgs 19:20; 20:5; 22:19; but see the negative response in Num. 14:27). Now YHWH's response is directly to Solomon's 'prayer and supplication' (*tĕpillātĕkā wĕ'et-tĕḥinnātĕkā*). These were offered in 1 Kgs 8:22–53, where 'prayer and supplication' (*tĕpillâ* and *tĕḥinnâ*) often stand together (vv. 28, 38, 45, 49; cf. v. 54) and alone ('prayer' in v. 29; 'supplication' in vv. 30, 52), and the related verbal roots (*pll* and *ḥnn*) are used both separately and together throughout (vv. 28–30, 33, 35, 42, 44, 47–48; cf. vv. 54, 59).

YHWH's response echoes Solomon's prayer in significant ways. He consecrates 'this house that you have built' (8:13, 27, 43, 44, 48) by 'putting my name there' (*lāśûm šĕmî šām*), a synonymous rendition of the periphrastic reflex 'for my name to be there' (8:16; *lihyôt šĕmî šām*; see Richter 2002: 43–52). Moreover, YHWH affirms his 'eyes and heart will be there' (8:29, 52). YHWH's words reveal he has truly heard Solomon's prayer.

As in ch. 3, YHWH's response goes beyond Solomon's prayer. YHWH advises Solomon that by 'putting his name there' – an action that Solomon's prayer and its preliminaries has assumed on the basis of the promise to David (8:16–20, 29, 43–44, 48) – he has effectually 'consecrated' the temple (1 Kgs 9:3, 7; cf. 2 Chr. 7:16, 20; 30:8; 36:14), a grace elsewhere applied to people (Num. 3:13; Jer. 1:5), places (Josh. 20:7) and things (Exod. 28:38; Lev. 22:2–3; 2 Kgs 12:18). The consecration goes beyond Solomon's request, for it is 'for ever' although it does not preclude YHWH's casting the house away (vv. 7–8). YHWH's response also supersedes Solomon's request, for Solomon notes YHWH's attention involves his eyes being open towards the temple (8:29, 52). YHWH, however, affirms both his eyes *and* heart are attentive, revealing the God who truly listens and responds to his people's prayers.

4–9. The Dtr phraseology of this section ('walk before me with integrity of heart and with uprightness'; cf. 1 Kgs 2:4; 3:6; 'statutes and judgments'; cf. Deut. 4:1, 5, 8, 14; 12:1; 1 Kgs 11:33; 'shall not lack a man upon the throne of Israel'; cf. 1 Kgs 2:4; 8:25; 'establish the throne of your kingdom over Israel for ever'; cf. 2 Sam. 7:13; 'statutes and commandments'; cf. Deut. 6:2; 10:13; 1 Kgs 11:34; 2 Kgs 17:13; 'go and serve other gods and bow down to them'; cf. Deut. 11:16; Josh. 23:7; 1 Kgs 22:54; 2 Kgs 17:35; 21:3, 21; 'I will cut off Israel from the land'; cf. Deut. 4:26; 6:15; Josh. 23:13–16; 1 Kgs 13:34; 'I will cast from me'; cf. 2 Kgs 13:23; 17:20; 'a proverb and a byword'; cf. Deut. 28:37; Jer. 24:9) characterizes the Dtr theology of dynasty, temple and land possession traced throughout Kings.

Solomon is emphatically addressed, 'As for *you*, if you . . .', and the first condition echoes Solomon's prayer. Walking before YHWH, as did the previous generation, is necessary to continued possession of the Davidic throne (8:25; 9:4). To 'walk before YHWH' is synonymous with torah observance ('all I commanded you'; 'statutes and judgments'), and is continuous with David's charge to Solomon (2:3–4), YHWH's words to Solomon (6:12) and Solomon's own petition concerning the Davidic covenant (8:25). In each instance the condition is stated positively: obedience to torah results in the full blessings of the Davidic covenant, including dynastic continuity. However, given the questions already raised concerning the extent of Solomon's torah obedience, one cannot help but hear the implicit negative word: disobedience will result in dynastic failure and covenant punishments.

The negative condition (vv. 6–7) is also emphatic ('*you* and your sons') and expands upon the requirement of torah obedience. Here the 'you' is plural (the pluralization is carried through the verbs of v. 6) and has in view the whole people Israel. Of course, 'Israel' would include Solomon and his sons, and thus Solomon cannot escape personal responsibility.

The consequences of turning aside from YHWH are crucial (denoted by the inf. abs. construction): 'if you ever turn aside' (*'im-šôb tĕšubûn*). Turning aside is torah disobedience that leads one to 'go and serve other gods and bow down to them'. Here is the heart of Deuteronomistic worship: YHWH alone is the object of worship (Deut. 12; Josh. 24; 1 Sam. 12:14–15, 24–25). Certainly, Solomon's great prayer emphasized this intent for temple worship; now the warning against deviation is clearly expressed. Deviation brings terrible consequences signalled by the 'if–then' construction of vv. 6–7. First, Israel will be cut off from YHWH's gift of land, as was threatened since Israel's entry (Deut. 28:36; 29:24–28) and remarked upon as recently as Solomon's prayer (8:40). The second consequence is that the temple will be cast away by YHWH and reduced to rubble (vv. 7–9; cf. Mic. 3:12; Jer. 26:18). The people's disobedience binds their fate together with the fate of the land and the temple – two identifiers of their chosen status before YHWH. The interwoven nature of the fate of Israel–land–temple becomes apparent, as vv. 7–8 frequently mention each in interrelated judgment.

In return for their disobedience Israel, a nation brought to great glory, renown, rest and prosperity during the era of Solomon (4:20–34; 5:4), will become a 'proverb (*māšāl*) and byword (*šĕnînâ*) among all peoples', a typical expression of covenant curse (Deut. 28:37; Jer. 24:9). The phrase also signals the irony of Solomon's life. He knew many proverbs (*māšāl*; 4:20), but this proverb regarding the future destruction of his people he does not learn nor heed (11:1–11).

As foreigners are mouthpieces to praise Solomon and YHWH (e.g. Hiram, the Queen of Sheba), now foreigners voice Dtr's retributive theology. Hissing expresses shock, amazement and derision (Jer. 18:16; 19:8; 29:17; 50:13; cf. Lam. 2:15–16; Mic. 6:16), and the question and answer (see Deut. 29:24–28; Jer. 22:8–9) expresses incredulity and the meetness of covenant justice. Because a people rescued out of Egypt by YHWH serve other gods, covenant calamity at the hand of YHWH is their due and the grand temple does not forestall the consequence.

9:10–14

Different in tone from the preceding section, the temporal notation places the section in the same time frame as the first (see discussion in 'Form and structure' above). Vv. 10–11 provide background information to the main action, which is Hiram's viewing of the deeded cities and his reaction to them. This main action begins with the cons. plus impf., 'Hiram went out' (v. 12)

Hiram's twenty-year provision of building materials and gold (vv. 10–11) is paid to him in annual grain and oil (5:11–12) as well as the gift of twenty Galilean towns (v. 11). The amount of gold Hiram had provided (6,614 to 15,432 pounds [3 to 7 metric tons]) is mentioned only after he views the cities and expresses his outrage (v. 14), although one might expect the detail when the gold is first mentioned (v. 11). The delay juxtaposes the extravagant provision of gold with the unsatisfactory cities – a rhetorical strategy that heightens Hiram's outrage.

The cities are in Galilee. 'Cabul' may be the town in eastern Asher of Josh. 19:27, or the administrative centre of Khirbet Rosh Zayit north-east of Kabul, for which the archaeological record provides evidence of activity during the Solomonic era (Gal 1990). Solomon's gift to Hiram reflects political and economic realities of the era. Phoenicia was expanding eastwards from the coast, and cities were exchanged in the border territory between Phoenicia and Israel along the Galilee/'Acco Plain boundary. Yet despite these historical realities, Dtr characterizes Solomon negatively. YHWH has just reminded Solomon that land is a gift (9:7; cf. Josh. 1:3, 6). Unlike Naboth after him (1 Kgs 21), Solomon holds YHWH's gift cheaply by giving it away, particularly to a non-Israelite.

Hiram's displeasure is evident in the name he gives the territory (Cabul, 'nothing' or 'worthless'). The covenant terminology 'my brother' suggests Solomon has wilfully subverted an agreement for payment. If so, Solomon has, as in 5:1–12, usurped the agreement to his advantage, placing Hiram in a subservient position.

9:15–23

15–19. The projects cited in v. 1 and enumerated here precipitate corvée labour. In Jerusalem, projects include fortifying and extending city walls around the temple–palace complex north of the City of David. Excavations provide several possible identifications of the Millo: a stepped-stone structure acting as a retaining wall, fortifications for the Jerusalem acropolis or fill in a shallow saddle between the City of David and the temple area (Domeris 1984: 26–28; Shiloh and Geva, *NEAEHL* 2:703–704).

The cities outside Jerusalem protect strategic economic routes. Hazor guarded Israel's northern boundary, Megiddo the inland route through the Jezreel Valley, and Gezer the Via Maris at its junction to Jerusalem. Continuing the enumeration of cities in a north–south axis, Beth-horon guarded the road from Gibeon through the Aijalon Valley; Baalath (Kiriath Jearim [Josh 15:9; 1 Chr. 13:6]) controlled access to the coastal plain; and Tamar, south-west of the Dead Sea, protected the road south to the port at Elath (Aharoni 1963, 1967; Cohen 1979). In addition, store cities (for provisions through taxation and tribute), and military-post cities served Solomon's administration. Finally, marking Solomon's international influence (4:21, 24), his building projects extended to Lebanon and 'all the land of his dominion'.

The list sounds dangerous notes. The king is obviously amassing wealth, including horses – against the proscriptions of Deut. 17:16–17. The mention of Gezer sparks a digression on its acquisition from Pharaoh. The association with a foreigner (especially from Egypt) cannot be approved by Dtr. Moreover, Pharaoh's daughter has elsewhere shadowed the narrative so that, in the midst of a portrayal of Solomon's glory, his wealth and his wife prevent the portrait of an unmitigated golden age.

20–23. The corvée force (*mas*) comprised two parts. The first was non-Israelite, and permanently enslaved (*mas-ʿōbēd*; cf. Exod. 3:8, 17; 13:5; 23:23; 43:11; Deut. 7:1; 20:17; Josh. 3:10; 9:1; 11:3; 12:8; 24:11; Judg. 3:5). These individuals were supervised by five hundred and fifty of Solomon's men. The smaller supervisory force for this group (v. 23), in comparison to the Israelite corvée force (5:16), suggests a relatively small enslaved force. The second part of the corvée was Israelite, and not enslaved (*ʿābed*; v. 22) but served on a temporary shift basis, particularly on the temple and palace projects (5:13–14). In addition, Israelites served in various supervisory and military capacities within the administration (v. 22; Mendelsohn 1962; Mettinger 1971:128–132; Soggin 1982).

The passage is not alarmed at enslavement per se; no anti-slavery sensibility intrudes on the ancient text. The point at issue is that of *ḥerem*, the destruction of the inhabitants of the land (Deut. 7:2; 20:17). The descendants of the inhabitants whom the Israelites were not able to destroy (*ḥrm*) are those Solomon enslaves for his building projects (vv. 20–21). The reminder of Israel's failure at this point adds little to the understanding of corvée. It does, however, provide a negative evaluative note: Solomon's labour force is possible because of Israelite non-compliance with deuteronomic law. The negative evaluation is furthered because the corvée is necessitated in part by a house for Solomon's foreign wife. Thus Israel's earlier disobedience is compounded by Solomonic administrative practice.

9:24–25

The conclusion brackets the long section begun at 3:1. According to 3:1, Solomon's Egyptian wife remains in the City of David until the temple and palace complex are completed. She takes up residence in 9:24 and the notation thus confirms the temple project is completed. But it does not mark that completion positively, for she will draw his heart away from the God of the temple. Her presence at this point in the narrative is, as it was in 3:1, a shadow upon both Solomon and the temple project.

The conclusion also notes Solomon offers burnt, peace and incense offerings at the temple's altar. These offerings are part of the three-times-yearly pilgrim rituals for all Israel of Unleavened Bread, Weeks and

Tabernacles (Exod. 23:14–19; 34:18–26; Deut. 16:1–17). Solomon leads the whole people in worship at the Jerusalem temple and by this measure all seems in order. Yet the narrative has repeatedly shown the flaws in Solomon's heart and this defect calls into question the propriety of his role as worship leader (2 Chr. 26:16–21). Despite Solomon's wisdom, his great kingdom and temple, all is not in order.

Explanation

A chapter to prepare for building the temple (ch. 5). Two chapters to build and furnish it (chs. 6–7). Another chapter to institute its rituals and dedicate it in prayer (ch. 8). But on all Solomon's preparation and work YHWH provides no comment. The only validation Solomon's great temple receives is contained in one brief verse in which YHWH states he has 'consecrated this house . . . by putting my name there' (9:3); the action itself is accomplished in an equally brief statement (8:10–11). The brevity of the response is almost lost in the magnitude of the account of the temple preparation, building and dedication until one understands that YHWH's response is the only response that makes Solomon's work of any value. Without it, the temple is just a building, however grand.

YHWH's brief remark on his consecration of the building is in contrast to the lengthy exhortation he then delivers to Solomon. For continuance of the Davidic dynasty, the life of the people in the land and YHWH's presence in the temple, they must not abandon YHWH to serve other gods, but continue in the fullness of his covenant life. There is a deep reality that must colour Israel's life, and that is the reality that their life and institutions are built upon and upheld by YHWH's presence and empowerment. But for Israel there always exists the danger that the external realities – temple, nationhood, throne – become all that is attended to, while the deeper reality of YHWH's presence and his consecration that gives value to the externals is ignored. Thus is a new idolatry borne.

This is, of course, Israel's story. The trading of deep realities for externals. So Moses receives the law while Israel jeopardize their blessings and sins at the foot of the mountain. Later the land is received as gifted by YHWH, but in the experience of its material goodness the gift becomes the sole reality and YHWH is disregarded (Deut. 6:10–12). At another point, Israel face defeat before the Philistines. Rather than seek the mind of YHWH, their puzzled discernment suggests that it is the absence of YHWH's ark that has precipitated the defeat. The ark is sent for and it is accompanied by Hophni and Phineas, priests who have no regard for YHWH and have made holy elements means only of personal satisfaction (1 Sam. 2:12–17). Using the ark as a talisman, they venture again into battle but are once more defeated. The ark is captured, and Hophni and Phineas killed (1 Sam. 4:1–11). Notably, YHWH does not appear in the narrative; his presence is absence. Forgetting the deeper reality that the ark represents, disregarding the God of the covenant whom the ark signifies and trusting only in the external reality of the symbol, Israel is defeated.

It is this very fault that YHWH takes so much of 1 Kgs 9 to address. Solomon and the people are urged to walk in covenant life so that the presence and grace of YHWH may continue to indwell and empower their national and religious life. It is important to note that YHWH's urging is not brought to a pristine, sinless king or people. On the contrary, much of the chapter reveals that alongside the building that YHWH has consecrated lives a king who repeatedly walks outside the covenant life of God's chosen people. He blithely gives away land that was deeded to Israel by YHWH's promise (v. 11) – and does so to a non-Israelite. In this, Solomon is markedly contrasted to Naboth, who refuses to give YHWH's land away and for his adherence to covenant standards loses his life (1 Kgs 21). Solomon pursues relationship with Pharaoh of Egypt, turning again to the land of enslavement from which YHWH had rescued Israel so that they might worship YHWH freely. He marries Pharaoh's daughter, breaking the prohibition against foreign marriages. He increases in wealth and horses against the laws for the king. He requires store cities for his wealth and the corvée labour force is a reminder of Israel's failure to clear the land.

The juxtaposition is incredible. YHWH has consecrated a temple, gracing it with his presence, while urging Israel to walk circumspectly under the covenant so that YHWH does not abandon the temple. And he consecrates the temple even while Solomon walks outside the covenant. But this is precisely the grace of YHWH, who chooses to dwell in the midst of – even consecrating – his broken people and their institutions.

Repeatedly in 1 – 2 Kings, kings, people and priests trade the deep reality of YHWH's presence for externals. For instance, shortly after the temple narrative Solomon is shown to have turned from YHWH towards foreign alliances and foreign gods (1 Kgs 11). He is perhaps no better than Jeroboam (1 Kgs 12 – 13) who, though granted a great promise of a dynasty should he walk in obedience to YHWH, manufactures religious realities of his own making. Ahab makes externally advantageous foreign alliances, but through them allows Baal worship into Israel. This leads Israel to rely on Baal falsely for the externals of food, rain – and even life itself. In response to this, on Mount Carmel Elijah prepares a sacrifice to YHWH before a people who have been captured by Baalism. There, in the midst of the people's unbelief, YHWH sanctifies the offering and reveals his glory. Only then do the people acknowledge that 'YHWH, he is God!' (1 Kgs 18:30–39). This trading of the deep realities for the externals is also what Jeremiah addresses in his famous 'Temple Sermon' (Jer. 7:1–29). In his charge that Israel trusts in 'The temple of YHWH, the temple of YHWH, the temple of YHWH' (v. 4), he exposes their trust in the external reality: the building, and their disregard of the deeper, true reality – YHWH's consecration of that building, which signifies his presence and blessing in Israel's midst. When both the northern and southern kingdoms fall, it is their attention to misplaced allegiance given to external realities that is cited for YHWH's actions against his people (2 Kgs 17:7–23; 21:10–16; 24:3). By worshipping false gods and worshipping YHWH in ways contrary to the covenant they trade allegiance to YHWH for allegiance to externals. And, without YHWH's blessing upon those externals, Israel's trust is a trust in false things that cannot save. Yet, even in the utter extremity of YHWH's judgment, he continues in faithfulness to his people, remaining their God despite their allegiance to externals.

Such examples of trading the deep realities for the externals are found throughout the OT, and continue into the New. And, for any who inhabit God's church or read its history, the same story is repeated time and again. It is true, then, that YHWH dwells in the midst of a broken people and institutions.

Perhaps there can be no other way for YHWH to presence himself in the midst of his people, unless he is willing to do so in the midst of waywardness and sin. This is manifest most clearly in the incarnation. In it a tabernacle was prepared – a human body (Heb. 10:5). In him is the full presence of God. The God-Man lived to do what Solomon, the kings or the people never did. He came to do YHWH's will written in the law (Heb. 10:6) and, never faltering in that, remains YHWH's true presence.

This is the hope of 1 Kgs 9. The temple is built, dedicated and consecrated by YHWH's presence, all while the narrative has (both implicitly and explicitly) made Solomon's sins clear. But even there YHWH stakes his tent to be with his people. Though that tent is cast as the people abandon YHWH (vv. 7–9), YHWH's intentions are clear. As always, his desire is to be with his people, a holy God and a holy people. And in the end the temple points to its own deeper reality: God tabernacled in the temple of his Son and, through his indwelling life, in the church.

1 KINGS 9:26 – 10:29

Translation

9:26King Solomon built a fleet of ships in Ezion-geber, which is beside Elath^a on the shore of the Reed Sea in the land of Edom. 27And Hiram dispatched his servants, experienced seamen, with the fleet alongside Solomon's servants. 28They came to Ophir and acquired from there 420 talents of gold and brought it to King Solomon.

10:1The Queen of Sheba, hearing of Solomon's fame redounding to YHWH, came to test him with difficult questions. 2She came to Jerusalem with a very large retinue, with camels bearing spices, much gold and precious stones. She came to

Solomon and spoke to him about all that was in her mind, ³and Solomon explained all her questions to her; there was nothing concealed from the king that he could not explain to her.

⁴When the Queen of Sheba saw all Solomon's wisdom, and the house that he had built, ⁵and the food of his table, the seating arrangement of his officials, the attendance and attire of his waiters, his cupbearersᵃ, and his burnt offeringsᵇ he offered in YHWH's house, she was totally breathless. ⁶She said to the king, 'The report was true that I heard in my land concerning your words and wisdom. ⁷I did not believe the reportᵃ until I came and saw with my own eyes. Indeed, the half was not told me! You surpass in wisdom and prosperity the reportᵇ I have heard. ⁸How fortunate are your menᵃ! How fortunate are these servants of yours who stand continually before you, attending to your wisdom. ⁹May YHWH your God be blessed, who delighted in you to place you upon the throne of Israel. Because of YHWH's eternal love for Israel he has set you as king to do justice and righteousness.'

¹⁰She gave to the king 120 talents of gold, and a very great quantity of spices, and precious stones. Never again did such an abundance of spices come in as those the Queen of Sheba gave to King Solomon. ¹¹(Also the fleet of Hiram, which supplied gold from Ophir, brought very many almug trees and precious stones from Ophirᵃ. ¹²The king made of the almug trees supportsᵃ for YHWH's house and the king's house, and lyres and harps for the singers. Such almug wood has not come in nor been seen until this day.) ¹³King Solomon granted to the Queen of Sheba every wish that she requested, besides what he gave to her according to the bounty of the kingᵃ. Then she returned to her own land, she and her servants.

¹⁴The weight of gold that came to Solomon in one year was 666 talents of gold, ¹⁵apart from the taxesᵃ of the merchantsᵇ, and the profit of the traders, and all the Arabᶜ kings, and the governors of the land. ¹⁶King Solomon made two hundred large body shields of beaten gold with 600 *shekels*ᵃ of gold on each shield, ¹⁷and three hundred small shields of beaten gold with 3 minas of gold on each shield. The king put them in the house of the forest of Lebanon. ¹⁸The king also made a large ivory throne, and overlaid it with fine gold. ¹⁹There were six steps to the throne. The throne's top was roundedᵃ in the back, and there were armrests on either side of the seat, with two lions standing beside the armrests. ²⁰There were twelve lions standing at either end of the six steps. Nothing had been so made for any other kingdomᵃ.

²¹All the drinking vessels of King Solomon were gold and all the vessels of the house of the forest of Lebanon were of pure gold. None was of silver – in Solomon's time it was not considered valuable. ²²ᵃFor Solomon had ships of Tarshish on the sea along with Hiram's ships. Once every three years the ships of Tarshish came bringing gold and silver, ivory, apes and baboons.

²³King Solomon was greater than all the kings of the earth for riches and wisdom. ²⁴All the earth sought audience with Solomon to hear his wisdom that God had placed in his heart. ²⁵Year by year each brought his gift: articles of silver and articles of gold; clothing, perfume and spices; horses and mules.

²⁶Solomon gathered chariots and horsemen. He had one thousand four hundred chariots, and twelve thousand horsemen. He stationed them^a in the chariot cities, and with the king in Jerusalem.^b ²⁷The king made silver in Jerusalem as common as stones, and cedars as numerous as the sycamores that are in the lowland. ²⁸The source of Solomon's horses was Egypt^a and Kue. The king's traders took them from Kue at a certain price: ²⁹a chariot could be imported from Egypt at 600 shekels^a of silver, and a horse at 150 shekels^a. In this way, they exported them^b to all the kings of the Hittites and the kings of Aram.

Notes on the text

9:26.a. Reading with some MSS, LXX, Vg, *'ēlat* for MT *'ēlôt*.

10:5.a. *ûmašqâw* ('cupbearers'; cf. Gen. 40:1–23 [nine times]; 41:9; Neh. 1:11).

5.b. *wĕ'ōlātô* MT points as a f. sg. const. noun with 3 m. sg. suff., 'his burnt offering', but here read with Syr, Vg as a pl. 2 Chr. 9:4 reads, *'ălîyātô*, 'his upper chamber'. Another possibility is to read as inf. const. *wĕ'ălōtô*, 'his going up', as descriptive of the pomp and ceremony of procession to the temple (Gray 1970: 258). Despite the difficulty of a foreign queen's seeing the cultic ritual (which difficulty the chronicler mitigates), the ritual is the climactic expression of Solomon's wisdom (v. 4).

7.a. Glossing MT 'reports' to agree with the sg. form in v. 6.

7.b. Reading *'el-haššĕmû'â* as *'al- haššĕmû'â*.

8.a. Reading with MT 'your men' (*'ănāšêkā*) against many modern commentators (De Vries 2003: Gray 1970: 258; Montgomery 1951: 217), who read, 'your wives' (*nāšêkā*) with LXX, Syr. 'Men' and the following 'servants' are not a tautology, but consider different groups of males surrounding Solomon.

11.a. The second occurrence of 'from Ophir' is absent from LXX and 2 Chr. 9:10. It is retained to emphasize the transportation distance and thus the costliness of the trees.

12.a. The hapax legomenon *mis'ād* is difficult to translate with certainty. English versions (NASB, NET, NIV, NRSV) use 'support', probably following LXX, ὑποστηρίγματα, 'supports, underprops'. The parallel passage (2 Chr. 9:11) has a different word, *mĕsillôt*, 'roadways, tracks'.

13.a. Deleting the second occurrence of 'Solomon', as in Syr, Vg, A, Par.

15.a. Reading *mē'anšê* as *mē'ānšê*, 'taxes, fines', with LXX^BL, Tg. A similar meaning is found in 2 Kgs 23:33, and a more general meaning of 'pay a penalty' at Prov. 19:19.

15.b. *hattārîm* is qal act. part., here translated from root *twr*, 'spy out, reconnoitre, seek out'. By parallel to the following phrase, *ûmissaḥar hārôkĕlîm*, 'the profit of the traders', it is translated as 'the taxes of the merchants'. The root is not without dispute (see Gray 1970: 264, who proposes *tgr* [merchant], from Aramaic and Arabic cognates).

15.c. Correcting *hā'ereb*, 'the evening', to *hā'ărab* ('the Arabs'; as in 2 Chr. 9:14, Syr, Vg). LXX reads 'the other side', that is, 'over the River' (*hā'ēber*).

16.a. The missing unit of weight, by comparison to the small shields, should be shekels.

19.a. Commentators (De Vries 2003; Gray 1970; Montgomery 1951) repoint *'āgōl* , 'round', to *'ēgel*, 'calf', and suggest the back of the throne had an image of a calf that Dtr expunged by repointing the noun. Thrones did have rounded backs (Jones 1984a: 228) and footstools.

20.a. Reading the pl. 'kingdoms' as sg. with 2 Chr. 9:19, LXX.

22.a. MT 9:15, 17b–22 follow this verse in LXX.

26.a. Reading with the versions, and 2 Chr. 9:25, *wayyanniḥēm*, 'he stationed them', for MT *wayyanḥēm*, 'and he led them'.

26.b. LXX adds 5:1a following this verse.

28.a. 'Egypt' (*mṣrym*) is the MT reading (cf. 2 Chr. 9:25). Several scholars correct to Musri (*muṣrî*) here and v. 29 (see Crown 1974–5; Jones 1984a: 230–231; Montgomery 1951: 226–228). The emendation is based on inscriptional evidence in which Que and Musri together provide horses, and seeks to address several perceived difficulties of historical reconstruction.

29.a. 'shekels' is supplied for meaning.

29.b. 'them' is provided as an object for 'they exported'. The antecedent of 'they' is ambiguous but here understood to be the traders of the king.

Form and structure

Solomon's international wisdom is the scope of this chapter. The origin of the chapter's component parts and its redactional history are unclear, although several identifiable forms and traditions are present in the chapter. Reports concerning Hiram's fleet activity (9:26–28; 10:11–12; 10:22) and enumerations of Solomon's wealth and manufacturing (10:14–21, 26–29) may be traditions taken from the Book of the Acts of Solomon. Editorial comments such as 'Never again' and 'has not been seen' (vv. 10, 12, 20) may represent reflection upon these earlier sources. The summative statement (vv. 23–25) has the same hyperbolic praise of Solomon found in 4:20–21 (see discussion under 'Form and structure', 1 Kgs 4). The sustained narrative of the Queen of Sheba's visit, while a retelling of a historical event, does so with forms suggestive of legend: the queen is unnamed; no date is given for the visit; the result is eulogistic praise of Solomon.

The passage has four main sections. The first section (9:26–28) pursues continuing cooperation between Hiram and Solomon. Its focus on international rather than national matters removes it from 1 Kgs 9. The kings' joint venture broadcasts the report of Solomon's greatness, precipitating the southern queen's visit.

The second section recounts that visit (vv. 1–10, 13), with an inter-polated comment on Hiram's fleet activity (vv. 11–12). The narrative is carefully crafted, focusing on Solomon's wisdom:

A   Introduction (vv. 1–3): report; arrival of retinue and gifts; display of wisdom
   B   The queen's observation (vv. 4–5): Solomon's wisdom
   B'   The queen's words (vv. 6–9): Solomon's wisdom praised
[Interpolation: Hiram's fleet activity, vv. 11–12]
A'   Conclusion (vv. 10, 13): gifts exchanged; the queen returns home

The third section (vv. 14–22) elaborates Solomon's great wealth and courtly grandeur. Two statements concerning the source, type and value of Solomon's wealth (vv. 14–15, 22) form an inclusio around the dis-position of that wealth on shields (vv. 16–17), throne (v. 18–20) and utensils (vv. 21).

The final section (vv. 23–29) eulogizes Solomon. Mention of the lavish gift of horses leads to an additional notation of Solomon's wealth in horses, chariots and horsemen (vv. 26–29).

Several leitmotifs connect the chapter and highlight its themes. The primary leitmotif is that of people and wealth 'coming' (bw') to Solomon (vv. 28 [twice], 1, 2 [twice], 7, 10, 12, 14, 22, 25). In the first section the fleet comes (bw') to Ophir and brings (bw') wealth to Solomon. In the second section the queen comes (bw') to Jerusalem to test Solomon's wisdom and brings (bw') abundant wealth (v. 10). The third section details the items made by Solomon with the wealth brought (bw') to his court (vv. 14, 22). The fourth section, like the second, has people come for Solomon's wisdom, and bring (bw') wealth to him. The hyperbolic nature of the passage places Solomon and Jerusalem as the world's centre to which come all peoples and wealth.

A second leitmotif is that of 'wisdom' (ḥōkmâ; vv. 4, 6–8, 23–24). Several times this leitmotif occurs as the world 'hears' of Solomon's wisdom (verbal forms in vv. 1, 6–8, 24; nominal forms in vv. 1, 7). Thus when the report of Solomon goes into the world, the queen and all peoples come to hear Solomon's wisdom (vv. 1, 6–7, 24). The queen lauds those whose service enables a continuous hearing of that wisdom (v. 8). The source of this wisdom is identified as YHWH (v. 24), confirming that the king who requested a 'listening heart' (3:12) receives wisdom and is then sought out by others who listen.

The leitmotif of abundant wealth reveals Solomon's greatness. The word 'gold' appears fifteen times throughout the four sections (vv. 2, 10, 11, 14 [twice], 16 [twice], 17 [twice], 18, 21 [twice], 22, 25). The gold is excessive and of high quality. There is 'much gold' (v. 2); it is lavishly applied (vv. 16–17) and both 'fine' (mûpāz; v. 17) and 'pure' (sāgûr). Other articles also characterize Solomon's wealth (e.g. spices, precious stones, many servants, ivory and rare wood).

The leitmotif of wealth returns to the leitmotif of wisdom. The queen explicitly connects Solomon's wisdom and wealth by remarking his 'wisdom and prosperity' are greater than the reports of it (v. 7). The narrator also connects his 'riches and wisdom' (v. 23), and Hiram's fleet brings wealth (vv. 26–28, 11–12, 22) because of the covenant previously contracted through Solomon's wisdom (5:12).

A final motif is the use of superlative statements to characterize Solomon's wealth. It sets his monarchy at a unique pinnacle (vv. 10, 12, 20). Solomon's wisdom and generosity are superlative (vv. 3, 7, 13), leave the queen breathless (v. 5) and attract 'all the earth' (v. 24). Gifts are superlative (vv. 2, 10–11, 22), gold and precious cedar are overabundant (vv. 21, 27) and goods made for Solomon's house are of finest quality (vv. 16–21). His court is an emporium of wealth and wonders, affirming the fullness of YHWH's promise (3:4–15). Yet while the world marvels at Solomon, the benefit of his wealth accrues only to him, with no mention of benefit to Israel (as in 3:28; 4:20, 25). This change of focus cautions against reading the wisdom and wealth of Solomon as an untarnished golden age.

Comment

9:26–28

The fleet is at Ezion-geber near Elath (Deut. 2:8; 2 Chr. 8:17) at the head of the Gulf of Aqaba. An early site identification at Tell el-Kheleifeh (Glueck 1965; Glueck and Pratico 1993) has been set aside in favour of the natural harbour of Jezirat Far'on to the south-west; marine archaeology confirms the identification (Lubetski 1992; Zorn 1992). Important trading routes terminated at Ezion-geber, and its construction coincides with developing Phoenician shipping interests.

The Gulf of Aqaba was at times named the 'Reed Sea' (*yam sûp*), but the name is most famously associated with the water crossed by Israel as they fled Egypt (Exod. 13:18; 15:4; the term 'Red Sea' is the Greek rendition, although the origin of the designation is uncertain [Mihelic 1962b]). The name 'Reed Sea' given the Gulf negatively associates Solomon's activity with the exodus tradition. Against the strictures of Deut. 17:16–17 Solomon's quest for wealth returns him to Egypt and his alliance with foreigners compounds his actions as non-Deuteronomistic (Deut. 7:1–6).

Solomon's servants work alongside Hiram's seamen. They return from Ophir with vast quantities of gold (450 talents totals 28,660 to 59,525 lb (13 to 27 metric tons). Ophir is known in the biblical tradition for its gold (Job 28:16; 22:24; Ps. 45:8[9]; Isa. 13:12) and extra-biblical evidence affirms Ophir as a source (Maisler 1951). Variously located in Africa, Arabia or India, its most probable locations are Somalia or Arabia (van Beek, *IDB* 3:605–606; Christidès 1970; Wiseman 1980; Baker, *ABD* 5:26–27).

10:1–13

1–3. The queen arrives from Sheba, in south Arabia or Africa (Harvey 1962; Kitchen 1997b: 128) to honour Solomon's reputation and establish trading partnerships (Kitchen 1997b: 138). Annalistic records from the eighth-century Assyrian kings Tiglath-pileser III and Sargon attest to Arabian queens and their gifts of tribute (*ANET* 283, 286; cf. Abbott 1941). Contextually, the 'fame' or report she has heard of Solomon is his wealth and trading might (9:26–28), and his wisdom (4:31).

She poses 'difficult questions' (*ḥîdôt*; the word is elsewhere parallel to *māšāl* ['parable'; Ps. 78:2; Prov. 1:6; Ezek. 17:2]). In Judg. 14:12–19 *ḥîdôt* are part of an elaborate contest and, as there, Solomon answers. Solomon answers 'all that was in her mind' and 'all her questions' with 'nothing concealed' that he 'could not explain', showing that he wins the contest of wits hands-down.

4–10. The queen praises Solomon, connecting his wisdom to what she observes in his palace: his table and servants, and numerous officials (Gillmayr-Bucher 2007: 139). She also links his wisdom to the temple by citing his burnt offerings, whose extravagance matches that displayed in the palace (v. 5). The legendary nature of the story is apparent in that a foreigner – and a woman – is witness to temple offerings. The notice of Solomon's wisdom evidenced in the temple is the last explicit coupling of 'wisdom' and 'temple' in 1 Kgs 1 – 11. 'Wisdom' (*ḥkm*) appears only once more in 11:41, and there the temple is only implicitly referenced.

She is overwhelmed – but not speechless – by his wisdom. Her speech (as Hiram's; 5:7) showcases Dtr's monarchic theology. Her experience (vv. 6–7) and the ongoing experience of those who hear Solomon's wisdom (v. 8) constitute her praise. Her praise extends to YHWH. By his delight in Solomon and his love for Israel, and for the purposes of justice and righteousness in Israel, he has enthroned Solomon.

Her lavish praise is demonstrated in the great gifts she presents (v. 2). Gold heads the list and is the leitmotif for wealth and wisdom throughout this passage. Later the queen's experience will be repeated in the second encomium on Solomon's wisdom (vv. 23–25). There, too, people 'come', 'hear' Solomon's 'wisdom' and 'bring' gifts of wealth. The pattern reiterates the fulfilment of the promise to Solomon of honour and riches (3:13).

11–13. The interpolation regarding Hiram's fleet disrupts the narrative and might better be placed after v. 13, forming (with 9:26–28) a bracket around the queen's visit. Its current place in the narrative reveals that

Solomon was rich before the queen's arrival and his abundant generosity to her cannot deplete his wealth. Further increasing Solomon's wealth is the inclusion of rare and valuable almug trees. Grown in both Ophir and Lebanon (2 Chr. 2:7), the identity of the tree is uncertain (Zohary 1982: 125).

The queen leaves with Solomon's lavish gifts and with 'every wish (*ḥēpeṣ*) that she requested' fulfilled – referring back to the display of wisdom in the contest. Despite attempts to make her 'wish' an allusion to a sexual liaison (Ullendorff 1962–3), the term is used of a variety of interactions. Elsewhere in Solomon's narrative it is used in similar contexts of trade relations (5:22–24; 9:11; cf. the usage in 9:1 and 10:9, both non-sexual). The narrative stresses only her monarchic power and wealth that cannot compete with Solomon's, and it is her non-sexual interaction with Solomon that makes her (as 'the foreign woman') powerfully distinctive in Solomon's narrative (Gillmayr-Bucher 2007). She showcases Solomon's wisdom that issues in wealth, and she voices Solomon's right to, and purpose upon, the throne.

10:14–22

14–15. Solomon's powerful administration is demonstrated by reference to his great wealth. His annual gold income is about 55,116 pounds (25 metric tons). This great wealth need not be dismissed out of hand as an exaggeration, for it is comparable to ancient accounts of wealth in Mesopotamia, Assyria and Egypt. Against this background, Solomon's great wealth is certainly feasible (Millard 1989). Additionally, taxation accrues from several common ancient sources (Montgomery 1951: 220). Several groups, including merchants, Arabian kings and the 'governors of the land' (*paḥôt*; mentioned alongside foreign kings, administrators of foreign territories who trade through Israel may be in view), pay for access to trade routes through Israel. As well, profits from royal traders (*rôkĕlîm*; perhaps the *sôḥărê hammelek* [king's traders] of v. 28) fill the king's coffers (Noth 1968: 229; DeVries 2003: 139).

16–22. Various artefacts demonstrate Solomon's wealth. Costly 'fine' (v. 18), 'pure' (v. 21) gold is showcased in shield work. Larger rectangular body shields (11–22 lb [5–10 kg]) and small, round bucklers (3–6 lb [1.5–3 kg]) are manufactured (Sellers 1962), and similar extant artefacts suggest the probability of the account (Millard 1994, 1997). Although both were used in battle (large shields: 1 Sam. 17:7; 1 Chr. 12:9, 24, 35; Jer. 46:3; Ezek. 38:4; small shields: Judg. 5:8; 2 Sam. 1:21; 2 Kgs 19:32; Jer. 46:9), Solomon's gold shields may be for ceremonial use (1 Kgs 14:25–28).

The material of Solomon's throne is notable (v. 20). Its large wood construction is overlaid with fine gold and ivory inlay. Six steps set the throne on an imposing seventh level, perhaps signifying the Babylonian mythological concept of the Divine Cosmos of which the king stood as guarantor (Gray 1970: 266). The throne's rounded back (see 'Notes on the text') and lion-embellished armrests correspond to depictions of ANE thrones (*ANEP* 332, 458). The lions on the steps represent sphinxes, or the 'lion of the tribe of Judah', that honour Solomon's tribe.

The final items, the golden drinking vessels, are pointedly *not* silver, as it is considered too common to be used for items intended to display the king's wealth (Millard 1997: 36–37). The gold and wealth are brought by the Tarshish fleet of heavy vessels designed for extended ocean voyages. The imports suggest destinations in Africa or Arabia (DeVries 2003: 140), or as far as the western Mediterranean (Jon. 1:3; 4:2; Ps. 72:10; Ezek. 38:13). The Phoenician colony of Tartessus in south-west Spain (from which 'Tarshish' may derive) is a possibility (Baker, *ABD* 6:331–333). The destination may intentionally be ambiguous, evoking a mythical, far-off 'ends of the earth' intended to show the reach of Solomon's influence.

10:23–29

23–25. 'All the earth' attends Solomon. The leitmotifs of 'come', 'wisdom', 'hear' and 'gold' found in the queen's visit also here summarize Solomon's superlative wisdom (see 'Form and structure'). Now not just the queen (v. 9) but all the earth credits Solomon's wisdom to YHWH (v. 24). They too bring gifts, yearly expanding Solomon's treasury in quantity and kind. His wealth, summarized in v. 25, has expanded throughout the chapter: to the gold of 9:28 is added by tribute spices and precious stones (vv. 2, 10), almug trees (v. 11), silver, ivory, apes and baboons (v. 22), and finally clothing, perfume, horses and mules (v. 25). Such tribute items are attested in the ancient world. The Black Obelisk of Shalmaneser III (ninth century BC), in which King Jehu (2 Kgs 9 – 10) bows in tribute to his Assyrian overlord, depicts tribute payments offered by Shalmaneser's vassals that include exotic animals (such as camels, elephants and apes), precious metals, ivory and garments.

26–29. The horses (v. 25) direct the superlative eulogy in one final direction: that of military strength. The number of chariots differs from the chronicler's parallel account (2 Chr. 9:25) and is difficult to comport with 1 Kgs 4:26. Regardless, the point is clearly to demonstrate Solomon's wealth in chariots and horses, great enough to require cities to house the military (see 9:19). The superlative regarding silver and cedar is provided as further proof of wealth.

Eulogistic praise diverges to an apparently historical footnote on Israelite horse and chariot trading with Egypt and Que, and with specific foreign kings (Ikeda 1982; Schley 1987). His far-reaching trade (both receiving and selling horses) shows his economic dominance: he truly is a king 'greater than all the kings of the earth for riches and wisdom' (v. 23). Additionally, the purchase price is high, revealing Solomon's great wealth (Ikeda 1982: 225, 229–230).

Several scholars emend Egypt (*miṣrāyim*) in vv. 26, 29 to read Musri (*muṣrî*), and suppose the region of Cappadocia north of the Taurus Mountains, and proximate to Que (see 'Notes on the text'). On a historical level, however, both Egypt and Que did have such commodities for trade (Tadmor 1961; Ikeda 1982; Schley 1987) and the MT should stand. The mention of Egypt reveals more than the geographic extent of Solomon's trade. The verses call Solomon's eulogized wisdom into question, for, according to deuteronomic law, the king is not to amass wealth, nor travel to Egypt to multiply horses (Deut. 17:16; Barclay Burns 1991: 38; Hays 2003: 173; Sweeney 2007: 152).

Explanation

The Queen of Sheba stands with a company of peoples in the Old and New Testaments who, as foreigners, give praise to YHWH. Hiram has done so (5:7[21]). Rahab gives praise (Josh. 2:9–11) that is both encouragement to Israel waiting east of the Jordan, and explanation for Israel's victories in the land. Nebuchadnezzar praises YHWH's sovereignty and dominion over all nations (Dan. 4:34–35). The psalter proclaims YHWH's praise in the Gentile nations (Pss 67, 87) and Isaiah's eschatological vision anticipates praise offered by many nations (Isa. 2:2–3; cf. Mic. 4:1–2). Matthew's report of the magi's visit, their testimony of God's king and their worship before the child stand in this same tradition (Matt. 2:1–12). The culmination of such praise occurs in Rev. 4. There YHWH is praised for redeeming those from 'every tribe and language and people and nation' (v. 9) and this multitude joins in offering praise to YHWH (v. 13). If that final scene notes the fulfilment of the covenant with Abraham that promises blessing for all nations, then these foreigners throughout the Old and New Testaments are its foreshadowing.

As women, the queen and Rahab are uniquely placed among those OT foreigners who praise YHWH. In the context of the canon, being identified as a foreign or strange woman holds significant negative overtones. This is especially true in the light of Proverbs, where the foreign woman leads young men astray and is the antithesis of wisdom, who in Proverbs is personified as a woman. By the criteria of foreignness and gender, both Rahab and Sheba are suspect. Each, however, breaks the negative stereotype by her words and actions, which show them to be women of wisdom, even though foreigners (Gillmayr-Bucher 2007).

Though a woman, Sheba is distinct from Rahab, for she is also a queen. This is a role not exercised in Israel but found in other nations. As a woman she comes with difficult questions and reveals herself (against the negative stereotype) to be wise. But as a queen she is portrayed as a typical ANE monarch in position, wealth and wisdom. Not a liminal woman, a servant maid or a wife, she stands on equal footing to Solomon. Portrayed as Solomon's equal, her words have rhetorical power that the narrator uses to highlight Solomon's wealth and wisdom. The rhetorical power of her words is heightened when juxtaposed to 1 Kgs 11. There foreign wives draw Solomon away from YHWH; Sheba neither marries Solomon nor seduces his heart. Instead, she attests to YHWH first in that she visits Solomon as one whose reputation redounds to YHWH's praise (v. 1), and secondly in that she credits YHWH with Solomon's wisdom (v. 9).

The queen's words provide a second avenue to theological reflection. She sees Solomon's wealth and praises his wisdom. Both are greater than she has been told. She sees them as evidence of YHWH's favour upon his rule, confirming the fulfilment of his promise (3:12–13). On this count she upholds the positive portrayal of Solomon.

Her words also contribute to the ambiguous portrait of Solomon explored in this commentary. She remarks that YHWH has set Solomon upon his throne 'to do justice and righteousness'. Yet, as noted in the 'Comment' section for this chapter, the narrative emphasis lies upon Solomon's wealth: acquired through trade, taxation, tribute and gifts. His wealth returns him to Egypt and increases his stables. It is noted that the benefit accrues to his comfort and reputation, and extends only to his court (v. 8) but not (as was the case in past chapters) to his people. Where, in this, is his 'justice and righteousness'? Indeed, in just two short chapters, his injustice will be cited as reason for secession (12:4). Thus the queen's words serve as narrative critique, highlighting the absence of the kingly attributes of righteousness and justice in Solomon's reign. Solomon is wise and rich, but does not exercise those gifts in kingly fashion for his people.

That the exercise of justice and righteousness is the ideal for Israel's monarch is clear from Ps. 72. It is the final psalm of the second book of the psalter, and provides several intertextual touch points with this narrative. It speaks of the king's justice (*mišpāṭ*) and righteousness (*ṣĕdāqâ*) in judging the people (vv. 2, 7; cf. vv. 12–14), prosperity in the land because of the king's reign (vv. 3, 6–7, 10), and the attendance of monarchs – including those of Sheba – with tribute (vv. 9–11, 15). The resonance of the psalm and narrative is noted in the ascription. Tradition reads the psalm as being 'Of Solomon'.

The psalm is a prayer, asking that God endow the king with these attributes. These gifts are rightly YHWH's to bestow (as apparent from 1 Kgs 3:12–13) because these qualities are inherent in YHWH himself. He is the just and righteous one. He has created the world on these foundations, and his desire revealed throughout the canon of Scripture is for the reign of justice and righteousness (Nardoni 2004).

Ps. 72 is a reminder that as YHWH's appointed ruler the wise king exercises justice and righteousness. In this the earthly king reflects the true king of Israel: YHWH (1 Sam. 8:7). As Israel's king, YHWH delivered them out of Egypt, covenanted with them as their suzerain at Sinai, granted them land and even allowed their request for an earthly king, all under his just and righteous rule.

The psalmist intercedes for these qualities in the king's rule, and in this he, as much as Dtr's portrayal of Solomon, voices both critique and hope. Both acknowledge that human kingship has imperfect justice and righteousness; both uphold the ideal. Perhaps in both instances Dtr and the psalmist recognize in the frailty of the human institution what Israel rejected but truly desires: the kingship of God ruling in righteousness and justice over all nations. They recognize that in the fulfilment of the ideal

All nations will be blessed through him,
and they will call him blessed.
(Ps. 72:17b)

And with the nations they join in saying:

Praise be to YHWH God, the God of Israel,
Who alone does marvellous deeds.
Praise be to his glorious name for ever;
May the whole earth be filled with his glory.
(Ps. 72:18–19)

With Dtr and the psalmist, God's people today recognize the desperate need for this justice and righteousness in the world. With them we wait in hope for the full reality of YHWH's rule and take up the conclusion of Ps. 72, saying, 'Amen and Amen'. Let it be so.

1 KINGS 11:1–43

Translation

[1]King Solomon loved many foreign women along with Pharaoh's daughter – Moabites, Ammonites, Edomites, Sidonians, Hittites – [2]from the nations that YHWH had said to the sons of Israel, 'You shall not intermarry with them and they shall not intermarry with you[a]. Surely[b] they will turn your heart after their gods.' To them Solomon clung in love. [3]He had seven hundred wives, royal princesses, and three hundred concubines, and his wives turned his heart.

[4]When Solomon became old, his wives turned his heart after other gods, and his heart was not wholly devoted to YHWH his God as the heart of his father David had been. [5]Solomon went after Ashtoreth, the goddess of the Sidonians, and after Milcom, the abomination of the Ammonites. [6]Solomon did evil in the eyes of YHWH, and was not true to YHWH as David his father had been. [7]Then

Solomon built a high place for Chemosh, the abomination of Moab on the mountain facing Jerusalem, and for Molech the filth of the Ammonites. [8]Thus he did for all his foreign wives who burned incense and sacrificed to their gods.

[9]YHWH was angry with Solomon because his heart had turned from YHWH the God of Israel who had appeared[a] to him twice [10]and had commanded him concerning this thing not to go after other gods (but he did not keep that which YHWH had commanded[a]). [11]So YHWH said to Solomon, 'Because this is how it is with you, and you have not kept my covenant and my statutes[a] that I commanded you, surely I will tear the kingdom from you and give it to your servant. [12]However, I will not do it in your days on account of David your father; from the hand of your son I will tear it[a]. [13]Only I will not tear[a] away all the kingdom; I will give one tribe to your son on account of my servant David and on account of Jerusalem, which I have chosen.'

[14]Then YHWH raised up an adversary to Solomon: Hadad the Edomite. He was of the royal line in Edom. [15]Earlier, when David was in Edom, while Joab the commander of the army was going up to bury the slain, he struck every male in Edom. [16]For six months Joab and all Israel stayed there until he had destroyed every male in Edom. [17]But Hadad fled, he and certain Edomites from his father's servants with him, to go to Egypt (now Hadad was a young boy *at the time*). [18]They set out from Midian and came to Paran. They took men with them from Paran and came to Egypt to Pharaoh king of Egypt. He provided him a house, ordered[a] food for him and gave land[b] to him. [19]Hadad found great favour in Pharaoh's sight. He gave him his own wife's sister as a wife – the sister of Queen[a] Tahpenes. [20]Tahpenes' sister bore to him Genubath his son and Tahpenes weaned him in Pharaoh's house. So Genubath lived in Pharaoh's house among Pharaoh's sons. [21]When Hadad heard in Egypt that David slept with his fathers and that Joab the commander of the army was dead, Hadad said to Pharaoh, 'Release me so that I may go to my land.' [22]Pharaoh answered him, 'But what have you lacked with me that you are seeking to go to your land?' He answered, 'Nothing, but do release me.'

[23]Then God raised up against him *another*[a] adversary, Rezon son of Eliada who had fled from his lord Hadadezer king of Zobah. [24]He gathered men to himself and became commander of a marauding band after David slew *Zobah's men*. They went to Damascus and dwelt there and he became king[a] in Damascus. [25]He was an adversary to Israel all Solomon's life, adding to the harm that Hadad did[a]. He abhorred Israel and ruled over Aram.

[26]Now Jeroboam son of Nebat, an Ephraimite[a] from Zeredah (the name of his mother was Zeruah, a widow), was Solomon's servant, but he raised his hand against the king. [27]This is the matter over which he raised his hand against the king. Solomon built the Millo; he closed the breach of the city of David his father. [28]Jeroboam was a competent man and Solomon noticed the young man, that he got work done. So he appointed him over all the carriers from the house of Joseph.

[29]It happened at that time that Jeroboam went out from Jerusalem and Ahijah the Shilonite, the prophet, found him on the road. He was clothed in a new mantle

and the two of them were alone in the open country. ³⁰Then Ahijah grasped the new mantle that was on him and tore it in twelve pieces. ³¹He said to Jeroboam, 'Take for yourself ten pieces, for thus says YHWH the God of Israel, "Behold! I am about to tearᵃ the kingdom from the hand of Solomon and give you ten tribes ³²(but one tribeᵃ will remain his on account of my servant David and on account of Jerusalem, the city which I have chosen from all the tribes of Israel) ³³because they have forsakenᵃ me and bowed downᵃ to Ashtoreth the god of the Sidoniansᵇ, Chemosh the god of Moab and Milcom the god of the sons of Ammon. They have not walkedᵃ in my ways to do what is right in my eyes, and my statutes and judgments, as did David his father.

³⁴"'I will not take all the kingdom from his hand, but I will make him a prince all the days of his life on account of David my servant whom I chose, who kept my commandments and my statutes. ³⁵I will take the kingship from the hand of his son and I will give it to you – ten tribes. ³⁶But to his son I will give one tribeᵃ so that there will be a lamp for my servant David always before me in Jerusalem the city that I have chosen for myself to establish my name there. ³⁷But you I will take and you will reign over all your soul desires and you will be king over Israel. ³⁸It will come about that if you listen to everything that I command you, and you walk in my ways, and you do what is right in my eyes, keeping my statutes and commandments as David my servant did, then I will be with you and I will build for you a sure house just as I built for David, and I will give Israel to you. ³⁹So I will humble David's descendants on account of this, only not for ever.'"

⁴⁰Then Solomon sought to kill Jeroboam. Jeroboam rose and fled to Egypt, to Shishak king of Egypt. He remained in Egypt until the death of Solomon.

⁴¹Now the rest of the acts of Solomon, and all that he did, and his wisdom – are they not written in the Book of the Acts of Solomon? ⁴²The days that Solomon reigned in Jerusalem over all Israel were forty years. ⁴³Then Solomon slept with his father and he was buried in the city of his father David, and Rehoboam his son became king after him.

Notes on the text

2.a. *lō'-tābô'û bāhem wĕhēm lō'-yābô'û*, 'you shall not intermarry with them and they shall not intermarry with you', draws upon Deut. 7:3 and prohibits intermarriage. Deut. 7:3 uses the more specific root for marriage, *ḥtn* (cf. 1 Kgs 3:1).

2.b. *'ākēn* (surely) as a strong asseverative. The prohibitive μή of LXX ('lest'; *pen*) does not capture the certainty of the wives' influence.

9.a. Reading the pf. *hannir'â* as a part., and the art. as a relative pr. (JM §145e).

10.a. LXX, Syr, Vg supply the object anticipated by the context ('which YHWH had commanded *him*').

11.a. MT *bĕrîtî wĕḥuqqōtâ*, 'my covenant and my statutes', deviates from the usual 'my commandments and my statutes'.

12.a. In vv. 12–13 LXX reads 'take' for MT 'tear'. The violence of MT better marks the serious nature of Solomon's sin.

13.a. See n. 12.a above.

18.a. MT *wĕleḥem 'āmar lô*, 'and food he said for him', makes little sense. Here, reading *'āmar* with Arab., 'ordered', 'assigned'. See Montgomery 1951: 246; *HALOT* 658.

18.b. *'ereṣ* as a property or estate.

19.a. The title 'Queen' translates *haggĕbîrâ*, the f. form of *gĕbîr* ('lord'; Gen. 27:29, 37). Often applied to the queen mother (1 Kgs 15:13; 2 Chr. 15:16; 2 Kgs 10:13; Jer. 13:18; 29:2), here the context cites the wife of the ruling king.

23.a. 'another' is supplied by context.

24.a. 'he became king' reads with LXX[L], correcting MT's pl. 'they became king'.

25.a. Following LXX, supplying the verb *'āśâ* , 'the harm that Hadad *did*'.

26.a. Reading *'eprātî* as gentilic 'Ephraimite', as in Judg. 12:5; 1 Sam. 1:1.

31.a. The part. *qōrēa'*, 'I will tear', here expresses a near future; the nuance of nearness is emphasized by the particle (*hinnî*, 'behold'). The following pf. plus waw cons. continues the near-future sense (JM §119n).

32.a. Here and in v. 36 LXX reads 'two tribes' to bring the total number of tribes to twelve (see 'Comment').

33.a. MT 'they have forsaken', 'they have bowed' and 'they have not walked' (3 m. sg. in the versions) emphasize the corporate identification of the people with the king.

33.b. *ṣidōnîn* as a corruption of *ṣidōnîm*, 'Sidonians'.

36.a. See n. 32.a above.

Form and structure

1 Kgs 11 prepares for the transition from united to divided monarchy. It judges Solomon for his sins, which are now explicitly named and credited to his 'heart turned from YHWH' (v. 9). Jeroboam is introduced (11:26–40) as the last and paramount of three adversaries brought as judgment against Solomon.

The chapter is divided into four sections. The first (vv. 1–13) names Solomon's sins and YHWH's judgment; the second (vv. 14–25) concerns two of three adversaries raised up against Solomon. The third adversary, Jeroboam, is the focus of the next section (vv. 26–40). Finally, notice is given of Solomon's death (vv. 41–43).

The initial verses (11:1–8) reveal Solomon's heart and the reasons for YHWH's judgment. With 1 Kgs 3:1–3 they bracket Solomon's narrative and negatively characterize the king. In 1 Kgs 3 Solomon marries Pharaoh's daughter; the closing bracket now includes other foreign women. In 3:3 Solomon 'loves' YHWH; the only other place where Solomon 'loves' is in 11:1 – but now the 'love' is for these foreign women. In 3:1 the king's intention to build the temple is mentioned (although the mention is not wholly positive; see 'Comment'); in 11:7–8 the temple project is denigrated as Solomon builds temples to foreign gods. Finally, 3:3 records the king's positive attitude towards torah obedience, obedience explicitly compromised in 11:10.

The conflict between loving foreign women, torah obedience and the state of Solomon's heart is made apparent in two parallel sections as follows:

A   Solomon loves foreign women (v. 1)
    B   Foreign women described as from nations forbidden to Israel (v. 1)
        C   The law against such alliances is cited (v. 2)
A'   Solomon clings in love to foreign women (v. 2b)
    B'   Foreign women are described according to number and rank (v. 3a)
        C'   The law's warning is actualized: Solomon's wives turn his heart (v. 3b)

Loving foreign women, Solomon's heart is turned and the outcome is also presented in parallel fashion:

A   General condition: Solomon's wives turn his heart (v. 4a)
    B   Solomon's heart is not like David's heart (v. 4b)
        C   Specific proof evidenced in pursuit of other gods (v. 5)
A'   General condition: Solomon did evil in YHWH's eyes (v. 6a)
    B'   Solomon's heart is not true as was David's (v. 6b)
        C'   Specific proof evidenced in building high places for his wives' gods (vv. 7–8)

The parallel structures of vv. 1–8 inextricably link Solomon's downfall to his wives, his attitudes/heart and his ensuing actions (particularly temple building), thus returning the narrative to its opening concerns.

After YHWH's judgment, three related episodes show opponents raised up against Solomon: Hadad (vv. 14–22), Rezon (vv. 23–25) and Jeroboam (vv. 26–40). Each narrative, the core of which represents a historical remembrance, is now artfully presented as irrefutable proof of YHWH's word against Solomon that he would tear the kingdom from him (v. 11). YHWH's judgment is partially realized in Hadad and Rezon, and fully realized in Jeroboam. Jeroboam's import to the ongoing history is reflected in the length of his account compared to that of Hadad and Rezon.

The transitional chapter ends with the first of many notices of a king's death. Much more could be said about Solomon's acts and wisdom from the Acts of Solomon, highlighting the selective representation of his forty-year reign. His death transitions the kingship to Rehoboam his son and anticipates the fulfilment of YHWH's judgment against Solomon (v. 35).

Comment

11:1–13

1–3. Pharaoh's daughter, a cipher of Solomon's blemished rule (3:1–3; 7:8; 9:24), now appears in the company of 'many foreign women', 'princesses' (v. 3) from nations surrounding Israel. Such alliances commonly established international ties, and Solomon's international reach is reflected in his harem.

The gravity of Solomon's action is revealed in its transgression of deuteronomic law (Brettler 1991: 91–92; Knoppers 1997). First, Solomon marries 'many foreign women' despite the warning that they will 'turn (*nṭh*) your heart', a close parallel to the 'many women' who will turn (*sûr*) the king's heart (Deut. 17:17). Secondly, the nationality of these women bears little resemblance to the prohibition against intermarriage in Deut. 7:1–3 (the lists share only the Hittite designation), but Joshua's prohibition includes 'these nations that remain' (Josh. 23:7), and thus includes Solomon's wives. Thirdly, in 1 Kgs 3:1, Solomon marries (*ḥtn*) a foreign woman. In 11:2 the intermarriage is literally expressed as having sexual relations ('go in to'; *bô' bĕ*; cf. a similar expression in Deut. 22:13; Josh. 23:12; Judg. 16:1; cf. Gen. 6:14; 16:2, 4; Ezek. 23:44). Prohibitions against intermarriage (*ḥtn*) are found in Deut. 7:3 and repeated in Josh. 23:12, where the prohibition is further explicated as 'you shall not go in' (*bô' bĕ*). Finally, Solomon is described as clinging in love to his foreign wives (v. 3; *dābaq . . . lĕ'aḥăbâ*) even though he loved ('*hb*) YHWH initially (3:3). Joshua warns Israel to cling to YHWH (Josh. 23:8; cf. Deut. 10:20; 11:22; 13:5; 30:20) rather than the nations (Josh. 23:12), and to love YHWH (Josh. 23:11). Israel's wrongly placed love will ultimately cause Israel to perish from the land (Josh. 23:13). Therefore, by Deuteronomistic standards of torah obedience, Solomon's actions place him and his nation in grave danger.

4–8. The hearts of Solomon and David are contrasted (v. 4; cf. 1 Kgs 1:29, 48; 2:1–4). Solomon 'went after' foreign gods (v. 5) and 'turned his heart' towards them (vv. 2–4 [three times]), actions that meant service and worship of these other gods (Deut. 6:14; 8:19; 11:28; 13:3; 28:14; Judg. 2:12, 17, 19). Solomon's heart is not wholly devoted as was his father David's. In this he is like the Israelites who, after a faithful generation, went astray (Josh. 24:31). Ironically, the king whose name (Solomon;

šĕlōmōh) evoked 'peace' (šlm) had a heart not at peace (i.e. 'wholly committed'; šlm) to YHWH.

'Ashtoreth' derogatorily combines the name 'Astarte' with the vowels of the Hebrew noun 'shame' (bōšet;Wyatt, DDD 112–113) and provides a comment on the shamefulness of Solomon's actions. Astarte, Canaanite goddess of fertility and warfare, is known from the Ras Shamra texts in association with the god Baal. Milcom (v. 5) and Molech (v. 7) are separate Ammonite gods, each with separate cult sites (cf. 2 Kgs 23:10; Jer. 32:35; Heider, DDD 584; Puech, DDD 575–576). They are here denigrated as an 'abomination'. Solomon may not have directly participated in worship (v. 8), but his accommodation is implicit participation and reveals his heart turned from YHWH.

9–13. Despite YHWH's appearing twice to Solomon (3:5; 9:2), the king perversely disobeys. The disobedience is doubly noted: YHWH commands (ṣwh) but Solomon rejects what YHWH commands (ṣwh; v. 10). Solomon's heart is turned (v. 9) and is not right before YHWH (9:4), resulting in high places and worship opposed to the law (9:6). YHWH's anger is strong (v. 9; 'np; see Deut. 1:37; 4:21; 9:8; cf. v. 20; 2 Kgs 17:18) and will result in captivity, as Solomon himself prayed (8:46; cf. 2 Kgs 17:18). For now YHWH issues a judgment oracle removing the kingdom from Solomon (v. 11). The oracle is typical, moving from accusation ('because . . .') to judgment ('surely I will . . .'; Westermann 1967: 142–168).

The emphatic 'surely I will tear' makes explicit the judgment implicit in 2:4; 8:25; and 9:4–5. Like the judgment given Saul (1 Sam. 15:28), the kingdom will be torn (qr') from Solomon and given (ntn) to Solomon's servant. The judgment is twice mitigated (by the restrictive 'however' ['ak] in v. 12, and by 'only' [raq] in v. 13). First, it will be enacted upon Solomon's son for the sake of Solomon's father, David. The father–son language is that of the Davidic covenant (2 Sam. 7:14) upon which the mitigation is predicated. Secondly, the kingdom will not be wholly removed from Solomon on account of David – now described not as Solomon's father but as YHWH's servant. Solomon failed to continue as servant to YHWH (8:59), and therefore his kingdom will pass to his own servant (v. 11). The mitigation also applies in recognition of Jerusalem, the city chosen by YHWH for his own dwelling (Deut. 12:5, 11; 16:6) and seat of the Davidic king.

11:14–25

14–22. YHWH uses three individuals as instruments of judgment. The instrumentality of Hadad and Rezon is signalled in that they are 'raised up' (qwm) by YHWH (v. 14) or God (v. 23) as adversaries (śāṭān) to Solomon. A śāṭān can be a celestial figure (Num. 22:22, 32; 1 Chr. 21:1; Job 1:6, 9, 12) or, as here, human military and political opponents (1 Sam. 29:4; 1 Kgs 5:18).

Hadad bears a name elsewhere used of the royal line of Edom (Gen. 36:35; 1 Chr. 1:46). The kingdom south-east of the Dead Sea continues as Israel's historic enemy (2 Sam. 8:11–14) despite the presence of an Edomite princess in Solomon's harem. Hadad had escaped to Egypt; his return begins a lengthy adversarial relationship that belies the hyperbolic peace of 1 Kgs 4:21–25.

23–25. Like Hadad's story, Rezon's abbreviated tale follows the same structure of introduction, flight and time in a foreign land. 2 Sam. 8:3–11 provides the background to Rezon's story (cf. 1 Sam. 30:8; 2 Sam. 3:22; 6:23; 13:20; 24:2). During ongoing conflict with David and internecine fighting with Hadadezer, Rezon is enthroned in Damascus. He mounts adversarial activity against Solomon, while Hadad harries Solomon from the south-east. The final comment regarding Rezon's abhorrence of Israel could be said of Hadad as well. Together the two adversaries plague Solomon throughout his reign, but the conflict is not mentioned until judgment is passed upon Solomon to illustrate narratively the immediate effect of YHWH's word.

11:26–40

26–28. Jeroboam is not introduced as an adversary (*śāṭān*), nor is he raised up (*qwm*) by YHWH, but he is nonetheless YHWH's instrument of judgment. His patronym is given only here, and Nebat is otherwise unknown. Nebat is dead and Jeroboam is thus identified by his widowed mother (DeVries 2003: 150). The naming of Jeroboam's mother also serves to foreshadow his coming kingship, for mothers of monarchs (at least in the south) are commonly named (e.g. 1 Kgs 14:21; 15:2; 22:42; 2 Kgs 8:26 *et passim*). That he is identified as Solomon's 'servant' brings to mind YHWH's judgment that Solomon's servant would be king (v. 11).

Elevated during work on the Millo (9:10–15) to official status within the construction bureaucracy (9:23), he is placed over the carriers (cf. 5:15) that are provided from 'the house of Joseph', that is, his own tribe of Ephraim (Josh. 17:17). The specifics of Jeroboam's rebellion are obscure but may well involve dissatisfaction among the northern tribes for Solomon's treatment of his workforce; certainly, 1 Kgs 12:4 makes this probable. But the reasons for the rebellion are left unexplored in favour of the prophetic word. Solomon's response to Jeroboam follows immediately after the oracle (v. 40), suggesting that, in the narrative world, historical exigencies such as rebellions and workforces are irrelevant. Rather, Solomon's action against Jeroboam seeks to forestall or prevent the prophetic word of YHWH.

29–40. 'At that time', that is, during Jeroboam's career, he is sought out by Ahijah. Ahijah is from Shiloh (1 Kgs 14:1–4), previous home of the ark and tent (Josh. 18:1; 1 Sam. 1 – 4). His ministry (1 Kgs 11 – 14) initiates

a paradigm of prophetic involvement in the appointment and dethronement of northern monarchs. The oracle begins with the typical 'Thus says
YHWH', with the added specification 'the God of Israel' signifying that
while YHWH's judgment creates a divided kingdom, his covenant commitment to all Israel remains.

A prophetic sign-act accompanies the oracle. Whether its power is
merely persuasive, or is an efficacious part of the divine oracle (Matheney
1968; Stacey 1990: 79–82, 262–282; Block 2001; Friebel 2001), certainly
word and sign-act together express the judgment given in vv. 11–13. Ahijah
tears Jeroboam's new mantle, representing the twelve tribes, into pieces,
and ten of those tribes mark the extent of Jeroboam's rule. By a wordplay,
tearing the mantle unleashes the destruction of Solomon's kingdom, for
the consonants of both 'mantle' (*šlmh*) and 'Solomon' (*šlmh*) are identical
(Walsh 1996: 143).

Ten tribes for Jeroboam and one tribe (Judah) for Solomon leaves one
tribe uncounted (vv. 31–32, 35–36). Attempts to improve YHWH's maths
offer Levi as the 'missing' tribe due to its dispersion throughout the land
(Jones 1984a: 248; Sweeney 2007: 160). The location of Simeon in the
midst of Judah (Josh. 19:1–9) may account for that tribe's inclusion into
Judah, or (given the inclusion of Benjamin with Judah in 1 Kgs 12:21)
Benjamin may be considered assimilated into Judah (DeVries 2003: 151;
Nelson 1987: 72). Mathematics may simply not be the point here;
rather, it is the fact of YHWH's wresting the bulk of the kingdom from
David's son.

A similar sign-act is found in 1 Sam. 15:27–28, where Saul seizes (*ḥzq*)
and tears (*qr'*) Samuel's robe (*mě'îl*). The pattern repeats here, although
the garment is now owned by the king to be and is torn (*qr'*) by the
prophet. The ownership of the mantle is ambiguous in the MT and many
English translations seek clarification by stating Ahijah had the new
mantle (NASB, NET, NIV, NRSV, RSV). The mantle, however, belongs to
Jeroboam. He is focalized as the primary participant in vv. 29–30, and
pronominal suffixes ('the mantle that was on *him*') are best understood
in reference to that primary participant. Further, the qal action 'grasp'
(*tpś*) followed by the *bě* prep. (as here) occurs ten times in the MT. Six of
those occurrences attach the *bě* prep. to the direct object grasped (as here)
and involve vigorous action, such as would be expected if one were seizing
a mantle not one's own (Chun 2006: 271–272).

The oracle utilizes three key linguistic elements. Jeroboam is invited to
respond to the enacted prophecy by 'taking' (*lqḥ*) ten pieces of the torn
robe (v. 31), symbolizing that not all the kingdom will be 'taken' from
Solomon (v. 34). Nevertheless, YHWH confirms he will 'take' the kingship
from Solomon's son (v. 35) and give it to Jeroboam, whom YHWH will
'take' and place as king (v. 37). Legitimate leadership is bestowed by
YHWH and Jeroboam remains a passive receptor. The second linguistic
element punctuates the oracle multiple times. The phrase 'on account of'

(vv. 32 [twice], 34, 36, 39) reveals that YHWH acts according to his promise to David (2 Sam. 7:13; 23:5); it is not undone by judgment against Solomon.

The prophecy looks backwards to the Davidic covenant in 2 Sam. 7, and to Solomon's acts for which he is judged, and in which the people participated ('They have forsaken . . . they have walked'). Yet YHWH does not fully remove power from Solomon, who remains a 'prince' (*nāśî*') because of David (v. 34). The term is different from that (*nāgîd*) used of Saul (1 Sam. 9:16; 10:1), David (1 Sam. 13:14; 25:30; 2 Sam. 5:2) and initially of Solomon (1 Kgs 1:35), and suggests that as a result of his sin Solomon is accounted a different type of leader than originally appointed.

The prophecy also looks ahead to one tribe retained on David's behalf (v. 32), establishing a 'lamp' (v. 36). The lamp (*nîr*) is a motif throughout Kings (1 Kgs 15:4; 2 Kgs 8:19). David was once referred to as a lamp (*nēr*; 2 Sam. 21:17; cf. Ps. 132:17) and the continuing dynasty in Jerusalem embodies YHWH's promises given to David.

YHWH also looks ahead to Jeroboam's rule (vv. 37–38). If he will 'walk . . . as David my servant did', then he will also receive a sure house (*bayit ne'ĕmān*). The promise uses the language of the established (i.e. sure) house (*ne'man bêtkā*; 2 Sam. 7:16) promised to David, but with a significant difference. The continuance of Jeroboam's dynasty is wholly dependent on Jeroboam's obedience. Conversely, while David's house could be disciplined for its disobedience (as the present prophetic word reveals) its surety is not dependent upon obedience.

In a last glance into the future, YHWH anticipates a time when the humbling of David's house will be completed (v. 39). Whether the whole kingdom will then be returned to David cannot be known at this point in the narrative.

Although the prophetic word is given to Jeroboam, in the narrative the response to it comes from Solomon. As one who disregards torah, he now seeks to subvert YHWH's word by killing its instrument. Jeroboam escapes to Egypt and his safety there signals his favour with Pharaoh Shishak (identified with Sheshonq I, 940–919 BC; see Horn 1967). Despite Solomon's marriage alliance with Egypt, two of his enemies are harboured by the regime. Jeroboam's future exodus from Egypt will be in accord with YHWH's word.

11:41–43

The notice of Solomon's death incorporates details that become common in subsequent death notices. Length and place of reign, and burial and succession details are provided. The irony of Solomon's notice is that his wisdom is once again mentioned in 'all he did'. Yet his wisdom without obedience is not enough – and perhaps was never wise at all. YHWH's approval is not guaranteed. It is always dependent upon the attitudes of the heart demonstrated in worship and observance of torah. These are the very places where Solomon fails.

Explanation

The chapter reveals YHWH's equal commitment to the unconditional Davidic Covenant and to the Mosaic law to which the Davidic kings are subject. Under the Davidic Covenant, kings – and specifically Solomon – are disciplined for their wrongs (2 Sam. 7:14). The kings' experience of the blessings of the covenant, and even the uninterrupted succession to the throne, is regulated by this discipline (Waltke 2007: 661).

The threat of discipline under the covenant is apparent in David's charge to Solomon as he urges his son to keep the torah of Moses (1 Kgs 2:3–4). In a 'reverberant cautionary note' (Walsh 1996: 154) YHWH four times revisits this same issue with Solomon (3:11–14; 6:11–13; 9:3–9; 11:11–13). Each speech in the downward spiral of Solomon's rule adds further details regarding disciplinary action or potential benefits for king and people under the Davidic Covenant. In the first the promise includes long life for Solomon. In the second the promise assures YHWH's presence among the Israelites, particularly as that presence relates to the temple. The third calls successive generations to torah obedience, and disobedience is for the first time defined as serving other gods (9:6). Failure under these conditions will be met with rejection of both temple and people. The fourth speech demonstrates Solomon's failure under these conditions. As a consequence, discipline is enacted and the kingdom will be torn from Solomon's hand. One anticipates the fulfilment of judgment against temple, people and dynasty will also be enacted, which of course occurs as 1 – 2 Kings draws to a close.

The disciplinary action tendered in these passages does not, however, negate the unconditional covenant YHWH initially granted David. Though its monarchic representatives may be disciplined and even removed from the throne, YHWH's commitment to an eternal rule of David does not waiver (2 Sam. 7:13, 16; 2 Sam. 23:5; Ps. 89:3–4, 28–37[4–5, 29–38]). The situation is very different in Jeroboam's case, however. For Jeroboam, the continuance of the dynasty is dependent upon only his actions (v. 38).

With the collapse of the kingdom and the exile of the monarchy Israel had to wonder how YHWH's unconditional promise could still remain. That Jehoiachin lives in exile at the end of 1 – 2 Kings suggests the possibility of a restored monarchy and nation. The psalmist's anguish, however, reveals that the possibility was viewed as slim, if not impossible (Ps. 89:38–51[39–52]). YHWH is feared to have abandoned Israel and their king, renouncing the covenant with David.

Yet in the psalmic and prophetic literature Israel's hope for YHWH's anointed king remains. Pss 2 and 110 each look to a mysterious king who is installed as YHWH's anointed, and whose reign extends from Mount Zion to the ends of the earth. This king is certainly more than Solomon, or even any of the good kings of the Davidic line, and reveals the hope for an ideal future king. Isaiah also speaks to this hope in passages such as Isa. 9:2–7[1–6] and 11:1–9, where the future king, bearing the spirit of God and even bearing his names (9:6[5]; 11:2), takes up David's throne. From that throne the ideal king rules justly and righteously according to torah, and extends his rule of peace over all the earth – far beyond the boundaries realized in Solomon's own era. Similar echoes of an ideal king flicker throughout the prophetic corpus, revealing Israel's continuing hope in what YHWH promised David (Jer. 23:5–6; Mic. 5:2–5a; Zech. 9:9–10).

The NT writers understand that in Jesus Christ a king has come who answers all the OT hopes for the continuance of the Davidic Covenant. He also fulfils the ideal of those hopes, as he alone of all kings walks in complete obedience to the torah. He is the 'son of David' (Matt. 1:1; 9:27; cf. Rom. 1:3) to whom are applied messianic titles from the psalms (Heb. 1:5, quoting Ps. 2:7; Acts 4:25–26, quoting Ps. 2:1–2) and who as God sits upon Israel's throne (Heb. 1:8–9, quoting Ps. 45:6–7[7–8]). He is named by all the Gospels as Israel's king (Matt. 2:2; 27:11, 37; Mark 15:2, 26; Luke 23:3, 38; John 19:19).

Although Solomon loses the kingdom through torah disobedience, Christ comes to do the will of the Father. Finally, in him is one of the line of David who can claim the throne and do so without any possibility of facing disciplinary action for his sins. Thus Jesus Christ stands as an antitype to Solomon and indeed all the kings throughout 1 – 2 Kings who, even though under the grace of an unconditional covenant, were not able to hold the throne in true righteousness and justice, obedient to torah. As YHWH, Jesus Christ is the true king of Israel and, without sin, holds the throne of David without end, fully realizing all the benefits of the Davidic Covenant for his subjects.

1 KINGS 12:1–33

Translation

[1]Rehoboam went to Shechem, for all Israel had come to Shechem to make him king. [2]Now when Jeroboam son of Nebat heard *of it* (he was still in Egypt where he had fled from the presence of King Solomon), he remained in Egypt[a]. [3]They sent and summoned him, and Jeroboam and all the congregation of Israel came[a] and spoke to Rehoboam, [4]'Your father made our yoke hard but you, now, lighten the hard labour of your father and his heavy yoke that he put upon us, and we will serve you.' [5]He replied to them, 'Go away for three days, then return to me.' So the people departed.

⁶King Rehoboam took counsel with the elders who had served his father Solomon when he was alive. 'How do you advise to answer this people?' ⁷They said to him, 'If today you will be a servant to this people and will serve them, and answer them, and speak good words to them, then they will be your servants for ever.' ⁸But he ignored the counsel of the elders that they gave him and he took counsel with the young men who had grown up with him who served him. ⁹He said to them, 'What do you advise that weᵃ answer this people who have spoken to me, saying, "Lighten the yoke that your father put upon us."' ¹⁰The young men who grew up with him answered him, 'Thus you should say to this people who have spoken to you, saying, "Your father made our yoke heavy but you lighten *it* for us!" Thus you should speak to them, "My little finger is thicker than my father's loins! ¹¹Now my father imposed upon you a heavy yoke but I will increase your yoke. My father rebuked you with whips but I will rebuke you with scorpions!"'

¹²Jeroboam and all the people cameᵃ to Rehoboam on the third day, just as the king had said, 'Return to me on the third day.' ¹³The king answered the people harshly, for he ignored the counsel of the elders that they had given him. ¹⁴He spoke to them according to the counsel of the young men, saying, 'My father made your yoke heavy but I will increase your yoke. My father rebuked you with whips but I will rebuke you with scorpions.' ¹⁵So the king did not listen to the people, for the turn of eventsᵃ was from YHWH so that he might establish his word that YHWH had spoken by the hand of Ahijah the Shilonite to Jeroboam son of Nebat. ¹⁶When all Israel saw that the king had not listened to them, the people answered the king, 'We have noᵃ share in David, no inheritance in the son of Jesse! To your tents, O Israel! Take care of your own house, O David!' So Israel departed to their tents. ¹⁷ᵃBut the sons of Israel who dwelt in the cities of Judah, Rehoboam ruled over them.

¹⁸King Rehoboam sent Adoramᵃ who was over the forced labour, and all Israel stoned him with stones, and he died. King Rehoboam managed to mount the chariot to escape to Jerusalem. ¹⁹So Israel has been in rebellion against the house of David until this day.

²⁰It came about when all Israel heard that Jeroboam had returned, they sent and summoned him to the assembly and they made him king over all Israel. There was none who followed after the house of David except the tribe of Judah alone.

²¹And Rehoboam came to Jerusalem and assembled all the house of Judah and the tribe of Benjamin, one hundred and eighty thousand chosen men, warriors, to fight with the house of Israel to restore the kingdom to Rehoboam son of Solomon.

²²Now the word of God came to Shemaiah the man of God, saying, ²³'Say to Rehoboam son of Solomon king of Judah, and to all the house of Judah and Benjamin, and to the rest of the people, ²⁴"Thus says YHWH, 'You shall not go up nor fight with your brothers the sons of Israel. Return each to his house for this thing has come about through me.'" Then they heeded the word of YHWH and turned to go *home* according to the word of YHWH.

²⁵Then Jeroboam built Shechem in the hill country of Ephraim and dwelt in it; he went out from there and built Penuel. ²⁶Jeroboam said to himself, 'Now the

kingdom will return to the house of David. [27]If this people goes up to offer sacrifices in the house of YHWH in Jerusalem, then the heart of this people will return to their lord – to Rehoboam king of Judah – and they will kill me and return to Rehoboam king of Judah.'[a] [28]So the king took counsel and made two calves of gold. He said to them, 'It is too much for you to go up to Jerusalem. Behold your gods, O Israel, who brought you up from the land of Egypt!' [29]He placed one in Bethel and the other he set in Dan. [30]Now this thing became a sin, for the people went *to worship* before the one as far as Dan[a]. [31]He made shrines on high places[a] and priests from among all the people[b], who were not from the sons of Levi.

[32]And Jeroboam made a festival in the eighth month, on the fifteenth day of the month, just like the festival that was in Judah. He went up to the altar; thus he did in Bethel, sacrificing to the calves that he had made. He placed in Bethel the priests of the high places that he had made. [33]On the fifteenth day of the eighth month, in the month that he had devised out of his own heart[a], he went up to the altar that he had made in Bethel. He made a festival for the sons of Israel and he went up to the altar to burn incense.

Notes on the text

2.a. LXX, Vg and 2 Chr. 10:2 read, 'and he returned from Egypt' (*wayyāṣob mimmiṣrāyim*). See 'Comment'.

3.a. LXX lacks 'they sent and summoned . . . all the congregation of Israel came', mitigating the difficulty in MT that includes Jeroboam in the rebellion (vv. 2–3, 12) only to have him seemingly return (from Egypt?) and be summoned after the rebellion (see 'Comment' and Gooding 1967).

9.a. LXX, Syr, Vg read, 'I answer'; 'we' is the communicative pl.

12.a. MT K *wayyābô* is corrupt and should read *wayyābô'û*, 'they came', as in two MSS, LXX*. The Q (*wayyābô'*, 'he came') is incorrect; the subject is pl. LXX omits 'Jeroboam and', consistently removing Jeroboam from the consultations with Rehoboam.

15.a. 'turn of events' (a hapax legomenon from root *sbb*, 'to turn'; cf. 2 Chr. 10:15 for an alternative spelling. See Machinist 1995).

16.a. Reading *mā* as a negation (*HALOT* 552; WO'C 1990: 326–327) rightly sets the exclamation into parallel lines.

17.a. The verse is missing from LXX[L]. Gray (1970: 302–303) suggests it is displaced in MT from after v. 20, where it better suits the context.

18.a. 'Adoram', possibly 'Adoniram' of 4:6 (but see 2 Sam. 20:24).

27.a. The redundant 'and return to Rehoboam king of Judah' is omitted in LXX. MT emphasizes Jeroboam's greatest fear.

30.a. Reading with the more difficult MT, LXX[B]. LXX[L] reads, 'before the one at Bethel and'. Citing only the furthest shrine emphasizes Jeroboam's determination to prevent Jerusalemite worship.

31.a. Deleting the marker *'et* in MT before the indefinite construct chain and reading the const. sg. *bêt* as a composite pl.: 'shrines on high places' (2 Kgs 17:29, 32; GKC §124r).

31.b. 'from among all the people' reads *miqṣôt* as 'out of their totality', 'from the whole population' (see Gen. 47:2; Judg. 18:2; Ezek. 33:2; and particularly Num. 22:41; cf. *HALOT* 1121). AV wrongly reads the 'lowest of the people', from one meaning of the noun *qāṣâ*, 'end, extremity'.

33.a. Reading with Q *millibbô*, 'from his heart', for MT K *millibbōd*, 'on his own'.

Form and structure

The chapter relates the events of the secession (vv. 1–24) and its aftermath (vv. 25–33) in which Jeroboam seeks to consolidate his kingdom, only to plant the seeds of its downfall.

The first part follows a discernible structure:

> Narrative introduction (vv. 1–3a)
> Convocation at Shechem (vv. 3b–20)
> > First interview led by Jeroboam (vv. 3b–5)
> > > Rehoboam consults with the elders (vv. 6–7)
> > > Rehoboam consults with the young men (vv. 8–11)
> > Second interview led by Jeroboam (vv. 12–17)
> Narrative conclusion (vv. 18–20)

Following the narrative conclusion (vv. 18–20), vv. 21–24 relate events from the perspective of Judah. In this section 'house of Judah' is used (vv. 21–22) as a contrast to the 'house of Israel' and 'sons of Israel' (vv. 21, 24), highlighting the division of the kingdom into two houses or nations.

The final section of the chapter (vv. 25–33) switches focus to events in the 'house of Israel'. Jeroboam is central and each of three sections features him as subject (vv. 25, 26–31, 32–33). Events are told from Jeroboam's perspective, but Dtr firmly controls the perspective, judging Jeroboam's actions by Deuteronomistic standards (v. 30).

Several motifs are apparent in the chapter. The primary motif is that of fulfilment of YHWH's word (*dābār*), signalled by the repeated use of the root *dbr*. It appears nine times in nominal form ('word, thing, answer') and eleven times in verbal form – often in places where the more usual root *'mr* might be expected to indicate speech (e.g. vv. 3, 7, 10, 14, 16). In vv. 15, 24 the inevitability of YHWH's word is made explicit.

A concomitant second motif is that of listening or hearing (the verbal root *šmʿ* occurs five times). Jeroboam 'hears' of the Shechem convocation (v. 2) but does not move to claim the kingship; only when Israel 'hears' of his return is he made king (v. 20). Rehoboam's part in the chapter is not to 'hear' and he subsequently loses his kingship (vv. 15–16). Finally, it is the 'house of Judah' that 'hears' the word of YHWH (v. 24). Their 'hearing' acknowledges that YHWH's word is accomplished.

A third motif is seeking 'counsel' or 'advice'. The nominal form of the root *y'ṣ* occurs three times (vv. 8, 13–14), while the verbal form occurs six times (vv. 6 [twice], 8–9, 13, 28). Rehoboam takes counsel with many, but treats the people harshly (*qšh*). In this way he echoes Solomon's hard (*qšh*) yoke and labour. Jeroboam, too, takes counsel, with even more devastating results (v. 28). His actions provide a final motif. In vv. 28–33 the verb *'šh* (to make) occurs nine times (vv. 28, 31 [twice], 32 [four times], 33 [twice]) as Jeroboam makes the calves, shrines, priests, festivals and altar.

Jeroboam's actions (vv. 25–33) seek to consolidate his rule. They also provide a hinge to ch. 13. Three times in vv. 32–33 Jeroboam 'goes up to the altar', the object of the man of God's judgment in ch. 13. Further, the similar phraseology of 12:30–31 and 13:33–34 serve as a frame that holds vv. 32–33 with ch. 13 (see 'Comment' at 13:33–34).

The LXX provides an alternative account of Jeroboam, and then includes a retelling of the MT account in which he conspires for the kingdom (LXX vv. 24a–z). Opinions as to the historical reliability of the accounts vary (Montgomery 1951: 252–254; Gooding 1967; Gray 1970: 289), but each presents Jeroboam with a particular *tendenz* suited to the aims of the variants (Gordon 1976). The *tendenz* of the MT reveals a conviction YHWH's word will be accomplished. The secession is his plan, and human actions, while free, work to that word's accomplishment.

V. 19 is a later commentary on the events but the compositional history cannot be certainly ascertained. The events of vv. 1–24 reflect a Judahite perspective that includes few details of the secessionists but provides details of Rehoboam's court (including a prophetic word). The castigation of Jeroboam's religion, although not blindly Davidic, suggests a perspective supportive of the Solomonic temple. It acknowledges the secession as YHWH's will (vv. 15, 24) but still expresses hope for a restored Davidic house (vv. 17, 19).

Comment

12:1–2

Shortly after Solomon's death Rehoboam journeys to Shechem (11:43), an ancient worship site in the Ephraimite hills (Gen. 12:6; 33:18–20; cf. Deut. 11:29–32; 27:1–26 and Josh. 24). Rehoboam is summoned by 'all Israel', which term denotes the whole nation in 1 Kgs 1 – 11 (six times), most recently in 11:42. Yet while the nation summons Rehoboam for investiture, every subsequent occurrence in the chapter of 'all Israel' specifies the northern tribes alone.

Ready contention suggests dissension simmered throughout Solomon's reign, sparked by measures such as corvée labour, taxation and cities ceded to Pharaoh (9:10–14; Sweeney 1995: 614–615). Given this climate, Rehoboam must procure the support of all Israel, instituting covenantal agreements with the tribes such as David had forged (2 Sam. 5:3; cf. 2:4), and that continued during the co- and sole-regency of his son.

The narrative aside reveals Jeroboam's decision to remain in Egypt, apparently in response to the investiture. His response establishes a pattern by which he does not attempt to gain the throne promised by YHWH.

12:3–20

3–5. 'Sent and summoned' out of Egypt, Jeroboam like Moses in the face of oppressive power speaks for Israel. An undisclosed group ('they') summons him, either 'all the congregation of Israel' (v. 3) or a select subgroup. He is similarly 'sent for and summoned' (v. 20) to become king. He is only a respondent to both summons, but is not seeking to fulfil YHWH's word.

The 'congregation of Israel' (*qĕhal yiśrā'ēl*), a representative body of the tribes, presents their request to Rehoboam; Jeroboam's familiarity with Solomon's labour policies makes him a probable spokesman. Solomon's taxation (1 Kgs 4) and conscripted labour (1 Kgs 5:13–18; 9:15–23) are characterized as 'hard' or 'obdurate' (*qšh*; cf. Deut. 10:16; 2 Kgs 17:14), and 'heavy' (*kbd*) or difficult to bear (cf. Exod. 17:12). A request for a just lightening of hard labour (*'ăbōdâ*) is made, with a pledge to serve (*'ābad*) the new king. The request could form the basis of a new covenant agreement desired by Rehoboam. The interview closes with all parties apparently negotiating in good faith; security for Rehoboam's crown is possible – only the presence of Jeroboam and the recollection of the prophet's words threaten that.

6–11. Rehoboam seeks counsel from two groups. The 'elders' elsewhere give advice to monarchs during crises (2 Sam. 17:4, 15; 19:11; 1 Kgs 20:7–9), served Solomon (v. 6) and were represented at significant national events (8:1). The 'young men' (*yĕlādîm*) are contemporaries of Solomon (v. 8) and thus grown adults (14:21). The term is technical, analogously derived from Egyptian sources, and designates privileged royal and non-royal members of the household who serve the king (Malamat 1963b; D. Evans 1966). Literarily, *yĕlādîm* contrasts the wiser, more experienced elders (N. Fox 1996).

He 'took counsel' and requested 'advice' from both groups (vv. 6, 8–9), but poses a different question to each. The elders are asked 'how' he should reply, and they counsel acquiescence 'today' to reap benefits 'for ever' (lit. 'for all days') – counsel that shows considerable political acumen from those who perhaps advised Solomon's oppressive policies. Rehoboam is to 'answer them' and to 'speak good words'. The latter phrase is covenantal in tone (Frisch 1991: 417–418) and the elders apparently envision a covenant enshrining the tribes' request in exchange for ongoing loyalty and contribution of labour. Hoping to ensure the prophetic word that one tribe 'will be (*hyh*) a lamp for my servant (*'abdî*) David always' (*kol-hayyāmîm*; 11:36), the counsel concludes Israel will be (*hyh*) servants (*'ăbādîm*) for ever (*kol-hayyāmîm*; v. 7). They do not realize YHWH's promise is not dependent upon their expediency, but upon his divine will – a tenet Jeroboam also forgets at the chapter's end.

The question posed the young men specifically seeks 'what' should be answered (v. 9). His identification with his contemporaries ('what should we answer') suggests a pre-commitment to their advice. He communicates Israel's request in an abbreviated form, which, divorced from its context of oppression and proffered service, appears a baseless complaint. Though the young men's answer reveals some awareness of the oppression, it lacks the expediency of the elders. Instead, they speak folly wrapped in three proverbial sayings (vv. 10–11). The 'wisdom' plays into the hands of the divine will, for it moves Israel to rebellion.

Their first proverb vulgarly struts Rehoboam's virile strength. Rehoboam's 'little finger' (i.e. his penis; Noth 1968: 267) is stronger than Solomon's loins. Their second and third proverbs continue the boast. 'My father . . . but I' promises to increase the heavy yoke, replacing Solomon's 'whip' with Rehoboam's 'scorpion' (perhaps a whip with embedded sharp objects). Their sarcasm and selfishness is evident.

12–17. The young men's arrogance contrasts Israel's acquiescent return 'just as the king had said'. Any hope of honest dealing is dashed when Rehoboam, like Solomon, answers the people 'harshly'. His answer repeats the foolish impudence of his contemporaries – that he sanitizes it is the only glimmer of wisdom.

Rehoboam's failure is that he does not 'listen'. Like Pharaoh before him (Exod. 7:13; Provan 1995: 104–105), his failure facilitates the 'turn of events' (v. 15), described as fulfilment of YHWH's word. All Israel recognizes the failure and responds with a proverb of their own arising out of the historic conflict between the northern tribes and the house of David (2 Sam. 20:1). To the proverb is added a damning summation, 'Take care of your own house, O David!' The departure of the tribes 'to their tents' is mitigated by a northern remnant remaining in Judah. They represent hope for a future reunification of rule over all tribes (11:39).

18–20. Adoram (probably an alternative form of Adoniram [4:6] and possibly the same official named in David's administration [2 Sam. 20:24]) is sent to effect reconciliation. Rehoboam's inept choice of negotiator meets Israel's hatred of the forced labour policy and Adoram dies. Rehoboam's escape is achieved only by persistent effort (attested by the hith. verb *'mṣ* with the following *lamed* preposition [as in Ruth 1:18]). His narrow escape affords opportunity for a second editorial comment.

That the rebellion continues 'until this day' reveals hope in the prophetic word (11:39) that some day the situation will be reversed.

V. 20 is the climactic moment for Jeroboam. In v. 3 an undisclosed group 'sent and summoned': now 'all Israel . . . sent and summoned' him upon his return from Shechem. The 'assembly' (*hā'ēdâ*), a representational body for national, legal and cultic purposes, makes him king. Fulfilment of the prophecy proceeds by the power of YHWH's word; Jeroboam remains passive throughout. A final mention of Judah's being left to David's house aligns the event unmistakably with the prophetic sign, where one piece of the torn robe remains for David's sake.

12:21–24

The prophet Shemaiah forestalls military intervention. Acceptance of the prophetic word confirms Judah's acceptance of events as YHWH's will. Strangely, while Rehoboam is specifically addressed by the prophet (v. 23), he is not specifically noted in the acquiescence. This is a subtle jab at his inability to lead his people wisely.

The division of the united kingdom into two houses is marked by the contrastive 'house of Judah' (vv. 21, 23) and 'house of Israel' (v. 21). Yet, while now separate houses, the northern house remains 'your brothers the sons of Israel'. The continuing relationship not only motivates the cessation of military activity against Israel; it also bodes well for the future reunification of this 'family' under Davidic rule.

12:25–33

25. Jeroboam first fortifies existing centres (Toombs 1992: 1184; Magen 1993: 1353). Shechem, 40 miles (65 km) north of Jerusalem and identified with modern Balatah, controls east–west trade routes and routes to Judah. Penuel, east of the Jordan near the Jabbok (Slayton 1992: 223), is a stronghold over cis-Jordanian tribes. Jeroboam associates his new rule with traditional locations that reach back as far as the patriarchs (Gen. 12:6; 32:30; 33:18–20; 35:1–4; Josh. 20:7; 21:21; 24).

26–31. Jeroboam's second action begins with his inner musing. He three times fears the people's 'return' (*šwb*; vv. 26, 27 [twice]) to the house of David. His fear is unfounded, for YHWH has made it clear no reunification will occur (vv. 21–24). And, while Rehoboam sought to 'restore' (*šwb*) the kingdom, at YHWH's word to 'return' (*šwb*), Judah does return (*šwb*) home. Further fears abound for Jeroboam: if the people consider Rehoboam their 'lord' (v. 27), and yet killed his representative (v. 18), Jeroboam's own life is not safe. Despite the prophetic word that transfers the northern tribes to him, he doubts its certainty.

Like Rehoboam, Jeroboam 'takes counsel' as a king (2 Kgs 6:8; 1 Chr. 13:1; 2 Chr. 25:17; 30:2; 32:3). Whatever counsel is given, Jeroboam is alone the subject of the chapter's remaining verbs. He is responsible for what 'became a sin' for Israel. Jeroboam was urged by prophetic word to do 'as David my servant did' ('*śh*; 11:38). In vv. 28–33 Jeroboam will 'do' ('*śh*) nine things, all arising from anxiety over the veracity of YHWH's word; in fact, the only mention of YHWH in the passage occurs in the context of human anxiety (Knoppers 1995: 99).

Whereas Jeroboam returned from Egypt in the role of Moses, now he is cast in the role of Aaron (Aberbach and Smolar 1967). The nature of Jeroboam's calves can be explored grammatically, historically and literarily. He makes the calves and proclaims, 'Behold, your '*ĕlōhîm*'; the noun is plural, as is the plural verb in the phrase 'who brought you up from the land of Egypt'. The reference may be to many 'gods', but the plural form is also regularly used of Israel's God. Grammar may not decide what the calves are meant to represent (other gods or YHWH God), but either the production of multiple gods or the image of YHWH violates covenant commands (Exod. 20:3–4; Deut. 5:7–8).

Historical evidence suggests bull iconography was used and accepted before the common cherubim iconography in Jerusalem (Cross 1973: 197–202; Halpern 1976; Curtis 1990; C. Evans 1995: 201–205). Both representations were used as supports to YHWH's throne. If so, Jeroboam is an archaizer, not an innovator, who returns the north to pre-Davidic, pre-Jerusalemite forms of worship.

Literary investigation reveals a very different story. However historically probable that Jeroboam presents the calves as legitimate iconography evoking YHWH's throne, to Dtr Jeroboam's actions are aberrant and sinful (v. 30). Characterizing them as 'other gods' ('*ĕlōhîm 'ăḥērîm*; 14:9), they are a clear violation of covenant commands (Exod. 20:3; Deut. 5:7) and part of Israel's sinful history (Deut. 6:14; 7:4; 8:19 *et passim*; Josh. 23:16; 24:16; Judg. 2:12, 17; 1 Kgs 9:6; 11:4, 10). Further, Jeroboam's words 'Behold, your gods, O Israel who brought you up from the land of Egypt!' literally evoke the Exodus passage. Only in these two passages does the expression employ the plural verb (elsewhere the confession employs the singular verb '*lh*, 'he brought up' [Judg. 6:13; 1 Sam. 12:6; 2 Kgs 17:36; Jer. 16:14; 23:7], or the concomitant *yṣ*', 'he brought out' [Exod. 16:6; Deut. 1:27; 6:12, 23; 7:8, 19; 1 Kgs 9:9; 2 Chr. 7:22]). The exceptional nature of the Exodus and Kings passages marks the words 'not as misunderstanding, but invective . . . . Aaron's calf perverts Sinaitic religion; Jeroboam's calves not only imitate but extend that perversion' (Knoppers 1995: 101).

Jeroboam sets the calves at northern and southern boundaries, shrewdly selecting sites with history as worship centres (Bethel in Gen. 12:8; 13:3–4; 28:10–22; 35:7, 15; Dan in Judg. 18 – 19). Additionally, Bethel stakes a claim on the frontier with Judah and provides a convenient deterrent to cultic traffic to Jerusalem. Both sites violate the command to worship YHWH only at the place of YHWH's choice: now the Jerusalem temple (Deut. 12:2–28; 1 Kgs 9:3).

Jeroboam introduces further cultic changes: shrines (lit. 'houses') on high places return worship to pre-temple locations (1 Sam. 9:12; 10:5; 1 Kgs 3:2) now negatively appraised (1 Kgs 14:23; 15:14; 22:44). Jeroboam's high places are judged (1 Kgs 13:2, 32–33) along with all subsequent northern high places (2 Kgs 17:9). Non-Levitical priests are appointed in violation of Deut. 18:1–8. The act may be further evidence of archaizing tendencies, instituting the ancient practice of priests, replacing the first-born dedicated to YHWH (Exod. 13:1; Num. 3:11–13, 40–44; 8:16–13). But regardless of Jeroboam's intention, the act is characterized as wholly sinful (13:33–34).

32–33. A new section begins with the third 'and Jeroboam' in which a final new innovation – a festival – is introduced. It attempts to supplant an existing festival celebrated in the seventh month and requiring attendance in Jerusalem (Exod. 23:16; Deut. 16:13; Lev. 23:33–34). Jeroboam's festival is tied to the later northern harvest and is celebrated in the eighth month. The move returns the date to earlier northern practice, displaying Jeroboam's archaizing tendency in the new cult (Talmon 1958: 55–58). The festival is mentioned three times (vv. 32, 33 [twice]) and it is derided as derived from 'his own heart' (v. 33).

Punctuating the denunciation of vv. 32–33 is the threefold 'he went up to the altar', Jeroboam's final negative action. Regardless of any imitation of Solomon's dedicatory celebrations and offerings before the altar (8:22, 62), the action is reserved for the high priest alone (Exod. 30:1–10; cf. Num. 16; Lev. 10:1–3; 2 Chr. 26:16–21). Moreover, he ascends an altar in Bethel, sacrifices to the calves and does so in the wrong month. He also ascends to 'burn incense', the common rendering of the hiph. stem of the verbal root *qṭr*. Such offerings can be licit or illicit (Clements 2004); given the location, object and timing of the action, here it can only be illicit.

The repeated reference to Jeroboam's going 'up to the altar' anticipates the next chapter, where the man of God confronts Jeroboam at the altar.

Explanation

The outworking of the secession illustrates the dual reality of YHWH's sovereign will and human freedom. YHWH's will for secession is revealed in Ahijah's prophetic word (11:30–39), but in 1 Kgs 12 human actions and words are foremost. Pointedly, the narrative explicitly refrains from insinuating YHWH into their decisions; nowhere does he coerce the outcome or the actors. Yet twice in the chapter the narrator notes human activity works in accord with YHWH's will (vv. 15, 24).

YHWH's will is worked in the free actions of the players. Rehoboam takes counsel, and chooses the counsel to heed. The spurned northern tribes respond to Rehoboam in anger and secede, when they could have continued acquiescently. The southern tribes heed the prophet and, when disobedience was an all-too-common response, forgo military retaliation.

YHWH is not unaware that human freedom may move in directions opposed to his revealed will. Thus Jeroboam is granted freedom to choose to walk in YHWH's commandments (11:38) – a freedom that must necessarily encompass an equal freedom to neglect those commandments. It is the latter eventuality that Jeroboam chooses (12:26–33). Yet YHWH's workings with his people encompass even this.

The interweaving of human freedom and YHWH's sovereignty is revealed throughout Scripture. Abraham and Sarah, while in receipt of the promise of offspring, freely choose to attempt to fulfil YHWH's promise through Hagar (Gen. 16). Though these free actions are presented as sinful and create relational tragedies, they are not able to circumvent YHWH's promise. YHWH decrees that Sennacherib will devastate Judah (2 Kgs 19:25–26), and he does so (18:13) but remains free to act beyond YHWH's decree, which he likewise does (19:22–24). Yet, even in the midst of Sennacherib's free actions (for which he is judged: 19:27–28), YHWH's will is accomplished and Judah and Jerusalem are humbled.

1 Kgs 12 evokes elements of the exodus narrative (Aberbach and Smolar 1967). Like Moses, Jeroboam champions his people against a monarch's oppressive regime; like Aaron, he makes golden calves. Similarly, the two passages engage YHWH's sovereignty and human freedom. YHWH's will is to deliver Israel. Towards this end he commits to harden Pharaoh's heart (Exod. 4:21; 7:3), but also Pharaoh by his own will hardens his own heart (8:15, 32; 9:34). Already in his first encounter with Moses his choice is apparent, for he disdains YHWH, refuses Moses' request and inflicts Israel with hard labour (Exod. 5:1–21). Of course, the correspondence between the two accounts is not complete. Nowhere does YHWH vow to harden Rehoboam's will against the northerners' request. But in each, humans act and speak in ways consonant with YHWH's stated will and that eventuate in that will's fulfilment.

Free human action cannot undo YHWH's will. Similarly, human inaction is unable to subvert it. Thus Jeroboam gains the throne passively, an attitude that especially marks those destined by YHWH to the throne. Though anointed (1 Sam. 10:1), Saul remains passive to kingly appointment until the people thrust it upon him (1 Sam. 10:19–22; 11:15). David repeatedly refuses to claim the crown by assassination (1 Sam. 24:6; 26:10–11); only when Saul dies does David step into his anointed role. Solomon is passive en route to the throne and it is gained by others' actions. It seems that an ideal is set up that is particularly observable in the southern kingdom, in which an approved throne is received with a significant element of passivity. In the northern kingdom several kings gain thrones by coup, but even in these cases YHWH has, by prophetic word, appointed the king to rule (1 Kgs 16:1–4; 2 Kgs 9:6–10). Appointment to monarchy reveals YHWH's control of the monarchic office: it is his to bestow and the recipient's to receive, but (ideally) never grasp.

This pattern is a repetition of the monarchy's initial institution: YHWH alone approves and bestows it in response to the people's request (1 Sam. 8:6–8). Ironically, his bestowal responds to human freedom – the request for a king was the people's desire. YHWH's acquiescence does not subvert his will; it is part of his sovereign design for Israel. It is through the vicissitudes of monarchy, its failures and cessation in exile, that Israel returns to hope in the sovereignty of YHWH, recognizing that his throne alone can fulfil their hope for covenant faithfulness and righteousness. It is through human monarchy that YHWH tutors his people back to what they had freely resigned, and to what was most meet for their life as YHWH's covenant people: the rule of YHWH.

1 KINGS 13:1–34

Translation

[1]Then behold, a man of God came from Judah to Bethel by the word of YHWH while Jeroboam was standing upon the altar to burn incense. [2]He cried out against the altar by the word of YHWH, and he said, 'O altar, altar! Thus says YHWH, "Behold, a son will be born to the house of David, named Josiah. He will sacrifice upon you the priests of the high places who burn incense upon you. They will burn human bones on you."' [3]He gave a sign in that day, saying, 'This is the sign that YHWH has spoken. Behold, the altar will be broken and the ashes that are upon it will be spilled out.'

[4]When the king heard the word of the man of God, which he cried out against the altar of Bethel, Jeroboam stretched out his hand from the altar, saying, 'Seize him!' But his hand that he had stretched out against him withered, and he was not able to draw it back to himself. [5]The altar was broken and the ashes from the altar were spilled out according to the sign that the man of God gave by the word of YHWH. [6]The king answered and said to the man of God, 'Please entreat the face of YHWH your God and pray on my behalf that my hand will be restored to me.' And the man of God entreated YHWH, and the king's hand was restored to him, and it was as before.

[7]The king spoke to the man of God, 'Come[a] home with me and eat[a], and I will give you a gift.' [8]The man of God said to the king, 'If you should give me half your house, I would not go with you nor would I eat bread, or drink water in this place. [9]For so he[a] commanded me by the word of YHWH, saying, "You shall not eat bread or drink water, and you shall not return by the way which you came."' [10]So he left by another way and did not return by the way he had come to Bethel.

[11]There was a certain prophet, an old man, dwelling in Bethel. His son came and told[a] him all the things which the man of God had done that day in Bethel, and the words that he had spoken to the king. When they had recounted[b] them to their father, [12]their father said to them, 'Which way, then, did he go?' Now his sons had seen the road that the man of God who had come from Judah had taken. [13]So he said to his sons, 'Saddle the donkey for me.' They saddled the donkey for him and he mounted it [14]and went after the man of God. He found him sitting under an oak tree and said to him, 'Are you the man of God who came from Judah?' He replied, 'I am.' [15]He said to him, 'Come home with me and eat bread!' [16]But he replied, 'I am not able to return with you, nor go with you. I cannot eat bread, nor drink water with you in this place, [17]for he spoke to me by the word of YHWH[a], "You shall not eat bread, nor drink water there, nor return by going in the way which you came."' [18]He said to him, 'I also am a prophet like you. An angel has spoken to me by the word of YHWH saying, "Bring him back with you to your house that he may eat bread and drink water."' But he deceived him. [19]So he turned back with him and ate bread in his house and drank water.

[20]As they were sitting at the table, the word of YHWH came to the prophet who had brought him back. [21]He cried out to the man of God who had come from Judah, saying, 'Thus says YHWH, "Because you have disobeyed YHWH's declaration, and have not kept the commandment that YHWH your God commanded you, [22]but have returned, and have eaten bread, and have drunk water in the place about which he said to you, 'Do not eat bread, nor drink water,' your corpse shall not come to the grave of your fathers."'

[23]After he had eaten bread and drunk *water*, then he saddled[a] for him the donkey belonging to the prophet who had brought him back[b]. [24]As he went along, a lion found him on the way and killed him. His corpse was cast on the road with the donkey standing beside it, and the lion also standing beside the corpse. [25]And behold, men passed by and saw the corpse cast on the road with the lion standing beside the corpse. They came and reported *it* in the city in which the old prophet lived.

[26]Now when the prophet heard, who had turned him back from the way, he said, 'It is the man of God who rebelled against YHWH's declaration, so YHWH gave him to the lion which tore him, and killed him according to YHWH's word, which he spoke to him.' [27]Then he spoke to his sons, saying, 'Saddle the donkey for me!' And they saddled *it*. [28]He went and found his corpse thrown on the road with *the* donkey and the lion standing beside the corpse. The lion had neither eaten the corpse nor torn the donkey. [29]So the prophet picked up the corpse of the man of God and placed it on the donkey and brought him back to the old prophet's city, to lament and bury him. [30]He placed his corpse in his own grave and they lamented over him, 'Alas, my brother!' [31]After he had buried him, he said to his sons, 'When I die, you shall bury me in the grave in which the man of God has been buried. Beside his bones, place my bones. [32]For the thing will surely come to pass which he cried out by the word of YHWH against the altar that is in Bethel, and against all the houses of the high places in the cities of Samaria.'

[33]After this matter, Jeroboam did not turn from his evil way but made priests of the high places from among all the people. Whoever desired, he ordained and

he became a priest[a] of the high places. [34]And this matter[a] became sin to the house of Jeroboam, to remove and destroy *it* from the face of the earth.

Notes on the text

7.a. The paragogic heh on the imp. ('come', 'eat') may be honorific when addressed to God, a father, a priest or a prophet (JM §48d).

9.a. The identity of 'he' in 'for so he commanded me by the word of YHWH' is assumed to be YHWH, although no antecedent account specifies how, or by whom, the communication came. Some commentators clarify the identity and read the gen. 'of YHWH' as nom.: 'for so YHWH commanded me by/with the word' (Gray 1970: 324). The text is commonly emended following LXX, Vg, to passive pu., 'for so I was commanded by the word of YHWH' (DeVries 2003: 165). The *lectio difficilior* is retained here.

11.a. 'his son . . . told' as the spokeman for the many sons later in the verse. LXX, Syr, Vg change to pl. The *lectio difficilior* of the MT is retained as original.

11.b. The temporal 'when they had recounted' is read with the main clause of v. 12, where the pl. 'sons' continues.

17.a. 'he spoke to me by the word of YHWH' requires only a change of pointing to MT's awkward (although not impossible) 'a word *came* to me by the word of YHWH'. See 'Comment'.

23.a. 'he saddled for him' the direct antecedent for 'he saddled' is the individual who 'ate and drank', which suggests the man of God. The context, however, suggests it is the Bethel prophet who saddled the donkey. Syr attempts to rectify the difficulty by reading 'they saddled'.

23.b. *lannābî' 'ăšer hĕšîbô* could be taken as a further identification of the person for whom the donkey is saddled: the man of God from Judah who has just been identified (*wayyaḥăbāš lô*). AV, RSV and NASB so translate. But nowhere else is the man of God from Judah called a prophet. The awkward parenthetical comment (omitted from some LXX* versions) is better read as here: a *lamed auctoris* (with NRSV, NIV; cf. DeVries 2003: 165). The comment further identifies the donkey that will play a key role in the following event as belonging to the Bethel prophet.

33.a. 'he became a priest' reads MT's pl. as sg., according to the context and with LXX, Syr, Vg.

34.a. Reading with LXX, Syr, Tg 'this matter' rather than MT 'by the matter'.

Form and structure

The chapter begins with the sequence 'Then, behold . . . he came . . .' (*wĕhinnēh* + part./suff. conjugation). The grammatical formulation links the ensuing narrative into an already-existing one (Simon 1976: 100; Gross 1979: 101; Van Winkle 1996: 104).

The identity of that already-existing narrative is, however, strongly debated among commentators and is often considered lost or an intentionally omitted opening (e.g. Simon and Gross). In this commentary 12:32–33 provides the needed opening, serving as a hinge between 1 Kgs 12 and 13 (see 'Form and structure', 1 Kgs 12).

1 Kgs 13 has two component parts (vv. 1–10, 11–32) followed by a summative statement of Jeroboam's continued sins (vv. 33–34). Historical-critical studies question the unity of the passage, although no agreement exists as to whether the narrative is a pre-Dtr story adopted by Dtr with possible later additions (Montgomery 1951: 261; Noth 1968: 293; Gray 1970: 321; Lemke 1976: 304; Dozeman 1982; DeVries 2003: 168–169), or whether the narrative is a post-Dtr composition (Eissfeldt 1965: 290; Van Seters 1999). Additionally, scholarly opinion varies on the relationship of the chapter (particularly v. 2) to its fulfilment in 2 Kgs 23:16–18 (Lemke 1976; Simon 1976; Lemke 1980: 34; B. Long 1984: 145). While the compositional history cannot be recovered with certainty, historical critics often recognize the coherence of the present narrative (Gray 1970: 321; Gross 1979; B. Long 1984). The man of God from Judah appears in both parts, and other connections bind them into a coherent whole. First, motifs are repeated throughout the narrative; several are clustered at its open and close, suggesting literary framing. The 'altar' appears eight times in vv. 1–6 and reappears in the old prophet's eulogy (v. 32); only in vv. 2 and 32 is the specific phrase 'against the altar that is in Bethel' found. Similarly, 'he cried out' appears both in the first part (vv. 2, 4) and the eulogy (v. 32), as well as at a crucial juncture in the narrative's second part (v. 21).

The 'word of YHWH' is a motif voiced by the narrator, the man of God and the prophet (vv. 2, 5, 9, 17–18, 32). Another consistent motif is that of the word 'turn' or 'return' ($\check{s}wb$), found sixteen times in various formulations ('restore', 'draw back', 'bring back', etc.; vv. 4, 6 [twice], 9–10, 16–20, 22–23, 26, 29, 33 [twice]). All but one of the occurrences (v. 29) refers to responses to the powerful word of YHWH and demonstrates the word's power to effect certain outcomes. That Jeroboam ultimately does 'not turn' anticipates negative outcomes implicit in the prophetic word of 11:38.

The final motif is that of eating/drinking. The king's invitation for the man of God to eat ($s'd$, v. 7) begins a series of utterances in which the focus is on eating ($'kl$) and drinking ($\check{s}th$) (vv. 8–9, 15–19, 22–23, 28). The motif moves the plot from moment to moment and the subtle differences in the expression of the phrase characterize the individuals in the drama. The rhetoric tension created is explored in the 'Comment' section below, and highlights the overriding theme of obedience to YHWH's word.

Finally, the unity of the chapter is apparent in the parallel structure of the core encounter of each section, set out below (see Mead 1999; Wray

Beal 2012). The parallels suggest the core encounters are an intentional pair (vv. 1–10, 20–25), speaking to similar issues.

Jeroboam 'standing upon the altar' (v. 1)	Bethel prophet and man of God 'sitting at the table' (v. 20)
Man of God 'cried out against the altar' (v. 2)	Bethel prophet 'cried out' to the man of God (v. 21)
Prophetic announcement, 'Thus says YHWH' (v. 2)	Prophetic announcement, 'Thus says YHWH' (v. 21)
Sign given: the altar will be torn down (v. 3)	Sign given: the man of God will not come to the grave of his fathers (v. 22)
The altar is 'broken' (v. 5)	The man of God's body is 'cast' down (v. 24)
'By the way' (*bdrk*) repeated three times (vv. 9–10)	'By the way/road' (*bdrk*) repeated three times (vv. 24–25)

Comment

13:1–10

1–3. Jeroboam's initiatory sacrifice is the culminating act of his alternative cult. Here the altar is presented as that cult's focal point. The man of God delivers his judgment oracle against it as a synecdoche for the whole cult. The altar later appears as a symbol of the cult's enduring potency, which is destroyed through the more enduring and greater power of YHWH's word (2 Kgs 23:15–17).

The man of God arrives in Bethel through the instrumentality of the word of YHWH. The phrase 'by the word of YHWH' (*bidbar yhwh*) is almost exclusive to this narrative (seven instances), appearing elsewhere only twice in the DH (1 Sam. 3:21; 1 Kgs 20:35 [in similar prophetic contexts]) and three times outside the history (2 Chr. 30:12; Ps. 33:6; Jer. 8:9). The cluster in 1 Kgs 13 emphasizes the power of YHWH's word, and the divine origin and authority of the prophet's oracle (Lemke 1976: 314).

The man of God from Judah and the prophet from Bethel, who appears later in the narrative, are representatives of YHWH and, for literary identification only, are consistently 'the man of God' who is from Judah, and 'the prophet'. The two terms are interchangeable (see for Moses [Deut. 33:1; 34:10], Elijah [1 Kgs 17:18; 18:22] and Elisha [2 Kgs 3:11; 5:8]) and do not differentiate the men by office, cultic allegiance or function. The phrase 'man of God' appears most frequently in the Elijah–Elisha cycle and the present tradition may likewise be northern. The man of God receives no other appellation in the narrative, although once it is significantly modified. Known as the 'man of God from Judah' or simply as the 'man of God', after the oracle is delivered he is specifically identified as 'the man of God who rebelled' (v. 26).

In true prophetic form the man of God 'cries out' (*qr'*; cf. Jon. 1:2; 3:2; Jer. 3:12; 7:2; Isa. 40:2; 58:1) and declaims, 'Thus says YHWH.' Strangely, Jeroboam is not himself addressed. Rather, having devised the cult 'out of his own heart' (12:33) the altar is apostrophized as the embodiment of Jeroboam's disobedient heart. No reason for the judgment is provided by the prophet, yet such detail is unnecessary in the narrative, for not only has the introduction (12:32–33) provided a summative statement of the sins, but all of 12:25–33 has indicated Jeroboam's sins. In the light of this, the prophet provides the expected judgment.

The judgment is unusual in that it names the three-centuries-distant King Josiah as its executor. Given the power of YHWH's word demonstrated in this chapter, there is no reason to deny that such a distant phenomenon could occur. Comparison of the oracle to the event (2 Kgs 23:15–20) indicates that the fulfilment did occur. A sign (*môpēt*) authenticates the oracle. Although signs are not always a guarantee of a prophet's ministry (Deut. 13:1–3), this sign occurs in the context of rejecting Jeroboam's cult in favour of YHWH and serves as a true authenticating sign.

4–6. As Pharaoh reacted against Moses' signs (Exod. 4:21; 7:3; 11:10), so Jeroboam rejects the sign and its attendant word. Attempting to apprehend the man of God, he is struck by YHWH's power. The prophet's oracle is further authenticated before the king's eyes as the ashes and sacrificial fat spill from the broken altar. By the rubrics of Lev. 6:10–11, Jeroboam's sacrifice is invalidated and his holy place desecrated.

The dual signs cause Jeroboam to accede to the oracle's authenticity. As before (12:26–27), he attends to his own well-being – not now by devising an alternative cult, but by entreating the prophet to restore his hand. His entreaty is an admission that his royal power (which he sought to safeguard through the institution of the alternative cult) has been bested by YHWH's royal power. Had he remained in submission to YHWH's original word to him, Jeroboam's power would have remained intact.

7–10. Ultimately, Jeroboam does not repent (v. 33) and his invitation cannot be construed as such. His motivation behind the invitation is not provided; whether it evidences a desire to receive a blessing or an attempt to cancel the curse is uncertain.

The king's command that the man of God come (*bô'*) to his house (*bayit*) for food and a gift elicits a response mirroring the king's vocabulary. Not for half the king's house (*bayit*) will the man of God go (*bô'*) to eat bread or drink water in 'this place' (*bammāqôm hazzeh*). Protesting against associating with the king in the place of the alternative cult, the man of God justifies his refusal by paraphrasing YHWH's command – the key component of the passage. The paraphrase notes YHWH's prohibition is commanded (*ṣiwwāh*) but does not repeat that command with the imperative forms that would be expected – this is left for the Bethel prophet's account of YHWH's word (v. 22). The missing imperatives suggest that even in this opening encounter the man of God softens YHWH's word.

The man of God departs in obedience: YHWH's command was that he not return (*šwb*) by the way (*baderek*) he came. The man of God leaves by another way (*bĕderek*) and does not return (*šwb*) by the way (*baderek*) he had come.

13:11–32

11–19. The 'prophet' (also the 'old prophet' vv. 11, 18, 20, 23, 25–26, 29 [twice]) is introduced as one who dwells in Bethel. After his deception, he is the prophet 'who brought him back' (vv. 20, 23, 26). The change of identification coincides with the core encounter of the second part of the narrative (vv. 11–32). The prophet affects the man of God's disobedience to YHWH's word, and his identity is tied to that crucial theme.

Bethel is a long-time Yahwistic cult site. Despite Jeroboam's recent innovations there (and the uncertainty about which god his cult honours, see 'Comment' at 1 Kgs 12:25–33), there is no a priori reason for the prophet not being Yahwistic. No differentiation exists between the terms 'man of God' and 'prophet' by which to determine legitimacy or allegiance (see 'Comment' at 13:1–3). The prophet, like the man of God, speaks a word of YHWH.

The prophet's son (see 'Notes on the text') relates the activities of the man of God (vv. 11–12) and the prophet sets out to meet him, effecting a very clever deception. He first identifies with the man of God in prophetic experience. If the man of God knows the veracity of YHWH's word to him, can he doubt YHWH's word to the prophet? Secondly, he attests that an angel (*mal'āk*), a legitimate messenger in the DH (Mead 1999: 200), has spoken 'by the word of YHWH'. Thirdly, he uses the vocabulary of eating bread, echoing (but transforming) YHWH's commandment (vv. 9, 15–17). The narrator reveals the deception so the audience immediately knows the man of God faces an invitation to disobedience, which is the point of the whole narrative. More, the text broaches no exploration of the motivation for the deception; the issue is simply beside the narrative point. Obedience to YHWH's word is paramount, regardless of alternative versions others offer. The man of God should commit to obey what he has heard from YHWH.

The man of God's response when compared to his response to Jeroboam (vv. 8–9, 16–17) takes up the same vocabulary regarding not returning (*šwb*), eating (*'kl*) or drinking (*šth*). But he significantly softens YHWH's word. When he recounts YHWH's command (v. 17), he remembers it not as commanded (*ṣiwwāh*) him (v. 9), but only spoken to him (v. 17). The weakening makes the man of God fruitful ground for deception. Having downgraded YHWH's command simply to a word spoken to him, he turns back, eats and drinks.

20–25a. Encircled by two accounts in which the prophet journeys to find the man of God (vv. 11–18b, 25b–32), this passage is the crux of the tale of the prophet and the man of God. In the very act of eating and drinking, the prophet delivers an authentic oracle. As the man of God cried out (*qr'*; v. 2) against the altar, now the prophet cries out (*qr'*), against the man of God, using the typical prophetic formula 'Thus says YHWH'.

The judgment of death and non-burial is pronounced for one reason only: disobedience against YHWH's commandment (*miṣwâ*; v. 21). As the man of God related (v. 9), and the prophet now affirms (v. 21), the commandment (*miṣwâ*) was commanded (*ṣiwwāh*; the root is the same). The prophet emphasizes this by using an imperatival form, indicating YHWH's commands 'Do not eat bread!' and 'Do not drink water!' (v. 22) have been violated. For this, the man of God is summarily judged. Within the space of two verses he is given the prophet's donkey, sent on his way and killed by the lion. Ironically, the man of God who three times indicated he must not return 'by the way' he had come (*baderek*; vv. 9–10) is now found 'on the way' (*baderek*; v. 24) and his corpse is cast 'on the road' (*baderek*; v. 24) so that all who pass by see it cast 'on the road' (*baderek*; v. 25).

25b–32. The narrative denouement provides commentary on the fulfilment of the prophetic word. The prophet hears of the corpse on the road and is so certain of YHWH's judgment he immediately identifies the corpse, interpreting the events as fulfilment of YHWH's word against the rebellious man of God. Mirroring his first journey to find the man of God, the prophet sets out. He finds the man of God, who ate, killed by a lion who – against nature – has not eaten. The lion is an illustration of what the prophet should have done

Returning the man of God to his own grave in Bethel, the prophet honours the man of God by creatively fulfilling the prophecy (v. 22). The man of God *is* buried, but not in his father's tomb (v. 22). The prophet then raises lament over the body. He affirms he truly spoke YHWH's word against the altar, now expanding upon that word to include every shrine on the high places in all the cities of Samaria. The request for joint interment is in acknowledgment that the man of God delivered YHWH's true word. So the prophet honours what was obedient in the man of God.

13:33–34

The prophet's reference to the altar in Bethel (v. 32) returns the narrative to its opening scene. Jeroboam, 'after these things' – both the things experienced by him in Bethel and those witnessed in the intervening narrative – does not change his mind. The man of God did not return (*šwb*) as instructed but was turned back (*šwb*) by the prophet, and now Jeroboam does not turn (*šwb*) from his evil way (v. 33). Jeroboam continues to transgress the deuteronomic law of worship as he did in 12:26–33. His disobedience will be judged as was the man of God's, but in Jeroboam's sin is the destruction of his household.

Explanation

This chapter brings to the forefront the ineluctable nature of YHWH's word, demonstrating it through a paradigm of prophecy and fulfilment. The judgment against Jeroboam's altar works in tandem with the narrative of the man of God and the Bethel prophet, and the core of each narrative (vv. 1–10, 20–25) brings a prophetic word that is subsequently fulfilled.

In the first, the prophecy against the altar is slated for fulfilment by Josiah, three hundred years later. The prediction is astounding, both in naming the king and in placing the fulfilment in the distant future. To provide supportive validation, the prophet announces one sign and performs another. The fulfilment of both enables confidence that the word against the altar has similar power of fulfilment.

The second part of the narrative further validates the certainty of the word against Jeroboam's altar. It similarly issues a prophetic word that is fulfilled, although with a gracious mitigation in the honour accorded the man of God and the prophet's wish for shared interment – more of this mitigation later. The prophetic judgment is enacted against the man of God solely for his disobedience, and the narrative takes care to emphasize the issue of obedience at every step. The judgment for his disobedience suggests that the judgment against the altar, though long years away, will likewise occur.

The prophecy against Jeroboam's altar falls at the beginning of the divided kingdoms; its fulfilment comes almost at the end of the monarchic period (2 Kgs 23:15–18). Thus the history is bounded by a schema of prophecy and fulfilment, inscribing upon the narrative a theology of history in which YHWH's word guides history and has power of inevitable fulfilment.

So fundamental is this theology to the monarchic history that its schema is easily traced, as von Rad demonstrated in his programmatic essay (1953: 74–92). Thus repeated notices of the fulfilment of the prophetic word are found in Kings, as shown in the table below.

Prophetic Word	Fulfilment
2 Sam. 7:13	1 Kgs 8:20
1 Kgs 11:29–39	1 Kgs 12:15b

Prophetic Word	Fulfilment
1 Kgs 14:6–16	1 Kgs 15:29
1 Kgs 16:1–7	1 Kgs 16:12
Josh. 6:26	1 Kgs 16:34
1 Kgs 22:17	1 Kgs 22:35–36
1 Kgs 21:21–26	1 Kgs 21:27–29; 2 Kgs 9 – 10
2 Kgs 1:6	2 Kgs 1:17
2 Kgs 21:10–15	2 Kgs 24:2
2 Kgs 22:18–20	2 Kgs 23:30

Of course, the power of YHWH's word to effect its fulfilment is not limited to a theological exposition in the DH but extends throughout the canon of Scripture. From the fulfilment of YHWH's word 'Let there be light' through to Isaiah's repeated assurances of YHWH's powerful word (Isa. 44:24–26; 46:8–10; 48:3; 55:11), Scripture upholds YHWH's word as effecting what it proclaims. For an exilic nation contemplating the negative history of kingship and the national fate of exile, such a theology reassures. YHWH has fulfilled the judgments against Jeroboam – and now against Solomon – but he will as surely fulfil the promises given David of an everlasting dynasty. The exile, then, is not the last word.

There is another way in which the narrative of the man of God and the prophet brings the theology of YHWH's word to bear upon an exilic people. Fruitful discussion traces the interactions of YHWH's spokesmen as analogues to the nations Israel and Judah within 1 – 2 Kings (see Barth 1957: 393–409; Lemke 1976; Walsh 1989: 367–368; Bosworth 2002). Each spokesman mirrors his kingdom in his actions and the narrative outcomes. Thus unfaithful Israel initially receives a witness from faithful Judah, warning of YHWH's judgment against disobedience. Yet Judah is not safeguarded from Israel's error: should they, too, walk in disobedience they will receive a like judgment. Like the man of God from Judah, the southern kingdom is 'buried' in a foreign land. And, as the prophet from Bethel experienced (2 Kgs 23:17–18), only those northern Israelites who geographically identify with Judah and are thus taken with them to burial in their Babylonian exile will be saved.

YHWH's word through his servants – the man of God to Jeroboam, and the prophet to the man of God – is true. Disobedience to torah (particularly in its expression of worship practices) by individuals (Jeroboam) and nations (Israel and Judah) is met with judgment. YHWH will be true to his word, destroying the works of the false cult, bringing dynasties to naught and casting nations into exile (1 Kgs 9:6–9; 11:38; 13:2; 14:10–16). But, in the place of death, YHWH will also remain true to mitigate his judgment in remembrance of the faithful promises given David.

1 KINGS 14:1–31

Translation

¹ªAt that time Abijah son of Jeroboam sickened. ²Jeroboam said to his wife, 'Arise, and disguise yourself so that they will not know you are the wife of Jeroboam. Go to Shiloh; behold, Ahijahª the prophet is there. He spoke concerning me that I would reignᵇ over this people. ³Take in your hand ten loaves of bread, and cakes, and a jar of honey and go to him. He will tell you what will happen to the boy.' ⁴So Jeroboam's wife did so. She arose, and went to Shiloh and came to Ahijah's house.

Now Ahijah could not see, for his eyes were dim due to his age, ⁵so YHWH said to Ahijah, 'Behold, the wife of Jeroboam is coming to seek a word from you concerningª her son, for he is sick. Thus and so you shall say to her. It will be that when she arrives she will be unrecognizable.' ⁶And so it was, when Ahijah heard the sound of her feet entering at the door, he said, 'Come in, wife of Jeroboam! Why then do you pretend to be another woman? – for I am sent to you with a hard *word*. ⁷Go, say to Jeroboam, "Thus says YHWH, the God of Israel, 'Because I raised you up from the midst of the people, and made you ruler over my people Israel, ⁸and tore the kingdom from the house of David and gave it to you; but you have not been like my servant David who observed my command-ments, and who walked after me with all his heart, doing only what was right in my eyes, ⁹but have done more evil than all who were before you, and have gone and made for yourself other gods and molten images, provoking me to anger, and have cast me behind your back; ¹⁰therefore, behold, I am bringing calamity uponª the house of Jeroboam and I will cut off from Jeroboam those who urinate against the wall, restricted and abandoned, and I will burn up the lastᵇ of the house of Jeroboam as one burns dung until it is gone. ¹¹The one belonging to Jeroboam who dies in the city the dogs will eat, and the one who dies in the field the birds of the heavens will eat,'" for YHWH has spoken!

¹²'Now you, arise; go to your house. When your feet enterª the city, the child will die. ¹³All Israel will lament for him, and will bury him, for this one alone of Jeroboam's *house* will come to a grave because in him has been found in the house of Jeroboam something pleasing to YHWH the God of Israel. ¹⁴YHWH will raise up for himself a king over Israel who will cut off the house of Jeroboam.

'This todayª – then what indeed is next? ¹⁵YHWH will strike Israel just as a reed is shakenª in the water, and he will uproot Israel from this good land that he gave to their fathers. And he will scatter them beyond the river *Euphrates* because they have made their sacred poles, provoking YHWH to anger. ¹⁶And he will give up Israel because of Jeroboam's sins that he committed, and that he caused Israel to sin.'

¹⁷Then the wife of Jeroboam arose and departed, and came to Tirzah. She was entering the door of the house when the boy died. ¹⁸All Israel buried him and lamented for him according to the word of YHWH that he had spoken by the hand of his servant Ahijah the prophet.

[19]Now the rest of the acts of Jeroboam, how he waged war and how he ruled – behold, they are written in the Book of the Chronicles of the Kings of Israel. [20]The time that Jeroboam reigned was twenty-two years; he slept with his fathers and Nadab his son reigned in his place.

[21]Now Rehoboam son of Solomon reigned in Judah. Rehoboam was forty-one[a] years old when he became king and he reigned seventeen[a] years in Jerusalem, the city that YHWH had chosen from all the tribes of Israel to set his name there. His mother's name was Naamah the Ammonitess. [22]Judah[a] did evil in the eyes of YHWH and they provoked him to jealousy more than their fathers had done with their sins that they committed. [23]They also built for themselves high places, and pillars, and sacred poles upon every high hill and under every leafy tree, [24]and there were also male cult personnel[a] in the land. They practised all the abominations of the nations that YHWH had dispossessed from before the sons of Israel.

[25]In the fifth year of King Rehoboam, Shishak[a] king of Egypt came up against Jerusalem. [26]He seized the treasures of YHWH's house, and the treasures of the king's house; he seized everything – he even seized the gold shields that Solomon had made. [27]So King Rehoboam made replacement shields of bronze, and committed them into the hand of the commanders of the guard who kept the doorway of the king's house. [28]As often as the king entered YHWH's house, the guards took them up, then returned them to the chamber of the guards.

[29]Now the rest of the acts of Rehoboam and all he did, are they not written in the Book of the Chronicles of the Kings of Judah? [30]And there was war between Rehoboam and Jeroboam continually. [31]Then Rehoboam slept with his fathers and was buried with his fathers in the city of David. And the name of his mother was Naamah the Ammonitess. And Abijam his son reigned in his place.

Notes on the text

1.a.–20. Verses are omitted from LXX*; a variation of the MT is found at 12:24g–n. Hexaplaric texts preserve yet another variant.

2.a. Variant spelling of 'Ahijah' (vv. 2–4a, cf. ch. 11 as *'ăhiyyah*; vv. 4b–18 as *'ăhiyyāhû*). Possibly representing variant traditions, or narrative linguistic variance.

2.b. MT *lĕmele*, 'for a king', is read for sense with LXX[O], Syr, Tg and Vg, *limlō*, 'to reign'.

5.a. Reading *'al*, 'concerning', for MT *'el*, 'to'.

10.a. Reading *'al*, 'upon', for MT *'el*, 'to'.

10.b. *'aḥărê* taken not as a prep. but subst., meaning, 'back, end'; here, 'last' (Gray 1970: 335; Montgomery 1951: 272).

12.a. Reading *bĕbō'â* as the inf. plus prep., *bĕbô'*, 'when [your feet] enter'.

14.a. The final phrase translates a notoriously difficult line in MT for which the versions give little assistance. Masoretic accents suggests *zê hayyōm*, 'this is the day; this today', completes the preceding phrase, and Gray (1970: 335) follows Kittel by emending the text to *bayyōm hahū'*, 'on that day', so that YHWH will 'cut off the house of Jeroboam on that day'. The present translation follows the Masoretic pointing and *HOTTP* 322; cf. DeVries 2003: 176.

15.a. The simile is not transparent: *how* is a shaken reed like Israel struck by YHWH? *BHS* suggests a lacuna, *wĕhitnôdĕdû*, so that Israel is both 'struck' and 'shaken' as a reed is shaken (so Gray 1970: 335; cf. similarly DeVries 2003: 176).

21.a. The years forty-one and seventeen are sixteen and twelve in LXX 12:24a. See the discussion on chronology in the book of Kings in the introduction.

22.a. Various LXX texts read, 'Rehoboam did evil', and may alter the subsequent verb ('they provoked') to 3 m. sg. (so LXX^A), and the pr. suff. ('their fathers') to 3 m. sg. (so LXX^B); cf. 2 Chr. 12:14 in which Rehoboam is implied. Rehoboam may have been an original reading, but vv. 23–24 are concerned with the state of Judah, so v. 22 is read similarly. That the pattern of regnal formulae indicates the king did evil or good suggests that 'Judah', as *lectio difficilior*, should stand.

24.a. The inarticulate singular *qādēš* here as a collective, although the term, with the article, is also used collectively at 1 Kgs 22:47. The collective may include male and female individuals (so DeVries 2003: 185; Provan 1995: 122), although the appearance of *qādēš* with *qĕdēšâ* in Deut. 23:18 [17] argues against this.

25.a. 'Shishak', according to Q, and along with Tg, Syr, Vg and K in 11:40.

Form and structure

The Jeroboam narrative climaxes with a prophetic word (1 Kgs 14:1–20). Then the history refocuses on the southern kingdom (14:21–31). Narrative alternation between the kingdoms continues almost without interruption through 1–2 Kings and communicates the importance of both kingdoms to YHWH's purposes.

The chapter is strategically linked to Jeroboam's earlier narrative. First, in chs. 11 and 14, Ahijah prophesies regarding Jeroboam's dynasty, utilizing similar phraseology. Secondly, the narrative connects parabolically to 1 Kgs 13, for both the man of God and Jeroboam are judged for disobedience; in each account burial and lament signify the authenticity of the prophetic word (13:29–30; 14:18). Thirdly, chs. 11–14 reveal an escalation in sinfulness, moving from implicit possibility (11:38) to a reality instituted by Jeroboam, which the people pursue (12:30). Jeroboam adds further malfeasance (12:31–33) and refuses repentance (13:34). His sins become greater than any before him (14:9), causing YHWH to destroy Jeroboam's house and cast Israel aside (14:10–11, 15–16).

A narrative framework (14:1–6, 17–18) encloses the oracle. The frame focuses on the life of Jeroboam's child, while the oracle focuses on the dynasty. The dual focus need not flag variant traditions but reveals narrative progression, for it is the child who represents dynastic succession. His fate provides a natural segue into dynastic concerns.

The oracular word is in typical prophetic style. Judgment oracles first provide reasons for YHWH's judgment (introduced by *ya'an 'ǎšer*, 'because'; vv. 7, 15; *ya'an* alone in v. 13) before announcing YHWH's action (introduced by *lākēn*, 'therefore'; v. 10). This pattern is followed in the first prophetic word (vv. 7–11); the second (vv. 13–16) reverses the elements (Gowan 1971: 172–174).

A closing regnal summary (vv. 19–20; cf. vv. 29–31) follows the narrative's conclusion. The summary provides specific information in a format followed for most subsequent monarchs. Sources such as the books of the Chronicles of the Kings of Israel and Judah are cited, from which selective enumeration of the 'rest of the acts' of the king is made. Much more could be said and the selection is constrained by the author's theological interests. The Chronicles were perhaps archival and available directly or via intervening sources to Dtr (Haran 1999). A notice of death and burial is included together with a notice of succession.

Rehoboam's reign begins with a regnal introduction (vv. 21–24) and almost without exception successive reigns are bracketed by opening and closing summaries (Campbell 1986: 139–202; B. Long 1985: 159–164). Specific information is included in opening summaries, although the pattern varies for northern and southern monarchs. First, the king's accession date is provided, synchronized to his northern or southern counterpart. Secondly, the kings' age at accession is provided for southern monarchs (with the exception of Abijam [1 Kgs 15:1–2] and Asa [1 Kgs 15:9–10]). For both kingdoms the length and place of reign is then provided. Then the name of the queen mother is cited for southern kings (with the exception of Jehoram [2 Kgs 8:16–17] and Ahaz [2 Kgs 16:1–4]). For both kingdoms a theological appraisal concludes the introductory summary, evaluating the king's worship practices. Kings are often compared to preceding kings: southern kings to David, and northern kings to Jeroboam.

Rehoboam's reign (vv. 21–31) has a tripartite structure. Its introductory and closing regnal summaries vary the typical pattern (see 'Comment'). These surround a notation of Pharaoh Shishak's incursion against Palestine and Jerusalem, which, in context, appears as punishment for Rehoboam's doing 'evil in the eyes of YHWH'.

Comment

14:1–4a

The temporal marker 'at that time' ties the judgment of ch. 14 closely to Jeroboam's perseverance in disobedience (13:33–34); YHWH's commandments cannot be mocked long. Ahijah's age and blindness (v. 4) suggest some years have passed since he last appeared (ch. 11).

Sickness precipitates enquiry of the prophet (1 Kgs 17:17–24; 2 Kgs 1:2–4; 5:1–19; 8:7–15; 20:1–11), and the expression of thankfulness through gifts (1 Sam. 9:6–10; 2 Kgs 5:15, 22–23; 8:8). Ahijah calls Abijah a 'child' (*yeled*; v. 12), a term applied to both infants and toddlers (Gen. 21:8; Exod. 2:3; Ruth 4:16; 1 Kgs 3:25) and also older children and grown men (Ruth 1:5; 2 Kgs 4:18). Jeroboam and the narrator refer to Abijah as a 'boy' (*nāʿar*; vv. 3, 17), a more limited term applied to adolescent boys and men (Gen. 22:12; Judg. 8:20; 1 Sam. 20:21; 2 Sam. 18:5). The child's name means 'My father is YHWH', perhaps reflecting Jeroboam's early (and brief) submission to YHWH, or it is an arrogant allusion to Jeroboam's own sense of greatness. Though he will soon die, the narrative poignantly records his name.

Poignant, too, is Jeroboam's wife, who seeks a word of life, but becomes the messenger of death. Never named, her anonymity is upheld through her silence and through Jeroboam's command that she disguise herself (*šnh*). Fearing the prophet's censure, he hopes to dupe him into providing a favourable oracle. She brings a commoner's gift, but the ten loaves recall the loss of the kingdom bestowed upon Jeroboam with ten pieces of cloak.

Jeroboam commands her to 'Arise (*qwm*) . . . go (*hlk*) . . . go (*bwʾ*)', actions repeated in the narrative. At Jeroboam's command, her feet enter (*bwʾ*) at Ahijah's doorway (v. 6) and the prophetic word is given. Ahijah commands her to 'Arise (*qwm*) . . . go (*hlk*) . . . enter (*bwʾ*) (v. 12). She 'arose (*qwm*) . . . and departed (*hlk*) . . . and came (*bwʾ*) to Tirzah' and, in the act of entering (*bwʾ*) the door of her house, the child dies (v. 17). The message to Jeroboam is clear: YHWH is indeed bringing (*bwʾ*) calamity upon the house of Jeroboam (v. 10).

14:4b–18

4b–11. Like Eli, Ahijah lives in Shiloh and is 'unable to see' due to old age (1 Sam. 3:2; 4:15). Unlike Eli, Ahijah 'sees' because of YHWH's word to him. YHWH provides details, including an appropriate response adumbrated with a typical 'thus and so' (*kāzōh wĕkāzeh*) used to summarize speech or events (Judg. 18:4; 2 Sam. 11:25). Until Ahijah delivers the oracle, a response only to the enquiry regarding the child is anticipated. YHWH also reveals the woman's disguise, highlighting its folly before YHWH's prophet.

Her disguise (like Saul's before her, 1 Sam. 28:8–12) is revealed in the prophet's presence. Ahijah communicates YHWH's judgment, commissioning Jeroboam's wife as messenger. The word against the dynasty encompasses the life of the son and, because of this, Jeroboam's wife is given no opportunity to make her request. Ahijah does provide an answer (vv. 12–13) that serves to work out the prophecy just given (vv. 7–11).

Ahijah gives two commands, 'go (*hlk*) and say', and though the wife remains narratively silent, she is commissioned to speak YHWH's word. The first-person speech of the oracle emphasizes the immediacy of YHWH's presence. The typical 'Thus says YHWH' (occurring thirty-three times in 1 – 2 Kings) identifies YHWH for the first time since the prophetic word to Jeroboam (11:31) as 'the God of Israel' (only eight of the thirty-three prophetic announcements in 1 – 2 Kings contain this addition). Thus at the moment the northern king is judged comes a reminder that YHWH remains king over all Israel, despite the fate of its rulers.

The many reasons for judgment can be categorized according to what YHWH has done for Jeroboam, and how Jeroboam has responded. Often the language of Ahijah's original oracle is utilized. First, YHWH raised up (*rwm*) Jeroboam (cf. 11:26–27, in which Jeroboam's raised [*rwm*] hand introduced him as YHWH's agent against Solomon). Secondly, YHWH made Jeroboam ruler (*nagîd*; v. 7) over Israel, as Solomon was over Judah (1 Kgs 1:35). Thirdly, YHWH tore the kingdom (*wā'eqra' 'et-hammamlākâ*) from David's house (11:35). Finally, YHWH reminds Jeroboam that this choice was for the purpose of giving (*ntn*) the kingdom to him (11:35).

Jeroboam has responded in increasingly heinous ways to YHWH's gracious action. He has not been like YHWH's 'servant David' who observed his commandments, 'walked after me with all his heart' and did 'only what was right in my eyes' (11:32–34). Jeroboam was called to these standards (11:38–39), but failed. He has done 'more evil' and has 'made (*'śh*) other gods'. Jeroboam made 'molten images' (*massēkôt*) and the word 'images' (*massēkôt*) identifies the golden calves (*'eglê zāhāb*) of 1 Kgs 12:28 with Aaron's calf (*'ēgel massēkâ*; Exod. 32:4, 8; cf. 34:17). The violation of the first two commandments (other gods; images) has provoked (*k's*) YHWH's anger. In Deuteronomistic writing YHWH is 'provoked' by idols and the worship of other gods; Jeroboam's sins 'provoke' YHWH (e.g. Deut. 4:25; 9:18; 32:16–21; Judg. 2:21; 1 Kgs 15:30; 16:2, 7, 13, 26; 2 Kgs 21:6; 22:17). Most heinous of all, Jeroboam has cast YHWH behind his back.

For Jeroboam's evil (*r'*; v. 9) YHWH will bring corresponding calamity (*r'h*; v. 10) upon Jeroboam's house, and the son who represents the continuing dynasty will die. Three graphic pictures reveal YHWH's disgust over Jeroboam's evil.

First, though leaders in Israel, the men of Jeroboam's house will be destroyed. The collocation rendered as 'those who urinate against the wall (*maśtîn beqîr*), restricted and abandoned (*'āṣûr we'āzûb*) in Israel' is notoriously difficult to translate. *maśtîn beqîr* appears with *'āṣûr we'āzûb* in 1 Kgs 21:21 and 2 Kgs 9:8, and on its own in 1 Sam. 25:22, 34 and 1 Kgs 16:11. *'āṣûr we'āzûb* also appears in Deut. 32:36 and in a slightly different form in 2 Kgs 14:26. The derogatory 'urinaters against the wall' accords with the reference to Jeroboam's house as 'dung'. The phrase *'āṣûr we'āzûb* is a synonymous and proverbial description of universality: all of Jeroboam's house will be cut off (Saydon 1952; see also Kutsch 1952; Cogan 1988: 107; Talmon and Fields 1989).

The scatology is extended in a second picture: Jeroboam's house is completely burned as unclean dung (Ezek. 4:9–15). Finally, graphic imagery of non-burial and mutilation expresses a common ANE fear (*ANET* 538; Cogan and Tadmor 1988: 107; cf. Hillers 1964: 68). Literally fulfilled in the case of Jezebel (2 Kgs 9:34–37), it expresses utter disdain for Jeroboam's house. Successive houses are similarly derogated for continuing Jeroboam's sins (1 Kgs 16:4; 21:22–23).

12–18. Concerning Abijah's fate, Jeroboam's wife is commissioned to 'arise . . . go . . . enter'. Tragically, should she obey, her child will die. To Abijah's judgment is added a mitigation similar to that granted the man of God (1 Kgs 13). In only these narratives in 1 – 2 Kings is one lamented (*spd*; 13:29–30; 14:13, 18) and buried (*qbr*; 13:29, 31; 14:13, 18). The mitigation in Abijah's case is due to 'something pleasing' in him – whether a recognition of the innocence of youth, or his conscious attention to YHWH's will cannot be ascertained (Wray Beal 2012).

A distant future deportation as the final judgment on Jeroboam's sins is envisioned. It brings amazement and consternation at the dire events (v. 14b). The phrase may be Ahijah's own interjection, or possibly a scribal note erroneously incorporated into the text. Israel's end will be a violent uprooting as a reed from 'good land' – here, land given by YHWH.

A new reason for the uprooting is introduced: the asherah or sacred pole, that is, the wooden cult symbol or representation of the mother goddess Asherah, consort of El. In popular Israelite religion Asherah was possibly considered as YHWH's consort (Day, *ABD* 1:483–487; de Moor 1977; Wyatt, *DDD* 99–105). The wooden poles were 'made' (1 Kgs 14:15; 16:33; 2 Kgs 17:16; 21:3, 7) and 'planted' (Deut 16:21) as symbolic trees. Specifically prohibited (Deut. 7:5; 12:3; 16:21), the prohibition was constantly disregarded in 1 – 2 Kings, as attested by the sixteen references to Asherah or her cult symbol found there. The people, not Jeroboam, are charged with making sacred poles. Here (as in 2 Kgs 17:7–23), Jeroboam sins, the people follow, and both are responsible for Israel's demise.

The narrator notes the child's death, and lamentation affirms Ahijah's word. The affirmation anticipates the full execution of all Ahijah has spoken.

14:19–20

The usual material comprises the closing regnal summary (see 'Form and structure') with an additional notice of the length of Jeroboam's reign. Usually included in the opening summary, it is appended here because

Jeroboam's reign began in the midst of a narrative that provided no opportunity for an opening summary (cf. similarly at 1 Kgs 2:11; 11:42; 2 Kgs
10:36).

14:21–31

21–24. Jeroboam's reign is juxtaposed to Rehoboam's, which began before
the kingdom split (see 1 Kgs 12). For this reason, no synchronization to
Jeroboam's reign is included (see 'Form and structure'). Rehoboam's age
indicates he was born before Solomon's accession (11:42); his mother was
one of Solomon's foreign wives. YHWH's relationship to Jerusalem (Deut.
12:5, 11, 18, 21, 26; 1 Kgs 8:16, 44; 11:13, 31) is a reminder that his commitment does not change, regardless of the actions of Jerusalem's king
and people.

Judah does evil and provokes YHWH, as had Israel (v. 9). Rehoboam's
later indictment (15:3) suggests his participation. Judah's sins (vv. 22–24)
account for the double mention of the foreign Naaman (vv. 21, 31). It is
Solomon's error in marrying foreign women that bears this fruit in his son
and the nation.

Judah continues to build high places. Associated with foreign worship
practices after the temple's completion (11:7–8; 12:13–31; 2 Kgs 17:9–12;
21:3), kings who do not remove them receive limited approval (1 Kgs 15:14;
22:44; 2 Kgs 12:3; 14:4; 15:4, 35; 16:4). Judah also built pillars (*maṣṣēbōt*)
as cult symbols of the storm and fertility god Baal (Day, *ABD* 1:545–549;
Herrmann 1999), and sacred poles (see 'Comment', v. 15), both of which
are proscribed in the deuteronomic code (Deut. 7:5; 12:3; 16:21–22).

Baal posed a threat to godly worship before entry to the land (Num.
25:1–9). The threat intensified during the monarchy, particularly under
Ahab (1 Kgs 16:31–33) and Manasseh (2 Kgs 21:3). Asherah and Baal were
often paired (Judg. 3:7; 6:25–32; 1 Kgs 16:32–33; 18:19; 2 Kgs 17:16; 21:3)
and were worshipped alongside YHWH. Baal may have syncretized with
YHWH, and Asherah may have been considered his consort (Day, *ABD*
1:548). Worship sites were located 'upon every high hill and under every
leafy tree' (2 Kgs 17:10; Jer. 2:20; cf. 2 Kgs 16:4; Jer. 3:6, 13; Hos. 4:13)
and were especially associated with Asherah. At these cult sites fertility
rites occurred (Ackerman 1992: 152–163).

Judah also appointed non-sanctioned cult personnel (*qādēš*). The term is
rare in the OT (sg. forms at Deut. 23:17; 1 Kgs 14:24; 22:46; pl. forms at 1 Kgs
15:12; 2 Kgs 23:7; Job 36:14). Long-held belief that these personnel were
cultic prostitutes has been largely set aside. Sexual practices may have been
part of ancient (and non-sanctioned Israelite) religion, but not prostitution
conducted under the auspices of the cult. In Ugaritic texts *qdšm* appear as
'a type of male cult personnel associated with priestly functions' (Kelle: 2005:
129; cf. Fisher 1976; Westenholz 1989; van der Toorn 1992; Bird 1995; Kelle

2005: 123–137). It is not primarily their sexual role, but their function within a non-Yahwistic or syncretized cult, that most alarms the Dtr.

Judah's provocations have escalated beyond that of their fathers (v. 22), and they even go beyond all previous generations by participating in the abominations of the nations (v. 24). These abominations reappear in 1 – 2 Kings and include but are not limited to the non-sanctioned worship practices and personnel enumerated here. At all times, however, the abominations are considered the greatest affront to YHWH that can be committed (2 Kgs 16:3; 21:2–11; 23:13; cf. Deut. 18:9–12; 27:15; 32:16). The gravity of these sins when practised by the nations resulted in their expulsion from the land. One must wonder whether the same fate awaits Judah.

25–28. The narrative contextualizes Shishak's campaign as a direct result of the actions in vv. 22–24. As in the time of the judges, foreign oppression communicates divine punishment (Mullen 1992: 235). It is a fine mark of irony that the instrument of YHWH's judgment strips YHWH's temple. Jerusalem's wealth is stripped, too, although the 'everything' is hyperbole, for enough remains to craft replacement shields. Their use is restricted to temple processions as a mark of their value in impoverished Jerusalem.

Shishak, the founder of Egypt's XXII dynasty, advanced into Palestine in 926/925 BC, Rehoboam's fifth year (DeVries, *IDB* 1:587). The invasion has extra-biblical attestation that notes 154 towns razed in Palestine (excluding Jerusalem) (*ANET* 242–243). Shishak moved north from the Negeb, traversed the coastal plain and moved inland from Gaza towards Gibeon. Rehoboam's tribute left Jerusalem otherwise unscathed as Shishak proceeded north towards Megiddo, returning via the Via Maris to Egypt. Shishak pursued political and economic aspirations against the unstable new states of Judah and Israel as he sought to expand his own territories and acquire control over lucrative east–west and Red Sea trade routes (Mazar 1957; Kitchen 1986; Malamat 1982: 203–204; Redford, *ABD* 5:1221–1222; Marx 1999).

29–31. Rehoboam's closing regnal summary is typical (see 'Form and structure'), except for the mention of his mother (see v. 21 above). A note regarding continuing warfare with Israel reveals the prophetic word (12:22–24) limited, but did not exclude, ongoing hostilities.

Explanation

The prophetic word against Jeroboam's house reveals God's righteous judgment upon sin. In the long years until that judgment's fulfilment in exile is also seen God's grace.

For violating the strictures of YHWH's initial word (11:38–39) Jeroboam voids the dynastic promise. Surprisingly, judgment is extended to all of Israel, and looks to the distant future (vv. 15–16). Thus in this chapter is the full programme for Israel's history. Jeroboam's dynasty ends –

proleptically in the death of Abijah and finally in the overthrow of Nadab (15:25–31). Every successive dynasty, however, participates in Jeroboam's sins and comes under similar judgment (16:1–4, 7; 21:20–29; 2 Kgs 9:7–10). With two exceptions (Shallum, 2 Kgs 15:13; Hoshea, 2 Kgs 17:2) every northern king explicitly (or implicitly; see Elah, 1 Kgs 16:13) walks in Jeroboam's sins. The indictment of Jeroboam's sins in 2 Kgs 17:16, 21–23 is long anticipated; the northern kingdom's conclusion fulfils what YHWH promised, revealing his unswerving abhorrence of sin.

The justness of Abijah's death might be difficult for a modern audience to comprehend. Upon him is visited the father's sins (Exod. 34:7) and his death is a clear message the dynasty will end. But his death provides some mitigation in the face of YHWH's judgment (see 'Comment' above). He alone of all Jeroboam's house is honoured in death.

The mitigation granted Abijah is a window through which YHWH's mercy shines. That window continues open as the history progresses, for, having given his word against the nation, YHWH does not abandon his covenant people. Instead, in mercy he continually urges them back to covenant life. YHWH's desire for Israel's repentance is profoundly expressed through the prophets.

Elijah and Elisha demonstrate YHWH's ongoing covenant commitment. At a time when the Omrides have added Baal worship to Jeroboam's sins (1 Kgs 16:31–33), God seeks to draw Israel away from Baal and back to himself. Their ministries are characterized by a concern for life for God's people (e.g. 2 Kgs 4, 6), and even for the foreigner to whom Israel was to be a blessing (e.g. the Sidonian window, 1 Kgs 17; Naaman, 2 Kgs 5). Elijah and Elisha repeatedly provide the means of life and even life itself, care for the oppressed, and mediate the covenant.

In the canonical prophets, too, YHWH reveals his unwillingness to abandon Israel. Hosea and Amos address early eighth-century Israel during the rule of Jeroboam II. Though Jeroboam's great-grandfather had eliminated Baal worship in Israel (2 Kgs 10:28), by Jeroboam's time it has resurfaced (Hos. 2:13, 17). Additionally, Jeroboam II continues to lead Israel in the way of his namesake (2 Kgs 14:24). Yet, despite this downward spiral, YHWH calls his people to repentance (Hos. 2:7, 14–15; 14:1–3; Amos 5:4–6, 14–15). His compassion is raw (Hos. 11:8–11; 13:14), and his commitment to covenant envisions a future of restoration and blessing (Hos. 14:4–8; Amos 9:11–15). Despite the word given Jeroboam I of Israel's demise, YHWH's grace continues to seek after his people.

A similar phenomenon of grace in the midst of judgment appears in Judah's history, too. The judgment against Jeroboam includes exile from the land (14:15–16) and echoes the judgment promised Solomon (9:6–9). Judah's sins under Rehoboam (vv. 22–23) include sins for which Jeroboam and Israel are indicted (vv. 9, 15). By making these close comparisons, the narrative uses the judgment levelled against Israel as a reminder of the judgment promised Judah. The prophetic judgment against Jeroboam also warns Judah to heed YHWH or experience a fate similar to Israel's (cf. 1 Kgs 6:11–13; 9:6–9).

In 1 – 2 Kings no other prophetic warning is delivered to Judah from Solomon to the fall of the northern kingdom. Instead, the word to Jeroboam, and Israel's fate, serves as that warning. In the same way, the peroration on the fall of the northern kingdom serves as a warning to Judah (see 'Comment', 2 Kgs 17).

Judah is graced several ways and their life in the land endures longer than does Israel's. They have YHWH's commitment to the Davidic covenant (1 Kgs 15:4; 2 Kgs 8:19). They have righteous kings who impede Judah's descent into sin. The canonical prophets attest that Judah too is repeatedly urged back to covenant life. They also have the experience of Israel. It was lived out before them and warned them, if they would heed it.

The warnings and judgments experienced by Israel and Judah are now part of the canonical record. For people under the New Covenant, upon whom the 'ends of the age have come' (1 Cor. 10:11), the witness of the OT still speaks, warning those who would heed it. YHWH's judgment has now fallen upon Christ, but the people of the New Covenant are still called to covenant obedience and may still face discipline. The law of the Spirit remains an imperative as was the law for Israel and Judah: 'if you love me, you will keep my commandments' (John 14:23; 15:1–4). YHWH still works by grace, calling his people – by community experience and history, by Scripture, by the Spirit – to walk in the covenant.

1 KINGS 15:1–32

Translation

¹In the eighteenth year of King[a] Jeroboam son of Nebat, Abijam began to reign over Judah. ²Three years he reigned in Jerusalem and his mother's name was Maacah the daughter of Abishalom. ³He walked in all the sins of his father that he committed before him, and his heart was not wholly devoted to YHWH his God like the heart of David his father. ⁴Nevertheless, for David's sake YHWH his God gave him a lamp in Jerusalem, setting up his son after him, and establishing Jerusalem ⁵because David did what was right in YHWH's eyes and did not turn aside from all that he commanded him all the days of his life, except in the matter of Uriah the Hittite.

⁶Now there had been war between Rehoboam and Jeroboam all the days of his life. ⁷The rest of the acts of Abijam and all which he did, are they not written in the Book of the Chronicles of the Kings of Judah? And there was war between Abijam and Jeroboam. ⁸Abijam slept with his fathers[a] and they buried him in the city of David. And Asa his son reigned in his place.

⁹In the twentieth[a] year of Jeroboam king of Israel, Asa king of Judah began to reign. ¹⁰He reigned forty-one years in Jerusalem, and his grandmother's[a] name

was Maacah daughter of Abishalom. [11]Asa did what was right in the eyes of YHWH, like David his father. [12]He put away the male cult personnel from the land and he removed all the idols that his fathers had made. [13]Even Maacah his grandmother[a] – he removed her as queen mother because she had made an abominable image for Asherah[b]. Asa cut down her horrid image and burned it in the Kidron Valley. [14]But they did not remove[a] the high places. Nevertheless, Asa's heart was wholly devoted to YHWH all his days. [15]He brought his father's dedicated items[a], and his own, *into* YHWH's house: silver, and gold, and utensils.

[16]And there was war between Asa and Baasha king of Israel all their days. [17]Baasha king of Israel went up against Judah and built Ramah to prevent anyone coming or going to Asa king of Judah. [18]Asa took all the silver and gold that remained in the treasuries of YHWH's house and the treasuries of the king's house and gave it[a] into the hand of his servants. King Asa sent them to Ben-hadad the son of Tabrimmon, son of Hezion king of Aram, who dwelt in Damascus, saying, [19]*Let there be*[a] a treaty between me and you, *as* there was between my father and your father. Behold! I have sent to you a gift of silver and gold. Go, break your treaty with Baasha king of Israel, that he may withdraw from me.' [20]Now Ben-hadad listened to King Asa and sent the commanders of his armies against the cities of Israel. He struck Ijon, and Dan, and Abel-beth-maacah, and all Kinneroth, besides[a] all the land of Naphtali. [21]When Baasha heard of it, he stopped building Ramah and stayed in Tirzah. [22]King Asa made a proclamation in all Judah – none was exempt – and they took up the stones of Ramah and its timber with which Baasha had been building. With them King Asa built Geba of Benjamin, and Mizpah.

[23]Now the rest of all the acts of Asa, and all his power, and all that he did, and the cities that he built, are they not written in the Book of the Chronicles of the Kings of Judah? However, in his old age he was diseased in his feet[a]. [24]And Asa slept with his fathers and was buried with his fathers in the city of his father David, and Jehoshaphat his son reigned in his place.

[25]Nadab the son of Jeroboam began to reign over Israel in the second year of Asa king of Judah. He reigned over Israel two years [26]and did what was evil in the eyes of YHWH. He walked in the way of his father and in his sin that he caused Israel to sin. [27]Baasha son of Ahijah, of the house of Issachar, conspired against him; Baasha struck him down at Gibbethon of the Philistines while Nadab and all Israel were laying siege against Gibbethon. [28]So Baasha killed him in the third year of Asa king of Judah and reigned in his place. [29]As soon as he became king, he struck all the house of Jeroboam; he did not leave to Jeroboam any that had breath until he had destroyed it according to the word of YHWH, which he had spoken by the hand of his servant Ahijah the Shilonite, [30]on account of the sins of Jeroboam, which he sinned and which he caused Israel to sin, by his provocation[a] with which he provoked YHWH the God of Israel to anger.

[31]The rest of the acts of Nadab and all that he did, are they not written in the Book of the Chronicles of the Kings of Israel? [32]And there was war between Asa and between Baasha king of Israel all their days.

Notes on the text

1.a. MT *lammelek*, 'King X' (as in 2 Kgs 11:10; 12:7; 18:9, 13; 22:3; 23:23; 25:2, 8), puts title before name. All other synchronizations read 'X king of Israel/Judah'. As the first, this unique formulation should stand.

8.a. A LXX insertion at this point notes, 'Abijam slept with his fathers *in the twenty-fourth year of Jeroboam*'. The insertion is suspect as such synchronization is not an element of closing regnal summaries nor does the length of Jeroboam's reign accord with the notice in v. 20.

9.a. LXX reads 'twenty-four years', apparently taking up again the LXX insertion in v. 8.

10.a. Here reading 'mother' as 'grandmother'. See under 'Comment'.

13.a. See n. 10.a above. See further in 'Comment'.

13.b. *mipleṣet lā'ăšērâ* could be rendered either 'an abominable image for Asherah', that is, an image representing Asherah, or 'an abominable image of the asherah', that is, an image of the sacred pole, which itself images Asherah. It borders on the nonsensical to make an image of an image (Ackerman 1993: 389) and the chronicler (2 Chr. 15:16) understood the image was of the goddess, reading *lā'ăšērâ mipleṣet*, 'for Asherah an abominable image' (cf. de Moor 1977: 443; Day, *ABD* 1:485).

14.a. In LXX, Syr and Vg 'they did not remove' reads *hēsîr*, 'he did not remove', thus blaming Asa.

15.a. Reading with K, LXX, Syr, Tg and 2 Chr. 15:18 'his dedicated items' (*qādāšayw*), rather than Q *qādšê*, which piously reads, 'the dedicated items of YHWH's house'.

18.a. The 3 m. pl. reading 'and gave them', grammatically correct in Hebr., is changed for sense to 'and gave it'.

19.a. MT is glossed optatively ('Let there be'; so Jones 1984a: 286; Fritz 2003: 167), rather than indicatively ('There is'; so Gray 1970: 352; DeVries 2003: 191).

20.a. *'al* not *'ad*, 'as far as', as in LXX. *'al* can mean 'in addition to', 'together with' (*HALOT* 826–827:6 b, c).

23.a. LXX^L specifically links Asa's diseased feet to evil-doing ('in his old age Asa did evil and was diseased' . . .). MT more subtly critiques the king (see 'Comment').

30.a. LXX^L, Vg read *běka'sô*, 'by his provocation', with a cop. 'and by his provocation' differentiating the sins from the provocations. The terms refer to the same activity of making idols and worshipping other gods, the content of Jeroboam's sins.

Form and structure

The deaths of Jeroboam (14:20) and Rehoboam (14:31) pass the dual kingdoms to their successors. The narrative now begins a characteristic alternation between northern and southern kingdoms. The alternations are not always strictly chronological (1 Kgs 15; 2 Kgs 11 – 16), and occasionally focus on one kingdom (e.g. much of 1 Kgs 16 – 2 Kgs 10 focuses on the northern kingdom). The reign of several kings may be related in a single chapter (as in 1 Kgs 15) and regnal summaries generally bracket each reign. The repetitious nature of the summaries can be reviewed in 'Form and structure', 1 Kgs 14. Deviations to the pattern are dealt with in the 'Comment' section below.

The narrative treats the reigns of Abijam and Nadab without going into much detail. Treatment of Abijam includes a theological explanation for dynastic continuance despite ongoing sin. Nadab's reign focuses on Baasha, the individual appointed to overturn Jeroboam's dynasty (14:14). Asa's reign reports on warfare with Baasha of Israel even though Baasha's reign is not introduced until later (15:33). He is featured in Asa's reign because his defeat by Asa illustrates YHWH's approval of the southern king.

The conflict between Asa and Baasha is introduced with the notation that 'there was war between Asa and Baasha . . . all their days' (v. 16). Similar notations are found in vv. 6–7 and 32, and suggest excerpts from annalistic sources. They bind the three reigns together thematically, and reveal the presence of conflict during the first fifty years of the divided kingdom.

Comment

15:1–8

Abijam succeeds his father Rehoboam. His name 'My father is Yam' is a reference to the Ugaritic sea god. 2 Chr. 13:1 reads 'Abijah', meaning 'My father is Yah(weh)', an ideologically motivated change. Although Jeroboam was enthroned shortly after Rehoboam, and Rehoboam reigned seventeen years (14:21), Abijam's reign is synchronized to Jeroboam's eighteenth year – at least one year too long. The discrepancy is accounted for by the different systems of dating in the two kingdoms; Jeroboam's eighteenth year is calculated by the accession year system, which counts the first partial year of a reign as one year (see Introduction).

Abijam's mother, Maacah, is the daughter of 'Abishalom' (a variant of 'Absalom'). Absalom, David's son, is not intended, as his daughter was Tamar (2 Sam. 14:27).

The Deuteronomistic indictment of Abijam charges he 'walks' (cf. 1 Kgs 2:3; 6:12; 8:58; 9:4; 11:5) in 'all the sins of his father' (14:9, 22) and is not 'wholly devoted' (1 Kgs 8:61; 11:4; 15:14) as was David before him who 'did what was right in YHWH's eyes'. David did not 'turn aside' (*swr*) from YHWH's commandments and thus showed his commitment to the deuteronomic law (Deut. 17:20). Keeping the commandments is a prominent concern in Kings (1 Kgs 2:3; 3:14; 6:12), reflected particularly in one's attitude towards other gods (9:6).

David serves as a paradigm for southern kings (1 Kgs 11:33, 38; 14:8; 15:11; 22:43; 2 Kgs 10:30; 12:2; 14:3; 15:3, 34; 16:2; 18:3; 22:2). His paradigmatic value is not dependent on a perfect life (cf. Uriah), but one oriented to YHWH's ways, especially regarding worship. YHWH's commitment to David's line does not waiver, despite the failures of Solomon, Rehoboam and Abijam. The dynasty remains as a lamp in Jerusalem (11:34–36).

The military incursions begun by Rehoboam (14:30) continue despite the prophetic word (12:23–24). This struggle for control of the border region characterizes the first years of the two kingdoms.

Abijam's rule ends with an unremarkable summary. The succession of his son confirms YHWH's promise of a continuing lamp in Jerusalem.

15:9–24

9–15. The typical regnal introduction lacks only the king's age at accession. Asa's forty-one-year reign is the second-longest Judean rule (Manasseh's is longer; 2 Kgs 21:1) and spans the rule of seven Israelite kings (excluding Tibni's claim). The unusual mention of Asa's grandmother Maacah suggests her power at court. Exercised during her son's short reign, it continues into Asa's (Montgomery 1951: 274; Spanier 1994: 193; DeVries 2003: 187).

Asa is compared favourably to David, as he 'does right' in YHWH's eyes through his reforming measures. He banishes the non-orthodox cult personnel (*qĕdēšîm*; see 'Comment' at 14:24) and destroys the idols (*gillulîm*), that is, the pillars (*maṣṣēbôt*) or sacred poles (*'ăšērîm*) Rehoboam and Abijam made (14:23; 15:3). The derogatory term *gillulîm* is from the root for 'dung' (*gālāl*) and shows utter contempt for such cultic deviations (Lev. 26:30; Deut. 29:17; 1 Kgs 21:26; 2 Kgs 17:12; 21:21; 23:24). The term's vocalization also follows that of *šiqqûṣ(îm)* – filthy abominable objects created for the cult (1 Kgs 11:5, 7; cf. Deut. 29:17, where both terms stand in parallel). Their destruction by Asa is a word of high approval.

Asa's reform includes his deposition of Maacah from her position as *gĕbîrâ* (great lady). The role of the *gĕbîrâ* is difficult to define, but extra-biblical occurrences suggest a position of respect and honour, and possible political, social and religious influence. The *gĕbîrâ* is probably the most powerful woman at court, although not necessarily the queen mother (Andreasen 1983; Ben-Barak 1991; Ackerman 1993; C. Smith 1998; Bowen 2001). The term occurs only fifteen times in the OT, with three meanings: 'mistress' over a maidservant (Gen. 16:4, 8–9; 2 Kgs 5:3; Isa. 24:2; Ps. 123:2; Prov. 30:23), queen or wife of a king (1 Kgs 11:19; Isa. 47:5, 7), and 'great lady' (some of whom are also queen mothers: 1 Kgs 15:13 [2 Chr. 15:16]; 2 Kgs 10:13; Jer. 13:18; 29:2). 'Great lady' is applied almost exclusively to southern women; only Jezebel (2 Kgs 10:13) is called a 'great lady', but by southern royals.

Maacah is removed for her participation in the Asherah cult. She makes a 'horrid image' (*mipleṣet*) of the goddess, a phrase found only here and in the parallel 2 Chr. 15:16. A related noun from the same root (*plṣ*) describes a reaction of shuddering horror (Isa. 21:4; Ezek. 7:18; Ps. 55:5[6]; Job 21:6); the one verbal occurrence describes a powerful earthquake (Job 9:6). An image of the goddess breaks the commandments and is a crime of such proportions that Asa's drastic action is justified and applauded.

Despite the kudos for Asa's reform, the high places are not removed. Since the temple's construction they are considered non-orthodox places of worship particularly associated with foreign gods (1 Kgs 11:1–8). Blame for the oversight is deflected from the king to the people by citing 'they' did not remove the high places. Similar deflection becomes common in the evaluation of other reforming kings who are otherwise approved (Jehoshaphat [1 Kgs 22:43(44)], Joash [2 Kgs 12:3(4)], Amaziah [2 Kgs 14:4], Azariah/Uziah [2 Kgs 15:4] and Jotham [2 Kgs 15:35]). Despite the deflection, the kings are implicated and experience some sort of punishment during their reign (Mullen 1992: 234–235).

Despite this failure Asa's wholehearted devotion to YHWH 'all his days' contrasts him to Abijam and Solomon, and aligns him with David (11:4; 15:3). The final evidence of the state of Asa's heart is the dedicated items for YHWH's house that replace those delivered to Shishak (14:26). As Solomon dedicated items as the final element in temple building (1 Kgs 7:51), so Asa's dedicatory gifts are the final element of his reform. Their loss to an enemy (v. 18) is punishment for Asa's failure to remove the high places.

16–22. Like his evaluation, the events of Asa's reign are mixed. Warfare continues between Asa and Baasha, who gains Israel's throne in Asa's second year (by the accession-year system). Samuel's home town of Ramah (1 Sam. 7:17) is 5 miles (8 km) north of Jerusalem and controlled by Israel since the secession (Arnold, *ABD* 5:614). The city's location on major routes gave it control over the region; its fortification by Israel presents a serious threat to Judah.

Asa sent the wealth of the temple and palace treasuries to Ben-hadad of Aram in hope of forging a treaty. The treaty achieves the hoped-for result, but, though pragmatic, is not to be considered positively for several reasons. First, it is a response to a threat of land loss (vv. 16–17). This threat recalls the negative cycles of sin and judgment in the period of the Judges. The present threat implies a negative judgment on Asa's reign, despite praise for his reforms.

Secondly, Asa looks to a foreign king for deliverance, rather than trusting YHWH. He sends a 'gift' (*šōḥad*), a word used often in legal contexts for a bribe (Exod. 23:8; Deut. 10:17; 16:19; 1 Sam. 8:3; Ezek. 22:12). Within 1 – 2 Kings the word is found again only in 2 Kgs 16:8, where Ahaz appeases another foreign king and thus confirms his wholly negative evaluation. On these grounds, while Asa is not as severely evaluated as Ahaz, his payment of a *šōḥad* reveals whom he trusts, and cannot contribute to his honour in the Deuteronomist's eyes.

Thirdly, loss sustained to the treasuries of temple (*'ôṣĕrôt bêt yhwh*) and palace (*'ôṣĕrôt bêt hammelek*) is a consistent negative measurement against Judahite kings (Mullen 1992). The phrase occurs seven times throughout the corpus, with some slight variations (1 Kgs 14:26; 15:18; 2 Kgs 12:18[19]; 14:14; 16:8; 18:15; 24:13). Four times it refers to payment to a foreign king, twice to plunder by foreign kings, and once to seizure of plunder by an Israelite king. In every narrative the kings are either wholly disapproved or the loss occurs at the end of a line of disapproved kings. Alternatively, the king is approved, but the loss signals error on his part (Hezekiah), or the approval is qualified because the high places are not removed (Asa, Jehoash, Amaziah). Temple and palace funds are a litmus test of the state of Judah: when they are plundered or paid out, it signals disapproval and judgment by YHWH, primarily due to cultic short-falls or non-trust of YHWH.

Tabrimmon, whose name ('Rimmon is good') honours the Syrian god of thunder (2 Kgs 5:18), ruled before Ben-hadad (Viviano, *ABD* 6:305). Hezion has sometimes been identified with Rezon (1 Kgs 11:23–24; see Nelson 1992). A treaty existed between Tabrimmon and Asa's father. Ben-hadad, with whom Asa made a treaty in the early ninth century, should not be confused with Ben-hadad of the late ninth century (2 Kgs 13:3–7) and is unlikely to be identified with the Ben-hadad of 1 Kgs 20, 22 and 2 Kgs 5 – 7, despite the difficulties of identifying that king (Dearman 1983; Pitard 1988, *ABD* 1:663–665; Halpern 1994; see 'Comment').

There is no reason to doubt the existence of a treaty between Tabrimmon and Abijam, even though his son Ben-hadad was allied with Baasha. Asa's gift procures a shift of treaty alliance and Ben-hadad's officers come against cities in the northernmost part of Israel (Ijon, Dan, Abel-beth-maacah), Kinneroth on the western shores of Galilee, and the tribal area of Naphtali north-west of that (Knauf 1998; Fritz 2003: 167). The threat must be credible, for Baasha withdraws his troops, returns and remains in Tirzah; whether he engages Ben-hadad is outside narrative concerns, but seems probable.

Tirzah, an old Canaanite city originally captured by Joshua (Josh. 12:24), was Jeroboam's city (14:17) and the capital until Omri's purchase of Samaria (15:33; 16:8, 15, 23). It is 7 miles (11 km) north-east of Shechem and stands on a rocky ridge. It commands the main thoroughfare through the Jordan Valley to the western mountain district, and the major north–south route from Beth-shan to Shechem. Today it is identified as Tell el-Far'ah (Manor, *ABD* 6:573–757; de Vaux, *NEAEHL* 2:433).

Baasha's withdrawal enables Asa to reassert sovereignty over his border. With temporary forced labour he reverses Baasha's work on Ramah and strengthens Geba (Arnold, *ABD* 2:921–922) and Mizpah (Arnold, *ABD* 4:879–881), 7 miles (12 km) north of Jerusalem. They serve as watchposts along Benjamin's northern border.

23–24. The closing summary follows the usual pattern with an additional note regarding Asa's diseased feet. This seems at odds with the positive achievements in the summary; that the note begins with the adversative *raq* (but, however) confirms this. The note tempers the positive evaluation of Asa's reign.

15:25–32

25–26. Nadab comes to the throne in Asa's 'second year' by the non-accession year system. By the accession year system Nadab begins to reign during Asa's first year, and rules for a period of one year and some months. The negative evaluation of Nadab establishes the pattern by which all northern kings are measured. All northern kings are evil because they walk in the way of Jeroboam, committing the same sins for which he was indicted (14:9, 16). These are cultic sins, particularly the golden calves and the alternative cult.

27–30. Nadab's reign and his narrative are surprisingly short in comparison to Jeroboam's; there is just enough narrative time to fulfil YHWH's word against Jeroboam's house.

During military operations against Philistine Gibbethon, on the western edge of the Judean hills (Peterson, *ABD* 2:1006–1007), Baasha strikes down the king. The details of the assassination and subsequent action against Jeroboam's house are minimal. It is enough that the narrative notes these events have occurred 'according to the word of YHWH' by Ahijah, and that they are judgment against the sins of Jeroboam. Theologically, the political realities or personal conflicts behind the coup matter not at all.

Baasha 'conspires' against Nadab (v. 27). Conspiracy is primarily a northern phenomenon in 1 – 2 Kings. The verb 'to conspire' (*qšr*) occurs fourteen times in the context of nine successful conspiracies against monarchs (1 Kgs 15:27; 16:9, 16, 20; 2 Kgs 9:14; 10:9; 12:21; 14:19; 15:10, 15, 25, 30; 21:23–24). Of these nine conspiracies, six are against northern kings and only three against Davidic kings. The preponderance of conspiracy in the northern kingdom cannot be attributed to their commitment to charismatic, occasional leadership. In the ANE (and thus in Israel) all leadership was charismatic, that is, appointed by the gods (Thornton 1962–3), and dynastic (Ishida 1977: 25). In the record of the DH the preponderance of conspiracy in the north reflects upon the sinfulness of the kings.

Baasha the son of Ahijah of Issachar (not the prophet of Shiloh) 'conspires against' and 'strikes' (*qšr* and *nkh*) the king, a coupling of action in the overthrow of each subsequent northern dynasty. Such action is judged as blameworthy (1 Kgs 16:7).

31–32. Nadab's death is narrated, but as the last king of a sinful dynasty his closing summary omits any notice of death or burial: the sinful dynasty ends, completely and utterly, signalling the fulfilment of the prophetic word (14:10–13). Similar omission is found in the closing summary of subsequent kings whose reign ends a sinful dynasty.

So complete is the obliteration of Jeroboam's house that the closing summary's reference to ongoing warfare mentions its continuance in Baasha's reign. No mention is made of warfare during Nadab's reign. It is as if the house of Jeroboam is eradicated from the storyline.

Explanation

'Life gets tedjous, don'tch it?' was the refrain of a comic song on an old record my parents owned. In a twanged-accent the singer complained about the tedium of life – the round of boring activities without any variance. Its sentiment certainly brings something to the understanding of the theology of this passage.

The chapter moves rapidly over twenty years and the monarchic record of three kings (four, counting Baasha). In comparision, Jeroboam and Rehoboam each ruled approximately twenty years in narratives spanning several chapters. Solomon's forty years take eleven chapters. The narrative accelerates through 2 Kgs 15 – 16, emphasizing repetitive elements with little variance. Regnal formulae, with increasingly familiar phrases, fire off monarchic eras with, at times (see Abijam's reign), virtually nothing by way of additional narrative.

In the north the sins of Jeroboam continue unabated and the first instance of conspiracy is enacted against Nadab. The repetitive pattern of Jeroboam's sins and dynastic instability will only increase in tempo in 1 Kgs 16. War between the two kingdoms continues through the chapter as they disregard the prophetic word (1 Kgs 12:22–24). In the south a new pattern emerges in which a good king follows upon the reign of a bad king and introduces cultic reform. That pattern, though less consistent than the pattern of the north's continuous adherence to Jeroboam's sins, is repeated (Hezekiah follows Ahaz [2 Kgs 18:3 and 16:2]; Josiah follows Manasseh and Amon [2 Kgs 22:2 and 21:2, 20]). The repetitions of ch. 15, especially as they continue into ch. 16, 'get tedjous'.

The tedium of warfare and cultic sin arises from the ongoing apostasy in God's people. It is this continuum that opens the theological crux of the passage – the reality is that there is little new to be said about sinfulness. Its patterns are set in human self-will and pride, and consistently turn from the goodness of YHWH to sin.

Thus one does not rightly read Gen. 3 – 11 without recognizing that the sinfulness of the garden is repeated: in Cain, in Lamech, in the wickedness of Noah's time, in Noah himself, in Babel. And, lest one misconstrue the patriarchal narratives as unmarred relief from repetitive sin, Abram lies regarding Sarai (Gen. 12:11–13), Isaac repeats the lie (Gen. 26:7) and Jacob – that trickster – lies to his father (Gen. 27:24) and is lied to in return (Gen. 29:23).

As a nation, Israel's sinfulness is anything but inventive. From the day YHWH brought them up from Egypt they forsook him and served other gods (1 Sam. 8:8). They made and worshipped the calf in the desert (Exod. 32:5–6), replayed that tune with Canaanite tones through Jeroboam's sin, and continued to worship other gods throughout the monarchy. Even after the exile the reconstituted north kept to other gods (2 Kgs 17:24–41) and escapees from Judah safeguarded their idols in Egypt (Jer. 44:8–10). The repetition is only too apparent in Israel's own enumeration in Ps. 106.

At the same time as sin was played out in terms of worshipping other gods, it also manifested in social ills for which the prophets repeatedly took the people to task (Isa. 1:16–17, 21–23; Jer. 5:1; Amos 5:10–15). Despite Israel's desire to walk in the commandments of YHWH (Josh. 24:14–22), they walked in the tedium of sin. Paul's wretched recognition of its presence – despite the law and one's desire to fulfil it (Rom. 7:7–25) – as readily describes Israel's ancient experience as the experience of the church to whom Paul wrote.

Just as 1 Kgs 15 begins repetitive cycles of sinfulness that maintain – and worsen – throughout the history, the chapter also reveals that sinfulness is not inevitable. Asa's rule follows three generations of apostasy, yet he is not destined to become the fourth. Instead, Asa 'did what was right in the eyes of YHWH, like David his father' (v. 11), living out the substance of David's charge to Solomon to 'keep the charge of YHWH your God, to walk in his ways, keep his statutes, his commandments, his judgments and his testimonies as written in the torah of Moses' (1 Kgs 2:3).

The narrative does not record what prompted Asa to walk in the covenant. Perhaps he took to heart the commands laid upon the king to read and meditate upon the law so as to revere YHWH and follow his torah (Deut. 17:18–19). Perhaps he then recognized Judah's actions were contrary to the law and wished to right them. Perhaps YHWH's words of commitment to David, or his vowed presence in Jerusalem's temple, which Asa may himself have experienced, prompted his heart towards YHWH.

While the narrative leaves unanswered the impetus for Asa's faithfulness, his faithfulness reveals that, common though sin may be, the king is not inevitably bound to it. A willing heart can be captured by the covenant and express itself in willing obedience. As predictable as sinfulness is, its cycle can be broken by righteousness. There is always hope, even in the downward spiral of sin Israel and Judah lived through, that YHWH may break in, working through an obedient heart, and reforming a recalcitrant people.

As sin can be traced through the Scriptures, so YHWH's inbreaking can similarly be traced. Thus Noah found favour in YHWH's eyes and through him the cycle of sin was interrupted and a way forward to a new hope found. Joshua attended Moses upon the mountain and did not go down to join the idol feast (Exod 24:13–14; 32:15–17). By his ongoing devotion before YHWH (Exod. 33:11) he was marked as a new leader to bring Israel into a new life in the land (Exod. 34:9). Josiah, who turned to YHWH with 'all his heart, soul, and strength in accordance with all the torah of Moses' (2 Kgs 23:25), reformed Judah's worship, even pulling down the high places and – though for a brief time only – restoring covenant between the people and YHWH (2 Kgs 23:3). And Ezra returned to Jerusalem with a dual legacy: devotion to YHWH's torah, and the power of YHWH's hand upon him, and in that legacy led the people into new hope after the exile (Ezra 7:1–10). YHWH is always able, through those who turn to him wholeheartedly, to break into the prevailing cycles of sin.

YHWH's inbreaking into the cycles of sin through people such as these is powerful, yet never wholly complete or assured. Asa's reform left the high places standing; Josiah's reform could not reverse the judgment upon Manasseh's sin; post-exilic Judah still needed the urging of prophets to walk in YHWH's commands. Though adhering to YHWH, all these could still echo Paul's cry 'wretched man that I am, who will save me?'

Paul answers his own cry of wretchedness with thanksgiving to the last king of Israel – Jesus Christ. He is the one righteous king who fully and finally broke the cycle of sin, ending its power. And, as Paul goes on to attest, those whose lives are placed under his sovereign rule are without condemnation. Sin may still be repeated in the lives of this king's subjects, but to no avail. They are instead set free to walk in his righteousness and continue his work of tearing down the structures and powers of sinfulness.

1 KINGS 15:33 – 16:34

Translation

[15:33]In the third year of Asa king of Judah, Baasha son of Ahijah began to reign over all[a] Israel at Tirzah; *he reigned* twenty-four years. [34]He did what was evil in the eyes of YHWH, and he walked in the way of Jeroboam and in his sin that he caused Israel to sin.

[16:1]It happened that the word of YHWH came to Jehu son of Hanani, against Baasha, saying, [2]'Because I raised you up from the dust and made you ruler over my people Israel, but you have walked in the way of Jeroboam and have made my people Israel sin, provoking me to anger with their sins[a], [3]behold, I will burn up[a] Baasha and his house, and I will make your house[b] as the house of Jeroboam, son of Nebat. [4]The one belonging to Baasha who dies in the city the dogs will eat, and the one belonging to him who dies in the field the birds of the heavens will eat.'

⁵Now the rest of Baasha's acts, and what he did, and his might – are they not written in the Book of the Chronicles of the Kings of Israel? ⁶So Baasha slept with his fathers and he was buried in Tirzah. And Elah his son reigned in his place.

⁷Furthermore, by the hand of Jehu son of Hanani the prophet the word of YHWH came to Baasha and to his house, both concerning all the evil that he did in the eyes of YHWH, provoking him to anger with the work of his hands, and becoming like the house of Jeroboam, and also because he destroyed itᵃ.

⁸In the twenty-sixth year of Asa king of Judah, Elah son of Baasha began to reign over Israel in Tirzah. *He reigned* two years. ⁹His servant Zimri, commander of half the chariots, conspired against him. Now he was in Tirzah, getting drunk in the house of Arza, who was in charge of the palace in Tirzah. ¹⁰Zimri entered and struck him and killed him, in the twenty-seventh year of Asa king of Judah and reigned in his place. ¹¹When he began to reign, as soon as he was seated upon his throne, he struck all the house of Baasha; he did not leave to him any who urinate against the wall, neither his kinsmen nor his friendsᵃ. ¹²Thus Zimri destroyed all the house of Baasha according to the word of YHWH that he had spoken againstᵃ Baasha by the hand of Jehu the prophet ¹³on account ofᵃ all the sins of Baasha, and the sins of Elah his son, which they sinned, and which they caused Israel to sin, provoking YHWH the God of Israel to anger with their idols. ¹⁴The rest of the acts of Elah and all that he did, are they not written in the Book of the Chronicles of the Kings of Israel?

¹⁵In the twenty-seventh year of Asa king of Judah, Zimri reigned seven days in Tirzah. The people were encamped against Gibbethon, which belonged to the Philistines. ¹⁶When the people who were encamped heard, 'Zimri has conspired and also struck the king,' all Israel made Omri, the commander of the army, king over Israel that day in the camp. ¹⁷Omri, and all Israel with him, went up from Gibbethon and besieged Tirzah. ¹⁸When Zimri saw that the city was captured, he entered the citadel of the king's palace and burned the king's palace over him with fire, and he died ¹⁹on account of his sins that he sinned, doing what was evil in the eyes of YHWH, walking in the way of Jeroboam and in his sin that he committed, causing Israel to sin. ²⁰Now the rest of the acts of Zimri, and his conspiracy that he carried out, are they not written in the Book of the Chronicles of the Kings of Israel?

²¹Then the people of Israel were divided in half; half of the people followed Tibni son of Ginath to make him king, while half followed Omri. ²²But the people who followed Omri prevailed over the people who followed Tibni son of Ginath; Tibni died, and Omri became king.

²³In the thirty-first year of Asa king of Judah, Omri began to reign over Israel; *he reigned* twelve years; in Tirzah he reigned six years. ²⁴He bought the hill of Samaria from Shemer for 2 talents of silver. He fortified the hill and called the city that he built Samaria, after the name of Shemer, the owners of the hillᵃ.

²⁵Omri did what was evil in the eyes of YHWH; he did more evil than all who were before him. ²⁶He walked in all the way of Jeroboam son of Nebat, and in his sinsᵃ that he caused Israel to sin, provoking YHWH the God of Israel to anger

with their idols. [27]The rest of the acts of Omri, and all[a] that he did, and his might[b] – are they not written in the Book of the Chronicles of the Kings Israel? [28]Then Omri slept with his fathers and was buried in Samaria, and his son Ahab reigned in his place.

[29]Ahab son of Omri began to reign over Israel in the thirty-eighth year of Asa king of Judah. Ahab son of Omri reigned over Israel in Samaria twenty-two years. [30]Ahab son of Omri did what was evil in the eyes of YHWH more than all who were before him. [31]And, as if it had been a light thing for him to walk in the sins of Jeroboam son of Nebat, he married Jezebel daughter of Ethbaal king of Sidon and went and served Baal and worshipped him. [32]He erected an altar for Baal in[a] the house of Baal, which he built in Samaria. [33]Ahab made a sacred pole and continued to act so as to provoke YHWH the God of Israel to anger more than all the kings of Israel before him. [34]In his days Hiel the Bethelite rebuilt Jericho. With the loss of Abiram his firstborn he founded it, and with the loss of Segub his youngest he set up its gates, according to the word of YHWH, which he had spoken by the hand of Joshua son of Nun.

Notes on the text

15:33.a. LXX* omits the modifier in 'all Israel'. Uncommon in regnal formulae (but see 1 Kgs 12:16, 18, 20; 14:13, 18; 16:16; 18:19; 22:17; 2 Kgs 3:6), its inclusion in MT notes the usurper's success.

2.a. MT 'with their sins' (*běḥaṭṭō'tām*) reads in LXX, 'with their idols' (Hebr. *běhablêhem*), a harmonization to vv. 13, 26.

3.a. Reading with MT as a hiph. *mab'îr*, 'cause to burn up', rather than LXX ἐξεγείρω (Hebr. *mē'îr*, 'will stir up').

3.b. After the third-person reference to Baasha, 'your house' returns to the second-person address of v. 2. LXX*, Syr, Tg recognize the awkwardness and read, 'his house' (οἴκου αὐτοῦ). V. 4 again refers to Baasha in the third person. Perhaps the difficulty lies in the fact that the words are both YHWH's address to Jehu about Baasha as well as Jehu's address to Baasha.

7.a. 'and because he struck it' reads *wě'al 'ăšer-hikkâ 'ōtô* as explanatory (so DeVries 2003: 195; Sweeney 2007: 197) rather than concessive ('though he struck it'; so Gray 1970: 361; cf. Montgomery 1951: 282, 289).

11.a. Reading pl. 'friends' with Syr, Tg, Vg, against MT sg. 'friend'.

12.a. Reading *'el*, 'to Baasha', as *'al*, 'against Baasha'.

13.a. Reading *'el* as *'al*.

24.a. MT reads *'ădōnê hāhār*, 'owners of the hill'. The pl. form suggests not one owner, but a clan or community (Gray 1970: 367).

26.a. Reading with K 'sins', against Q 'sin'. Both forms are stock Dtr terminology for Jeroboam's actions, although the pl. form is more frequently used (sg. in 1 Kgs 12:30; 13:34; 15:26, 34; 16:19, 26 [Q]; 2 Kgs 13:2; pl. in 1 Kgs 14:16; 15:30; 16:19 [Q], 31; 2 Kgs 3:3; 10:31; 13:6, 11; 14:24; 15:9, 18, 24, 28; 17:22).

27.a. With several Hebr. MSS, LXX and Syr, inserting 'and all' to read, 'and all that he did', as in v. 14.

27.b. Removing, with LXX*, Syr, the second 'that he did' (*'ăšer 'āśâ*) as a dittography.

32.a. LXX has the prep. 'in the house of Baal', and is so read here. Absence of the *bě* prep. would suggest an apposition: 'He erected an altar . . . [that is] the house of Baal'.

Form and structure

1 Kgs 15:33 – 16:34 chronologically covers the reign of five northern kings (six, including Tibni). Asa's forty-one-year reign ends and Jehoshaphat is enthroned during Ahab's reign (1 Kgs 22:41). Regnal summaries bracket each reign and follow the usual pattern; variations are treated in the 'Comment' section. Tibni's reign has no formulae, marking his unsuccessful bid for power. Ahab's summary begins a narrative block concluded at 1 Kgs 22:39–40 with a regnal summary, although Ahab's dynasty remains in focus until 2 Kgs 9 – 10. The block encompasses much of the Elijah corpus and paints Ahab as ranking in evil alongside Jeroboam.

Besides the regnal summaries, other literary forms are present. A prophetic oracle concerning Baasha in 16:1–4 is patterned after that given Jeroboam (14:7–11). Its fulfilment also bears a striking resemblance to the previous oracle's fulfilment. The oracle includes an additional explanation for judgment on Baasha (16:7), perhaps incorporated from a variant tradition (DeVries 2003: 195; Sweeney 2007: 199). Barring this addition, the oracles to Jeroboam and Baasha carry similar form and content to those at 1 Kgs 21:21–24 and 2 Kgs 9:8–10, thus thematically uniting the judgments against Jeroboam, Baasha and Ahab.

Notices of prophetic fulfilment at 16:12–13, 34 make explicit YHWH's power inherent in the prophetic word. Further, the second notice cites Josh. 6:26 and unites the monarchic history with a larger corpus.

Finally, details concerning warfare (16:9–11, 15b–18, 21–22) and building projects (16:24) arise from an annalistic source such as the Chronicles of the Kings of Israel and reveal the troubled transfer of dynastic power and the stability provided by Omri's new capital.

Comment

15:33 – 16:7

33–34. Baasha attains the throne in Asa's third year and reigns from Tirzah, north-east of Shechem (see discussion at 15:21). The city's location enables easy communication and troop movement during the years of warfare with Asa and Ben-hadad. Despite ongoing warfare, the summary focuses on evils identical to those previously espoused by Nadab (15:26; v. 34; cf. 16:2). Although there is a change of dynasty, the sins of Jeroboam are repeated and typical.

16:1–7. The prophetic word must be heard as a response – not to Baasha's conspiracy related in 1 Kgs 15 – but to his sins in the preceding summary. Nothing is known of Jehu, beyond his patronymic. If he is the same Jehu who prophesied to Jehoshaphat after Ahab's death in 853 BC (2 Chr. 19:2), and if the word to Baasha was near the end of his reign (886 BC), at least thirty-five to forty years pass between the prophetic episodes.

The oracle begins typically with *ya'an 'ăšer* (because) and lists reasons for judgment. The list begins from YHWH's perspective and cites what he has done for Baasha in terms reminiscent of the oracle given Jeroboam (14:7–11). Like Jeroboam, Baasha was 'raised up' by YHWH and 'made ruler' (14:7). Jeroboam was raised up from 'the people', but Baasha is raised 'from the dust'. A contrast is probably intended between Jeroboam's acclamation (12:20) versus Baasha's usurpation (15:27–28), but, however they gained the throne, both are set over 'my people Israel' (14:7). Baasha responds to YHWH's initiative by walking in the way of Jeroboam, that is, all the cultic sins for which Jeroboam is judged, particularly the sin of the golden calves (14:9; cf. 16:13, 26). Like Jeroboam he leads YHWH's people into sin (14:16), provoking YHWH to anger (14:9; cf. 15:30; 16:7, 13).

Not only the reasons but the judgment itself reflects the oracle against Jeroboam. Both houses will be 'burned up' (*b'r*) and consumed like dung. The utter contempt for both houses is apparent, for dogs and birds will consume their members (14:11).

Besides citing sources, the closing summary cites other actions by Baasha. These are vague, although Baasha's 'might' (v. 5) suggests both his coup and his military actions. While Baasha receives the oracle regarding non-burial, he (like Jeroboam) does not experience the judgment himself. Notice of his death and burial is provided and non-burial is visited upon the dynasty in his son.

The explanatory comment provides an additional reason for judgment and introduces a tension that continues in the rule of every successive usurper who conspires and 'strikes' (*nkh*) his predecessor. The tension is already anticipated in v. 2, for, how is it that one raised up by YHWH is subsequently judged for the means by which that individual achieves the throne? The tension will become particularly pointed in Jehu's narrative where he is specifically called upon to 'strike' (*nkh*) Ahab's house, yet the narrative judges him for exactly that action of 'striking' (see 'Comment' and 'Expanation', 2 Kgs 9 – 10). The very least that can be said is that Baasha's actions contrast the smooth transition of southern rule through the dynastic line, virtually without opposition.

16:8–14

The opening summary lacks any theological appraisal. Such appraisal is provided in v. 13, where it explains YHWH's judgment against Elah through Zimri. The appraisal is typically negative and links Elah's sins to those of his father and thus to Jeroboam's sins.

Both Baasha and Elah cause Israel to sin and provoke YHWH to anger (vv. 2, 13). The provocation is now specifically focused on the idols (*hăbālîm*). Certainly, the golden calves are in view, although the sacred (asherah) poles (14:15) may also be intended. The calves have been called 'molten images' (*massēkôt*; 14:9); *hăbālîm* (m. sg. pl. of *hebel*, 'breath, vanity') emphasizes the futility of Israel's worship. The term *hăbālîm* is found three times in the DH (cf. Eccl. 1:2; 5:7; 12:8; Jer. 8:19; 10:8; 14:22; Jon. 2:8). Two occurrences in this chapter (vv. 13, 26) define Israel's sin as being the worthless idols. The third occurrence is in Moses' litany against Israel's desert sins. These include the worship of *hăbālîm* (Deut. 32:21), which incites YHWH's punishment. Much later, reflecting on the sins for which Israel is exiled, Dtr notes that Israel followed after vanity (*hebel*) and became vain themselves (2 Kgs 17:15). In the making of idols (*hăbālîm*), Israel's empty vanity has never changed. From desert wanderings to Assyrian exile, they have turned their heart towards emptiness; towards *hăbālîm*.

Elah's account extends the comparison previously drawn between Jeroboam/Nadab (see vv. 1–4 above). Like Jeroboam's son Nadab, Baasha's son Elah reigns for only two years (v. 8; 15:25) and the reign is similarly ended by conspiracy (*qšr*; v. 9; 15:27). A usurper strikes (*nkh*) each king during a military campaign against Gibbethon (vv. 10, 15; 15:27), followed by complete annihilation of the overthrown house (v. 11; 15:29). In each instance it is particularly noted the assassination fulfils YHWH's word (v. 12; 15:29). The comparisons across the dynasties suggest the repetition of Jeroboam's sins will be met with a repetition of Jeroboam's judgments.

Elah's servant Zimri effects judgment upon his master. The lack of patronymic suggests his family is inconsequential in Israel. His consequence is attached to his command over half of Elah's chariots. Arza may have played the role of co-conspirator; if so, his authority over the royal estates (similar positions were held throughout the monarchic era in both north and south; see 1 Kgs 4:6; 18:3; 2 Kgs 10:5; 15:5) made him a powerful ally.

The realpolitik of disaffection over land loss in northern Israel (15:20), or factions among the military (note that Omri is immediately proclaimed Zimri's challenger) are possible, but unexplored. Instead, the efficacy of YHWH's word is the only reason provided for the coup (v. 12). Zimri's complete annihilation of Baasha's house fulfils the prophetic judgment (v. 3). Baasha's house walks in Jeroboam's ways and faces the same complete judgment (14:10).

No notice of death or burial is included in the closing summary, because Baasha's son bears the dynastic judgment of death and non-burial. For obvious reasons the notice of succession is absent.

16:15–20

Zimri rules seven days during Asa's twenty-seventh year (884 BC). As in Elah's reign, theological evaluation in the opening summary is delayed (until v. 19). That Zimri's brief reign faces the same judgment as kings who promoted Jeroboam's cult reveals the theological agenda of the summaries. Each northern king is connected in a 'dynastic line' of sin that stretches from Jeroboam to the exile. Each king walks in the way of Jeroboam their 'father', and Zimri is no exception.

Zimri, assumedly with his chariot company, holds Tirzah. The armed forces besieging Gibbethon (a military object as early as Baasha's reign; 15:27) react immediately to the coup. 'All Israel' (troops at Gibbethon who take upon themselves the role of the representative body [Gray 1970: 364; Walsh 1996: 216; Berlyn 2005: 225]) acclaim Omri.

Omri, like Zimri, has no patronym and is probably from an insignificant family. Despite his name's possible Amorite origin (*HALOT* 850), a foreigner was unlikely to be acclaimed king (Deut. 17:15). The name appears in later texts as Israelite and from Issachar (1 Chr. 7:8; 9:4; 27:18). Omride association with Jezreel in Issachar (1 Kgs 21; 2 Kgs 9; cf. Berlyn 2005: 229) affirms a tribal connection. Omri's powerful house becomes synonymous with Israel even after its overthrow; Assyrian inscriptions of Shalmaneser and Tiglath-pileser in the ninth–eighth centuries attest to Israel as the 'house of Omri'; even Jehu (who overthrows the Omrides) is a 'son of Omri' (*ANET* 282, 284).

Omri is 'commander of the army' (*śar ṣābā'*) like Abner before him (2 Sam. 2:8). He leads the siege of Zimri in Tirzah, and Zimri is either taken by surprise (perhaps anticipating greater support following Elah's assassination) or is simply unable (given Tirzah's exposed site and his lesser military might) to withstand the siege. As the walls are breached, he shuts himself in the fortified keep and torches it. The narrator explains his death by the recitation of the usual sins.

Both as a man assassinated and as the last of his line, the closing summary provides no death and burial notice nor succession notice.

16:21–28

21–22. Although acclaimed king by his troops, for approximately half of his eleven-year reign Tibni's faction opposes him. Various foreign and Israelite originations are suggested for Tibni's name (see *HALOT* 10043;

Gray 1970: 364; Jones 1984a: 294; Berlyn 2005: 227–228). Regardless of his origin, his claim upon the throne divides the whole populace – whether along tribal, ethnic or social boundaries cannot be determined. At some point during the struggle, Tibni's power wanes while Omri's waxes. Tibni's death whether by natural or violent causes leaves Omri's claim undisputed.

23–28. During Asa's thirty-first year (by the non-accession-date system; 880 BC), and having reigned in Tirzah an actual five years, Omri gains undisputed rule over Israel. Together with the years in Samaria he rules for a total of eleven years (the extra year in the text reflects the counting of the northern non-accession-date system).

He purchases Samaria as his new capital, a site eminently defensible, standing 299 feet (91 m) above the surrounding valley. Its Hebrew name 'Hill of *Šōměrôn*', that is, 'Watch-mountain' or 'Lookout-mountain' (Kaufman 1992: 915), reflects its situation. The purchase price exceeds the value of barren land, and archaeological evidence exists of a prior, developed Canaanite village producing and selling olive oil. Communal ownership by a clan or family is apparent, as Shemer is cited in the plural as the 'lords' or 'owners'. Its location at the intersection of major trade routes provides Omri ready sources of income to offset not only the losses of Baasha's era (15:18–20) but of the civil war with Tibni (Stager 1990: 98–104; Sweeney 2007: 204).

The purchase made the hill Omri's personal possession and provided a neutral place from which to stabilize his rule, much as David did through the personal acquisition of Jerusalem. Evidence of building projects at the site under Omri's rule together with subsequent building efforts by Ahab demonstrate the site's ongoing importance to the dynasty (Avigad, *NEAEHL* 4:1303).

Despite the military and building efforts of Omri's reign, he is evaluated solely on religious criteria. As all Israelite kings, his evaluation is negative. Omri, however, is credited with greater evil than those before him, placing the northern kings in a downward spiral of sinful activity. Omri's house will be particularly remembered as instrumental in leading Israel astray.

His death and burial in Samaria mark the city as the new capital. The succession of his son Ahab brings dynastic stability that continues to 2 Kgs 9.

16:29–34

Ahab's twenty-one-year rule from Samaria commences in Asa's thirty-eighth year (non-accession-dating; 873 BC). Ahab's importance is signalled by the triple mention of 'Ahab son of Omri' (vv. 29 [twice], 30). Not only does he lead the powerful 'house of Omri' for the greatest length of time (ruling longer than any northern king except Jehu), but his religious activities indelibly mark the northern kingdom.

The opening evaluation is much expanded, and characterizes Ahab as more evil than any previous king (vv. 30, 33) by exceeding Jeroboam's sins (vv. 31–32). Like Solomon, he marries a foreign princess (contra Deut. 7:1–6) through whom Baal worship is introduced. Contempt for Jezebel is signalled by her name. Originally spelled 'ĭzĕbūl (Where is the prince?), the Hebrew vocalization 'îzebel is a play upon the word 'dung' (zebel; cf. 2 Kgs 9:37). Her father, Ethbaal, ruled Tyre and Sidon for thirty-two years. His Phoenician name (Ittobaal) means 'Baal exists' and Jezebel may have been appointed priestess of Baal, the god of agricultural fertility, of thunder and rain (Viviano, ABD 2:645; Yee, ABD 3:848–849).

Through his marriage Ahab serves and worships Baal, building him a temple and altar in Samaria. Additionally, Ahab continues to make sacred poles for Asherah so that the male and female Canaanite deities are equally present in Israel. Yet Ahab's commitment to Baal cannot be fully measured, for he elsewhere works in cooperation with YHWH's prophets (1 Kgs 18:17–20), consults them before battle (22:6–8), repents at their rebuke (21:27), and his sons' names are theophoric (Ahaziah, Jehoram; see Angel 2007). Regardless, his evaluation interprets his actions as wholly evil and sets him above all previous kings in his provocation of YHWH. The influence of these practices is so widespread that for several chapters Baal, the god of Ahab and Jezebel, is YHWH's antagonist.

An archival note remembers the curse against the rebuilding of Jericho (Josh. 6:26). The loss of Hiel's sons due to natural or accidental causes evidences the power of the curse; the evidence that the deaths were infant sacrifices interred in the walls to invoke protection of the city is possible but inconclusive (Montgomery 1951: 288; Gray 1970: 370; DeVries 2003: 205; Sweeney 2007: 206–207).

Hiel's activities do not specifically implicate Ahab, but stand as a further negative evaluation of his reign. Even if Ahab did not instigate the building project, it is a fitting reflection on Ahab's reign. First, both Hiel and Ahab build (bnh; vv. 32, 34), in each instance contrary to YHWH's stated will (per Josh. 6:26 and Deut. 7:5; 12:2–7, 11–14). Secondly, Hiel's actions activate ancient prophecy in the same way that Ahab's actions will activate an older prophecy (14:10–16; 21:21–24).

Finally, the verse is a proleptic comment on Ahab's reign. The context of Joshua's prophecy includes one man (Achan) whose non-covenantal actions threatened the ongoing covenant life of Israel (Josh. 6–7). Similarly, Ahab's non-covenantal actions will threaten the covenant life of the whole nation. The archival notice, concerned as it is with YHWH's word, fittingly introduces narratives also concerned with YHWH's word through his prophet, Elijah (17:1–19:21). Even more, the notice suggests that, as the word spoken through Joshua long ago is effected, so too will the word spoken through Elijah the prophet be effected. The power of YHWH's word cannot be undermined (Conroy 1996; Sweeney 2004).

Explanation

The cycles of sinfulness that began in 1 Kgs 15 (see 'Explanation' there) continue unabated – and accelerated – in 1 Kgs 16. Coup follows coup, and, finally, years of civil war ensue in which the competing claims of Omri and Tibni split the northern populace. The chapter spirals into national chaos, and it is apparent that Israel must find a strong leader or dwindle under the tyranny of civil strife.

Omri's victory holds promise that strong leadership will end dynastic instability inherent since the north seceded. The Omride dynasty does endure, with four kings ruling more than forty years. The era is prosperous, and politically and militarily powerful. Yet success in realpolitik for Omri – and his better-known son – does not enable a new age for Israel. The sins of Jeroboam continue and Israel's covenant life remains in crisis, even worsening under Ahab's Baalism.

In this bleak scene the prophetic word regarding the rebuilding of Jericho – accompanied though it is by human tragedy – addresses Israel's crisis. It provides hope that is sustained through the Omride era (to 2 Kgs 10) that YHWH's word alone is capable of returning Israel to their covenant life. The ministries of Elijah and Elisha, which run parallel to the Omride crisis, show the hope is not vain as they urge YHWH's people back to covenant life.

YHWH's word similarly stands as a word of hope whenever God's people experience times of crisis and their covenant life is threatened. This is particularly apparent at the end of Israel's history, when the northern kingdom has gone into captivity, and the southern kingdom is threatened.

Ezekiel, writing from Babylon in this time of crisis, speaks to a people who are under threat of losing land, temple and national identity. His prophetic vision of the valley of dry bones speaks hope that includes return to land, unification as a nation, restoration of kingly rule over that unified nation and – as the primary sign of covenant life – YHWH's sanctuary and presence signifying the covenant (Ezek. 37).

Jeremiah joins Ezekiel, prophetically affirming these covenant realities in the Book of Consolation (Jer. 30 – 33). The book provides hope both at the institutional level for national Israel, as well as at a deeply personal level for those who – even though faithful – experience judgment meted out to Israel.

On the eve of Jerusalem's fall Jeremiah purchases a field, as YHWH has instructed (Jer. 32:1–16). He then prays, rehearsing YHWH's deliverance of Israel out of Egypt, his gift of the land, and the disaster of exile for their disobedience (32:17–23). As surely as these events occurred, Jeremiah now understands the city will be taken at YHWH's command (32:24). In the light of this, Jeremiah is perplexed at the command to purchase land in the midst of crisis (32:25). YHWH affirms Jeremiah's observation: the city will indeed be taken (32:26–35), but one day be restored and the people returned. They will once again purchase fields and their fortunes will be restored (32:36–44). YHWH's word speaks first to Jeremiah's personal crisis, assuring him that his land purchase is not in vain. YHWH's word also speaks hope to Israel, for Jeremiah's purchase is only a token of what will come for Israel. The enacted parable, and YHWH's word, enabled Israel's hope during the exilic years.

In the NT the church experiences no national crises, for it goes beyond national identifiers, comprising all nations. Though thus not threatened with foreign conquest or exile, the church does experience various crises. One is addressed in John's Apocalypse, where the church, like John on Patmos, suffers at the hands of Roman power. John reminds the church that its covenant life in Christ endures beyond earthly powers. Even in the face of violent persecution this knowledge enables the church joyfully to sustain worship of YHWH.

John concludes his prophetic word by assuring the church of its Lord's impending return. As the Alpha and Omega, the First and Last, he rules over all who persecute the church, and is the church's hope in the midst of such persecution (Rev. 22:12–16). John's final warning against adding to the prophecy (22:18) is a reminder that, in the light of Christ's certain return, no other words are necessary to sustain a people in crisis. Christ's affirmation that 'Yes, I am coming soon' (v. 20) is enough.

The Apocalypse, with its closing warning, takes on additional meaning in the canon. Closing Christian Scripture, its warning can also be taken as a warning not to add to any of Christian Scripture. The canon is God's word to his people, sufficient for the church's life. And, as the word regarding Jericho and Hiel sustained hope through the Omride era, the words to Ezekiel and Jeremiah through the exile, and John's words sustained a suffering church, so the whole canon sustains the church through ongoing crises, internal and external. As the Word of God that abides for ever (Isa. 40:6–8), Scripture endures through the years. It continually speaks 'Comfort, comfort' to God's people (Isa. 40:1) and lifts their eyes to hope in YHWH, because in the Scriptures the 'mouth of YHWH has spoken' (Isa. 40:5). No crisis ultimately overcomes what YHWH has said.

1 KINGS 17:1–24

Translation

[1]Now Elijah the Tishbite, of the settlers of Gilead[a], said to Ahab, 'As YHWH the God of Israel lives, before whom I stand, there shall be neither dew nor rain these years except by the word of my mouth!' [2]And the word of YHWH came to him,

saying, ³'Go from here and head eastwards and hide yourself in the wadi Kerith, which is east of the Jordan. ⁴You shall drink from the stream, and I have commanded the ravens to sustain you there.' ⁵He went and did according to the word of YHWH, and went and dwelt in the wadi Kerith, which is east of the Jordan. ⁶The ravens brought to him bread and meat in the morning, and bread and meat in the evening, and he drank from the stream.

⁷It happened after some time that the stream dried up, for there was no rain in the land. ⁸Then the word of YHWH came to him, saying, ⁹'Arise! Go to Zarephath, which belongs to Sidon, and stay there. Behold, I have appointed there a widow to sustain you.' ¹⁰So he arose and went to Zarephath. He came to the gate of the city and, behold, there was a widow gathering sticks. He called to her and said, 'Bring me a little water in a jar that I may drink.' ¹¹She went to fetch it but he called to her and said, 'Bringᵃ me a piece of bread in your hand.' ¹²She said, 'As YHWH your God lives, I have no breadᵃ, only a handful of flour in the bowl, and a little oil in the jug. See – I am gathering a couple of sticks that I may go in and prepare it for me and my son that we may eat it and die.' ¹³Elijah replied to her, 'Don't be afraid. Go in; do as you have said. Only first make me a little loaf from it and bring it out to me. Then for you and your son you shall make *something* afterwards. ¹⁴For thus says YHWH the God of Israel, "The bowl of flour will not be used up, and the jug of oil will not be emptied" until the day YHWH sends rain upon the face of the earth.' ¹⁵So she went and did according to Elijah's word, and she ate, she and he and her householdᵃ many days. ¹⁶The bowl of flour was not used up and the jug of oil was not emptied, according to the word of YHWH, which he spoke by the hand of Elijah.

¹⁷It came about after these things that the son of the woman, the mistress of the house, sickened. His sickness became very severe until there was no breath left in him. ¹⁸She said to Elijah, 'What is there between me and youᵃ, O man of God? ᵇYou have come to me to bring my sin to remembrance and to kill my son.' ¹⁹He said to her, 'Give me your son.' He took him from her bosom, and took him up to the upper room where he was staying, and laid him upon his bed. ²⁰He called to YHWH and said, 'O YHWH, my God. Have you indeed brought tragedy upon the widow with whom I am staying by killing her son?' ²¹Then he stretched himself upon the child three times and he called to YHWH and said, 'O YHWH my God! Please let the life of this child return toᵃ him!' ²²ᵃYHWH listened to the voice of Elijah, and the life of the child returned toᵇ him and he lived. ²³Then Elijah took the child, and brought him down from the upper room into the house, and gave him to his mother, and Elijah said, 'See, your son is alive.' ²⁴The woman said to Elijah, 'Now I know that you are a man of God and the word of YHWH in your mouth is truth.'

Notes on the text

1.a. MT introduces Elijah as 'the Tishbite', with a further identifier: 'of the settlers (*mittōšābê*) of Gilead'. LXX appears to misread MT with the tautologous 'the Tishbite, from Tishbe (*mittišbê*) of Gilead'.

11.a. The imp. form *liqḥî*, 'bring', is unusual, especially as the form in v. 10 (*qĕḥî*) is the common imp. form. Other instances of the imp. verb with lamed are found in Ezek. 37:16; Prov. 20:16; Exod 29:1. It may be an 'authentic North-Israelite form' (DeVries 2003: 213).

12.a. *mā'ôg*, 'bread, something baked', appears only here and in Ps. 35:16. A small cake or loaf may be intended (see v. 13, *'ugâ*; Montgomery 1951: 297).

15.a. Reading with Q and the versions 'she and he and her household'.

18.a. *mah-lî wālāk*, lit. 'what between me and between you' (cf. Judg. 11:12; 2 Kgs 3:13; 2 Chr. 35:21) signals avoidance and a disavowal of a claim forwarded by one party against another (similarly, Mark 1:24).

18.b. Some Hebr. MSS and Tg include the *kî* particle before 'you have come', explicitly linking her two exclamations as cause and effect. As translated, the cause and effect are implicit, with the emphasis on the highly emotive and accusatory nature of her statements.

21.a. *'al* is read correctly here as *'el*. The confusion of terms is common.

22.a. See n. 21.a above

22.b. LXX omits MT vv. 22–23 up to 'and Elijah took the child' and provides variant abbreviated readings such as 'and it was so; and the child cried out [or 'revived']'. MT accentuates the miraculous element and should stand. The miracle is the narrative point; it evidences Elijah's connection to YHWH.

Form and structure

1 Kgs 17 introduces Elijah, who in chs. 17–19 serves as YHWH's prophet to challenge Ahab and Baal. 1 Kgs 21 in the LXX follows immediately after chs. 17–19, grouping together all Ahab's interactions with Elijah. In ch. 21 Elijah appears again vis-à-vis Ahab, where he confronts royal power. In MT Elijah's actions in ch. 21 are grouped with the actions of other prophets (chs. 20, 22). The grouping of the chapter in MT thus divides Ahab's reign neatly into two groups of three chapters: YHWH's contest through his prophet Elijah against Baalism (chs. 17–19), and YHWH's contest through Elijah and other prophets against royal power (chs. 20–22).

Elijah's introduction at this point in 1 – 2 Kings and his prominence in these chapters must be explained. Further, even though Elijah is taken to heaven in a fiery chariot, his anointing is granted to Elisha, who continues Elijah's ministry (2 Kgs 2; see also 1 Kgs 19:15–18). Elisha's ministry does not conclude until his death in 2 Kgs 13. Thus the ministry of Elijah and its continuance in Elisha spans nineteen chapters of the biblical text (1 Kgs 17 – 2 Kgs 13).

The ministries of Elijah and Elisha are contemporaneous with the dynasty of Ahab; indeed, Elijah appears in 1 Kgs 17 immediately as Ahab takes the narrative stage (1 Kgs 16:29–34). These prophets therefore stand at a crucial juncture in Israel's history. At a time when Israel is seduced by the Baalism of Ahab and Jezebel and turns as a nation away from YHWH, it is Elijah and Elisha who serve as YHWH's covenant mediators. They repeatedly call Israel back to covenant loyalty. Their miracles are accomplished in the very areas that Baal attempts to claim for himself: the provision of rain, crops and life itself. Only when the dynasty of Ahab is overthrown at the behest of Elijah and Elisha (see 'Comment', 2 Kgs 9:1–3) does their ministry effectively end; Elisha makes only one more appearance before his own death (2 Kgs 13:14–21).

The import of these characters is a response to the ongoing and powerful Baalistic threat to Israel's covenant life. YHWH is not willing to let Israel go; instead he calls Elijah and Elisha to fight on his behalf for the very life of his nation. For an exilic people to whom these narratives eventually speak in the completed history, YHWH's covenant commitment is clearly communicated. Though now in Babylon because of covenant disobedience and rejection of YHWH, and though they may face their own temptations to submit to the gods of their captors, they may have confidence that YHWH desires to keep his people within covenant life. In Babylon he will recall them to that life as he did long ago on Mount Carmel.

The character of Elijah is a unifying element in 1 Kgs 17 – 19, and in each chapter his prophetic authority is revealed. Through motif and analogy, Elijah's authority is connected to that of Moses (see 'Comment'); the connection affords theological reflection on the loss of covenant life under Ahab. Another unifying element in chs. 17–19 is Israel's drought. Pronounced by Elijah (17:1), it ends at his word (18:41–45). Chapter 19 then explores Elijah's response to the events. Throughout the drought is emblematic of YHWH's power to control the rain versus Baal's ineffectual power.

Other motifs connect chs. 17–19. The motif of food and drink is ubiquitous (17:4–6; 9–11; 18:4–5, 41; 19:5–8, 21). Likewise, journeys punctuate each chapter: to Kerith, Zarephath, Carmel, Jezreel, Horeb and Elisha's home town. Each chapter climaxes with a journey to a high place: an upper room (1 Kgs 17), Mount Carmel (1 Kgs 18), the mount of God (1 Kgs 19), and is resolved when Elijah descends from the high place.

Each chapter also shares a structural pattern (Cohn 1982: 343–349). An announcement issues in a journey for Elijah that involves a dual encounter (with the ravens and the widow in ch. 17, Obadiah and Ahab in ch. 18, and an angelic being in ch. 19). A miracle at a high place leads to a conversion of sorts: the widow affirms the prophetic authority in ch. 17, the Israelites affirm YHWH's sole claim upon them in ch. 18, and Elisha responds and thus affirms his calling as a prophet in ch. 19.

While the chapters work together as a unit, each contributes a discrete message. 1 Kgs 17 begins with an oath report (v. 1), which together with v. 24 frames the chapter. The oath includes Elijah's self-assertion that he is YHWH's spokesperson, a claim the woman's words and actions question. Through three scenes (vv. 2–6, 7–16, 17–24) that move with increasing intensity through a pattern of imperative command and compliance (see 'Comment'), the woman finally affirms that Elijah acts for YHWH; that indeed the word in Elijah's mouth is YHWH's own, and is true (v. 24). Thus Elijah's self-presentation in v. 1 that he speaks on behalf of YHWH is confirmed.

The component parts of the chapter represent prophetic legend traditions perhaps preserved by a prophetic school associated with Elijah. During Jehu's dynasty these traditions were taken up into the narrative to legitimate his coup and thus found their way into the DH (Gray 1970: 371–377; DeVries 1978: 112–127; White 1997). Further, vv. 8–16, 17–24 resemble two episodes in the life of Elisha (2 Kgs 4:1–7, 8–37). That a relationship exists between the stories is recognized by most scholars; however, the exact nature of that relationship and the direction of dependence are disputed (White 1997: 11–17). Certainly, each has been crafted to communicate the concerns of each prophet's ministry.

Comment

17:1–6

Following Ahab's great sins, Elijah appears unannounced and with little personal information provided. 'The Tishbite' (cf. 21:17, 28; 2 Kgs 1:3, 8; 9:36) may suggest a town or area called 'Tishbe', which tradition locates north of the Jabbok River (Walsh, *ABD* 6:577–578). He is also identified as one of the 'settlers of Gilead' east of the Jordan, possibly immigrants or foreigners dwelling in the territory bounded by the Jabbok and Yarmuk.

Elijah's oath ('as YHWH the God of Israel lives') makes a claim that no rain will fall except by his word. Elijah's claim aligns his words with YHWH's power, which alone controls the rain. While the self-attestation is of prophetic status, the claim is at this point only Elijah's. Neither YHWH nor the narrator has yet identified Elijah as a prophet.

Until the chapter proves Elijah's claim, one remains uncertain of its validity, although narrative cues suggest Elijah's self-attestation is true. While he is not specifically called a prophet, he appears in response to Ahab's sins (16:29–34), particularly his introduction of Baal worship. Elijah's words challenge the belief that Baal is sovereign over rain and storm and are what one might expect of YHWH's prophet. Additionally, Elijah's oath follows the reference to the oath made in Joshua's day (16:34; cf. Josh. 6:26), identified in 16:34 as YHWH's word. Is Elijah's oath also to be identified as YHWH's word? The chapter takes up this question.

Elijah swears that dew (*ṭal*) and rain (*māṭār*) will be withheld. The significant words reappear only when the judgment is lifted (17:1; 18:1). Elsewhere within the narrative rain is *gešem* (17:7, 14; 18:44–45). In

Deuteronomy *ṭal* and *māṭār* are evidence of YHWH's covenant blessings (Deut. 33:28 [*ṭal*]; Deut. 11:11, 14; 28:12 [*māṭār*]), and the absence of *māṭār* is the specific evidence of YHWH's anger when Israel abandons the covenant for other gods (Deut. 11:17; 28:24). Thus Elijah's pronouncement enacts a covenant curse upon Israel because they have broken the covenant.

The narrator moves quickly to affirm Elijah's self-attestation. He is immediately addressed in the standard prophetic formula 'the word of YHWH came to him'. Elijah's challenge to Baal is also a challenge to his royal patrons and makes him liable to their wrath. Hidden at the wadi Kerith (east of the Jordan in north Gilead [Younker, *ABD* 1:899]), the king's wrath cannot find him, nor can Ahab plead for rain before YHWH's time. As proof positive that power belongs to YHWH and not Baal, the drought will last much longer than a one-yearly cycle (18:1), the agricultural period associated with Baal's ability to bring the rains once again.

YHWH commands Elijah to 'go, turn east, and hide'. There YHWH commands for Elijah's sustenance. Despite drought and the land's limited resources, water and food are provided ('I have commanded [*ṣiwwîtî*] . . . to sustain you [*lĕkalkelkā*] there [*šām*]'; v. 4). Like Moses long ago, Elijah the new prophet of power will be fed morning and evening with bread and meat (Exod. 16:8–12). Elijah immediately obeys YHWH's command, doing 'according to the word of YHWH' and the stream and ravens similarly obey YHWH and provide water and food.

17:7–16

The lengthening drought eventually dries up the sustaining water. To provide for the prophet, YHWH again commands Elijah to 'go'. The prophet obeys and removes to Sidon, a city in Baal's own territory. Yet even there YHWH's sovereignty is complete and he provides for his prophet. The Hebrew wording is identical to v. 4, although the order of the words differs. The difference emphasizes the astounding location of the provision ('I have appointed [lit. 'commanded', *ṣiwwîtî*] there [*šām*] . . . to sustain you [*lĕkalkelkā*]'; v. 9). YHWH appoints the foreign widow to provide bread for the prophet. This occurs in the midst of increased drought, for, while at the wadi Kerith Elijah received a twice-daily ration, now he asks only for a 'little' water and a 'piece' of bread (vv. 10–11).

In the encounter with the widow Elijah takes up YHWH's role of commanding action. He twice commands her to 'bring' food, but her response suggests she is not as convinced of YHWH's sovereign power as is his prophet. She complies when the request is for water, but baulks at the request for food. Her response begins by echoing Elijah's first words in the narrative by which the drought began. She says, 'As YHWH your God lives', but then states her reluctance: she has only enough to eat, and then die. Here is the crux of her problem: she lives in the territory of Baal, who supposedly rules the rains. By these rains grain is raised, flour provided and thus life sustained. If Baal is god, as she supposes, she would be unwise to offend him by turning to YHWH of Israel. And if YHWH truly is the living God (vv. 1, 12), does not the famine belie his claim? Her hesitancy expresses her uncertainty of YHWH's power of life. This episode and the next answer the widow's concern.

Elijah responds with further commands, now beginning with a word of assurance. She must 'not fear' and must 'go in . . . do . . . make . . . and bring'. The command that she provide his food before serving herself and her son is a great test of her faith. He provides a final assurance in a prophetic word: 'Thus says YHWH the God of Israel'. The promised provision will come to her not through Baal, but through the foreign prophet of the foreign God who is also lord in Sidon and of the widow. The widow responds, but she acts in response to Elijah's word (v. 15). She is not yet convinced that Elijah stands as YHWH's prophet and that 'the word in his mouth is truth' (v. 24). It is the narrator who equates Elijah's word to YHWH's (v. 16) so that, despite the widow's reservations, the narrator makes it clear that she is in actuality responding to YHWH. The outcome is that the prophetic word is effected and the 'bowl of flour was not used up; the jug of oil was not emptied' (vv. 14, 16).

17:17–24

The woman's words have questioned whether YHWH is indeed the Lord of life (v. 12). In this scene the threat of death actualizes and YHWH proves his power over death, for he alone is the Lord of life. The proof also reveals Elijah's identity as the prophet who speaks YHWH's words, thus establishing his credentials for the ensuing contest on Mount Carmel.

Differences suggest this pericope may well arise from a tradition other than that of vv. 7–16. The 'widow' (*'iššâ 'almānâ*; vv. 9–10) is now introduced as 'mistress of the house' (*ba'ălat habbāyit*). Elijah does refer to her in v. 20 as the *'almānâ*, but the different appellations are striking. Further, the widow of vv. 7–16 faces desperate lack, and speaks only of herself and her son (v. 12), while the mistress rules over a house substantial enough for an upper room. Despite the differences, narrative connections remain. The mistress's house is not wholly unanticipated (see v. 15), and each section presents the woman as mother. Regardless of possible disparate sources, the pericopes are intentionally connected by the temporal phrase 'after these things' (v. 17).

Death becomes a reality as the boy sickens until there is 'no breath left in him'. The phrase could refer to actual death, or that the child lies at the point of death (Lasine 2004: 121). Determining the boy's state is further complicated by realities of the ancient world in which severe sickness was a liminal phase considered death. It was only after a period of days that death was wholly confirmed (Lasine 2004: 121–122). Certainly within the narrative world, both the woman and Elijah believe the child is dead (vv. 18, 20), and elsewhere the loss of 'breath' describes real death (Deut. 20:16; Josh. 10:40; 11:11, 14; 1 Kgs 15:29). YHWH has thus far sustained life in a time of famine. The challenge now goes further – can he recall life that has ceased?

The woman accuses the man of God of visiting her sins upon her son. Elijah accuses YHWH only of killing the child (v. 20) but refrains from the charge of visiting parental sins upon the child (as YHWH has elsewhere done; 14:10–12). Elijah focuses only upon the narrative point: the issue of life and death. He leaves the mechanism of death unaddressed.

Elijah commands the woman to give him the child and he retires to the upper room, laying the child upon his bed. He immediately and boldly calls upon YHWH, turning to the one who has already revealed his power as the Lord of life. The dual address 'O YHWH my God' (*yhwh 'ĕlohāy*; vv. 20–21) suggests the close relationship he has as prophet to the deity.

Besides evoking the relationship of YHWH and his prophet, Elijah's petition invokes YHWH to act as Lord of life. Elijah first reminds YHWH that this same widow 'with whom I am staying' has obediently opened her home to Elijah. Secondly, he asks if YHWH has indeed brought tragedy by 'killing her son' (*lĕhāmît 'et-bĕnāh*; v. 20), echoing the woman's own charge (*lĕhāmît 'et-bĕnî*; v. 18). His query is open-ended, anticipating that death is not YHWH's final word. Finally, Elijah requests YHWH to return life to the child – significantly, in a narrative filled with imperative commands, Elijah does not here command YHWH. Rather, his petition grants YHWH sovereign freedom. YHWH attends to the prophet, exerts his power of life and the child quickens.

Elijah's words are punctuated by the strange action of laying himself upon the child three times. The actions may be explained historically as a form of medical procedure (Kiuchi 1994: 74–75), shamanistic sympathetic magic (Lasine 2004: 123–125) or an attempt to remove uncleanness through atoning or purifying actions (Kiuchi 1994: 78). Whatever the possible historical background to Elijah's actions, they quickly yield to the real issue of the encounter, which is YHWH's life-giving power. Elijah began by acknowledging death (v. 20) and requesting life (*nepeš*; v. 21), and the narrative summation records that YHWH listened, the boy's life or soul (*nepeš*) returned and he lived (*ḥyh*; v. 22). The term *nepeš* denotes several realities around the central concept of life. It can signify breath (Job. 41:13), or the soul together with the body (Isa. 10:18), which is the centre of feeling and perception (Song 1:7; Job 23:13). It often signifies life (Gen. 9:14; Lev. 17:11; Deut. 12:23; 1 Sam. 20:1; 2 Sam. 14:7; 1 Kgs 19:10; Prov. 7:23; see *HALOT* 2:711–713; Waltke, *TWOT* 2:587–591).

The denouement highlights the transformative power of YHWH, the God of Life. Elijah returns the boy, proclaiming him alive (*ḥay*), and this

declaration spurs the woman to her own proclamation. In her initial accusation against Elijah (v. 18) she accuses him of bringing death and calls him
a 'man of God'. Now it is the evidence of resurrected life that leads her
to call him a 'man of God'. She asserts what she has been reluctant to
assert throughout the narrative, that is, that YHWH's word in Elijah's
mouth (*bĕpîkā*) is true. By this she concedes to Elijah the identity of a
prophet. It is indeed YHWH's word spoken through Elijah's mouth (*lĕpî*)
by which the rains ceased (v. 1). It is by YHWH's word spoken through
Elijah that food was provided (vv. 14–15). Now, most telling of all, life is
returned to one dead. These are the proofs that Elijah is a prophet of
YHWH whose word is life. It is this credential that enables Elijah to engage
with power and authority King Ahab and his prophets.

Explanation

The concern of this chapter is *life*. The land experiences famine; food is
scarce and life is threatened both in YHWH's land and in the land of the
Sidonian Jezebel whose god Ahab imported. Even more pointedly, the boy
dies and the mother grieves. In this context YHWH sustains life, provides
food for the prophet and the foreigner (vv. 4, 14, 16) and restores the
boy's life (vv. 21–22). It is not surprising, then, that the oath formula 'As
YHWH the God of Israel lives . . .' (vv. 1, 12) is used twice. The oath
highlights the point: YHWH is life, and effects life in others.

YHWH's concern for life is reflected in his name. Revealed to Moses
when death threatened Israel's life, it speaks of YHWH's continual
existence. God responds to Moses' request for his name, 'I am (*'ehyê*) who
I am (*'ehyê*); I am (*'ehyê*) has sent you' (Exod. 3:14). This repetitious
statement employs the verb 'to be' (*hyh*) and is followed by the deity's
name, YHWH (*yhwh*; Exod. 3:15). It is the repeated sound of the verb 'to
be' that has 'by mere suggestion tied Yahweh to *hyh* irrevocably' (McCarthy
1978a: 316). YHWH is named as the ever-living one and as such he rescues
his people from Egypt into covenant life.

YHWH's power of life is evident before this event. At creation all living
creatures have the 'breath of life' (Gen. 1:30; 6:17). This includes the
human creatures into whom God breathes the breath of life (Gen. 2:7). It
is YHWH's breath of life that sustains his creatures' life (Ps. 104:29; Job
34:14–15). YHWH also works at the practical level to sustain life. During
famine he sustains Israel's life in Egypt (Gen. 50:19–20) and continually
sustains life in the wilderness with food and water (Exod. 16 – 17; Ps.
105:40–41). By this power he similarly sustains Elijah and the woman.

As life-giver it is somewhat surprising that he invokes death-dealing
famine in this narrative. Under the covenant, Moses repeatedly reminds
Israel that the covenant is for life. By it Israel possesses and lives in the
land (Deut. 4:1, 40; 5:33; 6:1–2, 24; 8:1–3) whose abundance ensures life.

Even more, the covenant calls Israel to choose life (Deut. 30:15–20). This life is not simply enjoyment of the land's abundance but is the relationship with YHWH who is their life (Deut. 30:20). As Israel commits to this covenantal choice, YHWH's life extends not only to them, but through their priestly role (Exod. 19:6) they mediate YHWH's life to all nations. In this chapter the sustaining life given to the Sidonian woman and her household is evidence YHWH's concern extends beyond Israel.

Participation in YHWH's covenant means Israel is to partake of and reflect the character of YHWH, being holy as he is holy (Lev. 19:2). Covenant obedience expresses their participation, by which they experience the covenant's benefits. Covenant disobedience expresses their refusal to respond and participate in the proffered covenant life. For this, several consequences are possible, one of which is famine (Deut. 11:13–17; 28:22–24; 29:23–27).

The famine that opens Elijah's narrative shows the chapter's real concern is with covenant life. It is threatened because the people have turned to Baal and have credited him with the power of life, of rain, of crops (Hos. 1:5; cf. Jer. 2:7–13). It is no narrative accident that the invocation of famine follows immediately Ahab's introduction of Baal to Israel (1 Kgs 16:31–33). Famine is an expected outcome of disobedience under the covenant. But that YHWH moves so immediately to send his prophet to call Israel back to covenant shows his commitment to life. Even though the covenant curses were prescribed (Deut. 28), YHWH is merciful and gracious and unwilling that Israel should linger long outside covenant life. It is this that precipitates his immediate action.

For the exilic community who received these narratives, the tale of Israel's discipline under the covenant must ring true. Babylon is their own 'time of famine' in which they feel the threat of loss of life. But in the same way that Elijah by YHWH's power returns life, so God's people in Babylon will find hope for quickened life. This hope will come to them as it did to the widow woman through the prophetic word. Messages from Jeremiah called the people to hope for return and renewed covenant life (Jer. 29, 30 – 33); Ezekiel brought visions of dead bones restored and given life by YHWH's breath (Ezek. 37). If famine is unable to hold sway in Sidon, it is equally unable to hold sway in Babylon, for in all places YHWH is sovereign and his word is the powerful word that alone effects life from death.

Finally, in 1 Kgs 17 YHWH communicates his commitment to life in two arenas. The first is the arena of the physical, the mundane. Food is provided by ravens. Life is restored to a physical body. There is no supra-materiality here. Having breathed the breath of life into human form, YHWH works with the stuff of human existence to sustain it. Secondly, YHWH communicates his commitment to life through his word. It is YHWH's word that sends Elijah to wadi Kerith and the sustenance provided there by YHWH's command. It is YHWH's word through his prophet that commands a 'little water' and a 'piece of bread' (v. 10), and then assures of ongoing plenty

(vv. 14, 16). And it is the prophet's petition that invokes YHWH to restore life. By this the woman is converted from doubt to faith in YHWH's prophet and YHWH's word.

The coalescing of YHWH's own living self, his commitment to life, the material arena of that life and the power of YHWH's word finds full expression in the incarnation. John introduces his Gospel with these very themes. The Word comes as one who is himself life, indeed is YHWH. The Word has given life in the creation of all things. This powerful Word of God himself becomes material stuff: incarnated as a human yet in whom the full glory of YHWH resides.

Later, John makes the astounding claim 'this is eternal life, that they may know you, the only true God, and Jesus Christ whom you have sent . . . and now, glorify me with the glory I had with you before the world began' (John 17:3). The means of this glorification is, of course, the crucifixion. When Judas leaves the gathered disciples to betray Jesus to death, symbolic 'night' comes immediately on the heels of his departure (John 13:30). In this context Jesus declares that the Son of Man is now glorified (John 13:31). The glorification of the crucifixion is not the final word, however. The resurrection of Jesus' physical body becomes the great attestation of the power of God in his Word, Jesus Christ, proving that YHWH truly is the Lord of life.

In the events John records regarding the Word – enfleshed, crucified, resurrected, ascended – a similar call for recognition as met the Sidonian woman comes anew. She recognized YHWH's power in the life he granted. This confirmed her understanding of the word. John's Gospel calls its audience to the same – though ultimately greater – recognition.

1 KINGS 18:1–46

Translation

[1]After many days, the word of YHWH came to Elijah in the third year, saying, 'Go, show yourself to Ahab and I will send rain upon the face of the earth.' [2]So Elijah went to show himself to Ahab. Now the famine was severe in Samaria, [3]and Ahab summoned Obadiah, who was over the house. (Obadiah greatly feared YHWH; [4]When Jezebel was destroying the prophets of YHWH, Obadiah took one hundred prophets and hid them, fifty men in a cave[a], and sustained them with bread and water.) [5]Ahab said to Obadiah, 'Go throughout the land to all the springs of water and to all the wadis. Perhaps we may find grass to keep the horses and mules alive, and not have to kill[a] some of the animals.' [6]They divided the land between them to pass through it. Ahab went one way by himself, and Obadiah went the other way by himself.

[7]Now Obadiah was on the road, when suddenly Elijah met him. He recognized him and fell upon his face and said, 'Is this you, my lord Elijah?' [8]He said to him,

'It is I. Go; say to your lord, "Behold, Elijah *is here*."' [9]He said, 'How have I sinned that you are giving your servant into the hand of Ahab to put me to death? [10]As YHWH your God lives, there is not a nation or kingdom to which my lord has not sent to seek you. When they said, "He is not here!" he would make the kingdom or nation swear that they[a] had not found you. [11]Now you are saying, "Go; say to your lord, 'Behold, Elijah *is here*.'" [12]It will happen, my lord, that I will depart from you and YHWH's spirit will carry you someplace I do not know. I will come to tell Ahab, but he will not find you. Then he will kill me, although your servant has feared YHWH from my youth. [13]Has it not been told to my lord what I did when Jezebel killed YHWH's prophets? How I hid some of YHWH's prophets, one hundred men by fifties[a] in a cave, and sustained them with bread and water? [14]Now you are saying, "Go; say to your lord, 'Behold, Elijah *is here*.'" He will kill me!'

[15]But Elijah said, 'As YHWH of Hosts lives, before whom I stand, surely today I will appear to him!' [16]So Obadiah went to meet Ahab and told him and Ahab went to meet Elijah.

[17]When Ahab saw Elijah, Ahab said to him, 'Is this you, you troubler of Israel?' [18]He said, 'I have not troubled Israel, but you have, and your father's house, because you have forsaken[a] YHWH's commandments and you have followed[a] the Baals! [19]Now then, send; gather all Israel to me at Mount Carmel, *along* with the four hundred and fifty prophets of Baal and the four hundred prophets of Asherah, who eat at Jezebel's table.' [20]So Ahab sent among all the sons of Israel and he gathered the prophets to Mount Carmel.

[21]Then Elijah drew near to all the people and said, 'How long will you waver between two opinions? If YHWH is God, follow him, but if Baal, follow him!' But the people did not answer him a word. [22]Elijah said to the people, 'I alone remain a prophet for YHWH, but the prophets of Baal are four hundred and fifty men. [23]Let them give us two bulls, and they shall choose one bull for themselves. They shall cut it up and put it upon the wood – but they shall not set fire *to it*. Then I will prepare one bull and I will put it upon the wood – but I will not set fire *to it*. [24]Then you shall call upon the name of your god, and I will call upon the name of YHWH, and the god who answers with fire, he is god.' And all the people answered and said, 'The word is good.'

[25]Elijah said to the prophets of Baal, 'Choose for yourselves one bull and prepare *it* first, for you are the majority. Then call on the name of your god, but do not set fire *to it*. [26]They took the bull which he gave to them. They prepared *it* and called on the name of Baal from morning to noon, saying, 'O Baal, answer us!' But there was no sound and no answer. And they danced on the altar that they had made[a]. [27]At noon Elijah mocked them, and he said, 'Call with a loud voice, for he is a god! Maybe he is musing, or has turned aside[a], or gone on a journey! Perhaps he is asleep and must be awakened!' [28]So they called with a loud voice, and according to their ritual they cut themselves with swords and lances until blood poured out upon them. [29]As noon passed, they prophesied until the offering of the oblation, but there was no sound; no one answered; no one paid attention.

[30]Elijah said to all the people, 'Draw near to me!' And all the people drew near to him. He repaired the altar of YHWH, which had been torn down. [31]Elijah took twelve stones according to the number of the tribes of the sons of Jacob (to whom YHWH's word had come, saying, 'Israel will be your name'). [32]With the stones he built an altar in YHWH's name. He made a trench around the altar, large enough to hold two seahs[a] of seed. [33]Then he arranged the wood, and cut up the bull, and placed *it* upon the wood. [34]He said, 'Fill four water jars and pour *them* upon the offering and the wood.' Then he said, 'Do it again,' and they did it again. Then he said, 'A third time!' And they did it a third time. [35]The water went all around the altar and the water even filled the trench.

[36]At the time of the offering of the oblation, Elijah the prophet drew near and said, 'O YHWH, God of Abraham, Isaac and Israel. Let it be known this day that you are God in Israel, and I am your servant and by your word[a] I have done all these things. [37]Answer me, O YHWH; answer me, that this people may know that you, O YHWH, are God and that you have turned their hearts back!' [38]Then the fire of YHWH fell and consumed the offering, and the wood, and the stones, and the dust, and licked up the water that was in the trench. [39]And all the people saw and they fell on their faces and said, 'YHWH, he is God! YHWH, he is God!' [40]Elijah said to them, 'Seize the prophets of Baal; do not let one of them escape!' They seized them and Elijah brought them down to the river Kishon and slaughtered them there.

[41]Elijah said to Ahab, 'Go up; eat and drink, for there is the sound of pelting rain.' [42]Ahab went up to eat and drink and Elijah went up to the top of Carmel and bowed to the ground and put his face between his knees[a]. [43]Then he said to his young man, 'Go up! Look towards the sea.' He went up and looked and said, 'There is nothing.' He said 'Go back' seven times. [44]On the seventh time he said, 'Behold, a cloud as small as a man's hand is rising from the sea.' Then he said, 'Go up; say to Ahab, "Hitch up! Go down! The rain will not hold back!"' [45]Meanwhile, the heavens blackened *with* clouds and wind, and there was a heavy rainstorm. But Ahab rode and went towards Jezreel. [46]And the hand of YHWH was upon Elijah and he girded his loins and ran in front of Ahab to the entrance of Jezreel.

Notes on the text

4.a. MT reads, 'in the cave', that is, one cave. LXX[BO] 'in two caves', assuming it is illogical to hide two groups in one cave. Montgomery (1951: 309) proposes the article signifies a cave complex (cf. similarly at v. 13).

5.a. Reading with MT (and LXX) the unusual hiph. form of *krt* (*wĕlô' nakrît*, 'not have to kill'), rather than ni. form (*wĕlô' nikrat*, 'not be deprived of'), as proposed by *BHS* and Gray (1970: 387).

10.a. 'they had not found you' agrees for sense with the 3 m. pl. form of the preceding verb, 'they said'. MT reads 3 m. sg.

13.a. 'by fifties' captures the sense of MT's 'fifty men by fifty'.

18.a. The double indictment is both collective ('you [2 m. pl.] have forsaken'), and particular ('you [2 m. sg.] have followed'; 2 m. pl. in LXX^min, Syr, Tg, Vg). The particularity is a reminder of the regnal evaluation of 16:31–32.

26.a. Reading MT 3 m. sg. *'āśâ* as 3 m. pl., 'they had made'.

27.a. *kî śîaḥ wĕkî śîg lô*. A translation of 'musing' (*śîaḥ*) comes from Sirach; LXX's ἀδολεσχία, reflects the usage. *śîg* is a hapax legomenon, possibly 'go away', 'go to the side', 'expulsion' or 'defecation' (*HALOT* 1319). The phrase may be a hendiadys for Baal turning aside to defecate (so Rendsburg 1988). Walsh (1996: 249) argues that the hapax is simply wordplay along the lines of 'helter-skelter', and translated as 'he's busy, in a tizzy'. However translated, the phrase is a scathing taunt against Baal's inability to answer.

32.a. A seah measures approximately 13 quarts (15 l); 2 seahs (26 qt [30 l]) is hardly a large volume. Possibly the area of land seedable by such a quantity is in view, although that measure (approximately 4,921 sq ft [1,500 sq m]) is exceedingly large and difficult to equate with the 12 jars of poured water (v. 34).

36.a. 'by your word' reading a sg. noun with Q against pl. K.

42.a. 'between his knees' reading a pl. noun with Q against sg. K.

Form and structure

1 Kgs 18 continues the conflict between Baal and YHWH (in chs. 17–19). Narrative continuity is sustained through shared structural elements, motifs and themes (see 'Form and structure', 1 Kgs 17).

The chapter's introduction (vv. 1–2a) is followed by two sections. The first (vv. 2b–20) concerns the promised rain, although the section closes without rain falling. Instead, the narrative segues to a second section, the contest on Mount Carmel (vv. 21–40). Only the concluding verses see the promised rain (vv. 41–46). The two sections can be understood through complex compositional theories, but no agreement exists whether the compilation arose in pre-Dtr prophetic circles (Gray 1970: 383), during the Jehuite dynasty (Sweeney 2007: 223–224; White 1997: 32), at the time of post-Dtr prophetic additions (McKenzie 1991: 90–98) or even during the late sixth century BC (Otto 2003: 504). The lack of agreement undermines the value of seeking such redactional history. The unity of the finished product may more easily be credited to a careful author, although even a redactional history does not detract from the narrative's unity.

Both narrative sections reveal YHWH as Israel's covenant Lord (K. Roberts 2000). The absence of dew and rain (17:1) are covenant punishments precipitated by Ahab's false worship, and the promise of rain (18:1) brings hope of covenant renewal. Such renewal is effected as Elijah challenges Israel to return to YHWH (vv. 21–40). Several allusions to Elijah as the new Moses contribute to the covenant theme (see 'Comment').

The rain narrative (vv. 2b–20) has three scenes with two primary characters interacting in each (vv. 2b–6, 7–16b, 16b–20). Using a pattern of command and response the three scenes echo the introduction in which Elijah is commanded to go (*hlk*) and show (*r'h*) himself to Ahab. In the first scene Ahab commands Obadiah to go (*hlk*), and Obadiah goes (*hlk*). In the second scene he meets Elijah, who commands Obadiah to go (*hlk*) to his master, a command Obadiah twice repeats before going (*hlk*) to Ahab. Elijah also promises to appear (*r'h*) to Ahab, taking up the narrative's initial command (v. 1). Finally, Ahab sees (*r'h*) the prophet in the final scene.

The scene closes not with rain but a new set of commands whereby Ahab is to send (*šlḥ*) and gather (*qbṣ*). This initiates the contest narrative, which also proceeds through three scenes featuring two main characters: Elijah and the people (vv. 21–24, 30–40), and Elijah and the prophets of Baal (vv. 25–29). YHWH and Baal are also unmistakably present as they are repeatedly named or mentioned (Baal in vv. 21–22, 24, 25 [twice], 26–28, 40; YHWH in vv. 21–22, 24, 30–32, 36 [twice], 37 [twice], 38, 39 [twice]).

The pattern of command and response continues, now with the verbs 'answer' (*'nh*) and 'call' (*qr'*). Elijah commands but the 'people did not answer (*'nh*) him'. Elijah announces the contest in which the god who 'answers' (*'nh*) by fire is god, and the people do 'answer' (*'nh*; v. 24). Elijah commands the prophets to prepare their offering and 'call' (*qr'*) on their god. Baal is enjoined to 'answer' (*'nh*), but no answer (*'nh*) is given. Elijah once again issues the command to 'call' (*qr'*), but the scene ends with 'no sound and no answer' (*'nh*). Finally, Elijah petitions YHWH to 'answer' (*'nh*). Only as the contest concludes do the people answer (*'nh*) Elijah's initial command to follow YHWH (v. 21).

The contest complete, the narrative returns to the drought (vv. 41–46). Once again command and response patterns the interaction between two characters, centring on 'going up' (*'lh*). Ahab is commanded to 'go up, eat and drink' (v. 41). Elijah's young man is commanded to 'go up and look' (v. 42). A final command to the servant to 'go up' delivers instructions to Ahab, and Ahab obeys, proving he, too, is now willing to follow YHWH's prophet.

Comment

18:1–20

1–2a. Proven a prophet in ch. 17, this chapter opens with the prophetic formula 'the word of YHWH came to Elijah'. After 'many days', that is, the drought's third year, Elijah is commanded to 'go and show' (*lēk hērā'ê*; imp. verbs) himself to Ahab, that YHWH would send (*'etnâ*; coh. verb) rain (*māṭār*). The verbal sequence (coh. following imp.) indicates rain follows as a result of Elijah's action. The rain is *māṭār* (as at 17:1) rather than *gešem* (17:7, 14: 18:44–45), and reveals the chapter's strong covenant associations (see 'Comment' at 17:1). Two scenes ensue before Elijah meets Ahab.

2b–6. The lengthy famine has depleted all crops and reserves (Beck 2003: 295), endangering the king's livestock. Ahab is unaware that covenant infidelity is responsible for the drought and he blames Elijah (v. 17). The king and prophet meet after a series of movements: Ahab summons (*qr'*) his steward (v. 3), who meets (*qr'*) Elijah (v. 7) and then returns to meet (*qr'*) Ahab (v. 16). Only then does Ahab meet (*qr'*) the elusive prophet (v. 16).

Obadiah is 'over the house' (a role known in both kingdoms [1 Kgs 4:6; 16:9; 2 Kgs 10:5; 18:18, 37; 19:2]) and is responsible for the king's household and estates, including livestock. Although he serves the apostate king, he is true to his name ('servant of YHWH') for he rescues YHWH's prophets from Jezebel. Despite further personal risk, he sustains (*kwl*) them with bread and water – as the ravens and the widow earlier provided for Elijah.

By contrast, Ahab does not serve YHWH. He does not seek YHWH's help in famine. Jezebel seeks to 'destroy' (*krt*) YHWH's prophets, but, rather than intervene, Ahab worries about having to 'kill' (*krt*) livestock. King and servant move in opposite directions – figuratively regarding the prophets of YHWH and literally, as they set off throughout the land (v. 6).

7–16. Several elements of Obadiah's characterization in this initial meeting parallel him to the Sidonian woman (ch. 17) and both serve crucial functions in forwarding the plot: the Sidonian woman affirms Elijah's prophetic identity; Obadiah facilitates the prophet's meeting with Ahab. Both charge Elijah with visiting their sin upon them and bringing death (17:18; 18:9); both initially resist Elijah's command (17:12; 18:9–14); both invoke the oath 'As YHWH your God lives' as part of their reluctance (17:12; 18:10); both receive Elijah's assurance (17:13–14; 18:15).

Obadiah's obeisance and submissive 'my lord' (v. 7) cannot disguise his reluctance to obey Elijah. His reluctance is communicated by his twice-repeated, incredulous, 'Go; say . . . "Elijah is here"' (vv. 11, 14) and his fear of death (*mwt*; v. 9) should he, like the surrounding nations, be unable to produce Elijah. His fear is emphasized as he says Ahab may kill (*hrg*; v. 12) him, and then repeats his concern (v. 14). This is the same word used of Jezebel's actions (*hrg*; v. 13); his fear is also directed towards the queen.

Reassuring Obadiah, Elijah's response (v. 15) also reconfirms his prophetic status: he 'stands before' YHWH who is a God of life, not death – a further assurance to Obadiah. Obadiah has thus described YHWH in his own oath (v. 10), but the power of death at Ahab's court overshadows that conviction in his mind. He believes he will die, not live. As further reassurance Elijah asserts he will 'appear' (*r'h*) before Ahab, returning the narrative to YHWH's command (v. 1). Obadiah responds to Elijah, proving that even in a court of death, Obadiah is truly Elijah's servant (v. 9).

17–20. Elijah digresses from the immediate issue of rain to the under-lying issue of covenant faithlessness. Ahab labels Elijah a 'troubler' (*'ôkēr*; qal part.) of Israel, attributing the drought to his malice. The implications of the label are telling. In the DH the word in the qal stem is used of two arch-villains: Saul (1 Sam. 14:29) and Achan (Josh. 6:18; 7:25). Both were covenant breakers and Ahab classifies Elijah with them, possibly acknow-ledging the covenant is at stake. Elijah turns the accusation back on Ahab. His covenant sins are responsible for the drought and Elijah prepares for a contest that will reinstate the covenant and return the rain.

Many individuals have been commanded to 'go' (vv. 1, 5, 8, 11, 14). Now Ahab is to 'send' (*šlḥ*) and 'gather' (*qbṣ*) all Israel and the Baal and Asherah prophets to Baal's mountain. Ahab's obedience is partial, signalling his continued resistance. He sends only *'among* all the sons of Israel' and gathers only 'the prophets'. The full four hundred and fifty Baal prophets are not mentioned; the Asherah prophets not at all. Ahab, the worshipper of Baal, may have felt a home-court advantage and considered the whole Baal and Asherah contingent unnecessary.

Elijah sets the contest for Mount Carmel in the Phoenician/Israelite border territory. The high seaside mountain enjoys abundant rain and lush vegetation. It had long been used as a site sacred to Baal the slayer of the sea, god of storm and rain, and giver of abundant vegetation (W. Herrmann 1999; Beck 2003: 298–299). An ancient altar to YHWH now lies in ruins (v. 30).

18:21–40

Elijah 'draws near' (*ngš*) to the people (vv. 21, 30) as he will later to the altar (v. 36). Like Moses (Exod. 19 – 24, 32 – 34) he will mediate the covenant. Like Moses (and Joshua) he urges the people to choose their god (Exod. 32:26; Josh. 24:14–24). In the pluralistic Baal cult such a choice is not necessary, but in the monotheistic YHWH cult there can be only one God. The people must choose YHWH or Baal; to do neither is 'waver[ing] between two opinions' (*posĕḥîm 'al-šĕttê hassĕ'ippîm*). The qal verb 'wavering' is elsewhere used in the ni. to describe Mephibosheth's lameness (2 Sam. 4:4), and later, its pi. form will explain the ritual dance of Baal's prophets (v. 26). The Israelites limp upon two *sĕ'ippîm*, forked sticks or crutches between which they are metaphorically caught. Israel's refusal to 'answer (*'nh*) him a word' suggests they are unwilling to give up their worship of Baal and return their choice to YHWH.

The contest is designed to press the people to choose. For the players there is only Elijah for YHWH (an exaggeration for effect, for Obadiah has saved at least one hundred of YHWH's prophets) against the four hundred and fifty for Baal. The contest procedure is given, and only the god who answers (*'nh*) will be acknowledged god – the outcome will dictate the people's choice. Before, the people answered not a word; now they answer (*'nh*) 'The word is good'. Their acquiescence now suggests a willingness to consider Elijah's initial question.

The contest proceeds in two rounds, each ending with the leitmotif 'answer'. In round one Elijah commands (the verbs are imperative) the prophets first to 'choose' (*bḥr*), 'prepare' (*'śh*) and 'call' (*qr'*). His commands are obeyed, for Elijah is in control – especially as he provides the bull, which they then 'take' (*lqḥ*). Elijah shrewdly lets the Baal prophets sacrifice first, lest YHWH's dramatic response forestall the Baal sacrifice. In that scenario the people might in future wonder if Baal may have acted in similar power. Elijah ensures an order of events that will demonstrate the greatest display of Baal's impotence and YHWH's power.

The prophets work hard invoking Baal from 'morning to noon'. Ritual dances intensify their effort. The dances (*yĕpassĕḥû*; v. 26) share the same verbal root as the people's 'wavering' (v. 21), tying people and prophets together in their devotion to Baal. Baal's silence is complete, with not only 'no answer' (*'nh*), but 'no voice'.

Round two begins with Elijah's mockery (v. 27). There has been no 'voice' (*qôl*) of Baal, so Elijah commands they call with a loud 'voice' (*qôl*). Perhaps, Elijah taunts, Baal is 'musing' or 'turned aside' (probably a euphemistic taunt that Baal is busy in the bathroom; Rendsburg 1988). If the terms are a hendiadys, they indicate Baal's meditative (or intestinal!) preoccupation. The taunt about the journey or Baal's slumber snidely uses the myth of Baal's yearly descent to the underworld of Mot where he is held powerless until the growing season begins (W. Herrmann 1999). Elijah mocks that Baal's inability to return or answer from his underworld imprisonment shows he is no god at all.

The prophets, as if agreeing with Elijah's assessment of Baal's pre-occupation or absence, 'call' upon their god until the time of the evening offering (Exod. 29:38–41; Num. 28:3–8; 2 Kgs 16:15; Ezra 9:4–5; Dan. 9:21). Their intensified rituals draw blood as they 'prophesy' (*nb'*), a word used to describe the actions of YHWH's prophets. Here it contrasts inefficient ecstasy (J. Roberts 1970) and the simple, word-centred actions of Elijah. To their ecstasy Baal gives no sound, answer or attention. Despite the home-court advantage, Team Baal fails. By Elijah's contest criterion (v. 24) Baal is proven no god.

Elijah now prepares for his sacrificial petition. As before, Elijah commands the people to 'draw near' (*ngś*) and their immediate response reveals a growing openness to YHWH's prophet. Like Moses, Elijah prepares an altar of twelve stones (Exod. 24:3–8), which is twice named by YHWH's covenant name (vv. 30, 32). The covenanted ancestor Jacob, who received the covenant name Israel, is evoked as a reminder of the people's covenant identity. The offering is prepared and placed on the altar surrounded by the 30-litre capacity trench. The Israelite's willingness to expend valuable water further reveals their new obedience to YHWH's prophet. The twelve jars, as the twelve stones, are sharp reminders of YHWH's covenant with the twelve tribes of Israel.

Without the histrionics of the Baal prophets, Elijah simply calls upon God. He invokes the patriarchs, naming Israel (rather than the usual Jacob) as a reminder of the people's covenant nature. The central petition is that YHWH 'answer' Elijah (*'nh*; v. 37). If YHWH does not answer, the contest will be a draw. If he does answer, YHWH must be acknowledged and known as God in Israel, having turned the people's hearts in repentance (vv. 36–37). Elijah's own status as YHWH's servant would also be confirmed, thus saving him from retribution at the hands of Baal's prophets, Jezebel, Ahab or even the people.

Elijah petitions an 'answer', and YHWH answers with action, sending the lightning over which Baal is supposed to have power. It wholly consumes offering, altar, water and even dust. YHWH's falling (*npl*) fire causes Israel to fall (*npl*) in obeisance as they answer Elijah's original question, 'YHWH, he is God! YHWH, he is God!' Thus Elijah's petition that YHWH answer so that the people 'know' and repent is met.

Testing the people's new commitment, Elijah commands they seize Baal's prophets. The response is immediate and the prophets are 'slaughtered' (*šḥṭ*) by Elijah (the verb is m. sg.), an action again reminiscent of Moses (Exod. 24:5; 32:27; cf. Josh. 24:14). 'Slaughter' (*šḥṭ*) most often describes sacrificial acts (Lev. 3:2; 4:24; 17:3; 22:28 *et passim*; cf. Exod. 24:5), which usage fits the present cultic context. The slaughter of Jezebel's prophets turns on its head her plan to dispatch YHWH's prophets. Royal power and cult are bested by YHWH's servant, securing Israel's devotion to their true God.

18:41–46

Returned covenant commitments herald the return of rain. Narratively absent during the contest, Ahab reappears to await the rain petitioned by the 'troubler of Israel'. Elijah commands Ahab to 'go up' (*'lh*) and 'eat and drink'. He is to represent Israel in a ritual meal under the renewed covenant (K. Roberts 2000), as had the elders, priests, Moses and Aaron under the original covenant (Exod. 24:11). Like the people, Ahab now immediately and completely obeys. So responsive is YHWH to the renewed covenant that Elijah anticipates 'pelting rain' (*hămôn haggāšem*). Its abundance is indicated by its tumultuous noise (*hămôn*), such as associated with a panicked military camp (1 Sam. 14:19) or tumultuous waves (Jer. 10:13).

Elijah, too, 'goes up' (*'lh*). As with Moses, the covenant is renewed on the mountain top (Exod. 34:2). There Elijah fervently prays, repeatedly commanding his young man to 'go up' (*'lh*), certain that the prophetic rain (v. 41) will come. It will sweep in from the sea in a final slight to Baal,

who in Canaanite mythology conquered the sea god. Now YHWH has
conquered Baal and summons the rain from the sea.

Elijah takes the sign of the small cloud as a harbinger. After many in
the scene have 'gone up' (vv. 41, 42 [twice], 43 [twice], 44), the appearance
of the cloud motivates Elijah's command that Ahab hitch up and 'go down'
(*yrd*). The narrative communicates Ahab's rapid obedience by skipping
over his trip down the mountain. He is pictured en route, fleeing the heavy
rainstorm. The mountain-top covenant renewal is complete. YHWH sends
rain, a covenant blessing.

Elijah's final prophetic act speeds him under YHWH's power to Jezreel.
The covenant restored and the rains released, Elijah need no longer hide
from Ahab. He accompanies him to the city, ready for his next interaction
with the king.

Explanation

'YHWH, he is God! YHWH, he is God!' (v. 39). The dramatic contest on
Mount Carmel, communicated through a delightfully artful narrative, works
to this one purpose: that Israel would know that YHWH alone – not Baal
– is God (v. 37). The conviction that YHWH is God and that there is none
other is not a late development in Israel only expressed in Isa. 40 – 55.
Despite critical arguments for the late development of Israelite monotheism from early polytheistic Canaanite worship, the biblical attestation
shows that Abraham and those after him worshipped one God (see Routledge
2008: 85–101 for a review of the theories of development of Israelite monotheism, and an argument for early monotheism). Abraham does come from
a background of polytheism and himself worships other gods (Josh. 24:2),
but his call (Gen. 12:1–3) represents a departure from his family's worship
practices. In that call a new god summons the patriarch, although Abraham
may not initially understand the uniqueness of this God's self-revelation.
Abraham may have known and perhaps worshipped the Mesopotamian
god *'El* and may have initially construed this new God in old terms, for he
formulated *'El* -names for the God who had called him (Gen. 17:1; cf. 28:3;
35:11; 43:14; 48:3; Exod. 6:3). But this new God is identified as Abraham's
own, the 'God of your father Abraham' (Gen. 28:13). In time this newly
revealed deity is adopted by successive patriarchs.

The God of Abraham, Isaac and Jacob is continuous with the God
revealed to Moses by the name YHWH (Exod. 3:6, 13–15; 6:3). This name
does appear in the narrative before this encounter with Moses (e.g.
throughout Gen. 2; 17:1; 21:1) and is evidence of the writers' conviction
that YHWH was the same God worshipped by the patriarchs and active
in the story before them (Moberly 1992: 55–67). It is Moses who enshrines
YHWH's command that there be no other gods before Israel (Exod. 20:3;
Deut. 5:7). In Deuteronomy Moses reinforces YHWH's exclusive claims

upon which the Mount Carmel contest is based: 'you were shown these things that you might know that YHWH is God . . . there is no other . . . Acknowledge and take to heart this day that YHWH is God . . . there is no other' (Deut. 4:35, 39). This may be understood at this point as practical rather than theoretical monotheism, that is, while not denying the possibility of other gods, it asserts that for Israel no other gods were to be considered. YHWH had selected Israel, and they were to deal with him alone (Routledge 2008: 97).

This provides the background for the exclusive claim YHWH makes upon Israel at Carmel and that comes to full expression in Isaiah. YHWH is incomparable (Isa. 40:18, 25; 42:8; 46:5) and there is no god apart from him – true theoretical monotheism (Isa. 44:6–8; 45:5–6, 14, 18, 21–22). His awesome power is shown in creation (Isa. 40:26; 42:5; 45:12). Such power surely encompasses the demonstration at Carmel. For these reasons Israel is to worship him alone.

The Mount Carmel contest demonstrates YHWH's call to exclusive worship by displaying his power. That power is positively revealed in the divine pyrotechnics that consume the offering. But it is also displayed by contrast to the negative portrayal of Baal. Baal is ineffective (as in Judg. 6:31), unable to answer or defend himself. Such false gods are worthless (Jer. 2:5; 10:8; 14:22; 51:17) and in fact no gods at all (Jer. 2:11; 5:7). Their only existence is as idols manufactured of wood, stone and metal, which cannot see or understand. So powerless, they cannot stand on their own and require nails to support them (Isa. 40:18–20; 41:7; 44:9–20; 45:20; 46:1–2, 6–7).

The choice is set before Israel: allegiance to an ineffectual god of wood and stone or allegiance to the living God (note also the portrayal of YHWH as lord over life in 1 Kgs 17), who is effectual. He sees and hears his people and has the power to deliver them (Exod. 3:7–8) and make them his own through covenant (Exod. 19:1–6). Their misplaced allegiance to Baal threatens that covenant and so YHWH attends to his people and, through the work of his prophet at Carmel, delivers them once again to covenant life.

YHWH's exclusive claims and the power that imbues them present Israel with implacable choice: either YHWH is God and should be worshipped, or he is not (v. 21). The covenant calls them continually to 'choose this day whom you will serve' (Josh. 24:15). The chapter reveals two individuals who have already made that choice, exercising it under very different circumstances: Elijah, the prophet of YHWH, and Obadiah, who serves an apostate king (v. 3). Others within and without Israel likewise make that choice under very different circumstances: Naaman the foreigner (2 Kgs 5), Daniel in captivity serving conquerors, prophets under Manasseh's reign of terror (2 Kgs 21:10), Huldah during Josiah's reform (2 Kgs 22), Stephen as the stones threaten his life (Acts 6), Euodia and Syntyche in the midst of personal battles (Phil. 4:2).

The assertion is always the same: 'Hear, O Israel: YHWH our God, YHWH is one.' And acknowledgment of that truth is likewise the same: 'Love YHWH your God with all your heart, with all your soul and with all your strength. These commandments that I give you today are to be upon your hearts.' This is the crux of covenant life. Sadly, although this is proven powerfully in this chapter, it is a lesson that Israel (and Judah her southern neighbour) fails to remember as 1 – 2 Kings progresses.

Once in exile the nation must recognize in 1 Kgs 18 their own history of wrong choices and limping between options. Their history shows they repeatedly turned from YHWH and, by the final years of Judah's life in the land, they had chosen many gods (2 Kgs 17:7–13, 16–20; 21:2–9) and trusted in foreign nations (Jer. 27:1–15). They looked to these to deliver them from the approaching Babylonian forces. But Judah's gods and foreign alliances failed to deliver them from Babylon. Like Baal on Carmel they had no power before YHWH's might and sovereign will. Judah became the sacrifice upon the covenant altar, Jerusalem was burned and her people exiled. It is finally in the place of exile that YHWH's people remember the truth, 'YHWH, he is God! YHWH, he is God!'

1 KINGS 19:1-21

Translation

[1]Ahab told Jezebel all that Elijah had done, and that[a] he had killed all the prophets with the sword. [2]Jezebel sent a messenger to Elijah, saying[a], 'Thus may the gods[b] do – and even more – if by this time tomorrow I do not make your life as the life of one of them.' [3]Then he was afraid[a], and arose and fled for his life. He came to Beersheba, which belongs to Judah, and he left his servant there, [4]but he went one day's journey into the wilderness. He came and sat under a certain broom tree and asked for his life that he might die. He said, 'It is enough; now, O YHWH, take my life for I am no better than my fathers.' [5]Then he lay down and slept[a]. Suddenly, an angel was shaking him. He said to him, 'Get up and eat!' [6]He looked, and at his head was a loaf baked over hot stones, and a jug of water, and he ate and drank, and then lay down again. [7]The angel of YHWH returned a second time and shook him. He said, 'Get up! Eat! For the journey is too long for you.' [8]So he got up and ate and drank and went in the strength of that food forty days and forty nights as far as the mountain of God, Horeb. [9]There he entered the cave and spent the night there.

And behold, the word of YHWH came to him. He said to him, 'What are you doing here, Elijah?' [10]He answered, 'I have been very zealous for YHWH the God of Hosts, for the sons of Israel have abandoned your covenant[a]. Your altars they have torn down, and your prophets they have killed with the sword. Now I remain – I alone – and they seek my life to take it.' [11]Then he said, 'Go out and stand on the mountain before YHWH.' And behold, YHWH was passing by, and a great and mighty wind was tearing the mountain and shattering the rocks before YHWH. YHWH was not in the wind. And after the wind, an earthquake; YHWH was not in the earthquake. ¹²And after the earthquake, a fire; YHWH was not in the fire. Then, after the fire, a sound of gentle silence. ¹³When Elijah heard *it*, he wrapped his face in his cloak and went out and stood at the entrance of the cave. Then, behold, a voice came to him and said, 'What are you doing here, Elijah?' ¹⁴He answered, 'I have been very zealous for YHWH the God of Hosts, for the sons of Israel have abandoned your covenantᵃ. Your altars they have torn down, and your prophets they have killed with the sword. Now I alone remain and they seek my life to take it.'

¹⁵YHWH said to him, 'Go; retrace your journey through the wilderness of Damascus. Enter and anoint Hazael king over Aram. ¹⁶And Jehu son of Nimshi you shall anoint as king over Israel, and Elisha son of Shaphat, from Abel-meholah, you shall anoint as prophet in your place. ¹⁷It will be that the one who escapes from the sword of Hazael Jehu shall kill, and the one who escapes from the sword of Jehu Elisha shall kill. ¹⁸Yet I will reserve seven thousand in Israel – all the knees that have not bowed to Baal, and every mouth that has not kissed him.'

¹⁹So he departed from there and found Elisha son of Shaphat. Now he was plowing with twelve yoke of oxen before him, and he was with the twelfth. Elijah passed over to him and threw his cloak upon himᵃ. ²⁰He left the oxen and ran after Elijah and said, 'Let me kiss my father and my mother and then I will follow after you.' He said to him, 'Go; return; for what have I to do with you?' ²¹So he returned from following him and took the yoke of oxen and slaughtered itᵃ. With the oxen's equipment he boiled their fleshᵇ and gave to the people and they ate. Then he arose and went after Elijah and served him.

Notes on the text

1.a. The second *wĕ'ēt kol-'ăšer* in MT is a dittography and should read only *wĕ'ăšer*, 'and that'.

2.a. LXX begins Jezebel's speech 'If you are Elijah and I am Jezebel'. The meaning of their names ('YHWH is my God' and 'Where is the Prince [Baal]?') is part of the challenge she issues. It is difficult to account for the phrase as original to MT and it is not included here.

2.b. *'ĕlōhîm*, 'gods', is pl. and matches pl. verbs in MT. LXXᴮ has sg. verb forms as Jezebel's reflection on Baal's primacy. In MT Jezebel invokes the pantheon, or Dtr makes an ideological assessment of her religion.

3.a. 'he was afraid' (*warrirā'*) reads with MSS, LXX, Syr, Vg against MT, 'he saw' (*wayyar'*).

5.a. MT 'under a certain broom tree' is elided as a secondary gloss taken up from v. 4 (Montgomery 1951: 317).

10.a. Here and in v. 14 reading with MT 'abandoned your covenant' against LXX 'abandoned you'.

14.a. See n. 10.a above.

19.a. Reading *'ēlāyw*, 'to him', as *'ālāyw*, 'upon him'.

21.a. That Elisha does not slaughter all twelve pairs of oxen but only the twelfth is indicated by the 3 m. sg. pr. suff. on the verb 'he slaughtered it' (*wayyizbāḥēhû*).

21.b. MT's *biššēlām habbāśār*, 'he boiled them, the flesh', includes the verb with 3 m. pl. pr. suff. ('he boiled them'), together with the appositional explanatory gloss ('the flesh'). The apposition is omitted in LXX.

Form and structure

1 Kgs 19 is bound to chs. 17–18 by themes, structures and motifs (see 'Form and structure', 1 Kgs 17). A complex editorial history that combines individual units is posited in ch. 19. The introduction may be a secondary addition, as Jezebel is the focus of the introduction (vv. 1–3a), but is not again present (B. Long 1984: 197; Jones 1984a: 326). The theophany doublets (vv. 9–14) may be due to redacted tradition, although redactional priority of each theophanic element is disputed (Gray 1970: 405; Würthwein 1970: 153, 160–161; Cross 1973: 193; B. Long 1984: 200). The prophetic commission (vv. 15–18) is partially executed in the prophetic call narrative (vv. 19–21) but Elijah's actions there do not precisely reflect the commission; this is taken as further evidence of redactional layers. Yet the possibility of individual traditions present in the narrative does not hinder the ability to read it as a thoughtful and cohesive product.

The introduction (vv. 1–3a) links ensuing events to ch. 18, in which Elijah kills Jezebel's cult prophets. Although Jezebel does not continue as an actor in the narrative, all Elijah's actions and the commission he is given respond to the reality of Jezebel and her cult. Following the introduction, the narrative sets in motion three journeys (vv. 3b–8, 9–18, 19–21). The first journey (vv. 3b–8) is marked by itinerary notations (vv. 3b, 8) and each of the three journeys ends with a dual encounter. As the first journey ends at Beersheba, an angel appears to Elijah twice (vv. 5, 7). As the second journey ends at Horeb, YHWH twice speaks to Elijah (vv. 9–11, 15), with the theophanic vision separating the encounters.

The voice of YHWH and the theophanic vision results in a prophetic commission (vv. 15–18) and sets Elijah on a third journey that brings him to Elisha (v. 19). His first encounter with Elisha (vv. 19–20) results in Elisha's own journey (v. 20). Elisha breaks with his old life and his second encounter with Elijah is his commitment to serve him. This 'encounter' extends beyond the confines of 1 Kgs 19.

Several linguistic motifs connect the chapter as a whole. First, the motif of 'life' (*npš*) appears throughout vv. 1–14 (vv. 2 [twice], 3, 4 [twice], 10, 14). Elijah's life is threatened by Jezebel, which precipitates his journey and is the crux of his complaint to YHWH. The complaint's irony is acute, for Elijah's ministry is as mediator of YHWH's life (17:21–22; *npš*); he is witness to the power of the living God (17:1, 12; cf. v. 22); he has experienced life through the provision of food. Further, YHWH's servant Obadiah feared for his life (vv. 9, 12, 14) in the face of Jezebel's threats; now that role is taken up by Elijah, even though he has broken the power of Jezebel's prophets (and god) and slaughtered them at the Kishon. Faced with Jezebel's threat, Elijah forgets these realities concerning life.

A second strong motif pictures Elijah as a new Moses, most profoundly in the theophanic encounter at the holy mountain (see 'Comment'). In both instances the narratives are set in the context of covenant breaking and renewal. The comparison of the two prophets is instructive of the narrative purposes of 1 Kgs 19.

A third motif is striking in its imperfect presentation. Both 1 Kgs 17 and 18 have a strong narrative thread of command and compliance. Elijah commands and is obeyed; Elijah is commanded and he obeys. Often the obedience is narrated in similar terms as the command. In ch. 19 the pattern is abortive. For instance, the angel commands Elijah to 'get up' (*qwm*) and 'eat' (*'kl*), but no concomitant notice of Elijah's 'getting up' is given, although he does 'eat'. The angel commands Elijah a second time to 'get up' (*qwm*) and 'eat' (*'kl*), the prophet complies in identical terms, but then engages in a journey never commanded and apparently not intended by YHWH. YHWH himself commands Elijah to 'stand' (*'md*) before him on the mountain, but compliance is delayed. When Elijah does 'stand' before YHWH, it is pointedly not 'on the mountain', but only at the entrance of the cave. Finally, Elijah is commanded to 'go' (*hlk*) and 'return' (*šwb*). He does 'depart' (*hlk*), but no notation is given that he 'returns'. Rather, the double command to 'go' (*hlk*) and 'return' (*šwb*) is repeated by Elijah to Elisha (v. 20). Even the commission Elijah is commanded to perform is only partially completed in this chapter. Thus the command and response motif so apparent in chs. 17–18 is virtually absent from ch. 19. This builds the theme of the prophet's attempt to abandon his prophetic role.

Comment

19:1–8

1–3a. The restored covenant is quickly threatened when Ahab relates *all* that Elijah had done, *all* the details by which *all* the prophets were killed (*hrg*). Jezebel, an agent of death, previously sought to kill YHWH's prophets (*hrg*; 18:13; cf. 18:12, 14) and is enraged. Her oath invokes *'ĕlōhîm*, a word that can be used to invoke YHWH (e.g. 1 Sam. 3:17; 2 Sam. 3:35). The context, however, leaves no doubt she invokes her foreign god (cf. 1 Kgs 20:10), for her death threat is against the life (*nepeš*) of the Lord of life's prophet. Both she and Elijah are in Jezreel (18:46) and the queen must be slow to execute her command. In that time Elijah interprets her past actions and present oath as a real threat and flees to preserve his life (*nepeš*). Sadly, he forgets how YHWH proved himself Lord of life and sovereign over the impotent Baal. In the past his interactions with Ahab were filled with bold authority (17:1; 18:1–2, 18–19); now he caves before Baal's patroness.

3b–8. His fear sends him to the southern extreme of Judah (Judg. 20:1; 1 Sam. 3:20; 2 Sam. 3:10; 17:11; 24:2, 15; 1 Kgs 4:25 [5:5]), well out of Jezebel's territory. He seems intent on leaving behind the venue of his prophetic ministry. He also leaves behind his servant, another reminder of a prophetic ministry that, after Carmel, seems ineffective. There still remain adherents of Baal – and adherents with power to pursue YHWH's prophet. If Elijah anticipated a complete victory and a glorious remembrance of his own name, he is sadly mistaken. In the light of these disappointments and the concomitant necessity of ongoing conflict with Baal, one can understand Elijah's desire to abandon ongoing ministry.

He runs into the wilderness (*bammidbār*) of Beersheba, but his fear is not lessened. Instead, he despairs of life (*nepeš*), asking that it be taken (v. 4). The contrasts to Hagar's flight to the wilderness are striking. She left her son to die under a certain bush (*taḥat 'aḥad haśśîḥîm*; Gen. 21:15); Elijah sat down himself under a certain broom tree (*taḥat rōtem 'eḥāt*). Hagar feared to witness her son's death; Elijah welcomes death. 'It is enough,' says Elijah; he, like Hagar, has reached the end of his rope. The death wish evokes another, stronger, parallel given the many allusions to Moses in 1 Kgs 17 – 19 (Jones 1984a: 330). In Num. 11:15 Moses' overburdened complaint petitions YHWH to kill him. Elijah is another overburdened prophet, who perhaps considers his ministry a failure, and so he too petitions death from YHWH. His cry that he is 'no better than my fathers' may cite not filial, but prophetic, relationship.

Elijah's wearied sleep is interrupted by a dual encounter (vv. 5b–6, 7–8). Jezebel had sent a messenger (*mal'āk*) threatening death (v. 2); now YHWH twice sends an angelic messenger (*mal'āk*) providing life. The miraculous provision of food (a loaf ['*ulâ*; v. 6]) and jug [*ṣappaḥt*; v. 6]) had previously sustained the prophet (1 Kgs 17: 12–14, 16) and shows YHWH (despite Jezebel's bluster) remains the same agent of life. Elijah half-heartedly eats, although his compliance is not identical to the command. The second command adheres more closely to the command-and-compliance pattern. Commanded to 'get up' (*qwm*) and 'eat' ('*kl*), Elijah does precisely that (v. 8) but then embarks on a journey of his own devising.

The journey to Sinai ('Horeb' three times in Exodus [3:1; 17:6; 33:6] and exclusively in Deuteronomy) takes forty days and nights. The number is symbolic and recalls Moses' time on the mountain (Exod. 34:28; cf. 24:18). In Moses' case, as Elijah's, the sojourn on Horeb takes place after the slaughter of apostates (Exod. 32:28; 1 Kgs 18:40). Of course, the allusion is here anticipatory: will YHWH once again appear to his servant in theophanic form (Exod. 34:5–7)?

19:9–18

9–14. Elijah enters 'the cave' (*hamm'ārâ*). The article on the noun indicates a particular cave is in view, and evokes the cleft (*nĕqārâ*) of Moses (Exod. 33:22). In each of 1 Kgs 17 – 19 the narrative climax occurs at a geographical high point: an upper room, Mount Carmel, and now the most holy of the three, Horeb. The location is specified several times. In v. 9 it is twice referenced as 'there' (*šām*) and YHWH asks what Elijah is doing 'here' (*pōh*; vv. 9, 13). However holy the site, the journey (*derek*; v. 7) intended by the angel was not Horeb but Damascus (v. 15), in service of Elijah's prophetic ministry. Yet even in this misguided place YHWH encourages his prophet, meeting him in the midst of his fear, and commissioning him once again to take up his prophetic ministry. The typical address of prophetic ministry 'The word of YHWH came to Elijah' reveals that, despite Elijah's flight, he is still YHWH's prophet.

Elijah responds to YHWH's queries with the identical response (vv. 10, 14). He claims zeal (*qn'*) for YHWH, as do Phinehas before him (Num. 25:11) and Jehu after him when faced with Baal worship (2 Kgs 10:16). Elijah also describes himself as utterly alone against hostile forces (v. 10; 'I remain – I alone'), which leads him to fear for his life (*nepeš*). His identification as alone and threatened is surely based on faulty memory arising from his exhausted or depressed state. He asserts that Israel has abandoned YHWH's covenant, but Mount Carmel saw that covenant reinstituted. He asserts that YHWH's altars have been torn down, but he himself has just rebuilt one (18:30). He asserts that YHWH's prophets have been killed with the sword, but Obadiah has saved them and Baal's prophets have instead been killed (18:13, 40). Elijah's recall of the facts is displaced by his fear for his life at the hands of Jezebel. The prophet, who in Sidon and on Mount Carmel acted and spoke with trust and authority, now cowers and complains. His complaint takes the form of a lament in which he protests his innocence, complains about his prophetic ministry and implicitly petitions divine aid (see e.g. Jer. 11:18–20; 15:15–18; 17:14–18; 20:7–12; Num. 11:10–15; Exod. 33:12–16).

YHWH's answer to Elijah is his theophanic presence. Elijah is to 'go out' (*yṣ'*) and 'stand' (*'md*) on the mountain, but the prophet who claims he 'stands' (*'md*) before YHWH (17:1; 18:15) does not immediately comply. When he eventually does 'go out and stand' (v. 13), his fear moves him only to the cave's entrance.

In addition to the common theophanic elements of wind and earthquake (Exod. 19:16; 20:18; Deut. 4:11; 5:24), additional elements evoke the theophany in Exod. 33 – 34. Both Moses and Elijah are to stand before YHWH (Exod. 33:21–22; 34:6; 1 Kgs 19:11). YHWH's hand shields Moses (Exod. 33:22) while Elijah wraps his face in his cloak before YHWH's presence. In both, YHWH's word follows the theophany. Elijah may attempt to distance himself from his ministry but the parallels reveal he is truly a 'prophet like unto Moses'.

The natural elements herald YHWH's presence, but three times it is made clear that YHWH 'was not in' the natural elements (v. 11–12). Instead, after these phenomena he appears in utter silence or as a small breath of wind (*dĕmāmâ daqqâ*; contra Lust 1975: 110–115). It is a small (*daqqâ*) sound like the stillness (*dĕmāmâ*) of Ps. 107:29 and Job 4:16. The silence of this theophanic presence is not a transition to a new theophanic form, particularly as it is preceded by the familiar elements of fire, earthquake and wind. Rather, the uniqueness of this theophany is traced to the context of 1 Kgs 18 – 19 in which Elijah bested Baal, the god of thunder and storm. YHWH does command these natural elements: they can presage his appearance. But lest YHWH be conflated with Baal, he pointedly awaits the passing of these elements before revealing himself. When YHWH comes, he comes as he wills: in storm or in silence.

15–18. Elijah is not convinced by YHWH's power and remains untransformed and still fearful. But YHWH does not attempt further to convince his prophet. Rather, as he not infrequently does in response to Jeremiah's complaints (e.g. 10:21–23; 15:19–21; 17:19–27), he recommissions his prophet. YHWH commands Elijah back upon his journey (v. 7). The command to 'go' (*hlk*; v. 15) is immediately complied with (v. 19). He is to anoint new people to kingly power (Hazael, Jehu) and prophetic authority (Elisha) who will be instrumental in judging the house of Ahab and effecting YHWH's judgment upon continuing apostasy.

Elijah learns two significant things from YHWH's words. First, Elisha will be 'prophet in his place' and will take up the fight after him. He will execute the commission regarding Jehu and Hazael and thus continue the prophetic ministry. The second thing that Elijah learns is that he is not alone as he feared. YHWH's faithful number, seven thousand people, is a conventional indefinite number of saga (Gray 1970: 412). Those who remain faithful are well above the fifties hidden in caves by Obadiah. The ongoing battle against Baal will no longer be the purview of just one powerful (albeit susceptibly weak) prophet. It will be enjoined by a large remnant and a successor prophet. While nowhere else is the prophetic mantle inherited by anointing, here at this crucial juncture in Israel's covenant life the prophetic ministry will be visibly passed from Elijah to Elisha. This assures that YHWH continues to fight on behalf of his people against the alluring forces of Jezebel's god.

19:19–21

As commanded in v. 15, Elijah does 'go' (*hlk*), but there is no note of his 'retracing' (*šwb*) his steps. That compliance awaits vv. 20–21 and Elisha's actions. Thus the final scene not only facilitates the transfer of the prophetic mantle, ensuring an ongoing prophetic ministry, but it also demonstrates that the ministry of Elisha takes up and completes that which Elijah leaves unfinished.

To find Elisha in Abel-meholah (v. 16) en route to Damascus, he travels through Jezebel's territory – at least to this extent has Elijah's confidence in YHWH been restored. Abel-meholah is situated in the western Jordan Valley across from the vicinity of Succoth (Edelman 1992: 11–12; cf. Judg. 7:22; 1 Kgs 4:12).

Elisha is identified here by his patronym (v. 16; 2 Kgs 3:11; 6:31) but he becomes the 'man of God' (2 Kgs 5:8) and 'prophet' (2 Kgs 9:1). Both the patronymic and the twelve yoke of oxen suggest a family of some means. Elijah was commissioned to anoint (*mšḥ*) Elisha, but he does not pour oil upon Elisha. Instead, he throws his cloak (*'adderet*) upon Elisha and this potent symbol of the prophetic ministry (2 Kgs 2:13–14) bestows the call.

The exchange between the two men reveals the interconnections of their ministry. YHWH had commanded Elijah to 'go (*hlk*) and retrace his steps (*šwb*)' (v. 15). Elijah, however, only 'goes' (*hlk*). Elisha 'follows' (*hlk*) the prophet (v. 20) and Elijah's response to him repeats YHWH's original command to 'go (*hlk*) and return (*šwb*)'. Elisha fills in the lacuna by 'returning' (*šwb*; v. 21). Similarly, his ministry will also echo and complete Elijah's ministry.

Elijah's 'What have I to do with you?' places the responsibility for response solely upon Elisha, with no manipulation by the prophet. The call is uncompromising: Elisha must choose, but in choosing he becomes committed. One wonders if this sense of the unrelenting nature of the call has become real for Elijah through the dual encounter at Horeb.

Elisha's request to 'kiss' (*nšq*; v. 20) his parents utilizes a term found in 1 – 2 Kings only in vv. 18 and 20 of this chapter. The action indelibly breaks Elisha's current ties and connects him to the seven thousand faithful Israelites who have not 'kissed' (*nšq*) Baal (v. 18). Elisha signals his complete break with his former calling by slaughtering one 'yoke of oxen' and burning its equipage (v. 21). This is the twelfth pair with which he was earlier associated (v. 19) and it may be his alone. The shared meal highlights a specific aspect of Elisha's ministry in which he brings provision for the common people of Israel. Breaking with his former life, he goes to serve (*šrt*) Elijah as Joshua served Moses (Exod. 24:13; 33:11; Num. 11:28; Josh. 1:1). Describing the apprenticeship in these terms is a further indication of the interconnectedness of Elijah and Elisha's ministry. As Joshua succeeded Moses and continued his ministry, one anticipates the same for Elisha.

Explanation

Elijah's complaint and the lament he gives are comparable to those of Moses and Jeremiah in Num. 11:1–17 and Jer. 11:18–20 (see 'Comment').

Further comparisons suggest complaint and even the desire to escape one's appointed prophetic role are vocational hazards for prophets. 1 Kgs 17 – 19 has drawn several parallels between Elijah and Moses; the fact that Elijah complains from Horeb makes the comparison here particularly pointed. The parallels between this and the ministry of Jeremiah are not so pointed, but are equally instructive towards our understanding of the prophetic ministry.

Both Moses (Num. 11:15) and Elijah seek death at YHWH's hand, and Jeremiah laments the day of his birth (Jer. 15:10; 20:14–18). Death is considered a preferable option in the face of severe opposition. Opposition arises from various quarters: all the people (Num. 11:12; Jer. 11:1), leaders and (for Jeremiah) even the king (Jer. 29, 36). Perhaps most troubling for the prophets is that in each case opposition arises from within the covenant – that is, those from whom one hopes to receive support and understanding. In each instance the opposition revolves around covenant life: the people distrust YHWH's role as covenant provider (Num. 11) or, in Jeremiah's case, the people reject Jeremiah's charge of covenant unfaithfulness that includes Baal worship (Jer. 11:1–13).

Since the inception of the covenant the people's desire to walk in it stands side by side with their rebellion against it (Exod. 32; Deut. 5:27; 31:16–21, 29; Josh. 24:14–27; Judg. 2:10–19). For this reason the need for a prophet 'like unto Moses' (Deut. 18:18) who mediates the covenant does not end. And, given the depth of the people's rebellion, it is not surprising that this prophetic role is a task almost beyond endurance.

Faced with seemingly unbearable opposition, YHWH's refusal to release his prophets is striking. Elijah is instructed to anoint a new prophet as his successor, but that instruction is part of Elijah's recommissioning: Elijah returns to prophetic ministry, re-established and continuing for an indefinite period (1 Kgs 21; 2 Kgs 1).

There is no indication in the text as to why YHWH does not release his burnt-out and discouraged prophets. Perhaps it hinges on the unusual circumstances of their callings: Jeremiah while in the womb, Moses despite his many protests. There is something in these individuals that made them meet for just this ministry, and YHWH's claim upon their lives cannot be erased. Even Elijah (who appears with no introduction or call narrative) has his ministry of prophetic word indelibly confirmed (1 Kgs 17) before the great covenant challenge (1 Kgs 18).

YHWH does not allow these individuals to settle into their self-pity or perpetuate their desire for death or release. He meets them there and engages them at their point of discouragement. Through that encounter they are enabled to return and minister – under situations no less onerous or non-responsive. Something much larger than their own understanding or ease is at stake, to which they have been called. They are called to mediate the covenant, and covenant life is not just for the comfort of Israel. It *is* their life and to break covenant *is* death (Deut. 30:19). And the intent of the covenant is that YHWH might through Israel work his purposes of blessing for all the nations (Gen. 12:3; Exod. 19:6). There is something 'greater than the prophet' here and to this the prophet is called without repentance.

YHWH does more than deliver a cosmic pep talk, for he does not leave his prophets without resources. Time for rest is given to Elijah, and needed nourishment for his body; God does not treat him as an automaton who can exist without such human needs attended to. But, even more, Elijah stands on the mountain and YHWH himself meets him. Moses will not depart without YHWH's own presence (Exod. 33:15) and, hid in the cleft of the rock, he sees YHWH pass by (Exod. 33:21–23; 34:5–8); Jeremiah's call contains the assurance YHWH is with him to rescue him (1:8). In each case YHWH proves his own character of Emmanuel, God with us. From the daily walk with Adam in the garden, to his presence given to a trickster on the run, to a 24/7 cloud-and-fire accompaniment to a rebellious people, YHWH is the God who is with his people. He proves this repeatedly in the lives of his prophets.

Having seen the ineffectiveness of Baal to answer his prophets, YHWH's effective appearance to Elijah must call him again to YHWH's purposes and power to accomplish them. It is this reality of YHWH's presence with his prophets that alone makes the unbearable task – the undoable task – both bearable and doable.

But YHWH also provides another assurance. Elijah is reminded that seven thousand others do stand with him. He is not alone (19:18), and another prophet is given as apprentice to walk with him (v. 21; 2 Kgs 2). Moses was granted Aaron, and his burdens were also shared with seventy elders (Num. 11:16–17; cf. Exod. 18:13–26). And Jeremiah had Baruch (Jer. 36) and a cadre of supporters who remained committed to YHWH's covenant (Ebed-melech [38:7–13], Ahikah, Achbor, Micaiah and Shaphan [26:22–24; 36:11–15] among others). With this company the prophet's task refocuses and his ministry is once again embraced, even though its difficulties remain.

How instructive, then, to consider Christ's own role not just as prophet, but also as priest and king. Christ conducted this ministry under an opposition much more crushing than that faced by any of Moses, Elijah or Jeremiah. He, too, longed for his cumulative ministry moment to pass from him but chose to set his face towards the father's own will, and not his own (Matt. 26:39). He knew physical torment, exhaustion, indescribable pain and thirst in his final hours. And all this while forsaken by YHWH (Matt. 27:46). Despite all this, he walked with set face to the cross, enduring the shame, so as to complete his father's will.

There are many Elijahs who today find their varied ministries on behalf of the church and world utterly beyond their own power. Burnt out, exhausted, tired of the unresponsive crowd, at the point of opting out. Perhaps time is needed: refreshment, nourishment, redirected or renewed ministry balance. But renewed ministry also comes in the recognition that it is not accomplished alone. There is a great company who have not bowed their knee to Baal, who are refreshment on the road. And in the company's midst is the one who carries his cross – and calls the company to the same task. The company walks with YHWH in their midst as Emmanuel, the Suffering Saviour. Only in this is ministry empowered and accomplished with joy.

1 KINGS 20:1–43

Translation

[1]Now Ben-hadad king of Aram gathered all his army, and thirty-two kings were with him as well as horses and chariots. He went up and besieged Samaria and attacked it. [2]He sent messengers[a] to the city to Ahab king of Israel [3]and said to him, 'Thus says Ben-hadad, "Your silver and your gold are mine, and the best of your wives and children are mine."' [4]Then the king of Israel answered and said, 'According to your word, my lord, O king! I am yours, and all that is mine!'

[5]The messengers came back and said[a], 'Thus says Ben-hadad, "Truly, I sent to you, saying, 'You shall deliver to me your silver and gold, your wives and your children'; [6]nevertheless, about this time tomorrow I will send my servants to you. They shall search your house and the houses of your servants and all that is pleasing in your eyes they shall put in their hand and take away.'" [7]Then the king of Israel summoned all the elders of the land, and he said, 'Take note and see how this man is seeking trouble, for he sent to me for my wives and my children, and for my silver and my gold, and I did not refuse him.' [8]All the elders and people said to him, 'Do not listen or concede!' [9]So he said to the messengers of Ben-hadad, 'Say to my lord the king, "All the terms you first sent to[a] your servant I will do. But this thing I am unable to do."' Then the messengers went and brought back word.

[10]Ben-hadad sent to him and he said, 'Thus may the gods do to me and more if the dust of Samaria will be enough to provide even a handful for all the people who follow me.' [11]The king of Israel answered and said, 'Say, "Let not the one who girds on his armour boast as one who takes it off!"' [12]Now it happened when he heard this word that he was drinking, he and the kings, in the tents[a]. He said to his servants, 'Get ready to attack!' So they attacked the city.

[13]Now a certain prophet approached Ahab king of Israel and said, 'Thus says YHWH, "Have you seen all this great multitude? Behold, I am giving it into your hand today so you will know that I am YHWH."' [14]Ahab said, 'By whom?' And he said, 'Thus says YHWH, "By the young men of the leaders of the provinces."' And he said, 'Who shall begin the battle?' And he said, 'You.' [15]He mustered the young men of the leaders of the provinces – there were two hundred and thirty-two. After them, he mustered the troops[a]; all the army[b] was seven thousand. [16]They went out at noon.

Now Ben-hadad was drinking himself drunk in the tents[a], he and the kings – thirty-two kings – helping him. [17]The young men of the leaders of the provinces went out first. Then Ben-hadad sent and they reported to him, saying, 'Men have come out from Samaria.' [18]He said, 'If they have come out for peace, take them alive! Or if they have come out for battle, take them alive!' [19]Now these had come out from the city: the young men of the leaders of the provinces, and the army that followed them. [20]Every man struck his opponent and Aram fled while Israel pursued them. Ben-hadad king of Aram escaped on horseback with horsemen. [21]The king of Israel went out and struck the horses and chariots and inflicted Aram with a great defeat.

[22]The prophet approached the king of Israel and said to him, 'Come, strengthen yourself; take note, and see what you must do, for in the springtime the king of Aram will come up against you.' [23]The servants of the king of Aram said to him, 'Their god is a mountain god; therefore they were stronger than us. But if we fight them on the plain, surely we will be stronger than they. [24]Now do this: remove each of the kings from his place, and put officials in their place. [25]You should muster an army for yourself like the one that you lost[a] – horse for horse, and chariot for chariot. Let us fight them[b] on the plain; surely we will be stronger than them.' He listened to their voice and prepared accordingly.

[26]Next spring, Ben-hadad mustered Aram and went up to Aphek for battle with Israel, [27]and the sons of Israel were mustered and provisioned, and went to meet them. The sons of Israel encamped opposite them like two little flocks of goats, but Aram filled the land. [28]Then a man of God approached and said to the king of Israel[a], 'Thus says YHWH, "Because Aram has said, 'YHWH is a god of the mountains but he is not a god of the valleys,' I will give all this great multitude into your hand. Then you will know[b] that I am YHWH."' [29]They encamped opposite each other seven days. On the seventh day the battle began and the sons of Israel struck Aram – one hundred thousand foot soldiers in one day. [30]The survivors fled to Aphek, into the city, and the wall fell upon twenty-seven thousand men of the survivors. Ben-hadad fled and entered the city, *into* an inner room.

[31]His servants said to him, 'Behold, we have heard that the kings of the House of Israel are certainly kings who honour covenants. Let us put sackcloth on our loins and ropes on our heads[a] and go out to the king of Israel. Perhaps he will spare your life.' [32]They girded sackcloth on their loins and ropes on their heads and came to the king of Israel. They said, 'Your servant Ben-hadad says, "Please spare my life!"' And he said, 'Is he still alive? He is my brother.' [33]The men were watching for a sign, and they quickly took it from him[a] and said, 'Ben-hadad is your brother.' He said, 'Go; bring him.' Ben-hadad came out to him and he had him come up into the chariot. [34]He said to him, 'The cities that my father took from your father I will return. You shall establish bazaars for yourself in Damascus, just as my father established in Samaria.' *And he said*[a], 'I for my part[b] will release you with a covenant.' So he made a covenant with him, and released him.

[35]Then a certain man of the sons of the prophets said to his companion by the word of YHWH, 'Strike me, please!' But the man refused to strike him. [36]He said to him, 'Because you have not obeyed the voice of YHWH, behold, as you are

leaving me, a lion will strike you!' So he went from his side, and a lion met him and struck him down. ³⁷Then he sought out another man and said, 'Strike me, please!' and the man struck him, hitting and injuring him.

³⁸The prophet went and waited for the king on the road. He disguised himself with a bandage[a] over his eyes. ³⁹As the king was passing by, he cried out to the king and said, 'Your servant went out from the midst of the battle and behold, a man turned aside and brought a man to me. He said, "Guard this man; if he goes missing, your life shall be forfeit instead of his life, or you shall pay a talent of silver." ⁴⁰It happened as your servant was busy here and there, he disappeared.' The king of Israel said to him, 'So your judgment shall be; you yourself have determined *it*.' ⁴¹Then he quickly took off the bandage[a] from his eyes and the king of Israel recognized him that he was from the prophets. ⁴²And he said to him, 'Thus says YHWH, "Because you released from your hand[a] the man I had devoted to destruction[b], your life shall be forfeit for his life, and your people forfeit for his people."' ⁴³Then the king of Israel went to[a] his house resentful and vexed, and came to Samaria.

Notes on the text

2.a. *mal'ākîm*, 'messengers', lacks the DDO and may be explicative. It is missing in LXX*.

5.a. Omitting the first *lē'mōr*, 'saying', as a dittography, and retaining the *kî* particle as an affirmative. LXX has *ἐγώ* for MT's *lē'mōr kî*, which may reflect a *Vorlage*, *'ānōkî*.

9.a. *šālaḥtā 'el* as sending instructions via messengers (*HALOT* 1514).

12.a. 'in the tents' (*bassukkôt*) rather than the more usual *'ōhālîm*, 'tents'. 'In Sukkoth' (*bĕssukkôt*) may be intended, necessitating only a change in pointing.

15.a. With some MSS, LXX*, Vg, omitting 'all' in MT 'all the troops'.

15.b. MT 'all the sons of Israel' (*kol-bĕnê yisrā'ēl*) refers to the army; the number is too small for the whole people. So LXX, 'every son of might' (*kol-ben-ḥayil*).

16.a. As in n. 12.a above, LXX reads 'Sukkoth' in v. 16.

25.a. 'which you lost' reads *hannōpēl mē'ōtāk* as *hannōpēl mē'ittĕkā* with Ed.

25.b. Reading with MSS, Syr, Tg *'ittām* for *'ōtām* after intransitive verb.

28.a. Deleting the second 'and he said' with some MSS, LXX, Vg.

28.b. 'you will know' reads pl. *wîda'tem* as sg. *wîdā'tā* with LXX and with v. 13.

31.a. Reading sg. 'head' as pl. See v. 32 and multiple MSS, LXX, Syr, Vg.

33.a. Reading 'took it from him' (*wayyaḥlĕṭûhā mimmennû*). This reads the interrogative heh in MT (*wayyaḥlĕṭû hămimmennû*) with the preceding word as 3 f. sg. suff., as do some MSS and Q^Occ. The suffix specifies the king's word.

34.a. LXX^L makes explicit the change of speaker with 'and the king of Syria said to Ahab'.

34.b. 'for my part' arises from the contrastive waw and emphatic *'ănî*.

38.a. The hapax *'ăpēr* as 'bandage' per LXX, Tg, rather than 'dust' (*'ēper*), as in Syr, or even 'turban' (*pĕ'ēr* per *BHS*).

41.a. See n. 38.a above.

42.a. 'your hand' as 2 m. sg. with LXX^BL, Vg.

42.b. 'the man I had devoted to destruction' glosses 'the man of my destruction'.

43.a. 'to his house' reads *'el* for *'al*.

Form and structure

1 Kgs 20 – 22 stand together as a unified witness against kingly power in military and social contexts. While the LXX places ch. 21 after ch. 19 and thus provides a continuous narrative of Elijah's ministry, MT places ch. 21 in the context of the Aramean wars and alongside that of unnamed prophets (chs. 20, 22). These unnamed prophets represent the faithful remnant of 1 Kgs 19:18.

Ahab is only infrequently named as the Israelite king (1 Kgs 20:2, 13–14), and textual evidence suggests the presence of a gloss, especially when compared to the more consistent 'king of Israel' (thirteen occurrences) and 'the king' (three occurrences). This is one reason the texts are thought to be literarily displaced from a historic location in another king's reign. The international climate and events of either the late Omride era (during Jehoram's reign, so DeVries 2003: 251) or the Jehuite era (during either Joash's or, more particularly, Jehoahaz's rule, so J. Miller 1966, 1968a) are suggested as better historical locations for the narratives in both 1 Kgs 20 and 22.

Several lines of reasoning underpin these suppositions. First, epigraphic evidence cites no Ben-hadad in Ahab's era, although texts from the Jehuite era mention him. Secondly, Ahab is presented in the text as a threatened vassal, yet epigraphic evidence such as the Mesha Inscription (*ANET* 320–321) and the Assyrian Monolith Inscription (*ANET* 278–279) suggest Ahab is a powerful ruler on the international scene at this time. Aram's threat, it is argued, is historically accurate during the reigns of Jehoram and Jehu, and the biblical text confirms Aram's power at that time (2 Kgs 5 – 8, 13).

The arguments answer some questions raised by the biblical text, but only introduce others. Wholesale historical revision and literary displacement err on several counts (contra J. Miller 1966, 1968a; *pace* Provan et al. 2003: 263–266). First, lack of epigraphic evidence of Ben-hadad in Ahab's era is not conclusive. The name may be a throne name used by several kings but is not always present in epigraphic texts (see 'Comment' below); more, the selective nature of epigraphy may itself overlook such a king. Secondly, a revisionist reading disregards the ongoing discord between Israel and Aram that began as early as Baasha's era (1 Kgs 15:16–22) and probably continued during Omri's era (20:34) and provides the background for Israelite–Aramean conflict during Ahab's reign. Moreover, such discord does not discount periods of relative peacefulness or even alliance against common enemies (as suggested by the Monolith Inscription; Mazar 1986: 166).

As a historiographical record of the time of Ahab the chapter may have arisen in prophetic circles possibly during the Jehuite era (see 'Form and structure', chs. 17–18). Yet whatever the narrative's compositional history, its present careful structure is part of its communicative power. The structure is broadly outlined as follows:

> A Dialogue between Ben-hadad and Ahab; tribute demanded (vv. 1–12)
> > B Warfare between Ben-hadad and Ahab at Samaria (vv. 13–21)
> > B' Warfare between Aram and Israel at Aphek (vv. 22–30)
> A' Dialogue between Ahab and Ben-hadad; covenant renewed (vv. 31–34)
> > > C Epilogue: outcomes and judgment (vv. 35–43)

Within a brief narrative framework (vv. 1, 12), Ben-hadad and Ahab engage in three interactions through messengers (vv. 2–4, 5–9, 10–11), each initiated by Ben-hadad. The interactions move from the polite phrases of treaty language (vv. 2–4) to peremptory aphorisms that precipitate war (vv. 10–11). Corresponding to the opening dialogue, the closing dialogue also proceeds through three interactions (vv. 31, 32–33a, 33b–34) that move Ben-hadad from hiding to direct interaction with Ahab.

Together, the opening and closing dialogues effect a transfer of roles. In the opening dialogue Ben-hadad is the overlord, but in the closing dialogue Ahab becomes overlord. It is the centre two sections that facilitate the switch in the overlord–vassal relationship. Each of B and B' relate separate military encounters using an identical structure.

	In Samaria	In Aphek
A. Consultation		
1. Prophet with Israel	vv. 13–14	v. 22
2. Servants with Aram		vv. 23–25
B. Muster of troops		
1. Israel	v. 15	v. 27a
2. Aram		v. 26
C. Preparation for battle	vv. 16–19	vv. 27b–29
(Additional prophetic oracle for Israel v. 28)		
D. Battle	v. 20a	v. 29b
E. Outcomes	vv. 20b–21	v. 30

Through the battles Ahab becomes the overlord. One wonders, then, why the epilogue judges Ahab so severely. The point of the epilogue arises from a narrative leitmotif. The leitmotif *šlḥ* (to send) occurs ten times throughout the narrative (vv. 2, 5–7, 9–10, 17, 34 [twice], 42). Most often Ben-hadad sends messengers to Ahab. In v. 34 Ahab 'releases' (*šlḥ*) Ben-hadad because he makes a covenant with him. For this, Ahab is judged (v. 42).

The epilogue is in the form of a petitionary narrative (Schipper 2009). In it a prophet poses as a petitioner whose inattention enables a prisoner of war to go free. He represents Ahab, whose inattention to holy war laws enables the prisoner (Ben-hadad) to go free. Ahab's failure on points of deuteronomic law means that, despite his victory, he is judged on the familiar refrain of covenant obedience.

Comment

20:1–12

1. No epigraphic evidence attests to a Ben-hadad in Ahab's era. Ben-hadad son of Tabrimmon (Ben-hadad I) is Baasha's contemporary (1 Kgs 15:18) but he is unlikely to be alive, as fifty-eight years have passed (1 Kgs 15:33; 16:23, 29). Ben-hadad I may be the king to whom Ahab's 'father' Omri lost cities (v. 34), although Omri's narrative gives no witness to this. 'Father' may be more generically used of the royal predecessor Baasha, who did lose cities to Ben-hadad I (1 Kgs 15:18–20).

Literary displacement of the passage to the Jehuite era (see 'Form and structure') equates Ben-hadad in 1 Kgs 20 with Ben-hadad in 2 Kgs 13 (J. Miller 1968a; Dearman 1983; Pitard 1988, *ABD* 1:663–665). That position, however, requires the revisionism argued against above (see 'Form and structure') and is therefore untenable. Epigraphy (Shalmaneser's Monolith Inscription, *ANET* 278–279) names Adad-idri (Hebrew; Hadadezer in Aramaic) as Ahab's Aramean contemporary. The two kings act as allies at Qarqar in 853 BC, the year of Ahab's death. 'Adad-idri' appears nowhere in the biblical text, but may well be the Ben-hadad of 1 Kgs 20 – thus Ben-hadad II. Kings often have dual names or throne names (for instance Jehoahaz is also known as Ahaziah [2 Chr. 21:17; 22:1]) and Ben-hadad may be Adad-idri's throne name.

Although allies during the Qarqar offensive of 853 BC, shifting political realities show Adad-idri/Ben-hadad and Ahab were at times enemies (1 Kgs 20, 22). Such an explanation attends to the historiographical integrity of the narrative, the occasional nature of both epigraphic and biblical sources, and the political complexities of the era (Cross 1972; Dearman 1983: 99; Provan et al. 2003: 263–266). Thus three Ben-hadads appear in the biblical text: Ben-hadad I (1 Kgs 15), Ben-hadad II (1 Kgs 20, 22; 2 Kgs 8) and Ben-hadad III (2 Kgs 13).

Ben-hadad begins the action by 'besieging' Samaria. He is not fully encamped against the city, as access remains open (v. 7) and the threat of sending servants 'tomorrow' (v. 6) suggests the messengers travel a considerable distance. The reference to Ben-hadad's activities in the 'tents' (*bassukkôt*) could be read as 'in Sukkoth' (*běssukkôt*), a city 31 miles (50 km) east. Near the juncture of the Jordan and Jabbok, it commands major routes conducive to Ben-hadad's southern campaigns (Yadin 1955).

Thirty-two kings and tribal leaders support Ben-hadad. The coalition is much larger than Ben-hadad III's ten kings of the Zakir Inscription (*ANET* 655–656).

2–10. Ben-hadad repeatedly 'sends' (*šlḥ*) to Ahab (vv. 2, 5–6, 10), and his initiative shows he holds the power. Ahab concedes to Ben-hadad's power with a favourable initial response (v. 4), but when he refuses (vv. 7, 9), war ensues (vv. 13–30). By the end of the war Ben-hadad has lost power and the kings' roles are reversed (vv. 31–34); it is Ahab who will 'release' (*šlḥ*) Ben-hadad.

Ben-hadad makes a theoretical claim over Ahab's household and wealth, and Ahab's acquiescence (vv. 4, 9) suggests an agreement regarding overlord rights. Ahab calls Ben-hadad 'my lord, O king' and himself 'your servant' (v. 9), courtly speech that characterizes a vassal–overlord relationship either already existent or now set in place (Tsevat 1952–3: 107–108). Ben-hadad is the clear winner of the first interaction.

Messengers are 'sent' a second time and speak on behalf of Ben-hadad, who tests his control over Ahab by asserting ('truly, I sent') that his original request was not theoretical. Ahab is now directed to relinquish ('deliver'; *ntn*) all to ensure submission. Ben-hadad then heightens the demand by threatening wholesale looting: he shall 'send' and 'all that is pleasing in your eyes' shall be taken. The threat calls for total surrender.

The severe demand sparks consultation with the 'elders of the land' (cf. Prov. 31:23), a more widespread representative body than the 'elders of the city' (Judg. 8:16; 1 Sam. 16:4). The abbreviated conversation represented here charges Ben-hadad is 'seeking trouble' rather than asserting overlord rights. Unlike Ben-hadad, who listed material wealth as his first demand (v. 3, 5), Ahab mentions the people first (v. 7), which speaks well of him – if that is the only criterion for evaluation. The elders' unanimous and immediate support also speaks well of Ahab. The reply to Ben-hadad affirms the treaty through its language ('my lord', 'your servant'), but declines to meet Ben-hadad's troubling request.

Ben-hadad sends a third time but reduces negotiation to threat and parry. Sounding suspiciously like Jezebel (19:2), he vows retaliation that will reduce Samaria to less than rubble. His boast reveals his reliance upon his army's might. Ahab's aphoristic response 'Don't count your chickens before they hatch' shows considerable pluck; Ben-hadad's response, issued while carousing with his men in the tents (or in Sukkoth; see 'Comment', v. 1, and 'Notes on the text', vv. 12, 16), commits him to war.

20:13–30

13–21. Despite Ahab's previous negative interactions with prophets, now an unnamed prophet brings a victory oracle. Oracular revelation of battle tactics occurs in holy war contexts (1 Sam. 14:36–37; 23:1–4, 10–12), and the phraseology of the passage echoes such contexts. YHWH will deliver the enemy 'into your hand' (see Deut. 2:24, 30; 3:2; 7:24; 20:13; 21:10; Josh. 6:2; 8:1, 18; 10:8; Judg. 4:7, 14; 7:7–9; 1 Sam. 23:4–5; 2 Sam. 5:19); the battle's outcome is 'so you will know that I am YHWH' (see Exod. 6:7; 7:5; 10:2; 14:4; 16:12).

Against the 'great multitude' is sent an advance strike force of 232 'young men' (*nĕʿārîm*). *nĕʿārîm* is the usual word for young men (perhaps here armour bearers [Judg. 9:54; 1 Sam. 14:1] or servants of the 'leaders of the provinces' [2 Sam. 13:17], but certainly not elite trained troops). Ahab musters an army of seven thousand to follow them and the number evokes the faithful remnant in Israel (19:18). Victory will be gained through YHWH's people and by his power.

Ahab's unexpected noon strike has the element of surprise. Both vv. 17 and 19a indicate in virtually identical terms that the young men set out first. The frame encloses simultaneously occurring events related in vv. 17–19 (B. Long 1987: 391), so we see the action in both camps. Ben-hadad's reply to his scouts' report (v. 18) reveals his arrogance (or drunkenness) and the misperception of his grave situation. That the information is sent for and reported suggests the king is at a distance – perhaps at Sukkoth. Trusting in his mighty army, he commands complete victory: Israel is to be 'taken alive', regardless of their intentions.

The battle takes only one verse (v. 20), demonstrating the depth of Ben-hadad's self-deception and the height of YHWH's power. Ben-hadad and a few horsemen are the only ones to escape. The final summative verse restates the action of the battle, repeatedly emphasizing Israel's power. Ahab 'struck' (*nkh*) Aram and 'inflicted' (*nkh*) a great 'defeat' (*nkh*).

22–30. The second battle also begins in consultation. The prophet (the 'certain prophet' of v. 13) warns the first battle was victorious but not decisive and commands preparation ('Come', 'strengthen', 'take note', 'see'). Ben-hadad also engages in consultation – not with a prophet – but Ben-hadad's servants can only surmise. They do so poorly, for they assume victory was due to YHWH's limited mountain power (the decisive battle occurring in the mountainous area around Samaria, and perhaps even between Samaria and Sukkoth; Yadin 1955), and suggest a new battlefield outside YHWH's perceived realm. Additionally, they counsel Ben-hadad to raise a replacement army headed not by foreign kings but by civil officials (*paḥôt*) directly loyal to Ben-hadad.

The springtime muster is the usual time for battle (2 Sam. 11:1), and Aphek, south and east of the Sea of Galilee at the border of Aram and Israel, is the battlefield (Frankel, *ABD* 1:275–277). The stakes are high.

Ben-hadad's overlordship is in question, as is YHWH's territorial power and reputation. The narrative makes the high stakes clear, for Ben-hadad musters not just his army (v. 1) but Aram (v. 26), and not just against Samaria (v. 1) but Israel (v. 26). They fill the land, while Israel, perhaps seven thousand strong (v. 15), is a 'little flock'. The tension mounts as the mustered armies encamp for seven days.

The oracle of the 'man of God' (perhaps a different prophetic figure from the 'certain prophet' of vv. 13, 22) echoes the first oracle, but its differences reveal the battle is for more than military dominance. First, victory will go to Israel to prove Aram's conception of YHWH's power is erroneous. YHWH's reputation will be upheld! Secondly, the victory will cause all Israel (the 'you' is now pl., rather than sg. as in v. 13) to know their God. Both these outcomes are achieved through holy war, as indicated in the phrases 'all this great multitude' and 'you will know, etc.' (see v. 13).

The brief engagement sees Israel again 'strike' (*nkh*) Aram decisively and they flee to their city of Aphek (Fritz 2003: 206). Holy war continues there and, as at Jericho, Aphek's walls fall on the seventh day. Ben-hadad flees into the city's inner strongholds to secure his safety.

20:31–34

A final three interactions (Ben-hadad and servants, v. 31; servants and Ahab, vv. 32–33a; Ahab and Ben-hadad, vv. 33b–34) forge a new covenant between Ahab and Ben-hadad. The reputation of Israelite kings' covenant loyalty (*ḥesed*) prompts counsel that Ben-hadad repent and sue for his life.

Ahab responds as expected. He refers to Ben-hadad in covenant terminology ('he is my brother') and the servants quickly grasp at this sign. They affirm the covenantal relationship of brotherhood and the king issues an invitation to Ben-hadad, taking him up into the chariot. Under this new covenant the power roles are reversed. Now Ben-hadad is the inferior and he shows this by pledging the return of captured cities (see 1 Kgs 15:18–20) and inviting re-established trade. Now the overlord, Ahab, affirms only he will 'release (*šlḥ*) you with a covenant', and does (twice, v. 34).

Ahab's magnanimity and covenant loyalty seem positive traits. However, the narrative epilogue reveals that, in the context of holy war, they are wrong.

20:35–43

Another prophet brings a negative word for the king of Israel, who, by the 'release' (*šlḥ*) effected in v. 42, is identified as Ahab. The prophet speaks 'by the word of YHWH' (*bidbar YHWH*), a phrase found in 1 – 2 Kings only here and in 1 Kgs 13 (vv. 1–2, 5, 9, 17, 18, 32). The lion as a figure of judgment against disobedience (v. 36; 13:24) also connects this passage to that of 1 Kgs 13, and in both the issue is disobedience to the prophetic word. Once the man refuses to strike the prophet, he is himself struck by the lion, according to the word of YHWH.

In the story the prophet agrees to extreme terms of payment for neglect of the prisoner: forfeiture of his life through enslavement, death or a high ransom. The judgment Ahab pronounces redounds upon his own actions: for neglect of Ben-hadad the king will forfeit his life and kingdom. Ahab's actions align him with both the disobedient man who refused to obey the word of the prophet (v. 35) and the inattentive warrior whose neglect freed the captive (v. 40).

No specific commandment for Ben-hadad's destruction appears in the chapter, but the context of holy war suggests Ahab *should* have followed the precepts for such wars. A double entendre appears in the term 'devoted to destruction' applied to Ben-hadad. Literally, it reads the 'man of my destruction' (*ḥermî*), but a homonym translates it as 'the man of my net' (Stern 1990: 45; Schipper 2009: 266, n. 5). By the precepts of holy war, the foreign king was caught in YHWH's 'net' and should be 'destroyed' (Deut. 20:16–18; cf. Agag, 1 Sam. 15:8–23; Achan, Josh. 6:18; 7:12, 15).

Ahab's victory and magnanimous action towards Ben-hadad set him (and the reader!) up; the judgment is unexpected (as it was in 1 Kgs 13). Ahab is judged because he has neglected Deuteronomistic norms for holy war and the payment is high: not only is Ahab's life forfeit (indicating death, as in the case of Achan [Josh. 7:25], or loss of kingship, as in the case of Saul [1 Sam. 15:26–29]), but Israel will be forfeit to Aram. Ahab's victory over Aram will be short-lived.

Irked that he was wholly taken in by the ruse, Ahab responds not in repentance, but in high dudgeon. He returns to Samaria 'resentful and vexed', and this attitude prevails in his response to Naboth.

Explanation

The concept of holy war can be a difficult one to comprehend. Our era knows the horrific excesses of religious fanaticism, and too often holy war in the OT is viewed through such a lens. Sensibilities recoil from the idea Israel expressed such fanaticism or that YHWH could commission his people thus against an enemy. Even more difficult is the OT concept of YHWH himself leading the army, and the placement of such warfare under the banner of religious activity. In the concept of holy war the distance of the OT world from our own is acutely felt.

All of life in the ANE was religious, and thus warfare was ideally conducted at the behest and under the auspices of a nation's deity. Israel was often involved in defensive warfare and at times initiated war that was not under the rubric of holy war (Num. 14:39–45; see Emery, *DOTP*

1:877–881). 'Holy war' indicates those wars specifically directed by YHWH. He was the army's commander and required particular attention to the preparation, conduct and aftermath of battle (Longman and Reid 1995: 31–47). Each of the elements acknowledged the presence of YHWH in the midst of the army.

Preparatory phases could include oracular consultation (as preceded each of the battles with Aram), sacrifice (1 Sam. 13:8–10), consecration of the army (Josh. 3:5; 5:2), and at times the making of vows (Num. 21:2; Judg. 11:31–32; 1 Sam. 14:24). The army marched into battle with the ark at its head, symbolic of YHWH's presence leading the battle (Josh. 6:3–7; 1 Sam. 4:4; 2 Sam. 11:11). Songs of praise accompanied the army (Num. 10:35–36; 2 Chr. 20:20–23). Victory came through YHWH's presence, and therefore Israel was not to rely upon military strength or weaponry (Deut. 20:1–4; Judg. 7:2; 1 Sam. 17:4–7). The 'great multitude' of Aram (v. 13) that 'filled the land' (v. 27) versus Israel's 'little flock' (v. 27), or its army of seven thousand and strike force of 232 young men (vv. 15–16), were no deterrent to victory. The aftermath of battle likewise acknowledged the victory was YHWH's. Praise was offered (Exod. 15; Judg. 5; Ps. 98), and the spoils belonged to YHWH unless otherwise directed. This could include towns, plunder, inhabitants and livestock. Such items were considered 'devoted to YHWH' or ḥērem and destroyed (Deut. 20:10–18; Josh. 6:24–25; 7:1–26; 1 Sam. 15:8–33; Emery, *DOTP* 1:383–387).

The presence of several of these elements makes 1 Kgs 20 an unmistakable holy war. Ahab fails to reckon the spoils belong to YHWH, and he is judged on the deuteronomic law of ḥērem.

In holy war YHWH directs Israel's battles as the divine warrior. YHWH can be pictured several ways throughout the OT; for example, as husband (Hos. 1 – 2; Ezek. 23), shepherd (Ps. 23) or mother (Isa. 42:14; 45:9–14; 66:7–13). The divine warrior image is prominent throughout Old and New Testaments. In the OT YHWH acts as divine warrior in three primary phases (Longman and Reid 1995). First, YHWH delivers Israel from their enemies. The stellar example is the deliverance from Pharaoh's army, although numerous other examples appear (Exod. 15:1–5; Josh. 10:12–14; 2 Kgs 6:8–23). In this context Israel conducts holy warfare. Secondly, when Israel violates the covenant, YHWH fights against them (Josh. 7:1–12; Judg. 2:16–23; Jer. 21:3–7). Finally, even after the exile, the OT anticipates YHWH's eschatological deliverance of his people (Dan. 7; Zech. 14).

Each of these phases of warfare demonstrates YHWH's sovereign power and arises from his covenant commitment to Israel. When Israel acts according to the covenant torah, YHWH fights on their behalf (Deut. 28:7; Lev. 26:7); when they violate the covenant, YHWH works through his prophets (e.g. Elijah and Elisha), and the nations (e.g. Aram, Assyria, Babylon) to fight against Israel (Deut. 28:25; Lev. 26:17; Jer. 21:1–7). Ultimately, YHWH's covenant commitment extends to the end of time, redeeming Israel from all their enemies.

1 Kgs 20 works within 1 – 2 Kings as a reminder that although YHWH fights on Israel's behalf against their enemies, that does not privilege them to carry out covenant abuses with impunity. In the case of Ahab such abuses are brought to judgment. In the same way, although YHWH frequently fights on behalf of Israel and Judah in 1 – 2 Kings (2 Kgs 3:18–24; 6:8–23; 7:3–20; 13:14–19; 14:25–27; 18:9 – 19:36), ultimately their covenant disobedience brings them to judgment. Of note in the story of both Ahab and the nation is the fact that YHWH continues to fight on behalf of his people *even while* they are disobedient under the covenant. This is truly a sign of YHWH's grace extended to his people, forestalling judgment while he works to woo Israel back to covenant relationship.

Ahab's fate in 1 Kgs 20, communicated in parabolic form through the prophet, serves the exilic community as a parable of the nation's fate. In this it is not dissimilar to 1 Kgs 13, to which it has several connections (see 'Comment' above, vv. 35–43) and which also presents a parable of the nation's fate (see 'Explanation', 1 Kgs 13). Reading 1 Kgs 20 in exile, the community could reflect on its own history in which YHWH continued to fight on its behalf. Yet the nation was ultimately judged due to its ongoing covenant disobedience. In this the parable has explanatory power of the exilic experience. It would also call the exilic community from presumptuous reliance on YHWH's covenant faithfulness towards relational obedience within the covenant.

The divine warrior theme is not concluded as the OT closes. In Jesus Christ the divine warrior comes in the flesh and engages battle. The cross becomes the antitype of the Red Sea deliverance (1 Cor. 10:1–4). In it Christ takes the battle to cosmic heights, for there the principalities and powers are finally defeated and the divine warrior is raised to reign supreme over the cosmos (1 Cor. 2:2–8; 15:24; Col. 2:15; Eph. 1:19–23). Yet, though enthroned, the battle is still engaged by his disciples as they await the consummation of Christ's kingdom at his second coming. His disciples are now of every tribe, tongue, people and nation, but the battle is no longer fought on human battlefields. Identified with Christ through baptism, the church takes up weapons of righteousness against the foes of Christ (Eph. 6:12–17; 1 Thess. 5:8; Rom. 6:13, 23; 13:12; 2 Cor. 6:7; 10:3–5; Longman and Reid 1995: 91–179). But as for Ahab so for Christ's disciples: the battle still belongs to YHWH and is conducted in his power, still recognizes the enemies of God's kingdom and still calls for undivided allegiance to the divine warrior in whose name the church stands.

1 KINGS 21:1–29

Translation

[1]After these things, it happened that Naboth the Jezreelite[a] owned a vineyard that

was in Jezreel beside the palace of Ahab king of Samaria. [2]Ahab spoke to Naboth, 'Give me your vineyard. It will be my vegetable garden, for it is close beside my house. I will give you a better vineyard in its place, or, if you prefer[a], I will give you its value in money.' [3]But Naboth replied to Ahab, 'YHWH forbid that I should give you the inheritance of my ancestors.' [4]Then Ahab entered his house resentful and vexed over the word that Naboth the Jezreelite had spoken to him when he said, 'I will not give you the inheritance of my ancestors.' He lay upon his bed and turned away his face and would not eat food.

[5]Jezebel his wife came to him and said to him, 'Why is it that your spirit is troubled and you are not eating food?' [6]He answered her, 'Because I spoke to Naboth the Jezreelite and said to him, "Give me your vineyard for money, or, if you prefer, I will give you a vineyard in its place." But he said, "I will not give you my vineyard."' [7]Jezebel his wife said to him, 'Now you yourself are king over Israel! Get up! Eat food! Let your heart be glad. I will give you the vineyard of Naboth the Jezreelite.'

[8]She wrote letters in Ahab's name, sealed *them* with his seal and sent the letters to the elders and nobles who lived with Naboth in his city[a]. [9]She wrote in the letters, saying, 'Proclaim a fast and seat Naboth at the head of the people. [10]And seat two worthless men before him and have them testify against him, saying, "You cursed[a] God and king." Then take him out and stone him to death.' [11]The men of his city – the elders and nobles who lived in his city – did just as Jezebel had sent to them, as written in the letters that she had sent to them. [12]They proclaimed a fast and seated Naboth at the head of the people. [13]Two worthless men came in and sat before him, and the worthless men testified against Naboth[a] before the people, saying, 'Naboth cursed God and king.' And they took him outside the city and stoned him to death with stones. [14]They sent to Jezebel, saying, 'Naboth has been stoned to death.'

[15]Now when Jezebel heard that Naboth had been stoned to death, Jezebel said to Ahab, 'Arise; take possession of Naboth the Jezreelite's vineyard, which he refused to give you for money, for Naboth is not alive, but dead.' [16]When Ahab heard that Naboth was dead, Ahab arose to go down to the vineyard of Naboth the Jezreelite to possess it.

[17]Then the word of YHWH came to Elijah the Tishbite, saying, [18]'Arise; go down to meet Ahab the king of Israel who *lives*[a] in Samaria. Behold, *he is* in the vineyard of Naboth where he has gone down to possess it. [19]You shall say to him, "Thus says YHWH, 'Have you murdered, and also taken possession?'" And you shall say to him, "Thus says YHWH, 'In the place where the dogs lapped up the blood of Naboth, the dogs shall lap up your blood, even yours.'"'[a]

[20]Ahab said to Elijah, 'Have you found me, O my enemy?' And he said, 'I have found you. Because you sold yourself to do evil in the eyes of YHWH, [21]behold, "I am bringing calamity upon you, and will consume you with fire, and cut off from Ahab everyone who urinates against the wall, restricted and abandoned in Israel. [22]And I will make your house like the house of Jeroboam son of Nabat, and like the house of Baasha son of Ahijah, because[a] of the provocation with which you provoked *me*, and because you caused Israel to sin." [23]And also

concerning Jezebel YHWH has spoken, saying, "The dogs will eat Jezebel by the wall of Jezreel. [24]The one belonging to Ahab who dies in the city the dogs will eat, and the one who dies in the field the birds of the heavens will eat."' [25](Surely, there was no one like Ahab who sold himself to do evil in the eyes of YHWH because Jezebel his wife incited him. [26]He acted very abominably by going after idols according to all that the Amorites had done, whom YHWH had dispossessed before the sons of Israel.)

[27]When Ahab heard these words, he tore his clothes and put sackcloth on his body and fasted. He lay in sackcloth and went about downcast. [28]Then the word of YHWH came to Elijah the Tishbite, saying, [29]'Have you seen how Ahab has humbled himself before me? Because he has humbled himself before me I will not bring the calamity in his days; in the days of his son I will bring the calamity upon his house.'

Notes on the text

1.a. 'the Jezreelite' is MT; LXX[BA] has 'the Israelite'. LXX also omits 'in Jezreel', perhaps to ease the tension created by the vineyard located in Jezreel, when Samaria is noted as the place of Ahab's death (see 21:19 with 22:38; see further in 'Comment').

2.a. MT *'im ṭôb bĕ'ênêkā*, 'If you prefer', may be better represented by some MSS that add cop. ('or if . . .'). Syr makes the 'or' explicit, as in v. 6.

8.a. 'in his city' (*'ăšer bĕ'îrô*) is omitted in LXX*. MT expresses the details: a 'legal fulness' (Montgomery 1951: 334).

10.a. 'you cursed' euphemistically reads on ideological grounds, 'you blessed' (*bēraktā*). LXX*, Syr, Vg read as 3 m. sg. and include the subject 'Naboth'. MT captures the immediacy of the accusatory moment.

13.a. MT reads, 'and the worthless men testified against him, against Naboth, before the people'. The reading adopted here conflates the 3 m. sg. pr. suff. ('against him') with the indicated DDO, Naboth.

18.a. 'who lives in Samaria' (*'ăšer bĕšōmĕrôn*) reads literally, 'who is in Samaria', which contributes to the question of where the vineyard is located (see 'Comment').

19.a. LXX adds at the end of the verse, 'and the harlots shall wash in your blood', influenced by 22:38.

22.a. Reading *'al* for *'el*.

Form and structure

In the LXX 2 Kgs 21 follows ch. 19, so that the Elijah narratives are grouped consecutively. The MT locates ch. 21 within a context of royal power exercised in military (chs. 20, 22) and social (ch. 21) spheres (see 'Form and structure', 1 Kgs 17). Within that context Elijah serves with other prophets (chs. 20, 22) to challenge the abuse of royal power. The placement of ch. 21 alongside narratives of other prophets demonstrates the truth of YHWH's word at Horeb. Elijah does not stand alone. Others have not bowed the knee to Baal, and he ministers in that company.

The chapter relates the monarch's abuse of power (vv. 1–16 [B. Long 1984: 224; Walsh 1996] or, alternatively, extending to v. 20 [Montgomery 1951: 332 (to v. 20a); DeVries 2003: 255]) and YHWH's response (vv. 17–29). The strongly Deuteronomistic language within the judgment oracles, the multiple oracles (vv. 19 [twice], 28), the difficult flow of the judgment section with its several themes and varied voices, as well as the surprising mitigation of judgment (vv. 27–29) suggest a process of compositional accrual, but no consensus delineates the original narrative, nor the composition's history (see Jones 1984b; B. Long 1984: 224 for brief reviews). In its present form (perhaps originally Jehuite propaganda), the prophetic narrative condemns Ahab's rule.

The narrative is carefully structured with a double chiasm, and several connecting motifs. Following the temporal introduction, the first chiasm concerns the disposition of Naboth's inheritance, and mirrored elements reveal interactions between the same characters:

A   Ahab and Naboth: request and denial (vv. 1–4)
  B   Jezebel and Ahab: promise to obtain (vv. 5–7)
    C   Jezebel and the leaders: instructions for exercise of royal power (vv. 8–10)
    C' Jezebel and the leaders: the vineyard obtained through royal power (vv. 11–14)
  B' Jezebel and Ahab: promise delivered (v. 15)
A' Ahab and Naboth: vineyard possessed (v. 16)

The second chiasm highlights the judgment at its centre and similarly mirrors interacting characters:

A   YHWH and Elijah: the word of judgment (vv. 17–19)
  B   Elijah and Ahab: the encounter (v. 20a)
    C   The judgment through the prophet (vv. 20b–24)
    C' The judgment through the narrator (vv. 25–26)
  B' Ahab: the response to Elijah's words (v. 27)
A' YHWH and Elijah: the word of mitigation (vv. 28–29).

Key motifs shape the chapter. Naboth, the central character, is repeatedly named (seventeen times), including six times after his death and twice in the judgment section. Pointedly, he is identified as the Jezreelite (six times), a reminder that the king seeks the ancestral inheritance held in that city.

The ancestral inheritance is a second motif. Naboth always refers to the land as the 'inheritance (naḥălâ) of my ancestors' (vv. 3–4), indicating he values land bestowed per covenantal allocations (Josh. 13:6–7). By contrast, Ahab and Jezebel refer only to the land as 'the vineyard' (eight times in vv. 2, 6–7, 15–16): a tradable commodity. The divergent views regarding the nature and ownership of land (see 'Comment') are explored through two related linguistic motifs. First is the motif of possession (*yrš*). Naboth possesses (*yrš*) an inheritance granted by YHWH its true owner (Lev. 25:23). YHWH gives the land for Israel's possession (Gen. 15:7–8; Deut. 1:8) and thus Naboth refuses Ahab. Jezebel commands Ahab to 'possess' the land, and he does (*yrš*; vv. 15–16). He obtains it against covenant provisions, and so YHWH's judgment also speaks of possession (*yrš*; vv. 18–19). The second motif is of 'giving' (*ntn*). Ahab commands Naboth to 'give' the land. Jezebel asserts she can 'give' the land to Ahab. Naboth's understanding of land makes him unable to 'give' it. Finally, because Ahab and Jezebel insist Naboth 'give' the land, YHWH's judgment against Ahab 'gives' (translated 'make' [*ntn*; v. 22]) Ahab's house over to destruction. In all, ten occurrences of 'give' (*ntn*; vv. 2–4, 6–7, 15) are used by Ahab, Jezebel and Naboth.

The final motif is that of eating and fasting. Ahab wants Naboth's vineyard so he can eat vegetables. Naboth's refusal leads Ahab to fast (v. 4). Jezebel notices his fasting (v. 5), urges him to eat (v. 7), while concocting a plan that involves Naboth in fasting (v. 9, 12) so that ultimately Ahab can eat from his garden (v. 15). Dogs lap up Naboth's blood (v. 19), and ensuing judgment ironically sets dogs to feast upon Ahab, Jezebel and his descendants (vv. 19, 23–24). Finally, Ahab repents and fasts (v. 27), which leads to mitigation of the judgment.

Comment

21:1–16

1–7. 'after these things' situates the account in the context of the Aramean wars. The chapter introduces each main character by birthplace: Naboth is a Jezreelite (v. 1), Elijah is the Tishbite (v. 17), Ahab is the 'king of Samaria' (cf. 2 Kgs 1:3). As he is later identified by his official title of 'king of Israel' (v. 18), it seems that Samaria designates his birthplace (Na'aman 2008: 204). The mention of Jezreel and Samaria in v. 1 also anticipates Ahab's desire to purchase Naboth's vineyard in Jezreel. Omri has already bought Samaria (16:24) and Ahab simply follows his example.

Jezreel (present-day Zer'in) is 9 miles (15 km) east of Megiddo, on a strategic ridge at the eastern entrance to the Jezreel Valley. A strongly fortified base for cavalry and chariotry with a moat, tower (2 Kgs 9:17) and guarded gate (2 Kgs 9:31), it also had a royal residence but no monumental buildings (Ussishkin 1997).

Ahab desires to replace the vineyard's long-term viticulture with a yearly 'vegetable garden' (*lĕgan-yārāq*). The phrase is a negative one for it is found elsewhere only in Deut. 11:10 (*kĕgan hayyārāq*), describing Egypt, the land of Israel's slavery. Further, Israel is a vine under God's special care (Isa. 3:14; 5:1–2; Jer. 12:10; cf. John 15:1–8). Both allusions negatively characterize Ahab's intent.

The offer to purchase ('give me'; cf. Gen. 23:4, 9) is generous and is not inherently illegal (YHWH judges the means of possession, not the purchase per se), but laws regulated the sale of land, particularly patrimonial holdings (Lev. 25:23–28; Deut. 25:5–10). Naboth's oath regarding his inheritance rests on these laws, which reflect the reality of YHWH's ownership of the land (v. 23). Israel possesses it because of covenant promises made to Abraham (Gen. 17:8), fulfilled in Israel's entry into the land (Josh. 1:2–4), and witnessed by Israel's division of the land along tribal lines (Josh. 13 – 21).

Ahab is vexed as before by the constraints of the law (cf. 20:42–43) and abides it with bad grace. Jezebel asks the cause of Ahab's 'troubled' (*sārâ*; v. 5) spirit and Ahab reprises Naboth's refusal, changing it significantly by removing the religious convictions upon which Naboth's refusal is grounded. This makes Naboth appear arbitrary and churlish. The narrative leaves open a provocative construal of Ahab's response. Jezebel has in the past acted decisively against YHWH's people and law (e.g. 18:4; 19:1–2). Does Ahab now hope to elicit similar action? If so, Ahab's passive pout is really masterful manipulation. In the end it is fully comprehended and judged by YHWH.

Jezebel's response emphasizes the king's position ('Now *you yourself* are king') is entitlement to act as he wishes. She operates out of a view of royalty informed by the Sidonian court and broader ANE practice at odds with the Israelite view of *primus inter pares* (Andersen 1966: 46, 50). In a string of imperative commands she urges her husband to get up, eat up and cheer up – not because Ahab will act with kingly prerogative, but because she will. She will 'give' the vineyard.

8–14. The core of the narrative follows Jezebel's actions through letters 'sent' (vv. 8, 11 [twice], 14). As in 1 Kgs 20, where Ben-hadad 'sends' and comes to grief, so too will Jezebel, although she initially meets with great success. Her strategy is to convene a kangaroo court disguised as lawful prosecution.

She writes in Ahab's name, and under his authoritative seal, although the messengers know whom to report to (v. 14). She conscripts the elders (*zĕqēnîm*) who represent the people and the heads of influential families (*ḥōrîm*) from Naboth's city. Their ready complicity against their compatriot suggests the power Jezebel exercises (or the fear she arouses), and the degree to which the law can be compromised in Omride Israel.

Fasting was practised at times of great national crisis (2 Chr. 20:3; Jer. 36:9; Esth. 4:16) and humble repentance (see vv. 27, 29; Lev. 16:29, 31), and thus the call to fast alerts the people to the critical nature of the gathering. Blasphemy against God was punishable by execution, and blasphemy against the king probably carried the same penalty (Lev. 24:16; Exod. 22:28 [cf. Isa. 8:21; 2 Sam. 16:5–9]). The crime is so horrendous the MT employs a euphemism ('you blessed'; cf. Ps. 10:3; Job 1:5, 11; 2:5, 9) rather than risk committing the offence of blaspheming God and king in the scroll.

The legal charade includes two witnesses as required by the law (Deut. 17:6; 19:15). The witnesses are dubious, for even Jezebel calls them 'worthless men' – a term one cannot imagine her using in actuality (as it would expose the charade) and suggests a narrative technique to alert the reader to Jezebel's infamy. The men are literally called 'sons of Belial', a term elsewhere employed of priests who did not know God (1 Sam. 2:12), those who incited people to worship other gods (Deut. 13:13) or broke laws of hospitality and sexuality (Judg. 19:22).

The acquiescence of Naboth's fellow-citizens is complete and their heinous actions follow her instructions using virtually identical verbal forms. They proclaim the fast and seat Naboth at the head of the assembly as one of the unsuspecting townspeople; were he brought on trial, he would stand (e.g. 1 Kgs 3:16; Andersen 1966: 56–57). The tables are turned on him when the false witnesses testify. He is judged and, according to the law, the whole assembly executes him. The kangaroo court proceeds exactly as Jezebel instructed. They need only send a report to satisfy her promise to Ahab.

15–16. Jezebel previously had urged Ahab to 'get up' and 'eat'; now she urges him to 'get up' and 'take possession'. Her proposed rationale is Naboth's death and probably refers to some legal precedent upon which the legal charade rests. Had such confiscation been illegal, the whole charade seems pointless: why purport to follow the law only to flout it in the end? Why not simply confiscate the land initially? Rather, biblical (2 Sam. 16:4; Ezra 10:8; cf. Ezek. 45:8; 46:18) and extra-biblical evidence suggests that in cases of treason the deceased offender's property ceded to the crown (Sarna 1997: 122–125). Thus, to the end, Jezebel's charade operates under the guise of the law. Of course, YHWH is the key witness to the charade and through his prophet will expose it.

21:17–29

17–19. As in 1 Kgs 17:2 and 18:1 Elijah enters the narrative when 'the word of YHWH came to Elijah'. Despite Elijah's protestation in ch. 19, he remains YHWH's prophet.

The first scene with Elijah is closely tied to the preceding scene between Jezebel and Ahab. In a play on Jezebel's imperative that Ahab 'arise and take possession' (*qûm rēš*) YHWH commands his servant to 'arise and go down' (*qûm rēd*). And, while Ahab went to 'take possession' (vv. 15–16), YHWH tells Elijah to find Ahab 'taking possession' (v. 18) and to confront his 'taking possession' (v. 19).

Ahab will be judged for his actions in his monarchic role over YHWH's people, and so Elijah is instructed to go down and meet the 'king of Israel' rather than the 'king of Samaria' (v. 1). Ahab is in Naboth's vineyard in Jezreel, but in the same verse Ahab is described as 'in Samaria' (see 'Notes on the text'). As argued in v. 1, each of the main characters is introduced by his birthplace. Thus Samaria in v. 18 should be similarly understood: Ahab was born and lives in Samaria.

Both the reason for judgment and the judgment itself are introduced by the authoritative 'thus says YHWH'. The reason for judgment exposes what has really occurred in Jezebel's scheme. Ahab has not only taken possession, but he has murdered (*rṣḥ*) to do so. His implication in the crime strongly suggests that (at the least) he turned a blind eye to Jezebel's actions or (at the most) manipulated her towards the very actions she took. In any case, YHWH now exposes the action as one prohibited in the Ten Commandments (Exod. 20:13; Deut. 5:17). Ahab once again fails in respect of torah. His judgment aligns with *lex talionis*: what was suffered by Ahab's victim will now be dealt out to Ahab himself. The blood carelessly lapped by dogs introduces a carnivalesque element, heightening YHWH's utter disgust for this wicked king. The carnivalesque element resurfaces when Ahab's dynasty falls (2 Kgs 9 – 10; see 'Comment').

20–26. Ahab earlier greeted Elijah as the 'troubler of Israel' when the issue was one of national covenantal failure (18:17). Now the greeting 'O my enemy' reveals Ahab's awareness of personal sin. But Elijah does not deliver YHWH's judgment against that sin, at least not at first. Rather, as YHWH's prophet, he interprets Ahab's sin in the light of deeper realities. The oracular word substantially repeats the words spoken to the dynasties of Jeroboam and Baasha. Ahab has 'done evil' (v. 20; 14:9; 16:7) 'in the eyes of YHWH' (v. 20; 14:8; 16:7), and has 'provoked YHWH and . . . caused Israel to sin' (v. 22; 14:9; 16:2, 7). In judgment, YHWH will bring 'calamity' (v. 21; 14:10), 'consume' (v. 21; 14:10; 16:3), 'cut off' Ahab's house (v. 21; 14:10) and expose their remains to the 'dogs and birds' (v. 24; 14:11; 16:4).

Elijah's role as YHWH's prophet is further signalled in vv. 20–24. As YHWH's prophet, he speaks of him in the third person (v. 20). But Elijah also speaks of YHWH in the first person (an immediate oracular word; vv. 21–22) and nothing marks the shift of perspective. In this Elijah simultaneously speaks on his own and as YHWH's mouthpiece. The overlapping voices of Elijah and YHWH extend even further. In vv. 23–24 the words are here represented as Elijah's, but ambiguity exists. They can also be understood as the narrator's words (see B. Long 1984: 226; Walsh 1996: 331) and certainty is impossible. Yet even if the words are the narrator's (in an aside that continues through v. 26), they accord with those spoken by YHWH and his prophet. All three together condemn Ahab.

Finally, the narrative aside of vv. 25–26 has in view both the Naboth incident, as well as Ahab's cultic sins. Ahab's evil is 'going after idols' (v. 26), and in this Jezebel is implicated (cf. 16:31–33). Further, she urged him to 'possess' (*yrš*) Naboth's land, and now his evil is despicably that of the Amorites whom YHWH had 'dispossessed' (hiph. form of the root *yrš*). No wonder she receives a particular notice of judgment (v. 23). In a freakish extension of the judgment of non-burial (v. 24) she will be eaten by dogs near the wall of Jezreel, the very city in which her scheme against Naboth was perpetrated.

27–29. The phrase 'when Ahab heard these words' recalls v. 15. There, when Jezebel heard the words of Naboth's death, she acted quickly – in further sin. Now Ahab acts quickly – in repentance. So unexpected is the repentance that one suspects Ahab's torn clothes, sackcloth and fasting (all common signs of repentance, 2 Kgs 22:11, 19; Jon. 3:6) are meant to hoodwink YHWH. But YHWH sees what lies behind actions and proclaims the repentance genuine.

A second time (vv. 17, 28) YHWH's word comes to Elijah. The judgment is mitigated, not by lessening, but by postponement. As in the case of Solomon and Jeroboam, judgment for cultic sin falls upon successive generations.

Explanation

The incident of Naboth's vineyard explores royal power exercised in the arena of social justice. It is rightly gathered with chs. 20 and 22, which, in military contexts, also explore royal power (see 'Form and structure', ch. 20). In none of the chapters does the narrative stray far from the underlying issue of covenant life: prophets abound, communicating YHWH's will and chastising the king's disregard of covenant law.

The king is judged for his abuse of social power (vv. 17–19), but this judgment is immediately couched in the underlying issue of covenant sin regarding the worship of YHWH (vv. 20–26). Ahab does evil, provokes YHWH by causing Israel to sin and goes after idols. Like Jeroboam and Baasha, Ahab is judged for wrong worship directed to the wrong God (the calves, Baal); his worship should be Deuteronomistically informed, and exclusively to YHWH. In this chapter social injustice goes hand in hand with wrong worship, demonstrating the implicit link between belief and practice. As the king worships, so he acts.

The judgment pronounced against Ahab anticipates its execution. While Ahab dies in 1 Kgs 22, the judgment against his house is not executed until 2 Kgs 9–10. Until that time there are several narrative moments when one might well expect the judgment will take place (2 Kgs 3, 6–7). The anticipatory tension builds the theme of the inviolability of YHWH's word. Elijah's ministry began by demonstrating his prophetic credentials; what he prophesies comes to pass. Even though delayed, judgment against Ahab is still certain.

The judgment pronounced by Elijah rests upon the covenant law. Biblical kings were charged as the representatives of YHWH and as such were to be familiar with covenant law, and uphold it before the people (Deut. 17:18–20). They were to act with justice and righteousness (Ps. 72; Isa. 11:3–5; 16:5; Jer. 22:2–5; 23:5–6), a characteristic for which Solomon is lauded (1 Kgs 3:28). Justice and righteousness were laid upon kings who led by example as YHWH's under-regents. They represented a God wholly just and unerringly righteous (Exod. 34:6–7; Deut. 32:4; Ps. 33:5; 89:14; 97:2). It is not surprising, then, that as kings fail in the exercise of justice and righteousness, the people also walk in similar covenant failure.

Repeatedly, the prophets condemn the people for injustice (Isa. 1:15–17, 23; 10:1–2; Jer. 5:1–2; Hos. 4:1–2; Amos 2:6–7; Mic. 3:1–3; 6:6–12) that was a breaking of covenant laws. The fault lay not simply in Israel's failure to adhere to a list of prescribed actions, however, for a more fundamental failure prompted their injustice.

YHWH had called them to exclusive covenant relationship with a God holy, just and righteous. Forging covenant with Israel at Sinai, YHWH revealed his holy character as the living God who saves (Exod. 19:1–6; 20:2). Out of that character follows the Ten Commandments (Exod. 20:3–17) and indeed all the subsequent covenant law. Knowledge of, and service to, YHWH enabled Israel to 'be holy as he is holy' (Lev. 20:26). Concomitantly, each step away from that covenant relationship distorted their view of YHWH and introduced Israel to other gods who were not holy, just or righteous. In worshipping those gods Israel became like them. Thus injustice is evidence of the deeper issue: fundamental failure in their relationship with the God to whom they are united and by whom they live.

The deuteronomic code is fully aware of the necessity of continued relationship with the living God, who saves and sought to perpetuate the covenant anew in each generation. In the recitation of the Ten Commandments Deuteronomy addresses the current generation (the 'you' and 'us' of Deut. 5:1–5) as if they themselves stood at Horeb with Moses. Reading the law every seventh year (Deut. 31:9–13), each generation heard the 'you' and 'us' and that rhetorical device joined them to the first generation at Horeb. They acknowledged through the covenant their union with the saving God, and gave him exclusive worship. It is that living expression of, and habitation in, the covenant's ongoing story that ensures Israel's continued identity as the holy people of a holy God. From that identity came their expressions of justice, that is, their ethic. They are to act out of whose they are.

The NT people are grafted in to that identity through the work of God in Christ (Rom. 11:17). They too read the deuteronomic law as their own and are rhetorically addressed as the 'you' and 'us' called to covenant life with the living God who saves. That covenantal life is, however, experienced differently, for the NT people of God come into covenant relationship through Christ. By his work, by his indwelling Spirit and by his presence through the word of the Gospels, the church lives life with God, grafted in to his people and his narrative. In this identity of word and Spirit the face of YHWH is known and worshipped (John 1:14, 18). Out of that worship the NT's ethic finds its ongoing expression of YHWH's power, truth and love (Holmes 2012).

1 KINGS 22:1–50[51]

Translation

[1]For three years there was no war between Aram and Israel. [2]In the third year Jehoshaphat king of Judah went down to the king of Israel. [3]The king of Israel said to his servants, 'Do you know that Ramoth-gilead is ours but we do nothing to take it from the hand of the king of Aram?' [4]And he said to Jehoshaphat, 'Will you go with me to battle at Ramoth-gilead?' Jehoshaphat replied to the king of Israel, 'I am as you are; my people as your people; my horses as your horses.' [5]And Jehoshaphat said to the king of Israel, 'Please seek YHWH's word first.' [6]So the king of Israel gathered the prophets, about 400 men, and said to them, 'Shall I go against Ramoth-gilead for battle or shall I refrain?' They said, 'Go up, for the Lord[a] will deliver[b] into the king's hand.' [7]Jehoshaphat said, 'Is there no other prophet of YHWH here[a] that we might enquire of him?' [8]The king of Israel said to Jehoshaphat, 'There is still one man by whom to enquire of YHWH, but I hate him for he does not prophesy anything good concerning me, only evil: Micaiah son of Imlah.' And Jehoshaphat said, 'Let not the king say so.' [9]The king of Israel summoned an official and said, 'Quickly bring Micaiah son of Imlah.'

[10]Now the king of Israel and Jehoshaphat king of Judah were sitting each upon his throne, arrayed in robes at the threshing floor at the entry of the gate of Samaria, and all the prophets were prophesying before them. [11]Zedekiah son of Kenaanah made for himself iron horns. He said, 'Thus says YHWH, "With these you shall gore Aram until they are destroyed."' [12]All the prophets were prophesying the same thing, saying, 'Go up to Ramoth-gilead and be successful, for YHWH will deliver[a] into the hand of the king.'[b]

[13]Now the messenger who had gone up to summon Micaiah said to him, 'Now look, the prophets' words are altogether favourable towards the king. Please let your word be as the word of one of them and speak favourably.' [14]Micaiah said, 'As YHWH lives, whatever YHWH will say to me, that will I speak.' [15]He came to the king and the king said to him, 'Micaiah, shall we go to Ramoth-gilead for battle or shall we refrain?' He said, 'Go up and be successful, for YHWH will deliver into the hand of the king.' [16]But the king said to him, 'How many times have I adjured you to speak to me nothing but truth in YHWH's name?' [17]Then he said, 'I saw all Israel scattered upon the mountains like sheep without a shepherd. And YHWH said, "These have no masters; let them return each to his

house in peace."' [18]The king of Israel said to Jehoshaphat, 'Did I not say to you, "He will not prophesy good concerning me, but only evil"?'

[19]He said, 'Therefore, hear[a] the word of YHWH: I saw YHWH sitting upon his throne and all the host of heaven standing around him, on his right and his left. [20]And YHWH said, "Who will deceive Ahab that he may go up and fall at Ramoth-gilead?" And one said this while another said that. [21]Then a spirit went out and stood before YHWH and said, "I will deceive him." Then YHWH said to him, "How?" [22]He said, "I will go out and be a spirit of deception in the mouth of all his prophets." He replied, "You will deceive him, and also succeed. Go out and do it." [23]And now, behold, YHWH has put a spirit of deception in the mouth of all these your prophets, and YHWH has declared disaster concerning you.'

[24]Then Zedekiah son of Kenaanah approached and struck Micaiah on the cheek and said, 'How[a] did YHWH's spirit pass from me to speak to you?[b]' [25]Micaiah said, 'Behold, you shall see on that day when you enter an inner room to hide yourself.'

[26]Then the king of Israel said, 'Take Micaiah and return him to Amon the ruler of the city and to Joash the king's son [27]and say, "Thus says the king, 'Place this man in prison and feed him rationed bread and water until I come in peace.'"' [28]Micaiah said, 'If you indeed come in peace YHWH has not spoken through me.' And he said, 'Hear, O people, all of you.'[a]

[29]Then the king of Israel and Jehoshaphat king of Judah went up to Ramoth-gilead. [30]The king of Israel said to Jehoshaphat, 'I will disguise[a] myself and go[a] into battle, but you wear your robes.' So the king of Israel disguised himself and went into battle. [31]Now the king of Aram had commanded his thirty-two chariot captains, saying, 'Do not fight with small or great but only with the king of Israel.' [32]So when the chariot captains saw Jehoshaphat, they said, 'Surely, he is the king of Israel,' and they turned[a] to fight against him, and Jehoshaphat cried out[b]. [33]But when the chariot captains saw that he was not the king of Israel, they stopped pursuing him. [34]Then someone randomly drew the bow and struck the king of Israel between the plates of his armour. He said to his chariot driver, 'Turn around; get me out of the front lines for I am wounded.' [35]The battle raged that day, and the king was propped up in the chariot opposite Aram. He died in the evening and the blood of the wound pooled in the bottom of the chariot. [36]As the sun set, a cry passed through the army, 'Every man to his city, and every man to his land!' [37]So the king died. He came to Samaria and they buried the king in Samaria. [38]They washed[a] the chariot at the pool of Samaria, and the dogs lapped up his blood, and the prostitutes washed *in the bloody water*[b], according to the word of YHWH that he had spoken.

[39]Now the rest of the acts of Ahab and all that he did, and the house of ivory that he built, and all the cities that he built, are they not written in the Book of the Chronicles of the Kings of Israel? [40]Then Ahab slept with his fathers and Ahaziah his son reigned in his place.

[41a]Now Jehoshaphat son of Asa began to reign over Judah in the fourth year of Ahab king of Israel. [42]Jehoshaphat was thirty-five years old when he began to reign and he reigned twenty-five years in Jerusalem. His mother's name was

Azubah daughter of Shilhi. [43]He walked in all the way of Asa his father; he did not turn from it, doing what was right in the eyes of YHWH. [44]However, he did not remove the high places[a]; the people still sacrificed and burned incense on the high places. [44[45]]Jehoshaphat made peace with the king of Israel. [45[46]]Now the rest of the acts of Jehoshaphat and his mighty power that he demonstrated and how he waged war, are they not written in the Book of the Chronicles of the Kings of Judah? [46[47]]The remnant of the male cult personnel who remained from the days of his father Asa he removed from the land. [47[48]]There was no king in Edom; a governor was king.

[48[49]]Jehoshaphat made ships of Tarshish to go to Ophir for gold but they did not sail, for they were wrecked at Ezion-geber. [49[50]]Then Ahaziah son of Ahab said to Jehoshaphat, 'Let my servants go with your servants in the ships,' but Jehoshaphat was not willing.[50[51]]Then Jehoshaphat slept with his fathers and he was buried with his fathers in the city of David his father. Then Jehoram his son reigned in his place.

Notes on the text

6.a. Reading *'ădōnāy* with MT as original against *yhwh* in multiple MSS, Tg. LXX reads *κύριος*. The argument that *'ădōnāy* is a polemic against non-Yahwistic prophets using the divine name founders; the same prophets use 'YHWH' in vv. 11–12 with no MSS evidence attesting otherwise.

6.b. Lack of object for MT 'will deliver' contributes to the passage's ambiguity.

7.a. *ha'ên pōh nābî' layhwh 'ôd* is ambiguous and may also mean 'Is there not here a prophet of YHWH still?', that is, the prophets are not Yahwistic. The translation used shows Jehoshaphat considers the prophets to be Yahwistic. Their allegiance is ambiguous throughout the passage.

12.a. LXX[BL] interprets, providing the object, 'the king of Aram'.

12.b. MT follows v. 6, 'into the hand of the king'. LXX reads, 'into your hand'.

19.a. 2 Chr. 18:18 (cf. v. 14) addresses both kings with pl. 'hear'. MT addresses Ahab alone, with a sg. verb.

24.a. *'ê-zeh* is read adverbially, 'in what manner; in what way'.

24.b. Reading MT *'ôtāk* as *'ittāk*.

28.a. 'Hear O peoples, all of you' is absent from LXX*. It does appear in 2 Chr. 18:27 and makes sense in the Kings context (Bodner 2003), and thus cannot be ruled out (as is commonly done) as a late scribal gloss taken up from Mic. 1:2.

30.a. The infs. (*hithappēs wābō'*) are read as first person ('*ethappēs wĕ'ābō'*) with LXX, Syr, Tg.

32.a. In LXX and 2 Chr. 18:31 the officers 'surround' (*wayyāsōbbû*) the king. MT's 'turned' (*wayyāsuru*) emphasizes the moment at which the ruse works and Ahab is left supposedly safe.

32.b. Chronicles pointedly answers the cry of the godly king, noting that 'YHWH helped him, and diverted them away'. LXX similarly notes, 'and YHWH saved him'.

38.a. Reading with LXX, Vg as pl., 'they washed'.

38.b. 'in the bloody water' follows LXX 'in the/his blood': a further slur on the king's character.

41.a. LXX^L omits 41–50[51], moving directly to Ahab's son; LXX* omits 46–49[47–50], including vv. 41–44, 46–51[41–43, 45–50], following 16:28.

43[44].a. 'He did not remove (*hēsîr*) the high places' is read with LXX against MT *sārû*, 'they did not abandon'. LXX pointedly evaluates the king.

Form and structure

Ahab's reign ends with a typical closing regnal formula (22:39–40), ending an extended focus on the northern kingdom (since 1 Kgs 15:25). A brief interlude turns to the southern monarch, Jehoshaphat (vv. 41–50[51]), before the narrative again focuses on the northern kingdom (v. 51[52] – 2 Kgs 8), beginning with Ahaziah's reign. The division of the monarchic history into two scrolls (see §2, '1 – 2 Kings in the canon', in the Introduction) awkwardly divides Ahaziah's narrative. The narrative is rejoined here, including vv. 51[52]–53[54]) with 2 Kgs 1.

1 Kgs 22 fulfils prophetic oracles against Ahab (20:42; 21:18–19), although full execution of prophetic judgment against Ahab's house is left until 2 Kgs 9 – 10. The prophetic word has proven ineluctable thus far and there can be no doubt that the whole prophecy will come to pass. Until that time Ahab's evil influence remains.

Several elements suggest chs. 20 and 22 are paired as bookends to the chapters on the Aramean conflict and royal power (chs. 20–22). Besides the references to the Aramean wars, the reference to the thirty-two kings in the first war (20:1, 16) works as an inclusion with the thirty-two captains of the final war (22:31). Battles are all preceded by prophetic consultation (20:13–14, 22, 28; 22:5–28), and in both chapters an 'inner room' provides refuge (20:30; 22:25). Ahab in both chapters disregards torah, forgoing holy war proscriptions in ch. 20 and disregarding YHWH's prophet in ch. 22.

As in ch. 20, alternative historical reconstructions argue the chapter is better read as a record of another king's reign (see 'Form and structure', ch. 20). The parallels with the battle in 2 Kgs 3 and against Ramoth-gilead in 2 Kgs 9 are one argument for relocating the chapter to Jehoram's reign (DeVries 2003: 266; Gray 1970: 416–418). Other reconstructions place the events in the reign of Jehoahaz (2 Kgs 13) with ch. 22 serving as the third of that king's campaigns against Aram (2 Kgs 13:19; see Jones 1984b; J. Miller 1966, 1968a). Yet another reconstruction retains Ahab as the king but considers Assyria the antagonist, thus allowing for the Israel–Aram coalition of the Monolith Inscription (Na'aman 2005b). As noted in the discussion at ch. 20 (see 'Form and structure'), the reconstructions all disallow the historiographical integrity of the biblical text, the complexities of shifting alliances, and the selective nature of both biblical and epigraphic reportage (see Provan et al. 2003: 263–266).

The chapter's narrative unity (Moberly 2003: 16–17 contra DeVries 2003: 259–272; Walsh 1996: 342) coheres around a typical battle report including battle preparations (with oracular consultation) (vv. 2–28), the battle proper (vv. 29–36) and outcomes (vv. 37–38).

Comment

22:1–40

1–28. The covenanted peace between Ahab and Aram (20:31–34) is undisturbed for three years. Additionally, an alliance binds the previously hostile northern and southern kingdoms (14:30; 15:6, 16–22) through the marriage of Ahab's daughter Athaliah to Jehoshaphat's son Jehoram (2 Kgs 8:18). The Aramean (chs. 20, 22) and Assyrian threat in the north and Jehoshaphat's maritime interests (v. 48) make alliance politically, militarily and financially beneficial. The alliance is not one of vassalship, but Jehoshaphat's support of Ahab in the face of prophetic warnings and his entry into battle as a decoy (v. 30) indicate he is the alliance's weaker member.

Ahab is identified as the king of Israel (v. 20). He queries his military advisors regarding Ramoth-gilead. One of Solomon's administrative centres (4:13) and perhaps one of the cities Ben-hadad was to have returned (20:34), it lies between the Yarmuk and Jabbok rivers east of Jordan. As its name suggests, it is on the heights (*rāmôt*) near the Aramean–Israelite border and is identified with modern Tell Ramith (Arnold, *ABD* 5:620–621). Ahab considers Ramoth-gilead rightly Israel's and his assertion that Israel 'does nothing' (the hiph. as here, can mean delay in possessing territory [Judg. 18:9]) reveals his desire to 'do something'. His servants agree. His Judean ally pledges military support.

Jehoshaphat's request to 'enquire of YHWH' (*dĕrāš . . . et-yhwh*; vv. 5, 7–8) is used in 1 – 2 Kings for concerns such as illness, torah disobedience and battle (2 Kgs 3:11; 8:8; 22:13, 18; cf. a variant at 1 Kgs 14:5). An oracle prior to battle is expected in the ANE (the phrase to 'ask of YHWH' [*šā'al bĕyhwh*] is likewise common [Judg. 1:1; 20:27–28; 1 Sam. 14:36–37; 23:1–4; 2 Sam. 5:19]; Block 2005: 196–198).

Prophets are summoned who appear to speak YHWH's word (vv. 11–12, 24) and whom Jehoshaphat apparently accepts as legitimate (v. 7). Their allegiance, however, is kept ambiguous throughout. They may be Yahwistic, servants of a syncretized and nationalistic version of YHWH (as instituted by Jeroboam), or prophets of Baal and Asherah who purport to speak YHWH's word. In any case, the prophets are 'Ahab's' (vv. 22–23) and monarchic support provides a powerful opportunistic motive to prophesy what Ahab desires to hear.

Further evidence amplifies the prophets' ambiguous allegiance. Ahab 'gathered the prophets' (*wayyiqbōṣ et-hannĕbî'îm*), a phrase found elsewhere only at 18:20 of the 400 Asherah prophets (cf. the parallel account in 2 Chr. 18:5). Those prophets did not respond when summoned earlier (18:19, 22); the allusion suggests they now respond to Ahab. The prophets' oracle is equally ambiguous. They cite the 'Lord', but do not identify which Lord will deliver, nor who or what will be delivered (see 'Notes on the text'), nor even into which king's hand victory will be given. The prophecy allows that Ahab will be delivered to the king of Aram. Ahab, already being determined to 'do something' and go up against Ramoth-gilead, assumes a favourable oracle. He thus plays into the deception YHWH lays for him.

Jehoshaphat's request for a second oracle need not suggest suspicion but is a common ANE practice of eliciting a second confirmatory oracle (Na'aman 2005b: 467). To placate Jehoshaphat, and despite antipathy towards Micaiah, Ahab summons him. That he can quickly be fetched (v. 9) and be 'returned' to prison (v. 26) suggests he may already be imprisoned for contrary oracles.

An interlude reaffirms the oracle (vv. 10–12). The kings, enthroned and in royal garb at the threshing floor (*gōren*) used for public meetings (Gen. 50:10; 2 Sam. 6:6; Ruth 4; Job 29:7–17), present an official court scene. The prophets 'prophesy' (hith. of *nb'*), a term used both of pagan prophets (18:29) and YHWH's prophets (22:8; cf. Num. 11:25, 27; Jer. 29:27). Part of the usual paraphernalia of ANE prophecy (Dion 1999), Zedekiah's iron horns evoke Deut. 33:17 in an effort to encourage Ahab to battle. All the prophets confirm Zedekiah's message, clarifying v. 6 with the additional phrase 'and be successful', which suggests the battle will be Ahab's. Yet still, whether the prophets are speaking truth or pandering to Ahab's desire cannot be known.

A good company man, the messenger who summons Micaiah urges a favourable message. Micaiah affirms he is ruled by YHWH's word. Interestingly, he makes no commitment to speak what is true; in the eventuality he speaks both what is false *and* what is YHWH's word.

Micaiah reiterates the oracle sent by YHWH's spirit (v. 21), but the uncharacteristically favourable oracle raises suspicions. Ahab's frustrated 'how many times' reveals ongoing conflict with Micaiah. When Ahab presses for the truth (and perhaps now in receipt of YHWH's further word), Micaiah prophesies Israel will lose its king (shepherds are common metaphors for kings [2 Sam. 5:2; Zech. 13:7; Ps. 78:72]). Israel itself will return in peace since the nation's fate remains in YHWH's hands, and not the king's folly. Ironically, the truthful revelation does not convince Ahab

(v. 18). He remains intractable in his previous assessment of Micaiah and in his commitment to engage in battle.

Micaiah's vision responds to Ahab's intractability. YHWH and his courtiers, the 'host of heaven' (at times indicative of astral deities [2 Kgs 21:5; 23:4], or stars [Gen. 2:1; Deut. 4:19; 17:3; Isa. 34:4], but here YHWH's angelic servants [Ps. 103:21]), invisibly parallel Ahab's court. In YHWH's court prophets can receive his message (Isa. 6:8; Jer. 23:18–22). YHWH calls for a messenger to deceive or entice (*pth*) Ahab to his doom. The pi. verb (vv. 20–22) carries nuances of seduction (Exod. 22:15) or wooing (Hos. 2:14), persuasion (Judg. 14:15; 16:5), enticement (Prov. 1:6; 16:29) and deliberate deception and lies (2 Sam. 3:25; Ps. 78:36–37; Prov. 24:28). The lie already given (vv. 11–12, 15) reveals deception is intended.

'The spirit' (*hārûaḥ*; v. 21) who volunteers is YHWH's own spirit of prophecy (cf. v. 24) by which prophets prophesy (1 Sam. 10:6; 2 Sam. 23:2; 2 Chr. 20:14; Ezek. 11:5; Mic. 3:8; cf. Chisolm 1998: 15–16). The spirit accomplishes the ruse as a 'spirit of deception' (*rûaḥ šeqer*), describing the effect of the spirit's actions. The deception is effected in Ahab's prophets and Ahab himself throughout the narrative (Block 2005: 206). Ahab's prophets have spoken by YHWH but have not told the truth (Chisholm 1998). YHWH is sovereignly free to use prophetic deception to accomplish the judgment already pronounced against Ahab (20:42; 21:19). Ahab desires to attack Ramoth-gilead and has continually shown himself intractable against YHWH's word. YHWH uses Ahab's own commitments to undo him. All this to the prophesied end: disaster for Ahab.

Micaiah's vision elicits two responses. Zedekiah's credibility is impugned and he attacks physically. His astonished question is particularly ironic, for the spirit *has* passed from Zedekiah to Micaiah, but Zedekiah has no inkling of it, nor that Micaiah is now the spirit's tool. Micaiah has seen the truth (v. 17) and waits for what Zedekiah will 'see' (v. 25) to prove it. Like Ben-hadad (20:30), Zedekiah will hide in an 'inner room' (v. 25) until the word comes to pass. Then, as a false prophet, he will be liable for a capital crime (Deut. 18:20–22).

Ahab's response is more practical. He imprisons Micaiah again to ensure he can face the king's wrath when he returns. He anticipates he will return 'in peace' (v. 27) even though Micaiah's oracle claimed that fate only for Israel (v. 17). Micaiah's parting challenge sets Ahab's return as the proof Micaiah has prophesied falsely. The king calls his court as witness to the challenge (v. 28; Bodner 2003). Choosing sides with Zedekiah against Micaiah, Ahab proceeds to battle where only one word will prove true.

Nothing further is heard of Zedekiah or Micaiah, as their narrative roles are finished. Ahab's fate and the proof of YHWH's word is the ongoing narrative's focus.

29–36. Despite the lengthy narrative preparation, the actual battle narration is brief. Although Ahab rejects Micaiah's oracle, his disguise suggests some level of unease. He hopes to pit himself against YHWH's word, despite YHWH's victorious interactions with the king since ch. 17. The disguise is doomed, signalled by the verb 'to disguise' (v. 30 [twice]; hith. of ḥpś). Elsewhere in the DH only at 1 Sam. 28:8 and 1 Kgs 20:38 (a similar theme but a different verbal root appears at 1 Kgs 14:2) it is always kings who disguise themselves, the disguise is always ineffectual and always results in an oracle of doom (or its fulfilment) against the king.

Jehoshaphat's royal robes will make him Aram's target. His acquiescence shows his inferior role in the alliance (and his stupidity). Jehoshaphat is saved from Aram only by his cry (theologized as a prayer in 2 Chr. 18:30), which reveals his true identity. By YHWH's power the 'random' bowshot finds Ahab and enters the armour's weak point. Ahab withdraws from the battle line but does not flee, while his troops fight on. His life lingers but he exsanguinates in the evening and the troops quit the field. And so YHWH's word is fulfilled: Israel's master is no more, and Israel returns home safely (v. 17).

37–40. The resumptive 'So the king died' begins a litany of YHWH's victory over Ahab's presumption. Ahab dies. He is taken to Samaria and buried. His chariot is washed at the pool and the dogs lap his blood as per the prophetic word (21:19). And, as a final derogatory comment, prostitutes bathe in the bloody water. It may only be that the pool was a usual place for such bathing or it may reflect a belief that a king's blood empowered life and fertility (Gray 1970: 455; Jones 1984b: 372). In either case, the association with liminal women reveals the low esteem in which Dtr holds Ahab. All of this has occurred according to YHWH's powerful word.

The difficulty in the fulfilment is of course that the blood is lapped up in Samaria (the location is noted three times, vv. 37–38), when the prophetic word indicates Jezreel, the place of Naboth's death (21:19). The narrative is unconcerned about the discrepancy (and one cannot imagine no editor saw it). Rather than attempting to match prophecy and fulfilment by relocating Naboth's death to Samaria (as is common in commentaries), or translating the original prophecy to read 'Instead of dogs licking up Naboth's blood, they will lick up yours' (so Provan 1995: 160), this discrepancy reveals the living nature of the prophetic word. The central thrust of the prophecy is realized and the variation of circumstances is inconsequential; indeed, it is a hallmark of prophecy in the ongoing fulfilment of YHWH's judgment against Ahab's house (Miscall 1989; Walsh 1996: 358).

The closing regnal formula contains common elements. Ahab's building projects include Jericho (16:34), Jezreel and Megiddo (Ussishkin 1997). The 'house of ivory' refers to royal residences highly decorated with ivory panelling or furniture, as attested in archaeological findings from Samaria (Shanks 1985: 45–46). The beauty of such works is overshadowed by the reality of the social oppression they represent (Amos 3:15; 6:4), and the notation further evidences Ahab's wicked rule.

Finally, the succession notice states that Ahab 'slept with his fathers'. If the phrase refers to a king's peaceful death, there is an obvious disjunct with Ahab's demise (DeVries 1978: 97; 2003: 269; Na'aman 1997: 168; but see 2 Kgs 1:17–18; 14:22 and 'Comment' there). The phrase can also mean the succession passes uneventfully to the king's son (Bright 2000: 247, n. 55; Sweeney 2007: 262). Ahab dies in battle and 'rests with his fathers' because dynastic succession proceeds without hindrance.

22:41–50[51]

Jehoshaphat rules from the fourth year of Ahab to the fifth year of Jehoram (2 Kgs 8:16) during the kingship of Ahab, Ahaziah and Jehoram. The opening regnal formula contains the usual elements (see 'Form and structure', 1 Kgs 14) and Jehoshaphat is evaluated positively in typical Deuteronomistic language. The continuing exception is that the high places remain. Since the temple's completion, they are illegitimate places of worship (see 'Comment', 1 Kgs 15:11–15).

Jehoshaphat's peace with Ahab is evident in the coalition against Aram, and sealed in the marriage of Jehoshaphat's son Jehoram to Ahab's daughter Athaliah. The peace repairs the breach in north–south relations (14:30; 15:6–7, 16–22). The peace (šālôm) Jehoshaphat brokers evokes the name of Solomon (šĕlōmô), and Jehoshaphat's reign evokes Solomon in other ways. His governorship over Edom ensures access to the port of Ezion-geber and, like Solomon, Jehoshaphat makes Tarshish ships and traffics for gold (see at 9:27–28; 10:22). As Hiram proposed a working relationship with Solomon, now Ahaziah makes a similar proposal. The relationship promised financial benefit to the north; Jehoshaphat's refusal indicates he now relinquishes any inferior status in the alliance. But, however laudable such a show might be, the inclusion of the shipwreck is a negative theological comment on Jehoshaphat's alliance with the Omrides.

Explanation

It is an uncomfortable conclusion: YHWH deceives Ahab. He sends his own spirit of prophecy to Ahab's prophets who speak the spirit's lie. Micaiah commits to speaking what YHWH tells him and repeats the same lie. Only when prompted to speak the truth does he give the unfavourable oracle. YHWH's deception works, however, and Ahab is enticed to battle and death.

YHWH's deception appears to stand in stark tension with biblical affirmations of YHWH's inability to lie (Num. 23:19; 1 Sam. 15:29), and affirmations of his truthfulness (Ps. 31:5; Tit. 1:2). Can YHWH both deceive and remain truthful? And, if he can do both, are his applications of deception or truthfulness arbitrary? How can such a God be trusted, much less worshipped as perfect and holy?

The discomfort engendered by Ahab's deception is further increased in the face of other instances of deception at YHWH's hand. A few examples, explored in a summative fashion, may suffice (for a fuller discussion of the passages and the difficulties inherent in their interpretation, see Chisholm 1998. Chisholm draws conclusions similar to those forwarded here).

In Ezek. 14:1–9 YHWH poses a hypothetical situation: a prophet provides an oracle to idolators. The context however indicates idolators should receive no such attention but only YHWH's judgment. In giving the oracle the prophet is deceived (v. 9a), and deceived (v. 9b) by YHWH (the root is *pth*, as in the Micaiah narrative [vv. 20–22]). Why might YHWH engage in such deception? That the prophet engages idolators in the face of YHWH's promised judgment suggests a prior willingness to compromise his prophetic word. Openness to syncretism with idolators leaves him vulnerable to YHWH's deception. The deception builds on the underlying sin and facilitates YHWH's judgment against the prophet.

Another interesting passage is Jer. 4:10. There Jeremiah accuses YHWH of deceiving (the root is *nš'*) the people through the prophetic message of peace. Elsewhere (Jer. 14:14–15; 23:16–18, 32), YHWH disavows these prophets as not speaking his message and having no part in the divine counsel. It may be that Jeremiah is mistaken in his accusation and the word of peace arises from false theology. But it may also be (as in Micaiah's story) that the prophets' false theology of peace made them agents of YHWH's deception. By it he moves Judah towards the certain judgment pronounced in Manasseh's reign (2 Kgs 21:10–15).

Other instances can be cited in which YHWH causes an action to be taken that results in the individual's downfall or destruction (although neither *pth* nor *nš'* is used): Eli's sons reject their father's advice (1 Sam. 2:25b), Absalom rejects Ahithophel's advice (2 Sam. 17:14), Rehoboam takes foolish advice (1 Kgs 12:15), Amaziah chooses to go to war (2 Chr. 25:20). In each case the one deceived has already shown some propensity against YHWH and his purposes. The outcome of YHWH's action is judgment against the individual.

This is certainly the case with Ahab. YHWH has already predetermined judgment against him (21:17–26) and, although Ahab repents (21:27–29), judgment is not commuted but delayed. Ahab has repeatedly shown himself intractable against YHWH. He has married a foreign princess and enshrined Baal worship while continuing Jeroboam's sins. He has disregarded YHWH's prophet on several occasions. He has enacted injustice and defied YHWH's covenant. Even after his repentance he returns to intractability: in the Micaiah narrative he resists the truthful prophetic oracle.

Given YHWH's ordained judgment against Ahab, and Ahab's entrenched disobedience, the deception plays upon Ahab's disobedience and facilitates the judgment. YHWH craftily uses an individual's perversity against that person as an example of the psalmist's observation that

> [w]ith the faithful you show yourself faithful,
> With the blameless you show yourself blameless,
> With the pure you show yourself pure,
> But with the perverse you show yourself crafty.
> (Ps. 18:26–27[25–26]).

YHWH acts towards people according to their own propensity, and those who oppose him he opposes. The deception plays out to their judgment and sin is called to account.

There is no loss to YHWH's truthfulness in such actions. YHWH's truthfulness is often spoken of in general terms. He is truthful as a judge (Pss 89:14; 96:13; Isa. 65:16), as an object of worship (Jer. 10:10), a defender of his people (Gen. 24:27; Exod. 34:6; Deut. 32:4; Ps. 30:9; Isa. 38:18–19), and as a source of beneficial instruction (Pss 19:9; 25:5, 10; 26:3; 119:142; Dan. 9:13). Likewise, he is truthful in the exercise of his prophetic decrees and unconditional promises (2 Sam. 7:28; 22:31; Ps. 45:19; Chisholm 1998: 27). Statements regarding his inability to lie (noted above) are attached to specific prophetic oracles. Thus Balaam, in reference to Balaam's oracle of blessing upon Israel, affirms that YHWH does not lie or change his mind (Num. 23:19), particularly as that blessing calls up the unconditional promises given Abraham; Samuel proclaims to Saul that YHWH does not lie (1 Sam. 15:29), indicating that, despite Saul's repentance, YHWH's rejection of the king is immutable.

Upholding YHWH's truthfulness in these contexts does not conflict with upholding YHWH's prerogative to act with sleight and deception against confirmed sinners. Set upon a path of destruction by their own way-wardness, their response to YHWH's deception simply confirms their waywardness. They are hoist on their own petard and brought to judgment.

Returning to Ps. 18 quoted above, reflection on its attribution to David sheds further light on the theology of YHWH's responses and speaks to the chequered lives of his people through all ages. Although David experienced YHWH as a crafty opponent able to catch him in his sin (v. 27[26]; 2 Sam. 12), YHWH never deceived David as a means of judgment. Despite David's many sins and despite suffering his sins' consequences, David's life was characterized by the willing praise of Ps. 18. It affirms love for YHWH, who is a shield and defender. It praises YHWH's way as perfect, his word as flawless, and gives him exclusive worship. David did sin, but his heart was attuned to YHWH and his ways.

That YHWH can act in deception should not leave his people wary, as if they stand before an arbitrary God. There is, instead, the knowledge that YHWH acts towards his people as they themselves act and deserve. As one's heart remains responsive to YHWH, as was David's, one is led in 'paths of righteousness for his name's sake'. Instead of fear there is praise, certainty of YHWH's commitment to his people and his sure promises. But to those who stand as YHWH's enemies he is a powerful opponent who – yet after many attempts towards redemption – will use even deception to execute judgment.

Finally, this chapter begins the judgment pronounced against Ahab in 1 Kgs 21, but the final dissolution of his house is not complete until 2 Kgs 9 – 10. During this time there is the possibility that Ahab's descendants might repent and turn again to covenant obedience, and it seems that at least Jehoram showed some attention to YHWH's ways (see 'Comment', 2 Kgs 3:2). Despite this, however, persistence in the sins of Jeroboam (and Ahab) remains, and judgment comes.

Both Solomon and Jeroboam receive words that caution against disregard of YHWH's covenant. To do so will bring disastrous consequences upon their own descendants and the nation (1 Kgs 9:6–9; 14:10–16). Their own lives end with those judgments in motion and their full execution anticipated. That YHWH forestalls the final judgment for many years grants each generation time for repentance and renewal. Sadly, however, although there may be moments of renewal, it is not lasting and covenant disobedience continues. Eventually, the ineluctable word of YHWH is fulfilled and each nation is destroyed and exiled. But in the same way that YHWH's word of judgment is ineluctable, so too is YHWH's word of hope: the promise given the Davidic king of an eternal dynasty, the promise that Israel is YHWH's possession and that he will not abandon it, the promise of return to the land. Each of these awaits fulfilment even though judgment comes. Such is the trustworthiness of YHWH's word.

1 KINGS 22:51[52] – 2 KINGS 1:18

Translation

22:51[52]Ahaziah son of Ahab began to reign over Israel in Samaria in the seventeenth year[a] of Jehoshaphat king of Judah, and he reigned over Israel two years. 52[53]He did evil in the eyes of YHWH and walked in the way of his father and mother and in the way of Jeroboam son of Nebat who caused Israel to sin. 53[54]He served Baal and worshipped him and provoked YHWH the God of Israel to anger, according to all that his father had done. 1:1Moab rebelled against Israel after the death of Ahab.

2Ahaziah fell through the lattice work of his upper room that was in Samaria and was injured. He sent messengers and said to them, 'Go; enquire of Baal-zebub the god of Ekron whether I will recover from this injury.'[a] 3But the angel of YHWH spoke to Elijah[a] the Tishbite, 'Arise; go up to meet the messengers of the king of

Samaria and say to them, "Is it because there is no[b] God in Israel that you are going to enquire of Baal-zebub the god of Ekron?" [4]Now therefore[a], thus says YHWH, "You will not come down from the bed to which you have gone up, but you will surely die."' Then Elijah departed.

[5]The messengers returned to him and he said to them, 'Why have you returned?' [6]They answered him, 'A man came up to meet us, and he said to us, "Go; return to the king who sent you and say to him, 'Thus says YHWH: Is it because there is no God in Israel that you are sending to enquire of Baal-zebub the god of Ekron? Therefore, you will not come down from the bed to which you have gone up but you will surely die.'"' [7]Then he said to them, 'What sort of man was it that came up to meet you and said these things to you?' [8]They said to him, 'He was a hairy man, with a leather belt bound about his loins.' And he said, 'It is Elijah the Tishbite.'

[9]So he sent to him a captain of fifty with his fifty. He went up to him and, behold, he was sitting upon the top of the mountain. And he spoke to him, 'O man of God, the king has said, "Come down!"' [10]Elijah answered and said to the captain of fifty, 'If[a] I am a man of God, may fire come down from heaven and consume you and your fifty!' Then fire came down from heaven and consumed him and his fifty.

[11]Then he again sent to him another captain of fifty with his fifty. He went up and said[a] to him, 'O man of God, thus says the king, "Come down quickly!"' [12]But Elijah answered and said to them[a], 'If I am a man of God may fire come down from heaven and consume you and your fifty!' And the fire of God came down from heaven and consumed him and his fifty.

[13]Again he sent a third[a] captain of fifty with his fifty. The third captain of fifty went up, and came and knelt on his knees before Elijah. He begged him and said to him, 'O man of God, please let my life and the life of these fifty servants of yours be precious in your eyes! [14]Behold, fire came down from heaven and consumed the first two leaders of fifty with their fifty. But now, let my life be precious in your eyes.' [15]Then the angel of YHWH spoke to Elijah, 'Go down with him[a]; do not fear him.' So he arose and went down with him to the king.

[16]He said to him, 'Thus says YHWH, "Because you have sent messengers to enquire of Baal-zebub the god of Ekron – is it because there is no God in Israel to enquire of his word? – therefore, you will not come down from the bed to which you have gone up, but you will surely die."' [17]So he died according to the word of YHWH that Elijah had spoken, and Jehoram[a] reigned in his place (in the second year of Jehoram son of Jehoshaphat king of Judah)[b], because he had no son. [18]Now the rest of the acts of Ahaziah that he did, are they not written in the Book of the Chronicles of the Kings of Israel?

Notes on the text

22:51[52].a. LXX[L] reads 'twenty-seventh year', indicative of the chronological difficulties in Kings.

1:2.a. *měhŏlî zê* ('this injury'; cf. 2 Kgs 8:8–9). LXX, Syr, Vg, Tg read, 'this my injury', which presupposes the consonantal suffix lost by haplography in MT.

3.a. The shorter spelling of Elijah (*'ēliyyâ*), only in vv. 3–4, 8; Mal. 3:23.

3.b. The double negative *bělî* + *'ēn* is emphatic; the addition of *min* makes it causative (GKC §152y).

4.a. The conj. on *lākēn* connects the consequence to the action.

10.a. Omitting the conj. on *'im* in conformity with v. 12 and several MSS, Syr, Tg, Vg.

11.a. MT 'he answered and said' (*wayya'an waydabbēr*) is read with LXX^L, 'he went up and said' (which presupposes Hebr. *wayya'al waydabbēr*). MT is possible (see v. 12), but the alternative fits the repetitious nature of the narrative (see. vv. 9, 13). 'he answered' is absent from LXX^B, Vg.

12.a. MT has Elijah respond to 'them'; LXX, Syr read, 'to him'. The larger delegation of v. 12 communicates the increasing urgency of the request.

13.a. 'Third' is read as m. sg. with LXX^B, Vg, and modifies the captain, not the fifty. It maintains the focus on the exchange between the captain and the prophet.

15.a. MT's DDO + suff. (*'ôtô*) makes no sense. Reading with LXX *μετ' αὐτοῦ* (*'ittô*).

17.a. LXX^Lmin Syr, Vg make explicit the relationship between Ahaziah and Jehoram with the addition 'his brother' after 'Jehoram'.

17.b. The synchronism to the reign of Jehoshaphat's son Jehoram is absent from LXX^L, perhaps due to the synchronism at 3:1, which differs (see 'Comment').

Form and structure

The division of Kings into two books produced two scrolls of equal length but divided the reign of Ahaziah. Here the narrative is rejoined. Following the brief focus on southern Jehoshaphat (1 Kgs 22:41–51), focus returns to the northern kingdom through ch. 8.

Ahaziah's regnal formulae are typical (see 'Form and structure', 1 Kgs 14); for slight variations see 'Comment'. The core narrative (vv. 2–17a) is a craftily told tale meant to entertain as well as instruct. Two compositional strata are discerned (generally, vv. 2–8, 17a and 9–16), with vv. 9–16 a later insertion. While vv. 2–8, 17a are credited with a historical kernel, vv. 9–16 are often considered historically dubious, legendary and even 'morally pointless' (Gray 1970: 459; cf. Jones 1984b: 375; Hobbs 1985: 4; Fritz 2003: 229). Not all argue for narrative disunity (Montgomery 1951: 348; DeVries 1978: 61–63), and thematic and linguistic motifs unite the supposed strata (Begg 1985).

The strongest connective threads are linguistic ones. The messengers (Ahaziah's in vv. 2–3, 5, 16; YHWH's in vv. 3, 15) are both *mal'ākîm*, the word for human and divine agents. Ironically, YHWH's messenger accomplishes his mission: Elijah is commissioned and YHWH's oracle is delivered to Ahaziah (vv. 6, 16) but Ahaziah's messengers abort their mission to accomplish YHWH's (vv. 5–6).

The second unifying linguistic motif is that of 'sending' (*šlḥ*; vv. 2, 6 [twice], 9, 11, 13, 16). Ahaziah repeatedly 'sends' (vv. 2, 9, 11), but he sends to no effect and his royal power is ridiculed in the face of YHWH's greater power. YHWH does not need to 'send' his prophet. He only 'speaks' to him (vv. 3, 15). His imperative commands are instantly and effectively obeyed. Thus in both sections of the narrative the motif of 'sending' reveals YHWH's greater power – a power that Ahaziah should acknowledge rather than sending to Baal-zebub.

A final linguistic motif is that of movement 'up' (*'lh*; vv. 3–4, 6 [twice], 7, 9, 11 [textual emendation], 13, 16) and 'down' (*yrd*; vv. 4, 6, 9, 10 [twice], 11, 12 [twice], 14, 15 [twice], 16). Ahaziah falls (*npl*; v. 2) and sends for an oracle. Elijah is to go up (*'lh*) and prophesy Ahaziah will not come down (*yrd*) from the bed to which he has gone up (*'lh*). The messengers repeat this same sequence of words (v. 6) when they report on the man who came up (*'lh*) to meet them. When Ahaziah discovers who came up (*'lh*) to meet them, he sends three captains up (*'lh*). The first two command the prophet to come down (*yrd*), but he refuses and sends fire down (*yrd*). The third captain also goes up (*'lh*) but kneels down (*kr'*), recounting the events of fire coming down (*yrd*), and begging for mercy. This change of action precipitates the angel's command that Elijah go down (*yrd*), and Elijah arises (*qwm*) and goes down (*yrd*). Upon meeting Ahaziah, he repeats the now familiar refrain that Ahaziah will not come down (*yrd*) from the bed to which he has gone up (*'lh*).

The narrative is a sorry return to Ahab's dynasty after the brief view of righteous Jehoshaphat. Ahaziah continues Ahab's devotion to Baal and his disregard for YHWH's prophet. This does not bode well for the ongoing Omride dynasty and one looks for the fulfilment of judgment given in 1 Kgs 21:21–22.

Comment

22:51[52] – 2 Kings 1:1

Ahaziah rules from Samaria, Israel's capital since Omri (1 Kgs 16:24). Ahaziah's two-year rule is tabulated by the non-accession-year system (in which a dying monarch's last year and the new monarch's first year are each counted as a full year). In real time, his rule is just over one year, starting sometime in 853 BC, Ahab's last year. Ahaziah gains the throne in Jehoshaphat's seventeenth year. His successor rules from Jehoshaphat's eighteenth year.

Following Jehoshaphat, who 'did right in the eyes of YHWH' (1 Kgs 22:43), that Ahaziah 'did evil in the eyes of YHWH' (v. 52) is a jarring reminder of the sins of the Omride dynasty. In stereotypical phrasing Ahaziah serves Baal (cf. 16:31) and thus provokes YHWH to anger (cf. 16:13, 26). In this his sins are those of both his father and mother, and (as is typical for northern kings), the sins of Jeroboam. Although his rule is brief, Ahaziah, like Jeroboam, causes Israel to sin (cf. 1 Kgs 14:16).

The translation here of 2 Kgs 1:1 follows the Hebrew in the ordering of the two clauses (NIV, NRSV read, 'after the death of Ahab, Moab rebelled', a reading that grammatically distances the rebellion from the preceding literary context of Ahaziah's reign). The present reading reveals the close connection (by a waw cons.) to the negative evaluation of Ahaziah and thus presents the loss of land control as a natural outflow of Ahaziah's sins. This is in marked contrast to Jehoshaphat, in whose righteous reign suzerainty over Edom is retained (1 Kgs 22:47). Moab's rebellion continues foreign conflict, demonstrating the necessity of torah obedience for a peaceful life in the land (Deut. 4:1, 25–28; Josh. 1:7–8; 1 Kgs 8:33). Ultimately, the pattern culminates in the exile.

Moab's rebellion begins in Ahaziah's reign and continues in Jehoram's reign (2 Kgs 3:5). The Mesha Inscription (*ANET* 320–321) appears to support the historicity of this rebellion, citing rebellion in the time of Omri's 'son' or 'descendants' (the term can be taken either way; cf. 2 Kgs 8:18, 26) following a period of forty years of Israelite domination. Omri's twelve-year reign and Ahab's twenty-two-year reign closely approximate this era of peace.

1:2–17a

2–8. The rebellion is introduced but the narrative segues to Ahaziah's sickness. The virtually identical opening at 2 Kgs 3:5 resumes the rebellion. The repetitive frame (2 Kgs 1:2; 3:5) is used to signal simultaneous events (B. Long 1987). Thus Ahaziah's sickness occurs during Moab's rebellion.

Ahaziah's sickness is the one event related from his reign. It is a canvas for the continuing theme of YHWH versus Baal, and the power of YHWH's prophet versus the monarch. Ahaziah falls through a lattice work (*śĕbākâ*; the same term describes the temple's netlike decorations; 1 Kgs 7:17; 2 Kgs 25:17), a window covering allowing breezes to cool an upper room. He seeks oracular assurance of recovery.

Given familial ties to the Baal cult, he sends to a local manifestation of Baal. 'Baal-zebub' literally means 'lord of the flies' (*zĕbûb* as 'flies' in Isa. 7:18; Eccl. 10:1) but is probably a caconymic for 'Baal-zebul', a name attested in Ugaritic myth for Baal (KTU 1.6 i 41–42) and meaning 'Lord Prince' (Day, *ABD* 1:545, 547; cf. Matt. 10:25; 12:24; Mark 3:22; Luke 11:15). Similar pejorative corruptions are found elsewhere in the biblical text (1 Kgs 11:5; see 'Comment'). He 'enquires' (*drš*) of the deity, just as elsewhere YHWH is enquired of regarding sickness (1 Kgs 14:5; 2 Kgs 8:8). The significance of sending to the Baal of a Philistine city is unknown; perhaps that particular manifestation of Baal was credited with saving or healing power (Fensham 1967). Theologically, the significance is apparent: not only does the king send to Baal, but he sends outside Israel, the territory particularly associated with YHWH. On both counts Ahaziah's actions are mistaken.

'Elijah the Tishbite' is introduced as he first appeared in YHWH's contest against Baal (17:1). Given his past actions, there should be no doubt that his appearance means trouble for Baal and his supporters. YHWH generally addresses Elijah directly, but here, as in 1 Kgs 19:7, the angel commissions him. As in each previous instance, the commission is abrupt (cf. 17:3, 9; 18:1; 19:5, 7, 15; 21:18) and Elijah immediately responds as YHWH's servant.

Narrative telescoping combines the angel's words to Elijah and his delivery of them to the messengers. This keeps the narrative moving rapidly to bring YHWH's word to Ahaziah. He is called the 'king of Samaria' (cf. 1 Kgs 21:1), a reference to his birthplace (Na'aman 2008: 204). The king's surprise suggests the messengers have returned quickly. Commissioned by Ahaziah, they readily abandoned that commission in the face of Elijah's authority.

That authority must have been especially compelling, because they know him only as 'a man' who met them. On the authority of an unidentified man, they deliver the judgment oracle. They preface the reason for judgment (sending to Baal-zebub, god of Ekron) and the judgment (death) with the messenger formula 'Thus says YHWH'. They repeat the oracle virtually word for word (with the appropriate exchange of 'going to enquire' [v. 4] with 'sending to enquire' [v. 6]). Ahaziah can have no doubt about his wrong and its consequences.

To test the oracle's authority Ahaziah attempts to identify the man. Commissioned to meet Baal-zebub (*ba'al zĕbûb*), they instead meet a *ba'al śē'ār*, a 'lord of hair'. Elijah is known by his hairiness – a wild beard or long, unkempt hair, as later Elisha will be known by his baldness (2:23) – and by some sort of distinctive leather clothing worn as a loincloth or belt. Ahaziah identifies his man: 'It is Elijah the Tishbite.' The full identification is key, for from his first appearance as Elijah the Tishbite (17:1) he has overcome all YHWH's foes, human and divine. Unfortunately, Ahaziah forgets this aspect of Elijah's identity and sends a second delegation, which proves as ineffectual as the first.

9–17a. Ahaziah's intentions towards Elijah are not benign. As elsewhere, kings have threatened prophets, particularly when they speak unfavourably

(1 Kgs 13:4; 17:2; 22:26; cf. 19:2). Ahaziah 'sends' (vv. 9, 11, 13) not messengers but soldiers − proof of his negative intentions. The rapid narrative reportage between soldiers and Ahaziah suggests the mountain is not as far as Carmel. A closer vicinity is probable, perhaps the mountains west of Samaria en route to Ekron (Gray [1970: 464]). The mountain top emphasizes that, while Ahaziah has gone *up* and will not come *down* from his bed of sickness by YHWH's word, Elijah has gone *up* and will not come *down* except by YHWH's word.

The three repetitions of the delegation is a common narrative technique by which events are enhanced for effect. Whether reflecting a historical accounting or using the technique of legend, it does much to mitigate against the horror of the deaths of so many, lending the story a darkly comic air (one imagines a classic Monty Python sketch). Throughout, Elijah remains stolidly immovable. He will not respond to the king's command, nor will he ramp up his rhetoric to match the increased rhetoric of Ahaziah's captains. Each captain acknowledges Elijah to be a 'man of God', yet it is only the third who acts appropriately towards Elijah. The first two captains repeat the disdainful words of Ahaziah, using the messenger formula 'Thus says X'. While the first captain's command is peremptory, 'Come down!', the second captain's command increases the urgency of the command: 'Come down quickly!' To each, Elijah responds exactly the same. As YHWH's man, he commands the 'fire of God' as at Carmel.

The third captain is sent in the same manner and, one can only assume, with the same message. But he alone of the captains and the king realizes the deference due a man of God. By acknowledging Elijah's authority and power as a man of God he wins his own life and that of his company. In response to the captain who acknowledges YHWH's prophet (and thus YHWH himself), the angel commands Elijah to action and Elijah immediately shows his own deference to YHWH by obeying.

The oracle is now delivered − by YHWH's prophet, not Baal-zebub's − and answers Ahaziah's initial query. What Elijah says differs in no significant way from prior iterations (vv. 3–4, 6), and bears all the hallmarks of the oracular word. The messenger formula comes first, ironically reminding Ahaziah which God he should have enquired of and is then followed by the classic form of a judgment oracle given to individuals. It provides first the reasons for judgment signalled by 'because' (*ya'an*), and follows with the word of judgment signalled by 'therefore' (*lākēn*; Westermann 1967: 142–168).

Ahaziah's authority throughout is proven ineffectual: he sends but cannot accomplish his mission; he cannot command YHWH's prophet. More, his cultic commitment is misplaced, seeking Baal rather than YHWH. As before, YHWH will not tolerate this misplaced allegiance and answers it with his authority. He sends his servant because he alone can command his prophet. In the end YHWH's word holds greater authority than Ahaziah's – for Ahaziah dies, according to the word of YHWH.

1:17b–18

Ahaziah's death is not followed by the usual order of the closing formula (see 'Form and structure', 1 Kgs 14). Rather, the succession notice to Jehoram immediately follows Ahaziah's death, perhaps because succession does not follow the usual father-to-son pattern. This unusual succession may also account for the lack of the phrase 'he rested with his fathers' (see 'Comment', 1 Kgs 22:40). The succession does not pass to Ahaziah's son, but to his brother (2 Kgs 3:1). Ahaziah's unusual death and the succession apparently also preclude the notice of death and burial.

The synchronization to the Jehoram of Judah's second year (v. 17) is expected in Jehoram of Israel's opening regnal summary. That is given in 2 Kgs 3, but the synchronization is not to Jehoram of Judah's second year but to Jehoshaphat's eighteenth year (3:1). The difficulty is clear: Jehoram of Judah succeeds his father Jehoshaphat (22:50), and Jehoram of Israel succeeds Ahaziah during the reign of Jehoram of Judah (1:17). Yet Jehoram of Israel's rule is synchronized to Jehoshaphat's (2 Kgs 3:1). Further complicating the difficulty, Jehoram of Judah ascends the throne in the fifth year of Jehoram of Israel (2 Kgs 8:16). The chronology of the monarchic era is extremely complex (see Introduction). The solution to this particular difficulty is that Jehoshaphat and Jehoram of Judah ruled as co-regents during Jehoshaphat's final years. Jehoram of Israel takes the throne in the eighteenth year of Jehoshaphat's rule (3:1), which is also the second year of Jehoshaphat's coregency with Jehoram of Judah (1:17). During Jehoram of Israel's fifth year, Jehoshaphat dies and Jehoram of Judah fully assumes the crown (8:16).

Explanation

'Is there no God in Israel'? The narrative tells of an Omride king's continuing allegiance to gods other than YHWH. In a time of distress the king turns to the false god of Ekron.

The chapter works in counterpoint with 2 Kgs 5, where it is a foreigner – and a worshipper of false gods – who discovers that there is indeed 'no God in all the earth except in Israel' (5:15). When read in counterpoint to 2 Kgs 5, Ahaziah's folly is brought into sharp focus.

The two chapters are not identical, however. Naaman seeks healing, while Ahaziah seeks only oracular assurance of recovery. The point of Ahaziah's narrative is not the healing ability of YHWH per se (as it is in 2 Kgs 5). Certainly, health and healing are ultimately God's jurisdiction

(Exod. 15:26), and he does intervene in healing power (Num. 21:8; 2 Kgs 20:5). Additionally, considerations for health are part of covenant law (Lev. 11 – 18), and prophets and priests participated in healing rituals (Lev. 12 – 13, 15; 1 Kgs 17:17; 2 Kgs 2:20–21; 4:32–35, 41; 5:3; 8:7; 20:1–7). These elements lie in the background of this narrative. Its intent is to pursue the question 'Is there no God in Israel?' (vv. 3, 6, 16).

Ahaziah's entrenched apostasy is instructive when compared to that of Israel's first king. When Jeroboam's son sickens, enquiry is made of Ahijah, YHWH's prophet (1 Kgs 14:1–3). Although Jeroboam institutes an alternative cult, he still maintains ties to true prophets. But after years of Jeroboam's sins and the worship of Baal, Ahaziah considers no such enquiry. More, Ahaziah must know of YHWH's work through Elijah that disproved Baal's power (1 Kgs 18). He has the recent history of prophets displaying YHWH's power against Aram and even his own father (1 Kgs 20 – 22). He does know of YHWH's prophet (v. 8) and thus does know of YHWH. But none of these affects his choice. YHWH is utterly dismissed and Ahaziah – though a king of YHWH's covenant people – turns readily to the powerless no-god.

He anticipates the later apostasy of his kingdom Israel. They turn to Baal and, even when receiving the covenant benefits from YHWH's hand, credit those to the false god (Hos. 2:5). Jeremiah, too, calls Judah to account for changing gods (Jer. 2:11). Their foolish apostasy is that they 'have forsaken [YHWH] the fountain of living water, and have dug their own cisterns, broken cisterns that can hold no water' (Jer. 2:13). Like Ahaziah, they turn from the real God who has shown his commitment and ability to help to what cannot help. And, like Ahaziah, the gods to whom they turn have no ability to 'heal' the sickened nation. It will be YHWH, who sends his people to the 'death' of exile, who alone can effect the cure. It is in the place of exile that healing takes place and YHWH's people are restored to new covenant life.

YHWH's power, being sovereign, has no relationship to whether his people believe in him or not. Ahaziah forgoes YHWH but that does not prevent YHWH from showing his power – the very power that Ahaziah needs. He proves it as his prophet exercises authority over Ahaziah's messengers. He proves it repeatedly as fire comes down to consume the hapless soldiers. He proves it ultimately when Ahaziah succumbs to death, just as YHWH said from the beginning. And, for the later apostate nation, YHWH's power remains YHWH's power: able to act on behalf of or against his people as his sovereign will directs. Belief is not the required arena for the exercise of God's power; apostasy does just as well.

When the Pharisees accuse Jesus of casting out demons by the power of Baal-zebub (Matt. 12:22–28; Mark 3:23–29; Luke 11:17–20), Ahaziah's story glimmers in the background, although the roles are reversed. The Pharisees parallel Jesus to Ahaziah: trusting in Baal-zebub instead of YHWH. This then would place the Pharisees in Elijah's role: the true prophet who knows YHWH's power. The reality is of course very different: the Pharisees are the apostate Ahaziah. Although they have seen Jesus' power exercised repeatedly, they will not acknowledge that before them stands 'God in Israel'. It is the people who read the evidence and wonder if indeed Jesus is the Son of God (Matt. 12:23). Regardless of the belief and disbelief held by these groups, God simply acts in power, doing what his sovereign will requires. The final act of God's power in Christ finds expression in the cross, resurrection and ascension. The cross, an instrument of torture, seems a foolish place for the display of God's greatest power but it is hidden there, nonetheless (1 Cor. 1:18–25).

God does not require belief for the exercise of his power. But, having exercised his power in the cross, he calls people to belief. The choice of Ahaziah remains: Is there a God in Israel or shall we turn to the gods of no-power?

2 KINGS 2:1–25

Translation

[1]It happened, when YHWH was about to take Elijah up to heaven in the whirlwind, that Elijah and Elisha set out from Gilgal. [2]And Elijah said to Elisha, 'Please remain here, for YHWH has sent me as far as Bethel.' But Elisha said, 'As YHWH lives, and as you yourself live, I will not leave you.' So they went down to Bethel. [3]The sons of the prophets who were in Bethel came out to Elisha and said to him, 'Do you know that today YHWH is taking your master from over you?' And he said, 'Indeed, I know. Be silent.'

[4]Then Elijah said to him, 'Elisha, please remain here, for YHWH has sent me to Jericho.' But he said, 'As YHWH lives, and as you yourself live, I will not leave you.' So they entered Jericho. [5]The sons of the prophets who were in Jericho approached Elisha and said to him, 'Do you know that today YHWH is taking your master from over you?' And he said, 'Indeed, I know. Be silent.'

[6]Then Elijah said to him, 'Please remain here, for YHWH has sent me to the Jordan.' But he said, 'As YHWH lives, and as you yourself live, I will not leave you.' So the two of them went on. [7]Then fifty men from the sons of the prophets went and stood at a distance opposite *them*. And the two of them stood by the[a] Jordan. [8]And Elijah took his cloak and rolled it up and struck the waters, and they were divided to one side and the other, and the two of them passed through on dry ground. [9]And when they had passed through, Elijah said to Elisha, 'Ask[a] what I shall do for you before I am taken from you.' And Elisha said, 'Please may[b] a double portion of your spirit *be given* me.' [10]He said, 'You have asked a hard thing. If you see me taken[a] from you, it shall be so for you; and if not, it will not be.'

[11]It came about as they were going along and talking, behold, a chariot of fire and horses of fire separated the two of them and Elijah went up in a whirlwind to heaven. [12]Elisha saw *it* and he cried out, 'My father, my father! The chariots of

Israel and its horsemen!' And he did not see him again. Then he seized his clothes and tore them in two pieces. [13]He took up Elijah's cloak, which had fallen from him[a], and he returned and stood upon the shore of the Jordan. [14]Then he took Elijah's cloak, which had fallen from him, and he struck the waters[a] and said, 'Where is YHWH, the God of Elijah, even he[b]?' He struck the waters and they were divided to one side and the other, and Elisha passed through.

[15]The sons of the prophets who were in Jericho opposite saw him and they said, 'The spirit of Elijah has rested upon Elisha.' And they went to meet him, and bowed to the ground before him. [16]They said to him, 'Behold now, there are with your servants fifty strong men. Let them go and seek your master lest the spirit of YHWH lifted him up and cast him on one of the mountains or in one of the valleys.' But he replied, 'You shall not send.' [17]They urged him until he was ashamed and said, 'Send.' So they sent fifty men and they searched three days, but did not find him. [18]They returned to him (now he was staying in Jericho) and he said to them, 'Did I not say to you "Do not go?"'

[19]Then the men of the city said to Elisha, 'Behold now, the location of the city is good, just as my lord observes, but the water is bad, and the land[a] is unfruitful.' [20]He said, 'Bring me a new jar, and put salt in it.' And they brought it to him. [21]He went out to the spring of water and threw the salt in it and said, 'Thus says YHWH, "I have purified these waters; may there never again come from them death or unfruitfulness."' [22]And the waters have been purified until this day according to the word of Elisha, which he spoke.

[23]Then he went up from there to Bethel; and as he was going up on the road, young men came out from the city and mocked him. They said to him, 'Go up, baldhead! Go up, baldhead!' [24]When he turned around and saw them, he cursed them in YHWH's name. Two she-bears came out from the wood and mauled forty-two of the young men. [25]He went from there to Mount Carmel, and from there he returned to Samaria.

Notes on the text

7.a. Syr makes the location explicit with the addition of *śĕpat*, thus 'by the shore of the Jordan', under the influence of v. 13.

9.a. LXX[B*] omits 'ask', which makes sense but lessens the immediacy of Elijah's translation; Elisha must ask now.

9.b. With LXX, Syr omitting the cop. on *wîhî-nā'*, 'please, may it be'.

10.a. The pass. pu. part. 'taken' (*luqqāḥ*) may appear without the preformative (GKC §52s).

13.a. The mantle has clearly fallen *from* Elijah (*nāpĕlâ mēʿālāyw*), emphasizing the continuance of the prophet's power. LXX has the mantle fall *upon* Elisha, emphasizing the transfer of power.

14.a. LXX[-BA], V[mss] add 'it did not part' (καί οὐ διέστη) after the first occurrence of 'he struck the waters', so that the waters did not part with the first blow.

14.b. MT *'ap-hû'*, 'even he', poses difficulties. It is here included with the preceding phrase, disregarding the MT accentuation, as do many interpretations. LXX simply transliterates the phrase, perhaps understanding it as a name, 'Elijah Apho'. The Jewish commentator Rashi and many English versions follow the accentuation and include the phrase with the following phrase. Thus 'when he also had struck'.

19.a. LXX[L] removes 'the land' so that it is the water that is both 'bad' and 'unfruitful'.

Form and structure

Regnal summaries set the narrative apart from the reigns of Ahaziah and Jehoram (1:17–18; 3:1–3), creating a narrative pause in which the prophetic office passes to Elisha. Elisha's ministry extends through the reigns of the northern monarchs Jehoram, Jehu, Jehoahaz and Jehoash (chs. 3–13), and his ministry completes the commission given Elijah at Horeb (1 Kgs 19:15–16; cf. 2 Kgs 8:7–15; 9:1–3).

The Elisha stories in chs. 3–13 probably originate in prophetic circles associated with Elisha. Many of the stories reveal the prophet's miraculous power exercised on behalf of individual Israelites or foreigners (e.g. chs. 2, 4–6). Others reveal Elisha's ministry on the larger stage of Israelite rule and polity (e.g. chs. 3, 6–9) (Gray 1970: 465). Whether the different types of narratives arose in different circles cannot be determined. The covenant concerns of Dtr make the stories of Elijah–Elisha (whose ministries were covenant centred) particularly pertinent to his theology.

The narrative has three units: vv. 1–18, 19–22, 23–25. Following an introduction anticipating the narrative's crisis point (v. 1a), an itinerary framework (B. Long 1991: 21) moves the prophets to the Jordan. The sons of the prophets challenge Elisha at Bethel (v. 3) and Jericho (v. 5), but the anticipated challenge at the Jordan is missing. Instead, a boundary marker is provided (the sons of the prophets stand 'at a distance opposite'; v. 7), while Elijah and Elisha cross the Jordan to the mysterious events that await them. Elisha's return crossing (v. 14) mimics that of Elijah (v. 8), and the boundary is similarly marked with the sons of the prophets 'opposite' him (v. 15). When they meet Elisha at the Jordan, the earlier missing challenge is supplied (vv. 16–17) and challenged in return by the new prophet (v. 18). The return itinerary revisits Jericho and Bethel and further proofs of prophetic power are provided. Finally, his return to the site of Elijah's great victory, and then to the royal city, concludes the narrative intent: Elisha is the new prophet, empowered and situated to continue Elijah's ministry.

The narrative structure works towards the focal point of Elijah's ascension and the transfer of prophetic office. Each element after that confirms the transfer of prophetic power:

Introduction (1a)
A   The journey begins at Gilgal (v. 1b)
  B   Journey to Bethel; first challenge (vv. 2–3)
    C   Journey to Jericho; second challenge (vv. 4–5)
      D   Journey to Jordan; boundary marker (vv. 6–7)
        E   Crossing of Jordan (took cloak, struck, divided to one side and the other) (v. 8)
          F   Ascension; double portion given and received (vv. 9–13)
        E'   Crossing of Jordan (took cloak, struck, divided to one side and the other) (v. 14)
      D'   Boundary marker; confirmation at the Jordan of succession (v. 15)
      [Missing third challenge and counter-challenge (vv. 16–18)]
    C'   Proofs at Jericho (vv. 19–22)
  B'   Proofs at Bethel (vv. 23–24)
A'   Journey ends at Mount Carmel and Samaria (v. 25)

The narrative shaping marks the import of the prophetic succession in the chapter. But this import is also marked by its uniqueness, for nowhere else does the prophetic office succeed from one to another. This succession is likened to that of Moses' leadership passing to Joshua. The mysterious disappearance of Moses the prophet (Deut. 34:10) and Elijah, the parting of the Jordan by the successor, and other allusions (see 'Comment' and 'Explanation' below) evoke the earlier narrative and suggest a similar continuity of ministry.

Comment

2:1–8

The introduction alerts the reader to Elijah's ascension, revealing that event as the narrative goal. With Elijah's ascension a given, the reader is left to wonder whether Elisha will now take up the prophetic role (1 Kgs 19:16, 19–21) and it is this upon which the narrative focuses.

The journey begins at Gilgal, near Jericho, the site closely associated with Israel's entry into the land (Josh. 4:19–20). The designation appears at first difficult, for it would send Elijah on a very circuitous route, and from the Jordan Valley to Bethel one would travel topographically higher, not 'down' as the narrative indicates (v. 2). An attempt to resolve these difficulties posits Jiljuleah, 7.5 miles (12 km) north of Bethel in the central highlands as an alternative Gilgal (Kotter, *ABD* 2:1023). However, that site is not higher in elevation than Bethel, nor does the valley between the two account for the command (contra Gray 1970: 474).

The other sites Elijah visits in the chapter (Bethel, Jericho, the Jordan) all feature prominently in Joshua's entry narrative. This makes the identification of Gilgal near the Jordan quite positive. In this case the circuitous route may indicate that Elijah already exercises authority over the sons of the prophets and travels to visit each centre (2:3, 5; 4:38). On a narrative and symbolic level the movement of Elijah 'down' to Bethel continues his movement 'down' begun in 2 Kgs 1:9, 11, 15 (see 'Comment' there). Finally, a command to go 'up' to Bethel (the notorious cultic site to which one goes 'up' to worship; Gen. 35:1; Judg. 20:18, 23; 1 Sam. 10:3; Hos. 4:15) would have been theologically inappropriate to issue to YHWH's great covenant prophet (Burnett 2010).

Elijah's persistent reluctance is met by Elisha's equally persistent oath (vv. 2, 4, 6), such as an inferior gives to a superior (Ziegler 2008). The persistence suggests each knows something of the purpose of the journey, if not the time and place of Elijah's departure. The travel itinerary takes the pair to Bethel and Jericho. At each way station the challenge of the sons of the prophets reveals they, too, are aware of the journey's purpose. Elisha's response confirms his knowledge of the imminent departure, and by enjoining silence he shrouds the event in mystery: some things should not be spoken of. The repetitive nature of vv. 2–6 builds suspense: when and where will Elijah be taken?

The 'sons of the prophets' (*běnê hanněbî'îm*) appear in 1 – 2 Kings particularly in association with Elisha, disappearing from the narrative with his passing (2 Kgs 2:3, 5, 7, 15; 4:1, 38 [twice]; 5:22; 6:1; 9:1; cf. 1 Kgs 20:35). They do not speak of themselves as Elijah's servants, but do accept the bestowal of his prophetic role, and self-identify as Elisha's servants (v. 15; 4:1). While at least one appears to be married and independently housed (4:1–7), others may live in community (6:1–6) and at least one functions as a prophet (9:6–10). They are supporters of Elisha, possibly united by shared prophetic ministry, but little can be posited towards a structured guild of prophetic or political enterprise (Hobbs 1985: 25–27; contra Porter 1981).

As the pair reaches the Jordan, fifty of the sons of the prophets from Jericho station themselves near but 'opposite' them. The phrase, repeated upon Elisha's return (v. 15), marks the separation of the earthbound group from the pair who enter the numinous realm of the whirlwind, across the Jordan. Elijah's cloak (*'adderet*), already a symbol of prophetic power (1 Kgs 19:19), is rolled or bundled to strike the waters, continuing the evocation of Moses (see at 1 Kgs 19), who long ago parted the Reed Sea with his staff of prophetic power (Exod. 14:16). As Israel at the Reed Sea and later at the Jordan, the pair cross over on 'dry ground' (*behārābâ*; see Exod. 14:21; Josh. 3:17) to the place of Moses' own mysterious death (Deut. 34:5–6).

2:9–13

Only when the boundary is crossed does Elijah directly refer to what all have known, which suggests he will be 'taken' imminently. Elisha's request for a 'double portion' (*pî-šěnayim*) refers to the customs of inheritance (Deut. 21:17) by which the birth order of the firstborn requires honour above his siblings. The custom focuses upon the heir's legitimacy, which is acknowledged through the amount of the bequest. Thus Elisha asks for appointment as Elijah's legitimate heir (Watson 1965) and signals this by the request for a double portion of the spirit experienced by Elijah.

The difficulty of Elisha's request is twofold: first, prophetic ministry is charismatic and thus by YHWH's appointment, not by heredity or designation. The request is not Elijah's to grant, but YHWH's. The closest parallel is the prophet Moses (Deut. 18:18; 34:10) who designated his successor by YHWH's direction. While Joshua is never called a prophet per se, he does function in prophetic roles (Oeste 2013) and, given the many parallels in Elijah's life to Moses' life, a correlation of Elisha to Joshua is not unexpected. The second difficulty to Elisha's prophetic succession is that a prophet should be one able to 'see' into the realm of God, and this is the difficult test Elijah sets for Elisha.

The two continue in conversation as they walk (v. 11, indicated by the part. + inf. abs. construction; JM §123m), when suddenly (signalled by 'behold' [*hinnēh*], v. 11) the fiery chariot and horses separate the pair and Elijah ascends to heaven in a whirlwind, a numinous phenomenon that often covers YHWH's presence (Job 38:1; 40:6; Jer. 23:19; Ezek. 1:4). Elisha does indeed 'see', although what he sees is not specified. Because he receives the prophetic anointing, he must at least see Elijah taken by the whirlwind, which is the criterion set by Elijah (v. 10). The recurrence of the verb 'see' (*r'h*) in vv. 10, 12 (twice) suggests this connection.

The first part of Elisha's cry 'My father!' exhibits his deep respect for Elijah and recognizes his prophetic leadership (J. Williams 1966: 344); the repetition reflects the intensity of the numinous moment. The second part of his cry 'The chariots of Israel (*rekeb yiśrā'ēl*) and its horsemen (*pārāšāyw*)', while not identical to the wording of the fiery chariot (*rekeb-'ēš*) and horses (*sûsê 'ēš*) that have accompanied the whirlwind, appears at first simply to note their appearance. Similar manifestations of YHWH's forces appear later in Elisha's story (6:15–17; 7:6–7) and may be one of the ways that YHWH is with his people in battle against flesh-and-blood chariots and horses (Deut. 20:1). The phrase, however, communicates much more than this acknowledgment. The term is a title, later applied to Elisha when he himself lies close to death (2 Kgs 13:14). It arises out of the holy war tradition (von Rad 1958: 100; P. Miller 1973: 134–135), acknowledging that the prophet and his message is the hand of YHWH – his weapon against the external and internal enemies of Israel. Elisha's career, bookended by these titular references, is not, surprisingly, concerned with warfare against flesh-and-blood enemies such as Aram and the spiritual enemy of Baal worship.

2:14–25

14–18. Earlier, Elisha had requested a double (*šěnayim*) portion; now in grief he tears his robes in two (*šěnayim*) and takes up the cloak, symbolizing the transfer of prophetic power. At the Jordan he repeats Elijah's action and strikes the waters, but only when he invokes the name of 'YHWH, the God of Elisha' and strikes again do the waters part, pointedly connecting Elisha's power to that of his predecessor. The crossing now evokes not the passage through the Reed Sea, but that of Joshua and Israel as they enter to take the land (Josh. 3). In the same way Elisha 'enters' to take the land for true Yahwism.

Recrossing the boundary from the numinous to the earthly, the prophets 'opposite' him meet him. They affirm his crossing as proof he possesses Elijah's spirit, do obeisance (v. 15) and indicate their new status as his 'servants' (v. 16). Not witnesses to Elijah's translation, they wonder if he has simply disappeared per his reputation (1 Kgs 18:12) and issue a challenge, filling the lacunae in vv. 6–7 (see 'Form and structure'). Ashamed at his adamancy, and to convince the group, Elisha consents. His own challenge in the face of the search results ('Did I not say, "Do not go?"') asserts his prophetic authority, and the sons of the prophets raise no further challenge.

19–25. Two final episodes affirm the transfer of the prophetic mantle, one issuing in blessing, one in cursing – both aspects of prophetic power. The first takes place in a city (Jericho, by context), which respectfully approaches Elisha, recognizing his authority. Like Moses (Exod. 15:23–25), Elisha heals the contaminated water, although the significance of salt is unknown. Its use in sacrifice suggests purificatory symbolism (Lev. 2:13; Gray 1970: 478), although it was also used to signify a city's utter destruction (Judg. 9:45). The importance of the episode lies in Elisha's proclamation of the prophetic word, his using the standard prophetic formula (as had Elijah, 1 Kgs 17:14; 21:19 [twice]; 2 Kgs 1:4, 6, 16). Significantly, it is a word of healing and blessing upon a city that earlier Joshua had cursed (Josh. 6:26). The power of the event is remembered in an etiological formula that affirms Elisha's prophetic power.

The second episode takes place as Elisha passes Bethel. He 'goes up' from Jericho but never enters Bethel (and thus cannot be construed as going up to worship at the notorious cult site; Burnett 2010: 295). Those who mock him are *ně'ārîm qěṭannîm* (v. 23) and later, *yělādîm* (v. 24). While both terms can refer to small boys, young men of unmarriageable age can also be indicated (*ně'ārîm qěṭannîm* in 1 Kgs 3:7; 11:17; *yělādîm* in 1 Kgs 12:8; Ruth 1:5; Dan. 1:4). The taunt is not merely childish mocking of 'male-pattern baldness' (Mercer 2002: 176–180), and its darker intent suggests the mockers are not merely children. Commenting on personal appearance is unusual in the OT; when it occurs, it is important to narrative purposes. Here Elisha's baldness is held up derisively in contrast to Elijah's hairiness (1:8): he is not Elijah, and they mock the succession that has occurred. Further, the narrative is reticent to have either Elijah (v. 2) or Elisha (v. 23) go 'up to Bethel', because the phrase indicates going up in order to worship (see at v. 1; cf. Hos. 4:15; Ps. 24:3). Thus here it is said Elisha goes 'up from Jericho' to avoid the association. The men's call to 'go up' may well taunt him to go up to worship at Jeroboam's cult site in Bethel (1 Kgs 12:26–33).

While the sons of the prophets and the city of Jericho honoured Elijah's spirit within YHWH's new prophet, the men of Bethel do not. Their denigration calls down a curse upon them; its immediate execution further affirms YHWH's prophet. The forty-two men mauled is a symbolic number, representing disaster and cursing (Judg. 12:6; 2 Kgs 10:14; cf. Burnett 2006: 93–95).

His prophetic authority confirmed throughout vv. 13–24, Elisha completes his itinerant journey. Mount Carmel, the site of Elijah's great victory, is visited and he ends at the royal capital, ready to address the continuing cultic offences of the Omrides and take up his own role as Israel's 'chariots and horsemen' – YHWH's weapon against his enemies – in 1 Kgs 3.

Explanation

The chapter is filled with allusions to the passage of leadership from Moses to Joshua. In both instances the transference of leadership occurs at a crucial moment in Israel's history. The passage also rings with echoes of Israel's entrance into the land under Joshua's leadership, and sets the stage for Elisha's ministry, which, in combating military and religious forces arrayed against Israel, effects a second conquest.

The analogy of Elijah to Moses has previously been made (see 1 Kgs 18 – 19) and is here furthered. Moses is presented in the tradition as a great prophet (Deut. 34:10). In his ministry to preserve the covenant life of Israel, Elijah truly is a prophet 'like unto Moses'. Like Moses who dies in Moab and is mysteriously buried by YHWH in an unknown grave (Deut. 34:5–6), Elijah also disappears east of the Jordan by YHWH's hand, leaving the prophet's disciples unable to find any trace of him. Moses does not live to see the conquest under Joshua, nor does Elijah live to see the full purging of the land of Baalism. And, as Moses appointed a successor before his death, so too will Elijah in terms that evoke the earlier appointment (Num. 27:18–23; cf. Deut. 34:9).

Joshua and Elisha are also presented in strongly analogical terms. Their very names identify them, for Joshua means 'YHWH saves', while Elisha means 'God saves'. The names evoke the holy war undertaken during their leadership and in which YHWH preserves his people. In their early ministries each 'serves' (*šrt*) his master (Exod. 24:13; 33:11; Num. 11:28; 1 Kgs 19:21). Upon taking up their master's role, each narrative provides proofs that they are received by the people (Josh. 1:16–18; 3:4; 2 Kgs 2:15 [and see further at 'Comment' on 2:15–25]).

When Elisha strikes the Jordan and walks through on dry land, Israel's crossing of the Jordan is evoked (Josh. 3) and Elisha effects a new 'entry' into the land. Yet, whereas Joshua's first act was to take Jericho and to curse it (1 Kgs 16:34), Elisha instead brings blessing through the cured waters. The cured waters point out another analogical contact between the conquest under Joshua and that under Elisha. In each narrative a contrast is drawn between faith and unbelief. Thus Israel trusts YHWH and has victory at Jericho, but Achan's sin mars the victory with judgment (Josh. 6 – 7). In the present narrative Jericho accepts YHWH's prophet and is blessed, while Bethel does not and is cursed (Satterthwaite 1998: 8–10).

The multiple analogies are not simply clever means to characterize Elisha. They shape the narrative towards its theological message. As in Joshua's time (Deut. 7:1–6; 12:2–4; Josh. 24:11–24), the greatest threat to Israel's existence is assimilation to the pagan worship in the land. This outcome Elijah has vigorously campaigned against, and it is Elisha who continues the contest. The sons of the prophets come to represent the remnant in the land that heeds YHWH's prophet and receives blessings; ultimately, the dynasty of Ahab represents those who do not heed the prophet and who receive judgment. Ahab's line continues the sins of Jeroboam and Ahab and, in the same way that Joshua was charged with eradicating the Canaanite inhabitants, Elisha replicates these actions, eradicating the house of Ahab by the hand of Jehu (2 Kgs 9 – 10).

Unfortunately, the analogical patterning is sustained in the long-term outcomes as well. The book of Joshua focuses upon the successes of Joshua's campaigns, but punctuates those successes with indications that the Canaanite remains in the land (Josh. 9; 13:1–5; 15:63; 16:10; 14:12–13, and esp. 23:4–13; cf. Judg. 1:19–21, 27–36). Israel settles with the Canaanites and takes up many of their worship practices. In the same way Elisha's actions are successful: Aram is defeated (2 Kgs 13:23–25; cf. v. 5), the Omrides are overthrown and Baal worship done away with (2 Kgs 10:28, 30). But the influence of Canaanite worship continues, for the sins of Jeroboam are not put aside (2 Kgs 10:29), the cult of Asherah remains (2 Kgs 13:6) and Baal worship resurfaces (Hos. 2:8).

Such analogical patternings are not unique to this chapter. Characters and events that stand in analogical relationship to other characters and events have already been explored in this commentary (see e.g. 1 Kgs 13). The narratives have been purposefully shaped to evoke a web of connections that inform and create meaning in new settings. In this way it is apparent the narratives are theologically informed writing: individuals and events from history people the narratives, but narrative concern is not primarily or only towards historical accounting. Rather, it is towards the communication of a message that reverberates repeatedly throughout all of Israel's history: YHWH has called a people out for himself, desires them to walk in his ways in fellowship with him, and will protect those people against debilitating forces, whether military or spiritual.

The weaving of such analogical connections surfaces in a powerful way in the ministry of Jesus. Jesus' name, like that of Joshua and Elisha, attests that 'God saves' (Matt. 1:21), and his ministry is heralded by John the Baptist's ministering in the power of Elijah (Matt. 11:14; 17:11–13; Luke 1:17). His own ministry echoes that of Elisha: gathering faithful followers (Matt. 10:2–4; Mark 3:14–19; Luke 6:12–16), feeding them by YHWH's provision (Mark 6:35–44; 8:1–10; cf. 2 Kgs 4:42–44), healing (Matt. 8:2–4; cf. 2 Kgs 5) and exercising life-giving power to a widow's son (Luke 7:11–17; cf. 2 Kgs 4:32–35).

Jesus is Elisha, but inasmuch as Elisha himself echoes the ministry of Elijah – in providing food and in raising the dead – Jesus stands as Elijah as well. Even more, as the new lawgiver (Matt. 5) Jesus is the new Moses, issuing the law of the kingdom of God. And, as one who fully conquers the forces arrayed against God, he is Joshua perfected, saving YHWH's people. The God represented in the NT is witnessed to by the apostles as none other than the God of the OT now incarnate among his people. The actions of Moses, Joshua, Elijah and Elisha all point ahead, showing God's character by how they act on his behalf. These actions are perfected in their source, Jesus the Christ.

2 KINGS 3:1–27

Translation

[1a]Jehoram son of Ahab began to rule over Israel in Samaria in the eighteenth year of Jehoshaphat king of Judah. He reigned twelve years. [2]He did what was evil in the eyes of YHWH, although not like his father and mother, for he removed the pillar of Baal that his father had made. [3]Nevertheless, he clung to the sins of Jeroboam son of Nebat, which he caused Israel to sin; he did not turn from them[a].

[4]Now Mesha king of Moab was a sheep breeder. He used to pay the king of Israel a hundred thousand lambs, and the wool of a hundred thousand rams. [5]But when Ahab died, the king of Moab rebelled against the king of Israel. [6]So King Jehoram went out from Samaria at that time and mustered all Israel. [7]As he went he sent[a] to Jehoshaphat king of Judah, saying, 'The king of Moab has rebelled against me. Will you go with me to fight against Moab?' He replied, 'I will go up. I am as you are; my people as your people; my horses as your horses.' [8]He said, 'Which way shall we go up?' And he replied, 'The way of the wilderness of Edom.'

⁹So the king of Israel, with the king of Judah and the king of Edom set out. They went around by this route for seven days and there was no water for the army or for the animals with them. ¹⁰The king of Israel said, 'Alas! For YHWH has summoned these three kings to give them into the hand of Moab.' ¹¹Jehoshaphat said, 'Is there not a prophet of YHWH here that we may enquire of YHWH by him^a?' One of the king of Israel's servants answered and said, 'Elisha son of Shaphat – who used to pour water on the hands of Elijah – is here.' ¹²And Jehoshaphat said, 'YHWH's word is with him^a,' and the king of Israel, Jehoshaphat and the king of Edom went down to him.

¹³Elisha said to the king of Israel, 'What do I have to do with you? Go to your father's prophets, or your mother's prophets.' And the king of Israel said to him, 'No; for YHWH has summoned these three kings to give them into the hand of Moab.' ¹⁴Then Elisha said, 'As YHWH of hosts lives, before whom I stand, were it not that I esteem the presence of Jehoshaphat king of Judah, I would neither look at you nor see you. ¹⁵And now, bring me a harpist.' (Now it would happen^a that when the harpist played, the hand of YHWH came upon him.) ¹⁶He said, 'Thus says YHWH, "This wadi will be^a full of pools." ¹⁷For thus says YHWH, "You shall not see wind, nor shall you see rain, but this wadi will be filled with water so that you shall drink: you and your livestock^a and your animals." ¹⁸This is trifling in YHWH's eyes, and he has also given Moab into your hand. ¹⁹You shall strike every fortified city and every choice city. Every good tree you shall fell, and all the water springs you shall stop up, and every good piece of land you shall spoil with stones.'

²⁰In the morning at the time of the offering, water suddenly began flowing from the direction of Edom and the land was filled with water. ²¹All Moab had heard that the kings had come up to fight with them. All who were old enough to put on armour^a were called out, and arrayed on the border. ²²They arose early in the morning and the sun was shining upon the water, and Moab saw the water opposite red like blood. ²³They said, 'This is blood! The kings have surely fought one another and each has struck his fellow. And now: to the plunder, O Moab!' ²⁴So they came to the camp of Israel and Israel arose and struck Moab and they fled before them. They went into the land^a, slaughtering Moab.

²⁵They overthrew the cities, and *on* every good piece of land each threw a stone and filled it. And every water spring they stopped, and every good tree they felled until only Kir-hareseth^a remained^b, and slingers encircled and struck it. ²⁶When the king of Moab saw that the battle was too strong for him, he took with him^a seven hundred swordsmen to break through to the king of Edom, but they could not. ²⁷Then he took his firstborn son who would reign after him and offered him up as an offering upon the wall. And great wrath came against Israel, and they departed from him and returned home.

Notes on the text

1.a.–3.a. A variant form of these verses appears in LXX at 1:18. In them Jehoram follows in the sins of his brothers and mother.

3.a. Reading *mimmennâ* (3. f. sg. suff. 'from it') as pl. suff., matching the pl. antecedent ('sins') and following LXX^{AL}, Syr, Tg, Vg.

7.a. The waw cons. plus impf. 'and he went and he sent' is read as non-consecutive action (JM §118k); 'and he went' is missing in LXX^L, Vg.

11.a. Reading MT *mē'ōtô* (DDO + *min* prep. and 3 m. sg. suff.) as *mē'ittô*, 'from/by him', with K of many MSS.

12.a. MT reads erroneously *'ōtô* (DDO + 3 m. sg. suff.) for *'ittô*, 'with him'.

15.a. MT *wĕhāyâ* is frequentative, relating past repeated practice. Because the moment of prophetic inspiration is not narrated, the verb is often amended to *wayhî*, 'and it happened that the harpist played', in order to fill the narrative lacuna.

16.a. The inf. abs. *'āśōh* is often translated as an imp. (GKC §113bb; JM §123u) but need not be; it can translate as absolute or abstract action (GKC §113a; Montgomery 1951: 361). An imp. translation ('*Make* this wadi full . . .') detracts from the wholly God-given nature of the miracle.

17.a. The *BHS* proposed emendation of *miqnêkem*, 'your livestock', to *maḥănêkem*, 'your armies', is unnecessary. The livestock are for food; the animals, burden bearers.

21.a. *ḥōgēr ḥăgōrâ*, lit. 'the ones who gird the girdle' – in this case, girding for battle.

24.a. MT *wayyabbû-bāh* represents a K–Q. The Q reads *wayyakkû- bāh*, 'and they struck it'. Here the reading follows the K, emending to include an elided aleph, thus *wayyābō'û-bāh*, 'and they went into it [the land]'. LXX partially attests to the K, reading 'and they went on, striking Moab as they went' (Montgomery 1951: 362, 365).

25.a. MT reads *qîr ḥărāśet* on the strength of MSS; cf. Isa. 16:7, 11; Jer. 48:31, 36. Some MSS read *qîr ḥărāśet*.

25.b. MT *'ad-hiš'îr 'ăbānêhā baqqîr ḥărāśet*, 'until only the stone walls at Kir-Haraseth remained', is confusing and best rendered *'ad-hiš'îr lĕbaddāh baqqîr ḥărāśet* ('until only Kir-Haraseth remained'; Montgomery 1951: 363; Hobbs 1985: 31).

26.a. Reading *'ittô* for *'ōtô*. See n. 12.a above.

Form and structure

Jehoram's opening regnal formula (vv. 1–3) returns the narrative to ordinary time after the interlude of Elisha's succession (see 'Form and structure', 2 Kgs 2). Jehoram's reign ends when he is assassinated during Jehu's coup (2 Kgs 9:24). So as not to impede the flow of that crucial narrative (see at 2 Kgs 9), no closing regnal formula is given.

Jehoram's reign begins with the common elements of a battle report (preparation including prophetic consultation, battle and outcome). The same battle report structure occurs in 1 Kgs 20, 22. Elisha's oracle is a central element of the battle report and resolves the dual crises of the Moabite rebellion and the lack of water:

A   Rebellion; alliance formed towards solution (vv. 4–8)
    B   Lack of water and request for prophetic consultation (vv. 9–12)
        C   Prophetic word to meet both crises (vv. 13–19)
    B'   Provision of water (v. 20) resolves need and precipitates . . .
A'   Battle with Moab (vv. 21–27)

It is striking that Elisha prophesies success in battle (vv. 18–19), yet the narrative ends in defeat for Israel (v. 27). Such perceived tensions between the prophetic oracle and the narrative proper have led to theories of dual sources. Some posit a battle report, with the addition of a later prophetic legend that theologizes the battle events (vv. 9b–17/19; Fritz 2003: 243; Jones 1984b: 391; B. Long 1973: 341). No consensus exists, however. Gray, for instance, holds that vv. 4–27 have the 'genuine ring of a good historical source' (1970: 469). While there may indeed be a compositional history behind the present narrative, the tensions within its present form are deliberate (Hobbs 1985: 32) and form part of the overall narrative message.

That message builds on the several connections forged between the chapter and 1 Kgs 22, in both of which a northern Omride and Jehoshaphat ally themselves against a foreign enemy. In both Jehoshaphat uses identical words to commit himself to the king of Israel (22:4; 3:7) and to call for YHWH's prophet (22:7; 3:11; the wording is virtually identical). The attitude of both Micaiah and Elisha is less than friendly towards the Omride king, yet each delivers a prophetic word promising the enemy will be delivered into 'the hand' or power of the king (22:15; 3:18).

YHWH had previously judged Ahab's dynasty (21:20–29) and Micaiah intentionally and by YHWH's design enticed Ahab to his fate at Ramoth-gilead, fulfilling the word of judgment against Ahab. The parallels in 1 Kgs 22 and 2 Kgs 3 must raise the following questions: Do the parallels include Elisha's speaking enticing words, as did Micaiah? Does Elisha prophesy victory for Jehoram knowing he will face defeat so that the judgment spoken against Ahab's son (21:29) will fall in this chapter upon Jehoram? Or, alternatively, is Elisha's prophecy intentionally selective and ambiguous so as to allow for the victories as well as the defeat? The answer to these questions, discussed in the 'Comment' section below, reveal that YHWH's word of judgment against Ahab (while not ultimately executed in this chapter) is still in force. And, unless another yet undisclosed son of Ahab is introduced, the anticipated judgment will fall upon Jehoram.

Comment

3:1–3

Ahab's son Jehoram, introduced in 2 Kgs 1:17, now takes centre stage. Most often called 'Jehoram', the variant 'Joram' also appears (8:25, 28–29; 9:14, 16). Jehoram of Judah son of Jehoshaphat (1:17), a contemporary of Jehoram of Israel, is also known by the variant 'Joram' (8:21, 23–24; 11:2). Context makes clear which king is in view, making the NIV's arbitrary decision to call the northern king Joram and the southern king Jehoram unnecessary.

The regnal formula contains the usual elements of synchronization, length and place of reign, and theological evaluation. The synchronization is to the eighteenth year of Jehoshaphat, although it was earlier synchronized to the second year of Jehoram of Judah (1:17). The dual chronology reflects a co-regency that Jehoshaphat in his latter years shared with his son (see further at 1:17). Jehoram of Judah's sole reign begins in the fifth year of Jehoram of Israel's rule (8:16).

Jehoram is less evil than his parents because he removes the pillar of Baal made by Ahab. The mention of Jehoram's parents is a reminder of judgment against them that awaits execution in the life of their son (1 Kgs 21:29). Ahab made an altar for Baal and sacred poles for Asherah (1 Kgs 16:32–33), and at some point made the pillar (*maṣṣēbâ*). Common in Canaanite worship, stone pillars were usually uninscribed and stood alone or in clusters as symbols of the deity or the deity's dwelling place. At one time considered neutral memorial stones in Israel (Gen. 28:18; 31:13; 35:14), they became proscribed due to their association with non-Yahwistic cults, especially those of Baal and Asherah (Exod. 23:24; Lev. 26:1; Deut. 16:22; cf. 7:5; 12:3; Gamberoni, *TDOT* 8:483–494). Jehoram 'removes' (*swr*) the pillar but he does not 'turn' (*swr*) from the sins of Jeroboam, thus doing evil in YHWH's eyes. The evaluation anticipates that in Jehoram's day – perhaps in the battle recounted in this chapter – the house of Ahab will be cut off.

3:4–19

4–8. The kingdom of Moab was originally subjugated under David (2 Sam. 8:2) and interrelations continued in Solomon's era (1 Kgs 11:7). With the division of the kingdom control passed to Israel, and in Jehoram's time Mesha, known as a 'sheep breeder' (*nōqēd*; cf. Amos 1:1), provided annual tribute of lambs' and rams' wool. The vast numbers are hyperbolic (as in 1 Kgs 4:21–24) and indicate Moab's utter subjugation. Ahab's engagements with Aram and Assyria in his latter years may have afforded Moab opportunity to gather strength; Ahab's death led to open rebellion (2 Kgs

1:1; 3:5) that began in Ahaziah's reign. His brief rule left the rebellion unaddressed.

The events of 2 Kgs 3 find a probable background, if not citation, in the Mesha Inscription (*ANET* 320–321). The stele credits Chemosh, Moab's god, with victories over Israel primarily north of the Arnon River, but also south towards the Zered. It cites events that could have occurred as early as Omri's reign and perhaps as late as Mesha's last years. Determining the inscription's date (before or after the events of 2 Kgs 3) is difficult (Liver 1967b; Sprinkle 1999).

Jehoram travels south to avoid the well-fortified northern reaches of Moabite power and mount an attack by southern desert routes. Moab's defence system along its southern and eastern flanks was not as strongly fortified as its northern defences, and was thus less able to withstand a concerted attack by an armed body (Liver 1967b: 27). En route, Jehoram solicits Jehoshaphat, allied through marriage to the Omride house (2 Kgs 8:18; cf. 'Comment', 1 Kgs 22:4), and Jehoshaphat answers as he did in 1 Kgs 22:4, pledging himself and his resources to assist Jehoram. By evoking the earlier episode, Jehoshaphat's answer strikes an ominous note: Will similar failure meet the kings in this undertaking? Will the prophetic word be similarly duplicitous? The ominous note is strengthened when Jehoshaphat pledges he will 'go up' (*'lh*), and Jehoram responds with a further query regarding the route by which they should 'go up' (*'lh*), both of which echo 'going up' to battle in the earlier episode (22:6, 12, 15).

9–12. The chosen route takes them south of the Dead Sea, and then towards the eastern reaches of Edom (Liver 1967b: 27; Gray 1970: 485). Edom stands in vassal relationship to Judah; a governor rules on Judah's behalf (1 Kgs 22:47). Edom does not attain sovereign power until 2 Kgs 8:20, and as a vassal is expected to assist its overlord.

By the lengthy route the kings hope to mount a surprise attack. But the route holds its own surprise, leaving the army without water. The kings of Israel and Judah respond to the crisis by confirming what is already known of their characters. In dismay, apostate Jehoram blames YHWH. His charge that YHWH has summoned the kings for deliverance into Moab's hand (vv. 10, 13) ironically foreshadows the final reversal of the narrative. His attitude of dismay and blame suggests he has already consulted a court prophet (as common in battles; 1 Kgs 20, 22). It is conceivable that Ahab's court prophets (22:6, 22–23) still serve Jehoram and that he has received from them a positive word regarding the battle's outcome. Given this chapter's parallels to 1 Kgs 22, such a consultation introduces a similar dynamic regarding the intents and veracity of the prophetic word (Long and Sneed 2004: 258).

By contrast Jehoshaphat, a true Yahwist (1 Kgs 22:43), immediately calls for YHWH's prophet. His words are virtually identical to 1 Kgs 22:7. That it is not Jehoram but an unnamed servant who alerts

Jehoshaphat to Elisha's presence lowers the assessment of Jehoram's character even further. The attitudes of the two kings – one wholly honouring YHWH, one suspicious of YHWH – are reflected in the narrative appellation granted each king from this point (v. 9) to the chapter's end. Jehoram is no more named, but called only the 'king of Israel'. His attitude towards YHWH is not significantly different from that of any other northern king. By contrast, the righteous Jehoshaphat is repeatedly called by name.

As prophetic oracles are often included as part of Israelite warfare, Elisha's presence in the camp is not unusual. He is identified by his service to Elijah, a reminder of the continuation of prophetic ministry. In their rush for clarification regarding the viability of the battle march, the kings attend on Elisha, going down to meet him.

13–19. Elisha's reception of Jehoram is less than cordial. Jehoram is not wholly devoted to YHWH and Elisha urges his attendance upon the cult prophets of Ahab and Jezebel (1 Kgs 18:19). Elisha is not moved by Jehoram's insistence the matter has to do with YHWH, but he is moved by the presence of the Yahwist king. His affirmation 'As YHWH of hosts lives, before whom I stand' directly repeats Elijah's words in 1 Kgs 18:15. This contrasts him with the prophets of Ahab and Jezebel and affirms his ministry continues Elijah's. Elisha's access to the prophetic state differs from Elijah's, however, for a harpist is called as the common means by which YHWH's power (the 'hand of YHWH'; v. 15, cf. 1 Kgs 18:46) comes upon the prophet (cf. 1 Sam. 10:5–6).

The actual interlude with the harpist is not related and the narrative moves quickly to the prophetic word. A dual 'Thus says YHWH' marks Elisha's first prophetic oracle. The fact of the miraculous influx of water is stated in absolute terms (v. 16; see 'Notes on the text'), and the mysterious and miraculous water source highlights the lack of human instrumentality. A rainstorm on the western reaches of the plateau could cause sudden flash flooding on the eastern, and generally rainless, slopes. Whatever the source, water comes suddenly, seemingly out of nowhere, and gives miraculous provision for troops and animals. The 'trifling' miracle will be proof of YHWH's ability to deliver Moab 'into your hands' contra Jehoram's conviction (vv. 10, 13). The prophet also gives details of their advance. The devastation in their wake outlines the usual procedures of warfare and should not be considered a violation of Deut. 20:19–10, a law concerned with Israel's ongoing food supply in the land of promise (Hobbs 1985: 37; Hasel 2002).

Elisha's oracle is true: Moab will be given into the hand of the coalition, but Elisha does not reveal all the truth. Moab will be given into Israel's hand only to a point – the final outcome of the battle is not revealed. Assured of victory, the kings enter battle and thus Elisha, like Micaiah before him (see 'Comment', 1 Kgs 22), has prophetically lured the Israelite king into battle, and perhaps to his death.

3:20–27

As Elisha predicted, life-giving water flows into the land in the early morning. Shifting perspective takes the reader to the Moab camp, which, hearing of the army's advance, had arrayed along the border. There is some desperation in the muster; with Moab's troops concentrated north of the Arnon, even the youngest able to wield weapons is called out. As Israel rises to drink, Moab rises and looks east to the invaders. The appearance of the water is presented in a clever wordplay: the water that flowed from Edom (*'ĕdôm*, 'red'), rich with red sandstone silt (Liver 1967b: 28), is struck by the sun's glancing rays and reflects back red (*'ădumîm*) as blood (*dām*). The Moabites put together a set of facts whose punning assonance ironically heightens their misperception.

Moab rushes upon the enemy camp thinking they have 'struck' (*nkh*) one another, but instead Israel rises and 'strikes' (*nkh*) Moab, slaughtering (*nkh*) them (v. 24). Moving through southern Moab, they do to the land, springs and trees what Elisha had prophesied, completing the prophetic word in reverse order (vv. 19, 25). Elisha's word that they would 'strike (*nkh*) every fortified city and every choice city' (v. 19) appears in fulfilment in significantly different wording and format (v. 25). First, no notice is given that they 'strike every fortified and choice city'. Instead, they 'overthrow' (*hrs*) cities and only slingers 'strike' (*nkh*) the capital Kir-hareseth (modern Kerak). Secondly, the action against the cities is stated in two separate phrases ('they overthrew the cities'; 'the slingers encircled and struck it') that envelope the actions against the land, springs and trees (v. 25). Israel is, theoretically, 'striking' Moab; Moab has to some degree been given into Israel's hand. But the misalignment between prophetic word and fulfilment should be a warning both to the Israelite force and to the reader: all is not as it seems!

Yet for a while the battle goes in Israel's favour. Rather than be taken, Mesha mounts an assault against Edom with a select and seasoned group. As a vassal, it is probable that Edom is the weakest part of Jehoram's force. Edom manages, however, to repel Mesha's attempt. Mesha's last effort is an appeal to Chemosh, Moab's god (Burns 1990: 188–190). As Israel was delivered at the time of the morning offering (*ka'ălôt*; v. 20), Mesha offers his son as an offering (*ya'ălēhû 'ōlâ*) in hope of deliverance.

The hope of deliverance arising out of sacrifice may be simply Moab's understanding of how Chemosh could be motivated. That understanding could certainly be false – both in respect of Chemosh's power and in respect of the efficacy of sacrifice to unleash that power. But as the narrative stands, the 'great wrath' against Israel follows on the heels of the sacrifice, suggesting the sacrifice precipitates the reversal.

The narrative, however, does not specify who effects the 'great wrath' and commentators draw varying conclusions. It is unlikely that Dtr, who has derogated Chemosh as the 'filth of Moab' (1 Kgs 11:7), would credit

Chemosh with any ability to effect such a reversal. The great wrath may be human anger (as in 1 Kgs 5:11; 13:19), as the Moabites are spurred by the dread sacrifice. But the term is most often used of YHWH's anger (Num. 16:46[17:11]; Deut. 29:28[27]; Josh. 22:20; 2 Chr. 19:2; Isa. 34:2; Jer. 21:5; Zech. 7:17). Certainly, YHWH is not motivated by child sacrifice, and has elsewhere made his repugnance of such actions apparent (Lev. 20:2; Deut. 12:30–31; 2 Kgs 16:3; 17:31; 23:10; Jer. 7:30–32; 19:3–5; Ezek. 16:20–21). If the wrath is indeed YHWH's, its link to the sacrifice is not that of response to appeasement. YHWH may unleash his anger immediately after the sacrifice as righteous indignation against the action – but one wonders, then, why the wrath is directed against Israel and not Moab. Perhaps the solution is that YHWH's anger is released at the moment when Israel's victory seems most secure. Only then is Moab driven to the extreme of the sacrifice. Such a moment is the point at which YHWH's action against Israel is most demonstrative of his ability to enact his judgment. The sacrifice spurs the Moabites on and they become YHWH's agents as he pours out his own wrath against Israel. The possibility that the wrath belongs to YHWH is a surprising but not wholly unexpected narrative twist given the chapter's echoes of 1 Kgs 22. The ambiguity remains, but YHWH's judgment on apostate Israel is clear.

YHWH has promised judgment will be meted out against Ahab's son. As in 1 Kgs 22, YHWH acts craftily towards the apostate king, using the stage of war to enact judgment. In both chapters the northern king joins Jehoshaphat, the prophet is solicited, an enticing oracle is provided and Israel goes to war. But while Israel was successful in battle in 1 Kgs 22, now the status quo is maintained with Moab. Only because Jehoram has mitigated Ahab's sin does he escape with his life. Where Ahab 'went up' but did not 'return' (1 Kgs 22:18, 28), Jehoram 'goes up' and does 'return' (vv. 8, 27). Once again the retributive oracle of 1 Kgs 21:21–29 is delayed (Long and Sneed 2004: 266).

Explanation

This chapter's several parallels to 1 Kgs 22 suggest that judgment should not be wholly unexpected. But after Israel's successful march, after the favourable prophetic word, after the miraculous water, after success on the battle line, the defeat surprises. Somehow the story has gone awry: how is it that YHWH abandons his people?

In 1 Kgs 22 the king is judged, but Israel, though scattered, returns home 'in peace' (1 Kgs 22:17). By comparison, in the absence of any specific word of judgment in 2 Kgs 3, judgment should fall against Jehoram of the house of Ahab. YHWH has challenged specific kings for so many chapters (Jeroboam [1 Kgs 14], Baasha [1 Kgs 16] and Ahab [1 Kgs 17 – 22]) that judgment against the nation is unexpected. And, given the nation's ongoing status of YHWH's covenant people, one might expect YHWH to stand on the side of his nation rather than array himself against it. Certainly, that outcome occurred as recently as 1 Kgs 20 and 22.

YHWH's covenant does not preclude judgment, and covenant unfaithfulness calls it forth (Deut. 28:15–68). It might be effected by defeat in battle (Deut. 28:25, 49–52) or at the hands of foreigners (Deut. 28:33; 36–37, 43–44, 49–52, 64–68). Such judgment is especially apparent during Israel's nationhood in the land of promise. Foreign invaders are instruments of judgment during the era of the judges (Judg. 3:7–8, 12; 4:1–2; 6:1; 10:6–7; 13:1). Similar judgments ensue throughout the era of Samuel and the early monarchy (see e.g. 1 Sam. 4 – 7, 17, 30). Although David achieves peace (2 Sam. 8, 10), the nations remain YHWH's instrument during the united monarchy (1 Kgs 11:11–25) and the divided kingdoms (1 Kgs 15, 20, 22; 2 Kgs 3, 7). Of course, ultimately it is through Assyria (2 Kgs 17) and Babylon (2 Kgs 25) that YHWH executes judgment against his people.

Despite clear covenantal warnings and the evidence of their own history, God's people often neglect their responsibilities before YHWH. The possibility of judgment is overshadowed in their mind by the expectation of covenantal privilege. The lengths to which YHWH goes to remind his people of covenantal realities and jar them from their complacency are particularly apparent in the work of the prophet Amos.

This prophet ministered in the northern kingdom approximately one hundred years after Jehoram's rule. In Amos 1 – 2 YHWH details the sins of the surrounding nations. Damascus, Gaza, Tyre, Edom, Ammon and Moab are each named as YHWH declares, 'for three sins of X, and for four, I will not turn back my wrath' (Amos 1:3, 6, 9, 11, 13; 2:1). Each nation is judged for sins against Israel, and the litany must evoke a sense of righteous satisfaction in Israel. Then, drawing the rhetorical circle even tighter, the prophet names Judah: 'for three sins of Judah, and for four, I will not turn back my wrath' (2:4). Israel's smugness must reach its zenith with these words: the nations are judged; Judah is judged; Israel is not.

But Israel must beware, for they are guilty of precisely those sins for which Judah is judged. And so the prophetic judgment finally turns from the nations and Judah to Israel. 'For three sins of Israel, and for four, I will not turn back my wrath' YHWH declares (2:6). Israel's complacency and misplaced sense of safety as the people of God is pointedly challenged. They cannot escape, for they too are one of the 'sinful nations' (9:8). Ironically, it is those very 'sinful nations' that are often the instrument of YHWH's judgment against his own nation.

Nothing inherent in Israel or Judah necessitated YHWH's choice of them (Deut. 7:6–8; 9:4–6). They were of the nations and only YHWH's gracious choice made them any different. That difference was not only for Israel's blessing (for abundant blessings were surely theirs under the covenant), but was to make Israel a blessing to the nations. When Israel forgot that calling and that covenant responsibility to YHWH and others, YHWH did not leave them without reminder.

YHWH's wrath against Israel, effected through Moab, is such a reminder. Israel as well as their king stand under judgment. These judgments are those prescribed under the covenant curses (Deut. 28:15–68). They are also the outworking of specific prophetic words that urge a return to covenant life and warn of further coming judgment (1 Kgs 14:10–11, 15–16; 20:42; 21:19–26; 22:17). Because YHWH's actions against Jehoram and Israel are the outworking of both general covenant curses and specific prophetic words, he has every right to act as he does in this chapter.

That Israel is blessed under the covenant must be held in balance with the realities of covenant commitments. Any sense of proprietary ownership of YHWH's blessing upon Israel qua Israel is the trap of presumption. It is the misunderstanding of a sovereign God by which one keeps him in one's back pocket to be summoned at will to do the proprietor's bidding. The trap of presumed proprietorial ownership of YHWH is not limited to ancient Israel but remains a pitfall for all God's people through all time. Particularly in today's era, and especially in the comfortable experience of North American Christianity, the sense of proprietorial ownership may indeed be great – YHWH may be expected simply to 'be there' for God's people to furnish greater blessing: financial, social, educational. This is, of course, the same lie that underlies a reading of Israel's encounter with Moab that cannot conceive of Israel's defeat.

To concede that Israel is defeated by YHWH in this chapter (in which YHWH has given many blessings) is to concede that YHWH is sovereign over his people. Towards them he acts with justice according to his word and his promise. More, his actions require no explanation of his timing or means so as to answer all questions. It is in the hope that Israel might concede this truth that they are not annihilated in this chapter. There is a gracious forestalling of the exercise of YHWH's full wrath. Judgment has been proclaimed and will be executed against Ahab's house. Judgment has been proclaimed and will be executed against Israel – unless they acknowledge their sovereign lord and realign themselves to their covenant commitments. This is the mercy of forestalled judgment for those who in their arrogance domesticate YHWH to be the God of perpetual blessing. In such instances the words of the ancient collect of confession are particularly appropriate: 'Cleanse the thoughts of our hearts by the inspiration of your Holy Spirit, that we may perfectly love thee, and worthily magnify thy holy name.'

2 KINGS 4:1–44

Translation

[1]Now a certain woman from the wives of the sons of the prophets cried out to

Elisha, saying, 'Your servant my husband is dead, and you know that your servant feared YHWH. Now the creditor is coming to take my two children as his slaves.' [2]Elisha said to her, 'What may I do for you? Tell me, what do you[a] have in the house?' She said, 'Your maidservant has nothing in the house except a jar of oil.' [3]He said, 'Go outside; borrow vessels from all your neighbours[a] – empty vessels – do not get just a few! [4]Then go and shut the door behind you and your sons and pour into all these vessels and, when full, set *each* aside.' [5]She departed from him and closed the door behind herself and her sons. They were bringing *the vessels* to her as she poured. [6]And when the vessels were full, she said to her son, 'Bring me another vessel.' But he said to her, 'There are no more.' Then the oil stopped. [7]She went and told the man of God and he said, 'Go; sell the oil and repay your debt[a] and you and your sons[b] can live on the remainder.'

[8]One day Elisha was passing through Shunem. A wealthy woman *dwelt* there and she urged him to eat a meal. And whenever he passed by he would turn aside there to eat a meal. [9]She said to her husband, 'Behold, I see that this is a holy man of God who passes continually by us. [10]Let us make a small walled upper room, and provide a bed for him there, and a table and chair, and a lamp so that when he comes to us he can stay there.'

[11]One day he came there and turned aside to the upper room and retired there. [12]He said to Gehazi his servant, 'Call this Shunammite.' He called her and she stood before him. [13]He said to him, 'Say to her, "Behold, since you have taken all this trouble for us, what may be done for you? Can anything be said on your behalf to the king or to the commander of the army?"' But she replied, 'I live among my own people.' [14]He said, 'But what may be done for her?' And Gehazi replied, 'Well, she has no son and her husband is old.' [15]So he said, 'Call her.' He called her and she stood in the doorway. [16]He said, 'At this season next year you[a] shall embrace a son.' And she said, 'No, my lord O man of God, do not lie to your maidservant.' [17]But the woman conceived and bore a son at that season the following year, as Elisha had told her.

[18]The child grew and one day went out to his father, to the reapers. [19]He said to his father, 'My head; my head!' He said to the servant, 'Carry him to his mother.' [20]He carried him and brought him to his mother. He sat upon her lap until noon and then he died. [21]She went up and laid him upon the bed of the man of God, closed *the door* on him, and went out. [22]She summoned her husband and said, 'Please send me one of the servants and one of the donkeys that I may run to the man of God and return. [23]He responded, 'Why are you going[a] to him today? It is not a new moon or Sabbath.' She said, 'It will be all right.' [24]So she saddled the donkey and said to her servant, 'Drive on! Don't slow the pace for me unless I tell you.' [25]So she set out and came to the man of God, to Mount Carmel.

When the man of God saw her at a distance, he said to Gehazi his servant, 'Look! There is the Shunammite! [26]Now run to meet her and say to her, "Is it well with you? Is it well with your husband? Is it well with your child?"' And she said, 'It is well.' [27]When she came to the man of God at the mountain, she seized his feet. Gehazi approached to push her away but the man of God said, 'Leave her be, for she is desperate; but YHWH has concealed it from me and has not told me.' [28]She said, 'Did I ask a son from my lord? Did I not say "Don't mislead me?"' [29]He said to Gehazi, 'Gird up your loins; take my staff in your hand, and go! If you meet anyone, do not greet him, and if anyone greets you, do not answer him. And set my staff upon the boy's face.' [30]The boy's mother said, 'As YHWH lives, and as you yourself live, I will not leave you.' So he got up and followed her.

[31]Now Gehazi went ahead of them and set the staff upon the boy's face, but there was no sound, and no response. He returned to meet him and told him, saying, 'The boy has not wakened.' [32]Elisha came to the house and the boy was dead, lying upon his bed. [33]He went in and shut the door on the two of them and prayed to YHWH. [34]He went up and lay upon the child and put his mouth on his mouth, his eyes on his eyes, and his hands on his hands, and as he bent over him, the child's flesh warmed. [35]He returned and walked back and forth once in the room, then he went up and bent over him. The boy sneezed[a] seven times and opened his eyes. [36]He called to Gehazi and said, 'Call this Shunammite.' So he called her and she came to him. He said, 'Take up your son.' [37]She entered and fell at his feet and bowed to the ground. Then she took up her son and went out.

[38]When Elisha returned to Gilgal, there was a famine in the land. The sons of the prophets were sitting before him and he said to his servant, 'Put the large pot on and boil some lentils for the sons of the prophets.' [39]One went out to the field to gather herbs and found a wild vine. He gathered wild gourds from it, filling *a fold of* his garment. He came and cut *them* up into the pot of lentils, without their knowing[a]. [40]They served up for the men to eat, but as they were eating the lentils they cried out and said, 'O man of God, there is death in the pot.' So they were unable to eat. [41]He said, 'Bring[a] some flour' and he threw it in the pot. He said, 'Serve *it* to the people that they may eat.' Then there was nothing harmful in the pot.

[42]Now a man came from Baal-shalishah and brought the man of God food from the first fruits: twenty barley loaves and fresh ears of corn in his sack. He said, 'Give *it* to the people that they may eat.' [43]And his servant said, 'What, shall I set this before one hundred people?' And he replied, 'Give *it* to the people that they may eat. For thus says YHWH, "They shall eat, and have some left over."'[a] [44]So he put it before them and they ate, and had some left over according to the word of YHWH.

Notes on the text

2.a. K *lky* is read with Q, *lāk* ('belonging to you'; 'for you'; Montgomery 1951: 370 cites K as a remnant of the northern Israelite dialect).

3.a. 'your neighbours' is pointed with Q *šĕkēnāyik*.

7.a. K *nšyky* is read with Q ('your debt').

7.b. K is read with Q 'and your sons'. The 2 f. sg. verb that follows ('shall live') agrees with the dominant subject, the woman.

16.a. Reading K *'ty* with Q, *'att*, 'you'.

23.a. *'tty hlkty* read with Q, *'att hōleket*, 'you going'.

35.a. LXX omits the verb 'the boy sneezed', thus reading that Elisha bends over him seven times. The omission makes Elisha's actions comparable to Elijah's (1 Kgs 17:21).

39.a. MT 'but they did not know' is usually translated with ignorance of the type of plant (so NASB, NRSV, NIV). But it is ignorance of the various cooks' actions that is in view.

41.a. Reading MT 'bring' without the cop. with MSS, Vrs.

43.a. The inf. abs. ('they shall eat and have some left over') can be used instead of the impf. in emphatic promises (GKC §113ee).

Form and structure

Four separate narratives turn Elisha's involvement from events of state (ch. 3) to the lives of individual Israelites. The stories probably find their origin in the company of the sons of the prophets, but whether originally intended to enhance Elisha's reputation through his miraculous powers (Gray 1970: 466–467), induce veneration of the man of God (Rofé 1989: 431–432) or encourage fellow prophets (DeVries 1978: 53) cannot be determined. In their present context consistent themes continue the polemic against Ahab's Baalism. The agents of death (debt-slavery, death and famine) experienced by YHWH's people under the Baalistic Omride dynasty are conquered by YHWH's power of life activated through his representative Elisha.

The chronological framework of the separate stories is indeterminate. The last two narratives (vv. 38–41, 42–44) both appear to occur during a time of famine, but the first (vv. 1–7) offers no time indication. The longer narrative (vv. 8–37) is marked only by the indeterminate 'one day' (vv. 8, 11, 18).

Strong connections of theme and wording hold the narratives of the two women together. Thus a poor woman and her sons want for food while a rich woman feeds Elisha and receives a son. Both women are asked in virtually identical terms 'What may I do for you?' (vv. 2, 13). In both narratives, events occur in a hostile 'outside' (vv. 3, 18, 21, 37; cf. v. 39) that are remedied behind closed doors (vv. 4–5, 21, 33). The rich woman engages the man of God at the doorway between these two realms (vv. 15, 21, 37). Further connections appear throughout the chapter: the provision for the poor woman leaves a 'remainder' (*bannôtār* from *ytr*; v. 7) that enables life and, similarly, the offering from Baal-shalishah is multiplied to provide a remainder (*wĕhôtēr* from *ytr*; v. 43) to sustain life. Present as background characters in the first narrative (v. 1), the sons of the prophets are active characters in the third narrative – and possibly the fourth as well, if they are included in 'the people' (vv. 41–43). In these three short anecdotes 'pouring out' and 'serving' (both *yṣq*) are crucial actions (vv. 4–5, 40–41) and, in the last two anecdotes, enable 'the people' (*'am*) to eat (vv. 41–43).

The interrelations among the narratives coalesce around the dominant themes of life and death, so that debt-slavery is relieved by life-giving oil (v. 7), a dead boy is returned to life (vv. 32–37), a deadly potage is purified (vv. 40–41) and food is multiplied to bring life to many (v. 43). The first two narratives bear obvious similarities to Elijah's own life-giving acts (1 Kgs 17). Unlike those narratives, Elisha the man of God is not referred to as a prophet. He only once pronounces 'according to the word of YHWH' (v. 44) and in this is contrasted to Elijah, who, in the parallel narratives repeatedly is instructed by, and speaks, YHWH's word. The contrast is deliberate and speaks to the different foci of the ministries of Elijah and Elisha. In this chapter Elisha is presented as a 'holy man of God' who, as his name indicates, shows that YHWH delivers (see 'Explanation' below).

A final structural element highlights the importance of Elisha's acts of life in the chapter. The annunciation of a child in the second narrative suggests, but then subverts, the commonly recognized annunciation type-scene in which (1) a woman is barren, (2) YHWH's messenger appears, (3) promises a son, (4) the event is confirmed despite doubt, and (5) the promised son is born and given a significant name. Yet in this chapter the woman is never described as barren (and may even have female children), no angelic messenger appears, the woman does not doubt but rejects the message, and the son is not only not named, but serves only as an occasion for Elisha's life-giving power (Shields 1993: 62–63; Roncace 2000: 115–116). Against anticipation, the child does not move the story forward in his own right. The events involving him highlight instead YHWH's power of life through his servant Elisha.

Comment

4:1–7

As Elijah provided for the Sidonian woman (1 Kgs 17:7–16), Elisha now provides for an Israelite widow, the wife of one of the group surrounding Elisha's ministry. Faced with the threat of debt-slavery (Exod. 21:17), the woman appeals to the man of God, apparently reliant upon YHWH's commitment to relieve the widow and orphan (Exod. 22:22–24; Deut. 10:18; 26:12–13; Ps. 68:5[6]). She never makes a direct request of Elisha but instead presents her past loss and anticipated future loss of children. She stresses her husband's relationship to Elisha as 'your servant' (v. 1 [twice]) and his character as one who fears YHWH, perhaps urging upon Elisha a moral obligation to his servant's family. Obadiah was previously described as a 'fearer of YHWH' (1 Kgs 18:3, 12), and midrashic texts identify him with the husband. The widow's tragedy is that the children of YHWH's servant (*'ebed*) will become the creditor's slaves (*'ăbādîm*). The loss of male support leaves the widow's future bleak.

Echoing Elijah's query (1 Kgs 2:9) and suggesting his ability to assist the widow (Gen. 27:37; 2 Sam. 21:3), he asks what he may do, and what she might have towards that end. The widow still sees with the eyes of past and anticipated loss and cites only her extreme poverty. She remains respectful, however, placing herself as Elisha's 'maidservant' and, as happened for the respectful inhabitants of Jericho (2:19–22), Elisha changes poverty to plenty. He urges her to extravagant action, collecting not just a few vessels. In the end the oil matches the extent of her extravagance, filling as many vessels as she had faith to gather. Later, Elisha will rebuke Jehoash for the littleness of his belief and action (2 Kgs 13:18–19), but no such rebuke is proffered here. Instead, the woman's extravagant action results in deliverance as Elisha pronounces her efforts sufficient to relieve her debt and live.

4:8–37

8–25a. The three scenes of this section, each marked by 'one day' (vv. 8, 11, 18), take place at the Shunammite's home. At the eastern border of the Jezreel Valley and 4 miles (7 km) north of Jezreel, Shunem is close to the route Elisha would take from Gilgal to Mount Carmel. Hospitality could be offered by men or women (Gen. 24:31; Exod. 2:20; 1 Sam. 25:18), and so her offer does not mark her husband as passive or insensitive. It is, however, wholly in keeping with her role as a woman in a Mediterranean culture, as the home was her sphere of influence and power and much of the narrative detail reflects this milieu (Hobbs 1993, 2001). The provision of hospitality enhances the honour of the host, making the guest part of the host's extended circle of kin and friends. Thus her hospitality to one perceived to be a 'holy man of God' may reflect some self-serving. The room she prepares on the rooftop would provide a cool respite in Elisha's journey and its generous appointments reflect the woman's wealthy status.

Elisha's offer to pay for received hospitality is an affront to cultural norms and an attempt to rebalance his indebtedness to her (Hobbs 2001: 25). Elisha appears discomfited by his indebtedness to the woman, and his interactions reflect some hubris on his part – which the course of events will set aside. First, he only twice speaks directly to the woman (vv. 16, 36) and most often maintains his distance via a third party. Secondly, the distance is maintained through the impersonal 'this Shunammite' (vv. 12, 36). Finally, he repeatedly has Gehazi 'call' her (qĕrā' lĕ; vv. 12, 15), a form often used to summon servants (Gen. 20:8; Num. 22:5, 21; cf. Roncace 2000: 112). His offer of assistance assumes a level of influence with both king and commander. Yet the woman is wealthy or great (gĕdôlâ; v. 8) and really does not need Elisha's influence; later she gains her own audience with the king (8:3). Her polite refusal that she 'lives among her own people' confirms her self-sufficiency. She needs nothing from the prophet.

The prophet insists on repayment and, in consultation with Gehazi alone (the woman has departed as she must be summoned again, v. 15), makes huge assumptions about what the woman needs (an act of hubris against the woman). Despite her assurance that her life is amply satisfied, Elisha promises she will bear a son in due season, in the springtime (lit. 'at this appointed time; at the time of living', *lammô'ēd hazzeh kā'ēt ḥayyâ*; similarly at Gen. 17:21; 18:14). The woman's remonstrance arises from the reality of her husband's age (v. 14). Like Sarah before her, she doubts the possibility of conception on physical grounds (Gen. 18:12–13). The prophet's word, however, is true, and the son is borne. Yet the narrative does not note the child's birth fulfilled YHWH's word, but only Elisha's word. Given the subversions to the annunciation type scene (see 'Form and structure'), and Elisha's attempts to rebalance power relations after the hospitality, the notation may signify that Elisha has acted not out of unselfish concern but for self-serving motives – he does not wish to stand obliged to her.

When old enough, the child 'one day' joins the workers in the field. He is stricken (perhaps by sunstroke) and the father's seeming unconcern reflects his role as a background character and a culture in which matters of health were a woman's sphere (Hobbs 1993: 96). When the boy dies, she lays him on the bed of the holy man to await his arrival, closes the door on that inner sanctuary, and ventures out into the public sphere. In Mediterranean society such public activity was undertaken by women on feast and holy days (Hobbs 1993: 93), making sense of the husband's surprise. She intently brushes her husband's objection aside, mounts the donkey and urges haste: she will 'run' to the man of God at Mount Carmel, 25 miles (40 km) distant.

25b–30. A better host than he was a guest, Elisha reaches out through his servant to the woman, even before she arrives. This action begins his journey from hubris to humility. As a guest the woman too breaks the codes of hospitality (as Elisha had done). She speaks untruthfully to her host's servant, enters the home uninvited and addresses her host accusatorially (Hobbs 1993: 96). Elisha extends welcome to the woman prostrate at his feet and prevents her removal. The next step of his journey to humility is his acknowledgment of the limits of his knowledge. The woman's reproach, echoing her objections over Elisha's earlier promise (vv. 16, 28), opens his understanding to her plight. Yet, resisting personal action, he dispatches Gehazi with instructions to travel without interruption to Shunem. There Elisha's staff is to transfer the prophet's power to the corpse.

Only when the woman uses the same words of commitment that Elisha used towards Elijah (1:2, 4, 6) does Elisha leave Carmel and follow the woman. Perhaps her words shame him to take responsibility for the life he himself promised. Or, reminded that his own commitment to Elijah eventuated in receiving the prophet's full power, he sets out to use that power on the boy's behalf.

31–37. Back at the Shunammite's home Gehazi's efforts bring 'no sound, and no response'; in the prophet's absence he is as ineffectual as Baal's prophets (1 Kgs 18:29). Elisha is confronted with the corpse in his own room. For the first time in this chapter he prays to YHWH and, while his prayer is not recorded (as was Elijah's in a similar circumstance [1 Kgs 17:20]), there is a clear acknowledgment that it is YHWH who reveals and conceals events (v. 27) and YHWH alone who can remedy them. His odd resuscitative efforts unite him closely to a defiling corpse (Num. 19:11) and the contact of eyes, mouth and hands – body zones that as a whole 'constitute the human being and are representative of his/her character and/or status' (Hobbs 1993: 97; cf. de Geradon 1958) symbolically unite him to the corpse, reducing his status through complete identification and defilement. These actions, twice undertaken, finally turn the man of God from hubris to humility. Twice Elisha 'bends' (*ghr*; v. 34–35) over the child, an action only elsewhere performed by Elijah (1 Kgs 18:42) at a similar moment of intense spiritual focus. The intensity emphasizes the scope of the miracle, and the defilement he is willing to undertake that life may ensue. Life returns in full force as the boy sneezes and the breath of life (Gen. 2:7) reanimates his corpse.

Despite Elisha's journey to humility, his character remains complex. He continues to distance himself from the Shunammite, summoning her through Gehazi as 'This Shunammite'. He himself though announces the reality of returned life – as he earlier had announced the reality of promised life. The woman falls at his feet, no longer in despairing supplication (v. 27) but in thankful acknowledgment of his power (v. 37). Her silence as she departs suggests similar complexity of character. The woman from Shunem and the man of God, with their varying motivations and goals, were caught up in an episode in which the life-giving power of YHWH is the focus. Ultimately, the complexity of their characters need not be resolved, for the characters are recorded primarily as witnesses to YHWH, the God of Life.

4:38–41

For the first time since Elijah was taken up Elisha returns to Gilgal. Ironically, the location that marked Israel's entry to the land of promise (Josh. 4:19–20), and all the hope of covenant life associated with that entry, now experiences the covenant curse of famine (Deut. 11:16–17; 28:3–6; cf. 16–19). As in Elijah's ministry when Baal worship brought drought and famine, so now in Elisha's ministry famine affects YHWH's people. In both instances there are those who remain faithful to YHWH (1 Kgs 19:18), but they, too, suffer the effects of covenant unfaithfulness.

The sons of the prophets gather before Elisha, perhaps for encouragement or teaching, and a shared meal provided by the man of God. The simple meal and the foraged field gourds (possibly the bitter fruit of *Citrullus colycinthus*, which may be fatal in large quantities [Gray 1970: 500]) suggest the extremity of famine. The problem that arises is a result of too many cooks in the kitchen. Elisha's servant (Gehazi?) puts the potage on, but another, unnoticed, adds the gourds without knowledge of their detrimental effect. The proof is in the pudding, so to speak, and the unknown addition is flagged as 'death'. Whether their concern is literal death or a bitter taste is irrelevant: the potage is rendered inedible.

The significance of the addition of flour to the potage is unknown – but its effect is immediate. The sons of the prophets eat, and the meal is shared with the 'people' (*'am*) – additional faithful Israelites, or a broader group. Elisha delivers YHWH's people, and the death experienced under Omride rule and Baal worship is cancelled by YHWH's life-giving power.

4:42–44

An offering from Baal-shalishah in northern Ephraim (Dyck, *ABD* 5:1153) is brought to Elisha, who, the context suggests, continues in Gilgal. Should the famine still persist there the offering would be particularly welcome. First fruits are generally brought to YHWH for a priestly offering (Lev. 23:10–11). Here the offering acknowledges Elisha's status as a 'holy man of God' (vv. 9, 42). Elisha twice commands his servant to 'give' (*ntn*) the food to the people (*'am*), who number one hundred. The servant is initially incredulous that the little would feed so many, but, as with the Sidonian woman, his incredulity is overcome by YHWH's word (1 Kgs 17:12–15). The sons of the prophets (who elsewhere have been designated in groupings of fifties [1 Kgs 18:4]) may be the 'people' who receive the food, or are part of a larger group of recipients. As occurred for the widow and her sons, the deliverance is overabundant, with some 'left over'.

Explanation

The parallels between Elisha's ministry in this chapter and that of Elijah's in 1 Kgs 17 are apparent: life is sustained through food, and restored through resurrection. The concentrated collection of vignettes in 2 Kgs 4 however extends Elisha's life-giving ministry beyond that of Elijah's in 1 Kgs 17. Elisha miraculously provides food for groups larger than a Sidonian household. He also cleanses food (vv. 38–41; cf. 2 Kgs 2:19–22). He not only raises a boy but prophesies the boy's nativity. And the abundant provision of oil brings life by relieving crushing debt.

The vignettes particularly differ from Elijah's ministry in 1 Kgs 17 in their exclusive concern with faithful Israelites rather than a foreign woman: sons of prophets, their widows and sons, a faithful Shunammite, and even the people ('am) of YHWH, which term denotes the covenant people. There is no ethnocentrism in Elisha's ministry, however, as, like Elijah, he ministers to foreigners (2 Kgs 5; 8:7–15). Neither is there social favouritism, for he attends to the wealthy Shunammite as well as the poor widow. But the chapter's focus on faithful Israelites is a reminder a remnant exists (1 Kgs 19:18). Under the shadow of an apostate king and the ineffectual Baal, the remnant finds life enabled by YHWH's faithfulness and life-giving power.

While this chapter focuses on YHWH's power enacted on behalf of the remnant, the larger context of Kings shows one cannot conclude that in all cases the faithful neither suffer nor die. Those in besieged Samaria experience both (2 Kgs 6:24–29); righteous kings suffer (2 Kgs 20) and encounter untimely death (2 Kgs 22 – 23); faithful prophets such as Jeremiah suffer for – and even because of – their ministries on YHWH's behalf. And there is a remnant of faithful people who yet are sent into exile in 2 Kgs 17 and 24 – 25. A few of these are known to us (e.g. Ezekiel), but many more are unknown. For the faithful who live among an apostate culture there is no guarantee of relief from that culture's realities.

For what purpose, then, does 2 Kgs 4 provide these collected vignettes of the remnant's deliverance from death? What do they reveal of YHWH, and what message might they communicate not only to a people in exile under foreign kings and gods to whom these stories are given, but to all God's people in similar hostile cultures?

The ministries of Elijah and Elisha are exercised under the threat of Baalism. Baal is falsely heralded as a life-giver, when the reverse is true. YHWH alone gives life; Baal gives only death. In worshipping Baal, all aspects of Israel's life falter under the power of death. Not only the gift of life itself, but Israel's economics, food distribution and even ecology are tainted and less than envisioned under YHWH's covenant. In a society experiencing death these vignettes reveal living faith in a living God and serve to call God's people in similar hostile cultures of death to living faith. The vignettes forcefully proclaim YHWH's 'Life!' in the face of Baal's death. From that conviction YHWH's people trust, and act. For an exiled people in Babylon's foreign culture under the power of foreign gods there is the reminder that even there YHWH's life holds and they are to have faith and act faithfully. While all might be taken from them by way of externals, even then the life of YHWH remains, sustains and calls those in exile to live a life of witness by and for the living God.

To speak of a hostile culture of death is to be reminded of Pope John Paul II's insightful naming of our own culture as a 'culture of death' (Paul 1995: §12; Leithart 2006: 184). Naming the gospel's proclamation of the unique sanctity, value and inviolability of all human life, he prophetically notes our own culture is arrayed against such life. Its commitment to means such as war, poverty, economic exploitation of the weak, the arms trade, environmental abuse for material gain, and more, shows our cultural underpinnings are hostile to life but open to material efficiency and gain. It is precisely in this hostile culture of death that John Paul calls the Christian church to speak for life, revealing its faith in a God who remains as powerful now as he was in Elisha's day.

Of course, there is ample witness for the church to speak against this culture's monolithic and pervasive values of death. In Jesus' great 'I am' sayings (John 6:35; 8:12; 10:7, 11; 11:25–26; 14:6; 15:1) he makes two related claims. First, the predication 'I am' is recognized as a restatement of the divine name of YHWH given on Sinai. That name is a statement of YHWH's eternal life in himself; he is the one who lives. That the association is intended and recognized is apparent because when Jesus claims 'I am' (John 8:58), his listeners recognize he identifies himself as YHWH and attempt to stone him for blasphemy. The claim reveals Jesus' identity as the same life-giving God active in the ministry of Elijah and Elisha (see 'Explanation', 1 Kgs 17). The second claim made in these 'I am' statements is that the life Jesus brings is not merely a future heavenly existence. Rather, the life he gives begins in this world, is full and abundant (John 10:10), and arises when one believes in Jesus' name (John 3:15; 20:31).

It is from the church's own life in the risen Christ that it proclaims what it knows to be so. Christ lives and provides life full and abundant, beginning now and extending beyond the grave. Out of this faith the church – individually and corporately – speaks and acts against death wherever it finds expression in our times.

2 KINGS 5:1–27

Translation

[1]Now Naaman was a commander of the army of the king of Aram. He was a great man before his lord and esteemed, for through him YHWH had given victory to Aram. The man was a mighty warrior[a], but he was a leper.

[2]Aram had gone out raiding and taken captive from the land of Israel a young woman and she served Naaman's wife. [3]She said to her mistress, 'If only my lord were with the prophet who is in Samaria! Then he would cure him of his leprosy.'

[4]So *Naaman*[a] came and told his lord, saying, 'Thus and so said the young woman who is from the land of Israel.' [5]The king of Aram said, 'Go then and I will send a letter to the king of Israel.' So he went and took with him 10 talents of silver, and 6,000 shekels of gold, and ten changes of clothes. [6]He brought the letter to the king of Israel, which read, 'And now, when this letter comes to you, note that I have sent to you Naaman my servant that you may cure him of his leprosy.' [7]When the king of Israel read the letter, he tore his clothes and said, 'Am I God, to kill or give life? For this man is sending to me to cure a man of his leprosy. Just consider and know that he seeks an opportunity *for battle* with me!'

[8]Now when Elisha the man of God heard that the king of Israel had torn his clothes, he sent to the king saying, 'Why have you torn your clothes? Let him come to me that he may know there is a prophet in Israel.' [9]So Naaman came with his horses[a] and his chariots[b] and stopped at the door of Elisha's house. [10]Elisha sent to him a messenger, saying, 'Go and wash seven times in the Jordan and your flesh shall be restored and cleansed.' [11]But Naaman was furious and left. He said, 'Behold – I thought for me he would surely come out and stand and call on the name of YHWH his God, and wave his hand over the place and cure the leprosy! [12]Are not Abanah and Pharpar, the rivers of Damascus, better than all the waters of Israel? Could I not wash in them and be clean?' So he turned and went away in a rage.

[13]But his servants approached and spoke to him. They said, 'My father, if[a] the prophet had told you to do some great thing, would you not have done it? How much more when he says to you, "Wash and be clean"?' [14]So he went down and dipped seven times in the Jordan according to the word of the man of God. And his flesh was restored like the flesh of a young child, and he was clean. [15]He returned to the man of God – he and all his company. He came and stood before him and said, 'Behold, now I know that there is no God in all the earth except in Israel. Now, please accept a gift from your servant.' [16]He answered, 'As YHWH, before whom I stand, lives, I will accept nothing.' He urged him to accept, but he refused. [17]Naaman said, 'If not, let two mule-loads of earth be given to your servant, for your servant will not again make an offering or sacrifice to other gods, but only to YHWH.' [18]But for this matter may YHWH pardon your servant: when my master goes to the house of Rimmon to worship there and he leans upon my hand and I bow down in the house of Rimmon[a], may YHWH pardon your servant in this matter.' [19]He said to him, 'Go in peace,' and he departed from him some distance.

[20]Now Gehazi, the servant of Elisha the man of God, said, 'Behold, my master has spared Naaman this Aramean by not taking from his hand what he brought. As YHWH lives, I will run after him and take something from him.' [21]So Gehazi pursued Naaman; and when Naaman saw him[a] running after him, he dismounted from his chariot to meet him. He said, 'Is it well?' [22]He said, 'It is well. My master sent me saying, "Just now[a] two men from the sons of the prophets have come to me from the hill country of Ephraim. Please give to them a talent of silver and two changes of clothes."' [23]Naaman said, 'Please, accept 2 talents.' He urged him, and bound 2 talents of silver in two bags, with two changes of clothing. He gave them to his two attendants and they carried them before him. [24]When he came to the hill[a], he took them from their hand and put them safely in the house. Then he sent the men away and they departed. [25]He entered and stood by his master and Elisha said to him, 'Where have you been, Gehazi?' He replied, 'Your servant went nowhere.' [26]He said to him, 'Did not my heart go with you when the man turned from his chariot to meet you?[a] Is this a time to accept silver and clothing, and olive groves and vineyards, and flocks and herds, and male servants and maid servants? [27]Therefore, the leprosy of Naaman shall cling to you and your descendants for ever.' And he went out from his presence leprous, as white as snow.

Notes on the text

1.a. LXX[L] omits *gibbôr ḥayil*, 'mighty warrior', but the phrase provides a contrast with *mĕṣōrā'*, 'leper', and should be retained.
  4.a. The subject of 'he came and told' is ambiguous. It may be an unnamed individual ('someone'). In the light of the king's address to Naaman in v. 5, it is here understood as Naaman. LXX reads, 'she [Naaman's wife] came and told her lord'.
  9.a. Reading 'horses' with Q.
  9.b. Sg. 'chariot' is read as a collective (Gen. 50:9; Deut. 11:4; 1 Sam. 13:5; 1 Kgs 10:26).
  13.a. After 'my father' (*'ābî*; missing in LXX*) 'if' (*'im*) is provided for sense, following LXX[L] (πάτερ εἰ).
  18.a. MT *bĕhištaḥăvāyātî bêt rimmōn*, 'when I bow down in the house of Rimmon', follows immediately upon 'and I bow down in the house of Rimmon'. Deleted as a dittography.
  21.a. Reading with two MSS and LXX *wayyir'ēhû*, 'and he saw him', for MT *wayyir'eh*, 'and he saw'.
  22.a. *'attâ zeh* as an adv. of time (cf. 1 Kgs 17:24).
  24.a. *'ōpel* here translated 'hill' refers to an undetermined area, assumedly in Samaria. Similar usage in reference to Jerusalem suggests the acropolis or citadel and surrounding quarters (Isa. 32:14; Mic. 4:8; cf. Gray 1970: 510).
  26.a. The interrogative is implied and need not be marked by the particle (GKC §150a).

Form and structure

Having demonstrated Elisha's power towards individual Israelites (ch. 4), this chapter returns again to the international scene. There, as prophet, Elisha mediates YHWH's miraculous power towards a foreign oppressor. The story is a strongly unified narrative (so Montgomery 1951: 373; see also Hobbs 1985: 59; B. Long 1991: 68), although vv. 15–19 can be understood as a later expansion (Jones 1984b: 412–413) and vv. 20–27 are often considered a later addition providing an etymology to explain Gehazi's name, understood as 'avaricious' (so Gray 1970: 508; see also Jones 1984b: 412–413; Fritz 2003: 258).
  Theories of compositional development often neglect the strongly integrative character of the whole narrative (as outlined by B. Long 1991: 68–69) that unites it through language, style, narrative reversals and contrasts. So, for instance, the opening and closing verses are united by leprosy (vv. 1, 27) and a great man (v. 1) finds a cure through the words of a young woman (*na'ărâ qĕṭannâ*; v. 2), while the prophet's servant is stricken. The powerful king is helpless to effect the cure (v. 7), while

YHWH's prophet mediates it effortlessly (vv. 8–9). He charges Naaman to a 'small' task (v. 13) that enrages the mighty man but makes sense to his servants and restores the great man's flesh to that of a 'young child' (*naʿar qāṭôn*; v. 14), making him the counterpart of the young woman who set him on his quest. Naaman's expression of faith (vv. 15–19) ends with the phrase 'he departed from him some distance', which implies that further action is in the offing (Gen. 35:16; 48:7) and the ensuing narrative is dependent upon the events of vv. 1–19.

The narrative's overall coherence is also apparent in its structure that twice seeks the cure with opposite results (vv. 1–7, 8–14). The first ends with a despairing declaration regarding the God of life; the second ends with YHWH's power displayed, which opens the narrative to a sustained declaration of praise towards the God of life (vv. 15–19). That declaration of praise is the first of two contrasting responses to the cure that echo one another in their component parts (vv. 15–19, 20–27). Naaman's humble allegiance attests to YHWH's sovereign power over all nations. Gehazi's response attests to his inability to accede to YHWH's open hand. It also stands as an ironic cipher of the northern kingdom's own rejection of YHWH's sovereign ways. The narrative can be outlined as follows:

A   A foreigner seeks for a cure (vv. 1–7)
    Problem (v. 1)
    Solution proposed (vv. 2–3)
    Proposal mediated to the king of Israel (vv. 4–6)
    The cure is not effected; the king despairs of God, the giver of life (v. 7)
A' Reprise: a foreigner seeks for a cure (vv. 8–14)
    Problem (vv. 8–9)
    Solution proposed (vv. 9–12)
    Proposal mediated (v. 13)
    The cure is effected by the word of the man of God (v. 14)
  B   Naaman responds to the life-giving God (vv. 15–19)
    The foreigner affirms YHWH's sovereignty (v. 15)
    A gift offered and refused (vv. 16–17)
    A chiasm of worship practicalities (v. 18)
      a. The 'matter' (*dābār*) of worship
      b. YHWH's pardon
      c. The master's worship (*hištaḥăwōt*) in Rimmon's house
      d. Leaning on Naaman's hand
      c' Bowing (*hištaḥăwāyātî*) in Rimmon's house
      b' YHWH's pardon
      a' The 'matter' (*dābār*) of worship
    The departure in peace

B'   Gehazi responds to the life-giving God (vv. 20–27)
       The problem (v. 20)
       A gift requested and received (vv. 21–24)
       The prophet's accusation and judgment (vv. 25–27a)
       The departure with leprosy (v. 27b)

By contrasting the king of Israel's brief and despairing acknowledgment of YHWH to Naaman's lengthy and humble acknowledgment, and by embedding a chiasm within Naaman's response, the narrative highlights that response as central to the chapter's message. Naaman fulfils yet another type scene of the foreigner who witnesses and praises YHWH's sovereign power (Exod. 18:7–12; Josh. 2:9–13; Dan. 4:31–34; similar, but lacking specific praise of YHWH's sovereignty, is 1 Kgs 10:6–9; 17:17–24).

Comment

5:1–7

An Aramean commander and Israel's enemy, Naaman is introduced in very complimentary terms. Attested in Ugaritic texts both as a proper name and as a royal epithet, 'Naaman' carries connotations of 'pleasantness'. Similar to the 'great woman' (*'iššâ gĕdôlâ*) of Shunem (2 Kgs 4:8), he is a 'great man' (*'îš gādôl*). He is also a *gibbôr ḥayil* (esteemed), a term that refers to greatness of wealth, reputation or (as here) prowess in battle (Judg. 11:1; Ruth 2:1; 1 Sam. 9:1; 1 Kgs 11:28). He is esteemed for the victories he has gained against Aram's historic enemy (see 1 Kgs 15, 20, 22), enabled by YHWH's hand. Yet, for all this, Naaman is a leper (*mĕṣōrā'*). The term is used of various curable and incurable skin conditions (see Lev. 13). If incurable or contagious, the sufferer was considered permanently unclean and lived in isolation (e.g. Uzziah in 2 Kgs 15:5; but see 'Comment' there). Naaman (and later, Gehazi) continues societal contact and thus his disease is perhaps some form of psoriasis, leucodermia or eczema, and certainly not the debilitating disease known in modern medicine as Hansen's disease (Harrison, *IDB* 3:111–113; Wright and Jones, *ABD* 4:277–282).

Although set during a peaceful interval with Israel, the border remains volatile owing to raiding parties (*gĕdûdîm*; cf. 6:23; 13:20; 1 Kgs 11:24), and it is one of these that captures the young woman (*na'ărâ qĕṭannâ*). There is no little providence in the fact she is placed with Naaman's wife, where she not only cares for the welfare of her foreign captor but also (despite the fact that YHWH has not kept her from captivity) affirms the power of YHWH through his prophet in the city of Samaria. If Naaman were only 'with' (lit. 'stand before', *lipnê*; v. 3) the prophet, he would be cured. The position of 'standing before' is a recurrent theme in the narrative (vv. 15–16 [a different construction occurs in v. 25]) and acknowledges the power of the one 'stood before'. The girl does not use the common term for healing (*rp'*), but *'sp*. The term is used of healing only in this narrative (vv. 3, 6–7, 11), and besides enhancing the singularity of the girl's witness, it also marks its persuasive power, for both the king of Israel and Naaman repeat the girl's unusual terminology.

The king of Aram (by narrative context Ben-hadad II [see discussion at 1 Kgs 20]) acts immediately on the girl's conviction. He sends not to the prophet but to the king of Israel (by narrative context Jehoram); perhaps he thinks the prophet is a court prophet whom the king controls. The lavish gift (772 lb [350 kg] of silver, 110 lb [50 kg] of gold, and clothing) reveals Naaman's great desire for health and (if furnished by the king) his valuation in his king's eyes. The narrative skips over the letter's introduction, signalling its core request with the common ANE form 'and now' (cf. 2 Kgs 10:2; Pardee 1982: 173). However Ben-hadad conceptualizes the relationship of Jehoram to Elisha, Jehoram knows he has no power to command the prophet, and so, reading (*qr'*) the letter, he tears (*qr'*) his clothing in grief and futility (an action he similarly undertakes when faced with famine [6:30]).

Jehoram's protest 'Am I God, to kill or give life?' arises out of his sense of futility (for only YHWH can heal leprosy [Num. 12:13]). It evokes another passage that opens up the meaning of Naaman's story. In Deut. 32:39 YHWH declares through Moses that 'I put to death and give life.' Moses makes this declaration in the context of affirming YHWH's utter sovereignty over other gods, and the inability of those gods to deliver or rescue YHWH's people. Elisha has shown many times over that it is YHWH and not Baal who holds the power of life (ch. 4). Jehoram's cry affirms this, but ironically so. While his rule has mitigated some aspects of Baal worship (3:2), it still continues (2 Kgs 10:18–28). Baal is worshipped as a giver of life through his supposed control of the rains and crops. Yet it will be Naaman, the foreign oppressor, who relinquishes another god to embrace YHWH, the God of life. Israel will maintain their worship of Baal and Jeroboam's gods. They refuse to know what Naaman comes to know: that 'there is no God in all the earth except in Israel' (v. 15).

5:8–14

The second phase of the quest begins when Elisha addresses the dual problem of the king's distress and Naaman's leprosy. Naaman is invited to come 'that he may know there is a prophet in Israel' (v. 8). When Naaman later acknowledges that 'there is no God except in Israel' (v. 15), Elisha's objective will be achieved. Naaman arrives in pomp, gifts and servants in tow, and stands expectantly at the prophet's door. Insult is heaped on insult when (disregarding Naaman's great status and wealth), Elisha not only does not appear, but sends a mundane prescription via a servant (possibly Gehazi). For restored flesh, Naaman is to 'wash' (*rḥṣ*; cf. vv. 12–13) seven times in the Jordan to be 'cleansed' (*ṭhr*; vv. 12–13, 14). This evokes the Levitical texts for treating leprosy, where washing (*rḥṣ*) is prescribed (Lev. 14:8–9) for cleansing (*ṭhr*; Lev. 13:7, 35; 14:2, 23, 32), followed by a seven-day quarantine. Of the two prescriptions, Naaman's cure is the less onerous, but it nonetheless offends his pride.

Naaman's fury reveals his sense of self-importance: he expects some miraculous display commensurate with his status – at the very least, the presence of the prophet invoking his God and gesturing over the affected area! As well, a conqueror's superiority cites the clear rivers that feed the oasis of Damascus (modern Barada and el-A'waj; R. Roth, *ABD* 1:6; Pitard, *ABD* 2:5–7; H. Thompson, *ABD* 5:303–304) as at least as good as any muddy Jordan. Angered at the wasted trip and personal slight, he departs enraged. Only the wise counsel of his servants (furthering the wise counsel of his wife's servant) urges him to consider the prophet's simple cure. He *has* come this far, a great (*gādôl*) man (v. 1) expecting some great (*gādôl*; v. 13) thing. Their cajoling convinces him to submit to the prophet's prescription and he dips 'according to the word of the man of God' (v. 14). The mighty man's submission and obedience to YHWH's prophet enable YHWH's cure. Exactly as the prophet promised (v. 10), he is cleansed (*ṭhr*) and his flesh restored (*šwb*) as a young child's (*na'ar qāṭōn*) – now, the 'great man' (*'îš gādôl*) is like the 'young woman' (*na'ărâ qĕṭannâ*; v. 2). Whereas the first scene brought the quest to a king's futile cry that he was not God, the second scene brings the quest to its completion – but as the next section reveals, a completion that shows the proud commander is like the young woman in more than the state of his flesh. He will burst into effusive praise, every bit as convinced of YHWH as was the young woman.

5:15–19

His flesh restored (*šwb*), Naaman returns (*šwb*) to the man of God. His words reveal that his 'turning' is not only physical, but includes his 'turning' to YHWH in repentance and faith (as the verbal root often connotes; see e.g. Jer. 3:7, 12, 14, 22; Hos. 3:15; 6:10). This turning is initially signalled in his stand 'before' (*lipnê*) Elisha.

The young woman had promised his cure if he stood 'before' (*lipnê*) the prophet (v. 3). When Naaman first arrived at Elisha's house, he 'stood at the door' – but the telltale preposition was not used. Only now, cleansed and restored in body and heart, does he stand before the prophet, as an inferior before a superior. Naaman thus acknowledges the prophet in Israel, but, as Elisha himself is merely a servant who stands 'before' (*lipnê*) YHWH (v. 16), Naaman rightly acknowledges not the prophet, but the prophet's master. Perhaps this sheds further light on why Elisha sent a messenger when Naaman arrived at his door, and was absent when the miracle occurred. His appearance could have led Naaman to conclude that the miracle was by his power alone. In Elisha's absence the miraculous power was credited to its true source. Healed and restored, Naaman acknowledges YHWH's sovereignty over all gods: no god exists but in Israel. What he does not know (but the reader does) is that YHWH's power is not limited to Israel's borders. He has already empowered the foreign commander against Israel (v. 1).

Gifts to prophets are common (1 Sam. 9:7; 1 Kgs 14:3) and Elisha himself elsewhere accepts them (2 Kgs 8:7–9). Naaman's offer reveals his new attitude of humility, for he refers to himself as 'your servant' (five times in vv. 15–18). Elisha's refusal appears intent on directing Naaman's thanks to YHWH alone: Elisha is YHWH's servant and accepts nothing, even when urged.

In the light of Elisha's refusal to grace Naaman by accepting the gift, Naaman pursues another sort of favour ('if not, then . . .'). The measure of Israelite soil will enable Naaman to build an altar to YHWH (Exod. 20:25) and perhaps serve as a 'tangible and material tie to the community of faith Elisha represents' (Fretheim 1999: 153). While he will no longer sacrifice to other gods, the demands of his position present a dilemma that the chiasm of v. 18 makes clear (see 'Form and structure'). The king of Aram will worship Rimmon, the Baal of Aram, also known as Hadad the head of the Aramean pantheon (Greenfield, *DDD* 377–382). Naaman will be expected to join the king in worship and therefore humbly asks YHWH's pardon upon 'your servant' (see Bb, b' in 'Form and structure') 'in this matter' (Ba, a' in 'Form and structure').

The request is a bold assertion of trust in YHWH's gracious forgiveness and, while Elisha does not give explicit consent, it must be implied in his command that Naaman 'Go in peace.' No judgment is levelled against the foreigner and he is free to set the worship of YHWH into the complex demands of his existing allegiances, even though they are tied to foreign worship practices.

5:20–27

Gehazi's response to YHWH's gracious healing is starkly contrasted to that of Naaman and Elisha. Whereas Naaman as 'your servant' (vv. 15–18) urges Elisha to 'take' (*lqḥ*) gifts (vv. 15–16), and Elisha as YHWH's servant swears he will not take (*lqḥ*) gifts (v. 16), the servant Gehazi swears only to take (*lqḥ*; v. 20 [twice]). Although he is Elisha's servant, he does not abide by his master's decision. Rather, he contemptuously calls Naaman 'this Aramean'. With equal insubordination he invokes YHWH's name in an oath that does not honour YHWH but only seeks personal gain. He swears that he will take (*lqḥ*) whatever he can get, and in this mocks Elisha's earlier oath (v. 16).

Naaman, the once-proud commander, dismounts to greet the pursuing servant of the prophet. The greeting 'Is it well?' is the same as Gehazi once directed towards the Shunammite (4:26). In the same way that her response to Gehazi was untruthful, Gehazi's response now is equally untruthful: 'It is well.' But though the Shunammite's lie was aimed towards the benefit of another person, now Gehazi's lie is aimed at his own benefit. His elaborate lie seeks to mask his greed under the guise of charity. Naaman's enthusiastic response shows his thankful devotion to YHWH remains intact. He urges Gehazi (as he earlier urged Elisha), generously doubling the gift. The gifts (154 lb [70 kg] of silver, and the clothing) are bundled up and sent off with two of Naaman's servants carrying them. There is no word of protest, and certainly no recorded word of thanks from Gehazi to 'this Aramean'.

Back in Samaria Gehazi secrets the goods in Elisha's house. He then presents himself to Elisha's presence, standing not 'before' (lipnê) Elisha, which would have signalled his submission to his superior (cf. vv. 3, 15 and 'Comment'), but 'by' ('el) Elisha. Certainly, Gehazi's actions prove he no longer stands in submission before his master. But despite the rupture in relations, Elisha remains the master and has omniscient knowledge of Gehazi's actions. Gehazi may protest with a further lie, but the prophet's own presence attended Gehazi's escapade ('did not my heart go with you?').

Elisha pointedly schools Gehazi through a rhetorical question. There are times to take gifts, but this is definitely a time to refrain from taking any gift: silver, clothing or any other boon. The transformation YHWH wrought in the foreigner's life is credited solely to YHWH, and Elisha's refusal of the gift reinforced that. Naaman responded rightly to YHWH, noting his incomparability and superiority. Gehazi responded wrongly, robbing YHWH of complete honour. For this, Gehazi is stricken with leprosy. Naaman left Elisha's presence 'in peace'; Gehazi leaves it 'white as snow'. Each departs bearing the measure of his devotion to YHWH.

Explanation

In a series of narratives about the prophet Elisha, this chapter's miracle is not the particular item of note – one has come to expect them! What is of note is that the miracle is granted a foreigner (and an enemy) and that the foreigner recognizes YHWH as the God of Israel (v. 15). This recognition contrasts the king's feeble response (v. 7) and apparently even exceeds Elisha's expectations for Naaman's visit (v. 8). Naaman's statement of faith and his commitment to worship YHWH completes a journey not only geographical but evangelistic. Responding out of his need to the young girl's witness, he moves through arrogance (v. 11), to incredulity (v. 12), to obedience (v. 14), to faith (vv. 15–18). Whether the destination was anticipated by Elisha or not, the prophet makes surprising allowance (in a Deuteronomistic text) for non-Deuteronomistic worship. His allowance acknowledges the complexity of worshipping YHWH within non-Yahwistic cultures, and an openness to extend the people of God beyond Israel's borders.

Naaman's journey to faith is part of the larger biblical witness to the inclusion of all nations in God's plan. Its expansive eschatological vision is anticipated even in the first chapters of Genesis. God's blessing rests upon his creation of humanity (Gen. 1:28) and, even when the increase of sin leads to the flood, he does not abandon his creation (Gen. 9:12–16). YHWH's desire that the nations should be blessed is furthered by the covenant made with Abraham, Israel and David. It is, of course, the promise made to Abraham that specifies blessing to 'all peoples on earth' (Gen. 12:1–3). The covenant with Israel at Sinai places their election as a chosen priestly nation in the context of YHWH's ownership of the whole earth (Exod. 19:5–6). As Israel live under the covenant, they mediate the promised blessing to those nations. Even the Davidic king, covenanted to YHWH (2 Sam. 7) is a source of blessing to the nations (Ps. 72:17).

Solomon's temple is an attestation to YHWH's commitment to the Davidic Covenant. It, too, has a place in drawing the foreigner to Israel's God. Foreigners are participants in its construction (1 Kgs 5:1–6[15–20]; 7:13–14), and its splendour (together with Solomon's court and wisdom) draws praise for Israel's God from the visiting queen (1 Kgs 10:9). Solomon's dedicatory prayer recognizes the place of the nations in temple worship as he petitions YHWH to answer the foreigner's prayer offered in it. Solomon reiterates the theme of blessing for the nations when he acknowledges answered prayer will lead the nations to know the God of Israel (1 Kgs 8:41–43).

The temple remains central to the eschatological vision that includes the nations in YHWH's plan. Isaiah envisions all nations streaming to it, submitting themselves to YHWH's teaching and partnering with Israel in worship (Isa. 2:1–5). YHWH's glory will shine over Mount Zion and, hearing the report of this glory, all nations will come to see for themselves, bringing their gifts and praise as the Queen of Sheba had earlier brought hers (Isa. 60:1–6; cf. Zech. 8:20–23).

But eschatological worship will occur (as in Naaman's case) in places other than the temple, or even Israel. Egypt, Libya and Greece are among the nations to whom YHWH's glory is revealed, drawing them to praise (Isa. 19:19–22; 66:19–21). Even in Israel's own era the events of their history as they are dispersed in exile draw the nations to the knowledge of God (Ezek. 36:23).

Despite this expansive eschatological vision, the realities of exile and return lead to a leavening of the vision's inclusive nature. The NT reflects a more exclusionary milieu in which the dividing line between Jews and Gentiles is strictly enforced. Thus the thought of a Gentile's entry into the temple draws Jewish wrath (Acts 21:28), a good Samaritan is an ethnic shocker (Luke 10:30–37) and the possibility and means of inclusion of Gentile believers tests the NT church (Acts 10, 15; Gal. 2:11–21).

It is in this milieu that the church upholds the OT eschatological vision. Christ sends his disciples to all nations (Matt. 28:18–20) and Gentiles are full members in the church (Eph. 2:11–22). It is the church – Jew and Gentile united together in the life of Christ – that stands as the new temple in the world, the place of prayer and God's blessing and presence (1 Cor. 3:16–17; Eph. 2:21). No longer centred in Jerusalem, the new temple is dispersed throughout the world heedless of national borders or identities. In the church the full eschatological vision is to be realized, drawing into Christ those of 'every tribe and tongue and people and nation' (Rev. 5:9–10).

In the final consummation of YHWH's plan to bless all the nations, the eschatological vision portrays the 'Lord God Almighty and the Lamb' as a temple lighting up the New Jerusalem. By their light all the nations walk, bringing new glory and praise (Rev. 21:22–26). It is this vision of God, instituted at creation and consummated in the new creation, to which Naaman's story witnesses. Bowing to YHWH – even while in the house of Rimmon – his praise is added to that of the nations. Perhaps Elisha had a glimpse of God's eschatological purposes and, rejoicing, he granted Naaman's request with a welcoming word of 'peace'.

2 KINGS 6:1–23

Translation

[1]The sons of the prophets said to Elisha, 'Look now, the place where we meet with you is too small for us. [2]Let us go to the Jordan and each take from there a beam, and let us build there for ourselves a place to meet.' And he said, 'Go.' [3]Then one said, 'Please go[a] with your servants.' And he said, 'I will go.' [4]So he went with them; and when they came to the Jordan, they began cutting down trees. [5]As one was felling a beam, the axe-head[a] fell into the water. He cried out and said, 'Alas, my master! It was borrowed!' [6]The man of God said, 'Where did it fall?' He showed him the place and he cut a stick and threw *it* there and made the axe-head float[a]. [7]He said, 'Pick it up for yourself!' So he stretched out his hand and took it.

[8]The king of Aram was warring[a] against Israel. He took counsel with his advisors saying, 'My camp will be in such and such a place.' [9]The man of God[a] sent to the king of Israel, saying, 'Be careful that you do not pass this place, for Aram is going down[b] there.' [10]So the king of Israel sent to the place of which the man of God[a] had told him. More than once or twice the man of God warned him[b] and he was on guard there.

[11]The heart of the king of Aram was enraged concerning this matter. He called his advisors and said to them, 'Will you not tell me who among us is for the king

of Israel?'[12]One of his advisors said, 'No one, my lord, O king. But Elisha the prophet who is in Israel tells the king of Israel the words that you speak in your bedroom.' [13]He replied, 'Go and see where he is that I may send and take him.' Then it was told him saying, 'Behold, he is in Dothan.' [14]So he sent horses and chariots and a great army there. They came by night and surrounded the city.

[15]Now the servant of the man of God rose early and went out and, behold, an army had surrounded the city with horses and chariots! And his young man said to him, 'Alas, my master; what shall we do?'[16]And he said, 'Don't fear! For there are more who are with us than with them[a].' [7]So Elisha prayed and said, 'O YHWH, open his eyes that he may see.' And YHWH opened the eyes of the young man and he looked, and the hill was full of horses and chariots of fire surrounding Elisha. [18]When they came down to him, Elisha prayed to YHWH and said, 'Please strike this people with blindness.' And he struck them with blindness according to the word of Elisha. [19]Elisha said to them, 'This is not the way, nor is this the city. Come, follow me, and I will lead you to the man whom you seek.' And he led them to Samaria.

[20]When they came to Samaria, Elisha said, 'O YHWH, open the eyes of these men that they may see.' So YHWH opened their eyes and they looked, and behold – they[a] were in the midst of Samaria! [21]The king of Israel said to Elisha when he saw them, 'Shall I strike; shall I strike[a], my father?' [22]And he said, 'You shall not strike; would you strike those whom you had captured with your sword and bow? Set food and water before them and let them eat and drink, and go to their lord.' [23]So he prepared a great feast for them and they ate and drank. Then he sent them off and they went to their lord. And the raiders of Aram no longer came into the land of Israel.

Notes on the text

3.a. 'Please go' is a double imp. phrase 'please be willing [first imp.] to go [second imp.]' (hô'el nā' wĕlēk) and reflects the request's urgency.

5.a. barzel, 'iron', signifies an axe-head (vv. 5–6).

6.a. 'made the axe-head float' reads hiph. with MT (wayyāṣep). Montgomery (1951: 382; cf. Gray 1970: 511; Hobbs 1985: 70) reads as qal with Vrs, 'the axe-head floated' (wayyĕṣāp).

8.a. The repeated action of Aram against Israel is signalled by the pf. hyh + ni. part. form (nilḥām; GKC §116r).

9.a. 'Man of God' in vv. 9–10 reads 'Elisha' in LXX*, identifying the as-yet unnamed prophet.

9.b. Repointing MT nĕḥittîm with HALOT 2:692 as nōḥătîm, 'going down [i.e. to battle]'. So Gray 1970: 514.

10.a. See n. 9.a above.

10.b. Reading with Q wĕḥizḥîrō, 'he warned him', rather than K, wĕḥizḥîrāh, 'he warned it [i.e. the place]'.

16.a. MT *'ôtām* is pointed *'ittam*, 'with them'.

20.a. Reading *wĕhinnê*, 'and behold', as *wĕhinnām*, 'and behold, they', with LXX, Syr, Tg.

21.a. MT *ha'akkê 'akkê* ('shall I strike, shall I strike'; hiph. impf. twice) captures the excited tension of the moment. Reading inf. abs. + impf. (LXX^L, Syr, Tg) or deleting the finite verb (LXX^L, Vg) is unnecessary.

Form and structure

The healing of the individual Aramean in 2 Kgs 5 begins a series of interactions with Aram as a nation (chs. 6–9). In this Aramean context Elisha continues to demonstrate that YHWH saves, attesting repeatedly to his own name, which means 'God saves'.

A brief interlude features the sons of the prophets (vv. 1–7). It is a reminder that Elisha ministers within the 'remnant' promised Elijah (1 Kgs 19:15–18) as well as internationally. The vignette joins others in which Elisha miraculously provides for the sons of the prophets (4:38–41, 42–44; cf. 2:19–22). Perhaps originally gathered by Elisha's followers, the vignettes reveal the prophet's power and reputation as YHWH's mediator.

The lengthy narrative of vv. 8–23 is carefully crafted (see below) and reveals the power and authority of the prophet on the international stage. In addition to the recounting of Elisha's legendary power, this narrative reveals a great comedic sensibility in which an army is bested by a single man, the mighty king of Aram is portrayed as inept, and first-person perspectives (signalled by the several *hinnê* markers; vv. 15, 17, 20) introduce surprising reversals.

The compositional integrity of the narrative is questioned, with vv. 15b–17 often considered a later theological elaboration, and vv. 18, 20 a later interpolation (Jones 1984b; Rofé 1999: 349–351; Fritz 2003: 264). But, as usual, no agreement exists on the extent of the interpolation, and Long's comment that this 'reflects the degree of arbitrariness in such judgments' and thus the 'wiser course [is] to discuss the tradition as it stands' seems eminently sensible (B. Long 1991: 83).

In its present form the narrative is remarkably crafted. At its core (D) is Elisha's power over Aram, executed through his word empowered by YHWH:

> A   The problem for Aram: Elisha knows their movements and 'sends' (*šlḥ*) to the king of Israel (vv. 8–10)
> > B   The king consults without understanding; Aram 'sent' (*šlḥ*) to 'go' (*hlk*), 'see' (*r'h*) and take Elisha (vv. 11–14)
> > > C   Elisha prays and his servant 'sees' (*r'h*) (vv. 15–17)
> > > > D   Elisha prays and Aram is blinded and 'led' (*hlk*; v. 19 [three times]) (vv. 18–19)

C'   Elisha prays and Aram 'sees' (r'h) (v. 20)
B'   The king 'sees' (r'h) and consults; Aram is hosted and 'sent'
     (šlḥ) to their lord (vv. 21–23a)
A'   The solution for Israel: Aram's raiding ceases (v. 23b)

Elisha's power is revealed not only through the structure that puts his power over Aram at the narrative centre, but is also communicated through repeated words. Elisha's knowledge enables him to 'send' (šlḥ) and warn the king of Israel. The king of Aram can 'send' (šlḥ) his army to capture Elisha, but is powerless – Elisha captures the army and 'sends' (šlḥ) them back to Aram. Further, the narrative begins with Elisha's seeing the troop movements, to which the king of Aram responds by commissioning his army to 'go' (hlk) and 'see' (r'h) Elisha. Elisha prepares for their arrival by first enabling his servant to 'see' (r'h) and then blinding the Arameans and 'leading' (hlk) them to Israel's king, where they finally 'see' (r'h) that Elisha has power not only to blind but also to deceive them. Finally, the king of Israel, 'seeing' (r'h) the captive army, yields to Elisha's power (as the king of Aram had not, but his army had), and the Arameans are 'sent' (šlḥ) back to Aram to tell the tale of Elisha's power over Israel's foes and her king. Aram learns the lesson, but only for a short time; in the subsequent chapter the lesson is forgotten in all-out war against Israel and their prophet.

Comment

6:1–7

Located near the Jordan, the prophetic group may be the one that earlier confronted Elisha (2:5). Now the long-established group has outgrown its meeting place and a new one in which to 'meet with' (yōšĕbîm . . . lĕpānêkā) the prophet is suggested. The phrase implies something other than dwelling space (which would use the same verbal root). Coupled with this preposition it indicates formal gatherings in which inferiors sit before a superior to listen, worship or be taught (Gen. 43:33; 2 Sam. 7:14; Ezek. 8:1; 14:1). Such gatherings feature in the relationship between Elisha and the prophets (4:38).

Urging the prophet to accompany them reveals their reliance upon and respect towards their master. In the event it turns out to be propitious, for the iron axe-head is somehow loosened from its handle and lost in the Jordan waters. Its wielder is alarmed, for not only is iron expensive, but the axe is borrowed and therefore doubly valuable. Elisha's query 'Where did it fall?' acknowledges he is not omniscient (see also at 4:2, 14, 27) but also focuses on 'the place' (v. 6), which is of course the Jordan. Knowing that Elisha has just healed a man through the Jordan waters, and that he has parted those same waters, the retrieval of the axe-head should pose no problem. It is effected by throwing in a stick (similar to miracles effected in 2:21; 4:41), an imitative miracle enabling the iron to float like the wood. Rationalizing the retrieval by suggesting Elisha fished it out or moved it within reach with the stick (Gray 1970: 511; Jones 1984b: 6) negates the supernatural power so prevalent in Elisha's ministry.

6:8–23

8–14. The king of Aram is unnamed throughout the narrative, as is the king of Israel. Gray sets the conflict in the era of Hazael or his son Ben-hadad, and particularly during the era of Jehu. He argues that the Judahite–Israelite alliance of Jehoram's reign enabled Israelite aggression against Aram and provides no context for Aram's 'warring against Israel' (v. 8). Rather, Gray argues the conflict of 2 Kgs 10:32 in Jehu's reign provides a more probable context for the raiding parties of the present chapter (Gray 1970: 513). However, in chs. 2–8, the kings are Jehoram of Israel and Ben-hadad II of Aram (see further in 'Form and structure', 'Comment', 1 Kgs 20). Periodic military action between Israel and Aram has occurred since 1 Kgs 15, and Aram's border conflicts (v. 23) and frequent warring (v. 8) may reflect the tenuous relationship between the two countries during Jehoram's reign.

Aram's repeated action against Israel includes at least marauding bands (*gĕdûdîm*; v. 23) such as captured the young Israelite girl (5:2). These may be cross-border skirmishes, or sorties from Aramean camps established within Israel (v. 8). From the camps larger actions are planned in which Aram 'goes down', that is, attacks Israel (cf. Jer. 21:13). In consultation with his advisors the camps are deployed in *pĕlōnî 'almōnî* (i.e. 'indeterminate locations' [cf. 1 Sam. 21:3]; the phrase may also indicate 'indeterminate persons' [Ruth 4:1]). But each move is foiled as 'the man of God' (identified as Elisha in v. 12) 'sent' (*šlḥ*) an alert to the king of Israel who in turn 'sent' (*šlḥ*) the alert to his own troops, enabling them to avoid the enemy threat or to counterattack successfully.

Israel's success raises the king of Aram's ire. His rage (from *sʿr*) has the violence of stormy seas and winds (Jon. 1:11, 13; Zech. 7:14), but is wrongly directed towards his own advisors, accusing them of treason. Sarcastically, he asks to be 'told' (*ngd*) the traitor's identity, revealing that, while the prophet knows what Aram is doing, the king of Aram is clueless about what the prophet is doing – so clueless, in fact, that even his advisors know what he does not! One advisor reveals that the prophet 'who is in Israel' (apparently the advisor has learned the lesson of Naaman; see 5:8) knows everything and 'tells' (*ngd*) it to Jehoram. No secret is hidden, for the prophet's power can reach into the most private of spaces. The advisor is not here attesting to some elaborate spy network headed by Elisha, which has infiltrated the king's private chambers, but metaphorically speaks of the reach of Elisha's powerful knowledge. The contrast with the knowledge of the king of Aram is acute.

The king charges that his servants 'go' (*hlk*) and 'see' (*r'h*) Elisha's whereabouts that he may 'send' (*šlḥ*) and kidnap him. His words further reveal his lack of knowledge, for once again others know what the king does not: Elisha is in Dothan. The king thinks he controls his troops, but his words will later come back on him and prove that it is Elisha who controls his troops (vv. 19–20). 'Told' (*ngd*) of Elisha's whereabouts, the king 'sends' (*šlḥ*) a great force against the lone prophet. Ironically, despite the evidence that Elisha knows Aram's troop movements, the king dispatches the force by night, thinking to mount a surprise attack. The king is truly blind.

15–17. Elisha is in Dothan, a town on the eastern edge of the Dothan Valley, 12 miles [20 km] north of Samaria on a major north–south trading route (Gen. 37:15–36; Dever, *ABD* 2:226–227). Whether resident there, or perhaps in transit from Carmel or Samaria, he is accompanied by his 'servant' (*měšārēt*; 4:43), a verbal designation (pi. part.) that earlier described Elisha's service to Elijah (1 Kgs 19:21). The expression 'behold!' (*hinnê*) captures the alarmed perspective of the servant when his early-morning chores are met with the Aramean army. His awareness of the numerical odds is evident: 'Alas, what shall we do?'

His master, however, is aware of an invisible but greater army and urges his young man, 'Don't fear!' The admonition arises from the context of holy war (Deut. 20:1–4) and, while there is no physical Israelite army to engage in battle, YHWH himself is present in the conflict. The fiery heavenly host attests to YHWH's power, but also evokes the chariots and horses of fire at Elijah's ascension. At Elijah's ascension Elisha's acknowledgment of the 'chariots of Israel and its horsemen' refers to the manifestation before him. But it may also be a title applied to the prophet Elijah, acknowledging that he, too, is part of YHWH's supernatural army against Israel's foes. The title, arising out of the holy war traditions (von Rad 1958: 100; P. Miller 1973: 134–135; see also 'Comment' at 2 Kgs 2:12), is later applied to Elisha (13:14). It affirms that he also serves as YHWH's weaponry against Israel's internal and external enemies. No wonder that Elisha needs no assistance to see the heavenly host – he is himself a soldier in it!

The servant is not as perceptive as Elisha. Elisha prays to YHWH and YHWH responds. The two references to YHWH, occurring so close together, are a reminder that while Elisha is YHWH's prophet, it is YHWH who enables the miraculous. The servant's eyes are opened and once again the narrative communicates his perspective when 'behold' (*hinnê*) he 'sees' (*r'h*) the supernatural power that surrounds YHWH's prophet. He stands as a contrast to the king of Aram, who is utterly unable to 'see' the realities of the supernatural realm in which the prophet serves.

18–20. The Arameans surrounding Dothan descend to take Elisha. The prophet-soldier again addresses YHWH in prayer, asking now that the enemies be 'blinded' (*sanwērîm*). Earlier the prophet's prayer was answered directly by YHWH. Now the prayer is answered 'according to the word of Elisha', attesting to the congruity between the prophetic word and YHWH's will. The term for 'blindness' occurs elsewhere at Gen. 19:11 and is a causative form of the root *nwr* (to be bright). The term cannot mean that the army was struck wholly blind, for they make their way, following Elisha's lead, to Samaria, 12 miles [20 km] away. Rather, *sanwērîm* suggests that the army was 'in a dazed condition' (Provan 1995: 199) as when one is dazzled by bright light. But because Elisha is able to lead them, unrecognized and unsuspected, to the Israelite capital, this suggests mental perception is also lost by the army.

Elisha's ruse to lead them to Samaria and the man they seek effectively answers the king of Aram's charge. He commanded his army to 'go' (*hlk*) and 'see' (*r'h*) Elisha. Now Elisha commands them to 'come' (*hlk*) so that he may 'lead' (*hlk*) them. He does 'lead' (*hlk*) them to Samaria, and once there prays yet again, using the exact words spoken over Elisha's servant, 'O YHWH, open their eyes . . . that they may see' (*r'h*). YHWH responds as before and they 'look' (*r'h*). For a third time, the viewer's first-person perspective is apparent through 'behold' (*hinnê*). Their surprise is great: they see Samaria, the enemy's capital and Elisha, the enemy's prophet. It is by Elisha's word and power that the king of Aram's commission is executed. Elisha controls the great army sent after him; by him, they 'go and see'.

21–23. The army's surprise is shared by the king of Israel. When he 'sees' (*r'h*) the army, his excitement is barely contained in the query that tumbles out. So rough are his words 'Shall I strike; shall I strike, my father?' that attempts have been made to bring a smoother elegance to the phrase (see 'Notes on the text'). But such attempts only dull the king's tongue-lolling excitement at his enemy delivered to his doorstep. The king is deferential, addressing Elisha as 'my father', yet he hopes to gain permission for wholesale slaughter.

Elisha, as he does for so much of his ministry, stands on the side of life. The reason he provides for not killing the captives suggests some rule of war by which prisoners, particularly those captured without battle, are spared and enslaved (Deut. 20:10–11; Montgomery 1951: 382; Jones 1984b: 428). Nor does Elisha invoke the *ḥērem* clause of holy war (Deut. 20:16–18), for the enemies are not inhabitants of the land of promise and, further, while the fiery chariots and horses are part of the holy war tradition, no battle has been engaged. YHWH wins through his prophet while Israel's battle gear lies silent.

It seems that Elisha has a better end for the hapless army. Wined and dined, they are 'sent off' (*šlḥ*). The king of Aram had 'sent' the army (*šlḥ*; vv. 13–14) to capture Elisha; now he returns them empty-handed but full-bellied, telling of the surprising events and attesting to the power of the prophet in Israel. No wonder the raiding bands stop coming into Israel. Aram now 'sees', and acts appropriately.

Explanation

The comedic effect of this passage stems from its gentle mockery of Aram. As the first of several interactions with the nation (chs. 6–9), it positions YHWH's dealings with Aram under the theological message communicated by that mockery. Throughout the chapter the king of Aram is shown inept: he thinks he sees, but is blind; he desires to know, and does not; he sends to no effect. His bumbling ineptitude is in contrast with YHWH's prophet who, by YHWH's power, succeeds where Aram fumbles.

The chapter narratively portrays a theological message also found elsewhere in the OT. In Ps. 2 YHWH, enthroned in heaven, both laughs (from root $śḥq$) and mocks (from root $l'g$) against the nations. He cuts them, not out of meanness or capriciousness, but for their conspiracy against both YHWH and his anointed king. Their rebellion is ludicrous on two counts: first, they seem unaware that YHWH both hears and sees their stance against him. Yet he listens in on their counsels and knows their plots. Secondly, they seem unaware of – or choose to challenge – his power to stand against them. Yet he can and does bring their rebellion to naught.

Underneath the nations' ill-advised actions is their fundamental misperception of YHWH's sovereign kingship. He is enthroned over all (v. 4), and even the concerted actions of nations cannot succeed against such a powerful and knowing overlord. They are a two-year-old trying to wrestle an Olympic champion – ridiculous to contemplate and painful to watch!

YHWH also directs laughter (from root $śḥq$) and mockery (from root $l'g$) against the nations in Ps. 59:8[9]. There a righteous sufferer petitions for YHWH's deliverance from the nations' conspiracies. As part of their actions they speak terrible things, thinking they have impunity: 'Who can hear us?' they muse (v. 7[8]). A similar issue pertains here as in Ps. 2: the nations labour under a misperception of YHWH's knowledge and his sovereign power.

The same mockery (from root $l'g$) is coupled with ridicule (bzh) and directed against Assyria in 2 Kgs 19:21. There Zion scorns Assyrian arrogance that lifts proud eyes against YHWH, the Holy One of Israel (vv. 22–24). YHWH's response against such ludicrous pride is to assert his eternal sovereignty that has preordained the nation's action against Zion. That sovereignty will now be exercised against misplaced Assyrian pride, directing them away from Zion (vv. 27–28) – in much the same way that YHWH's wrath overset the nations' plans in Ps. 2:5, 12.

In Isa. 40 YHWH's sovereign power to see, know and do is once again juxtaposed against the nations' inability. While the words 'laughter' and 'mockery' are not used, several images show the ludicrous futility of any nation's arraying itself against YHWH. As in Ps. 2, YHWH sits enthroned (v. 22). His power, exercised in creation (vv. 12–14, 26), is able to bring kings to nothing (vv. 23–24). So powerless are the nations before YHWH that they are grass before the breath of his word (vv. 6–8), a drop in the bucket and dust on the scales (v. 15), and grasshoppers (v. 22). In short, the nations are nothing in comparison to YHWH's power (v. 17). For all these reasons Isaiah reminds a beleaguered people that their idols are futile.

It is the juxtaposition of YHWH's sovereign power to the nations' futile power that is the source of humour in 2 Kgs 6. Aram takes the place held by the nations in Pss 2 and 59, 2 Kgs 19 and Isa. 40. Aram's efforts are doomed to the same failure because they work against the enthroned God and his amassed host. Through his prophet YHWH sends Aram home in shame and only then do Aram seem to acknowledge their opponent's power: they leave YHWH's people alone – at least for a while.

Two further words need to be said in this exploration of the mockery made of Aram. It is true that YHWH works against Aram in this chapter and thus mocks their futile actions. But YHWH's sovereignty can also enable the nations' success against Israel (e.g. in 2 Kgs 19; cf. 1 Kgs 22). With equal ease YHWH intervenes in the nations' internal affairs to effect his purposes. This is particularly pertinent for Aram, for YHWH deposes Ben-hadad and appoints Hazael (2 Kgs 8:7–15; cf. Isa. 45:1). These examples show the completeness of YHWH's sovereignty over the nations.

In 1 – 2 Kings one also discerns YHWH's sovereignty over his own nation of Israel. His commitment to Israel will not be mocked by their disregard of the covenant, and he will bring covenant judgments against their waywardness. Kings such as Solomon and Jeroboam are granted freedom to attend to, or disregard, covenant norms. In his sovereignty YHWH exercises both immediate and long-term judgment against these actions. Thus Solomon and Jeroboam hear chilling words of judgment (1 Kgs 9:3–9; 13:2–3; 14:6–16) that stand throughout the long history and come to pass by YHWH's will. It is ultimately through this judgment that Israel's own eyes (that have become as blind to YHWH's ways as Aram's) are opened.

The final word that must be said is that YHWH's sovereign power is not only exercised on the field of the nations: Isa. 40 has noted YHWH's power over creation, for instance. In 2 Kgs 6 YHWH's power is exercised in a way that is particularly highlighted in juxtaposition to the larger narrative of Aram that follows. The chapter begins with a small story: that of the recovered axe-head. Only seven verses, it is easily lost beside the doings of the nation. It is a needed counterpoint to that tale, for it speaks of sovereign power exercised on a very small, very personal, scale. A similar personal note is included in the majestic Isa. 40, where YHWH is likened to a tender shepherd who carries the lambs. Such intimate sovereignty is possible when a sovereign God hears and sees (as Aram did not), cares and acts for his people, however insignificant their need appears to be in the face of the nations.

While the focus of 1 – 2 Kings is upon the grand events of nation and monarch, it is not oblivious to the details of YHWH's intimate care within ordinary lives. This care is particularly apparent in the ministries of Elijah and Elisha, as life-giving intervention is granted to both foreign and Israelite widows and their children (1 Kgs 17; 2 Kgs 4), secret injustice is challenged (2 Kgs 21), waters are purified and poisoned food healed (2 Kgs 2:19–22; 4:38–41), food is multiplied (2 Kgs 4:42–44) and borrowed items miraculously restored (2 Kgs 6:1–7). Although Elijah and Elisha walk on a stage of national events, much of their ministry also works to reveal YHWH's sovereign yet intimate care. When the nation falls (2 Kgs 24 – 25), the narrative focus is upon the world stage, but, as one correlates the simultaneous events in the book of Jeremiah, one notes that during this dark time YHWH also directs his care towards his people. His prophet (Jer. 36:19, 26; 38:7–13; 39:11–14; 40:1–6), those who ministered to the prophet (Jer. 39:15–18; 45:1–5), and even the poor left in the land receive YHWH's sovereign care (Jer. 40:7–10; 42:7–12). The history in 1 – 2 Kings may be primarily an account of national events, but its attention to the mundane reveals YHWH's sovereign power is never limited to such events. Always YHWH's work is equally powerful on the scale of the intimate.

2 KINGS 6:24 – 7:20

Translation

6:24After this, Ben-hadad, the king of Aram, gathered all his army and went up and besieged Samaria. 25And there was a great famine in Samaria and, behold, they[a] laid siege against it until a donkey's head sold for eighty *shekels* of silver, and a fourth of a kab of dove's dung for five *shekels* of silver. 26As the king of Israel was passing by on the wall, a woman cried out to him, 'Help, my lord, O king!' 27He said, 'If YHWH does not help you, from where shall I help you? From the threshing floor or from the winepress?' 28And the king said to her, 'What is your trouble?' And she said, 'This woman said to me, "Give up your son that we may eat him today, and my son we shall eat tomorrow." 29So we cooked my son and ate him. Then I said to her on the next day, "Give up your son that we may eat him," but she has hidden her son.' 30When the king heard the woman's words, he tore his clothes. Now because he was passing by on the wall, the people could see sackcloth underneath[a] on his body. 31He said, 'Thus may God do to me, and even more, if the head of Elisha son of Shaphat remains on his *shoulders* today!'

32Elisha was sitting in his house and the elders were sitting with him. Now *the king*[a] had sent a man ahead of him. Before the messenger arrived, he said to the elders, 'Do you see that this murderer[b] has sent to take my head? Look, when the messenger comes, shut the door and hold him at the door. Is not the sound of his master's feet behind him?' ³³While he was talking with them, behold, the messenger came down to him. He said, 'Behold, this evil is from YHWH; why should I^a wait for YHWH any longer?'

^{7:1}Elisha said, 'Hear^a the word of YHWH! Thus says YHWH, "About this time tomorrow a seah of flour *will be sold* for a shekel, and two seahs of barley for a shekel in the gate of Samaria."' ²The captain upon whose hand the king leaned answered the man of God. He said, 'Behold, even if YHWH made windows in heaven, could this thing happen?' And he said, 'Behold, you will see with your own eyes, but will not eat from it!'

³There were four leprous men at the entrance of the gate. They said to one another, 'Why should we sit here until we die? ⁴If we say, "Let us enter the city," the famine is in the city and we will die there. But if we sit here, we will die. Now come, let us desert to the Aramean camp. If they spare us, we will live; but if they kill us, we will but die.' ⁵They arose at twilight to go to the Aramean camp. They came to the outskirts of the camp of Aram and, behold, no one was there! ⁶(Now YHWH had caused the Aramean camp to hear a sound of chariots, a sound of horses and a sound of a great army. They said to one another, 'Behold, the king of Israel has hired against us the kings of the Hittites and the kings of Egypt^a to come upon us.' ⁷So they arose and fled at twilight and abandoned their tents and their horses and their donkeys, *leaving* the camp just as it was, and they fled for their lives.)

⁸When these leprous men came to the outskirts of the camp, they entered one tent and ate and drank, and took from there silver and gold and clothes. They went and hid *them* and returned and entered another tent. They took *items* from there and went and hid *them*. ⁹They said to one another, 'We are not doing right – this day is a day of good news. If we are silent and wait until dawn, punishment will find us. Now, come; let us go and tell the king's household.' ¹⁰So they went and called to the city gatekeepers^a. They told them, 'We came to the Aramean camp and there was no one there, nor any human voice, only the horses and donkeys tied up, and their tents^b just as they were.' ¹¹The gatekeepers called^a and reported to the king's household within.

¹²The king rose in the night and said to his servants, 'Let me tell you what Aram has done to us: they know that we are hungry and they have gone out from the camp to hide themselves in the open country, saying, "When they come out from the city we will take them alive and enter the city."' ¹³One of his servants answered and said, 'Let men take five of the remaining horses that are left in the city, since they will be like all the multitude of Israel^a that have perished. But let us send and see.' ¹⁴So they took two chariots with horses and the king sent *them* after the Aramean army, saying, 'Go, and see.' ¹⁵They followed them until the Jordan, and all the road was filled with clothes and equipment that Aram had dropped in their haste. Then the messengers returned and reported to the king. ¹⁶Then the people went out and plundered the Aramean camp.

So it happened that a seah of flour *sold* for a shekel, and two seahs of barley for a shekel, according to the word of YHWH. ¹⁷The king set the captain, upon whose hand he leaned, over the gate, and the people trampled him in the gate and he died, just as the man of God had said who spoke when the king came down to him.

[18]It happened as the man of God had said to the king, 'Two seahs of barley *will be sold* for a shekel, and a seah of flour for a shekel about this time tomorrow in the gate of Samaria.' [19]And the captain had answered the man of God, 'Behold, even if YHWH made windows in heaven, could this thing[a] happen?' And he had said, 'Behold, you will see with your own eyes, but you will not eat from it.' [20]And so it happened to him, for the people trampled him in the gate of the city, and he died.

Notes on the text

6:25.a. *wĕhinnê*, 'and behold', read as *wĕhinnām*, 'and behold they', with two MSS, Tg.

30.a. 'underneath' is the translation for *mibbāyit*, 'from the house', that is, 'from within'.

32.a. Following LXX[L], *the king* removes any ambiguity of who sends the messenger; *BHS* proposes transposing the phrase 'Now *the king* had sent a man ahead of him' to the beginning of the verse for the same reason.

32.b. 'murderer' is lit. 'son of a murderer' (*ben-hamraṣṣēaḥ*) and could refer to Jehoram as Ahab's son. In the light of Jehoram's present intent to kill Elisha, it is intended as a slur against the king's character.

33.a. The first-person message may be the messenger, or even the king speaking. The king had followed after the messenger and on arrival may have delivered this message himself (vv. 32; 7:17). Many commentators change the word from *mal'āk*, 'messenger', to *melek*, 'king'.

7:1.a. 'Hear' is a pl. imp., addressing all who are present.

6.a. MT 'the kings of Egypt' (*miṣrāyim*). LXX[82], Syr, Tg[f] *hammiṣrîm* is often pointed to 'kings of the Musrites' (*hammuṣrîm*; so Montgomery 1951: 389; Gray 1970: 520) as geographically a more probable alliance (see also 'Notes on the text' at 1 Kgs 10:28).

10.a. 'Gatekeepers' pluralized with Syr, Tg, and in agreement with the following pr. and v. 11.

10.b. *wĕ'ōhālîm*, 'and tents', is read as *wĕ'ōhālêhem*, 'and their tents', with LXX.

11.a. *wayyiqrā'* is pluralized in agreement with the subject.

13.a. The duplicate phrase *'ăšer niš'ărû-bāh hinnām kĕkol-hămôn yiśrā'ēl*, 'which are left in the city since they will be like all the multitude of Israel', appears here and is removed as a dittography, following many MSS, LXX, Syr, Tg.

19.a. *kaddābār*, 'this thing', is read with the art. rather than the prep. with many MSS and v. 2.

Form and structure

The siege of Samaria is contextualized in the escalating conflict between Israel and Aram (chs. 5–7). The inclusion of 6:24–31 with the following verses is warranted, as the temporal phrase 'after this' (6:24) suggests a separate incident. More, different military settings are suggested: intermittent and guerilla warfare (6:8–23) and full military assault (6:24 – 7:20). The background is briefly sketched (vv. 24–25) and an initial panel reveals the problem for which the king has no solution (vv. 26–31) and concludes with a prophetic word of resolution (v. 32 – 7:2). In a second panel YHWH resolves the king's problem (vv. 3–16a) and notice is provided of the prophetic word's fulfilment (vv. 16b–20). The action moves across the panels in a chiasm from the king's palace (6:26 – 7:2), to the city gate (7:3–4), to the Aramean camp (vv. 5–9) and then reverts to the gate (v. 10) and the palace (vv. 11–15; Hobbs 1985: 87). Only then do the people experience deliverance.

The panels contrast their characters. The king's inability contrasts with YHWH's ability; the horrific pragmatics of the women contrast the rational pragmatics of the lepers. The threatening army of Aram becomes a comical dupe, hustling to vacate camp. Even the figure of Elisha, prominent in the first panel, disappears from the second. He reappears only when the narrator confirms his words fulfilled (vv. 16b–20). But in the disappearance of Elisha ('ĕlîšā', 'God saves') YHWH's invisible deliverance (yš'; 6:27) is prominent.

As for most of the Elijah–Elisha narratives, various theories of compositional redaction exist. Ultimately, the narrative must be broached as a unit of which structural and thematic sense can be made (B. Long 1991: 91). Set in the context of Jehoram's rule (see 'Comment'), the dire situation raises the ongoing question 'Is it at this time that the dynasty of Ahab will be overthrown in judgment (1 Kgs 21:29)?'

Comment

6:24 – 7:2

6:24–31. The intermittent conflict between Aram and Israel (2 Sam. 8:5; 1 Kgs 15:20; 20:1; 22:1–3; 2 Kgs 5:1; 6:8) once again leads to open warfare. The king of Israel is not named, but the narrative context suggests it is Jehoram. Certainly a siege fits in the growing Aramean–Israelite tension in chs. 5–8. Of the three kings known as Ben-hadad (found in 1 Kgs 20, 22; 2 Kgs 6, 8, 13; see 'Form and structure' and 'Comment', 1 Kgs 20), Ben-hadad II is Jehoram's contemporary (see Provan et al. 2003: 263–266).

Siege and famine are inevitable companions, and the people's desperation makes grotesque items valuable. An unclean donkey's head (Lev.

11:18; Deut. 14:3–8) sells for almost 2 pounds (1 kg) of silver, while approximately 2 pints (1 l) of dung is valued at 2 ounces (55 g) of silver. The dung was used for fuel, and possibly as a desperate bid for food. Certainly, it cannot be understood as euphemistic for the variety of seeds, herbs or pulses suggested by the commentators (Montgomery 1951: 385; Gray 1970: 555; Fritz 2003: 269); only the absolute absence of viable food sources can account for the cannibalism of the mothers.

The horrific reach of the famine is illustrated by the cannibal mothers in a scene enclosed by the notation that the king was 'passing by on the wall' (vv. 26, 30). The same cry for help (*hôšîʿâ ʾădōnî hammelek*) has elsewhere brought a king's immediate and intentionally helpful response: 'What is your trouble?' (*mah-lāk*; 2 Sam. 14:4–5; cf. 2 Kgs 4:13). Such a response is here delayed by the king's futile cry (v. 27), which evokes his earlier despair (5:7). Even though Jehoram follows in Jeroboam's sins (3:3), he knows that without YHWH's saving help (*yšʿ*) he cannot produce food from the 'threshing floor or wine press'.

'Threshing floor' and 'wine press' are elsewhere coupled as symbols of YHWH's abundance upon a covenant people (Num. 18:27, 30; Deut. 15:14; 16:13; Joel 2:24). Their emptiness tokens YHWH's judgment (Hos. 9:2). Jehoram may simply be using a common saying, but it is here charged with meaning, for the siege and resultant famine are YHWH's ongoing judgment meted out through Aram. YHWH's saving help (*yšʿ*) will be prophesied through Elisha, whose name means 'God saves'. Where the king could not save, YHWH does – precisely proving the king's lament.

The king finally invites the woman's petition but is unprepared for her pragmatic and shameless account of maternal cannibalism and her misplaced sense of justice. Whatever desperation drove the woman, and whatever emotion (if any) she felt, she has killed her son (if he was not already dead), boiled him up and shared him at table as part of a macabre scheme. Cannibalism is a sign of covenant disobedience (Lev. 26:29; Deut. 28:56–57; Ezek. 5:10) and betokens the 'upside-down world' realities experienced by the disobedient, who face YHWH's retribution (Lasine 1991). Jehoram's response (v. 30) mourns such realities and further emphasizes his impotence (as in 5:7). The onlookers see his mourning sackcloth (1 Kgs 20:31; 21:27; 2 Kgs 19:1; Jer. 4:8; 6:26), a glimpse that reveals Jehoram, though apostate, still turns to YHWH during calamity.

Yet, even as his reply to the mother suggests some blame is directed towards YHWH (v. 27), Jehoram seeks to wreak that blame upon YHWH's spokesperson. After all, Elisha let the Arameans go (6:23), enabling them to regroup and mount this debilitating siege. And Elisha has (to date) done nothing to alleviate the siege. Like Jezebel before him (1 Kgs 19:2) he swears on oath to have Elisha summarily executed.

6:32 – 7:2. The opposing forces of royal and prophetic power meet at Elisha's house. Whether in a permanent or temporary residence, Elisha can accommodate a meeting with the city elders. Perhaps seeking advice or petitioning intervention, their subsequent actions indicate their full support of the prophet. Prescient of the messenger's approach, Elisha urges the elders to bar the door. This is not an indication of cowering impotence (contra Hobbs 1985: 75), but a desire to hold any exchange until the king arrives. The messenger has been sent before the king (v. 32; 7:17) and Elisha desires to deliver his oracle to Jehoram. The king's reasons for appearing at the house are not stated but he may desire to witness the arrest and execution personally. Elisha knows the king's intent and names him a 'murderer'. His low opinion of Jehoram (3:14; 6:21–22) is confirmed.

A confusing tussle ensues at the barred door, with words exchanged through the barrier. Whether the messenger (*mal'āk*) speaks, or (by slight change to the word) the king (*melek*) himself delivers the message (see 'Notes on the text', v. 33), the first-person sentiment is clearly Jehoram's own (and not that of a despairing Elisha; so Hobbs 1985: 81). In short, he is fed up with YHWH, blaming him for the disaster and peeved that he does not save. His lament 'Why should I wait (hiph. impf. of *yḥl*) for YHWH any longer?' contrasts with the many places in the canon where the form is used by the righteous, who in dire circumstances affirm their hope (*yḥl*) in the covenant God (Pss 38:15[16]; 42:5, 11[6, 12]; 43:5; 130:5; Lam. 3:24; Mic. 7:7). As one who follows Jeroboam's sins, Jehoram is not among the company of the righteous, despite his sackcloth.

Elisha, using the formal messenger formula 'Thus says YHWH', is saved from the king's pique by a well-timed prophetic word. This marks the significance of YHWH's promise to reverse the economics of famine. Within a day fine flour as well as barley will sell for much less than noxious donkey heads and dung. Such abundance will be found in the 'gate of Samaria', the place of business. For the captain who voices his objection, the location will prove particularly important. His incredulous doubt denigrates both YHWH's power and his provision; it is a flat denial of the prophet's words and ministry that have repeatedly shown YHWH *does* save and provide. The captain's words begin with 'Behold' (*hinnê*), marking his perspective on YHWH's word. Elisha shoots right back with his own perspectival 'behold' (*hinnê*) that issues judgment against such unbelief.

7:3–20

3–11. Elisha disappears from the narrative while YHWH works behind the scenes (but in view of the reader, v. 6), leaving the characters to draw their own conclusions about the events. The work begins with four lepers (*mĕṣōrā'*) who, according to Lev. 13:46, live outside the city isolated from the healthy population. Due to the besieging army they have sought a modicum of refuge at the city gate. They consider their plight and, though it is no less desperate than that of the cannibal mothers, arrive at a far more reasonable conclusion. If they will die regardless, they might as well take their chances with the Arameans.

At twilight (the phrase can indicate either evening [Isa. 5:11; 21:4; Job 24:15; Prov. 7:9] or morning [1 Sam. 30:17; Ps. 119:147; Job 3:9]; v. 12 indicates an evening twilight) the men approach the Aramean camp. YHWH's timing is comically fine, for as the lepers approach from one direction the Arameans flee in the other (v. 7). The flight is so harried they abandon camp leaving behind goods and food, as well as animals such as chariot horses and burden bearers. The flight is precipitated by YHWH's supernaturally causing them to hear a large army, whether the fiery army of Dothan (6:17) or some other supernatural source. The Arameans wrongly identify the army as 'kings of the Hittites', that is, kings of the small states of the Neo-Hittite Empire located in northern Syria and 'kings of Egypt' (Houwink ten Cate, *ABD* 3:219–225; McMahon, *ABD* 3:231–233; Gelb, *IDB* 2:612–615; Astour, *IDBSup* 411–413). Because Egypt had a sole ruler, the Egyptian 'kings' may refer to lesser rulers (Konkel 2006: 452). Alternatively, 'kings of Musri' could be read as a geographically proximate and therefore probable ally of the Hittite kings (see 'Notes on the text' and 'Comment', 1 Kgs 10:28). Together the kings of the Hittites and Egypt represent powers against which Aram could never stand (Fritz 2003: 271).

However the attackers are identified, their effect on Aram is immediate and effective, leaving the lepers free to feast and forage. Mid-plunder they 'say to one another' (v. 3, 9) words that are as pragmatic as their earlier decision to desert to the Arameans. In the face of good news the lepers state they act wrongly and are liable to punishment. They resolve as before ('now come', vv. 4, 9) to apprise the king's household. They relay their good news to the gatekeepers. Pragmatic to the end, they offer no speculation (as did the Arameans) on the cause of their experience.

12–16a. Despite hearing Elisha's prophecy, the king does not consider the events YHWH's work; nor does he consult with the prophet. Rather, like the Arameans, he draws wrong conclusions and attributes the empty camp to a military ruse. He is apparently unwilling to take the supposed bait and, as in many of the Elisha narratives, it is the words of servants that move the plot to resolution (3:11; 5:3, 13; 6:12). The servant's logic is as unrelenting as the lepers' had been, for since death awaits those who remain in the city it is expedient to risk a few for the sake of the many.

The king acts sensibly, dispatching a reconnaissance team of two chariots each harnessed with two horses (the fifth [v. 13] may be an additional outrider, or perhaps 'five horses' is emblematic of a small number). They trace the Aramean retreat by the items dropped in haste, pursuing them to the Jordan. Whether the army crossed at the Jabbok or Yarmuk fords, the distance travelled is considerable and the scouts are certain the retreat is complete. The king acts upon the intelligence and the people receive the good news of the abandoned camp. Perhaps while it was still night, or in the breaking dawn, they plunder the camp. The siege is broken, and the famine over.

16b–20. Because YHWH's work was invisibly accomplished, various perceptions are offered throughout the narrative as to exactly what has occurred (e.g. vv. 6, 10, 12). Now the narrator takes special pains to confirm that what has occurred was indeed YHWH's work, accomplishing the prophet's word. The economics of famine are reversed 'according to the word of YHWH', and the captain trampled in the gate 'just as the man of God had said'.

To ensure full recognition that the events occurred as prophesied, a second rendition of the fulfilment notice is given (vv. 18–20). It happened 'as the man of God had said', followed by an almost verbatim account of the prophetic exchange (note the reversed order of the flour and barley), and a further fulfilment notice: 'and so it happened to him'. The events at the gate of Samaria (vv. 17–18, 20), during which foodstuffs sold cheaply and the doubting captain was trampled, prove the prophetic word, revealing that YHWH does in his mercy indeed 'save' (*yšʿ*) his people – even if they are not willing to 'wait any longer' (v. 33).

Explanation

There are three certainties as this narrative begins. First, the situation in Samaria is bleak, as demonstrated by the cannibal mothers. Secondly, the king is powerless to rectify the situation, as demonstrated by his despairing cry (6:27). Thirdly, the prophetic word is certain. This is demonstrated not only by the prophetic messenger formula (7:1), but by the history in 1 – 2 Kings of fulfilment of the prophetic word. Ultimately, the attestation of the fulfilment of the prophetic word (see 'Comment', vv. 16–20) shows YHWH has done what he promised. In this the narrative adds to the consistent theme throughout 1 – 2 Kings of the inviolability of YHWH's word (see Introduction, section 7.3).

What is not revealed in the prophetic word is how YHWH will accomplish the dramatic end to famine within a 24-hour period. With no details given and with the prophet's absence in vv. 3–15 precluding explanation, the characters draw their own conclusions as the events unfold. They surmise they experience a mercenary attack (the Arameans; v. 6) or a military ruse (Jehoram; v. 12). They remain agnostic but are open to explore possibilities (the servants; v. 13). They follow the evidence trail and conclude a full retreat has occurred (the charioteers; v. 15). To this might also be added the captain's denial (v. 2) and the lepers' unwillingness to proffer explanation (v. 10). The reader knows for certain that YHWH is afoot in the events only because of the narrative aside (v. 6). Surprisingly, not one character – not even the king, who heard the prophetic word – ventures the events are by YHWH's hand to fulfil his word.

The characters' obtuseness, given the repeated evidence at this point in Israel's history of God's inbreaking work and his commitment to his word, is striking. Certainly, the events take place in apostate Israel and this must account to some degree for their inability to perceive YHWH's hand at work.

In the worship of Baal, Israel turn to a god without power. Even though YHWH has in recent history shown himself present and powerful over Baal (1 Kgs 18), and Jehoram has put away the pillar of Baal (2 Kgs 3:3), Baal worship still continues with a strong following (2 Kgs 10:18–24). Moreover, Israel have not turned away from the idols of Jeroboam. The worship of idols that are dumb, sightless and powerless leads Israel to conceive of God in similar categories. It is not surprising, then, that the first consideration in the light of these unusual events is not that God is working in mysterious power. Having emasculated God, he does not feature as a logical explanation for the events.

However, it cannot be Israel's apostasy that is solely responsible for the many perspectives within this narrative – none of which acknowledges God's power at work. Throughout the history YHWH's faithful people have also received assurance of YHWH's action and have similarly misconstrued (or missed) his presence in the events around them. One could consider Hezekiah who, despite the prophetic word of YHWH's victories on Judah's behalf (2 Kgs 20:6) and the relief from siege (2 Kgs 19), still turns to Babylon seeking alliance (2 Kgs 20:12–13). The southern kingdom of Judah do not discern YHWH's hand of warning in the fall of the northern kingdom (2 Kgs 17). Though they have received several words of coming judgment (1 Kgs 9:6–9; 2 Kgs 21:10–15; Jer. 4:5–8; 21:3–7), not even Josiah's reform enables the southern kingdom to read YHWH's hand in its own history. Jeremiah in obedience to YHWH's word buys a field, but then in consternation and not a little bewilderment he prays for understanding. Jeremiah knows the city is besieged and thus his purchase and YHWH's word seem diametrically opposed. Jeremiah wonders how and where YHWH might be at work (Jer. 32:1–25). One might also consider the whole prophetic ministry of Jeremiah. By YHWH's commissioning word (Jer. 1:1–19) Jeremiah knows he will minister in power and that his ministry will be opposed. Yet Jeremiah spends considerable time looking for YHWH's hand in the trials the prophet endures (Jer. 15:10–18; 17:14–18). Even faithful Habakkuk, delivering the oracle proclaiming Judah's judgment at the hand of Babylon, struggles to perceive YHWH's hand working through historic events.

The misconstrual of YHWH's prophetic hand at work in the events of life is not limited to the OT. Even the appointed messenger John, who prepares the way for Jesus Christ, *the* prophetic Word of God, is not immune. As Jesus' ministry unfolds, he struggles to see in it the work of YHWH. He questions Jesus, 'Tell us, are you the one to come, or should we look for another?' (Matt. 11:2–6).

Faithfulness is no guarantee that, as the word of YHWH unfolds in the events of life, one will recognize his hand at work. There is in YHWH's work always the expression of his profound wisdom: his power to do beyond what we could 'ask or imagine' (Eph. 3:20–21). Working in subtle power and mysterious sequences, God is at work in ways that are often far beyond human comprehension. And, being beyond us, often his work is left unrecognized in the moment, credited to other mechanisms or simply overlooked. All that may be certain – as life unfolds for OT and NT saints – is that YHWH has spoken his word and will fulfil it. The outworking of that word may not be recognized until its completion, and perhaps only then can it be recognized, named and proclaimed.

This recognition and proclamation is the function of the completed account of 1 – 2 Kings. In exile those responsible for this work had time and distance from the events to ponder and draw out the theological implications of the monarchic history. Inspired by the Spirit, they rightly reckoned where and how YHWH's power was at work in past events. They attested to the fact that YHWH works in history to fulfil his word – whether or not his hand is correctly discerned in the moment. Not intended as only a bald recording of events, 1 – 2 Kings sought to reveal YHWH's work to an exilic people. Those exilic peoples might labour under various understandings of their own present situation. But the theological account of monarchic history would encourage them to trust that, in time, their present would also be theologically discerned. Accounts of where and how YHWH was at work would then stand as a witness to a future generation of the mighty acts of God, faithful to his word.

For the faithful under siege in Samaria, there may have been similar misperception of the powerful working of God in their midst. But despite such blindness, they, as all God's saints, are yet called to hold to and trust the word given. YHWH is a God who does what he says, and works to accomplish it even in the face of blind misperception of the very working of God.

The needs of the church today are as certain and as desperate as the famine of Samaria and the powerlessness of the king. But equally certain is YHWH's word. He has proclaimed that he will dwell in, discipline and cause his church to flourish. And so, knowing that it may not even recognize God at work in its midst, it prays this doxology, trusting God's mysterious power:

> Now to him who by the power at work within us is able to do abundantly more than we could ask or imagine, to him be glory in the church and in Christ Jesus from generation to generation, for ever and ever. Amen. (Eph. 3:20–21)

2 KINGS 8:1–29

Translation

[1]Now Elisha spoke to the woman whose son he had restored to life, 'Arise and go, you and your household, and sojourn wherever you can, for YHWH has called for a famine and surely it will come on the land seven years.' [2]So the woman arose and did according to the word of the man of God. She and her household went and sojourned in the land of the Philistines seven years. [3]At the end of seven years, the woman returned from the land of the Philistines and she went out to appeal to the king concerning[a] her house and her land. [4]The king was speaking to Gehazi, the servant of the man of God, saying, 'Tell me all the great deeds that Elisha did.' [5]He was recounting to the king how he had restored the dead to life when, behold, the woman whose son he had restored to life appealed to the king concerning her house and land. Gehazi said, 'My lord, O king! This is the woman and this is her son whom Elisha restored to life.' [6]The king questioned the woman, and she told him. The king appointed an official for her, saying, 'Restore all that was hers and all the revenue of the land from the day she left the country until now.'

[7]Now Elisha came to Damascus while Ben-hadad king of Aram was sick. It was told him, saying, 'The man of God has come here.' [8]The king said to Hazael[a], 'Take a gift in your hand, and go to meet the man of God. Enquire of YHWH through him[b], saying, "Will I recover from this sickness?"' [9]So Hazael went to meet him, and took a gift in his hand – forty camel loads of all good things[a] from Damascus. He came and stood before him and said, 'Your son Ben-hadad king of Aram has sent me to you, saying, "Will I recover from this sickness?"' [10]Elisha said to him, 'Go, say to him, "You will certainly recover,"[a] but YHWH has shown me that he will surely die.' [11]Then he fixed his gaze and stared *at him* until he was ashamed[a]; and the man of God wept. [12]Hazael said, 'Why is my lord weeping?' And he replied, 'Because I know the evil you will do to the sons of Israel. Their fortresses you will set on fire, and their young men you will kill with the sword, and their children you will dash to pieces, and their pregnant women you will rip open.' [13]Hazael said, 'But what is your servant, who is a dog, that he should do this great thing?' And Elisha said, 'YHWH has shown me you will be king over Aram.' [14]He departed from Elisha and came to his lord. He said to him, 'What did Elisha say to you?' He said, 'He told me that you will certainly recover.' [15]But on the next day he took the blanket[a], and dipped it in water and spread it over his face until he died. And Hazael became king in his place.

[16]In the fifth year of Joram[a] son of Ahab king of Israel, and Jehoshaphat was then king of Judah, Jehoram[a] son of Jehoshaphat king of Judah began to reign. [17]He was thirty-two years old when he began to reign and he reigned eight years in Jerusalem. [18]He walked in the way of the kings of Israel, just as the house of Ahab had done, for the daughter of Ahab was his wife. He did what was evil in the eyes of YHWH. [19]But YHWH was not willing to destroy Judah on account of David his servant, for he had promised to give him a lamp for his sons for ever.

²⁰In his days Edom revolted against the power of Judah and set a king over themselves. ²¹Joram crossed over to Zair and all the chariotry was with him. He arose in the night and struck Edom, which had surrounded him, and the commanders of the chariots and the army fled home. ²²So Edom revolted against the power of Judah until this day and Libnah also revolted at that time. ²³Now the rest of the acts of Joram and all that he did, are they not written in the Book of the Chronicles of the Kings of Judah? ²⁴And Joram slept with his fathers and was buried with his fathers in the City of David, and Ahaziah his son reigned in his place.

²⁵In the twelfth[a] year of Joram son of Ahab king of Israel, Ahaziah son of Jehoram king of Judah began to reign. ²⁶Ahaziah was twenty-two years old when he began to reign and he ruled one year in Jerusalem. The name of his mother was Athaliah, granddaughter[a] of Omri, king of Israel. ²⁷He walked in the way of the house of Ahab and did what was evil in the eyes of YHWH according to the house of Ahab, for he was son-in-law[a] to the house of Ahab. ²⁸He went with Joram son of Ahab to war with Hazael king of Aram in Ramoth-gilead, and the Arameans wounded Joram. ²⁹So Joram the king returned to Jezreel to be healed of the wounds that the Arameans had inflicted[a] *on him* in Ramah[b] when he fought with Hazael king of Aram. And Ahaziah son of Jehoram king of Judah went down to see Joram son of Ahab in Jezreel because he was sick.

Notes on the text

3.a. *'el* read as *'al* by context: 'concerning her house; concerning her land'.

8.a. Hazael is spelled variantly: *ḥzh'l* (vv. 8, 13, 15, 28–29; 2 Chr. 22:6), elsewhere *ḥz'l* (e.g. v. 9, and in some MSS in v. 8).

8.b. Reading *mē'ittô* with two MSS, and Vrs for MT *mē'ōtô*.

9.a. MT *wěkol-ṭûb* is read *mikkol-ṭûb* with LXX[L], Syr.

10.a. Reading the K *'ěmār lō' ḥāyô tiḥyê*, 'Say, "You will certainly not recover,"' with Q and Vrs as *'ěmār lô ḥāyô tiḥyê*, 'Say to him, "You will certainly recover."' The K seeks to remove the discrepancy with the next statement that the king will die.

11.a. Identification of the actors is problematic in the difficult phrase, which reads, literally, 'he caused his face to stand and he set until ashamed' (here translated, 'he fixed his gaze and stared *at him* until he was ashamed'). Hazael is unlikely to be emboldened to stare at a superior. The translation adopted here clarifies that Elisha stares (discerning Hazael's intention) until Hazael responds with shame. The change in actors (from Elisha to Hazael) is confirmed, as the next verb ('he wept') specifies the actor (Elisha, the man of God). Had Elisha been the actor throughout the sequence, this specification would be unnecessary.

15.a. The hapax noun *makbēr* is related to the noun *mikbār* ('open grating'; Exod. 27:4; 35:16 *et passim*). An absorbent open-weave blanket is meant.

.

16.a. Israelite Jehoram is called by the variant Joram (cf. 8:25, 28–29; 9:14, 16), possibly to differentiate from Judahite Jehoram (but see at 2 Kgs 1:17, where both are called Jehoram). Judahite Jehoram is also called by the variant Joram (8:21, 23–24; 11:2). Different traditions, or a deeper theological reason underlies the variants (see 'Comment', 8:21–24; cf. Provan 1995: 185).

25.a. LXX[L], Syr read 'eleventh'; see 9:29. Two dating systems are in place; see 'Comment'.

26.a. The text reads 'daughter of Omri' but should be understood in the sense of 'descendant', as Athaliah is also described as the daughter of Ahab (8:18).

27.a. Unless Ahaziah himself marries a daughter of Ahab, 'son-in-law' should here be construed in its broader sense of 'relation'.

29.a. Reading hiph. pf. 'had inflicted' for MT impf. with 2 Chr. 22:6; cf. 9:15.

29.b. 'Ramah' is an alternative for Ramoth-gilead (Arnold 1992c: 614).

Form and structure

Three distinct units (vv. 1–6, 7–15, 16–29) prepare for the long-anticipated demise of Ahab's dynasty (2 Kgs 9 – 10). With few detractors (Jones 1984b: 439; Fritz 2003: 272) the narrative of the Shunammite stands as a unified whole. It demonstrates the prophet's power and, by revisiting a previous narrative, serves as a reminder that the previous events of 1 Kgs 19:15–18 can similarly be reactivated.

The core narrative takes the form of an oracular enquiry during sickness (1 Kgs 14, 22; 2 Kgs 1) in which (1) a problem surfaces, (2) preparation for enquiry is undertaken, (3) an audience is granted, with initial dialogue followed by proclamation of an oracle, and (4) the oracle is fulfilled (B. Long 1973: 343; 1991: 105–106). Yet the standard form takes a surprising turn (vv. 10–13). The oracle regarding sickness is overtaken by Israelite concerns and is ultimately superseded by a royal succession oracle (v. 13), so that the narrative concludes with a standard royal succession formula (v. 15b). It is the transformation of the form that gives the narrative its power.

The annals of Shalmaneser III (*ANET* 280) note the usurpation of Aram's throne by Hazael, a commoner. Elisha is not mentioned. In the biblical text he has acted favourably towards Aram (2 Kgs 5; 6:8–23), providing a context for the present consultation. Granted narrative shaping, a historical core including a role for Elisha can be upheld (Gray 1970: 470 contra Jones 1984b: 441; Fritz 2003: 275). The narrative works well as a coherent whole (Gray 1970: 528; Hobbs 1985: 98–99), although the apparent contradictions within vv. 10–13 suggest redactional layering to some (Wurthwëin 1984: 318; Jones 1984b: 441; Fritz 2003: 275).

The chapter's final section turns to Judah, advancing the monarchic line in preparation for the events of 2 Kgs 9 with typical regnal formulae (see 'Form and structure', 1 Kgs 14). Ahaziah's opening formula bridges to the narrative of Jehu's coup, during which he dies. No closing formula occurs at that point; a brief notation suffices without unduly interrupting the coup narrative (9:29). Within the formulae, vv. 20–22 are probably adapted from annalistic sources similar to those found in Assyrian records (*ANET* 279–281).

Comment

8:1–6

The Shunammite's appeal arises from a string of events precipitated by Elisha's earlier counsel (vv. 1–2). She flees a famine brought by YHWH. The famine is not that of the preceding chapter (6:25; 7:4), which was localized in Samaria and a result of siege.

The identification of the Shunammite is apparent through the references to her son 'restored to life' (vv. 1, 5). Additionally, Elisha's concern for her survival recalls her own provision to him (4:8), and his injunction that she and her household sojourn elsewhere reverses her secure position 'among her own people' (4:13). Elisha addresses the woman as if she has authority over her household; perhaps her old husband has died, or Elisha acknowledges her prominent position (4:8) and his past interactions with her. Her sojourn in Philistia, located on a fertile coastal plain with adequate rainfall, would have ensured adequate food during the famine in Israel.

After seven years the woman returns to appeal (ṣʿq) to the king's justice, as others have done (1 Kgs 20:39; 2 Kgs 6:26). Her land has been expropriated in her absence, taken over by a relative, or has reverted to the crown (Fritz 2003: 273) to be held in trust (Gray 1970: 527). Her appeal within seven years follows similar laws for the reversion of property (Exod. 21:2). Her husband may be dead and she makes the claim on his behalf, or she may be the owner through family inheritance and thus the claim is hers to make.

The timing of her appeal is providential. As she approaches (vv. 3, 5), Gehazi relates Elisha's 'great deeds'. At the moment he relates the greatest deed of all, the evidence of that deed appears! The king turns to the woman, questioning her further on the story and, favourably disposed towards her, grants her petition. An official is assigned her case with directions to restore both her property and seven years of lost revenue. Thus, while the woman moves confidently among her own people and petitions the king (4:13), the stories of Elisha tip the king's response in her favour. His power is active through his reputation even in his absence.

8:7–15

Elisha travels to Damascus, perhaps to avoid Jehoram (6:31) or at YHWH's bidding. There is no indication he travels at Ben-hadad's behest (identified by narrative context as Ben-hadad II; see 'Comment', 1 Kgs 20:1). Given Elisha's reputation for healing the Aramean Naaman, the visit is fortuitous for the king.

Apprised of Elisha's approach, and in keeping with other scenes of prophetic enquiry, the king charges a messenger to 'go'. The 'meeting' with the man of God probably occurs while Elisha is still en route (1 Sam. 9:19; 2 Sam. 25:20; 1 Kgs 18:7; 21:18; 2 Kgs 1:3; 4:26). As in other enquiries, the messenger is prepared with a gift (1 Kgs 14:3; cf. 1 Sam. 9:7). The gift is very lavish, 'forty camel loads' (v. 9) of the rich commodities common to a trading city such as Damascus. The messenger is also charged to 'enquire of YHWH' (*wĕdāraštā ʾet-yhwh*), phraseology that delineates a 'prophetic enquiry schema' (B. Long 1973: 343; Wagner, *TDOT* 3:302–303; see similarly at 1 Kgs 14:5; 22:13, 18; 2 Kgs 3:11).

The commission and meeting are an ironic echo of Ahaziah's story (2 Kgs 1), for the foreigner acts more circumspectly than the native Israelite. Ahaziah sent messengers, whom Elisha 'meets', but the Israelite king sent to 'enquire of' Baal-zebub, not YHWH. Not surprisingly, the word to Ahaziah is he will 'surely die' – and he does. Ben-hadad, seeking YHWH, is told he will 'surely live' – but surprisingly dies.

The introduction of Hazael immediately draws attention back to Elijah's as-yet unfulfilled charge to anoint Hazael king over Aram (1 Kgs 19:15). Despite his importance in YHWH's plans, his introduction is without fanfare. He has no patronymic, and is only a messenger. Certainly, in order to seize and hold power he must have some standing within Aram, but even in official Assyrian documents he is remembered as a nobody and a usurper (*ANET* 280). Although he is lowly, his name means 'God envisions' (*ḥzh ʾēl*) and it is precisely because of YHWH's vision that everything changes for Hazael.

The oracular exchange progresses through a series of three questions and answers (vv. 9b–13), which are bracketed by Hazael's arrival and departure (vv. 9, 14). He 'stands before' Elisha as an inferior before a superior (1 Sam. 16:21; 2 Kgs 5:15), and maintains a humble stance, addressing Elisha as 'my lord' (v. 12) and himself as 'your servant' (v. 13). Even when told of the 'great things' he will do, he refers to himself as 'a dog', a self-deprecating reference not uncommon in biblical and extra-biblical sources (1 Sam. 24:14[15]; 2 Sam. 9:8; 16:9; cf. the sixth-century Lachish letters 2, 5–6 [*ANET* 322]).

His courtesy extends to his message. Using the typical messenger self-introduction formula ('PN [personal name] has sent me'; Exod 3:13; 7:16; 2 Kgs 5:22; Jer. 26:12), he calls Ben-hadad 'son' (with Elisha implied as 'father'; see 2 Kgs 2:12; 6:21; 13:14). In that context he presents the first question. Elisha's answer is contradictory: Ben-hadad will recover; Ben-hadad will die.

The dual reply has caused interpreters consternation for fear Elisha is lying. One solution proposes that Elisha's first word is his own, and the second what YHWH has 'shown him'. But Elisha is speaking throughout in the context of an oracular enquiry: all his words are YHWH's words. Another solution follows textual changes to mitigate what seems to be Elisha's lie (see 'Notes on the text'; a good summation of the various approaches can be found in B. Long 1991: 104; Provan 1995: 208).

But that Elisha might lie – or at least not tell the whole truth – should not cause such alarm. Other prophets have not told all the truth before (see 1 Kgs 22; 2 Kgs 3) while in full service to YHWH. Elisha may well be lying, and suggesting that Hazael communicate a similar lie to Ben-hadad (which, in the event, he does), all in service to YHWH's purposes. Or Elisha's words are true: Ben-hadad does recover but is then murdered. Or his words are contingently true: Ben-hadad dies only if Hazael acts on the second word (Tiemeyer 2005: 347–348).

Elisha, however, broaches no contingency. His fixed gaze measures Hazael, discerning his inner ambitions regarding kingship, Ben-hadad and Israel. Hazael's thoughts are less than innocent, and Elisha weeps. His tears precipitate the second question of the series and his answer reveals what he has discerned. The coming years of warfare (2 Kgs 9 – 13) will bring disaster for Israel and the atrocities are expressed in stereotypical language (Isa. 13:16; Hos. 13:16; Amos 1:13). Later Hazael and Aram will be judged for their actions (Amos 1:3–5).

Hazael's final question (v. 13) shows polite deference (but no refusal) towards the 'great thing' Elisha has prophesied (a very different kind of 'great thing' than previously related of Elisha [vv. 4, 13]). Elisha's final answer that YHWH has shown him suggests this information, like that of Ben-hadad's death (v. 10), has come to him through a particular vision or word from YHWH (Jer. 38:21; Amos 7:1, 4, 7; 8:1; Ezek. 11:25; Zech. 1:20; 3:1). The oracular enquiry precipitated by the king's health ends with a final and chilling word: Hazael will be king.

The finality of YHWH's word may account for the rapid denouement. Hazael returns and delivers a partial message. On the morrow he soaks a loosely woven blanket in water, making its fibers impermeable, and smothers the king. While the subject of these actions is not stated, the only narrative actor is Hazael. Gray's suggestion (1970: 532) that the blanket was hung over the king as a form of air conditioning and that it hid the fact of the king's death until the blanket was changed, entirely misses the point. Hazael fulfils the prophetic word, the king dies and Hazael 'became king in his place'. The surprising has happened. Now judgment against the house of Ahab can be executed and 'the one who escapes from the sword of Hazael Jehu shall kill, and the one who escapes from the sword of Jehu Elisha shall kill' (1 Kgs 19:17).

8:16–24

The last southern monarch introduced by a regnal formula was Jehoshaphat (1 Kgs 22:41–50). From his rule through to 2 Kgs 9 two further southern monarchs reign (Jehoram, Ahaziah); their reigns are now summarized before the narrative continues in 2 Kgs 9 during Ahaziah's reign.

Jehoram's regnal formula is typical: synchronization to the northern monarchy, his age at accession, and length and place of reign. As noted elsewhere (see 'Comment', 2 Kgs 1:17), Jehoram is co-regent with his father Jehoshaphat. The notation here of Jehoshaphat's rule suggests his abdication or death in this year and the commencement of Jehoram's sole rule. The southern monarch is compared to the kings of Israel and the house of Ahab, for he follows the sins of Jeroboam (1 Kgs 13:33–34; 14:9) and Ahab's cult of Baal and the sacred poles (1 Kgs 16:31–33). This is credited to the influence of Athaliah, Jehoram's wife, the daughter of Ahab and Jezebel. Tellingly, when the worship practices of Jehoram (1 Kgs 22:50; 8:16) of Judah and Jehoram of Israel (1:17; 3:1, 6) most closely resemble each other, they are both named by the same variant, 'Joram' (8:16–29; see Provan 1995: 184–185). Only on the strength of YHWH's faithful promise granted David will an ongoing 'lamp' or dynasty continue in Jerusalem (see 'Comment', 1 Kgs 11:36).

Despite the ongoing lamp, the Davidic dynasty is disciplined for covenant unfaithfulness (2 Sam. 7:14; 1 Kgs 9:7), losing dominion in Edom. Previously, a Judahite-appointed governor was granted authority in Edom and supported Judah (1 Kgs 22:47; 2 Kgs 3:9). Now Edom asserts independence and Judah barely escapes with their army at Zair (the location is disputed but may be Lot's hiding place of Zoar south-east of the Dead Sea in the Moabite hills; Liwak 1992: 1038–1039). From that time both Edom and Libnah (another border town in south-west Judah, possibly Tell Bornat near Lachish; Peterson, *ABD* 4:322–323) remain in revolt. The situation ensues 'until this day', that is, at least until the time of the tradition's source and possibly as late as the author's own time (Childs 1963: 279–292). The loss of control in both areas reveals the diminishing reach of the Davidic dynasty. Jehoram's rule ends typically, recounting source documents, death and burial, and succession.

8:25–29

Ahaziah's summary is also standard for southern kings. The synchronization to Joram's reign differs in 9:29 and reflects the different methods of calculating accession years in Judah and Israel (see Introduction). His mother, of the house of Ahab (see 'Notes on the text'), is an ominous addition to the Davidic house. As her later actions reveal (ch. 11), her evil effect extends beyond the realm of the cult and threatens the Davidic line.

Ahaziah's evaluation is couched in typical Dtr phrases and his relationship to the house of Ahab is cited as contributory to his misdeeds.

Vv. 28–29 adapt and summarize information originally narrated in vv. 14b–16a and provide a bridge to the following narrative, foreshadowing events in which Ahaziah dies. Ahaziah 'goes to war' (*wayyēlek . . . lammilḥāmâ*) with Joram against Aram, a phrase that elsewhere is used for attending in battle (Deut. 20:1; 21:10; Judg. 3:10; 20:14; 2 Sam. 21:17; 1 Kgs 8:44; 20:18; 1 Chr. 7:11; 2 Chr. 6:34). Given Judah's recent alliances with Israel (1 Kgs 22; 2 Kgs 3) and the strong family ties, the statement indicates actual engagement in battle (Cogan 1988: 99) rather than only a supporting political policy (Gray 1970: 536–537; Hobbs 1985: 104–105).

Explanation

As in 2 Kgs 7, this chapter deals with the fulfilment of YHWH's word spoken through his prophets. Here YHWH's powerful word continues, effective long after it is issued. By this power the prophetic word shapes and moves forward Israel's history to accomplish YHWH's will.

As in 2 Kgs 6, a short vignette introduces the chapter's theological focus. The narrative briefly revisits the Shunammite woman, revealing that the current events are part of an older story. The concern YHWH exhibited earlier in the woman's life is no less potent in the present instance, as through providential timing YHWH again intervenes to provide life to the faithful woman and her household.

In vv. 7–15 YHWH again works providentially. Elisha comes to Damascus during Ben-hadad's illness; Hazael is dispatched to meet the prophet. In the propitious meeting the unfaithful foreigner (a clear contrast to the Shunammite) finds no words of life. Instead, Elisha prophesies death – not only for the King of Aram (v. 10), but also for Israel by Hazael's hand (v. 12).

The word given Hazael effects the second of three commissions given in 1 Kgs 19:15–18. The anointing of Jehu will complete the final commission. The commissions are given in the context of Baal worship and point to its overthrow (1 Kgs 16:31–33; 19:18). Such worship was introduced by Ahab, and for these sins his dynasty is judged (1 Kgs 21:17–29). Judgment comes at the hand of Jehu, and in the context of war with Hazael (2 Kgs 9:1–10). Thus in the unfolding history the commission given Elijah (1 Kgs 19:15–18) is tied to the prophetic judgment against Ahab – the one facilitates the other. Within this larger context of judgment the anointing of Hazael finds meaning.

The conviction that the prophetic word shapes Israel's history necessitates the placement of the two accounts of Judahite kings alongside the anointing of Hazael. The Dtr author could have placed these accounts following Jehu's coup (2 Kgs 9 – 10). This would have presented two blocks with different focuses: the Omride dynasty from 1 Kgs 16 – 2 Kgs 10, and the southern kingdom accounts of Jehoram and Ahaziah together with Jehoash (2 Kgs 11 – 12). However, because Jehoram and Ahaziah are Omrides – the first by marriage to Athaliah, the second by birth (vv. 18, 26) – the narrative must present their reigns before the judgment executed against Ahab's house. As Omrides they too will fall under that judgment (2 Kgs 9 – 10).

There is a fullness of time to the prophetic word. When the time is right, it comes to pass. The narrative is shaped to provide all that is necessary for the full effect of the prophetic word: Elisha anointed (1 Kgs 19), Hazael anointed and southern Omrides noted (2 Kgs 8), Jehu anointed (2 Kgs 9). Judgment then comes as no surprise: it is prophesied, and the narrative has fully prepared for its execution.

In the same way the account of Ahab's house is itself part of a larger narrative driven by the prophetic word. The northern kingdom, founded by Jeroboam, had the possibility of YHWH's favour (1 Kgs 11:30–38). By his sin Jeroboam forfeited that favour and sealed his own, and the kingdom's, judgment (1 Kgs 14:6–16). All that occurs throughout Israel's history moves it towards that end. Whether experiencing YHWH's mercy or wrath, the sins of Jeroboam continue and the judgment is not lifted. When the northern kingdom eventually ends, many sins are enumerated as contributing to that event, but they do not supersede the first sins of Jeroboam (2 Kgs 17:5–23).

The northern kingdom, too, stands within a larger history that is likewise shaped by the prophetic word. It is Solomon's failure under covenant (1 Kgs 11:1–8; cf. 1 Kgs 2:2–4; 6:11–13) that calls forth the northern kingdom (1 Kgs 11:9–13) and accounts for the southern kingdom's demise (1 Kgs 9:4–9). Again the unfolding events of history inevitably move Judah to exile, and the prophetic word is fulfilled

The judgment against Solomon also stands in the larger prophetic history of the Davidic Covenant. Mediated by the prophetic word, it promises David an eternal dynasty (2 Sam. 7:4–17). The exile of Judah ends the dynasty: no king sits again upon the throne of David. But in the face of the repeated evidences of the prophetic word's veracity there is confidence that this word, too, will be fulfilled. Within the Christian tradition that word is fulfilled in the coming of Christ. Of the kingly line of David (Rom. 1:3; Matt. 1:1–16; 2:2), he takes up that throne at his ascension, never to relinquish it (Heb. 1:3–4; 2:9; Ps. 110:1).

The Deuteronomistic theology of the prophetic word prepares for this aspect of the gospel account. The prophetic word is sure and, in the fullness of time, the events of history move towards its fulfilment. But in the enthronement of Christ is demonstrated not simply the Deuteronomistic theology of the prophetic word, but the fulfilment of the word of YHWH given Abraham. Through Abraham's seed (Gen. 15:3–5; Gal. 3:8, 16) would come one to fulfil the promise granted Abraham, that all the families of the earth would be blessed through him (Gen. 12:3).

The pattern of the prophetic word outlined in 2 Kgs 8 is not limited to the Deuteronomistic history but remains throughout the Bible. This attests to the action in history of one whose word speaks the cosmos, the world and life itself into existence (Gen. 1). God's word is certain and by its power history itself is shaped towards the word's fulfilment. As history unfolds, old words are revisited and extended in new directions, culminating in the goal of history. Jesus Christ fulfils all history, and in him all God's words come to completion.

2 KINGS 9:1 – 10:36

Translation

⁹:¹Now Elisha the prophet summoned one of the sons of the prophets. He said to him, 'Girdᵃ up your loins and take this flask of oil in your hand and go to Ramoth-gilead. ²When you arrive there, look for Jehu son of Jehoshaphat son of Nimshi. Go in, get him up from the midst of his brothers, take him into an inner room, ³take the flask of oil and pour it on his head and say, "Thus says YHWH, 'I anoint you king over Israelᵃ.'" Then open the door and flee, and do not wait.' ⁴So the young man, the prophetᵃ, went to Ramoth-gilead. ⁵When he arrived, the commanders of the army were in session. He said, 'I have a word for you, O captain!' Jehu answered, 'For which one of us?' And he said, 'For you, O captain.'

⁶So he arose and entered the house and he poured the oil upon his head and said to him, 'Thus says YHWH, the God of Israel, "I anoint you king over the people of YHWH, over Israel!" ⁷You shall strike the house of Ahab your master, and I will avenge the blood of my servants the prophets and the blood of all the servants of YHWH at the hand of Jezebel. ⁸For the whole house of Ahab will perish and I will cut off from Ahab those who urinate against the wall, restricted and abandoned in Israel. ⁹I will make the house of Ahab like the house of Jeroboam son of Nebat and like the house of Baasha son of Ahijah. ¹⁰And Jezebel the dogs will eat in the territory of Jezreel and none will bury.' Then he opened the door and fled.

¹¹Jehu went out to his master's servants. They saidᵃ to him, 'Is it peace, Jehu? Why did this madman come to you?' He said to them, 'You know the kind and their speechᵇ.' ¹²They said, 'A lie! Tell us.' So he said, 'Thus and so he said to me, "Thus says YHWH, 'I anoint you king over Israel.'"' ¹³They hastened and each took his garment and laid it under him on the bare steps. They blew the shofar and said, 'Jehu is king!' ¹⁴Thus Jehu son of Jehoshaphat son of Nimshi conspired against Jehoramᵃ.

Now Jehoram with all Israel was defending Ramoth-gilead against Hazael king of Aram. ¹⁵Jehoram the king had returned to be healed in Jezreel from the wounds that the Arameans had inflicted[a] *on him* when he fought with Hazael king of Aram. Jehu said, 'If this is your desire, let no one leave the city to go report in Jezreel.' [16]Jehu mounted his chariot and went to Jezreel, for Jehoram was lying there, and Ahaziah king of Judah had come down to visit Jehoram.

[17]Now the lookout was standing upon the tower in Jezreel. He saw Jehu's company[a] as he approached and he said, 'I see a company.' Jehoram said, 'Take a horseman and send to meet them and he shall ask, "Is it peace?"' [18]So the horseman went to meet him and said, 'Thus says the king, "Is it peace?"' And Jehu said, 'What have you to do with peace? Turn in behind me.' The lookout reported saying, 'The messenger came to them[a] but has not returned.' [19]So he sent a second horseman. He came to them and said, 'Thus says the king, "Is it peace?[a]"' Jehu said, 'What have you to do with peace? Turn in behind me.' [20]The lookout reported, 'He came to them[a] but has not returned. And the driving is as the driving of Jehu son of Nimshi – for he drives like a maniac!'

[21]Then Jehoram said, 'Get ready!' and they readied[a] his chariot. Jehoram king of Israel and Ahaziah king of Judah went out, each in his chariot. They went to meet Jehu and found him at the property of Naboth the Jezreelite. [22]When Jehoram saw Jehu he said, 'Is it peace, Jehu?' And he said, 'What peace[a] – while the many harlotries and sorceries of Jezebel your mother remain?' [23]Then Jehoram reined about and fled while he called to Ahaziah, 'Treachery, Ahaziah!' [24]Jehu drew his bow with full strength and struck Jehoram between his shoulders. The arrow pierced his heart and he sank in his chariot. [25]He said to Bidkar his officer, 'Take him up and throw him on the property of the field of Naboth the Jezreelite. For remember[a] when you[b] and I rode together after Ahab his father and YHWH uttered this oracle against him: [26]"Surely I saw yesterday the blood of Naboth and the blood of his sons," says YHWH, "and I will repay you on this property," says YHWH. Now lift him up and throw him on the property, according to the word of YHWH.'

[27]When Ahaziah king of Judah saw *this*, he fled by the way of Beth-haggan. Jehu pursued after him and said, 'Him too! Strike him!' They struck him[a] in the chariot on the ascent of Gur, which is by Ibleam, and he fled to Megiddo and died there. [28]His servants carried him by chariot to Jerusalem and they buried him in his grave with his fathers in the city of David. [29](In the eleventh year of Jehoram[a] son of Ahab, Ahaziah had begun to reign over Judah.)

[30]Then Jehu came to Jezreel. Now Jezebel had heard and she painted her eyes with kohl and adorned her head and looked out of the window. [31]Jehu entered the gate and she said, 'Is it peace, Zimri[a], who murdered his master?' [32]He lifted his face to the window and said, 'Who is with me? Who?' And two or three eunuchs looked down at him. [33]He said, 'Throw her down!' And they threw her down and her blood splattered the wall and the horses, and he trampled her[a]. [34]He entered, and ate and drank, and said, 'Look after this accursed woman and bury her, for she is a king's daughter.' [35]They went to bury her but found no more of her than the skull, the feet and the palms of *her* hands. [36]They returned and reported to him, and he said, 'This is the word of YHWH, which he spoke by the hand of his servant Elijah the Tishbite, "In the territory of Jezreel the dogs shall eat the flesh

of Jezebel." ³⁷The corpse of Jezebel will be as dung on the face of the field in the territory of Jezreel so that no one can say, "This is Jezebel."'

¹⁰:¹Ahab had seventy sons in Samaria. Jehu wrote letters and sent to Samaria to the leaders of the cityᵃ and to the elders and to the guardians of the sonsᵇ of Ahab, saying, ²'Now, when this letter comes to you, since you have your lord's sons and the chariots and horses and a fortified city and weapons, ³choose the best and most capable of your lord's sons and set *him* upon his father's throne. Then, fight for your lord's house.' ⁴They were terribly afraid and said, 'Look; two kings could not stand before him, how can we stand?' ⁵The steward and the mayor and the elders and the guardians sent to Jehu, saying, 'We are your servants. Whatever you say to us, we will do. We will not make anyone king. Do what is good in your eyes.'

⁶He wrote a secondᵃ letter to them, saying, 'If you are for me and will obey my voice, take the heads of the men, your lord's sonsᵇ, and come to me at Jezreel about this time tomorrow.' (Now the king's sons were seventy men. They were with the great men of the city who were raising them.) ⁷When the letter came to them, they took the king's sons and slaughtered *them*ᵃ, seventy men, and put their heads in baskets and sent *them* to him at Jezreel. ⁸The messenger came and reported to him, saying, 'They have brought the heads of the king's sons.' And he said, 'Put them in two piles at the entrance of the gate until morning.'

⁹In the morning he went out and stood and said to all the people, 'You are innocent. Behold, I conspired against my lord and killed him. But who struck all these? ¹⁰Know then that there shall fall to the ground nothing of YHWH's word that YHWH spoke concerning the house of Ahab, for YHWH has done that which he spoke by the hand of his servant Elijah.' ¹¹Then Jehu struck all the remainder of the house of Ahab in Jezreel and all his great men and his acquaintances and his priests, until he left him no survivor.

¹²Then he aroseᵃ and went to Samaria. En route, while he was at Beth-eked of the shepherds ¹³he metᵃ the relatives of Ahaziah king of Judah. He said, 'Who are you?', and they answered, 'We are the relatives of Ahaziah. We have come down to visit the king's sons and the sons of the great lady.' ¹⁴He said, 'Take them alive.' So they took them alive and slaughtered them at the pit of Beth-eked, forty-two men. He spared none of them.

¹⁵He went from there and met Jehonadab son of Rechab *coming* to meet him. He greeted him and said to him, 'Is your heart upright, as my heart is with your heart?' Jehonadab said, 'It is.' *Jehu said*, 'If it is, give me your hand.' He gave *him* his hand and he took him up with him into the chariot. ¹⁶He said, 'Come with me and see my zeal for YHWH,' and he had him rideᵃ with him in his chariot. ¹⁷They came to Samaria and he struck all who remained to Ahab in Samaria until he had destroyed him, according to the word of YHWH that he spoke to Elijah.

¹⁸Jehu gathered all the people and said to them, 'Ahab served Baal a little; Jehu will serve him a lot.' ¹⁹And now, summon to me all the prophets of Baal, all his worshippers and all his priests. Let none be missing, for I will make a great sacrifice to Baal; whoever is missing shall not live.' But Jehu acted with cunning so that he might destroy the worshippers of Baal.

²⁰Then Jehu said, 'Sanctify[a] an assembly to Baal.' So they proclaimed *it*. ²¹Jehu sent throughout all Israel, and all the worshippers of Baal came and not a man was left who did not come. They entered the house of Baal and the house of Baal was filled from one end to the other. ²²He said to the keeper of the wardrobe, 'Bring out vestments for all the worshippers of Baal,' so he brought vestments out for them. ²³Jehu and Jehonadab son of Rechab entered the house of Baal. He said to the worshippers of Baal, 'Search carefully and see that there are no worshippers of YHWH here with you, but only worshippers of Baal.' ²⁴Then they entered to make sacrifices and burnt offerings. (Now Jehu had stationed eighty men for himself outside. He had said, 'Whoever allows any of the men whom I bring to your hand to escape, his life will be forfeit.')

²⁵When he had finished making the burnt offering, Jehu said to the guards and officers, 'Go in! Kill them! Let no one come out.' So they struck them with the edge of the sword and the guards and officers threw *them*[a] out and they went into the central shrine of the house of Baal. ²⁶They brought out the pillar[a] of the house of Baal and burned it, ²⁷and tore down the altar of Baal[a]. They tore down the house of Baal and made it a latrine[b] until this day. ²⁸Thus Jehu eradicated Baal from Israel.

²⁹However, the sins of Jeroboam son of Nebat, which he caused Israel to sin, Jehu did not turn from them – that is, the calves of gold that were in Bethel and Dan. ³⁰And YHWH said to Jehu, 'Because you have done well in doing what is right in my eyes, according to all that is in my heart you have done to the house of Ahab, your sons of the fourth generation will sit upon the throne of Israel.' ³¹But Jehu was not careful to walk in the torah of YHWH the God of Israel with all his heart. He did not turn from the sins of Jeroboam that he caused Israel to sin.

³²In those days YHWH began to cut off *land*[a] from Israel. Hazael struck them in all the territory of Israel. ³³From the Jordan eastward, all the land of Gilead, the Gadites and the Reubenites and the Manassites, from Aroer, which is by the wadi Arnon, that is, Gilead and Bashan. ³⁴Now the rest of the acts of Jehu and all that he did, and all his might, are they not written in the Book of the Chronicles of the Kings of Israel? ³⁵Then Jehu slept with his fathers and they buried him in Samaria. And Jehoahaz his son reigned in his place. ³⁶The time that Jehu ruled over Israel in Samaria was twenty-eight years.

Notes on the text

9:1.a.–3.a. Elisha's commands are imp. verbs ('gird', 'take', 'go', 'look') followed by waw cons. + pf. verbs continuing imp. sense ('go', 'get', 'take', 'pour', 'say', 'open', 'flee').

3.a. *'el-yiśrā'ēl* should read *'al-yiśrā'ēl*. A common scribal error, also at vv. 6, 12–14.

4.a. Is the young man a prophet, or a servant of a prophet? The first occurrence of *hanna'ar* is sometimes omitted (several MSS, LXX, Syr), leaving the second appositional; thus 'the young man, that is, the prophet', as here. Reading the second occurrence in const. with 'prophet' and appos-itional to the first, 'the young man' reads, 'the young man, that is, the young man of the prophet' (so two MSS, Tg, Vg).

11.a. Reading 'they said' for 3 m. sg. with Vrs.

11.b. 'their speech' from n. *śîaḥ*, meaning 'babble' (G. Cohen, *TWOT* 2:876). LXX translates 'idle talk', 'garrulity'.

14.a. The variant 'Joram' appears in MT vv. 14–16, 29; 'Jehoram' used here for uniformity.

15.a. Reading hiph. pf. 'had inflicted' for MT impf. with 8:29; 2 Chr. 22:6.

17.a. MT 'company' (*śip‘â*) refers to a multitude and is used of camels (Isa. 60:6), horses (Ezek. 26:10) and water (Job 22:11). LXX 'dust cloud' (κονιορτὸν; LXX^L adds 'of the multitude') describes the company's effect.

18.a. *‘ad-hēm* as primitive spelling for *‘ădêhem* (Montgomery 1951: 405).

19.a. Prefixing *šālôm* with interr.

20.a. The double prep. *‘ad-’ălêhem* need read only *‘ad-hem* or *‘ădêhem* (see v. 18; Burney 1903: 225; Cogan 1988: 110). See further at n. 18.a above.

21.a. 'they readied' reads pl. with LXX^-B, Syr, Vg.

22.a. Deleting the interr. on *šālôm* with LXX, Tg.

25.a. The versions read imp. *zĕkōr* as part. and expand to 'For I remember that I and you' (*kî zôkēr ’ănî kî ’ănî wĕ’attâ*). Though awkward, MT 'For remember! I and you' can stand (so Montgomery 1951: 406).

25.b. Deleting *’ēt* as dittog. of *’attâ*.

27.a. With Syr, Vg adding the hiph. impf. response 'and they struck him', missing by haplography from MT. LXX reads the imp. in 'Him too! Strike him!' as a 3 m. pl. hiph. impf., providing the response.

29.a. See n. 14.a above.

31.a. A reference to Zimri (1 Kgs 16:9–10), not a first-person pr. suffix with root *zmr* (using the third homophonic listed in *HALOT* 1:274), meaning 'my strong one, my protector' (so Parker [1978–9: 71–72], arguing Jezebel intends to seduce Jehu).

33.a. MT sg. 'he trampled' (contra Vrs. pl. 'they trampled her') maintains the brutal characterization of Jehu (Cogan 1988: 112).

10:1.a. MT 'leaders of Jezreel' is difficult, as Jehu writes from Jezreel. *yizrĕ‘e’l* is a probable corruption of *hā‘îr wĕ’ēl*, 'to the leaders of the city and to' (so LXX^L; cf. Burney 1903: 302; Montgomery 1951: 413; Gray 1970: 552).

10:1.b. Adding 'the sons of' with LXX^BL as the object of the guardians.

6.a. With LXX, MSS *šĕnê*, 'a second letter'. MT *šēnît* is adv., 'a second time' (GKC §100c).

6.b. In MT *rā’šê ’anšê bĕnê-’ădōnêkem* stands as an appos. 'the heads of the men, the sons of your lord' (GKC §131e). 'Men' is missing from several MSS, LXX^L, Syr, Vg.; some MSS read *bêt*, 'house', for *bĕnê*. Jehu's clever ambiguity centres on the dual meaning of 'heads' (lit. 'chief men').

7.a. 'they slaughtered *them*' takes the object from LXX*, Syr.

12.a. *wayyābō'*, 'and he came', omitted with LXX*. Conj. added to *hû'*. with LXX^L, Syr, Vg.

13.a. MT *wĕyēhû' māṣā'* is properly read *wĕhû' māṣā'* (Burney 1903: 303; Montgomery 1951: 414, citing S. Driver 1892: §169, n. 2), synchronizing to Jehu's stop in Beth-eked.

16.a. Reading MT *wayyarkibû*, 'and they had [him] ride', as sg. with LXX, Syr, Vg.

20.a. Tg, Syr 'call' (*qir'û*) an assembly as a theologically informed avoidance of 'sanctifying' (*qaddĕšû*). The convergence of 'sanctify' and 'call' can be seen in Lev. 23:36; Joel 1:14; and supported by Ugaritic sacrificial texts (Kuyt 1985: 109–111).

25.a. No stated object is provided for *wayyašlikû*, 'they threw out'. None is needed when contextually apparent (Hobbs 1985: 123, citing 2 Kgs 4:41; 6:6). *BHS* suggests replacing the second occurrence of 'guards and officers' with *'ōtām*, 'them'; Tg reads, 'the dead' (*hammētîm*).

26.a. Reading MT *maṣṣebôt* as f. sg. const. in agreement with the following pr. and MSS, Vrs. *BHS*, following Burney (1903: 306), suggests emendation to *'ăšērat* on the strength of 1 Kgs 16:33 and due to supposed difficulties of burning stone pillars. But the sacred poles (asherah) remain within Israel (2 Kgs 13:6) and stone can be shattered by heating and dousing with cold water (Gray 1970: 558).

27.a. *wayyittĕṣû 'ēt maṣṣĕbat habbā'al*, 'and tore down the pillar of Baal', is a possible repetition of the actions of v. 26 or v. 27b. LXX^L deletes the second action of v. 27. *maṣṣĕbat* is better emended to *mizbēaḥ*, 'altar'. Ahab made an altar (1 Kgs 16:32) and altars are often 'torn down' (Exod. 34:13; Deut. 7:15; 12:3; Judg. 2:2; 6:28; see Burney 1903: 306; Montgomery 1951: 416; Gray 1970: 558).

27.b. K. is pointed *lĕmaḥărā'ôt*, a hapax meaning 'latrine'. Q (*lĕmôṣā'ôt*) is euphemistic, 'withdrawal' or cognate 'be clean' (*HALOT* 2:559), that is, 'excrement'.

32.a. *land* is provided for sense and by context (v. 33); the pi. verb has the sense of breaking off, piece by piece.

Form and structure

The longest sustained narrative in 2 Kings relates the coup of Jehu. His anointing is the final outstanding element of Elijah's commission (1 Kgs 19:15–18). He is anointed to execute judgment against Ahab's house (1 Kgs 21:20–29) and as an outcome also precipitates a coup in Judah that threatens the Davidic dynasty (2 Kgs 11).

Jehu's coup takes place in the midst of the narrative. So as not to interrupt that account, and because his kingship is not by normal dynastic succession, the opening regnal formula is omitted. Its companion is presented at the end of Jehu's reign (10:29–36). Dtr's hand is acknowledged throughout, although redactional theories trace up to four compositional layers (DeVries 1978: 56, 67–69, 90, 119, 122; Gray 1970: 537–539). Such theories find little consensus and rest on quite subjective criteria for discerning redactional layers; whatever the text's prehistory, the final narrative remains the locus for interpretation (so B. Long 1991: 113–116) and there are proponents for the narrative's essential unity (Hobbs 1985: 111; Montgomery 1951: 399).

Recognizable forms appear throughout the narrative. An oracle with the common messenger formula 'Thus says YHWH' sparks the coup (vv. 3, 6) and a further oracle is remembered, although the form is anomalous (9:26). Several fulfilment notices declare the events transpire according to YHWH's word (9:26, 36; 10:10, 17). Several scenes reveal underlying ANE treaty forms. Jehu's meal after Jezebel's death, his meeting with Jehonadab, and his letters with the leaders each include covenantal elements (see further in 'Comment').

Several leitworts carry narrative themes. Šālôm occurs ten times (9:11, 17, 18 [twice], 19 [twice], 22 [twice], 31; 10:13), and once in a verbal form (9:26). Šālôm describes peace, wholeness and well-being experienced personally, relationally and nationally in full covenantal relationship with YHWH (BDB 1022; von Rad, TDNT 2:402–406; Good, IDB 3:704–706; Durham 1983: 276–277; Keber 1996:10). Often it is a greeting that anticipates an affirmative response (Gen. 29:6; 43:27–28; 1 Kgs 2:13; 2 Kgs 4:26; 5:21–22). Used in this narrative, the greeting is ironically charged (Olyan 1984: 666), for those who use it are unaware of the lack of šālôm in the land. Jehu's violent actions of non-šālôm intend to restore šālôm fully. However, his own rule continues the sins of Jeroboam and thus šālôm is aborted.

The 'house of Ahab' (bêt 'aḥ'āb) is the second leitwort. Of eleven occurrences in 1 – 2 Kings (2 Kgs 8:18, 27 [three times]; 9:7–9; 10:10–11, 30; 21:13), six appear in these two chapters. 1 Kgs 21:29 had promised judgment against Ahab's house and it is here executed.

This leitwort extends in another direction, for Ahab's introduction of Baal worship includes a 'house of Baal' (bêt habba'al) in Samaria (1 Kgs 16:31–32). Judgment against Ahab necessarily purges the 'house of Baal' (10:18–28). The phrase occurs ten times in the OT (Josh. 13:17; Judg. 9:4; 1 Kgs 16:32; 2 Kgs 10:21 [twice], 23, 25–27; 2 Kgs 11:18), six of which are found in Jehu's purge. In addition, 'Baal' is mentioned eleven more times in the purge (10:18–28) so that there can be no mistake: the house of Baal falls with the house of Ahab.

The final leitwort reveals the means of judgment. Jehu is commanded to 'strike' (nkh) the house of Ahab (v. 7) and the verb is used nine times more in the narrative (or ten; see 'Notes on the text', 9:27). Six times Jehu strikes Ahab's house (9:24; 10:11, 17), commands it be done (9:27; 10:25) and it is (9:27 [see 'Notes on the text']; 10:25), or queries who struck

Ahab's house (when it is obvious that he did; 10:9). The narrator uses the same verb to describe Jehoram's wounds 'inflicted' by Aram (9:15), and in a final irony Hazael is used in judgment against Jehu, 'striking' Israel (10:32). So crucial is the verb to Jehu's coup that it is used twice more in the preceding bridge (8:28–29).

The narrative is artistically shaped. It begins with Jehu's crowning and ends with a symbolic 'decrowning' as his rule is criticized on Deuteronomistic criteria. The coup progresses in two movements: the first from Ramoth-gilead to Jezreel, the second from Jezreel to Samaria. In the first movement the royal monarchs and the queen mother are executed; in the second the extended family of each member is executed. Each panel ends with scatological references that deride the arch-villain Jezebel and her 'relatives', the house of Baal (adapted from García-Treto 1990: 54):

A	Jehu is king (9:1–14a)	Crowning
	Movement from Ramoth-gilead to Jezreel:	
B	Jehoram killed (9:14b–26)	Israelite king
C	Ahaziah killed (9:27–29)	Judahite king
D	Jezebel killed; left as dung (9:30–37)	Alien queen
	Movement from Jezreel to Samaria:	
B'	Ahab's kin killed (10:1–11; cf. v. 17)	Israelites
C'	Ahaziah's kin killed (10:12–14)	Judahites
D'	Jezebel's 'kin' killed: Baal worshippers; temple made a latrine (10:15–28)	Alien god, followers
A'	Jehu's rule criticized (10:29–31)	Symbolic decrowning

Comment

9:1–14a

1–3. Elisha the prophet's words activate the prophetic commission given Elijah (1 Kgs 19:16). Although Elisha now carries the prophetic mantle (2 Kgs 2:14–15), the commission remains intimately tied to Elijah and he is the prophet of record throughout (9:25–26, 36–37; 10:10, 17).

The 'sons of the prophets' is a group of supporters of Elisha who may function (as here) in prophetic roles (see further at 'Comment', 2 Kgs 2:1–8). The several imperatival-force verbs (see 'Notes on the text', 9:1.a.–3.a) that command the young prophet convey both prophetic authority and the urgency of the events. Jehu's own direct speech contains predominantly imperatival verbs, revealing his self-understanding as acting under the same prophetic authority. The young prophet is to attend the battle at Ramoth-gilead (one of a series of conflicts with Aram; 1 Kgs 20, 22; Arnold, *ABD* 5:620–621), anoint Jehu and flee the potentially dangerous situation.

The double patronymic (9:2, 14; cf. v. 20) for Jehu ('YHWH is he') introduces the otherwise unknown character. The double name suggests Jehu is of a family of note, although its inclusion may be an attempt to bolster his claim to the throne. Contemporary inscriptions from Shalmaneser III refer to him as of the 'house of Omri' but, despite attempts to position Jehu as an Omride (Schneider 1996: 100–107), the inscription is only a favourable reference by an Assyrian overlord that supports and seeks to legitimate a usurper (Na'aman 1998a: 236–238).

4–10. The prophet immediately obeys Elisha. His arrival at Ramoth-gilead is viewed through his eyes (signalled by the *hinnê* marker; v. 5), where he is confronted by many military men from whom he must identify the unknown Jehu. His clever address to 'the captain' prompts Jehu's answer, singling him out as the leader. The inner room (1 Kgs 20:30; 22:25) affords privacy and safety. The anointing initially proceeds as directed but two slight changes 'begin to transform the . . . simple formula into a moment of high drama' (Cohn 2000: 66). First, he further identifies YHWH as 'the God of Israel', making clear it is YHWH (not Baal or any other) who is Israel's God, something Jehu honours in the destruction of the Baal cult. Secondly, he anoints Jehu 'over the people ['*am*] of YHWH', the sacral covenant people (van Groningen 1980: 676), an identity Jehu's rule is to uphold and protect.

The slight changes progress to wholesale additions to Elisha's original words (vv. 7–10a), which take up the focuses of Elijah's ministry – the house of Ahab, and Jezebel – and abuses and concerns previously addressed by YHWH (2 Kgs 21:17–24). First, Jehu is to 'strike' (*nkh*) the 'house of Ahab', now embodied in Jehoram 'his master'. Through this, YHWH will take vengeance for his servants the prophets – perhaps those killed during Ahab's rule (1 Kgs 18:4) – as well as 'all the servants of YHWH' killed at the hand of Jezebel – a probable reference to Naboth (1 Kgs 21:9–10). Secondly, the prophet reissues an oracular word (vv. 8–9) given against the dynasties of Ahab (1 Kgs 21:21–22), Baasha (1 Kgs 16:3–4) and, originally, Jeroboam (1 Kgs 14:10–11), pronouncing similar judgment against each dynasty for walking in the sins of Jeroboam. Thirdly, the young prophet does not repeat the curse of exposure contained in the patterned oracle (14:11; 16:4; 21:24) for its essence has already been fulfilled against Ahab (1 Kgs 22:38). Instead, the prophet formulates the curse against Jezebel (v. 10) whom he credits with many of the evils of Ahab's house (v. 7). The prophet's additions to Elisha's instructions (vv. 7–10) are an example of prophetic (re)interpretation for specific situations and times (something that Elijah has already demonstrated; see 1 Kgs 21:17–24). Despite the reinterpretation, the words are in service to YHWH and stand as true prophecy (Miscall 1989: 76–83).

11–14a. Jehu's compatriots greet him, asking after *šālôm*, ironically revealing they are unaware Ahab's house prevents *šālôm* in the land. They hold the prophet in contempt, calling him *mĕšuggā'* ('madman'; v. 11; see also Jer. 29:26; Hos. 9:7; see Parker 1978: 282–283), but enquire after his message. Despite the anointing oil on his head, Jehu attempts to sidestep their question, discounting the prophet's speech. Their insistence brings only the briefest of summations, signalled by 'thus and so' (Josh. 7:20; 2 Sam. 17:15; 2 Kgs 5:4), and reveals only the anointing. There is no reference to his own commitment to kingship, or the actions proscribed upon him against Ahab's house. He is guarded in revealing his own hand until the military leaders make their commitment known.

The response is hurried and decisive. The cloaks (Matt. 21:8) and trumpets (1 Kgs 1:34; 2 Kgs 11:14) are accompaniments to investiture, but the cry 'Jehu is king' (*mālak* personal name) is not the usual cry of acclamation (*yĕhî hammelek*; 1 Sam. 10:24; 2 Sam. 16:16; 1 Kgs 1:25, 31–39; 2 Kgs 11:12). Rather, it is that used when an individual seeks to establish a claim to the throne (2 Sam. 15:10; see Mettinger 1976: 132; Halpern 1981: 125–136). The military leaders fully support Jehu's claim and the narrator laconically draws the conclusion that Jehu conspires against Jehoram. The coup is set in motion.

9:14b–26

14b–20. The scene cuts to Jezreel, the fortress and central military base at the eastern edge of the Jezreel plain whose walls afford protection for a royal residence (Hunt, *ABD* 3:850; Ussishkin, *NEAEHLSup*:1838–1839). The bridge (8:28–29) has already summarized Jehoram's condition; the repetition of that information brackets the intervening material, signalling that it occurs simultaneous to Jehoram's convalescence in Jezreel. The mention of Jehoram and Ahaziah is ominous, for Jehu is commissioned against them. Jehu first secures Ramoth-gilead to ensure a surprise attack against Jehoram, then sets out for Jezreel, 44 miles (70 km) distant.

The chariot company is spied far off by the lookout, but viewed close up by the reader. Consequently, the lookout can interpret events only while the reader has the complete picture. The company's dust cloud alerts the lookout, and the king dispatches the first horseman to enquire after events at the front. Jehoram can have no suspicions of Jehu for he later goes out unarmed to meet him. Jehu gives a cryptic answer to the ironic greeting and his implication is that no agent of Jehoram can be associated with peace (L. Barré 1988: 73) – only the prophet-inspired rule of Jehu augers peace. Jehu's usurped authority commands the king's man; immediate obedience testifies to the reality of his authority as much as the unrelenting drive towards Jezreel. The lookout reports what he can see of the events and a second rider is dispatched with the same message and the same result. Now the company is close enough that the lookout reports the driving is none other than Jehu's. It is characterized by urgency, 'madly' (*bĕšiggā'ôn*), a word whose root (*śg'*) is the same as that used to describe the 'madman' prophet. In this way Jehu's actions are connected to the prophetic commission.

21–26. Jehoram interprets Jehu's ride as bringing crucial news from the front that cannot be entrusted to messengers. He rides out to receive the news himself and speed any return to the front, entirely without suspicion for his own safety (Nelson 1987: 201; L. Barré 1988: 75, contra Donner 1977a: 409). Ahaziah accompanies him, and perhaps other officers too, but this is not indicated, for only the kings are pertinent to narrative purposes.

Doom is intimated by the introduction of Naboth's property, mentioned several times in the passage (vv. 21, 25–26), but Jehoram remains unaware of the approaching prophetic events. He pursues his original question and now Jehu deigns to answer. His answer does not cite the deeds against Naboth or even the sins of Ahab, although both arise from what Jehu charges. Rather, Jezebel is named as the source of non-*šālôm* in Israel. Her 'harlotries and sorceries' are not to be taken literally but are metaphoric for worship of idols (in this instance Baal and Asherah), and participation in false cults (Montgomery 1951: 402; Cogan 1988: 110; B. Long 1991: 121) – a dual charge only elsewhere levelled against Nineveh (Nah. 3:4). As long as Jezebel's sins remain, Jehu charges, further acts against God's people (such as that against Naboth) will disrupt *šālôm*.

Jehoram finally realizes the danger. Fleeing, he alerts Ahaziah to 'treachery' (*mirmâ*), which from his perspective it is, but from YHWH's perspective it is just judgment against a disobedient house. In Jehu's urgency he 'strikes' (*nkh*) Jehoram with 'full strength' and Jehoram falls. Narrative action ceases while a fulfilment notice is provided by Jehu. He asserts his actions are under the prophetic word and refers to Bidkar as witness to a confirmatory earlier oracle given by Elijah at Naboth's field. The oracle, however, is nowhere recorded – does Jehu fabricate it, or is it a 'free recollection of an oracle of Elijah (1 Kgs. 21:19)' (so Hobbs 1985: 113)? The mention of Naboth's sons is also a new element to Naboth's story, although it is likely they would be killed to ensure no claim be made against the property. Certainly, it comports with the actions of Jezebel and Ahab in 1 Kgs 21 (Keil 1988: 343). Narratively, the mention of the sons serves as a justification for Jehu's intended slaying of Jehoram's sons, contextualizing the coming requital (10:1–7; so Miscall 1989: 79).

The notice of fulfilment provided, Jehoram is unceremoniously dumped on the field, presumably as carrion fodder. This, too, is understood by Jehu as fulfilment of the prophetic word (1 Kgs 21:19, 24).

9:27–29

Ahaziah flees south towards Beth-haggan (modern Jenin; Zertal 1992: 687) on the main road to Jerusalem. Of the house of Ahab, he too must be killed, and Jehu commands he be 'struck' (*nkh*). He is pursued and 'struck' (*nkh*) in the pass of Gur leading to the Dothan Valley, dies in Megiddo and is buried in Jerusalem. The details are sparse (and difficult to comport with those of 2 Chr. 22:9). Ultimately, Ahaziah serves in this narrative only to demonstrate the full extent of the prophetic word against the house of Ahab. In the next chapter the import of his death on Judah is explored. Rather than interrupt the flow of the narrative with a full closing regnal summary, only a brief notation is given. Its discrepant chronology (see 8:25) is due to the variant means in Israel and Judah for accounting regnal years.

9:30–37

The narrative's first panel ends at Jezreel. There Jezebel has already heard of the coup. Knowing that her time is limited, she prepares to greet Jehu – and her death – with queenly dignity. Although it has been argued that her toilette is aimed at seducing Jehu (Parker 1978–9: 67–78), this cannot be the case, for her words of greeting are not in a seductive tone. Her query after *šālôm* is high irony, for she is the one against whom the charge of non-*šālôm* is laid. She aligns Jehu with 'Zimri', the usurper whose reign lasted seven days and ended in suicide (1 Kgs 16:15–19). Her accusatory sarcasm contains the hope Jehu's coup will be similarly ignoble and short-lived.

Jehu ignores the queen's gibe and seeks for those willing to transfer loyalty to him. As with the military officers, only when the eunuchs reveal their commitment does Jehu issue orders. These are characteristically terse and instantly obeyed. The gruesome detail of her blood splattered against the wall provides a feminine counterpart to the prophetic oracles in which those who 'urinate against the wall' (v. 8) are destroyed (García-Treto 1990: 58), and introduces the scatology by which Jezebel is denigrated (see 'Form and structure').

Jehu disregards her and moves inside to eat and drink. The meal suggests a covenantal meal by which he seals a pact with the city elders (Gray 1970: 551; K. Roberts 2000: 632–644), and it may be his softened attitude towards Jezebel (v. 34) reflects a contractual condition. He makes allowance for her burial but the allowance serves only to reveal Jezebel's complete destruction – nothing remains for burial. He affirms that events fulfil the young prophet's curse (v. 10), which itself evokes Elijah's curse (1 Kgs 21:23–24), and fulfils YHWH's word through his servant Elijah. His assertion claims that none should doubt Jehu's coup is YHWH's will.

In addition to the macabre details of her bits and pieces left by the dogs, Jehu adds one more derogatory comment that Jezebel will be as 'dung' (*dmn*) on the face of the field – a scatological detail that neither prophet mentions. The word used is an unusual one (elsewhere 'dung' is *gll* [1 Kgs

14:10] or *ḥr'* [2 Kgs 18:27]). The unusual word may be a wordplay on the Arabic cognate of *dmn*, which is *zbl* ('dung'; Montgomery 1951: 291, 407). If so, the wordplay extends the scatological reference into a snide play upon Jezebel's name (*'yzbl*; see 'Comment' at 1 Kgs 16:31), which contains the element *zbl*.

10:1–11

Jehu now turns to the extended family and supporters of the dead monarchs. The 'seventy sons of Ahab' are not Ahab's actual children (indeed, some of them are Jehoram's sons: vv. 2–3, 6–7) but signify descendants of Ahab: his house. At least some of these 'sons' are still under age, for Jehu includes 'guardians' (*'ōmĕnîm*; as at Num. 11:12; Ruth 4:16; Esth. 2:17; Isa. 49:23) as recipients of the letters (vv. 1, 5; cf. v. 6).

In the first letter Jehu dispatches to the various leaders of the city (Wray Beal 2007: 105–106) he suggests they have a strong hand to resist him. He urges them to be faithful to their covenant obligations to the house of Ahab and defend a new Omride king. Of course, unstated in the letter is the threat that he now holds the crown, having successfully usurped power. The leaders are well able to read between the lines and are utterly afraid (the Hebrew double-intensifies the expression of fear; here 'terribly afraid'), and their capitulation is almost comical in its abject excess. They claim themselves to be Jehu's servants, not Ahab's, and commit to doing whatever he says. Although they have not fought for Ahab's house, neither will they make anyone king (despite Jehu's command). They will do what is 'good' (*haṭṭôb*) in his eyes (despite the fact they were to select the 'best' [*haṭṭôb*] of Ahab's sons for the throne). They have shrewdly discerned Jehu's real request to abandon their covenant obligations to Ahab and institute a new contractual relationship with him. The letter exchange, including declarations of subservience and loyalty, negotiates this new covenant according to ANE parameters (Kalluveettil 1982: 140–159).

Jehu accepts their proffered covenant with his words 'If you are for me', and presses his advantage with his next request – but what is it he really asks for? Does he ask for the literal 'heads' of the seventy, or the 'chief' men of the seventy? The word *rō'š* bears either interpretation (see 'Notes on the text'), as does his next command that they 'come' to him (with the heads, or with the leaders?). The request's ambiguity is intentional: Jehu does wish the sons dead, but he also desires deniability (which he asserts in the next scene).

The leaders interpret the ambiguous request as they were intended to and the seventy are killed and dispatched post-haste. One suspects the leaders in Samaria hope Jehu will no longer bother them, a hope dashed when Jehu arrives in Samaria with bloody consequences (v. 17). Jehu's anticipation of the heads' arrival shows in his utter lack of surprise, and they are laid at the city gates, following the Assyrian practice (*ARI* 2:546; *ANEP* 236) to ensure the population's submission. It works.

Jehu's words on the morrow are a study in manipulation. He credits the people with innocence regarding the events, allaying any fear of reprisal. He also credits himself with guilt regarding the conspiracy (which by now would be obvious to all). His admission is manipulative, for were he guilty of the sons' death, one assumes he would claim responsibility for that too. He does not, and leaves the conclusion open as to who 'struck' (*nkh*) the men. He thus absolves himself of this guilt while justifying the acts as fulfilling YHWH's word (v. 10 [twice]) spoken through his servant Elijah. He does not produce a specific prophetic word, but relies on a general application of the word against the house of Ahab. One must wonder how correct is his claim that YHWH's word applies to the wholesale slaughter of Ahab's relations.

Jehu's final act in Jezreel interprets YHWH's word against Ahab's house to its stretching point. He massacres all who claim allegiance to Ahab's house: great men, acquaintances, priests – even those related by allegiance rather than blood are not safe from Jehu.

10:12–14

The second panel (10:1–28) moves events to Samaria. Jehu encounters the extended 'house' of Ahab at Beth-eked, the 'house of binding', whose location though disputed lies en route between Jezreel and Samaria (Hunt, *ABD* 1:685). The relatives seem unaware of events, willingly acknowledging they travel to 'visit' (*lĕšālôm*; the word's final occurrence in the chapter) the royal family. The 'great lady' is probably Jezebel, although it may be some other powerful woman at court (see 'Comment', 1 Kgs 15:13).

The final occurrence of *šālôm* in ch. 10 proves fatal for the kinsmen of Ahaziah. Jehu utters his usual imperative command, it is summarily obeyed and the relatives of Ahaziah are slaughtered at the house of binding as was Ahaziah at the house of the garden (Beth-haggan). None are spared, as Ahab's house is systematically exterminated.

10:15–28

Jehu's second encounter en route to Samaria follows the same pattern as his meeting with Ahaziah's relatives. In both, Jehu 'went' (*hlk*; vv. 12, 15) and met (*mṣ'*; vv. 13, 15) individuals with whom he dialogues (vv. 13b–14a, 15b–16). The first encounter ends in a massacre, with none spared (vv. 14, 17–28). This second encounter, however, has a variant, for Jehonadab is not himself killed but serves as a witness to Jehu's great 'zeal' demonstrated in the carnage at Samaria.

15–17. Little is definitely known of Jehonadab son of Rechab. Nothing in the narrative suggests his membership in, or founding of, a nomadic, ultra-conservative Yahwistic group as is often argued. Nor can the much later text in Jer. 35 in which the Rechabites again appear be necessarily construed as denoting such a sect, nor be read back over two centuries as a description of Jehonadab (Pope 1962). With slightly more success he can be identified by his name. Names with the element *ndb* are often members of noble families, while the element *ben* (son of) may indicate he is a member of a guild, in this case of chariot makers ('Rechab' [*rēkāb*] suggesting 'chariot' [*rekeb*]) or metalworkers. 'Rechab' may even indicate his occupation as a chariot driver (Frick 1971; Knights 1993; Huffmon 2009).

Whatever Jehonadab's identity, it is his function in the narrative that is of importance. He serves as a bridge, connecting Jehu's journey to the events in Samaria where Jehonadab has a role. There he serves as a witness to Jehu's actions, a role similarly played by Bidkar (9:25), servants (9:36) and townspeople (10:10). Charged to come and see Jehu's 'zeal' for YHWH, Jehonadab's presence witnesses such zeal in Jehu's actions. Jehonadab is to see Jehu's 'zeal (*qin'â*) for YHWH', a characterization used of very few individuals. Phinehas shows 'zeal' when he kills an Israelite involved in foreign worship (Num. 25:11), but Elijah is the only other who is characterized as showing 'zeal for YHWH' (1 Kgs 19:10, 14). Like Elijah, Jehu's zeal is demonstrated against Baalism and thus continues Elijah's ministry.

In preparation for his role as witness, Jehu and Jehonadab form a pact or covenant. Jehu tests Jehonadab's allegiance and, when it is revealed, Jehu offers his hand. The phrase 'give me your hand' is elsewhere indicative of covenant making (Ezra 10:1–5, 19; 17:18; Lam. 5:6; 1 Chr. 29:24; 2 Chr. 30:8; see Kalluveettil 1982: 23). Further, Jehu takes Jehonadab 'up into the chariot', an indication of covenanted relationship (1 Kgs 20:33). The exchange signifies a union of minds, and Jehonadab's submission to Jehu.

Jehu's first zealous act in Samaria is to 'strike' (*nkh*) Ahab's remaining supporters. After each similar action Jehu has provided a prophetic word of justification (9:26–27, 36–37; 10:10). Now the narrator affirms Jehu's actions are 'according to the word of YHWH that he spoke by Elijah'. There may have been doubt regarding the veracity of Jehu's justifications before; now the narrator sets those doubts aside.

18–28. Jehu has purged the house of Ahab: its monarchs and queen, and its extended house. Now his final act is against the 'house' of the foreign queen by whom Baal worship entered Israel. The whole tenor of Jehu's coup suggests he will destroy the house of Baal and its worshippers, yet his actions on the surface appear to support the cult. The narrator's aside (v. 19) reveals Jehu constructs an elaborate subterfuge, and thus his actions and words are double-edged.

First, as expected of a new king, Jehu takes up the religious commitments of the capital city (Donner 1977a: 411–412; B. Long 1991: 139). He asserts he will 'serve' (*ya'abdenû*, from *'bd*) much more than Ahab 'served' ('*ābad*) Baal. This assertion, however, is negated by his true intent, which is to 'destroy' (*ha'ăbîd*, from *'bd*) the worshippers of Baal: the roots of 'to serve' and 'to destroy' sound identical, and underline Jehu's subterfuge. Further, both Jehu and the narrator call the ones to be destroyed 'worshippers' (qal part. of *'bd*, 'those who serve'; vv. 19–23), while the worshippers of YHWH are designated by a construct noun of the same root (v. 23). The distinction is subtle but crucial: only the second group is the true worshippers and only they will escape the purge. The Baalists, however, do not have their hearing so attuned; the segregating distinction slides by them, as did the true import of Jehu's segregation of the worshippers of Baal.

Secondly, Jehu promises a 'great sacrifice' (*zebaḥ gādôl*) to Baal (v. 19). Elsewhere in the DH the term denotes a sacrifice of false priests (1 Kgs 13:2; 2 Kgs 23:20). The Baalists apparently envision a sacrifice such as usually offered Baal; they do not perceive that they themselves are the sacrifice. Finally, Jehu's cunning appears in his call to 'Sanctify an assembly to Baal.' Using terminology familiar in the ritual world (see 'Notes on the text'), the Baalists are again assured Jehu supports Baalism. Of course, Jehu plans the exact opposite. The irony the Baalists do not perceive is that Deuteronomistic worship could never condone the worship of foreign gods as holy (Deut. 5:7–9; Josh. 23:66–68; 1 Kgs 14:9; 21:26 *et passim*). Jehu merely speaks their language to lure them to destruction.

His subterfuge endures through three phases of public preparation (vv. 18–21, 22–23a, 23b–24), and each phase ends with the notation that they 'entered' the temple. As each phase ends, one anticipates that the 'sacrifice' will take place, but each time it is put off and narrative tension builds. In the first phase Jehu gathers Baal's adherents, emphasizing that 'all' must attend', 'none should be missing' and 'not a man was left who did not come' (vv. 19, 21) – but the sacrifice is postponed. In the second, he further distinguishes them by vesting them in ritual garments, making them easy marks for the slaughter that will ensue – but again the sacrifice is postponed. In the third, he charges the Baalists to ensure the segregation is complete. Yet, while 'all' gather and are prepared for slaughter, Jehu secretly prepares eighty men, charged to let none escape.

The public and private preparations complete, the 'sacrifice' is quickly executed and Jehu issues three abrupt imperative commands that are obeyed to the full ('Go in! Kill them! Let no one come out'; v. 25). The Baalists are struck (*nkh*) and their bodies thrown out to degradation. The shrine of the house is desecrated and the pillar and altar destroyed (see 'Notes on the text'). The ultimate desecration is to turn the house of Baal into a latrine; as with Jezebel, the house's destruction concludes with scatological references.

Jehu's eradication of Baal worship is in reality neither complete nor lasting: archaeological evidence supports its continuance in Israel, and Hosea's eighth-century prophecy condemns it (e.g. 2:13). But here, to support the narrative concern with fulfilment of the prophetic word against all aspects of the house of Ahab, including the house of Baal, Jehu is remembered as 'eradicating' Baal from Israel.

10:29–35

The preamble to Jehu's final regnal assessment notes YHWH's approval of Jehu: he has done 'well', 'what was right in my eyes' and 'all that was in my heart' (v. 30). The terminology is astonishing, for Jehu is the only northern king who acts in these ways; in this his comparison resembles those southern kings who are compared favourably to David. By this criterion Jehu is approved, and for this receives a limited dynastic promise. However, the approval is not wide-ranging. It is given only in recognition of the judgment against Ahab effected by his coup.

The approval of Jehu is not the final, nor the prominent, word in the evaluation. Surrounding the one verse of approval is a twice-repeated, familiar refrain: Jehu returns to the sins of Jeroboam (vv. 29, 31). By this Deuteronomistic criterion Jehu is disapproved and this is the defining word on his career despite his 'successes' regarding Ahab.

Because Jehu continues to walk in Jeroboam's sins, his coup, which sought to restore *šālôm*, ultimately falls short. Israel still worships idols, and worships outside Jerusalem (1 Kgs 14:9). Evidential of Israel's ongoing sin and YHWH's disapproval, YHWH disciplines Israel through loss of land. It is highly ironic that, in a narrative in which Jehu has consistently 'struck' the house of Ahab, he now is 'struck' (*nkh*) by Hazael.

The narrative concludes with the typical regnal summary. Added is the number of years Jehu ruled, which would usually appear in the opening formula. Additionally, 'he did not turn from them' introduces a notation that henceforth is included in the introductory summary of northern kings until Pekah (15:28; cf. 2 Kgs 3:3; Campbell 1986: 144).

Explanation

Jehu's coup is an exciting narrative. It moves quickly, acts decisively and has intrigue. It is also exceptionally bloody. But while the narrative does not shy from depicting that, it makes no explicit comment against it. That comment is found elsewhere (Hos. 1:4) as Jehu's bloody excess is judged.

The narrative does show implicit signs that the progress of Jehu's coup and his character are considered less than favourably by Dtr (Wray Beal 2007). His character is by turns cunning, deceitful and manipulative. This portrayal does not necessitate disapproval of his actions, but Dtr takes no pains to sanitize Jehu: he is a fully dimensional character, not a glowing hero who fulfils the prophetic word. Jehu also at several points claims the prophetic word as justification for his actions – but it is not always clear whether he claims true words, or manufactures them for his own purposes. This uncertainty characterizes Jehu in ambiguous terms. Finally, Jehu conspires and strikes his master – an action that earlier drew YHWH's judgment (1 Kgs 16:7) – and that contrasts the righteous model of David, who refuses to strike Saul (1 Sam. 26:8–9) but waits upon YHWH's timing.

Added to these implicit characterizations by which Jehu is drawn in ambiguous terms are the explicit judgments he receives. He is fully approved for executing the prophetic word against Ahab's house, but he is fully disapproved for his continuance in the sins of Jeroboam. The tension of approval and disapproval makes Jehu an ambiguous character and points towards the passage's theological meaning. However much Jehu fulfils the prophetic word (and the implicit characterizations raise questions about even these actions of Jehu), it is his stance vis-à-vis Jeroboam's sins that determines how he is remembered. The narrative shows a ranking of considerations towards kingly evaluation, as it has throughout 1 – 2 Kings. Obedience to the prophetic word, success in battle, building projects – all these count as less than obedience to the deutero-nomic laws for correct worship. Any king who fails in this latter regard cannot be approved.

The purpose of the ambiguity surrounding Jehu's character becomes even clearer later in the history when Josiah conducts his great reform (2 Kgs 22 – 23). Comparison between the two kings highlights Josiah's righteousness and proves the centrality of Deuteronomistic worship in evaluating kingship. Both Jehu and Josiah are reformers and can be compared on that score. But the comparison goes deeper and rests upon an explicit comparison made between Manasseh and Ahab (2 Kgs 21). Manasseh is the unrighteous southern king (2 Kgs 21) who is twice compared to Ahab (vv. 3, 13) for introducing foreign worship to Judah that includes both Baal and Asherah worship (vv. 2–15). Additionally, only of Ahab and Manasseh is it stated that they 'acted abominably' or 'committed abominations' by going after 'idols' as the 'Amorites' had done (1 Kgs 21:26; 2 Kgs 21:11). If Ahab is the northern apostate, Manasseh is his southern counterpart.

Jehu reforms Ahab's sins; Josiah reforms Manasseh's sins, drawing the analogy further: if Jehu is the northern reform, Josiah is his southern counterpart. The analogy is reinforced when the reformers are more closely compared: both did 'right in the eyes of YHWH' according to 'all that was in [his] heart' (2 Kgs 10:30; 22:2); both remove Baal's pillar or vessels and burn them (10:26; 23:4); both depose idolatrous priests, although only Jehu uses duplicitous methods (10:25; 23:5). The differences between the two reformers is also instructive: Josiah destroys the Asherah (23:6) but Jehu does not; Josiah destroys the Bethel altar (23:15–16) but Jehu worships the calves there (10:29, 31); Josiah destroys the high places (23:19–20) but Jehu does not (10:29; cf. 1 Kgs 12:31).

While the reformers are drawn as analogues, it is where the analogy slips that is instructive. Both set out to reform, but it is Jehu's coup that falls short of its goal. Because the sins of Jeroboam remain, true šālôm is not attained. The temple built by the man of peace ('Solomon', šĕlōmô) is the place at which exclusive worship of YHWH must take place in the Deuteronomistic world view. Jehu fails in the pursuit of šālôm while Josiah restores it. Deuteronomistic worship is re-established by him not only in the Jerusalem temple, but is extended outwards as far as Bethel, the seat of Jeroboam's cult. What Jehu fails to do, Josiah completes.

A fundamental difference between the two reformers accounts for the different outcomes. That difference is the state of their heart. While Jehu fulfils all of YHWH's heart regarding the house of Ahab, he does not 'walk in the torah of YHWH . . . with all his heart' and so follows in the way of Jeroboam (v. 31). For this he is not approved. Of Josiah it is said that he 'turned to YHWH with all his heart and with all his soul, and with all his strength according to all the torah of Moses' (23:25). There is ambiguity in Jehu, but not Josiah. His heart is right and so his actions – and specifically his worship – are right and he is fully approved.

Josiah's reforms fully redress Jehu's failures regarding worship, but they also fully redress Solomon's failures. Like Jehu, Solomon's worship fails according to Deuteronomistic norms. As it was for Jehu and Josiah, so it is for Solomon: the issue lies with the heart. Solomon loved YHWH (1 Kgs 3:3) but he came to love his foreign wives (11:1–4) and thus his heart was turned away to their gods.

Each of Solomon, Jehu and Josiah can be viewed through their submission to the great commandment placed upon Israel to hear the law and 'love YHWH your God with all your heart' (Deut. 6:5). The failure to hear and love affects these kings' worship for good or ill. In analogy to Jehu and Solomon, Josiah's life is one that exhibits wholehearted love of YHWH, and he is approved without qualification (2 Kgs 22:2; 23:25). For Dtr a heart that does not love YHWH ends in wrong worship. It is this that ultimately matters, for one's heart and one's worship are the measures by which all other actions are weighed.

Josiah remains an encouragement to righteous leadership. His godly legacy flows from his undivided heart. Would that Jehu's life were heard as a cautionary tale.

2 KINGS 11:1–20

Translation

[1]When Athaliah the mother of Ahaziah saw that her son was dead, she proceeded to destroy all the royal family. [2]Jehosheba, King Joram's daughter, Ahaziah's sister,

took Joash, Ahaziah's son[a], and stole[b] him from among the king's sons who were being put to death. *She put* him and his nurse in the bedroom and they hid him from Athaliah so he was not killed. [3]He was hidden with her in the house of YHWH six years while Athaliah ruled over the land.

[4]In the seventh year Jehoiada sent and brought the commanders of the hundreds of the Carites and the guards. He brought them to him in the house of YHWH, made a pact with them and put them under oath in the house of YHWH. Then he showed them the king's son. [5]He commanded them, saying, 'This is what you shall do: the third of you who come on duty on the Sabbath shall guard[a] the king's house, [6]with one third at the Gate Sur[a], and one third at the gate behind the guards. You shall guard the palace[b]. [7]And your two divisions who go off duty on the Sabbath shall guard the house of YHWH for the king. [8]You shall surround the king, each with his weapons in his hand, and whoever enters the ranks shall be killed. Be with the king as he goes out and comes in.'

[9]So the captains of the hundreds did just as Jehoiada the priest commanded. Each man took his men who were coming on duty on the Sabbath together with those who were going off duty on the Sabbath, and they came to Jehoiada the priest. [10]The priest gave to the captains of the hundreds the spears[a] and quivers[b] that had belonged to King David, which were in the house of YHWH. [11]The guards stood, each with his weapon in his hand, from the south side of the house to the north side of the house, at the altar and the house, all around the king. [12]Then he brought out the king's son and set the crown on him and gave him the testimony. They proclaimed him king and anointed him, clapped hands and said, 'Long live the king!'

[13]Athaliah heard the noise of the guard *and of* the people and she came to the people in the house of YHWH. [14]She looked and, behold, the king was standing by the pillar, according to the custom, and the commanders[a] and trumpeters were beside the king with all the people of the land rejoicing and blowing trumpets. Then Athaliah tore her clothes and cried out, 'Treason! Treason!' [15]Jehoiada the priest commanded the captains of the hundreds appointed over the army. He said to them, 'Escort her out between the ranks and whoever follows after her put to death with the sword.' For the priest said, 'Let her not be put to death in the house of YHWH.' [16]So they laid hands on her, and when she came to the entryway of the horses at the king's house, she was put to death there.

[17]Then Jehoiada made a covenant between YHWH and the king and the people, that they would be YHWH's people, and between the king and the people. [18a]And all the people of the land went to the house of Baal and tore it down. Its altars and images they thoroughly broke in pieces, and Mattan the priest of Baal they killed before the altars. And the priest posted sentries over the house of YHWH. [19]He took the captains of the hundreds, and the Carites, and the guards, and all the people of the land, and they brought the king down from the house of YHWH. They entered through the Guard's Gate to the king's house, and he sat upon the throne of the kings. [20a]And all the people of the land rejoiced, and the city was quiet, for they had killed Athaliah with the sword at the king's house.

Notes on the text

2.a MT 'Ahaziah's son' (*ben-'ăhazyâ*) reads in LXX* 'her brother' (*ben-'ăhîhā*); the two readings are similar in appearance and the change could easily occur; LXX[L] conflates the readings.

2.b. Qal of *gnb*, 'stole', used of kidnapping in Exod. 21:16; Deut. 24:7; 2 Sam. 19:41[42]; (pu.) Gen. 40:15.

5.a. Reading MT *wĕšômĕrê*, 'the guards of', as *wĕšāmĕrû*, 'they shall guard', for sense (see v. 7). So Montgomery 1951: 424; Cogan 1988: 124.

6.a. The 'Sur' (*sûr*) Gate is unknown. 2 Chr. 23:5 reads the 'Foundation' (*yĕsôd*) Gate. Gray (1970: 571) suggests as possible 'Horse' (*sûs*) Gate in the light of vv. 16, 19.

6.b. The hapax *massâ* is omitted, with LXX as unintelligible.

10.a. 'Spears' (*hahănît*) read as pl. with 2 Chr. 23:9.

10.b. 'Shields' is often the translation of *šĕlāṭîm* (NASB, NRSV, NIV, NET) but LXX reads the items as 'spears and lances' (LXX[L] 'spears and quivers'). 2 Chr. 23:9 adds another item, *māginnôt*, 'shields' (thus 'spears, and shields [*māginnôt*] and *šĕlāṭîm*'). HALOT translates *šĕlāṭîm* as 'quivers' at Jer. 51:11; Ezek. 27:11; Song 4:4; and here.

14.a. MT *wĕhaśśārîm*, 'commanders, leaders', is *wĕhaššārîm*, 'singers', in LXX, Vg. 2 Chr. 23:13 appears to know the LXX and combines the two readings: 'with the commanders and trumpeters . . . the people rejoicing . . . blowing trumpets and the singers with instruments'. Gray objects to the people's possessing trumpets (but see 1 Kgs 1:40 for the people's playing musical instruments at a similar event) and removes the first occurrence ('and trumpeters') and reads, 'the people rejoicing and sounding of trumpets' (Gray 1970: 576).

18.a. *BHS* suggests transposing the verse after v. 20, that is, after all aspects of the king's investiture are completed. But the verse should remain as the appropriate action after the covenant made with YHWH.

20.a. MT ends at v. 20; English v. 21 is MT 12:1. MT is preferred, as MT 12:1 is better included as an element of the regnal introduction.

Form and structure

The death of Ahaziah at Jehu's hand sparks a bloody coup in the southern kingdom as Athaliah seizes power. The threat to the Davidic dynasty is set aside only when the priest deposes the imposter queen and her Baal cult. The parallels to the downfall of Jezebel and her cult are marked, but the southern coup is less widespread in its destruction.

Two sources are generally delineated in the critical discussion: one 'political' or 'official' (vv. 1–12, 18b–20) and one 'populist' or 'religious' (vv. 13–18a) (so Montgomery 1951: 418; Gray 1970: 566–567; Jones 1984b: 475–476). The delineation is based on factors such as the supposed repetition of Athaliah's death (vv. 16, 20), and variant spellings of her name (*'ătalyāhû* in vv. 2, 20; *'ătalyâ* elsewhere). The sources are also delineated by action either instigated by a politically motivated official group headed by the priest, or a religiously motivated populist group headed by the 'people of the land' (see further in 'Comment').

The narrative can be explained as arising from a single source (Cogan 1988: 131; Hobbs 1985: 135). As such, Athaliah's 'second' death is a summative statement rather than a disparate accounting. The variations in name are not uncommon (see e.g. Jehoram/Joram [cf. 2 Kgs 1:17 with 8:16, 21 *et passim*] or Joash/Jehoash in this chapter [vv. 2, 21(12:1)]) and names can appear in both forms even within one source (Athaliah in short form in vv. 1, 3, and long in v. 2). Finally, delineating a politically motivated official source and a religiously motivated populist source is untenable, for many of the characteristics credited to one source are present in both source traditions. For instance, the 'people of the land', supposedly indicative of the populist source (see above), also appear in the 'official' source (vv. 19–20) and a commanding 'official' presence appears everywhere in the narrative. Nor can political action be isolated from religious action, as both are tied together under Israel's national life forged in the Sinaitic and Davidic covenants.

The narrative follows a simple structure:

A   Introduction (vv. 1–3)
　　B   Davidic king re-established (vv. 4–12)
　　　　C   Imposter queen dethroned (vv. 13–16)
　　B'   Covenantal relationship re-established (vv. 17–19)
A'   Epilogue (vv. 20)

The problem is introduced in the introduction, and only the rescue of Joash anticipates the solution. Vv. 4–12 and 13–16 move from illegitimate to legitimate Davidic rule, culminating in Athaliah's death (v. 16), the last of a notorious family. With legitimate rule re-established, the narrative reasserts several covenantal relationships. Wholly Yahwistic, the covenants naturally lead to the destruction of the house of Baal. Once the wicked queen and her wicked cult are dethroned, the rightful king ascends the throne of David. The epilogue emphasizes, in terms reminiscent of the period of the judges, that Athaliah's demise results in rejoicing and quietness.

Comment

11:1–3

The regnal formulae at 10:34–36 and 12:1–3 mark this narrative as a distinct unit. It nevertheless remains intimately connected to the events of chs. 9–10. Ahaziah's death recalls 9:27–29 and anticipates the effect of that murder upon the southern kingdom. That Athaliah is an Omride (8:18, 26) anticipates that the fate prophesied against the Omrides similarly awaits her.

Athaliah seizes power and 'destroys' (*'bd*) all the royal family, mimicking the ferocity of Jehu, who likewise 'destroyed' (*'bd*) his enemies (10:19) and royal claimants. More than simple greed for power, the massacre removes any scion who might summon conservative Davidic and Yahwistic factions against her (as Jehoram himself apparently did; 2 Chr. 21:4). Athaliah rules over Judah for six years (v. 3), an anomaly in Israel where rule inheres in the male line. As both an Omride and a woman, her rule is illegitimate and Dtr never refers to her as a queen, nor provides regnal summaries for her 'reign'.

The 'all' massacred is hyperbolic, but correctly represents the dire state of affairs for the Davidic house. Only one escapes: Joash, rescued by Jehosheba his aunt. She is Jehoram's daughter and Ahaziah's sister. As his sister, she opposes her own mother, hiding the infant and his wet nurse in an inner room while the massacre sweeps by. As Jehoiada's wife (2 Chr. 22:11), her care for the child in the temple would raise no suspicions, especially if he were presented as Jehosheba's own son or an acolyte.

The temple is a holy place capable of sheltering the child. It is contrasted to areas outside its precincts where Athaliah rules 'over the land' (v. 3). Through the remainder of the narrative the temple's holiness is incrementally extended against the foreign queen, until ultimately the throne, land and people are cleansed for YHWH.

11:4–12

Jehoiada initiates his plan in Athaliah's seventh year. The chronological notation need not indicate a Sabbath year (a similar notation introduces the Sabbath year in Deut. 15:1; cf. Lev. 25:4), nor evoke a posited enthronement festival that Jehoiada uses as a backdrop for the planned events (contra Widengren 1957: 7; Gray 1970: 180). Rather, the notation is a common trope that introduces a climactic event in a series (one thinks of the seventh day of creation, or the seventh march around Jericho; see McCurley 1974: 67–73). The trope suggests Jehoiada's careful preparation for climactic re-establishment of the Davidic throne.

The priest (although not acknowledged as such until v. 9) has evident authority, for he gathers and commands several military units. The 'commanders of the hundreds' (a similar role elsewhere commands a larger group; 1 Sam. 22:7) command 'Carites' and 'guards'. Little else is known of the Carites beyond their loyalty to the Davidic house. Evidence is inconclusive for any relationship to the Cherethites of 2 Sam. 8:18; 20:23 (Q); 1 Kgs 1:38, 44. Nor is their identification supported by Carian mercenaries from south-west Anatolia who serve in foreign courts (Ehrlich, *ABD* 1:872). With them are the 'guards' (*rāṣîm*, lit. 'those who run') who elsewhere serve in several capacities (2 Sam. 15:1; 1 Kgs 1:5; 2 Kgs 10:25). Their assignment here at several of the citadel gates (v. 6) accords with service such 'guards' render elsewhere (1 Kgs 14:27).

It is twice noted that the priest's plan begins in the temple (v. 4 [twice]). From that holy locus the action moves progressively outwards, cleansing and restoring covenantal life (B. Long 1995). Priest and military enter a pact, a *bĕrît* (later translated as 'covenant'; v. 17), and only under this solemn and binding agreement does the priest reveal the king's son. His intention for this son is apparent, for he refers to Joash as 'king' (vv. 7, 8 [twice]) before he is crowned.

The description of Jehoiada's plan to deploy his forces (vv. 5–7) is unclear in the MT. However, it is clear the deployment is to afford ultimate protection to the king as he is brought to public attention. It involves three military units. The first, coming on guard duty, is dispatched by thirds to key stations around the palace (vv. 5–6). The location of the Gate Sur is unknown, as is the 'gate behind the guards', but deployment of forces to these locations is meant to provide an appearance of 'business as usual' (lest any suspicion be roused in the palace and Athaliah stave off the counter-coup). The remaining two military units, those who would normally be off guard duty, are stationed in the temple to guard the king (note the triple mention of 'king', vv. 7–8) wherever he goes. On high alert and armed, they are under orders to kill any who threaten Joash (similar construal of Jehoiada's plan is found in Hobbs 1985: 140; Cogan 1988: 127).

At the changing of the guard, when the extra activity would be least likely noticed, the plan is executed 'just as Jehoiada the priest commanded' (v. 9). The subsequent narration focuses upon the temple where the king will be revealed. The men are armed with spears and quivers (possibly the ones David took from Hadadezer [2 Sam. 8:7]). They were part of temple stores that included at least ceremonial shields (1 Kgs 14:26–27). The difficulty of translation for both these terms (see 'Notes on the text') has led to suggestions that the guards are given one spear and a shield that were David's own and that were to be given the young king as symbols of royal power (Gray 1970: 572–573; Jones 1984b: 480; Provan 1995: 222). Yet the items never appear in this guise at the coronation, and the context in which the items are given out is one of danger in which weaponry (and not symbols of royal power) would be expected.

The armed guards are deployed throughout the temple, from its outer reaches inwards towards the altar in preparation to surround the king. Commissioned by the priest, the guards function in the Levitical role of enclosing the sacred centre (Num. 1:53), thus 'converting the secret refuge (v. 3a) into a public, royal, and sacralized sanctuary' (B. Long 1991: 150).

Into this context of public holiness the Davidic king is introduced so that all the people present (v. 13) serve as witnesses. The king receives (presumably from Jehoiada) a *nēzer*, a diadem or headpiece signifying consecration and worn by kings (1 Sam. 1:10; Pss 89:39[40]; 132:18) and priests (Exod. 29:6; Lev. 8:9). He is also given the *'ēdût*, a word used of the divinely ordained laws of the covenant (Deut. 4:45; 6:17) that kings were charged to keep (Deut. 17:18–20; 1 Kgs 2:3; Ps. 132:12). The king receives a copy of this law, or a token reminder of his responsibility to keep it. The *'ēdût* may also signify a royal protocol of adoption, which in Israel is encapsulated in the Davidic Covenant, once again tying the *'ēdût* closely to the divine law the Davidic king is to uphold (von Rad 1966: 225–229; Gray 1970: 573–574; Hobbs 1985: 141).

The king is then proclaimed and anointed (the verbs are plural, signifying the corporate nature of these acts), and the people affirm the action with noise (clapping, instruments [vv. 13–14; cf. 1 Kgs 1:38–40]) and the traditional acclamatory cry 'Long live the king!' (1 Sam. 10:24; 2 Sam. 16:16; 1 Kgs 1:25, 31–39).

11:13–16

In order for the complete re-establishment of the Davidic throne, the imposter queen must be deposed. The action begins when Athaliah, intrigued by the noise, traces its source. What she encounters in the temple is viewed through her personal perspective (indicated by the word *hinnê*, 'behold'). She instantly recognizes a coronation has occurred (the word 'king' is twice used in v. 14), for, besides the crown, *'ēdût*, anointing oil and noise of the people and the military, she observes the king standing 'by the pillar' (*'al-hā'ammûd*). In the parallel Chronicles account (2 Chr. 23:13) the pillar is 'at the entrance' of the temple and probably signifies one of Jachin or Boaz (1 Kgs 7:21). Built by Solomon and placed at the temple porch, their names mean 'He [YHWH] establishes' and 'In strength', and signify YHWH's legitimation of the Davidic state (Meyers 1983: 167–178). As such, they would easily lend themselves to coronation customs and, as later occurs (v. 17), as part of covenant renewal (cf. 2 Kgs 23:3).

Her torn robe (*wāttiqra'*) anticipates her cry (*wāttiqrā'*; the two words sound very similar). Ironically, what she mourns as 'treason' or 'conspiracy' (*qšr*; cf. 2 Kgs 9:14) is really a covenantal act (vv. 4, 17). Jehoiada again commands and is obeyed and the captains of the army (a higher rank than the captains of hundreds) escort her from the holy premises. As the priest has said (and perhaps previously communicated to the troops), her death must not occur within the holy temple and thus offend the distinctions of holy and profane (B. Long 1995). She is led out and, once she reaches her own domain of the palace, is summarily executed.

11:17–21

Unlike Jezebel's execution, the narrative does not linger over Athaliah's death. It is enough that she is removed from the throne. Instead, the narrative immediately returns to the coronation scene where specific covenantal relationships, interrupted and corrupted by Athaliah's rule, are restored along with Davidic rule. Customarily, the king as possessor of the '*ēdût* would negotiate such covenant renewals (2 Kgs 23:3; before and after the monarchy the role was filled by Moses, Joshua and Ezra as custodians of the law [Widengren 1957]). Given Joash's age, Jehoiada takes the role. The custom, however, is not entirely refashioned, for the king still holds the '*ēdût*.

The covenant has several elements. It reasserts YHWH's covenant with the house of David (2 Sam. 7:11–16; 23:5; 1 Kgs 8:15–16, 25–26; 11:36–38) interrupted by Athaliah's rule. It also invokes the particular relationship of YHWH to his people. In this the phrase 'that they would be YHWH's people' echoes that of Deut. 27:1–10 [v. 9] (cf. Deut. 7:6; 14:2). The phrase takes up the Sinai moment during which the people became YHWH's people (Exod. 19 – 20). Finally, Jehoiada reinstitutes covenant between the king and people. Disrupted during the rule of a non-Davidide, such a covenant has appeared earlier in the history, delineating the king's rule and the people's acceptance (2 Sam. 5:3; 1 Kgs 12; 2 Kgs 23:3).

The natural response to the restored covenant relationship with YHWH is the destruction of the foreign god's house. Whether within the city confines (in palace or even in temple), or outside the city at a high place (Yadin 1978: 130 suggests Ramath-Rahel, 2 miles [3 km] south of Jerusalem), the people tear (*ntṣ*) it down. The action is that of Jehu (10:27) and the destruction, while not as bloody, is as thorough: temple, altars and images are destroyed. Whatever Mattan's pedigree (his name is construed as either Phoenician [Montgomery 1951: 423] or Semitic [Gray 1970: 581]), as priest of Baal he is likewise destroyed. Jehoiada follows up the purge by posting guards around the temple, forestalling any retaliatory action by the followers of the foreign queen and god and ensuring the continued sanctity of the temple precincts.

Participants in the coronation (vv. 13–14) and the purge (v. 18) are 'the people of the land', a term occurring between sixty and seventy times in the OT, and with various interpretative nuances (Nicholson 1965). At times in Kings the 'people of the land' are participants in deposing or installing a Judahite king (2 Kgs 11:14; 21:24; cf. 2 Chr. 36:1). The designation is not intended as a contrast to a group 'of the city', nor does it designate a particular class of rich elites wielding power in support of conservative politics, as is sometimes argued (Würthwein 1936). In monarchic Judah the 'people of the land' denotes all the enfranchised citizenry of Judah (Buccellati 1967: 162–166; Halpern 1981: 192–195; Healey, *ABD* 1:168–169).

After Baal is purged from Jerusalem, the 'people of the land' assemble with the chapter's other key participants. In a procession reminiscent of 1 Kgs 1:38–40 they conduct the king from holy temple to recently cleansed palace. Protected and crowned within holy precincts, invested with emblems of his holy rule, and under the holy offices of a renewed Davidic covenant, the king takes up his seat on the throne of kings (cf. 1 Kgs 1:46). The procession extends the temple's sacral space outwards into palace and city once again (B. Long 1995: 238) and it is no wonder that the people 'rejoice' and the city is 'quiet' (šqṭ). The state of the city is that experienced by Israel after conquering hostile territory (Josh. 11:23; 14:15), or after a judge empowered by YHWH purged foreign oppressors (Judg. 3:11, 30; 5:31; 8:28). YHWH has 'broken the scepter of the wicked' under whom the people were subdued, and there is rest (šqṭ) and rejoicing (Isa. 14:7). The final note of victory is a reminder that Athaliah is dead: killed at the king's house where now the true king sits enthroned.

Explanation

The chapter echoes Jehu's coup in several ways, particularly in the extinction of the foreign queen and her cult. Yet, unlike Jehu's coup, Jehoiada acts without any prophetic direction, and YHWH's voice does not appear in any guise in the chapter. The coup is solely directed by the priest, and derives its moral and theological power from the sacred space of the temple. In it the king is reinstalled and acknowledged, and covenants are reforged. Athaliah is escorted from the sacred space so that her death should not mar it. When the king ascends the palace throne after the false cult is deposed, he extends the temple's holy reach to that civic space. Finally, the people's rejoicing and the quieted land evidence the extension of the temple's holiness further outwards to the people and land.

The chapter is a good example of the maxim 'God's in his heaven, all's right with the world.' In this case, however, the 'rightness' flows from God's holy temple. By the presence of YHWH, the priest's actions are charged with his holiness (see B. Long 1995 for an exploration of the chapter's 'sacred geography').

There are several places, particularly in the psalter, that witness to the special character of the temple as the place of YHWH's power and holiness (e.g. Pss 63, 72, 84), and the account in which YHWH's glory inhabits the temple takes up the same theme (1 Kgs 8:10–11). 2 Kgs 11 presupposes this presence, but shows the extension of that holiness to sanctify other realms. There is in this action a reaching back to early ideals within the biblical narrative as well as a reaching forward to the narrative's eschatological consummation.

In the garden, the holy space inhabited by God's presence and power, all relationships are whole. Adam and Eve live openly as equals and image bearers, in harmony with their physical environment and with YHWH. All areas of life and creation are ordered rightly in YHWH's holy presence.

The sacred space of the garden is next encountered at Sinai. The holy mountain is bounded to prevent unintended intrusion on the sacral space (Exod. 19:12–13). The people are sanctified for proximity to the sacral space and only those specified are granted admission (Exod. 19: 3, 10–11, 24). In the sacred space YHWH communicates the law, extending his holiness outwards to the people.

The law makes provision for entry to the sacred space of the tabernacle (Exod. 25 – 31, 35 – 39; Lev. 1 – 27). YHWH's presence moves from the mountain top to the new cult site (Exod. 40) that will enable sacred space during the desert journey. As the locus for sacrifice, instruction and healing, the sacred tabernacle (like Sinai) extends YHWH's holiness outwards to the life of the community.

The holiness of the temple is also extended in judgment upon Israel. It is in the temple that Isaiah is confronted by YHWH's holiness. He immediately falls to his face, profoundly aware of his own uncleanness. From that holy encounter Isaiah is commissioned outwards to bring the message of judgment (Isa. 6:8–13). It is by this judgment at the hand of Assyria (and later Babylon) that the 'holy God will be proved holy' (Isa. 5:16). The temple's sacred space is only a result of YHWH's presence. YHWH abandons the temple during the exile to continue his commitment to dwell with his people, though in exile (Ezek. 1, 10).

The image of the temple's sacred space extending outwards remains alive in Israel's eschatological reflections and in the NT. Isa. 2 envisions a last-days temple on Mount Zion, raised far above all other mountains. Its influence extends beyond Mount Zion, drawing to it all nations. Like the tabernacle and the Solomonic temple, the eschatological temple extends YHWH's teaching outwards – only no mention is made of prophet, priest or king in the role of teacher; it springs immediately from YHWH himself (vv. 3–4) and restores peace between peoples. There is a return to the Edenic harmony experienced by Adam and Eve in YHWH's presence.

An extended exposition of the eschatological temple is found in Ezek. 40 – 48. There the temple is the centre of a perfected nation and land, and the whole temple area is counted as holy (Ezek. 43:12). Serving in this holy place are restored religious officials (priests and Levites) and a new civic official (the prince). Around the holy precincts the tribal allotments, land boundaries and city are measured in relation to the holy place, and from the temple flows life-giving waters. Finally, the city of Jerusalem, perfected in holiness, receives the new name 'YHWH is there'. Ezekiel's eschatological vision expands the Edenic holiness of relations between YHWH, his people and his land in grand directions. Nothing is left untouched by the extension of YHWH's holy presence in the restored temple.

This perfect Edenic city filled with YHWH's own presence is the basis for John's eschatological vision in the book of Revelation. Yet the holy city of John's vision – perfect in measurements and beautiful in construction – has no temple. YHWH's own presence and that of the slain Lamb, the Christ, fill the city. In them the presence of YHWH (once associated with the temple) extends to and fills the cosmic realms. Sin is defeated; false worship is done away with, as is death, mourning, crying and pain; the old order has passed away (Rev. 21:4–8, 27; 22:3). All nations feel the reach of this new 'temple's' holiness, for they walk by the light of God's glory and bring their own glory to it (21:24). Creation itself answers to God's holy presence as waters flow with life-giving power, trees bear fruit and the nations are healed by their power. Civic powers are done away with, for YHWH exercises all power from his throne (21:5; 22:3), giving assurance of the city's ongoing perfection.

The extension of the temple's holy reach in Jehoiada's countercoup acknowledges that the holiness and power of God extend beyond a sacred building. This anticipates an eschatological time when all comes under the power of YHWH's divine kingship exercised in holiness. Never again will the unrighteous seize power or hold God's people hostage, as did Athaliah. Because God will be in his heaven-on-earth, all will be right with the world.

2 KINGS 11:21 – 12:21[22]

Translation

11:21[12:1]a Jehoash was seven years old[b] when he began to reign. 12:1[2]In the seventh year of Jehu, Jehoash began to reign, and he reigned forty years in Jerusalem. His mother's name was Zibiah of Beer-sheba. 2[3]Jehoash did what was right in the eyes of YHWH all his days[a], for Jehoiada the priest instructed him. 3[4]However, the high places were not removed; the people still sacrificed and burned incense on the high places.

4[5]Jehoash said to the priests, 'All the silver of the holy offerings[a] that is brought into the house of YHWH – silver from the census, silver from each soul's valuation and all the silver each voluntarily brings to the house of YHWH – 5[6]let the priests take for themselves, each from his merchant[a], and repair the damage to the house wherever any damage is found.'

6[7]In the twenty-third year of King Jehoash the priests had not repaired the damage to the house. 7[8]King Jehoash summoned Jehoiada the priest and *the other* priests. He said to them, 'Why have you not repaired the damage to the house? Now, take no more silver from your merchants but give it for damages to the house.' 8[9]So the priests agreed neither to take silver from the people nor to repair damage to the house.

9[10]Jehoiada the priest took a chest and bored a hole in its lid. He put it to the right of the altar[a] as one enters the house of YHWH. The priests who kept the threshold put all the silver in it that was brought into the house of YHWH. 10[11]And whenever they saw that there was a lot of silver in the chest, the king's scribe and the high priest came, tied it up[a] in bags and counted the silver found in the house of YHWH. [11[12]]They gave the silver that was weighed into the hand of[a] the workers appointed over the house of YHWH, and they paid it out to the carpenters and builders who worked on the house of YHWH, [12[13]]and to the masons and stone-cutters to buy[a] timber and hewn stone to repair the damage to the house of YHWH, and for anything laid out on the house for repairs.

[13[14]]However, from the silver that was brought into the house of YHWH no silver basins, snuffers, bowls, trumpets, any vessel of gold or silver were made for the house of YHWH [14[15]]for they gave it to the workers and with it they repaired the house of YHWH. [15[16]]They did not require an accounting from the men into whose hand they gave the silver to pay the workers, for they dealt faithfully. [16[17]]The silver from the guilt offering and the silver from the sin offering[a] was not brought into the house of YHWH; it belonged[b] to the priests.

[17[18]]Then Hazael king of Aram went up and fought against Gath and captured it. When Hazael set his face against Jerusalem, [18[19]]Jehoash king of Judah took all the holy things that Jehoshaphat, Jehoram and Ahaziah, his fathers, kings of Judah, had consecrated, and his own holy things, and all the gold found in the treasuries of the house of YHWH and the king's house and sent *them* to Hazael king of Aram. Then he withdrew from Jerusalem.

[19[20]]The rest of the acts of Jehoash and all that he did, are they not written in the Book of the Chronicles of the Kings of Judah? [20[21]]Then his servants arose and conspired and struck Joash at Beth-millo[a], on the way down to Silla[a]. [21[22]]For Jozabad[a] the son of Shimeath, and Jehozabad[a] the son of Shomer, his servants struck him. He died, and they buried him with his fathers in the City of David, and Amaziah his son reigned in his place.

Notes on the text

11:21[12:1].a. Throughout, English versification is followed in brackets by MT versification.

21[12:1].b. The age of southern monarchs is often included in regnal introductions, although normally appearing after the synchronization. LXX[L] transposes v. 21[1] after the synchronization in 12:1[2].

2[3].a. *kol-yāmāyw* is the expression for 'all his life' (Deut. 22:19; 1 Kgs 15:14 [2 Chr. 15:17]; 2 Kgs 15:18; 2 Chr. 34:33; Eccl. 2:23; 5:16). In 2 Chr. 24:2 the limitation is only while Jehoiada lived (*kol-yĕmê yĕhôyādā'*).

4[5].a. The translation of the sources of income are various (a brief summation appears in B. Long 1991: 156). Here the 'holy offerings' subsume the following detailed offerings.

5[6].a. *makkārô* is often translated, 'his acquaintance', from hiph. part. of *nkr*. LXX[B], 'from his trade', suggests root *mkr*, 'to sell', from which this translation arises (see further at 'Comment').

9[10].a. A perceived problem of the altar placed near the threshold, together with LXX[A] transliteration ἀμμασβη, leads to the emendation *hammaṣṣēbâ* ('pillar'; Burney 1903: 314; Montgomery 1951: 432). The Greek is equivocal; it could also transliterate 'altar' (*hammizbēaḥ*; McKane 1959: 260–261).

10[11].a. 'tied up' reads 'emptied' (*wî'ārû*) in 2 Chr. 24:11. Montgomery 1951: 430 follows Torrey (1936: 255–257; cf. Oppenheim 1947) and envisions the later step of 'minting' or 'casting' (*wayyiṣrû*) the silver into ingots.

11[12].a. Maintaining K 'hand of' to coincide with v. 16, 'their hand'.

12[13].a. 'to buy' omits cop. with LXX.

16[17].a. 'sin offering' sg. with LXX. MT pl. 'they belonged' sg. with LXX, Syr, Vg, and in agreement with sg. 'silver'.

16[17].b. MT pl. 'they belonged' sg. with LXX, Syr, Vg and in agreement with sg. 'silver'.

20[21].a. LXX versions read variant names for both Millo and Silla, and disagreement among commentators exists over the locations, or whether the names are geographic or personal.

21[22].a. The similarity of the two names in MT leads many English versions to use LXX 'Jozacar' for the first name.

Form and structure

2 Kgs 12 is bracketed by the now-familiar regnal formulae (vv. 11:21 – 12:3[12:1–4], 19–21[20–22]). Within this bracket two events are related (vv. 4–16[5–17] and 17–18[18–19]). The selection of only two events from Jehoash's forty-year reign attests to Dtr's theological agenda; only these two events are selected to contribute to his message in 1 – 2 Kings.

The temple and its 'holy things' (*haqqŏdāšîm*; vv. 4[5], 18[19]) thematize each section, for it is the holy offerings that enable the repairs to the temple, and as tribute forestall Hazael's attack. The two episodes demonstrate approved and disapproved uses of the *qŏdāšîm*, and illustrate the mixed evaluation given the king in the regnal introduction.

The priority of temple matters in the two sections led Wellhausen to posit a prior temple history that included 2 Kgs 11 – 12, 22 – 23 (Wellhausen 1889: 293–294). While the theory has not generally been accepted, others have posited a source taken up or authored by priests before incorporation into the DH (Gray 1970: 582–583). However, given the critique of priests in the narrative, the theory is generally rejected (Montgomery 1951: 426; Hobbs 1985: 14; Na'aman 1998b: 337). Several features suggest the two sections are adopted by Dtr from royal archives (Hobbs 1985: 150; B. Long 1991: 160) and include the military report (vv. 17–18[18–19]), the king's institution of the repairs to the national shrine, and the presence of language regarding temple funds and repairs that is similar to that of official Assyrian letters (Hurowitz 1986; see further in 'Comment').

Jehoash's temple repairs are related in a fashion remarkably similar to that of Josiah's later work (22:1–7). In both the money is collected from the people by the identical temple functionaries (12:9[10]; 22:4), and the money is 'brought into the house of YHWH' (12:9[10]; 22:4). In both accounts the high priest prepares the silver for distribution (12:10[11]; 22:4) and it is given 'into the hand of the workers appointed over the house of YHWH' (12:11[12]; 22:5). The workers who receive the funding are described in virtually identical terms and in the same order in both accounts (12:11b–12[12b–13]; 22:6) and 'they did not require an accounting', for the workers 'dealt faithfully' (12:15[16]; 22:7). Finally, the purpose of the funding is stated in identical terms: to 'repair (*ḥzq*) the damage (*bedeq*) to the house of YHWH (*bêt yhwh*)' (12:5–12[6–13], 22:5–6). The more extensive rendering of the account in Jehoash's reign sets in place a system for renovation that Josiah follows (Hobbs 1985: 149; Na'aman 1998b: 338–339). Certainly, as Hobbs argues, the extensive similarities between the accounts are rightly credited to shared authorship and common historical circumstances (Hobbs 1985: 149). But in Dtr's theological history the parallels also highlight a narrative and theological link between the two kings. Jehoash is lauded not only for the reforms, but because they are proleptic of Josiah's greater reform.

The centrality of Jehoash's temple renovations to his overall rule is highlighted by a leitmotif that consists of two words: 'repair' (pi. of *ḥzq* occurs seven times in vv. 5–14[6–15]) and 'damage' (*bedeq*, in vv. 5–12[6–13], occurs six times with 'repair', and once alone). The frequency of occurrence focalizes the passage's primary concern around appropriate treatment of the temple arising from the holy offerings. The leitmotif does not appear in the second episode of Jehoash's reign, which can be accounted for by the different concern of that episode. Its absence, however, further tempers the approval granted Jehoash (see 'Explanation').

Comment

11:21 – 12:3[12:1–4]

The young king's lengthy reign of around forty years (835–797 BC) begins with a notation of his age at accession (11:21 in English texts). It is here included with the regnal introduction, where it would normally be found following the notice of synchronization. Placed prior to the synchronization, it ties this narrative to the preceding chapter (11:4), but the king's young age also explains Jehoiada's ongoing influence (v. 2[3]). That influence may have prompted the king's interest in temple affairs.

The long form of the king's name is consistent throughout the chapter and appears in its short form only in the final regnal summary and its notation of the assassination. This difference may arise from the different

sources upon which Dtr drew. For ease, 'Jehoash' will be used throughout
these comments. Jehoash's long reign of thirty-eight full years and two
partial years (835–797 BC; see DeVries, *IDB* 1:589) coincides with three
northern monarchs (Jehu, Jehoahaz and Jehoash; 2 Kgs 9 – 13).

The evaluation does not compare Jehoash either to his father or to David
(as is often done; see 1 Kgs 15:3, 11; 22:43). Jehoiada, mentioned in this
context, appears as a surrogate father, taking the place of the paradigmatic
David. He 'instructs' (*hôrāhû*) the child-king. The common root (*yrh*) is
shared by the words 'instructs' and 'torah' (*tôrâ*), and suggests the topic
for such instruction: the torah to which a king is subject (Deut. 17:19).
Jehoash is approved for 'doing what was right in the eyes of YHWH all
his days', although he does not remove the 'high places'. The negative
comment consistently tempers positive evaluations given southern
monarchs from Solomon to Hezekiah, who does remove the high places
(1 Kgs 15:14; 22:43; 2 Kgs 14:3–4; 15:3–4, 34–35). The comment that
Jehoash does right 'all his days' is different from the tradition of Jehoash's
failure after Jehoiada's death (2 Chr. 24; see 'Notes on the text'). Dtr may
have been unaware of the tradition, or selectively set it aside for polemical
reasons.

12:4–16[5–17]

4–8[5–9]. Jehoash's approach to the temple repairs is portrayed in a very
positive light. The king begins not with a description of neglect to the
temple or with blame for such neglect, but with a ready solution to provide
funding. Various sources of 'silver' (*kesep*; minted coinage does not appear
until the Persian era and silver in various forms, including jewellery and
graded nuggets, serves as currency [see Betylon, *ABD* 1:1079]) are to be
brought into the house of YHWH, all as 'holy offerings' (*qŏdāšîm*).

There are several sources of these holy offerings. The first two are listed
in a shorthand representation. The first, *kesep 'ôbēr*, 'silver from the
census', refers to the amount paid as one is counted or enumerated (lit.
'crosses over', *'ôbēr*). Such an accounting is outlined in Exod. 30:11–16.
The second, *'îš kesep napšôt 'erkô*, the 'money from each soul's valuation',
refers to payment of dedicatory vows (Lev. 27:1–8) redeemed by a valuation
(*'ērek*) of people (*napšôt*) (see Cogan 1988: 137; Provan 1995: 225). The
final source of the *qŏdāšîm* is voluntary offerings, literally, those 'laid upon
one's heart'.

Jehoash places these sources of income brought 'into the house of
YHWH' (v. 5 [twice]) into the care of the priests for the temple's repair.
Perhaps the damage is merely due to the passage of time (the temple is
now over 100 years old); more probably the damage has been caused by
the people's neglect and patronage of the house of Baal during the Omride
era. It may even be due to intentional damage or diversion of funding

under Athaliah's seven-year regime. The priests work with a 'merchant' (*makkār*; vv. 5, 7[6, 8]). The root of the word, and thus its translation and role in the text, are disputed ('acquaintance' in NASB, 'donors' in NRSV, 'constituency' in NKJV, and, closer to the translation taken here, 'treasurers' in NIV, NET). The term is best taken, as here, as temple personnel, for evidence of similar religious and secular personnel exists in the surrounding cultures. For instance, Ugaritic texts reveal *mkrm* (pl.) were merchants (Rainey 1963), and Ugaritic and Egyptian texts list them as temple personnel, possibly disposing of commodity offerings (Montgomery 1951: 432; Albright 1952: 251; Delcor 1962: 362–364). It is probable that the priests needed those skilled in valuing the silver and commodity offerings.

Finally, the offerings are in service of 'repairing' (*ḥzq*) any 'damage' (*bedeq*) to the temple, and the repetition of the terms throughout highlights the focus of Jehoash's efforts. Moreover, the combination of these terms, the joint responsibility between palace and temple for the funds, and key phrases ('silver . . . brought into the house of YHWH' [vv. 4, 9, 13, 16(5, 10, 14, 17)]; 'into the hand' [vv. 11, 15(12, 16)]; 'wherever any damage is found' [v. 4(5)]) are elements found in ANE administrative records regarding collection procedures for such temple repairs (Hurowitz 1986: 289–294). The account reflects not a building inscription as Na'aman 1998b suggests and as the debated 'Jehoash Inscription', which surfaced in 2001, attempted to affirm (Shanks 2003: 22–23, 69; Knauf 2003: 22–26) – after all, Jehoash is not building, but repairing. Rather, the procedures Jehoash introduces and that continue to the Josianic era (2 Kgs 22:1–7; see 'Form and structure' above) are consistent with the ANE cultural milieu regarding financing and executing temple repairs.

It is not known whether Jehoash institutes the collection early in his reign, but it is not until his twenty-third year that he becomes aware of the scheme's failure. His ignorance does not speak well of his administration. Nor does the neglect speak well of the priests' commitment to, or ability to perform, temple repair. Jehoash is now thirty, and while it would be extreme to posit he now 'wanted to emancipate himself and the state from priestly domination' (so Gray 1970: 586), there may be political reasons for his care for the temple. Israel, due to Aramean incursion, is becoming less stable, and Judah, now re-established under a Davidide, more so. As the primary symbol of YHWH's endorsement of the state and the dynasty's power, it is politically expedient to ensure that symbol's wholeness (Sweeney 2007: 352).

His first recorded challenge to the priests and his own mentor rightly labels him as 'King Jehoash' – his action is that of the dynastic head of state. His charge to the priests accuses them only of neglect or incompetence but falls short of a charge of corruption. Even the implication of corruption is belied (contra Cohn 2000: 82) by the priests' willingness to redress the wrong, and the permission that they continue to collect the funds. The flow of monies from the merchants to themselves is diverted to temple repair, and the priests stand aside for others more qualified to attend to the repairs.

9–16[10–17]. A series of steps is taken to ensure transparency and accountability in the new arrangements. Jehoiada prepares a receptacle for the offerings, probably at the behest of the king and as part of the larger plan. The location of the chest is debated, and the text is often emended (see 'Notes on the text'), but, following the MT, a good argument is made for its placement at the north gate of the inner court. There an altar stood at the threshold and on it priests prepared offerings for sacrifice and also 'kept the threshold' by guarding ingress to the holy precinct (McKane 1959: 263–265). The three threshold priests on duty (1 Kgs 25:18) deposited the silver offerings into the chest in the sight of all the worshippers.

The text next outlines a number of steps taken each time the chest filled with silver (vv. 10–16[11–17]), and the iterative account reveals the steps were actually taken and the chest was emptied several times. The participation of royal and temple personnel in counting the silver is apparently common ANE practice (Oppenheim 1947; Hurowitz 1986) and not to be taken as a sign the throne mistrusts the temple priests (so Provan 1995: 224).

Several individuals are named in the procedure. The king's scribe is a role appointed by Solomon (1 Kgs 4:3). The 'high priest' (v. 10[11]; 22:4, 8; 23:4), while designating an official by a term generally thought post-exilic (Montgomery 1951: 429; Gray 1970: 587), certainly indicates a functionary known in the pre-exilic era (Hobbs 1985: 153). A 'head priest' (kōhēn hārō'š) is indicated in 2 Kgs 25:18, and Ugarit knew of a 'high priest' (rb khnm; Gray 1970: 587).

The silver is sorted into incremental units, tied into bags and counted (v. 10[11]). Further disposition may include the process of minting into refined ingots to be used as temple treasury funds (Torrey 1936).The silver is entrusted to (i.e. placed in the power or 'hand' of, 'al-yad) supervisory workers indicated in vv. 11, 14–15[12, 15–16]. They in turn contract various workers for temple repair and disperse expenses particularly related to repair work (vv. 11–12[12–13]). The king's scribe and high priest did not require an accounting from the supervisory workers who 'dealt faithfully'. This is not an accusation against the priest's honesty (contra Hobbs 1985: 155; Cohn 2000: 82), but an emphasis on the meetness of the new scheme: talents and inclinations are well matched and the workers function appropriately and get the job done; the plan does not stall for years, but proceeds apace.

Two habitual exceptions are noted. First, the funds are not directed towards refurbishing implements used in temple service. Many of the items appear in the list of implements Solomon provided for the temple (though of a different metal, the basins and snuffers appear in 1 Kgs 7:50, bowls in 1 Kgs 7:40, 45, and possibly the vessels of gold or silver in 1 Kgs 7:51). Solomon provided them out of the king's revenue and a similar arrangement apparently remains in place. Certainly, the exception indicates the single-mindedness of the project, as funds are directed only to temple repairs. This exception ensures no delay.

The second exception concerns ongoing support to the priests from the guilt and sin offerings. The nature of these offerings is difficult to determine, as the phrases 'silver from the sin offerings' (*kesep ḥaṭṭā'ōt*) and 'silver from the guilt offerings' (*kesep 'āšām*) appear nowhere else. The sin (purification) offerings detailed in Lev. 4:1 – 5:13 and the guilt (reparation) offerings of Lev. 5:14 – 6:7[5:26]) may be intended. However, the sin offering outlined in Leviticus does not provide for an equivalent monetary substitution, as the phrase *kesep ḥaṭṭā'ōt* suggests. Whatever specific law the offerings refer to, the narrative point is that the priests are not punished or disadvantaged by the new scheme. Previously, the priests had accessed the monies intended for repairs (v. 8[9]), but now those funds are redirected to their intended purpose while still ensuring provision for temple personnel.

12:17–18[18–19]

The section begins with a temporal marker 'then' (*'az*) with impf. ('went up'). This does not necessitate consecutive action and the Aramean incursion could occur either in or shortly after Jehoash's twenty-third year (Rabinowitz 1984). This would be late in Jehu's reign or early in Jehoahaz's (2 Kgs 13:1), when Aram harries Israel (10:32–33; 13:3). Hazael's campaign against the coastal plain weakens both Israel and Judah by annexing trade and military routes. Gath (modern Tell es-Safi, 7 miles [12 km] south-east of Ekron and proximate to Judah [Seger, *ABD* 2:908–909]) is captured. Jerusalem's payment of tribute to deter Hazael weakens any possibility it might provide assistance to Israel against Aram.

Funds from temple and palace treasuries, earlier paid as tribute (1 Kgs 14:25–26; 15:18), have now been restored by several kings, including Jehoash. There is enough in the treasury to pay both the workers (vv. 9–16[10–17]) and the tribute (contra Rabinowitz 1984: 61–62; Lipschits 2006: 250–251). The tribute payment relieves Judah of an encroaching enemy but should not be regarded in a positive light. Payment of temple and palace treasures (especially to a foreign king) negatively characterizes a king. It reveals he does not trust in YHWH to deliver his people in time of war (Mullen 1992). Thus, while Jehoash's use of the *qŏdāšîm* with regard to the temple is laudable, his use of the *qŏdāšîm* (v. 18[19] [twice]) in this instance is not. The reprieve from Hazael is a short-term benefit only.

12:19–21[20–22]

The final summary includes the usual notations of sources, death and burial, and succession. In addition, a brief account of Jehoash's assassination at the hands of two servants is provided. Confusion exists in Kings and Chronicles regarding the names of the perpetrators (see 'Notes on the text'); in 2 Chr. 24:26 they are further identified as foreigners, probably seen as fitting instruments of recompense in the chronicler's portrait of an apostate Davidide. No reason is provided in the Kings account for the assassination (in Chronicles it is credited to Jehoash's execution of the priest's son). Following as it does Jehoash's military action and payment of temple riches, it evidences concern over his foreign policy, or disapproval of his use of temple funds. Assuming the assassination takes place in Jerusalem, 'Beth-millo' must be near the Millo, north of the City of David (see 'Comment', 1 Kgs 9:15), and en route to an unknown location, Silla (Montgomery 1951: 431; Hobbs 1985: 146; Cogan 1988: 136, 139).

Explanation

Jehoash 'does what was right in the eyes of YHWH all his days'. He is one of a few kings who though approved does not remove the high places, and this notation implies disapproval of the king. High places, while acceptable in the premonarchic era and until the establishment of the temple (1 Sam. 9:11–25; 10:5), are since the temple's dedication illegitimate worship sites. Only those kings who remove them are given unqualified approval (2 Kgs 18:4; 23:8). In Jehoash, once again a king succeeds and fails at the same time. His failure, however, does not negate the good he does for YHWH and his people. The combination of success and failure in the regnal summary highlights that YHWH acts graciously through his fallible people.

The narrative sustains this contrast of approved and disapproved actions, particularly through Jehoash's use of the holy offerings (qŏdāšîm), which are held in the temple. In the account of his temple repairs they fund the project (v. 4[5]). The account of the repairs stands as supportive evidence of the royal evaluation that Jehoash 'did what was right in the eyes of YHWH all his days'. In the second pericope the Aramean invader comes against Jerusalem, and Jehoash now uses the holy offerings (qŏdāšîm) held in the temple and royal treasuries to bribe Hazael's withdrawal. This action is wrong on several counts (see below). Foreign aggression against Israel is, in the Deuteronomistic purview, just retribution for cultic ills. And, the narrative makes clear, should a king fail regarding Deuteronomistic norms, that mindset opposed to YHWH will result in other actions of a disapproved nature. Worship and belief, without fail, truly do affect practice.

The narrative gives no explicit evaluation of Jehoash's payment of tribute to Aram. But the act is evaluated negatively through several implicit means. The first is simply the juxtaposition of the two accounts regarding the holy offerings. The absence of the word 'repair' (ḥzq) in the second account accentuates the different use to which the offerings are put. When faced with foreign opposition, YHWH's people are to trust YHWH will fight on their behalf, rather than to trust in the strength (qal of *ḥzq*) of their own hand (or bank account!).

The absence of the root *ḥzq* in the second pericope touches on this issue of trust in another implicit manner. When Joshua enters the land of promise, he is assured that YHWH will give the land to Israel. Jericho's walls fall, Ai is delivered into Israel's hand, the sun stands still, and northern and southern campaigns are successful – all by YHWH's hand. As the divine warrior, he fights on behalf of faithful Israel (Longman and Reid 1995). As leader of YHWH's people, Joshua is charged to 'be strong (qal of *ḥzq*) and courageous' (Josh. 1:6–7, 9). His strength is to arise from YHWH's promise to give them the land and to be with them in the face of opposing peoples. The leader is to direct his strength not to warfare, but to obedience of the law of Moses so that he will have success (vv. 7–8). It is not surprising that when Jehoash fails in the face of opposing foreign forces, no mention is made of *ḥzq*. In the matter of Aram, Jehoash is not strong. He does not trust YHWH as did Joshua before him and, though he wins a reprieve from Aram, it is not lasting (see 2 Kgs 16) and is gained at the expense of obedience and trust. This linguistic device rhetorically highlights the gravity of Jehoash's failure by placing it alongside Joshua's success.

The matter of tribute is also implicitly evaluated as one of several examples of a king who, though approved, yet fails regarding the high places. In the southern kingdom five kings in addition to Jehoash receive a positive evaluation that is then tempered by the cultic failure of not removing the high places: Asa (1 Kgs 15:11–15), Jehoshaphat (1 Kgs 22:43–44), Amaziah (2 Kgs 14:3–4), Azariah (2 Kgs 15:3–4) and Jotham (2 Kgs 15:34–35) (see Mullen 1992). In each instance the ensuing narrative records negative outcomes: Jehoshaphat makes an alliance with the house of Ahab, Azariah is afflicted with leprosy and Jotham is attacked by a foreign alliance (Rezin of Aram with Pekah of Israel). The remaining two kings (Asa and Amaziah) together with Jehoash pay tribute from the temple and palace treasuries to foreign kings – an action whose negative impulse is outlined above. Furthering the negative view of such payments, Asa, Amaziah and Jehoash stand with Rehoboam (1 Kgs 14:25–28) and Ahaz (2 Kgs 18:13–16), both of whom are wholly disapproved and who pay foreign invaders with temple and palace funds. Once again the Deuteronomistic world view is demonstrated. Those who do not worship YHWH exclusively, and in the Jerusalem temple, cannot be granted full approval. More, their reigns are marred by negative circumstances: invaders, illness and alliances with apostate kings. The payment of tribute is simply another example of the negative outcomes attendant upon aberrant worship.

Finally, Jehoash's reign is comparable to Josiah's (see 'Form and structure'). The repairs Josiah makes repeat virtually verbatim those of

Jehoash. The parallels naturally draw the two accounts together as comparables. Both Josiah and Jehoash are fully approved for their renovations. But Josiah is one of only two kings (Hezekiah is the other) who removes the high places (2 Kgs 23:4–20). These (and other) reforms demonstrate Josiah's whole commitment to the Deuteronomistic code. No disapproval is voiced of him either in the regnal summaries (as in Jehoash's case) or in the ensuing narrative. Particularly in the face of encroaching foreign armies (Assyria and Egypt; see 'Comment', 2 Kgs 22 – 23) Josiah offers no tribute from temple or royal treasuries.

In comparison to Josiah, Jehoash is much less than the ideal. The high places remain. This aberrance in worship affects other areas in which he is called to trust and serve YHWH. The tribute paid from the holy offerings evidences this.

Yet one cannot deny the approval under which Jehoash stands. Like many other kings and leaders he is less than perfect. Gracious as always, YHWH works in the midst of his imperfect people despite his promise of judgment for cultic sins (1 Kgs 9:6–9). Grace is offered, but should not be presumed upon. The ongoing presence of the high places is a reminder that none has come to correct the abuses instituted by Solomon. One is left to wonder whether such a one will ever come, and whether YHWH will continue to withhold his wrath on account of cultic ills until such a time.

2 KINGS 13:1–25

Translation

[1]In the twenty-third year of Jehoash son of Ahaziah king of Judah, Jehoahaz son of Jehu began to reign over Israel in Samaria. *He reigned* seventeen years. [2]He did what was evil in the eyes of YHWH and followed the sins of Jeroboam son of Nebat, which he caused Israel to sin; he did not turn from them[a]. [3]So YHWH's anger burned against Israel and he gave them continually into the hand of Hazael king of Aram and into the hand of Ben-hadad son of Hazael. [4]Jehoahaz entreated YHWH and YHWH listened to him. He saw Israel's distress[a], for the king of Aram oppressed[a] them. [5]Therefore YHWH gave Israel a deliverer and they escaped from the hand of Aram, and the sons of Israel dwelt in their homes as before. [6]Even so, they did not turn from the sins of the house of Jeroboam, which he caused Israel to sin, but walked[a] in them[b]; the sacred pole also remained in Samaria. [7]There was left[a] to Jehoahaz an army of not more than fifty horsemen and ten chariots and ten thousand foot soldiers, for the king of Aram had destroyed them and made them like the dust at threshing. [8]Now the rest of the acts of Jehoahaz and all that he did and his might, are they not written in the Book of the Chronicles of the Kings of Israel? [9]And Jehoahaz slept with his fathers and they buried him in Samaria, and Jehoash his son reigned in his place.

¹⁰In the thirty-seventhᵃ year of Jehoash king of Judah, Jehoash son of Jehoahaz began to reign over Israel in Samaria. He reigned sixteen years. ¹¹He did what was evil in the eyes of YHWH; he did not turn from all the sins of Jeroboam son of Nebat, which he caused Israel to sin, but walked in themᵃ. ¹²ᵃAnd the rest of the acts of Jehoash and all that he did, and his might with which he fought against Amaziah king of Judah, are they not written in the Book of the Chronicles of the Kings of Israel? ¹³And Jehoash slept with his fathers and Jeroboam sat upon his throne. Jehoash was buried in Samaria with the kings of Israel.

¹⁴Now Elisha had sickened with the illness of which he was to die. Jehoash king of Israel went down to him and wept over him, crying, 'My father! My father! The chariots of Israel and its horsemen!' ¹⁵Elisha said to him, 'Get a bow and arrows.' So he brought him a bow and arrows. ¹⁶He said to the king of Israel, 'Put your hand on the bow,' and he put his hand on it. Then Elisha set his hand upon the hands of the king. ¹⁷Then he said, 'Open the eastern window,' and he opened it. Elisha said, 'Shoot!' and he shot. Then he said, 'YHWH's arrow of victory; even the arrow of victory over Aram! You shall strike Aram at Aphek until it is destroyed.'

¹⁸Then he said, 'Take the arrows,' and he took them. He said to the king of Israel, 'Strike the ground!' and he struck three times, then stopped. ¹⁹But the man of God was angry with him and he said, 'You should have struckᵃ five or six times – then you would have struck Aram until it is destroyed. But now you will strike Aram only three times.'

²⁰So Elisha died and they buried him. Now Moabite raiders used to invade the land when the spring cameᵃ. ²¹Once, they were burying a man when they saw a raiding band, so they threw the body into Elisha's tomb. As soon as the body touched Elisha's bones, it came to life and stood on its feet.

²²Hazael king of Aram oppressed Israel all the days of Jehoahaz, ²³but YHWH was gracious and had compassion, and turned to them on account of his covenant with Abraham, Isaac and Jacob. He was not willing to destroy them or cast them from his presence until now. ²⁴Hazael king of Aram died and Ben-hadad his son began to reign in his place. ²⁵Then Jehoash son of Jehoahaz again took the cities from the hand of Ben-hadad son of Hazael, which he had taken in battle from the hand of Jehoahaz his father. Three times Jehoash struck him and he recovered the cities of Israel.

Notes on the text

2.a. The sg. pr. suff. 'from it' (*mimmennâ*) is translated as pl. so as to agree with the pl. const. antecedent *ḥaṭṭōʾt*, 'sins'. Also in vv. 6, 11.

4.a. 'distress' and 'oppressed' share the same root (*lḥṣ*), marking action and consequence.

6.a. Reading 'they walked' (*hālĕkû*) per context and with LXXᴮ, Tg, Vg.

6.b. The pr. suff. is understood as pl. (see n. 2.a above).

7.a. The subject of the verb *hišʾîr*, 'for there was left', is here understood as indefinite (Burney 1903: 316). Montgomery (1951: 434) makes YHWH

(v. 3) the subject and excises vv. 4–6 as an 'awkward intrusion'. Gray (1970: 596) gives 'he' as the subject, but whether this refers to YHWH or Hazael is unclear.

10.a. In the light of v. 1, thirty-nine years is expected here. LXX texts provide various numbers for the synchronization, including thirty-nine. The adjustment, however, then creates problems in 14:1. MT 'thirty-seven' should remain, reflecting the two dating systems in place in Israel and Judah at this time (see introduction). Syr reads 'thirteen' for length of reign.

11.a. The pr. suff. is understood as pl. (see n. 2.a above).

12.a.–13. These verses are found at the end of the chapter in LXX[L]. In MT they are repeated almost verbatim at 14:15–16. See further in 'Form and structure', 2 Kgs 14.

19.a. *lĕhakkôt*, 'you should have struck', is past paraphrastic use of the inf. (S. Driver 1892: §204). LXX's unnecessary emendation (followed by Gray 1970: 598) presupposes *lû hikkitā*, 'would that you had struck'.

20.a. MT *bā' šānâ*, 'a year came', makes little sense and versions and commentators propose several emendations. Here LXX ἐλθόντος τοῦ ἐνιαυτοῦ is followed ('when spring came').

Form and structure

Jehu was promised a dynasty lasting four generations (10:30). Here, after the hiatus tracing events in Judah, the narrative presents two of the dynasty's kings: Jehoahaz and Jehoash.

The chapter's structure and contents present many difficulties. For instance, Cogan (1988: 144) takes the allusions to the book of Judges as a later interpolation set off by a resumptive repetition (vv. 2, 6), but the extent of the interpolation is differently considered by various scholars (Gray 1970: 591; McCarthy 1973: 409–410; Jones 1984b: 498; Fritz 2003: 307).

Several difficulties are presented by the structure of the reign of Jehoash of Israel. It is represented initially only by opening and closing regnal summaries (vv. 10–11, 12–13), but after the closing summary he features in the following verses (vv. 14–25) and a second regnal summary appears at 14:15–16. The regnal summary that appears in vv. 12–13 contains the anomalous 'and Jeroboam sat upon his throne', found nowhere else in a regnal summary. Gray (1970: 593) argues the anomaly reveals the secondary nature of the summary, Sweeney that it reveals the pre-Dtr nature of the summary. Both agree it highlights the intentional placement of the summary at this point.

Other difficulties centre on the character of Elisha. His appearance comes suddenly after a long narrative absence and with little anticipatory context. For this reason Gray (1970: 466) considers vv. 14–21 originally appeared at 8:7–15. Yet more difficulties centre on Jehoahaz of Israel. Notations of YHWH's grace bestowed on him (vv. 4–5, 23) and the promise of a deliverer (v. 5), who seems to come in Jehoahaz's day, stand in apparent contradiction to the statement that Hazael oppressed Israel 'all the days of Jehoahaz' (v. 22). Gray (1970: 594) argues vv. 4–6 originally stood with the name 'Jehoash' and rightly belonged after v. 22.

These and other difficulties of structure and content have spurred numerous attempts to tease out the chapter's diachronic history and the theological or historical impetus behind each redaction (see Gray 1970; McCarthy 1973; Jones 1984b; Cogan 1988; Fritz 2003). Yet whatever textual development inheres behind the text, its present form can be explained as an authorial or redacted product of Dtr that, even with its difficulties – or because of them – enhances the chapter's overall message in its context in Kings.

Two elements inform the intentionally structured whole. The first is that of the passing of an era, and the second is the continuity that extends beyond that passing. The chapter includes the first two kings in Jehu's dynasty granted in 2 Kgs 10:30. Jehu's kingship was introduced in a prophetic word that also commissioned the anointing of Elisha and Hazael (1 Kgs 19:15–19). As the three men were introduced together, there is a narrative logic that ends the story of two of these characters in one chapter. Elisha's ministry continued that of Elijah, and with his passing the era of these two great prophets ends. The death of Hazael similarly closes an era in Israel's history first mentioned in 1 Kgs 19, and set in motion when Elisha commissioned Hazael to the throne of Aram (2 Kgs 8). But though Hazael dies, Aram's enmity towards Israel continues.

That Aramean hostility towards Israel continues beyond Hazael's death means that Israel's need for the 'deliverer' promised Jehoahaz (v. 5) also continues. Any deliverance under Jehoahaz does not last; the oppression continues under Jehoash. The deliverance Jehoash brings is also not complete: he strikes Aram only three times. Thus the chapter ends with the question unanswered as to whether a 'deliverer' can really be expected, and, if so, who that deliverer might be. The question continues beyond the lives of Hazael and Elisha and is answered only in 2 Kgs 14.

Comment

13:1–9

Jehoahaz begins to reign in 814 BC in Jehoash of Judah's twenty-third year (DeVries, *IDB* 1:598). This synchronization, together with the length and place of reign and the evaluation, completes the introduction. Like his father Jehu and all northern kings, Jehoahaz continues in the sins of Jeroboam; moreover, he 'does not turn from them', a notation included in the introductory summary of northern kings from Jehu until Pekah (15:28; cf. 2 Kgs 3:3; Campbell 1986: 144).

Unlike previous northern kings, the Jehuites live under the protection of a dynastic promise granted Jehu (10:30) and it is this that, despite increased Aramean aggression (2 Kgs 13 – 15), enables Israel's survival and occasional victory (13:24–25; 14:25–28). To explain further Israel's survival under Aramean pressure the narrative utilizes the paradigm found in the book of Judges. The paradigm moves from Israel's sin to YHWH's anger at that sin to judgment by foreign oppression to YHWH's gracious deliverance through a deliverer (vv. 3–6). Thus YHWH responds to Jeroboam's sin and his anger 'burns' (hrh) against Israel (v. 3; Judg. 2:14, 20; 3:8; 10:7). This anger is not unique to the Israelites' God; it is the same response of Chemosh, the god of Moab towards his people's sin (line 5 of the Moabite Stele, *ANET* 320). YHWH's delivery of his people 'into the hand of' (*wayyittēm bĕyad*) the enemy evokes the cycle of Judges (v. 3; Judg. 2:14; 6:1; 13:1; cf. the similar phrase 'sold into the hand of' [*wayyimkĕrēm bĕyad*] at Judg. 3:8; 4:2; 10:7).

In Judges YHWH's anger is turned aside when the people 'cry out' ($z'q$). Jehoahaz, however, 'entreats' YHWH (v. 4). The verb (pi. of hlh) has instructive narrative associations. Jeroboam 'entreats' the man of God (1 Kgs 13:6) – not an association particularly flattering to Jehoahaz. Better is the association to Hezekiah, who 'entreats' YHWH against the evil planned for Jerusalem (Jer. 26:19). Manasseh, too, 'entreats' YHWH and humbles himself (2 Chr. 33:12); any humility on Jehoahaz's part is not stated and can only be assumed. Finally, in the strongest association, Moses 'entreats' YHWH when the Lord's anger burns against Israel's false worship. Jehoahaz is subtly compared to Moses, and his entreaty, together with the 'distress' (*lahas*) of Israel under Aramean oppression (*lāhas*) moves YHWH as it does in Judges (v. 4; cf. Judg. 2:18; 4:3; 10:12).

As in Judges, YHWH provides a 'deliverer' (*môšîa'*, from $yš'$; Judg. 3:9, 15; 6:36; also 'judges' [*šôpĕtîm*] 'deliver' [*hôšî'*, from $yš'$] Israel in 2:16, 18). It is narratively ambiguous, however, whether this deliverer actually appears in Jehoahaz's time or in the future. Various 'deliverers' are proposed: Jehoahaz (Fritz 2003: 308), Jehoash (v. 25; Cody 1970: 336; Sweeney 2007: 355, 357) and Elisha (Gray 1970: 595). Even Adad-nirari III, an Assyrian ruler whose anti-Aramean actions draw Aram from Israel, is forwarded as a candidate (Haran 1967: 268; Mazar 1986: 167). An Assyrian deliverer is unlikely and no indication in the narrative confirms this. But there is an indication in the narrative that Jehoash in the intended deliverer: Elisha promises 'victory' (*tĕšû'â* [like *môšîa'*, also from $yš'$]; v. 17) through him. But Jehoash provides only partial relief, and deliverance is left to Jeroboam who finally 'delivers' ($yš'$) Israel (see 'Comment' at 14:27).

The final allusions to the book of Judges are less directly comparable but still evocative. Through the deliverer Israel 'escapes' (ys') from the hand of Aram (contra 'delivered ($yš'$) from the hand of' in Judg. 2:16, 18).

Escaping, they 'dwelt in their homes' (contra 'the land had peace', in Judges). The final echo is that oppression and deliverance do not turn Israel away from Jeroboam's sins (*pace* Judg. 2:16–19). The sins are instead worsened, for the sacred poles (unmentioned since 1 Kgs 14:15; 16:33; cf. 18:19) are reintroduced.

The continual oppression at the hand of Aram (v. 3) leaves Jehoahaz with significantly reduced chariotry (v. 7) when compared to Ahab's forces. At Qarqar they numbered two thousand chariots and ten thousand infantry, possibly a fraction of Ahab's available troops (*ANET* 278–279). Although the infantry comparables are not significantly different, the chariotry is. Nonetheless, the point is clearly stated: Aram's oppression renders Israel as useless as the chaff after threshing.

Jehoahaz's reign is focused on Israel's oppression and YHWH's gracious response of a promised deliverer. The allusion to the Judges paradigm suggests cyclical oppression both in, and after, Jehoahaz's reign. The final evaluation contains nothing but expected elements. His 'might' notes his ability to sustain Israel through the long years of warfare. He dies and the dynasty continues in Jehoash.

13:10–13

Jehoash rules for sixteen years (798–782 BC), including a co-regency with Jeroboam from 793 to 782 BC (from Jehoash of Israel onwards, both kingdoms use the non-accession dating system; DeVries, *IDB* 1:589; see also discussion in Introduction). The long and short forms of his name (shared with the Judean king in 2 Kgs 11 – 12) both appear in the MT. The long form appears in the opening summary (v. 10) and the second closing summary (vv. 15–16), but the short form (Joash) appears in the closing summary (vv. 12–13) and elsewhere in the chapter. For ease, the translation and comments below use the long form throughout.

Like his dynastic predecessors Jehoash is evaluated negatively as 'not turning' from Jeroboam's sins (v. 11). Additionally, Jehoash 'walked in them'; despite the dynastic grant given Jehu, neither he nor his descendants repent of Jeroboam's sins. The opening summary segues immediately to the closing summary, which references his 'might' raised against Amaziah and foreshadows the events narrated in the context of Amaziah's reign (14:8–14). Two effects are achieved by the immediate closure of Jehoash's reign. First, it leaves the telling of Elisha's death (vv. 14–21) outside the confines of regnal formulae. In a similar fashion Elisha's ministry was introduced outside regnal structures (2 Kgs 2; it falls between the close of Ahaziah's reign and the opening of Jehoram's reign). The effect is to show that Elisha's ministry is subject to no king. He does not appear enclosed in any king's story. Instead, kings appear as subjects within his story. Secondly, the immediate closure to Jehoash's reign leaves no occasion to demonstrate Jehoash as the 'deliver' promised in v. 5. Thus the anticipation for the deliverer is heightened. Who will he be? And when will he appear?

13:14–21

14–19. Elisha's ministry began in 1 Kgs 19 and now, approximately fifty years later, the aged prophet is near death. He may still reside in Samaria (2 Kgs 6:24, 32), or in the Jordan Valley (2 Kgs 2:18; 4:38; 6:4). That the king 'goes down' to him does not help to locate him, for the term is not specifically geographical. Elsewhere it is used of kings going down before battle to seek advice from Elisha (2 Kgs 3:12). Given the ongoing context of battle with Aram, and the word that Elisha gives Jehoash, that may be exactly what is intended here.

Jehoash's cry 'My father! My father! The chariots of Israel and its horsemen!' is much more than an expression of grief at the impending loss of Israel's prophet. The cry is identical to Elisha's when Elijah departed with whirlwind, fiery chariot and horses (2 Kgs 2:12). Similar phenomena also appear in Elisha's ministry (6:15–17; 7:6–7) but the cry references more than these phenomena. First, 'My father!' expresses respect for Elisha's prophetic leadership (Williams 1966: 344). The remainder is a title arising out of the holy-war tradition (von Rad 1958: 100; P. Miller 1973: 134–135) and recognizes the prophet as YHWH's weapon against the enemies of Israel (see also 'Comment', 2:12). Thus Jehoash expresses grief at the loss of such a powerful instrument, and despair at the loss of the oracular insights often given kings before battle (e.g. 1 Kgs 20:13, 28; 22:6–7; 2 Kgs 3:11–12; cf. 7:1).

In this context Elisha addresses the king's concern. He performs two sign-acts, or prophetic dramas, in each of which the king is a significant participant. It may be that Elisha's sickness prevents his own enactment of the signs; nevertheless, the prophetic power infuses them because the prophet directs them. The acts are not sympathetic magic, nor merely encouragement. They are part of the prophet's efficacious word, a powerful proclamation of what is willed by YHWH (Stacey 1990: 282; see also 'Comment' at 1 Kgs 11:30).

The command–response sequence (vv. 15–18) demonstrates Elisha's authority. As instructed, Jehoash brings the weapon to a weakened or bedridden Elisha. He then 'put his hand on the bow' (*harkēb yādĕkā 'al-haqqešet*). The verb *rkb* (here a hiph. form) usually refers to chariotry, but here suggests bringing the hand (possibly holding the arrow) up to the bow strings (*HALOT* 1233; Barrick 1985: 356). Elisha places his own hand on the king's, linking his prophetic power to the ensuing action. The arrow is shot out of the east window, signifying the general direction of an Aramean attack, and its significance interpreted: YHWH will grant full victory over Aram at Aphek, long a disputed border location south-east of the Sea of Galilee (1 Kgs 20:26; Frankel, *ABD* 1:275–277).

Unfortunately, the assurance of complete victory is undercut by the next sign-act, as Jehoash demonstrates a lack of belief in Elisha's words. His less than passionate demonstration rouses Elisha's anger. The smallness of Jehoash's belief limits, but does not negate, the first word of total victory (v. 17; *těšûʿâ*, from *yšʿ*): if Jehoash ultimately is not the 'deliverer' (*môšîaʿ*, also from *yšʿ*), there remains hope of another in that role.

20–21. Elisha dies and is buried, perhaps near Jericho or Gilgal. These locations are easily accessible to the yearly Moabite raids. The burial procession occurs some time after Elisha's death (for only the bones remain). The party's alarm at the approaching raiders provides an opportunity to show once more the life-giving prophetic power. Elisha's ministry has brought life to many through healed water (2:19–22), provision of food (4:1–7, 38–41, 42–44) and resurrection (4:32–35). Even though he is dead, Elisha's power remains. Its demonstration heightens hope his word of Aram's complete destruction will be fulfilled. Israel may yet find life free of Aram's oppression.

13:22–25

The last section of the chapter turns to events concerning Hazael, the third individual named in YHWH's commission to Elijah. The section begins with a backward glance at Hazael's oppression of Israel 'all the days of Jehoahaz'. The expression is difficult to take literally, for Hazael probably dies during the reign of Jehoahaz.

Hazael is mentioned in Assyrian inscriptions of Shalmaneser III in 838 BC (*ANET* 280). The Damascene king during Adad-nirari III's siege of 806 BC is called *marʿi*, 'my lord', probably a reference to Ben-hadad (*ANET* 281; Page 1968: 149). This would place Hazael's death before 806 BC and before Jehoahaz's death in 798 BC (Gray 1970: 601; Jones 1984b: 505). By this reckoning, it is difficult to argue that Hazael oppressed Israel 'all the days of Jehoahaz' (v. 22). Increasing the difficulty is the statement in v. 3 that both Ben-hadad and Hazael oppress Israel during Jehoahaz's reign. Perhaps v. 22 should be understood to mean Hazael oppresses Jehoahaz all his days *during which Hazael lived*. And if one considers that v. 3 describes Aramean oppression under Hazael and Ben-hadad during the reigns of Jehoahaz and Jehoash, the contradiction is at least mitigated.

The theological point is made regardless: Israel suffers under Aram. And, in the same way YHWH's grace moves him to alleviate Israel's suffering in vv. 4–5, so here grace is sounded. This grace is extended not on account of a promise given Jehu (see 'Comment', v. 3 above) but on the far older promise granted the patriarchs. The Abrahamic Covenant is referenced elsewhere in the DH only at Josh. 24:3 (cf. 1 Kgs 18:36) in the context of Israel's possession of the land. It features frequently in Deuteronomy (1:8; 6:10; 9:5, 27; 29:12; 30:20; 34:4) and is the basis of YHWH's gift of land to Israel (Gen. 12:1; 15:18). In the light of this covenant Israel remains in the land despite Aramean aggression.

Hazael's death marks the passing of an era, but his son continues the policy of oppressing Israel (v. 24). The passage closes with the fulfilment of Elisha's final prophetic word as Jehoash takes back cities taken from Jehoahaz. This recovery probably took place during the Assyrian advance against Aram under Adad-nirari III (811–783 BC) and the siege of Damascus in 806 BC. The Rimah Stele records tribute paid by Jehoash, Tyre and Sidon to Adad-nirari. Jehoash's gift may have enabled him to regain border cities without Assyrian interference (Page 1968; Cody 1970). Three actions are mounted against Ben-hadad according to Elisha's word. Cities are regained, but Aram is not overcome and continues in ch. 14 to harass Israel.

Explanation

This chapter takes up the ongoing story of Jehu's dynasty, granted for fulfilment of the prophetic word (10:30). Jehu's coup however was ultimately abortive in its failure to restore *šālôm*, and the continuing sin of Jeroboam leaves the northern kingdom under judgment, despite the promised dynasty.

Yet even upon these sinful people YHWH's grace is poured out. There are several evidences of YHWH's grace explored in the 'Comment' section above. These include the existence of the dynasty despite Jehu's cultic failures. The promise of a deliverer and the pattern of the book of Judges both recall YHWH's past (and repetitive) grace extended to an apostate people. The prophetic word of deliverance assures of YHWH's unwillingness to abandon his people – an unwillingness reiterated in the narrator's comment that YHWH 'was not willing to destroy' (v. 23). The life-giving ministry of Elisha operates even from the grave, recalling YHWH's desire that his people experience life, and whispering that YHWH's purposes have not changed. Finally, the recollection of the Abrahamic Covenant is a powerful reminder that YHWH's grace is long-standing, and predicated upon his unbreakable promises.

In these many ways YHWH shows himself gracious and merciful, even towards an apostate people. That YHWH so acts arises out of his character. In Exod. 34:6–7a is found the summative confession of this character. YHWH proclaims to Moses that he is

> YHWH! YHWH! A God compassionate and gracious;
> Slow to anger, and abounding in covenant mercy;
> Showing love to thousands
> And forgiving wickedness, rebellion and sin.

The proclamation of YHWH's fundamental character appears several more times in the OT (Num. 14:18; Joel 2:13; Nah. 1:3; Neh. 9:17; Jon. 4:2; Pss 86:15; 103:8; 145:8).

In several of the passages YHWH demonstrates his fundamental character in the midst of apostate Israel. Indeed, it is such a people who desperately need such a God. Thus Exod. 34 follows on the heels of Israel's great sin with the golden calf (Exod. 32 – 33). While interceding for the nation, Moses requests the revelation of YHWH's glory (Exod. 33:18–23). YHWH promises to do this and to proclaim his name. Exod. 34:6 is that proclamation; that he grants Moses' request for mercy upon Israel shows the outworking of that name in the context of Israel's sin. Interestingly, Moses predicates his plea for YHWH's mercy in part upon the covenantal promises given the patriarchs (Exod. 32:13). Those same covenantal promises are cited in 2 Kgs 13:23 as underlying YHWH's mercy.

In Num. 14:18, Joel 2:13 and Neh. 9:17 the divine character is also proclaimed in the context of Israel's sin. In the desert (Numbers), calling Israel to repentance (Joel) and in remembrance of Israel's past sins (Nehemiah) YHWH's character demonstrates his astonishing mercy that forestalls deserved judgment. In the psalter (Pss 86:15; 103:8; 145:8) the divinely gracious character precipitates the psalmist's plea for mercy, together with his praise. Finally, in Nah. 1:3 and Jon. 4:2 YHWH's characteristics of compassion, grace, longsuffering and mercy are extended beyond Israel to Nineveh, the great city of Assyria. Like Israel, Nineveh is sinful and called to repentance. Towards both, YHWH's gracious character is exhibited. Not only does this reveal his complete consistency, but also that he is Lord over all – all are called to be righteous under the God of Israel and all may similarly experience his divine character.

The revelation of YHWH's holy character speaks of his compassion, grace, longsuffering and mercy. It concomitantly reveals his opposition to sinfulness in all its forms. Moses learns this second aspect of YHWH's character immediately on the heels of the first in Exod. 34:7b:

> He does not leave the guilty unpunished,
> But punishes the children and grandchildren
>   for the sin of the ancestors,
> To the third and fourth generations.

YHWH's hatred of sin and his commitment to judge it shows up in interesting ways in 2 Kgs 13. First, Israel under Jehoahaz and Jehoash find themselves in a 'now and not yet' era. They stand under judgment for Jeroboam's sin, but judgment is forestalled due to YHWH's mercy. In part that hiatus is due to the promised dynasty: at least for four generations the nation will endure. Yet even the interim time is punctuated by judgment in the guise of foreign oppression. Secondly, the narrative's perspective is from the place of judgment. Despite the many reasons and ways YHWH's grace has forestalled judgment, the narrative notes that 'he was not willing to destroy them, or cast them from his presence *until now*'. It is the last two words that communicate present reality: *now* Israel is destroyed; *now* they are cast from YHWH's presence.

There is a reckoning for continuing in Jeroboam's sin. It is not erased but only forestalled by YHWH's grace. In the time of the 'now and the not yet', while Israel stand under judgment but await its consummation, they experience YHWH's grace. His grace is poured out upon them in numerous ways, many of them perhaps only clearly seen in retrospect. In that time of grace YHWH repeatedly issues a call to repentance. Through his prophets, through the deuteronomic law, through the discipline of foreign oppression prescribed under that law YHWH calls his people back to himself.

YHWH's character is that which places him in the midst of sinful people as he did when Moses interceded for Israel at Sinai (Exod. 33:1–6, 12–17). YHWH's commitment to his OT people arose out of the Abrahamic Covenant and was for the sake of the nations (Gen. 12:1–3). In Israel his servant YHWH desired to make himself known (Isa. 42:6–7; 49:6–7). In the NT YHWH's gracious presence in the midst of a sinful people comes to fruition in the incarnation of Christ, the true Israel. In him YHWH tabernacles among sinful humanity, forestalling judgment and calling all to repentance and belief in the Son. By the Spirit he indwells the church and in them his presence goes into all the nations (Matt. 28:16–20). His character remains the same, extending grace and mercy, and marking sinfulness for judgment. As with 2 Kgs 13, the period of YHWH's patient waiting remains undisclosed but in that time he calls all who will respond.

2 KINGS 14:1–29

Translation

[1]In the second year of Jehoash[a] son of Jehoahaz king of Israel, Amaziah son of Jehoash[a] king of Judah began to reign. [2]He was twenty-five years old when he began to reign, and he reigned twenty-nine years in Jerusalem. His mother's name was Jehoaddan of Jerusalem. [3]He did what was right in the eyes of YHWH, except not as David his father; he did according to all that Jehoash his father had done. [4]But the high places were not removed; the people still sacrificed and burned incense on the high places.

[5]When the kingdom was firmly in his power, he struck his servants who had killed the king his father. [6]But he did not kill the assassins' sons, as it is written in the book of the torah of Moses, which YHWH commanded, saying, 'The fathers shall not be killed on account of the sons, and the sons shall not be killed on account of the fathers, but each shall be killed for his own sins.' [7]He struck

Edom in the Valley of Salt, ten thousand men, and captured Sela in battle and called it Jokthe-el, *as it is* until this day.

[8]Then Amaziah sent messengers to Jehoash son of Jehoahaz son of Jehu king of Israel, saying, 'Come, let us face one another.'[a] [9]But Jehoash king of Israel sent to Amaziah king of Judah, saying, 'The thornbush in Lebanon sent to the cedar in Lebanon, saying, "Give your daughter to my son for a wife," but a wild beast in Lebanon passed by and trampled the thornbush.' [10]You have indeed defeated Edom and your heart has made you proud. Enjoy honour and stay at home. Why invite trouble so that you fall, you and Judah with you?'

[11]But Amaziah would not listen. So Jehoash king of Israel went up and he and Amaziah king of Judah faced each other at Beth-shemesh in Judah. [12]Judah was defeated by Israel and they fled, each to his home. [13]But Amaziah king of Judah son of Jehoash son of Ahaziah was seized by Jehoash king of Israel at Beth-shemesh. He came to Jerusalem and breached the wall of Jerusalem from the Ephraim Gate[a] to the Corner Gate, 400 cubits. [14]He took all the gold and silver and all the articles found in the house of YHWH and in the treasuries of the king's house, and hostages, and returned to Samaria. [15a]And the rest of the acts of Jehoash that he did and his might and how he fought with Amaziah king of Judah, are they not written in the Book of the Chronicles of the Kings of Israel? [16]And Jehoash slept with his fathers and was buried in Samaria with the kings of Israel, and Jeroboam his son reigned in his place.

[17]Amaziah son of Jehoash king of Judah lived fifteen years after the death of Jehoash son of Jehoahaz king of Israel. [18]And the rest of the acts of Amaziah, are they not written in the Book of the Chronicles of the Kings of Judah? [19]They planned a conspiracy against him in Jerusalem so he fled to Lachish. But they sent after him to Lachish and killed him there. [20]They brought him back on horses and he was buried in Jerusalem with his fathers in the City of David. [21]All the people of Judah took Azariah (he was sixteen years old) and made him king in place of his father Amaziah. [22]It was he who rebuilt Elath and restored it to Judah after the king slept with his fathers.

[23]In the fifteenth year of Amaziah son of Jehoash king of Judah, Jeroboam son of Jehoash began to reign over Israel[a] in Samaria. *He reigned* forty-one years. [24]He did what was evil in the eyes of YHWH; he did not turn from all the sins of Jeroboam son of Nebat, which he made Israel sin. [25]He restored the border of Israel from Lebo-hamath as far as the Sea of the Arabah, according to the word of YHWH the God of Israel, which he had spoken by the hand of his servant Jonah son of Amittai the prophet who was from Gath-hepher. [26]For YHWH saw the very bitter affliction of Israel[a] and there was no one[b] but the restricted and abandoned[c], and no helper for Israel. [27]But YHWH had not said he would blot out the name of Israel under heaven, so he delivered them by the hand of Jeroboam son of Jehoash. [28]Now the rest of the deeds of Jeroboam, and all which he did and his might, how he fought and recovered Damascus and Hamath for Israel[a], are they not written in the Book of the Chronicles of the Kings of Israel? [29]And Jeroboam slept with his fathers – with the kings of Israel – and Zechariah his son reigned in his place.

Notes on the text

1.a. MT 'Joash son of Joahaz' is a variant of 'Jehoash son of Jehoahaz' (13:10; cf. at vv. 13, 23, 27). MT 'Amaziah son of Joash' is a variant for 'Amaziah son of Jehoash' (2 Kgs 12). For consistency the long forms are used throughout.

8.a. 'face one another' is literally 'look one another in the face' (*nitrā'eh pānîm*). The hith. form for *r'h* appears only here and in v. 11 (2 Chr. 25:17, 21) and indicates hostile confrontation.

13.a. Reading *miššaʿar*, 'from the Gate', with LXX[L], Vg, Tg against MT *bĕšaʿar*, 'in the gate'.

15.a.–16. Appear in almost identical form at 2 Kgs 13:12–13. See further in 'Form and structure' and 'Comment' below.

23.a. Reading *ʿal-yiśrā'ēl*, 'over Israel', for MT *melek-yiśrā'ēl*, 'king of Israel', with many MSS, LXX, Tg.

26.a. MT reads, 'YHWH saw the affliction of Israel very rebellious', which is enigmatic. LXX has πικρὰν σφόδρα and assumes Hebr. *mārâ mĕ'ōd*, 'very bitter', which, being f., does not agree with the MS noun 'affliction' it modifies. Burney (1903: 320) emends *mārâ* to art. + MS *hammar*. Thus 'the very bitter affliction of Israel', which follows the meaning of the versions and gives good sense.

26.b. *'epes* as negation is rare in prose, but see examples at BDB 67.

26.c. *ʿāṣûr wĕʿāzûb* is a synonym for the helpless. It emphasizes the universality of Israel's need (see 'Comment' at 1 Kgs 14:10 and studies cited there; see also Cogan 1988: 161).

28.a. MT 'for Judah in Israel' is a *crux interpretum*; arguing for a Judahite state with Israelite overlordship is difficult historically and historiographically; NIV's 'for Yaudi' introduces a name unattested elsewhere in the Hebrew Bible. Montgomery omits 'for Judah' (1951: 446), which follows Syr.

Form and structure

Amaziah of Judah and Jeroboam of Israel are the subjects of this chapter and regnal formulae open and close each reign (vv. 1–4, 17–18; 23–24, 28–29). The unusual circumstances surrounding Amaziah's assassination and the succession to his son account for the additions to Amaziah's closing summary.

Amaziah's regnal formulae enclose two sections, the first of which (vv. 5–7) briefly reveals Amaziah's consolidation of his rule. The second (vv. 8–14) is a lengthier historical narrative in which action is initiated by Amaziah but whose focus is Jehoash. His reign was opened and closed in 1 Kgs 13:10–13 and his reappearance here continues to highlight the dynasty of Jehu and places Amaziah in a subordinate narrative role. So important is Jehoash within the narrative that a second closing regnal summary is provided for him (14:15–16) within the regnal framework for Amaziah. Only after Jehoash's reign is thus concluded does the narrative return to Amaziah with the unusual notation of his continuing reign (v. 17). Thus Amaziah's reign serves as a backdrop for the central and victorious role played by Jehoash.

Included in the chapter are several identifiable forms and sources. Archival sources underlie several verses (vv. 7, 22, 25a), and the emphatic pronoun 'he' (*hû'*) is indicative of the original source (Montgomery 1951: 439; Hobbs 1985: 176). The brief parable (v. 9) is similar in form to other more extensive examples (Judg. 9:7–21; Isa. 5:1–7) but despite its brevity its meaning is transparent. The reference to the 'book of the torah of Moses' is rare in Kings (v. 6; cf. 2 Kgs 23:6; cf. 'torah of Moses' in 1 Kgs 2:3; 2 Kgs 23:25). A quotation of Deut. 24:16 is provided and reveals the author's concern with the deuteronomic law code.

Finally, a brief notice of prophetic fulfilment provides reasons for YHWH's gracious deliverance of Israel despite their ongoing sin (vv. 25–27). YHWH's concern for the 'affliction of Israel' and his reticence to 'blot out' Israel's name recall the themes of 1 Kgs 13:4, 23. YHWH's decision to 'deliver' (*yôšî'ēm*, from *yš'*) Israel by the hand of Jeroboam reveals the 'deliverer' (*môšîa'*, from *yš'*) promised to Jehoahaz (13:5) and only partially experienced in the reign of Jehoahaz and Jehoash (see 'Comment', 2 Kgs 13).

Comment

14:1–22

1–4. Amaziah's twenty-nine-year reign begins in Jehoash's second year (796 BC) and ends in the fifteenth year of Jeroboam's sole rule (767 BC). The presentation of the dates for Amaziah, Azariah and Jeroboam (14:1, 23; 15:1) are on the face of it hopelessly misaligned and present a gap of twelve years between the end of Amaziah's rule (in Jeroboam's fifteenth year; 14:1, 23) and the start of Azariah's rule (in Jeroboam's twenty-seventh year; 15:1). Thiele (1983: 106–116; cf. DeVries, *IDB* 1:589–592) provides a solution that makes sense of the dates provided in the MT by positing a co-regency of Amaziah and Azariah beginning in 792 BC, as well as a co-regency of Jehoash and Jeroboam beginning in 793 BC. By this reckoning, the last fourteen years of Amaziah's rule are shared with his son, perhaps with Amaziah in enforced retirement after Israel's victory.

Amaziah is evaluated positively, yet not wholly so, for he does not compare favourably to David. Only two southern kings thus far have been compared to David. Asa was compared positively to David (1 Kgs 15:11) while Abijam was negatively compared to David because his heart was 'not wholly devoted to YHWH his God like the heart of David his father' (1 Kgs 15:3). This is the implication of the negative 'not like David' said of Amaziah. Amaziah does what Jehoash his father had done and the high places are still used for cultic purposes.

5–7. After Jehoash's assassination (12:20–21) Amaziah must consolidate his power, possibly against vying political or religious factions. Only once this is accomplished and the 'kingdom was firmly in his power' does he execute blood vengeance for his father's murder. Blood vengeance was an established ANE custom (Greenberg, *IDB* 1:321; Cogan and Tadmor 1988: 155) expressed in laws such as Num. 35:19 and Exod. 21:23. Amaziah's vengeance is not indiscriminate but is limited by the 'book of the torah of Moses' and includes an almost verbatim citation of Deut. 24:16. The citation places Amaziah in a positive light and is a piece with Dtr's focus on the deuteronomic law. The book of Deuteronomy refers often to 'this law' expounded by Moses (Deut. 1:5; 4:8; 27:3 *et passim*) or 'the/this book of the/this law' (Deut. 28:61; 31:26). Joshua is to follow the commands of 'this book of the law' (Josh. 1:8), which he later identifies as 'the book of the law of Moses' (Josh. 23:6). It is this same tradition that surfaces again when Josiah discovers 'this book of the law' in 2 Kgs 23:8, 11.

One brief verse is given to military action against Judah's historic enemy (2 Sam. 8:11–14; 1 Kgs 11:14–22). Judah once held authority over Edom (1 Kgs 22:47; 2 Kgs 3:9) but more recently that authority was lost (2 Kgs 8:20–22). Edom's rebellion 'until this day' suggests Amaziah is unable to subdue Edom wholly. David fought Edom at the Valley of Salt (2 Sam. 8:13), although its location is uncertain. A probable location is the area south of the Dead Sea (Younker, *ABD* 1:907; Cogan and Tadmor 1988: 155), which accords well with the site for Sela', modern es-Sela', northwest of Bozrah (Rainey 1976; Hart 1986). The battle is part of Judah's push towards the crucial port of Elath (v. 22), and the ten thousand men killed (a typological number indicating vast casualties) assures Judah's victory. Despite Judah's success, the brief note hurries the tale on to Amaziah's futile effort against the scion of Jehu (1 Kgs 13:25).

8–17. There is no apparent reason given in Kings for Amaziah's hostility (2 Chr. 25:5–20 provides political, economic and theological reasons). The temporal *'āz* plus perfect that begins the verse connects Amaziah's challenge to his victory over Edom (Rabinowitz 1984: 54). Messages are 'sent' between the kings (vv. 8–9) and Amaziah issues a call to 'face one another' (*nitrā'eh pānîm*), which, in the light of its use in v. 11, is a challenge to battle. Given Jehoash's greater military strength and recent victories over Aram (13:25), Amaziah's actions after one military victory indeed seem 'proud' (v. 10). The action takes place in Beth-shemesh 'in Judah', although elsewhere Beth-shemesh is 'in Israel' (Josh. 19:22, 38). Beth-shemesh is in the Sorek Valley along a contested Judahite–Israelite border (Cogan and Tadmor 1988: 158) and guards a major approach to Jerusalem

(Brandfon, *ABD* 1:696–698; Ferris, *ABD* 6:159–160). The identification suggests the narrative is told from a northern perspective.

Jehoash's wise parable is a common diplomatic form (extant examples are found in the Amarna letters; see *ANET* 486). He acknowledges Amaziah's initial victory and urges prudence rather than defeat. Amaziah does not listen, confirming his pride and imprudence. Whether he issues further challenges or marches out immediately, battle is engaged. Amaziah is captured in Judah's defeat – the first Davidide to face this ignominy. The solemnity of the event is marked by the use of Amaziah's full patronymic and title. Amaziah is soon released, for he continues to feature in the action in Jerusalem (vv. 17–21).

Jehoash exerts a conqueror's authority in Jerusalem: 656 feet (200 m) of the northern wall are breached and the temple and palace treasuries (replenished since 12:18–19) are plundered, removing resources for repairs. Hostages (*hatta'ărubôt*) are taken (perhaps of royal or noble family); the term occurs only here (see the parallel in 2 Chr. 25:24) and may be an Assyrian practice to ensure the good behaviour of the conquered monarch (Cogan and Tadmor 1988: 157; B. Long 1991: 167). Judah's power is significantly reduced and Jehoash returns to Samaria.

Within Amaziah's regnal summaries (vv. 1–4, 18–22) it is surprising to find a closing summary for Jehoash (vv. 15–16), especially when one has already been provided (13:12–13). Its inclusion by Dtr reveals the importance of the northern king in the narrative; even the remainder of Amaziah's reign is reckoned in relation to Jehoash's death (v. 17). The unique indication that Amaziah 'lived' (rather than 'ruled') after Jehoash's death hints that a co-regency may indeed be in place. Amaziah could have appointed a regent when he went to battle, or Jehoash may have required a co-regent alongside Amaziah as part of the terms of victory (Thiele 1983: 115; DeVries, *IDB* 1:592; but see the caution in Hobbs 1985: 185).

18–22. No reason for Amaziah's assassination is given. Retaliation for the lost battle is unlikely, as at least fifteen years have passed, but other political or military machinations may lie behind the event. For instance, Azariah does not avenge the assassination (as Amaziah did Jehoash's) and may be implicated. Likewise, Lachish is Judah's strongly fortified second city and seat of royal officials (Ussishkin, *NEAEHL* 3:905–907). That it affords Amaziah no protection suggests elements there complicit in, or amenable to, the coup. Amaziah is killed, his body returned by horse-drawn carriage and interred.

Azariah is made king by the 'people of Judah' (*'am yĕhûdâ*), that is, the general population of Judah (Cogan and Tadmor 1988: 157). Hobbs's suggestion (1985: 182) that the 'army' (*'am*) is involved aligns with the possibility of a military coup. If the event follows Amaziah's death and if a co-regency has been in place for fifteen years, Azariah's age of sixteen is very young (v. 21). Thus Thiele (1983: 115) argues that the verse retrospectively describes the appointment to the co-regency when the sixteen-year-old Azariah was 'made king' by the people.

In an unusual notation (v. 22) one event of Azariah's reign is related outside the boundaries of his own monarchic summaries (15:1–4, 6–7): he takes and rebuilds the port of Elath after 'the king slept with his fathers'. 'The king' is not Amaziah (no notice of his 'sleeping with his fathers' is given); it is Jehoash who 'sleeps with his fathers' (v. 16). That Azariah takes the port suggests Amaziah's weakness, and Jehoash's power had earlier prevented such action. Only after Jehoash's death is Judah strengthened to win again in battle (Na'aman 1993). Once again, the events of the southern monarchy stand in relation to its northern counterpart; the successful northern kingdom overshadows the south.

14:23–29

Following Thiele's solution to the chronological problems within the eighth-century monarchies, Jeroboam is co-regent with his father, Jehoash (793–782 BC), and then rules as sole monarch starting in Amaziah's fifteenth year (782 BC). Only by calculating his forty-one years (793–753 BC) to include both a co-regency and sole rule does the reign fit within the overall time frame for the northern kingdom (Thiele 1983: 116–118; DeVries, *IDB* 1:592). Like all Jehuite kings, he continues in the sins of Jeroboam.

Jeroboam follows in the ways of his namesake; he 'does not turn' from Jeroboam's sins and thus Israel's judgment stands. Paradoxically, his rule is the longest of any northern monarch (and only the Judahite reigns of Azariah and Manasseh are longer) and is economically and militarily strong. During his reign Aram's power is severely restricted, and Assyria from 783 to 745 BC diverted its attention from Israel to threats on its northern and southern borders (Hallo 1960: 44–46). In this window Jeroboam extends Israelite borders north of Damascus to Lebo-Hamath (v. 25). Though its location is disputed, modern Lebweh on the river Litani is probable (Aharoni 1979: 72–73, 344; but see Provan 1995: 239 for a location north of Tiphsah on the Euphrates). Jeroboam also 'recovered' Damascus and Hamath (v. 28), although the extent of Israelite control intended by this verse is uncertain. Israel had not held power there since David's time (2 Sam. 8:3–10), and restoration of trading centres in Damascus and Hamath may be in view (1 Kgs 20:34; Montgomery 1951: 444). Indeed, the text of v. 28 is 'hopelessly obscure and leaves the precise extent of Jeroboam's conquest uncertain' (Bright 2000: 257). But from its northern reaches, through the territories regained in the Transjordan, to the Sea of the Arabah, and perhaps into Moab (Aharoni 1979: 344), the territory approximates the extent of the kingdom of David and Solomon (2 Sam. 8; 1 Kgs 8:65).

That ideal borders are won by an apostate king of a nation under judgment creates a tension within Dtr's retributive theology and calls out several theological reasons for Jeroboam's success. First, YHWH 'delivers' Israel through Jeroboam and in this way the promise of a 'deliverer' originally given Jehoahaz (see 'Comment' at 2 Kgs 13:1–7, 19, 25) is now fulfilled. What was only partial in 2 Kgs 13, and left unfulfilled at that chapter's close, now reaches its fulfilment. It is Jeroboam who enables Israel to 'dwell in their homes as before' (13:5). The restoration of Solomon's ideal borders evokes the idyllic Solomonic empire as described in 1 Kgs 4:25[5:5]. Secondly, Israel's expanded borders are credited to the word of Jonah of Amittai, a prophet. Knowing the power of the prophetic word throughout Kings, its fulfilment here should not surprise. It is by the prophetic word that Jeroboam finds success. Thirdly, the deliverance occurs because of YHWH's own compassion over, and commitment to, Israel. In 13:4–5 YHWH 'saw' Israel's distress and gave a deliverer; this is echoed in 14:26, as YHWH 'sees' the affliction of Israel with none to help. As in the days of Moses, YHWH's compassion is roused when he 'sees' Israel's affliction, and deliverance is provided (Exod. 3:7; Deut. 26:7). All of this is in response to YHWH's gracious commitment not to 'blot out' Israel, just as Moses had petitioned (Exod. 32:32–33; Deut. 9:14).

Thus, though an apostate king of an apostate dynasty, Jeroboam (together with Jehoahaz and Jehoash) is the focus of these chapters. Because of the dynastic promise made to Jehu and the older covenant with Israel at Sinai (and before that, Abraham; 13:23), YHWH provides Israel a deliverer, and extends their boundaries. Because of YHWH's grace, Israel under the Jehuites live a 'charmed' life (B. Long 1991: 168).

In the light of Jeroboam's role in this extraordinary act of YHWH's mercy, little more need be recorded of his reign. Like all previous Jehuite kings Jeroboam 'slept with his fathers', but unlike the previous Jehuites, there is no record of his burial, perhaps a slight that recalls the fate of his namesake (1 Kgs 14:20). Zechariah, the fourth-generation Jehuite, succeeds Jeroboam.

Explanation

How easy it would be to draw erroneous conclusions from the northern kingdom's successes. The narrative reveals those successes in several ways: the northern kingdom overshadows the southern kingdom, overreaching it militarily. Amaziah's reign is structured so as to foreground the northern King Jehoash. Jehoash shows wisdom alongside Amaziah's proud imprudence. Jeroboam is the long-awaited deliverer. The prophetic word assures his success, and by him Israel's borders approximate those of the Davidic and Solomonic eras. If one were to measure a nation's righteousness or deservedness by material markers, the northern kingdom would be given top honours.

A more careful reading reveals the true story. The northern kingdom's success is in no way linked to their deservedness or righteousness – even the deliverer Jeroboam walks in the sins of his namesake. It is only by YHWH's graciousness and his commitment to ancient promises that Israel succeeds militarily or a deliver is given. The ongoing Jehuite dynasty remains only by YHWH's word, and the powerful prophetic word of Jonah comes by YHWH. It is by these gracious enactments on YHWH's part that Israel finds success.

The true story of Israel's success is also evident from the larger context. YHWH has repeatedly bestowed grace upon a sinful people – as recently shown in the reigns of Jehoash and Jehoahaz of Israel (2 Kgs 13; see 'Comment' and 'Explanation'). Equally evident is that YHWH has pronounced judgment upon Israel. According to Deuteronomistic norms they will face defeat and not success (Deut. 28:20, 25–26, 36, 49–57). The word given Jeroboam I likewise forecasts this end (1 Kgs 14:15–16).

Israel's remaining years as a nation (2 Kgs 15 – 17) reveal the same truth. In Jeroboam II Israel stands on the brink of the rapid slide to conquest and exile (2 Kgs 17). In the sixty years from Jeroboam to Hoshea, seven kings reign, dynastic instability is unparalleled, and increasing foreign conflict signals Israel's approaching demise. They fall to Assyria for the sins of Jeroboam and Ahab that have appeared throughout their history. There is no 'golden age' of righteousness in Jeroboam II's monarchy; he is as Israel has always been. His success comes not by Israel's righteous deservedness but by YHWH's grace.

But appearances can deceive one who does not carefully exegete events and their contexts. In a history in which retributive theology – the concept that good or bad actions elicit good or bad effects – is predominant, YHWH shows his freedom. He is in no way bound to abide by those concepts. That is what makes grace, grace: even the unrighteous can be blessed by YHWH's hand and for his purposes. If one measures only by pragmatics, then military success or victory, power and influence can be taken as proofs of deservedness. By these measures, no acknowledgment may be given of YHWH's grace extended to those who are under judgment. One must therefore judge with righteous judgment.

The dangers of judging appearances wrongly, and the necessity for righteous judgment, are not surprising in a history inhabited by a God who works freely as he wills. What one might expect and how one might measure appearances may not align with what YHWH is actually about. One need only imagine Samuel's befuddlement as the sons of Jesse pass before him. Something different than suggested by appearances was afoot by YHWH's design (1 Sam. 16). Job, too, shows that appearances may lead to wrong conclusions, especially when the measurement applied to those appearances by Job's comforters was likewise misconstrued. In Job's story YHWH was about something the human actors (and perhaps his readers) could never understand, and indeed is never explained. Ananias and Sapphira present an interesting NT example of a couple attempting to put forward a false appearance. By the Spirit Peter sees truly, and measures them by righteous judgment (Acts 5:1–11).

To 'judge with righteous judgment' brings to mind Jesus' own ministry. He charges that the people do not rightly judge his adherence to the law of Moses. Yet Jesus moves seamlessly with the law and fulfils the Father's will. The people measure appearances by the wrong measurement, and miss YHWH in the process.

YHWH's grace in 2 Kgs 14 is poured out on Israel before exile encroaches. It calls for the right reading of appearances. For those in exile in Babylon it must be apparent that neither Israel's success nor the grace that enabled it pardoned Israel from judgment. The chapter is equally cognizant that Judah is not free from sin (vv. 3–4) and so they, too, face judgment. In the extension of their life for over 100 more years, for the reprieve they experience during Hezekiah's reign (2 Kgs 18 – 19), for the restoration under Josiah's reign (2 Kgs 22 – 23) they must acknowledge that these, too, were by YHWH's grace. Perhaps it is only after YHWH has bestowed his grace and time has gone by, or only from the place of exile that one is able to see rightly. Appearances at the time can be deceiving. For Dtr true sight comes afterwards, from the place of personal experience, theological reflection and memory.

I am mindful as I write this of the church's propensity to judge by pragmatic appearances. True success is always by YHWH's grace, but do we measure success rightly? True success may by YHWH's grace be enabled in a sinful people, but do we seek his righteousness to align ourselves better with his gracious acts? There can be times and places of exile in the church, where it, like Israel, realigns its vision of where and how God works. How much better if exile never comes, if by submission to Word and Spirit the church sees rightly and walks righteously and the Son is glorified.

2 KINGS 15:1–38

Translation

[1]In the twenty-seventh year of Jeroboam king of Israel, Azariah son of Amaziah king of Judah began to reign. [2]He was sixteen years old when he began to reign and he reigned fifty-two years in Jerusalem. His mother's name was Jecoliah of Jerusalem. [3]He did what was right in the eyes of YHWH, according to all that his father Amaziah had done. [4]Only the high places were not removed; the people still sacrificed and burned incense on the high places. [5]YHWH struck the king and he was a leper until the day of his death. He lived freely in his house[a] and the

king's son Jotham was steward, governing the people of the land. ⁶Now the rest of the acts of Azariah and all that he did, are they not written in the Book of the Chronicles of the Kings of Judah? ⁷Then Azariah slept with his fathers and they buried him with his fathers in the city of David. And Jotham his son reigned in his place.

⁸In the thirty-eighthᵃ year of Azariah king of Judah, Zechariah son of Jeroboam reigned over Israel in Samaria six months. ⁹He did what was evil in the eyes of YHWH just as his fathers had done. He did not turn from the sins of Jeroboam son of Nebat, which he caused Israel to sin. ¹⁰Shallum son of Jabesh conspired against him and struck him in Ibleamᵃ and killed him. Then he reigned in his place. ¹¹Now the rest of the acts of Zechariah, behold, they are written in the Book of the Chronicles of the Kings of Israel. ¹²This was the word of YHWH that he spoke to Jehu, saying, 'Your sons to the fourth generation shall sit on the throne of Israel.' And so it was.

¹³Shallum son of Jabesh began to reign in the thirty-ninthᵃ year of Uzziah king of Judah, and he reigned one month in Samaria. ¹⁴Then Menahem son of Gadi went up from Tirzah and came to Samaria. He struck Shallum son of Jabesh in Samaria. He killed him and began to reign in his place. ¹⁵Now the rest of the acts of Shallum, and his conspiracy that he planned, behold, they are written in the Book of the Chronicles of the Kings of Israel. ¹⁶Thenᵃ Menahem struck Tiphsah and all who were in it, and its territory, from Tirzah. He struck it because it did not open *to him*, and all its pregnant women he ripped openᵇ.

¹⁷In the thirty-ninthᵃ year of Azariah king of Judah, Menahem son of Gadi began to reign over Israel. *He reigned* ten years in Samaria. ¹⁸He did what was evil in the eyes of YHWH; he did not turn from allᵃ the sins of Jeroboam son of Nebat, which he caused Israel to sin. ¹⁹In his daysᵃ Pul king of Assyria came against the land and Menahem gave to Pul 1,000 talents of silver to help strengthen the kingdom in his hand. ²⁰Menahem exacted the silver from Israel, that is, from all the wealthy – 50 shekels of silver from each one – to pay to the king of Assyria. So the king of Assyria withdrew and did not remain there in the land. ²¹Now the rest of the acts of Menahem, and all that he did, are they not written in the Book of the Chronicles of the Kings of Israel? ²²Then Menahem slept with his fathers and Pekahiah his son reigned in his place.

²³In the fiftieth yearᵃ of Azariah king of Judah, Pekahiah son of Menahem began to reign over Israel in Samaria. *He reigned* two years. ²⁴He did what was evil in the eyes of YHWH; he did not turn from the sins of Jeroboam son of Nebat, which he caused Israel to sin. ²⁵Then Pekah son of Remaliah his officer conspired against him and struck him in Samaria in the citadel of the palaceᵃ, and fifty Gileadites helped him. He killed him and reigned in his place. ²⁶Now the rest of the acts of Pekahiah, and all that he did, behold, they are written in the Book of the Chronicles of the Kings of Israel.

²⁷In the fifty-second year of Azariah king of Judah, Pekah son of Remaliah began to reign over Israel in Samaria. *He reigned* twenty years. ²⁸He did what was evil in the eyes of YHWH; he did not turn from the sins of Jeroboam son of Nebat, which he caused Israel to sin. ²⁹In the days of Pekah king of Israel,

Tiglath-pileser king of Assyria came and captured Ijon, Abel-beth-maacah, Janoah, Kedesh, Hazor, Gilead, Galilee and all the land of Naphtali, and he deported them to Assyria. ³⁰Then Hoshea son of Elah conspired against Pekah son of Remaliah and struck and killed him and reigned in his place. This occurred in the twentiethᵃ year of Jotham son of Uzziah. ³¹Now the rest of the acts of Pekah and all that he did, behold, they are written in the Book of the Chronicles of the Kings of Israel.

³²In the second year of Pekah son of Remaliah king of Israel, Jotham son of Uzziah king of Judah began to reign. ³³He was twenty-five years old when he began to reign, and he reigned sixteen years in Jerusalem. His mother's name was Jerusha the daughter of Zadok. ³⁴He did what was right in the eyes of YHWH; he did according to all that his father Uzziah had done. ³⁵Only the high places were not removed; the people still sacrificed and burned incense on the high places. He built the upper gate of the house of YHWH. ³⁶Now the rest of the acts that Jotham did, are they not written in the Book of the Chronicles of the Kings of Judah? ³⁷In those days YHWH began to send Rezin king of Aram and Pekah son of Remaliah against Judah. ³⁸Then Jotham slept with his fathers, and he was buried with his fathers in the city of David his father. Then Ahaz his son reigned in his place.

Notes on the text

5.a. 'freely in his house' reads *haḥopšît* (so the Q at 2 Chr. 26:21) adverbially. Translating 'freely' (as the noun clearly means in 1 Sam. 17:25; Job 3:19: Ps. 88:5[6]; *HALOT* 341–342) rather than 'separate', as it often is translated.

8.a. LXX texts have 'twenty-eight' and 'twenty-nine', evidencing the confusion surrounding the chronology within Kings. Similarly at vv. 13, 17, 23, 30.

10.a. MT *qābāl ʿam* often as 'before the people' with LXX^BO, Syr, Tg, Vg, but *qābāl* is a late Aramaism and MT would need an article on *ʿam*. Here read as a place, 'Ibleam', with LXX^L. Other assassinations in the chapter (vv. 14, 25) include a location (Cogan and Tadmor 1988: 171).

13.a. LXX has a different chronology. See n. 8.a above.

16.a. *ʿaz* with impf. indicating related temporally, but not necessarily consecution (Rabinowitz 1984).

16.b. MT's awkward *wayyak ʾēt kol-hehārôtêhāh*, 'he struck [. . .] and ripped open all its pregnant women', read as *wayyak ʾōtāh wĕkol-hārôtêhāh*, 'he struck it and all its pregnant women he ripped open'. Following the versions, the DDO takes a 3 f. sg. object suff., and a conj. is added. The article, probably a dittography, is removed.

17.a. LXX has a different chronology. See n. 8.a above.

18.a. *mēʿal* as *mikkol* with some MSS, LXX^L, Tg.

19.a. Final *kol-yāmāyw*, 'all his days', in v. 18 becomes *bĕyāmāyw*, 'in his days', and is moved to the beginning of v. 19 with LXX^L.

23.a. LXX has a different chronology. See n. 8.a above.

25.a. MT *'et-'argōb wě'et-hā'aryēh* ('Argob and the lion' or 'Argob and Arieh') makes little sense here and is deleted. No verb stands with the two accusatives. Stade (1886: 160) removes the names as a misplaced gloss from v. 29 and a corruption of place names (see 1 Kgs 4:13). His insight is generally followed today (Gray 1970: 625; Hobbs 1985: 188; Cogan and Tadmor 1988: 173). Geller (1976: 374–377) translates as a location 'near the eagle and the lion', assuming sphinxes in the Samaria palace. His evidence is slim textually and iconographically.

30.a. LXX chronology differs; see n. 8.a above.

Form and structure

Following the years of northern stability in the Jehuite era, 2 Kgs 15 shows a remarkable reversal. As YHWH's commitment to the Jehu dynasty ends with the fourth generation, the northern kingdom falls again into the pattern of consecutive coups last experienced in 1 Kgs 15 – 16. In the north four coups take place over twenty years. In the same period only two southern monarchs reign and succession passes without hindrance. The chapter's structure emphasizes the northern instability, for the continual shifts in the north are enveloped by the stable reign of the two Judahite kings.

The chapter has a rapid narrative pace served by the repetitive structure of the regnal formulae. These toll off each reign, with little additional information. Any additional information provided for a northern monarch either signals northern instability through another coup, or northern vulnerability before the encroaching Assyrian threat. Both contribute to Israel's decline. The sins of Jeroboam continue as Israel moves towards inevitable exile, and abbreviated closing formulae speed the narrative pace towards Israel's demise.

The southern monarchs are judged favorably, although the shadow of the high places remains. In the light of judgment on Israel for non-Deuteronomistic worship, they serve as a warning regarding Judah's fate. The chapter closes with Judah threatened by Rezin and Pekah, by YHWH's hand. This, too, serves to warn that Israel's judgment may similarly be visited upon Judah.

The events of the chapter find several references in extra-biblical witnesses, specifically Assyrian reportage of westward expansion. These historical touchstones at times bring clarity to the chronology of these rapid years but often raise questions that are not always answerable with the information currently available. Yet the narrative focus is not on a full explication of the events within their historical context. Rather, the narrative focuses on the theological reasons for the tragedy of Israel's final years: YHWH's favour has been withdrawn, the time for payment for

Jeroboam's sins draws near, and the instrument for YHWH's wrath is at hand in the Assyrian Empire.

Comment

15:1–7

Ahaziah's fifty-two-year reign (792–740 BC) is calculated from his co-regency at age sixteen, with Jeroboam's twenty-seventh year marking his sole regency. His lengthy reign coincides with Jeroboam's long reign and the significantly briefer reigns of Zechariah, Shallum, Menahem, Pekahiah and Pekah (Thiele 1983: 118–123; DeVries, *IDB* 1:589–592). In Kings he is generally named 'Azariah', although 'Uzziah' (with variant 'Uzziahu') also appears (vv. 13, 20, 32, 34). Elsewhere he is named Uzziah (2 Chr. 26 – 27; Amos 1:1; Hos. 1:1; Isa. 1:1; 6:1; 7:1). Azariah and Uzziah derive from two roots bearing a close semantic relationship meaning 'strength, victory' and should be considered variants (Jones 1984b: 519; Cogan and Tadmor 1988: 165; Sweeney 2007: 370) rather than being a personal and a throne name (Montgomery 1951: 446).

Azariah is approved for acting as his father, without the negative comparison made to David as happened for Amaziah. Wholesale approval is mitigated, as the high places remain (1 Kgs 3:2; 15:14; 2 Kgs 12:3; 14:4).

Juxtaposed to the failure to remove the high places is Azariah's leprosy, the sole event recorded for his reign (compare to Chronicles' much fuller account). The juxtaposition and the affliction's occurrence by YHWH's hand suggest a note of displeasure for the continuance of the high places (a similar note is sounded in the account of Asa's diseased feet; see 'Comment' at 1 Kgs 15:23). Not the debilitating disease known today as Hansen's disease, the leprosy was any number of curable or incurable skin diseases that rendered an individual unclean (Lev. 13; see 'Comment', 2 Kgs 5:1).

Like Gehazi and Naaman before him, Azariah's non-contagious disease did not require his isolation (see 'Notes on the text', v. 5), although he was released from governing responsibilities. These responsibilities were vested in Jotham, who served as steward over the king's estates (lit. 'over the house'; see 'Comment' at 1 Kgs 4:6, where the role first appears), and who as co-regent governed (*špṭ*) the Judean populace. Upon Azariah's death Jotham begins to 'reign' (*mlk*). Azariah's closing summary conforms to the usual pattern, although it should be noted that 2 Chr. 26:23 has a variant burial tradition. Interestingly, an Aramaic ossuary inscription of the Second Temple period refers to the removal of Azariah's bones and may be behind the chronicler's tradition (Sukenik 1931).

The lack of detail given for Azariah's reign is not due to a 'lacuna' in the traditions available to Dtr (so Montgomery 1951: 448). Rather, it highlights the stability of Azariah's reign during illness and co-regency. This stability is a contrastive backdrop to the successive instability of the northern monarchs. Whereas the earlier Jehuites experienced stability by YHWH's gracious acts, now that favour is lifted and it is the Davidides who are once again portrayed favourably – with, however, hints that their actions may yet lead them to the judgment that inevitably awaits the north.

15:8–31

8–12. Zechariah is the last of the Jehuite dynasty and his brief reign (compared to the consecutive twenty-eight-, seventeen-, sixteen- and forty-one-year reigns of his dynastic predecessors) signals how completely YHWH removes his blessing as the dynasty ends. The only event related from his reign is its abrupt end by an assassin's hand, and his demise is presented as proof of YHWH's fulfilled word to Jehu (10:30). YHWH's grace has favoured the dynasty and held back judgment, but now that judgment is released to sweep over the nation.

Ironically, the Jehuite dynasty ends at Ibleam, where Azariah of Judah was assassinated as the dynasty began (9:27). Shallum is known only as 'son of Jabesh', probably a patronym, as is common in the introduction of a new king. The reference to Jabesh is often taken to refer to his origins in Jabesh-gilead in the Transjordan (Ishida 1977: 173–176; Thiele 1983: 124; Cogan and Tadmor 1988: 178). From this are posited intertribal conflicts across the Jordanian divide that fired the rapid succession of rulers after Zechariah (thus Shallum was from Gilead, Menahem from Manasseh, Pekahiah from Gilead; see 'Comment' below, v. 14). There is merit in this argument; however, it does not wholly explain the assassination of Zechariah by a Gileadite. Zechariah's dynastic head was (if not himself from Gilead) supported by Elijah and Elisha, who were Gileadites, and tribal allegiance would militate against Zechariah's assassination; something more must be behind the assassination. Given the rising Assyrian threat, the various coups probably represent different policies vis-à-vis Assyria.

Zechariah's closing summary is abbreviated, with no notice of his death or burial. This pattern ensues through the closing formulae for all subsequent northern kings. Only in the case of Menahem is a notice of death provided.

13–16. Shallum's reign is embarrassingly brief (only Zimri's is shorter). As if to give as much narrative attention as possible to Shallum, his name precedes the (usually initial) synchronism. The brevity of his reign accounts for the lack of Dtr evaluation. The inclusion of the 'rest of his acts' follows the formulaic nature of the regnal summaries.

Menahem's coup arises out of Tirzah in Manasseh, Israel's capital from Jeroboam I to Omri (1 Kgs 14:17; 15:33; 16:8, 15, 23). If Tirzah is Menahem's home town, he is a Manassite. 'Son of Gadi', then, is his patronymic and not a reference to his tribal origins in Gad, east of the Jordan (Gray 1970: 622; Jones 1984b: 522; Cogan and Tadmor 1988: 171).

At the time of the coup Menahem takes severe action against Tiphsah. The town is on the northern extremity of Solomon's kingdom (1 Kgs 4:24[5:4]) and may be part of Israel's holdings as a result of Jeroboam's expansion (Haran 1967). The location's distance from Tirzah is thought to pose difficulties for such an expedition (Bright 2000: 271), and Tappuah (as in LXX[L]) on the Ephraim–Manasseh border south of Tirzah is considered a likelier location (Montgomery 1951: 450; Gray 1970: 623; Jones 1984b: 523). Action against Tiphsah, despite its distance, could be credited to attempts to strengthen Israel's northern boundaries in the face of the growing Assyrian threat. If this is the case, Tiphsah's unwillingness to 'open to Menahem' might signal they have allied with Assyria. Menahem's horrific punitive measure, then, serves as a dark lesson to the city, for such actions were used by nations such as Aram and Ammon (2 Kgs 8:12; Amos 1:13), and Assyria (Cogan 1983: 755–757; cf. Hos. 13:16[14:1]).

17–22. Menahem's reign (752–742 BC) is marked by one event: the payment of tribute to Pul, the throne name for Tiglath-pileser III (v. 29; ANET 272). Tiglath-pileser (745–727 BC) restored Assyria's fortunes and pursued a new policy of empire building that incorporated subdued nations into the Assyrian Empire as provinces under Assyrian governors. Often, loss of national status began with tribute payments and proceeded incrementally to loss of national independence (Aharoni 1979: 369; Jones 1984b: 525).

Menahem's policy represents a return to the pro-Assyrian stance of the Jehuite dynasty, and, if Shallum represented an anti-Assyrian party, suggests also the reason behind Menahem's coup. Tribute of 1,000 talents (7,716 lb [3,500 kg] of silver by a conservative measure) is raised; given the taxation rate, sixty thousand persons would be required. Royal contributions could reduce that significantly (Sellers, IDB 4:828–839; Jones 1984b: 526). The tribute is high but comparable to other tributes Tiglath-pileser notes in his Summary Inscriptions. Hulli of Tabal paid 1,000 talents of silver, and Metenna of Tyre 2,000 talents of silver; in both instances the high tribute can be explained by the fact they were usurpers whose tribute bought Assyrian support (Tadmor 1994: 171). A similar purpose may have motivated Menahem's payment, for he seeks to 'strengthen the kingdom in his hand', that is, strengthen his hold upon the kingdom (v. 19). This would be a concern of a usurper within an already unstable kingdom, especially if a rival claimant to the crown existed (see 'Comment' on Pekah below).

Menahem's payment, along with payments by Rezin of Damascus, and Tyre, is recorded in both Assyrian annals (ANET 283) and a stele inscription (L. Levine 1972: 40–42; Tadmor 1994: 154, 171). The annal is dated to 738 BC, well after Menahem's reign ends, although it may represent a collation of several of Tiglath-pileser's earlier campaigns back to 743 BC, when Menahem was in power (L. Levine 1972; Cogan 1973; DeVries, *IDB* 1:593; Thiele 1983: 125–126).

While Israel's payment may have strengthened Menahem's hold on the kingdom, it is a first step towards their ultimate incorporation into the Assyrian Empire. Menahem succeeds in buying time, and, 'resting with his fathers', passes the throne to his son. The appearance of stability is deceptive, and short-lived.

23–26. Pekahiah's rule is overturned in its vulnerable early years (Ishida 1977: 173–174) by an insider. Pekah, his officer (*šālîš*; 2 Kgs 7:2), is supported by a company of Gileadites. This group does not provide proof of Pekah's own tribal origins, nor is there evidence of a rival faction east of the Jordan seeking to supplant the Manassite Pekahiah (see 'Comment' at vv. 10, 14 above). It is more probable that Pekah's coup responds to Menahem's and Pekahiah's pro-Assyrian policy. Together with Aram Pekah institutes an anti-Assyrian policy (see 'Comment' at 2 Kgs 16:5–6; cf. Isa. 7). This supposition is borne out by Pekah's failure to submit tribute to Assyria (v. 29).

Pekahiah is struck down in a fortified portion of the palace (1 Kgs 16:18). The lack of detail regarding the events or the role played by the Gileadites focuses the passage on the rapid turnover of rule. The kingdom is now moving quickly towards its destruction. No dynasty is established by Pekah, and though he and Hoshea each rule longer than Pekahiah, they provide no relief for Israel.

27–31. Azariah's fifty-second year is 740 BC. This presents chronological difficulties, for if Pekah's twenty-year reign begins in that year it would not conclude until after Israel fell to Assyria (dated to 722 BC), and would leave no room for Hoshea's reign. One solution calculates Pekah's rule from 752 to 732 BC, making his rule concurrent with and rival to the rules of Menahem and Pekahiah (Thiele 1983: 129; cf. Oded 1972: 162–163; Cogan and Tadmor 1988: 179); another proposes that Pekah took the throne in 740 BC but sought to bolster his claim by calculating his regnal years back to Shallum, disregarding the reigns of Menahem and Pekahiah (DeVries, *IDB* 1:589). This dual dating for Pekah's reign (accession in 740 BC and regnal years 752–732 BC) provides a framework within which the remaining chronological problems find a reasonable resolution (see 'Comment' on chronology in 2 Kgs 17 – 18).

Pekah and Aram ally against Assyria and attempt to draw Judah into the alliance (v. 37; 2 Kgs 16; Isa. 7). Pekah's anti-Assyrian policy is not successful, however. In 734–732 BC (*ANET* 283) Assyria under Tiglath-pileser III subjugates the coastal plain and takes Damascus and much of Israel (Hallo 1960: 48–50; Donner 1977b: 425–427; Aharoni 1979: 371–374; Bright 2000: 274–275). Tiglath-pileser's policy of mass deportation (Oded 1979: 20) effects staggeringly high population displacement: upwards of fourteen thousand people as an accumulated aggregate from the Galilean campaign (Younger 1998: 208–213).

Hoshea's coup takes place in the twentieth year of Jotham's reign (732 BC) reckoned from the co-regency with his father (v. 5). The coup may be assisted by Tiglath-pileser, who claims he put Hoshea on the throne (*ANET* 284). Hoshea's immediate tribute to Assyria saves Israel from complete subjugation as an Assyrian province.

15:32–38

The history of the southern kingdom is advanced to the same point as the northern kingdom. Jotham's co-regency begins in Pekah's second year (750 BC) and is calculated as sixteen years (v. 32; fifteen actual years, as the first year of the co-regency is double-counted), ending in 735 BC. That he still reigns in his twentieth year (v. 30) suggests a further co-regency with Ahaz at the end of his life (borne out by the chronology given for Ahaz; see 'Comment' at 16:1; Thiele 1983: 132).

Jotham is favourably evaluated, although the caveat of the high places remains. The building of the upper gate leading into the temple courtyard (Jer. 20:2; Ezek. 9:2) is the one event recounted from Jotham's reign. It lauds his action but by recounting the fortification of Jerusalem also ominously foreshadows the Syro-Ephraimite threat (v. 37) and the larger Assyrian threat behind it. Despite Jotham's fortifications (see also 2 Chr. 27:3–4) Judah must still place their safety in YHWH's hands. Given their ongoing failure regarding the high places, such trust cannot be assumed as inevitable.

Explanation

The contrast of the experience of multiple disasters in this chapter to the experience of YHWH's grace recounted in 2 Kgs 13 – 14 is striking. Jehu's dynasty ends abruptly as YHWH's favour ends, followed by years of instability and brutality. Assyrian incursions press upon Israel despite tributary payment (vv. 19, 29), and deportation of the population begins (v. 29). The sins of Jeroboam remain constant throughout the reigns of successive northern monarchs, and each reign is narrated rapidly until that of Hoshea, Israel's last king.

Jeroboam II's reign is the final pause before the storm breaks upon Israel. It rages with increasing intensity until Israel fall (2 Kgs 15, 17) and fulfil YHWH's word spoken to Moses. As Israel stood on the east side of the Jordan, Moses charges them with the deuteronomic law as the means for life in the land. As the covenant is renewed (Deut. 29) Moses rehearses YHWH's past gracious acts: salvation from Egypt (vv. 2–3), sustenance through the wilderness and defeat of Israel's enemies (vv. 4–8). The covenant is renewed with Israel on behalf of the present and all future generations, and fulfils the ancient promises made to Abraham (vv. 9–15). Two possible threats are capable of undermining Israel's continued prosperous existence in the land: worship of foreign gods (vv. 16–18, 25–26), and personal complacency that presumes the covenant will ensure safety despite such false worship (vv. 19–21).

Throughout their history Israel err on both these counts. And, although they repeatedly experience YHWH's patient grace that does not release all the covenant curses upon them, that grace is now withdrawn from the northern kingdom. The tragedy of this withdrawal was communicated to Moses after the covenant was renewed. While standing before YHWH in the tent of meeting, Moses was told that the people would break the covenant and forsake YHWH. YHWH also forecast to Moses his anger and abandonment of his people. He would hide his face from them and, as a result, multiple disasters would come upon them (Deut. 31:15–18). Although Israel experienced disasters as a result of her sinfulness (e.g. the cycle of sin and foreign oppression in the book of Judges), it is only now in this chapter that YHWH fully turns his face from Israel and the promised multiple disasters take place.

The tragedy of YHWH's withdrawal of favour was also communicated to the people. Immediately as YHWH told Moses of Israel's impending failure and YHWH's withdrawn favour (Deut. 31:14–18), he urged Moses to enshrine these realities in a song to be taught Israel as a witness against them (31:19–22). The song communicates clearly YHWH's covenant commitment to Israel, Israel's rejection of YHWH for other gods, and YHWH's abandonment of his people as he hides his face from them (Deut. 32; see esp. v. 20). The enactment of this eventuality is set in motion in 2 Kgs 15.

There is no greater tragedy than a nation rescued out of slavery, cared for in every way and covenanted in love to YHWH who has saved them, only to have that people reject their saviour God. As the song is sung by successive generations it serves not only as a didactic warning, but as a lament over Israel's perversity.

In a similar way 2 Kgs 15 is a didactic warning. The witness of Israel's slide towards exile speaks of YHWH's abandonment of his people: he has turned his face from the northern kingdom. But that narrative is enclosed by two vignettes of southern kings. Though each king is approved, the high places remain and each king is chastised for such sins. Azariah is afflicted with leprosy and Jotham feels the bite of foreign oppression from Aram and Judah. As Kings continues, the chapter serves to warn Judah: they must beware, for Israel is abandoned on account of cultic sins. If Judah persists, they may face the same withdrawal of YHWH's face, with concomitant disasters.

But knowing the outcome of the history and Judah's fate, the chapter is also (like the Song of Moses) a proleptic lament for Judah. The crafters of the narrative, writing from exile, know that soon YHWH's face will also turn from a disobedient southern kingdom (1 Kgs 9:7; 2 Kgs 24:3).

In this light the grief of the chapter is profound, for it attests to the perversity of the whole nation. North and south likewise turn from their covenanted partner and – after centuries of his patient grace – receive the full extent of covenant punishment.

There is, however, a note of hope inherent in the lamentation in 2 Kgs 15 and Deut. 32. Though the northern kingdom is released from YHWH's care and rushes headlong to destruction, that nation remains YHWH's people. As for their sister, the southern kingdom, the covenantal promises remain despite the people's sinfulness. The Song voices this ongoing commitment on YHWH's part. Though YHWH will judge his people to the extremity of national and covenantal life, turning his face from them, he remains in covenant with them. As a God of life, he commits himself to bring life out of death, healing out of woundedness, and atonement for land and people (Deut. 32:36–43). Other prophets echo this same astounding promise (Jer. 30 – 31, 33; Ezek. 37). Israel (and later, Judah) is released to rush towards final destruction. But YHWH's word is that destruction is *not* final and that resurrection life will restore the nation.

As Israel are released from YHWH's favour in 2 Kgs 15 they embark on their own Via Dolorosa that ends in destruction and exile. To their didactic warning and lament must be added the additional note of ongoing promise and resurrection power. Israel's Via Dolorosa (and later, Judah's) leads to the death of the nation. But even such perverse sinfulness cannot trump YHWH's faithfulness. Israel's release to destruction becomes only another stage upon which YHWH's covenantal goodness will be demonstrated. Sin must be punished – even to death – but out of death will come new life.

2 KINGS 16:1–20

Translation

[1]In the seventeenth[a] year of Pekah son of Remaliah, Ahaz son of Jotham king of Judah began to rule. [2]Ahaz was twenty years old when he began to reign, and he reigned sixteen years in Jerusalem. He did not do what was right in the eyes of YHWH his God, as David his father had done. [3]He walked in the way of the kings of Israel and even made his son[a] pass through the fire according to the abominations of the nations whom YHWH had driven out before the sons of Israel. [4]He sacrificed and burned incense on the high places and on the hills and under every leafy tree.

[5]Then Rezin king of Aram and Pekah son of Remaliah king of Israel went up against Jerusalem to wage war. They besieged Ahaz but were not able to overcome *him*[a]. [6]At that time the king of Edom[a] recovered Elath for Edom. He cleared the Judeans from Elath and the Edomites[b] came to Elath and have dwelt there until today.

[7]Ahaz sent messengers to Tiglath-pileser king of Assyria, saying, 'I am your servant and son; come up and deliver me from the hand of the king of Aram and from the hand of the king of Israel who have risen against me.' [8]Ahaz took the silver and the gold that were found in the house of YHWH and in the treasuries of the king's house and he sent a gift to the king of Assyria. [9]The king of Assyria listened to him, and the king of Assyria went up to Damascus and captured it. He deported its people to Kir and put Rezin to death.

[10]Then King Ahaz went to meet Tiglath-pileser king of Assyria at Damascus. He saw the altar that was in Damascus and King Ahaz sent to Uriah the priest a model of the altar and the pattern for all its construction. [11]Uriah the priest built the altar according to all that King Ahaz sent from Damascus; thus did Uriah the priest make it before King Ahaz returned from Damascus. [12]The king came from Damascus and the king inspected the altar. The king then approached the altar and went up on it. [13]He burned his burnt offering and his meal offering and he poured out his libation, and he sprinkled the blood of the peace offerings on his behalf upon the altar. [14]And the bronze altar that was before YHWH he moved from the front of the house, from between the altar and the house of YHWH. He set it on the north side of the altar.

[15]Then King Ahaz commanded Uriah the priest, saying, 'Upon the great altar burn the morning's burnt offering and the evening's meal offering and the king's burnt offering and his meal offering and the burnt offering of all the people of the land and their meal offering and libation, and all the blood of the burnt offering and all the blood of the sacrifice you shall sprinkle upon it. But the bronze altar will be for me to enquire by.'[a] [16]So Uriah the priest did all that King Ahaz commanded.

[17]King Ahaz cut off the frames[a] of the stands and took the basins off them. He took the sea down from the bronze oxen that were under it and he put it on a stone base. [18]The Sabbath covering[a] that they had built in the house and the outer entry for the king he removed from the house of YHWH because of the king of Assyria.

[19]And the rest of the acts of Ahaz that he did, are they not written in the Book of the Chronicles of the Kings of Judah? [20]Then Ahaz slept with his fathers and was buried with his fathers in the City of David, and Hezekiah his son reigned in his place.

Notes on the text

1.a. LXX[127], Syr read, 'eighteenth' year.

3.a. LXX[L] and 2 Chr. 28:3 read, 'sons'.

5.a. 'to overcome *him*'. In the parallel account of Isa. 7:1 the object is provided in MT.

6.a. MT reads, 'Rezin, king of Aram'. 'Rezin' is removed as a later interpolation informed by the occurrence of 'Rezin' in v. 5. It is unlikely Aram would venture so far south on behalf of a third party. 2 Chr. 28:17 reveals

Edom was engaged against Judah during the era of the Syro-Ephraimite alliance and, on this basis, reading 'Edom' for Aram' (twice) with most commentators; the change is of only one consonant.

6.b. Reading with Q 'Edomites' for 'Arameans'. See n. 6.a above.

15.a. The significance of *lĕbaqqēr* (pi. inf. const. with lamed prep.; here 'to enquire by') is hard to discern (NASB, NRSV 'to inquire by'; NIV 'to seek guidance'; LXX 'in the morning' assumes Hebr. *labbōqer*). The only other instances of this formulation are in Ps. 27:4, variously translated as 'meditate' (NASB), 'inquire' [in his temple] (NRSV) and 'seek' [him] (NIV); and in Prov. 20:25 'inquiry' (NASB), 'reflect' (NRSV) and 'consider' (NIV). Two impf. occurrences have the idea of 'scrutinize' (Lev. 13:36; 27:33), and one pf., as 'attend to, look after' (Ezek. 34:11–12). See *HALOT* 1:151. Burney 1903: 327 translates, 'to enquire by', as in seeking an oracle, *possibly* through extispacy; Gray assumes extispacy (1970: 637).

17.a. Deleting the art. on the Hebr. const. noun ('the stands') for grammatical correctness. The wheeled stands and frames are described in 1 Kgs 7:27–43.

18.a. Reading *mûsak haššabbāt*, 'Sabbath covering', with Q. LXX supposes Hebr. *mûsad haššebet*, 'base for the throne'.

Form and structure

After the rapid succession of reigns in 2 Kgs 15, this chapter lingers over Ahaz, a Judahite king who 'walks in the way of the kings of Israel'. The chapter relates Ahaz's response to the Syro-Ephraimite threat introduced in his father's reign (2 Kgs 15:37) and his appeal to the king of Assyria. But, despite these pressing international security issues, it is Ahaz's alterations to the temple cult that are the chapter's concern and that are presented as evidence of Ahaz's wickedness.

The political events of Ahaz's reign are summarized in vv. 5–9. The temporal markers 'then' (v. 5) and 'at that time' (v. 6) commonly mark verbatim quotes from archival sources (Cogan and Tadmor 1988: 186), but the lack of detail suggests the summary nature of the notation. The brief attention paid to the events of secular history compared to the narrative space granted Ahaz's temple alterations (vv. 10–18) reveals the focus of the chapter. Political history serves only as a backdrop to religious history.

The lengthy temple narrative, similar in theme to 2 Kgs 12, suggests a common source, perhaps from a temple chronicle (Hobbs 1985: 216; Cogan and Tadmor 1988: 193). Gray (1970: 631) argues for a priestly redactor – possibly even Dtr himself – although the fact that Jones denies a priestly source (1984b: 532–533) reveals the subjectivity of such assessments.

Ahaz's actions in the temple are the central point of the narrative and this is apparent from the chapter's structure:

Introductory regnal summary
    A   Submission to the king of Assyria
        B   Instructions for temple alterations; compliance by
            Uriah
            C   Worship at the new altar
        B' Instructions for offerings; compliance by Uriah
    A' Submission to the king of Assyria
Closing regnal summary

Although submission to Assyria is related in succinct fashion, it is important to the narrative because it is the primary reason Ahaz's actions in the temple are negatively construed. While Ahaz fashions a new altar, that altar is not negative per se, for Josiah's great reform does not remove it. Neither are the sacrifices Ahaz institutes non-Yahwistic (see 'Comment'), nor is his priestly role at the altar's inauguration without positive precedent (2 Sam. 6:17–18; 1 Kgs 8:63). Rather, it is that these alterations are made in the context of a covenant relationship with Assyria – a relationship in which Ahaz places his trust in a foreign nation rather than YHWH for the salvation of Judah. The covenantal relationship with Assyria is preserved in the covenantal form that underlies vv. 5–9 (and that underlies similar covenants made by Judean kings in 1 Kgs 15:16–22 and 2 Kgs 18:18–19). The form, familiar from ANE texts, includes the following elements (Kalluveettil 1982: 122–123; B. Long 1991: 176):

1. Situation of difficulty: invasion (vv. 5–6)
2. Method of resolution: approach superior power for assistance (vv. 7–8)
   a. Propose political subservience (v. 7)
   b. Offer an inducement (*šōḥad*; see 'Comment', v. 8)
   c. Request military aid (v. 7)
3. Result: superior party brings aid and enemy is repelled (v. 9)

It is as a king who has pledged submission to Assyria – and whose submission is thus a sign of non-trust in YHWH – that Ahaz's altar and temple alterations are viewed.

Comment

16:1–4

Ahaz's rule is reckoned from 735 BC, Pekah's seventeenth year. That

Jotham is still ruling at the end of Pekah's twentieth year (15:27, 30) suggests a co-regency (735–732 BC) between Jotham and his son Ahaz. Ahaz's sixteen-year rule is thus calculated from the commencement of his sole regency (Thiele 1983: 133; DeVries, *IDB* 1:590, 593).

Ahaz's negative assessment 'he did not do what was right . . .' is markedly different from the usual positive assessment 'he did what was right . . .' followed by exceptions (as in 1 Kgs 22:43; 2 Kgs 12:2–3; 14:3; 15:3–4, 34–35). Even more damning in Dtr's economy, Ahaz walks 'in the ways of the kings of Israel', a comparison made previously only of Jehoram (2 Kgs 8:18). The regnal formula for only these two southern kings withholds the name of the queen mother, a characteristic of northern regnal introductions.

Jehoram's conduct is attributed to his marriage alliance; no explanation is given for Ahaz's conduct, making his deviance even more heinous because apparently without cause. Ahaz's sin is also worse than that of Israelite kings, for unlike any of them he practices abominations – particularly defiling sins (Lev. 18:24–30) – for which YHWH drove out the Canaanite nations. Ahaz makes his son 'pass through the fire (*heʿĕbîr bāʾēš*)', as does the later arch-villian Manasseh (21:6; cf. 17:17).

Passing children through the fire is an action listed together with other Canaanite divinatory rites in Deut. 18:9–13. Related texts suggest the rite was much more than simply a divinatory act – blameworthy as such an act was. Nor was the act merely symbolic in nature. 'Passing through' (*heʿĕbîr*) elsewhere refers to actual burning (Num. 31:23), and the immolation (*śrp*) of children is attested as a Canaanite practice (Deut. 12:31) that occurs in Israel (Jer. 7:31; cf. 2 Kgs 17:31). Several texts speak of passing children [through fire] to Molech (Lev. 18:21; 2 Kgs 23:10; Jer. 32:35) or giving children to Molech (Lev. 20:1–5), a netherworld deity. The horrific practice of child immolation and human sacrifice also finds archaeological support. This is the practice that fuels Dtr's abhorrence of Ahaz (Day 1989; Heider 1992, 1999; for a different reading see Cogan 1974: 77–78).

The usual caveat of the high places appears, although always before in Judean regnal summaries it is the people who worship at them (1 Kgs 22:43; 2 Kgs 12:3; 14:4; 15:4, 35). Specifying Ahaz's participation at the high places reveals the particular disapproval granted his reign. Even more, the reference to the 'hills . . . and leafy trees' implies the illicit sexual rites that occurred at such places (Ackerman 1992: 152–163).

16:5–9

Juxtaposed to the negative evaluation, the aggression of Aram–Israel and Edom is the familiar trope of judgment for wickedness at the hands of foreign aggressors (Mullen 1992: 235, 242). Indeed, the coalition's earlier action against Ahaz's father, Jotham, is explicitly by YHWH's instrumentality (15:37).

The coalition of Aram and Israel (often named the Syro-Ephraimite coalition) is an alliance spearheaded by Aram (notice that Rezin is named first in the text), and includes Israel and several smaller states such as Tyre, Gaza, Arabia, Edom, Moab and Ammon, which ultimately become tributary to Assyria (and are named in Tiglath-pileser's Summary Inscriptions 4, 7 and 9; see Tadmor 1994). The anti-Assyrian coalition sought to pressure Judah into standing with it against Tiglath-pileser. Isa. 7:1–6 suggests the plan includes the installation of a puppet king in Judah. The coalition began to exert pressure in 736–735 BC during the co-regency of Jotham and Ahaz. Pressure continued, and the attack against Jerusalem was mounted during Ahaz's sole regency (Na'aman 1991: 92–93, contra Oded 1972). Although the text does not give details, the attack against Jerusalem is unsuccessful.

The separate annalistic notice of Edom's action concerns the crucial port of Elath, held by Judah since Azariah's reign (14:22). It is retaken and held by Edom 'to this day', perhaps the Josianic (Cogan and Tadmor 1988: 193–194) or exilic (Hobbs 1985: 214) era, both times of renewed Edomite hostility towards Judah.

The two annalistic notices provide a snapshot of the coalition's action against Judah. In the parallel Isaianic account Ahaz responds with fear. A similar motive may lie behind the Kings account of Ahaz's appeal to Tiglath-pileser. The narrative silence in Kings regarding Ahaz's motive renders the king in a negative light: without reflection or excuse he gives voluntary submission to the 'king of Assyria'. This initial covenant is probably enacted in 734 BC during Tiglath-pileser's advance down the coastal plain and is noted in Assyrian records (*ANET* 282; see Cogan 1974: 65–67 for a suggested time line).

The narrative emphasizes the covenant position of inferiority and dependence into which Ahaz places Judah. Tiglath-pileser is four times called the 'king of Assyria', while Ahaz by contrast is 'your servant and son'. The conjoined terms 'servant and son' are not elsewhere used in the biblical text in a similar covenantal context, but are found in the Amarna letters (*ANET* 488), usually in a context requesting assistance (Kalluveettil 1982: 132).

Ahaz voluntarily enters a covenant relationship with a foreign king in the hope that king will 'deliver' (v. 7) Judah. In this Ahaz is in error, for YHWH alone is Judah's deliverance and the king should look to him for help. By forging this foreign alliance without YHWH's direction Ahaz demonstrates a lack of consideration and trust directed to YHWH.

Ahaz sends a 'gift' (*šōḥad*), a political bribe or inducement to covenant. The term preserves the negative connotation given it elsewhere (Exod. 23:8; Deut. 10:17; 16:19; 1 Sam. 8:3; 1 Kgs 15:19; Isa. 1:23; Ezek. 22:12) and adds to the negative characterization of Ahaz's actions. Completing the negative assessment, Dtr notes the funds are garnered from temple and palace treasuries (Mullen 1992). The bribe is successful, although the historical reality of Assyrian response to rebellion means action against the Syro-Ephraimite coalition is inevitable; Ahaz's plea for assistance is unlikely to be the sole instigating factor. Yet the Judah-centric narrative perspective makes exactly this point. Damascus falls in 732 BC after a two-year siege; these are also the years of Galilee's subjugation, and Pekah's assassination (see 15:29–30 and 'Comment' there; Bright 2000: 274–275). Rezin is killed, and Damascus is deported to Kir, possibly Aram's original homeland (Amos 9:7).

16:10–18

After the rapid succession of events in vv. 5–9, the narrative pace slows, focusing upon those elements of Ahaz's reign that are of greatest importance to Dtr – worship in the Jerusalem temple.

10–11. After Damascus falls, Ahaz travels there to meet Tiglath-pileser and affirm his vassal status. The official nature of the trip is signalled by the use of the title and name of both parties. There he sees the Damascene altar he later replicates. Because Assyria did not impose religious observance on subdued nations, the altar Ahaz sees is certainly not Assyrian, but Damascene, perhaps dedicated to Rimmon, the Aramean god (McKay 1973: 5–12; Cogan 1974: 74–77). However, although the altar is Aramean, its style is shared with Assyrian altar forms (Cogan and Tadmor 1988: 193; Smelik 1997: 274–275). Within this brief section 'Damascus' is named four times, highlighting the altar's foreign origin.

Ahaz's voluntary assimilation to the foreign form of altar is a great fault under the Deuteronomistic code. This fault is emphasized several ways. First, the narrative communicates the personal enthusiasm with which Ahaz acted: he 'saw' (*r'h*) the altar, and immediately sent a model (*dĕmût*) and plans (*tabnît*) for its replication in Jerusalem. He is only too ready to assimilate international fashions into the Jerusalem temple. Ahaz's assimilation to the Aramean altar is yet another example of his following the ways of the nations (v. 3).

His fault is emphasized, secondly, in that the altar stands as a symbol of Judean subservience to Assyria. Assyria had conquered Damascus and thus placed its god in subservient relationship to the gods of Assyria. By copying the Damascene altar, that same subservience is implied of YHWH to Assyria. More pointedly, Ahaz's treaty submission to Assyria submits both king and YHWH to Assyria and its god, Asshur. The Damascene altar may be the place at which Ahaz ratifies his treaty with Tiglath-pileser (McKay 1973: 7; Kalluveettil 1982: 123; Sweeney 2007: 384). Thus while Ahaz continues Yahwistic worship at the temple, such worship is conducted in subservience to a foreign king and god. This is the evil of Ahaz's altar.

Ahaz's enthusiasm is matched by the ready obedience of Uriah the priest, the 'trustworthy witness' of Isa. 8:2. The interaction between king and priest is marked by a pattern of command and compliance (as later in vv. 15–16). Acting in official capacities, 'King Ahaz sends' (*šlḥ*) to 'Uriah the priest' (v. 10), and 'Uriah the priest' does 'according to all' that 'King Ahaz sent' (*šlḥ*; v. 11). So marked is Uriah's compliance that the narrative has him complete his task before Ahaz's return.

12–16. The narrative pace slows still further to describe the inaugural sacrifices. Arriving from Damascus, Ahaz 'saw' (*r'h*; here 'inspected') the altar. Interestingly, this is also Ahaz's first action upon arrival in Damascus. Both in Damascus and Jerusalem Ahaz acts immediately after 'seeing'. He approaches the altar and then goes up on it to officiate at the inaugural sacrifices of whole burnt offerings, grain offerings, libations of oil or wine, and peace offerings (Lev. 1 – 3, 6 – 7; Num. 15:5; see Gaster, *IDB* 4:147–159). Sprinkled blood is applied to consecrate the altar (Lev. 8:15).

The offerings are wholly Yahwistic rather than Assyrian (and again in vv. 15–16), for animal and blood rituals are not part of Assyrian rites (Cogan 1974: 74–75; Cogan and Tadmor 1988: 192; Sweeney 2007: 384). The king acts in a priestly role in the dedication, as did David and Solomon before him (2 Sam. 6:17; 1 Kgs 8:5, 63–64). But though such action is legitimate for a king, Ahaz is not approved. Not only does he approach the altar as an apostate (vv. 2–4), but, unlike either David or Solomon, he has sold YHWH's people to a foreign king and god. The renovations he proposes place Yahwistic worship in submission to them.

The new altar affects the original bronze altar made by Solomon (1 Kgs 8:5). The bronze altar's position impedes access to the temple and Ahaz's solution is to reposition it from 'before YHWH' to the north (the right as one approaches the temple) of the new altar (McKane 1959: 262–263). Tellingly, however, that new altar is never spoken of as 'before YHWH'. To move the altar is grave business and this gravity is reflected in an unusual word order that places the noun ('bronze altar') before the verb ('he moved'; v. 14).

In its demoted position the bronze altar will be for the king's sole use. He will use it 'to enquire by' (*lĕbaqqēr*; v. 15). Exactly what is meant by Ahaz 'enquiring' is debated (see 'Notes on the text'). The action is similar to one who 'seeks' (*drš*) an oracle. 'Enquiring' could include (but does not require) cultic actions such as extispacy (2 Sam. 2:1; 1 Kgs 22:6–17; 2 Kgs 19:1–7; 22:11–20; Gray 1970: 637; McKay 1973: 8; Nelson 1987: 226; Sweeney 2007: 385).

Ahaz directs Uriah regarding the ongoing sacrifices. They are to be performed on the new altar, now called the 'great altar', and no longer on the smaller bronze altar. As in the instructions in vv. 10–11, the official nature of the exchange is marked by the formal title and name of each actor ('King Ahaz', 'Uriah the priest'). And, as before, the command and compliance pattern is established: King Ahaz 'commands' (*ṣwh*) Uriah the priest, and Uriah the priest 'did all that King Ahaz commanded (*ṣwh*)'.

Ongoing Yahwistic sacrifices of two basic types are included: morning burnt offerings (cf. 2 Kgs 3:20) and evening meal offerings (cf. 1 Kgs 18:29). Each is offered on behalf of king and people. Ahaz's instructions alter the established morning and evening burnt offerings specified in Exodus (29:38–42) and Numbers (28:2–8).

17–18. After instructions to build the altar, inauguration of the altar, and further instructions for its ongoing use, the narrative re-explores the question of submission to Assyria (see 'Form and structure'), thus couching all Ahaz's cultic changes within this context. He removes the decorative bronze frames from the ten wheeled stands crafted by Solomon (1 Kgs 7:27–38) and also removes the sea off its bronze stand of bulls (1 Kgs 7:25, 45). No bronze is mentioned in the initial tribute paid to Tiglath-pileser (v. 8). The removal may be towards further tribute, but such is not mentioned. It is more probable the alterations are part of the acculturation to the style of the Damascene temple. And, reading this verse in conjunction with v. 18, the changes are done 'because of the king of Assyria' – another voluntary assimilation to the style of worship of Ahaz's overlord.

Finally, for this same reason, the 'Sabbath covering' and 'outer entry for the king' are removed from YHWH's house. The identification of the first is debated. A hapax noun from the root *skk*, it has the sense of something that 'covers over' (*HALOT* 2:557), thus a covered walkway (NASB), lintel (NRSV) or awning (NIV, NET) apparently used only on the Sabbath. Despite the uncertainty of identification, it is clear both are removed 'because of the king of Assyria'. There is no hint of coercion; the act is one of deference. Possibly the items are symbolic of, or stylized to represent, the unique relationship of YHWH to the Davidic house. Their removal thus signals the demotion of that house in favour of the new Assyrian master. Whether for reasons of cultural assimilation or political pandering, Ahaz's wholesale reforms in the Solomonic temple are undertaken with a high hand. Ahaz shows no regard for the symbolic demotion of promises granted the house of David, and the God who grants them.

16:19–20

The chapter explicitly (vv. 1–4) and implicitly (vv. 5–18) disapproves Ahaz and nothing more need be said of his reign; it closes in typical fashion. Rule passes to Hezekiah, who will reverse his father's political and religious policies.

Explanation

In King Ahaz, Judahite kings first turn to the way of the kings of Israel and the abominations of the nations (v. 3). The reign of Ahaz is placed immediately before the fall of the northern kingdom. The north falls for covenant abuses, and for following in the sins of the nations (17:8, 11, 15). That Judah turns to the same ways stands as a warning. Should they continue in these sins, walking in the way of the nations, they will likewise fall.

Two particular events are related from Ahaz's reign: alliance with Assyria, and unauthorized renovations in the temple. Although different in type, each arises from the same rejection of covenant relationship with a holy God.

Behind the alliance with Assyria lies a rejection of YHWH's commitment to care for and protect his people. Whatever motivates Ahaz to the alliance, it shows he fundamentally disbelieves that YHWH is the divine warrior who covenanted to fight on behalf of his people. Despite ample evidence of such action in the past (Exod. 15:2–12; Deut. 2:31–37; 3:1–3; 7:1–2; Judg. 6:1–16; 1 Kgs 20, 22), Ahaz disregards this aspect of the covenant relationship and forges an alliance. Thus he rejects the God of the covenant, and alienates himself and his people from that God.

The same alienation and rejection of covenant relationship underlies his actions in the temple. Ahaz unilaterally and eagerly fashions something for the temple whose design is not approved by YHWH. Ahaz sends a 'pattern' (*tabnît*) of the Damascene altar. The uncommon word is used only a few times in relation to tabernacle and temple. The chronicler emphasizes the plans (*tabnît*) David provides Solomon for the temple structure, work and some of its items (1 Chr. 28:11–12, 18–19). Granted this text is later than the Deuteronomistic work, the specifications it commends reflect the temple's sanctity that should not be lightly violated.

Specifications for temple structures and furnishing originate from YHWH. Moses receives the pattern (*tabnît*) for the tabernacle's structure and furnishings (Exod. 25:9, 40) that include the ark, table and lampstand. The altar is specified in Exod. 27 and, although the word *tabnît* is not used, YHWH clearly sets a standard governing the altar's construction.

In Josh. 22 the word *tabnît* refers to the altar of burnt offering. When the Transjordanian tribes make a memorial altar, it is misinterpreted by the other tribes as supplanting the tabernacle altar. When confronted for their perceived violation, the Transjordanian tribes protest the copy or model (*tabnît*) was for memorial purposes only (v. 28). They affirm that to make a copy for the purposes of offering burnt sacrifices is rebellion against YHWH. The only altar appropriately used for burnt offerings is that which stands 'before his tabernacle' (v. 29). Thus the story of the model (*tabnît*) altar made in Josh. 22 reveals assumptions that no other altar of burnt offering is to be made lest it be used for false worship that supplants the tabernacle altar.

Tracing the usage of *tabnît* in respect of the tabernacle, temple and furnishings affirms the reading of Ahaz's narrative undertaken here. He makes an altar against the model specified by YHWH. He does offer Yahwistic sacrifices upon it, but does so as an idolater who sacrifices and burns incense on the high places. For all these reasons his alternative model (*tabnît*) is at fault.

The construction of the foreign altar against YHWH's approved pattern reveals an underlying rejection of norms set in place to facilitate covenant relationship between YHWH and his people. The temple, like the tabernacle and Sinai before it, is the place appointed for YHWH to meet with his people. Such a meeting without proper precautions and without proper delineation of holy space is potentially deadly. For this reason, the holy space of Sinai was protected (Exod. 19:11–12, 23) and zones of increasing holiness were delineated within the tabernacle and temple. Only those individuals and only those items of approved holiness are granted safe entrance inside these zones (Lev. 16), and attempts to overstep the barriers of holiness are punished by death (Lev. 10:1–3; Num. 4:15–20; 2 Sam. 6:6–7). Within holy space, rituals are carefully conducted in conformity to YHWH's specifications (Lev. 1 – 7, 16; 1 Kgs 8). It is to fashion an appropriately holy space that careful attention is given to the description of the structure, construction, furniture, implements and garments that must be used within holy precincts (Exod. 25 – 31, 35 – 39; 1 Kgs 6 – 7).

Additionally, holy space is not simply about protective barriers set up between a holy God and a sinful people. Holy space (Sinai, the tabernacle, the temple) is created so that a holy God can presence himself in the midst of a sinful people. Initiated by YHWH, the creation of holy space shows a holy God's desire for relationship with his chosen people. The people's participation in creating and maintaining holy space is one of the ways they indicate their desire for, and submission to, relationship with a holy God. They demonstrate trust that such a relationship is possible, and that observance of holy space is a necessary component to its enjoyment.

Thus the action Ahaz takes affects the temple's holy space. Without regard to YHWH's specifications for its protection, and without regard to his infringement upon holy space, he eagerly imports the new altar. By alliance with Assyria he rejects YHWH's commitment to preserve and defend his people. These attitudes lie behind his actions. As he enters the temple, there is no sense of Moses' holy awe before the holy space of a burning bush (Exod. 3:5). There is, instead, the cavalier innovation that attended David's initial attempt to transport the ark – with deadly results (2 Sam. 6:6–9). That YHWH does not similarly break out upon Ahaz is another witness to his longsuffering grace in the monarchic era, and his commitment of faithfulness to the Davidic house.

2 KINGS 17:1–41

Translation

¹In the twelfth[a] year of Ahaz king of Judah, Hoshea son of Elah began to reign in Samaria over Israel. *He reigned* nine years. ²He did what was evil in the eyes of YHWH, except not as the kings of Israel before him. ³Shalmaneser king of Assyria came up against him (now Hoshea was his vassal and had sent him tribute) ⁴because the king of Assyria found treachery in Hoshea in that he had sent messengers to Sais[a], to the king of Egypt and no longer sent tribute to the king of Assyria as he had done annually. The king of Assyria arrested him and confined him in prison. ⁵The king of Assyria invaded all the land and went up against Samaria and besieged it three years. ⁶In the ninth year[a] of Hoshea, the king of Assyria captured Samaria. He exiled Israel to Assyria and settled them in Halah and on Habor the river of Gozan and in the cities of the Medes.

⁷This happened because the sons of Israel had sinned against YHWH their God, who had brought them up from the land of Egypt, from under the hand of Pharaoh king of Egypt, and had feared other gods ⁸and walked in the practices of the nations that YHWH had driven out from before the sons of Israel, *and the practices* that the kings of Israel had introduced. ⁹The sons of Israel uttered[a] things that were not right against YHWH their God and they built for themselves high places in all their towns, from watchtower to fortified city. ¹⁰They set up for themselves pillars and sacred poles upon every high hill and under every leafy tree. ¹¹They burned incense there, on all the high places, like the nations that YHWH had exiled from before them; they did evil things, provoking YHWH to anger. ¹²And they served idols, concerning which YHWH had said to them, 'You shall not do this thing.'

¹³Yet YHWH warned Israel and Judah by the hand of every prophet and every seer[a], saying, 'Turn from your evil ways and keep my commandments, my statutes, according to all the torah that I commanded your fathers, and that I sent to you by the hand of my servants the prophets.' ¹⁴But they would not listen, and were stubborn like their fathers, who did not trust in YHWH their God. ¹⁵They rejected his statutes, and his covenant that he made with their fathers, and his warnings with which he warned them. They went after emptiness and became empty, and after the nations that surrounded them, concerning whom YHWH had commanded them not to act as they did. ¹⁶They ignored all the commandments of YHWH their God and they made for themselves molten images – two calves – and they made a sacred pole, and bowed down to all the host of heaven, and served Baal. ¹⁷They passed their sons and daughters through the fire, and they practised divination and sought omens[a]. They sold themselves to do evil in YHWH's eyes, provoking him to anger. ¹⁸YHWH was extremely angry with Israel and removed them from his presence. None was left except the tribe of Judah alone.

¹⁹But even[a] Judah did not keep the commandments of YHWH their God. They walked in the practices of Israel, which they had introduced. ²⁰So YHWH rejected

all the seed of Israel. He afflicted them and gave them into the hand of plunderers until he had cast them from his presence.

²¹When he had torn Israel from the house of David, they made Jeroboam son of Nebat king. Jeroboam enticedª Israel away from following YHWH and caused them to commit a great sin. ²²The sons of Israel walked in all the sins that Jeroboam committed; they did not depart from themª ²³until YHWH removed Israel from his presence, just as he had spoken by the hand of all his servants the prophets. So Israel were exiled from their land to Assyria until this day.

²⁴The king of Assyria brought *people* from Babylon and from Cuthah and from Avva and from Hamath and Sepharvaim, and settled *them* in the cities of Samaria in place of the sons of Israel. So they possessed Samaria, and dwelt in its cities. ²⁵It happened when they first settled there that they did not fear YHWH; therefore YHWH sent lions among them which killed some of them. ²⁶It was reportedª to the king of Assyria, 'The nations that you exiled and settled in the cities of Samaria do not know the custom of the god of the land. So he has sent lions among them and, behold, they are killing them because they do not know the custom of the god of the land.' ²⁷Then the king of Assyria commanded, 'Send one of the priests there whom I exiledª from there. He shall go and dwellᵇ there and teach them the custom of the god of the land.' ²⁸So one of the priests whom they had exiled from Samaria came and dwelt in Bethel. He taught them how to fear YHWH.

²⁹But each nation still made its own gods and put them in the shrines of the high places that the people of Samaria had made, every nation in the cities in which they lived. ³⁰The people of Babylon made Succoth-benoth, the people of Cuth made Nergal, the people of Hamath made Ashima. ³¹The Avvites made Nibhaz and Tartak, and the Sepharvites burned their children in the fire to Adrammelek and Anammelek, the gods of Sepharvaim. ³²Yet they also feared YHWH and appointed for themselves from among all the people priests of the high places, who acted for them in the shrinesª of the high places. ³³So they feared YHWH, but also served their own gods, according to the custom of the nations from among whom they had been exiled.

³⁴To this day they act according to their earlier customª; they do not fear YHWH, nor do they act according to their statutes and ordinancesᵇ or according to the torah and the commandment that YHWH commanded the sons of Jacob, whom he named Israel. ³⁵YHWH made a covenant with them and commanded them, saying, 'You shall not fear other gods, nor bow down to them, nor serve them, nor sacrifice to them. ³⁶But YHWH, who brought you up from the land of Egypt with great power and with an outstretched arm, him you shall fear, and to him you shall bow down, and to him you shall sacrifice. ³⁷And the statutes and the ordinances, and the torah and the commandment that he wrote for you, you shall be careful to do for ever, and you shall not fear other gods. ³⁸And you shall not forget the covenant that he madeª with you, and shall not fear other gods. ³⁹But YHWH your God only shall you fear, and he will deliver you from the hand of all your enemies.' ⁴⁰But they would not listen; instead, they did according to their earlier custom.

⁴¹Thus these nations both feared YHWH and served their idols; even their children and their children's children did just as their fathers did, until this day.

Notes on the text

1.a. LXX texts recognize the chronological difficulty of MT 'twelfth', and read variously 'tenth', 'fourteenth'. Gray conjectures 'second' (1970: 640).

4.a. MT *sô*', 'So', may identify a Pharaoh to whom Hoshea appeals (so NIV; see summary of identifications in Day 1992c). The alternative reading taken here identifies a place name (Egyptian *s'w*) mistakenly read by later Hebr. scribes as a king's name (so Cogan and Tadmor 1988: 195; Day 1992c). The place was Sais, and Pharaoh Tefnakht ruled from there.

6.a. MT *bišnat* is read *baššānâ* with some MSS.

9.a. MT hapax *wayḥappĕ'û* (here 'uttered') is often translated as a variant of the root *ḥph*, 'to cover', with the idea of 'doing secretly' (so NASB, NRSV, NIV). But the sins of Israel were anything but secret. Tg and Syr read, 'spoke against YHWH', cognate to Assyrian *khapu*, 'to utter' (G. Driver 1925: 89).

13.a. 'every prophet and every seer' reads against Q 'all the prophets of every seer' and LXX 'all his prophets, every seer', but with Syr, Vg. The reading moves final *waw* on *nābî'* to initial cop. on second *kol-*.

17.a. LXX[L] adds to the list of grievous sins 'and made an ephod and teraphim' after 'sought omens'.

19.a. Reading *wĕgam* for *gam* with LXX, Syr, Vg.

21.a. 'enticed from' (*wayyadda'* . . . *mē'aḥărê*) reads with Q. The hiph. + *min* prep. of the root *ndḥ* also appears in the context of other gods at Deut. 13:6, 11.

22.a. 'from them' reads MT sg. as pl. in agreement with the antecedent.

26.a. 3 m. pl. 'they reported' read as an impersonal form.

27.a. MT 2 m. pl. *higlîtem* read with LXX[L], Tg as 1 com. sg., 'I exiled'.

27.b. 'he shall go and dwell' as 3 m. sg. with LXX[L], Syr, Vg against MT 3 m. pl.

32.a. Reading MT 'shrine' as pl. with LXX[L], Vg.

34.a. MT 'their earlier customs' is read with LXX, Syr, Vg as 'their earlier custom', in agreement with v. 40.

34.b. Reading pl. 'ordinances' for sense.

38.a. Following LXX, Vg 'he made', rather than MT 'I made'.

Form and structure

The progress of the northern kingdom occupies much of 1 Kgs 11 – 2 Kgs 17. YHWH has shown gracious favour to deliver Israel (2 Kgs 13:5, 22–23; 14:27) but that ends with the rapid advance of Assyria. Six brief verses (vv. 1–6) report Samaria's fall and this brevity is countered by the lengthy reflection on Israel's demise (vv. 7–23). The chapter's second half repeats the pattern, reporting on foreign repopulation (vv. 24–33) and reflecting on the worship of those peoples (vv. 34–41).

The macrostructure of reportage followed by reflection suggests intentional arrangement. Further careful arrangement of the two reflections (vv. 7–23; 34–41) highlights the chapter's themes (see also Viviano 1987; Becking 2000: 218):

The first reflection varies an ABCA'B'C' pattern (vv. 7–23):
A Reason for exile: Israel has sinned against God and feared other gods (vv. 7–8)
  B Catalogue of specific sins (vv. 9–12)
    C YHWH's response: warning by prophets (v. 13)
A' Reason for exile: failure to listen, and rejection of statutes and covenant (vv. 14–15)
  B' Catalogue of specific sins (vv. 16–17)
    C' YHWH's response: removal of Israel from his presence (v. 18)
  B" Judah's sin: walking in the practices of Israel (v. 19)
    C" YHWH's response: rejection of 'seed of Israel' until cast 'from his presence' (v. 20)
Reprise of Israel's history (vv. 21–23):
A Reasons for exile: Jeroboam's sins (vv. 21–22)
    C YHWH's response: Israel removed 'from his presence' as spoken by prophets (v. 23a)
    D Israel remains exiled 'until this day' (v. 23b).

The chiastic structure of the second reflection differs considerably but reveals similar concerns:

A 'Until this day' 'earlier customs' followed; YHWH is not feared (v. 34)
  B YHWH's covenant commands: 'you shall not fear other gods' (v. 35)
    C Instead (*kî 'im*) fear YHWH who delivered out of Egypt (v. 36)
      D Be careful to do laws, and do not fear other gods (v. 37)
      D' Do not forget covenant, and do not fear other gods (v. 38)
    C' Instead (*kî 'im*) fear YHWH who will deliver (v. 39)
  B' They do not listen but (*kî 'im*) act according to 'earlier customs' (v. 40)
A' YHWH is feared and idols served 'until this day' (v. 41)

The two reflections concern different groups (Israel, the foreigners) but revolve around the same themes: salvation out of Egypt (vv. 7, 36), the covenant (vv. 15, 35), the call to fear no other gods (vv. 7, 35, 37–38), obedience to torah (vv. 13, 15, 34, 37), and the failure to listen (vv. 14, 40), which leads to covenantal disobedience (vv. 7–12, 15–17, 21–22, 34, 40–41). The similarity of themes across the different groups is key to the chapter's message (see 'Comment' and 'Explanation').

No agreement exists on the compositional history. Much of vv. 7–33 is attributed to Dtr, although whether Hezekian or Josianic remains in dispute (see McKenzie 1991: 140–142 for a summary). Similar disagreement also exists regarding the date and origin of vv. 34–40 with Hezekian, Josianic or late post-Dtr provenances forwarded (Sweeney 2007: 392; Cogan 1978). As has often been remarked in this commentary, the process of delineating and attributing such sources is subjective, and certain reconstruction of any possible history is impossible. The text before us reveals remarkable coherence and artistry, whether through a redactional process or a single author/editor. Focus upon the present form of the text and its theological message is the approach taken here.

Comment

17:1–6

One event is recorded of Hoshea's reign: Israel's fall. Hoshea is evaluated less negatively than most northern kings. The exception (*raq*; v. 2) granted him may be due, like Jehoram, to cultic reform (2 Kgs 3:2). Ultimately it does not matter, for the kingdom falls regardless. A closing summary for Hoshea's reign is absent; in its place is a lengthy sermon (vv. 7–41). It is a fitting commentary on the fate of Israel and the monarchy, marred by Jeroboam from its inception.

The synchronization to the twelfth year of Ahaz would begin Hoshea's reign in 720 BC. This is at odds not only with the synchronization at 1 Kgs 15:30 but with historical data – the last northern king would come to the throne after the kingdom fell. Thiele's proposal that Dtr misunderstood the dual dating of Pekah's reign (which moved his reign twelve years earlier; see 'Comment', 1 Kgs 15), and thus continued the twelve-year miscalculation in the dates provided in 2 Kgs 17 – 18, is not without flaws, but provides a solution that accounts for the historical information and requires no alteration of the MT (see further at Introduction; Thiele 1983: 134–138; for an alternative solution see McFall 1989). By Thiele's proposal, Hoshea reigns 732–723 BC.

The fall of Samaria in Hoshea's ninth year (723/722 BC) occurs after a three-year siege (cf. 2 Kgs 18:9–11) at the hand of Shalmaneser V (726–722 BC). The extra-biblical historical record, while not wholly clear, provides a viable context for the bibilical account. The Babylonian Chronicles record that Shalmaneser 'ravages' Samaria, referring either to initial attacks or the final siege. The Eponym Chronicle provides a three-year context (725/724–723/722) in which Shalmaneser's action against 'all the land', including Samaria, might occur. Although Shalmaneser's successor Sargon II also claims the conquest of Samaria, these claims are made late in his reign as he sought to legitimate his rule. His service under Shalmaneser (perhaps as a general) against Samaria makes such claims feasible. He may have been present at, or even have overseen, the siege (Tadmor 1958: 31, 36).

Israelite vassalage had begun under Tiglath-pileser III (see 'Comment', 2 Kgs 15:30). Early in Shalmaneser's rule Hoshea ceased paying tribute and sought alliance with an Egyptian king, probably Tefnakht who ruled from Sais and was the most powerful of the delta rulers during Hoshea's time. Though his western delta location places him further afield than his contemporary Osorkon in the eastern delta, he is not too distant to provide aid (as did later western delta rulers Neco [2 Kgs 23:29] and Hophra [Jer. 37:5–11]) (see Day 1992c; Christiansen 1989; contra Kitchen 1986: 372–375; Kang 2010).

Shalmaneser responds to Hoshea's act of rebellion and attacks Samaria, imprisoning and perhaps deporting Hoshea. Shalmaneser's death in 722 BC and the opposition Sargon II faces upon his succession leave the deportation incomplete. In 720 BC Sargon returns, deports twenty-seven thousand people (*ANET* 284) and resettles foreigners in Israel (v. 24; Oded 1979: 28–32). He rebuilds Samaria as an administrative centre for the new Assyrian province, Samerina (an evaluative summary of evidence and theories is found in Younger 1999).

17:7–23

7–13. The theological reflection on Israel's fall cites three general wrongs (vv. 7–8) followed by a catalogue of specific sins (vv. 9–12). First, Israel is exiled because they sin (vv. 7, 21–32) against the God who chose them for his own ('YHWH their God') and 'brought them up from the land of Egypt' (v. 7). The phrase is that of the Sinai Covenant (Exod. 20:1; Deut. 5:6) and contextualizes Israel's sins in *Heilsgeschichte*: salvation out of Egypt, covenant at Sinai, the gift of land (vv. 7–8, 14–15).

In response to God's saving act the Covenant first commands Israel to have 'no other gods' (*'ĕlōhîm 'ăḥērîm*; Exod. 20:3; Deut. 5:7), yet Israel fears (*yr'*) other gods (*'ĕlōhîm 'ăḥērîm*; v. 7; cf. vv. 21–22). This sin is restated at the end of the enumerated list (vv. 9–12), albeit in different terms: they served (*'bd*) abominable idols (*gillulîm*; v. 12; Deut. 29:17, cf. Lev. 26:30; 1 Kgs 21:26; 2 Kgs 21:11; 23:24). The pairing of 'fearing' other gods and 'serving' idols reverses a Deuteronomistic tenet: fear and service are rightly given exclusively to YHWH (Deut. 6:13; 10:12, 20; 13:4[5]; Josh. 24:14; 1 Sam. 12:14, 20, 24). Here exclusive loyalty to YHWH is shared with other gods.

The second general statement of Israel's wrongs is that they take up the practices (*ḥuqqôt*; v. 8) of the nations (cf. vv. 11, 15), which are forbidden them (Lev. 18:3; 20:23). For these practices the land's original inhabitants were cast out (Lev. 18:24–27) as Israel will be (Lev. 18:28), a reality the reflection acknowledges: YHWH exiled (*glh*) the nations (v. 11); now Israel themselves are exiled (*glh*; vv. 6, 23).

The third general statement of Israel's wrongs is that they walk in the ways of the kings of Israel (v. 8), later specified as the sins of Jeroboam and Ahab (vv. 16, 21–22). Israelite kings have repeatedly been charged with the 'sins of Jeroboam' and 'causing Israel to sin' (1 Kgs 14:16; 15:26, 34; 16:2 *et passim*). The reflection consistently charges 'they' or 'the sons of Israel' (vv. 7–12, 14–17), making clear the people share the kings' guilt for the exile.

After noting the sins in general terms, a catalogue is given (vv. 9–12). The sins are widespread, as the pronoun *kōl* ('all' [vv. 9, 11] and 'every' [v. 10 (twice)]) and the hendiadys 'from watchtower to fortified city' (v. 9; cf. 2 Kgs 18:8) indicate. The 'high places' are condemned not only because Jerusalem is the place to worship, but also because these places of worship are associated with other deities. The pillars and sacred poles signify the worship of both Baal and Asherah, and the reference to 'high hills . . . and leafy trees' implies the inclusion of prohibited sexual practices (see 'Comment' at 1 Kgs 14:23). Additionally, the burning of incense (pi. of *qṭr* is used [with the exception of Amos 4:5] of the illegitimate cult [1 Kgs 12:33; 13:1–2; 2 Kgs 17:11]) within a Yahwistic context is a common negative assessment (1 Kgs 22:43; 2 Kgs 12:3[4]; 14:4; 15:4, 35; 16:4). These, and other 'evil things' (v. 11), provoke (*k's*) YHWH's anger (1 Kgs 14:9, 15; 15:30; 16:2, 7, 13, 26, 33; 21:22; 22:59; 2 Kgs 23:9).

The reflection turns to the long history of YHWH's gracious warnings. His servants the prophets (vv. 13, 23; cf. 2 Kgs 9:7, 'my servants'; 1 Kgs 14:18; 2 Kgs 14:25; 21:10; 24:2, 'his servants'; 1 Kgs 18:36, '[Elisha] I am thy servant') call YHWH's people back to covenant, urging them to 'turn' (*šwb*) and walk in the 'commandments' (*miṣwōt*) and 'statutes' (*ḥuqqôt*) and all the 'torah' (*tôrâ*). In this the prophets echo the deuteronomic concern (Deut. 4:40; 5:31; 6:1, 17; 7:11) found throughout Kings (vv. 34, 37, cf. 15–16, 19; 1 Kgs 2:3; 3:14; 8:58, 61).

Suddenly, the warning turns to Judah. Judah is actually very much in focus through the catalogue of 'Israel's' sins (see 'Comment' at v. 19), but after this mention once again slips from explicit view.

14–20. Israel's response to YHWH's prophets (v. 14) begins the second accounting of their sins. They do not 'listen' (*šm'*) and thus are like their fathers (Deut. 5:1; cf. 6:3). Like them, Israel are 'stubborn' (lit. 'stiff of neck' [Exod. 32:9; 33:3, 5]) and reject (*m's*) the commandments, covenant and prophetic warnings (v. 13). They turn instead to 'emptiness' (*hebel*), that is, the 'other gods' (v. 7) and 'idols' (v. 12; cf. Deut. 32:21; 1 Kgs 16:13, 26; Jer. 8:19). *hebel* is that which is transitory (Ps. 144:4) or futile (Prov.

21:6; 31:30; Eccl. 1:2), and in serving *hebel* Israel become *wayyehbālû*, 'empty'.

Israel also go 'after the nations' (cf. vv. 8, 11), a reference to Deut. 18:9–13. That passage also rejects the abominable practices of passing children through the fire, practising divination and seeking oracles. Each of these is named in this summary of Israel's sins (v. 17). For these sins Deuteronomy notes the nations are driven from the land, which is now Israel's fate.

The second list of specific sins (vv. 16–17) indicts the people for Jeroboam's golden calves and Ahab's sacred pole and Baal worship. The people worship 'all the host of heaven', a reference to astral deities (appearing only in Kings in 2 Kgs 21:3, 5; 23:4–5), sacrificing their children in fire (see 'Comment' at 2 Kgs 16:3), practising divination and seeking omens. The coupling of 'practising divination' (not elsewhere specified in Kings) with 'seeking omens' points to a practice introduced by Manasseh, who is the king indicted for seeking omens (2 Kgs 21:6). Finally, relinquishing the covenant's freedom, they sell themselves to evil as did Ahab (1 Kgs 21:20, 25).

YHWH is again provoked to anger (vv. 11, 17) but now no prophets warn Israel. God enacts the covenant curses, casting Israel 'from his presence' (*mē'al pānāyw*), an action so grave it is twice more repeated (vv. 20, 23). So complete is Israel's exile that Judah is utterly alone (v. 18).

There is no hopeful reprieve in the mention of Judah's survival. They also do not keep the commandments (*miṣwôt*) and follow Israel's practices (*ḥuqqôt*), which were the practices (*ḥuqqôt*) of the nations (v. 8). Indeed, a close look at the list of Israel's sins (vv. 7–17) reveals Judah has committed many along with Israel. Some are explicitly credited to Judah alone (e.g. divination [2 Kgs 21:6], passing children through the fire [2 Kgs 16:3; 21:6], bowing to the host of heaven [2 Kgs 21:3, 5; 23:4–5, 12]; Viviano 1987: 552; Becking 2000; 221–228). The inclusion of Judah's sins in the catalogue stands as a warning to the nation. They must repent or similarly fall. Given Judah's ultimate exile and the absence of any reflective sermon at that point (2 Kgs 25), the passage is also a proleptic reflection.

YHWH's rejection (*m's*) of 'all the seed of Israel' (v. 20) includes Israel who 'rejected' (*m's*) YHWH (v. 15) and (in the light of Judah's exile) the southern kingdom as well. The plunderers (*šōsîm*; v. 20) appear elsewhere only in Judg. 2:14, 16, where the context is loss of land. The plunderers are embodied in Assyria and in the 'raiders' (*gĕdûdîm*) of 2 Kgs 24:2.

21–23. The possibility of Judah's repentance leads to a final retrospective, recalling the moment the kingdom is torn (*qr'*; 1 Kgs 11:30–31) from Solomon to humble David's descendants 'but not for ever' (1 Kgs 11:39).

Jeroboam's alternative cult entices Israel to a 'great sin' (*ḥăṭā'â gĕdôlâ*), a phrase found in the golden calf episode at Sinai (Exod. 32:21, 30–31). Israel's persistence in sin brings the third and final notice of their removal from YHWH's presence (v. 23). The prophetic word is cited once again (cf. v. 13) yet now with no call to repentance. Judgment falls and Israel is exiled to Assyria 'until this day'. Israel's demise should move Judah to consider their own life before YHWH.

17:24–33

The second report details the Assyrian policy of two-way deportation. It provides an ironic narrative reversal of Israel's entry into the land, as foreign conquered peoples from eastern and western reaches of the Assyrian Empire (Jacobsen, *IDB* 1:752; Haldar, *IDB* 2:516; Kapelrud, *IDB* 4:273) are settled in Samaria, taking Israel's place.

Ignorant of YHWH, the newcomers do not 'fear' (*yr'*), that is worship, YHWH. The term is used eleven times in the second half of the chapter (vv. 25, 28, 32–39, 41) and sets up a contrast between cultic ritual and exclusive worship of YHWH; it is only the second that provides the proper context for the first, as the experience of both Israel and the new foreign inhabitants proves.

The failure in worship results in the familiar judgment through lions (1 Kgs 13:24–32; 20:35–36). Interpreted as a failure of the 'custom' (*mišpāṭ*; vv. 26 [twice], 27, 33) for worshipping the Israelite God, Sargon sends a priest to 'go and teach'. A similar action is recorded on the Khorsabad Cylinder by which deportees are to be instructed in service to god and king (S. Paul 1969). The historical verisimilitude of the words must not overshadow the utter irony of the command: only one priest is allotted to teach all the deportees; more, that priest teaches from the cult site of Bethel, so notorious in Israel's downfall. While this sole priest 'taught them how to fear YHWH' (v. 28), no correct teaching can be expected from such a place.

The priest's teaching results only in a status quo, as the foreigners take up the same syncretistic practices by which Israel fell. Vv. 29 and 32 each begin with the same construction (*wayyihyû*) and signal simultaneous action, as is summarized in v. 33. On the one hand, the nations place their own gods in shrines previously used by Israel. On the other hand, they 'fear YHWH' and, like Israel, appoint their own priests 'from among all the people' (1 Kgs 12:31). This is the 'custom' (*mišpāṭ*) of the nations (v. 33). Sadly, it is also the custom of Israel, who 'feared other gods and walked in the practices of the nations' (vv. 7–8).

17:34–41

The final verses are bracketed by 'to this day' (*'ad hayyôm hazzeh*; vv. 34, 41) and reflect on the nations who now dwell in the land (the 'they' of v. 34; Knoppers 2007: 230–232). The reflection contrasts the nations' observance of earlier 'customs' (*mišpāṭ*; vv. 34, 40) of syncretistic worship to the exclusive worship of YHWH enjoined in the Sinai Covenant (v. 35).

The nations' syncretistic worship identifies them with Israel. Both worship other gods at the high places under their own priests (vv. 29–33). But the nations and Israel (the 'sons of Jacob') are further identified, as the nations are held accountable to the statutes, ordinances, torah and commandment of the Sinai Covenant (v. 34). As inhabitants in the land, rather than follow their earlier 'custom' (*mišpāṭ*), they are to follow the 'ordinance' (*mišpāṭ*; v. 34) of Sinai.

YHWH's covenant 'commands' (*ṣwh*) exclusive worship, stated in four negative statements, each introduced by the negative particle *lô'*. They are not to fear other gods, nor bow down to them, nor serve, nor sacrifice to them (v. 35). By contrast (signified by *kî 'im*; v. 36), YHWH, described in terms of his great saving act, is to be worshipped. The contrast is emphasized as it follows the same order of the negative statements of v. 35: *him* you shall fear; *to him* you shall bow down; *to him* you shall sacrifice. The contrast is further heightened by assonance: 'to him' (*lô*) sounds identical to the negative particle (*lô'*).

Exclusive Yahwistic worship is safeguarded by the same measures as already noted (vv. 34–36): (1) careful observance of the statutes, ordinances, torah and commandments (v. 37; the very thing the nations and Israel have failed to perform, vv. 13, 15–16, 34); (2) avoidance of other gods (vv. 37–38); and (3) remembrance of the covenant. Israel is enjoined (by the passage's second *kî 'im*; v. 39) to exclusive worship of YHWH – the outcome of which is deliverance from enemies, the very thing Israel (and Judah, should they persist in their ways) do not experience.

Sadly, the nations would not listen (*wĕlô' šāmē'û*; v. 40) to the covenant commands, a failure that is no different from Israel's (v. 14) . Both refuse the attitude of listening response and instead (the third *kî 'im* of the passage) walk in their earlier 'custom' (*mišpāṭ*; vv. 34, 40).

Not listening leads to syncretistic worship (v. 41), and the failure is lamented 'to this day'. If one wishes to know what Israel had been like, one need only look to the contemporary inhabitants of the land (Nelson 1987: 232). For Judah in exile the reportage and reflection of both halves of the chapter are a warning and a call to attentive listening and exclusive reverence of YHWH in the midst of a foreign land.

Explanation

This chapter is the nadir of 1 – 2 Kings. Unlike 2 Kgs 25, which offers a slight hope of restoration, this chapter paints without relief the tragedy that befalls Israel. It outlines in stark detail Israel's wholesale failure under the covenant: loss of land, loss of worship and loss of YHWH's kind attention as he turns his face away (vv. 18, 20, 23).

Israel's sins are many, but the chapter emphasizes (see 'Form and structure') that underlying all the catalogued sins are two primary failures: Israel does not follow the commandments, and Israel does not fear YHWH alone. Their rejection of YHWH as exclusive covenant partner encapsulates the first two of the Ten Commandments (Deut. 5:6–21), and from this failure stems every other sin Israel commit. Of course, the tragedy outlined in this chapter is not Israel's alone. Judah is warned against following Israel's sins (vv. 13, 19), and their later failure affirms the inability of all of YHWH's people to live as faithful covenant partners.

The chapter clearly indicates that the failure of Israel and Judah places them on par with the surrounding sinful nations (vv. 8, 11, 15). And, as explored in the 'Comment' section above, the entry of the nations into Israel's territory brings those nations into identification with Israel. They are to take up Israel's covenant life, but likewise fail for the same reasons Israel did: failure to follow the commandments, and failure to fear YHWH alone.

As a nation Israel's election to covenant life was not predicated upon any ability or characteristic within them. Moses makes clear that the covenant is only predicated upon YHWH's gracious sovereign choice (Deut. 7:7–8; 32:8–9). Only as YHWH singled them out from the nations did they become his treasured possession (Exod. 19:5–6). YHWH's initiative in this matter was an extension of his covenant made with Abraham (Gen. 12:1–3; 15; 17). By this covenant the covenanted nation was to be a light to the nations, drawing them to the God of the covenant (Isa. 60:1–3; Zech. 8:23). Through Abraham was to come blessing to all the nations.

Neither Israel nor Judah succeed in living the covenant life, and when the nations are brought into Israel's land they, too, are incapable of drawing near to YHWH. For this reason the tragedy of the failure of Israel, Judah and the nations in 2 Kgs 17 reveals the failure of this purpose of the nation's election. That is, the nation fails as the means by which YHWH's salvation is extended to the nations. Thus the failure of Israel and Judah is more than national loss of land and temple, and more than the reality of covenant punishments. It is a missional failure to shine YHWH's light so as to make him known among the nations.

Israel's failure did not arise because they did not commit to the covenant; repeatedly, they did so (Exod. 24:1–8; Deut. 29 – 30; Josh. 24:16–25). But even as covenant was affirmed, it was witnessed that the people would be unable to remain faithful to it (Josh. 24:19–23).

The larger biblical witness speaks clearly to the cause of covenant failure, and the disobedience of Israel, Judah and the nations. As the crown of YHWH's creation, humankind was made for relationship with their creator, to steward his earth and to reflect his glory. The experience of these realities was early connected to humanity's choice: obedience to YHWH's commands (Gen. 2:16–17), leading to ongoing relationship, or disobedience to YHWH's command, and rejection of relationship (Routledge 2008: 147).

Tempted to sin, the primal couple is ejected from the garden and experience disruption in all their relationships: to YHWH, to one another, to his creation. Gen. 1 – 11 demonstrates the expanding effects of sinfulness and, while the promises made to Abraham do lead ultimately to the defeat of such sinfulness (Gal. 3:6–18), sin continues as a destructive reality in YHWH's creation. Its pervasiveness is such that the psalmist proclaims that all are sinful and none are righteous (Pss 14:1–3; 53:1–3) – verses the apostle Paul cites as he builds his argument in the epistle to the Romans, that all fall under God's judgment because all are sinful (Rom. 3:1–20). Certainly, within 1 – 2 Kings (and the larger history of God's people in the land) the witness to the nation's sinfulness is paramount. Even the most revered of kings (Solomon, Jehoshaphat, Hezekiah) are not untainted by sin.

2 Kgs 17 unfolds the just judgment upon the northern kingdom (and the same judgment anticipated against the southern kingdom). It also communicates in no uncertain terms the depth and breadth of human sinfulness as found in YHWH's covenant people as well as the nations. From such a bleak picture one might conclude that no hope for remedy is possible. But at this very nadir of covenant life the prophets begin to speak of such a remedy. The remedy for sinfulness calls the nation not to more persistent covenant obedience (although obedience is still required), but calls for change in the people's hearts, the very place where obedience and disobedience are born, and sinfulness finds its root.

Thus Jeremiah (for whom the fall of Israel remains a national memory, and who lives through the fall of Judah) looks for a new covenant that solves the inherent problem of sinfulness that marred the first. This new covenant effects obedience because its laws are engraved upon receptive hearts, and knowledge of YHWH is widespread and lasting (Jer. 31:31–34; 32:38–41). From this inward change arises obedience to YHWH's laws that results in full relationship of covenant life. Ezekiel (who also suffers the realities of exile) similarly speaks of this dynamic change of heart effected by YHWH (16:59–63; 37:1–14). This new covenant is one that is everlasting (Isa. 55:3; 61:8; Jer. 50:5) and accomplishes the change of heart encouraged and hoped for in Deuteronomy (6:5; 30:6–8).

The NT witness reaffirms the inherent sinfulness of humankind that precludes obedience to YHWH's righteous ways. The heart of humanity remains disobedient and, without YHWH's gracious act, remains opposed to him. The New Covenant, effected through the life, death, resurrection and ascension of Jesus Christ is the means by which human hearts are softened and changed. Reconciled to God through Christ, those who believe are free to walk in the law of the Spirit of life in Christ (Rom. 3:21 – 6:23; 8:1–17; Gal. 4:1–7). In Christ the intent of the first covenant is fulfilled in the hearts and lives of a people ingrafted into the root of Israel

(Rom. 11:17–24). In the Christian proclamation 'Jesus is Lord' (Rom. 10:9: 1 Cor. 12:3; Phil. 2:11) YHWH is exclusively worshipped, and in the life of a believer yielded to the Spirit the commands of Christ are obeyed.

The tragedy inherent in 2 Kgs 17 is therefore not the final word, although the chapter itself speaks of no way forward. It is during this dark era that the prophets begin to speak of a way forward. Envisioning a new covenant graciously empowered by God himself, they look ahead to an experience of full relationship with YHWH characterized by loving obedience. Even more, they witness to an eschatological hope that includes the nations (Isa. 2:2–4; 60:1–3), overturning even this failure in 2 Kgs 17. One day the nations too would join Israel in exclusive worship and loving obedience rendered to YHWH. It is this vision John takes up as he describes the myriad nations gathered at YHWH's throne. With wonder they proclaim, 'Salvation belongs to our God who is seated on the throne, and to the Lamb!' (Rev. 7:10).

The wonder of this new covenant is that it alone can reverse the bleak reality of human hearts that turn to sinful disobedience. In its light even 2 Kgs 17 cannot remain wholly dark. Even there God's purposes remain and move towards fulfilment.

2 KINGS 18:1 – 19:37

Translation

^{18:1}In the third^a year of Hoshea son of Elah king of Israel, Hezekiah^b son of Ahab king of Judah began to reign. ²He was twenty-five years old when he began to reign, and he reigned twenty-nine years in Jerusalem. His mother's name was Abi^a, the daughter of Zechariah. ³He did what was right in the eyes of YHWH, according to all that his father David had done. ⁴He removed the high places and broke down the pillars and destroyed the sacred pole^a. He crushed the bronze serpent that Moses had made, for until those days the sons of Israel burned incense to it, and they^b called it Nehushtan. ⁵He trusted in YHWH the God of Israel, and neither before nor after him was there anyone like him among all the kings of Judah. ⁶He clung to YHWH; he did not turn from following him and he kept his commandments that YHWH had commanded Moses. ⁷YHWH was with him; whenever he went out, he prospered. He rebelled against the king of Assyria and would not serve him. ⁸He struck the Philistines as far as Gaza and its territory, from watchtower to fortified city.

⁹Now in the fourth year of King Hezekiah (it was the seventh year of Hoshea son of Elah king of Israel), Shalmaneser king of Assyria went up against Samaria and besieged it. ¹⁰They captured it at the end of three years in the sixth year of Hezekiah. It was the ninth year of Hoshea king of Israel when Samaria was captured. ¹¹The king of Assyria deported Israel to Assyria and settled them^a in Halah and on the Habor, the river of Gozan, and in the cities of the Medes ¹²because they did not

listen to the voice of YHWH their God but transgressed his covenant, all that Moses the servant of YHWH commanded. They neither listened nor obeyed.

[13]In the fourteenth year of Hezekiah, Sennacherib king of Assyria went up against all the fortified cities of Judah and seized them. [14a]Hezekiah king of Judah sent to the king of Assyria at Lachish, saying, 'I have done wrong. Withdraw from me; whatever you impose on me I will bear.' Then the king of Assyria imposed upon Hezekiah king of Judah 300 talents of silver and 30 talents of gold. [15]Hezekiah gave all the silver found in the house of YHWH and in the treasuries of the king's house. [16]At that time Hezekiah stripped the doors of the temple of YHWH and the doorposts[a] that Hezekiah king of Judah had overlaid, and he gave it[b] to the king of Assyria.

[17]Then the king of Assyria sent Tartan, the Rab-saris and the Rab-shakeh with a large army from Lachish to King Hezekiah in Jerusalem. They went up and came to Jerusalem[a] and stood at the conduit of the upper pool that is on the highway to the fuller's field. [18]They summoned the king, but Eliakim the son of Hilkiah the steward went out to them, with Shebna the scribe and Joah son of Asaph, the recorder.

[19a]The Rab-shakeh said to them, 'Say to Hezekiah, thus says the great king, the king of Assyria, "What is this confidence in which you trust?" [20]You say – but it is only words – I have counsel and strength for war. Now, upon whom do you rely that you rebel against me? [21]Now behold, you rely on the staff of this crushed reed, upon Egypt, which, if a man leans upon it, it will enter his hand and pierce it. Thus is Pharaoh king of Egypt to all who rely on him. [22]But if you[a] say to me, "We trust in YHWH our God," is it not he whose high places and altars Hezekiah has removed, saying to Judah and Jerusalem, "You shall bow down before this altar in Jerusalem"? [23]So now, wager with my master the king of Assyria and I will give you two thousand horses if you are able to put riders upon them. [24]How can you repulse one official of the least of my master's servants if you rely upon Egypt for chariots and horsemen? [25]Furthermore, is it without YHWH that I have come up against this place to destroy it? YHWH has told me to go up against this land and destroy it!'

[26]Then Eliakim son of Hilkiah, with Shebna and Joah, said to the Rab-shakeh, 'Please speak to your servants in Aramaic for we understand it. Do not speak with us in Judean in the hearing of the people who are on the wall.' [27]But the Rab-shakeh responded to them, 'Is it only to[a] your master and to you that my master has sent me to speak these words, and not to the men sitting upon the wall *destined to* eat their own dung and drink their own urine[b] with you?' [28]Then the Rab-shakeh stood and called in a loud voice in Judean. [a]He said, 'Hear the word of the great king, the king of Assyria! [29]Thus says the king, do not let Hezekiah deceive you, for he is not able to deliver you from my hand[a]! [30]And do not let Hezekiah make you trust in YHWH, saying, "YHWH will certainly deliver us and this city will not be given into the hand of the king of Assyria." [31]Do not listen to Hezekiah, for thus says the king of Assyria, make peace with me and come out to me. Eat, each of his vine and each of his fig tree, and drink, each of the waters of his well, [32]until I come and take you to a land like your own land: a land of grain and new wine, a land of bread and vineyards, a land of olive trees and honey. So you shall

live and not die. But do not listen to Hezekiah, for he will mislead you, saying, "YHWH will deliver us."'

³³'Has any of the gods of the nations ever delivered his land from the hand of the king of Assyria? ³⁴Where are the gods of Hamath and Arpad? Where are the gods of Sepharvaim, Hena and Ivvah? Have they delivered Samaria from my hand? ³⁵Who of all the gods of the lands has delivered their land from my hand, that YHWH should deliver Jerusalem from my hand?' ³⁶But the people remained silent and answered him not a word, for the king's command was, 'Do not answer him.' ³⁷Then Eliakim son of Hilkiah, the steward, and Shebna the scribe and Joah son of Asaph the recorder came to Hezekiah with their clothes torn and reported the Rab-shakeh's words to him.

¹⁹:¹Now when King Hezekiah heard *it*, he tore his clothes and covered himself with sackcloth and entered the house of YHWH. ²He sent Eliakim the steward and Shebna the scribe and the elders of the priests covered in sackcloth to Isaiah the prophet the son of Amoz. ³They said to him, 'Thus says Hezekiah, "This day is a day of distress and rebuke and humiliation, for children have come to birth and there is no strength to deliverᵃ. ⁴Perhaps YHWH your God will hear all the words of the Rab-shakeh whom his master the king of Assyria sent to reproach the living God and will rebuke the words that YHWH your God has heard. Therefore, offer a prayer on behalf of the remnant that remains."' ⁵So the servants of King Hezekiah came to Isaiah.

⁶Isaiah said to them, 'Thus you shall say to your master, "Thus says YHWH, 'Do not fear because of the words that you have heard with which the servants of the king of Assyria have blasphemed me. ⁷Behold, I am putting a spirit in him so that he will hear a report and return to his land, and I will make him fall by the sword in his land.'"'

⁸The Rab-shakeh returned and found the king of Assyria fighting against Libnah, for he had heard that he had left Lachish. ⁹When he heard concerningᵃ Tirhakah king of Cush, 'Behold, he has come out to fight with you,' he again sent messengers to Hezekiah, saying, ¹⁰'Thus you shall say to Hezekiah king of Judah, saying, "Do not let your God, in whom you trust, deceive you, saying, 'Jerusalem shall not be given into the hand of the king of Assyria.'" ¹¹'Behold, you have heard what the kings of Assyria did to all the lands, destroying themᵃ. Now will you be delivered? ¹²Did the gods of the nations that my fathers destroyed deliver them – Gozan and Haran and Rezeph and the sons of Eden who were in Telassar? ¹³Where is the king of Hamath and the king of Arpad and the king of the city of Sepharvaim, Hena and Ivvah?"'

¹⁴Then Hezekiah took the scrollᵃ from the hand of the messengers and read itᵇ. He went up to the house of YHWH and Hezekiah spread it out before YHWH. ¹⁵Hezekiah prayed before YHWH and said, 'O YHWH, the God of Israel who is enthroned *upon* the cherubim. You are God – you alone – of all the kingdoms of the earth. You have made the heavens and the earth. ¹⁶Incline your ear O YHWH and hear. Open your eyes O YHWH and see and listen to the wordsᵃ of Sennacherib, which he has sent to reproach the living God. ¹⁷Truly, O YHWH, the kings of Assyria have laid waste the nations and their land. ¹⁸They have putᵃ their gods to

the fire – for they are not gods but the work of man's hands, wood and stone – and have destroyed them. ¹⁹And now, O YHWH our God, save us from his hand so that all the kingdoms of the earth may know that you alone, O YHWH, are God.'

²⁰Then Isaiah son of Amoz sent to Hezekiah, saying, 'Thus says YHWH the God of Israel, "Because you have prayed to me concerning Sennacherib king of Assyria, I have heard."

²¹'This is the word that YHWH has spoken against him:
"She has despised you and derided you,
the virgin daughter of Zion.
She has shaken *her* head behind you,
the daughter of Jerusalem.
²²Whom have you reproached and blasphemed,
and against whom have you raised *your* voice
and lifted high your eyes?
Against the Holy One of Israel!
²³By the hand of your messengers
you have reproached the Lordᵃ
And you have said,
'With my many chariotsᵇ
I ascended the heights of the mountains,
to the far reaches of Lebanon.
I have cutᶜ down its tallest cedars and its choicest firs.
I have enteredᶜ its furthest shelterᵈ, its densest forest.
²⁴I have dug wells and drunk foreign waters.
And with the sole of my feet I have driedᵃ up all the rivers of Egypt.'
²⁵Have you not heard? From long ago I accomplished it,
from ancient days I fashioned it;
now I have brought it about –
that you shouldᵃ lay waste unassailable cities
into ruinous heaps of stones.
²⁶Their inhabitants were powerless.
They were dismayed and ashamed,
They were as the weed of the field,
and as the green plant
and as grass on the rooftop
is scorched before it is grown.
²⁷I know your sitting down,
and your going out and coming in,
and your raging against me.
²⁸Because your raging against me
and your arrogance has come up to my ears,
I will put my hook in your nose
and my bridle in your lips,
and I will turn you back by the way that you came."

²⁹'And this shall be a sign for you: you shall eat in this year what grows on its own, and in the second year what self-seeds^a from that, but in the third year sow and harvest, plant vineyards and eat their fruit. ³⁰And the surviving remnant of the house of Judah shall again take root downward and bear fruit upward. ³¹For from Jerusalem a remnant will go forth, and survivors from Mount Zion; the zeal of YHWH of Hosts will accomplish this.

³²'Therefore, thus says YHWH concerning^a the king of Assyria, "He shall not enter this city, nor shoot an arrow there, nor come against it with a shield, nor cast up an assault ramp against it. ³³By the way he came against it, he shall return. And he shall not enter this city," declares YHWH. ³⁴"For I will defend this city^a to save it for my sake and for the sake of David my servant."'

³⁵Then it happened in that night that the angel of YHWH went out and struck one hundred and eighty-five thousand in the Assyrian camp. When they arose in the morning, behold, all of them were dead. ³⁶So Sennacherib the king of Assyria departed, and went *home* and dwelt in Nineveh. ³⁷And it came about that when he was worshipping in the house of Nisroch his god, Adrammelech and Sharezer his sons^a struck him with the sword. They escaped into the land of Ararat and Esarhaddon his son reigned in his place.

Notes on the text

Chs. 18–19.a. Isa. 36 – 37's parallel account aligns in large degree. Most variants, being minor in nature, are not addressed in these notes. 2 Chr. 32's treatment is significantly different, abbreviating the narrative, and adding new materials (such as Hezekiah's preparations to defend the city).

18.1.a. LXX texts have variant chronologies, reading fourth and fifth years.

1.b. The short form of Hezekiah's name (*ḥizqiyyâ*) appears in vv. 1–16; the long form (*ḥizqiyyāhû*) appears in vv. 9, 17–37 as well as in chs. 19–20.

2.a. 'Abi' is probably an abbreviation for 'Abijah', as read at 2 Chr. 29:1.

4.a. With MT and following Montgomery 1951: 500 (cf. 2 Kgs 17:16; 23:3) sg. *hā'ăšērâ*. Vrs read pl.

4.b. 'they called it' reads pl. with Vrs.

11.a. MT *wayyanḥēm*, 'he led them', is read as *wayyanniḥēm*, 'he settled them' (root *nwḥ*). See BHS; Montgomery 1951: 501; Gray 1970: 672; Hobbs 1985: 244; cf. Gen. 2:15.

14.a.–16. Missing in Isaiah. Hobbs (1985: 255) argues that *wayyišlaḥ* at vv. 14, 17 suggests haplography.

16.a. The hapax *'ōmĕnôt*, 'doorposts', arises from the root *'mn*, 'to confirm, support' (BDB 52).

16.b. 'gave it' reads the 3 m. pl. suff. as sg. for sense.

17.a. In MT a second occurrence of 'they went up and came' occurs at this point. Here omitted, as in some MSS, LXX, Syr, Vg. Isa. 36:3 similarly does not repeat the phrase.

19.a.–25. Hezekiah is addressed almost exclusively throughout and the pronouns and verbs are sg. Only in v. 22, when the Rab-shakeh explicitly attempts to pit the people against Hezekiah, is the 'you' pl. Isaiah, LXX, Syr (and Vg in v. 23) blur this distinction, making the 'you' in v. 22 sg., and the verb 'wager' in v. 23 pl.

22.a. See n. 19.a.–25 above; only here in vv. 19–25 is the pl. 'you' employed.

27.a. Reading with BHS and Isaiah *ha'el*, 'is it . . . to', for MT *ha'al*, 'is it concerning'.

27.b. Q reads euphemistically, 'their filth', 'the water of their feet'.

28.a. *waydabbēr*, 'he spoke', is omitted with some MSS, Tg, Vg and Isa. 36:13.

29.a. With many MSS and Vrs, 'his hand' is read as 'my hand', as the king's first-person speech. LXX[B] supports MT.

19:3.a. MT *lĕlēdâ* as an inf. const. LXX presupposes part. *layyōlēdâ*, 'one who delivers'.

9.a. Reading the prep. *'al*, 'concerning', for MT *'el*, 'to'.

11.a. Montgomery (1951: 503) emends MT *lĕhaḥărîmām* from *ḥrm*, 'utterly destroy, place under the ban', to the root *ḥrb*, 'to devastate', arguing Assyria did not put conquered lands under the ban. No textual support exists and MT should stand. Sennacherib's rhetoric is a scare tactic.

14.a. *hassĕpārîm*, 'the letters', is read as sg. with LXX[L], Tg, and in agreement with the suffix in 'he spread it'.

14.b. *wayyiqrā'ēm*, 'and read them', with 3 m. sg. suff. with LXX[L], Isa. 37:14 (although with pl. noun), and in agreement with final suff. ('he spread it') in verse.

16.a. Isa. 37:17, Syr, Tg, Vg read, 'all the words'.

18.a. MT qal pf. *wĕnātĕnû*, 'they put', read as inf. abs. with Isa. 37:19 and per Montgomery (1951: 504), Gray (1970: 687).

23.a. Several MSS read 'YHWH' for 'Lord'.

23.b. Reading with Q 'my many chariots' (*bĕrōb rikbî*).

23.c. 'I have entered'; 'I have cut' reads MT simple waw as cons. with LXX, Vg.

23.d. Reading with Q 'its furthest shelter'.

24.a. As in v. 23, simple waw as cons., 'I have dried up'.

25.a. MT *ûtĕhî* read as juss. of purpose.

29.a. Reading *šāḥîs*, 'self-seeded', with Isa. 37:30. *sāḥîš* is unknown.

32.a. *'al* read for first *'el*.

34.a. *'el* read as *'al*, in 'this city' (*'el hā'îr*).

37.a. 'his sons' is omitted in MT, but noted in the *Mp.* and supported by many MSS, Vrs, Isa. 37:38.

Form and structure

Hezekiah's reign is delineated by regnal summaries (18:1–8; 20:20–21). Within those boundaries two addenda (20:1–11, 12–19) follow a lengthy narrative of Assyrian aggression against Hezekiah (18:13 – 19:37) and are treated in the next commentary chapter.

The account in chs. 18–19 has several clear divisions. The regnal summary is followed by a paragraph (vv. 9–12) that uses the language of 17:5–6 to explain Israel's exile by Assyria. It concludes (v. 12) with a pithy summation of 17:7–23. It is this same Assyrian power that now confronts Hezekiah (vv. 13–16). Each of vv. 9–11, 13–16 may arise from annals and follows the pattern of an invasion report in which an aggressor goes up against a foe, a siege or battle takes place, and an outcome is related (B. Long 1991: 194).

The brevity of Hezekiah's initial interaction with Assyria (vv. 13–16) reflects its annalistic source and contrasts with the lengthy account in 18:17 – 19:37 in which delegations are sent from Lachish (18:13 – 19:7) and Libnah (19:8-37). The contrast of the brief first encounter (vv. 13–16) to the expansive narrative style of subsequent encounters (18:17 – 19:37) has led to theories of two sources that describe the same event. Stade's 1886 article explored the phenomenon and labelled the two accounts A (vv. 13–16) and B (18:17 – 19:37).

Stade further divided the B source (B^1, 18:17 – 19:9a, 36–37; B^2, 19:9b–35), noting similar themes in each delegation. The B^1 source included the prophesied report of 19:7, which found its fulfilment in the report of Tirhakah in 19:9a, and the events of 19:36–37. This left the B^2 account as a separate source. With some minor secondary insertions it provides a later, more theological, reading of the tradition (see Childs 1967: 73–103).

Variant sources may underlie the present account. But this need not detract from its presentation of consecutive events. A brief initial interaction (vv. 13–16) proceeds to two subsequent delegations. The two delegations pursue repetitive arguments but are different in mode (a face-to-face encounter; a letter). And the arguments presented in ch. 19's letter are sharpened, as one might expect after the Judean response of ch. 18. It is unremarkable that the prophetic word (19:7) is not fulfilled immediately, for such is a common pattern in Kings. By this reasoning, 19:36–37 need not be appended to v. 9a to provide the fulfilment and conclusion to a putative B^1 account.

The structure and content of the two delegations is worth examination. The first, from Lachish (18:13 – 19:7), includes two speeches of the Rabshakeh (18:17–25, 26–36). The speeches utilize flowing logic, deftly addressing both Hezekiah and the assembled people. The speeches freely mix forms such as threat, taunt and argument. In this they model contemporary diplomatic disputations (Childs 1967: 80–82; B. Long 1991: 218).

The first speech (18:17–25) asks who is worthy of trust (*bṭḥ*), a key word that appears seven times in as many verses (vv. 19 [twice], 21 [twice], 22, 24, 29; cf. v. 5; 19:10). In it the Rab-shakeh raises five questions to pursue his thesis that Egypt and YHWH are unreliable military resources and Hezekiah should therefore submit to Sennacherib. The second speech (18:26–36) also deals with the question of whom to trust (v. 30), but pursues it through the theme of deliverance (*nṣl*; vv. 29–30, 32–34, 35 [twice]). In this speech the Rab-shakeh goes beyond arguing YHWH cannot be trusted for deliverance, and questions YHWH's ability to deliver.

The conclusion of the first delegation's interaction records the consultation with Isaiah and continues to 19:7. The Assyrian threat has twice utilized the prophetic messenger form 'thus says X' (vv. 29, 31). Isaiah now uses the same form (v. 6) and prophesies. Given the reliability of the prophetic word throughout 1 – 2 Kings, one anticipates fulfilment of this word. The fulfilment (19:35–37) confirms Hezekiah's trust in YHWH and YHWH's ability to deliver.

The second lengthy interaction begins with vv. 8–9a, launching the second delegation from Libnah as was the first from Lachish (18:14). Sennacherib's message revisits themes from the first delegation but nuances them so that the challenge is no longer between Sennacherib and Hezekiah, but Sennacherib and YHWH. The second delegation is succinctly reported, moving the narrative quickly to YHWH's response.

Hezekiah's receipt of the delegation is followed by his petition to YHWH (vv. 15–19). It is typical in form and includes an invocation (v. 15), complaint (vv. 16–18) and supplication (v. 19) (Jones 1984b: 577; Hobbs 1985: 270). The supplication pleads for deliverance, and restitution for YHWH's maligned reputation. The oracular response (vv. 20–34) takes up both concerns in three sections:

1. Taunt song (vv. 20–28) including:
   a. Introduction with messenger formula (vv. 20–21a)
   b. Jerusalem's taunt (vv. 21b–22)
   c. Sennacherib's boast (vv. 23–24)
   d. YHWH's sovereign power displayed (vv. 25–28)
2. Sign to Jerusalem promising renewal and restoration (vv. 29–31)
3. Oracle of salvation (vv. 32–34)

The three sections are clearly distinguished. The first and third are marked with the messenger formula 'Thus says YHWH', and the taunt song's clear poetic style differs from the prose of the sign section. Vv. 32–34 are often understood as the original ending to v. 20 (Jones 1984b: 578; Childs 1967: 96–97), and the intervening verses as later interpolations in two stages (vv. 21–28, 29–31). Yet, while the oracle has easily discernible sections, and may have a compositional history, such is not required and perhaps reflects modern sensibilities of what is appropriate form and flow for prophetic oracles.

The chapter ends with the deliverance of Jerusalem. Because of YHWH's sovereign power, Sennacherib 'returns' (*šwb*) home (v. 36; cf. vv. 7, 28) and is killed while worshipping his Assyrian god – who is himself without sovereign power to deliver the king. All this occurs according to the word of YHWH (19:7, 28).

Comment

18:1–8

All the elements of a southern regnal introduction are included for Hezekiah: synchronization of rule to the northern kingdom, age at accession, length and place of reign, mother's name, and theological evaluation of reign. The synchronization presents one of the most acute difficulties of the chronology in Kings. Synchronization to Hoshea's third year (cf. vv. 9–10) brings Hezekiah to the throne in 729 BC. The date does not accord with that given in v. 13, for the events of that year took place in 701 BC, requiring Hezekiah's accession in 715 BC.

Thiele argues that the dates given in vv. 1, 9–10 are 'late and artificial' (Thiele 1983: 174; see discussion at 2 Kgs 15) and that Dtr, misunderstanding the dual chronology of Pekah's reign, placed Hezekiah's reign twelve years too early. Thiele corrects this supposed error and begins Hezekiah's reign in 716/715 BC. Thiele's chronology makes sense of the numbers, but begins Hezekiah's rule long after that of Hoshea's and the fall of Samaria and is here rejected. McFall's solution of a co-regency with Ahaz (729–715 BC) and a twenty-nine-year sole regency (715–786 BC) is also not without difficulties, but does allow for the chronological accounting as presented, and for Hezekiah's rule during the final years of Hoshea's reign (McFall 1989).

Hezekiah is highly praised and compares to both Asa (1 Kgs 15:11) and Jehoshaphat (1 Kgs 22:43) for doing 'all that his father David had done'. He is praised beyond all previous and subsequent Judean kings (v. 5). If the reference is not hyperbolic rhetoric, it suggests the tradition arose before Josiah's account. In that account Josiah is praised far beyond Hezekiah.

Hezekiah's commitment to YHWH is demonstrated several ways. Like Asa, Hezekiah reforms Judah's cultic life, removing articles that had long been part of Israelite religion. The reform may have expressed Hezekiah's nationalism and his rejection of the Assyrian overlord. The reform should not, however, be construed as purging Assyrian cult practices imposed under her vassal state. McKay (1973) and Cogan (1974) give ample evidence that Assyria placed no such requirement upon their vassals. Additionally, 2 Chr. 29:3 suggests Hezekiah's cultic reforms may long have preceded the break with Assyria.

Many righteous kings failed to remove the high places (1 Kgs 22:44; 2 Kgs 12:4; 14:4). Hezekiah removes them and 'broke' (*šbr*) and 'destroyed' (*krt*) the Baal pillars and Asherah poles, actions that associate him with Moses (Exod. 34:13). Additionally, he 'crushed' (*ktt*) the bronze serpent as Moses had earlier crushed the calf (Deut. 9:21). Though made by Moses as a means of life (Num. 21:6–9), over time the serpent became part of the illegitimate cult. The object was not unique to Israel, and in the ANE serpent images were thought to hold apotropaic power or to symbolize the deity's fertility (Joines 1968). In a pun 'Nehushtan' joins the consonants and vowels for the words for serpent (*nāḥāš*) and bronze (*nĕḥōšet*), reflecting either the people's sense of familiarity towards an honoured object, or Dtr's contempt.

Hezekiah's attitudes confirm the aptness of the praise bestowed on him. Of all kings, only Hezekiah is specifically said to 'trust' in YHWH (v. 5), and this trust becomes the testing point of his encounter with Assyria (vv. 19 [twice], 21 [twice], 22, 24, 29; 19:10). Hezekiah also 'clings' (*dbq*) to YHWH, a particularly Deuteronomistic quality (Deut. 4:4; 10:20; 11:22; 13:4[5]; 30:20; Josh. 22:5; 23:8) often associated with faithful observance of the commandments of Moses. Hezekiah's commitment to YHWH is similarly measured (v. 6).

Like David before him YHWH is 'with' Hezekiah (1 Sam. 16:18; 18:12, 14; 2 Sam. 5:10), so that Hezekiah has success when he goes out to war (cf. 1 Sam. 18:5, 14–15). Hezekiah's action against Assyrian-controlled Philistia (v. 8), probably undertaken during a time of Assyrian political instability following Sargon's death in 705 BC (Oded 1977: 445), serves as an example of Hezekiah's success. In this light one anticipates success in any military conflict with Assyria precipitated by Hezekiah's cessation of the vassal tribute originated under Ahaz (see 'Comment', 2 Kgs 16:7).

18:9–12

Samaria's downfall is related in terms taken from 2 Kgs 17:5–6, here synchronized to the years of Hezekiah's co-regency. Besides the facts of the capture and deportation of Israel, an editorial comment links Israel's failure to their refusal to listen to YHWH (see 2 Kgs 17:14), and their transgression of the covenant mediated by Moses. By contrast, Hezekiah keeps Moses' commandments. His actions, so different from Israel's, suggest a different fate awaits their confrontation with Assyria.

18:13–16

Dating from Hezekiah's sole rule, the fourteenth year is 701 BC. In that year Sennacherib undertakes his third campaign against rebellion in the

Levant. This rebellion arose following Sargon's death in 705 BC (Hallo 1960: 56–59; Provan et al. 2003: 273). The Assyrian Annals (*ANET* 287–288) reveal that Assyria regains both Phoenicia and Philistia before turning against Judah, where, as the biblical text indicates, forty-six fortified Judean cities on the eastern borders of Philistia are taken. The action prevents Judah's military support to their Philistine neighbours and also leaves Hezekiah isolated in the capital.

Sennacherib boasts of shutting Hezekiah in Jerusalem 'like a bird in a cage' by setting earthworks to prevent egress from the city (*ANET* 288). Unlike the action against other Judean cities, the Annals fall short of claiming a siege against Jerusalem. Sennacherib has overrun the country, stripping its resources and blockading the city (Millard 1985: 70; Cogan and Tadmor 1988: 246–251; Edelman 2008: 402–403; Dalley 2004: 392; cf. 2 Kgs 19:32). A siege of Jerusalem is not certain (contra Hobbs 1985: 272–273). It is part of the Rab-shakeh's threat (v. 27), but ultimately no siege ramp is raised against Jerusalem (19:32).

Recognizing his vulnerable position, Hezekiah sends to Lachish, where Judah's strongly fortified second city (Ussishkin, *NEAEHL* 3:905–907) is under siege. A record of the successful siege appears in the stunning wall reliefs from the palace of Nineveh now displayed in the British Museum. Hezekiah pleads his guilt, using the word *ḥṭ'*, commonly used for cultic sin but also (as here) in contexts of political wrong (Gen. 20:9; Exod. 10:16; Judg. 11:27). He begs Assyrian withdrawal (*šwb*; cf. 19:28, 33) in exchange for an imposition of tribute payment; in the end it is not the tribute payment but YHWH's intervention that effects the withdrawal.

The Assyrian Annals confirm this payment, although the amounts differ slightly: 800 talents (61,729 lb [28,000 kg]) of silver and 30 talents (1,050 kg) of gold, together with various other tribute items. The larger amounts given in the Annals reflect differences in calculating weights or include additional annual payments. By the Annals the payment is made upon Sennacherib's return to Nineveh. The Annals reveal that Hezekiah is also required to release Padi, King of Ekron, a pro-Assyrian king whom he holds captive (*ANET* 287–288).

Hezekiah plunders temple and palace treasuries; even the temple doors and doorposts are stripped of gold. As in the case of other kings who paid voluntary tribute from the treasuries (Rehoboam [1 Kgs 14:25–28]; Asa [15:17–19]; Jehoash [2 Kgs 12:18–19]; Amaziah [14:11–14]; Ahaz [16:7–9]), Hezekiah's actions are negative (Mullen 1992). They reveal his lack of trust in YHWH to deliver Jerusalem. In the ensuing encounter with the Rab-shakeh Hezekiah is tested on this very point.

18:17 – 19:7

17–25. Despite Hezekiah's acquiescence, Sennacherib does not withdraw.

To explain his further aggression, theories of dual traditions are proposed (see 'Form and structure'), or the Rab-shakeh's envoy is moved to a subsequent Assyrian campaign. However, Sennacherib's annals are complete through 691 BC and reveal no further campaign by him into the Levant (Hallo 1960: 59). Reading the biblical text as a chronological account of one campaign, Sennacherib's envoy returns to Jerusalem to demand an additional indication of submission. Hezekiah, the prominent leader of the rebellion, is to surrender his city to his overlord (Provan et al. 2003: 273–274).

Once Sennacherib and Hezekiah are identified, the narrative consistently refers only to Sennacherib as 'king'. No honorific is provided for Hezekiah. This communicates the military superiority and power of Assyria over Hezekiah. The three envoys are identified by Akkadian titles: the Tartan is the highest official after the king, the Rab-saris is the chief eunuch, often dispatched on military duty at the head of the Assyrian forces, and the Rab-shakeh is the chief cupbearer or butler whose duties are restricted to the court and the king's person. His role here may be due to his linguistic facility in Judean (Tadmor 1983: 279; Cogan and Tadmor 1988: 229–230).

Exercising their position of power the envoys summon Hezekiah. He makes his own statement of power by not acquiescing and sending a delegation instead. Three Judeans, holding administrative roles current since Solomon's era (see 'Comment' at 1 Kgs 4:3, 6), match the Assyrian delegation. A well-chosen location places the Assyrian representatives at the conduit of the upper pool, north-west of the city walls and on high ground, enabling easy address to those on the city walls (see Excursus in Hobbs 1985: 260–262; Fritz 2003: 370).

The Rab-shakeh begins with a standard messenger formula, 'Thus say X'. His role as a trusted messenger is apparent, for he clearly speaks for Sennacherib (e.g. vv. 19b–20; cf. vv. 31–32). He also at times speaks of his own accord (e.g. vv. 23–24), or even obscures the addressor's identity, so that his words and Sennacherib's are indistinguishable (v. 25). All, however, represent the will of Sennacherib. He addresses Hezekiah (using verbs and pronouns in second-person singular). The public nature of his argument (v. 26) means his words are also intended for the delegation and gathered populace. At the point when he hopes to turn public sentiment against Hezekiah he addresses them in plural forms (v. 22). His disputation seeks to undermine their trust in anyone other than Sennacherib, and the theme is apparent through the multiple use of the key word 'trust' (bṭḥ; also translated as 'confidence' and 'rely'). Hezekiah has been lauded as one who 'trusted' YHWH (v. 5), but has already failed to do so (vv. 13–16). Will his trust hold in the face of the Rab-shakeh's disputation?

The disputation proceeds through five questions. The first (vv. 19b–20) questions reliance on military counsel and strength. The second (vv. 20–21) particularizes the source of that strength and scorns reliance upon Egypt. Such reliance will bring painful self-harm in the form of military defeat.

In the third (v. 22) the Rab-shakeh craftily addresses the assembled people, attacking any trust they might express in YHWH. He shows his awareness of Hezekiah's actions against the high places (v. 4), but assumes these are legitimate places of worship. Why, he argues, would a god aid a people who have ceased to worship him in these places? By such reckoning his logic is indisputable. The fourth question (vv. 23–24) returns to the offensive against Egypt, slighting their military power by highlighting the vast military resources available to Assyria. Two thousand horses could be Judah's if they would only throw their lot in with Assyria – a 'wager' the Rab-shakeh suggests would only benefit Judah. The aside about their inability to seat riders on the horses is a further slight, for Judah's forces have been seriously depleted by defections (*ANET* 288) in part out of alarm at Hezekiah's destruction of the high places. The final question (v. 25) presents the ultimate argument: Why should Judah trust in YHWH for deliverance when Assyria's successful actions are claimed to arise from YHWH's own command? It is, in the outcome, a truthful claim (19:25–26).

Unfortunately, Assyria has no limits to its hubris in insulting YHWH. This is revealed in the Rab-shakeh's next speech and to large degree accounts for Assyria's failure to take Jerusalem (19:27–28).

26–36. Attempting to forestall persuasion of the assembled people, the delegation urges Aramaic be used instead of the local Judean dialect (Gray 1970: 683). Aramaic was the language of diplomacy in the western Assyrian Empire. The Rab-shakeh denies the envoy's commission is only between the 'masters' in the conflict; rather, it involves the very people who will suffer greatly should any siege or warfare occur. His graphic language emphasizes the desperation of such straits.

Continuing his disputation, he takes up again the theme of misplaced trust (v. 30), arguing that Hezekiah attempts to deceive his own people by urging trust in YHWH. The irony is that, by the Rab-shakeh's words, Assyria is the one attempting to effect deception by urging YHWH not be trusted. Taking up again the messenger formula ('Thus says X') the Rab-shakeh delivers three negative commands from Sennacherib. The people are (1) not to let Hezekiah deceive them (for he is unable to deliver), (2) not to trust in YHWH (by implication because he also is unable to deliver; the specific statement of this is left until vv. 33–35), and (3) not to listen to Hezekiah.

In his first speech the Rab-shakeh has shown the folly of trusting YHWH. To that he adds Sennacherib's commands of what they should *not* do. Now he presents Sennacherib's four commands outlining what they *should* do. Again utilizing the messenger formula, the commands are given succinctly and rapidly to emphasize their sensibleness; only in compliance will they live. They must first make 'peace' – here using the word for 'blessing', perhaps referring to the gift of tribute to be paid (Scharbert, *TDOT* 2:298–299). Then they must 'come out' and surrender. Finally, rather than endure starvation (v. 27) they are commanded to 'eat' and 'drink' in safety.

Hyperbolic fullness is offered them once the people are deported to a land 'like their own land'. The hyperbolic imagery evokes the same security as that offered Solomon's subjects (1 Kgs 4:20, 25[5:5]). The final incentive is that the land of exile is described in the same terms with which Moses described the Land of Promise (v. 32; Deut. 8:7–9). All these positives can be theirs, if (in a final negative command) they will not listen to Hezekiah's assurance that YHWH will deliver.

The point of persuasion now moves beyond Hezekiah's affirmation of YHWH's *willingness* to deliver to YHWH's *ability* to deliver. The argument is simple: it cites lands in the eastern and western reaches of the empire whose 'gods of the nations' (v. 33) were impotent to deliver. Hamath and Arpad represent the west; Hena the east; Sepharvaim is variously placed in the east or west; Ivvah's location is unknown (Avalos, *ABD* 1:401; *ABD* 3:587–588; *ABD* 5:1090; Buhl, *ABD* 3:33–36; H. Thompson, *ABD* 3:137–138; Na'aman 2000a: 394–395). Even Samaria – whose God the Rab-shakeh must know is YHWH – was not delivered. If all these gods were unable to deliver from Assyria's might, how (the Rab-shakeh argues) can YHWH now deliver?

Certainly, the arguments have logic to them. Should the people buy into his presuppositions, they may well surrender. Their silence suggests they remain faithful to Hezekiah's command. Will they remain faithful to his trust in YHWH?

37 – 9:7. The Rab-shakeh's words send the delegation into mourning, signalled by their torn clothing (cf. 1 Kgs 21:27; 2 Kgs 5:7–8; 6:30; 22:11). When Hezekiah hears, he too mourns. But rather than simply despair that Assyria will win, he goes into the temple. From there he sends his envoys to the prophet Isaiah – an unusual appearance in Kings of one of the canonical prophets. The message is delivered by the envoy with another messenger formula and acknowledges two realities. First, a proverbial saying (similar to that found in Hos. 13:13) confesses Jerusalem's need is like that of a woman in labour whose strength fails (v. 3). At the hand of the Assyrian, Jerusalem's inability brings distress (cf. Jer. 16:19; Nah. 1:7; Hab. 3:16), rebuke and humiliation. Secondly, the message acknowledges the Assyrian challenge is really directed against YHWH (v. 4). It is his character and power that are reproached (*ḥrp*; v. 4; cf. 19:16, 22–23). Hezekiah petitions a response.

Isaiah, too, uses the messenger formula (v. 6; cf. 18:19, 29; 19:3). In the encounters between the two powers it is the message sent by YHWH's prophet that has true authority. YHWH assesses the Assyrian challenge not merely as 'reproach' (v. 4) but as 'blasphemy' (*gdp*, v. 6; cf. v. 22), that is, defiant action against YHWH (Num. 15:30). By including YHWH as one of the 'gods of the nations' (18:33–35) Sennacherib has denied his sovereignty. Now, mocking his trustworthiness and ability to save, he denies his power and covenantal character. In the face of this blasphemy YHWH urges Hezekiah to 'not fear'. Sennacherib's words are 'only words' (cf. 18:20) and will be undone by the sovereign God. When Sennacherib hears (*šāma‘*) a report (*šĕmû‘â*; v. 7), he will return to his own land and be killed. The content of the report is not disclosed and may include the news of Tirhakah (v. 9), news of the camp's decimation (19:35) or even an undisclosed report from Nineveh. Whether YHWH's message enables Hezekiah to 'trust' YHWH (18:5) is revealed in the subsequent exchange between Assyria and Judah.

19:8–37

8–13. The Rab-shakeh returns to report Hezekiah's continued resistance. It is left unstated whether the army (18:17) remains to press the Assyrian claim (so Hobbs 1985: 275) or withdraws to join the force at Libnah and against Tirhakah (so Kitchen 1986: 385–386). The exact location of Libnah in the Judean Shephelah (Josh. 15:42) is disputed, but a site east of Lachish en route to Jerusalem is well supported (Corney, *IDB* 3:123).

Sennacherib had previously defeated an Egyptian coalition at Eltekeh (*ANET* 287; Na'aman 1979: 65). Now Tirhakah heads a second Egyptian coalition against Assyria. Earlier scholarship argues that in 701 BC Tirhakah was only an infant. Thus the coalition he led is set against a later Assyrian incursion. The difficulty of this argument is that no such later incursion exists. It is now widely agreed that Tirhakah was already a young man in 701 BC. He became king in 690 BC and the ascription of the title 'king' reflects the perspective of the writer's own time (Kitchen 1986: 158–166, 383–388; Millard 1985: 63–64; Hess 1999: 29). The report of Tirhakah that Sennacherib 'hears' (*šm‘*; v. 9) may raise hope in Judah that Isaiah's prophecy is being fulfilled (18:7) – a hope that Sennacherib's successful action against Tirhakah quickly dispels.

The message is directed to Hezekiah alone (as indicated by the singular verbs and pronouns) and in the form of a letter (v. 14). It repeats arguments delivered by the Rab-shakeh, but now sharpens the attack to assert that YHWH, not Hezekiah (18:29, 32) is deceptive. Sennacherib mounts as proof the nations and cities whose gods were powerless against Assyria. The places are throughout the empire. Some have already endured Assyrian enforced deportations (see 'Comment' at 17:6, 24; 18:34). Some are newly mentioned: Haran, Rezeph and the 'sons of Eden' from northern Babylonia. All were captured by Assyrian monarchs from the ninth century onwards (Na'aman 2000a: 395; Fritz 2003: 374–375). Sennacherib argues that YHWH's assertions of protection are false and should be disregarded.

Sennacherib's point is well taken: no gods of the nations have withstood Assyria. But his claim to have 'destroyed' the nations (v. 11, from *ḥrm*, intending total destruction) overstates the case. Assyrian policy was deportation and resettlement rather than destruction. His claim serves as rhetoric to frighten Hezekiah into submission.

14–19. As before (v. 1), Hezekiah goes to the temple. He spreads the scroll 'before YHWH', a term that can denote specific locations within the holy precinct (several are denoted in Lev. 4: the entrance of the tent, before the curtain, at the altar, etc.). Like David before him (2 Sam. 7:18), although under very different circumstances, Hezekiah lifts his prayer to YHWH within the holy temple. He acknowledges YHWH, the God of Israel enthroned 'on the cherubim' (v. 15), and as the nation's representative petitions on behalf of its dire need (v. 19).

Key descriptors describe YHWH's sovereignty in terms echoed throughout the OT: he is enthroned on the cherubim (1 Sam. 4:4; 2 Sam. 6:2; Pss 80:1[2]; 99:1) and is thus not powerless as Sennacherib asserts. His uniqueness as the only God is proclaimed (Neh. 9:6; Pss 83:18[19]; 86:10), a quality that is similarly attested elsewhere (Deut. 4:35, 39; Isa. 42:8; 44:6). YHWH's uniqueness places him as the only God over all nations, a claim that directly opposes Sennacherib's theology. The final evidence of YHWH's unique sovereignty lies in his creative power in the heavens and earth. Elsewhere this creative power attests to his ability to provide help (Pss 121:2; 124:8) and give life (Neh. 9:6), which makes all things possible (Jer. 32:17).

Invoking such a God makes Hezekiah bold to plead YHWH act. He urges him (in imperative verbs) to 'incline your ear' and 'hear', to 'open your eyes' and 'see' and 'listen' (v. 16). The foreigner's words (note no honorific is used of Sennacherib) 'reproach' (*ḥrp*) YHWH, as Hezekiah has previously noted (v. 4) and YHWH will later acknowledge (v. 22). The reproach lies not only in Sennacherib's words but his actions. In conquering nations (v. 17), he asserts the power of Assyrian gods over the nations' gods. Against this Hezekiah has claimed YHWH's sovereignty (v. 15). In destroying foreign gods (v. 18), Sennacherib asserts Assyria's power over these gods. Instead, Hezekiah again asserts YHWH's sovereignty by noting the foreign gods are man-made and therefore powerless (v. 18). They are nothing in comparison to the only powerful God, YHWH of Israel.

Hezekiah voices his supplication in a final imperative: 'save us' (v. 19). The supplication is not solely for the relief of Jerusalem. It asks for the removal of the reproach Sennacherib has cast upon YHWH. In responding, YHWH will prove all the sovereign power Hezekiah has credited to him.

Hezekiah's prayer evokes Elijah's earlier prayer for the vindication of YHWH's sovereignty over Baal's presumed power (1 Kgs 18:24, 36). Hezekiah's prayer also evokes the exodus tradition. Like Sennacherib, Pharaoh challenged YHWH's sovereignty (Exod. 5:2) and YHWH acted to reveal his power among the nations (Exod. 14:4; Josh. 2:10–11).

20–28. YHWH's response through his prophet answers Hezekiah's plea. As Israel's sovereign king, YHWH directs the prophecy against Sennacherib the 'king of Assyria' (v. 20). Three voices are raised in the prophecy's first section; each works to elevate the power of YHWH and thus reveal the folly of Sennacherib's boast.

The first voice is that of Jerusalem, the 'daughter of Zion' (Isa. 1:8; 10:32; 16:1; 52:2) who, though threatened by Assyria, remains free and a 'virgin' (Leithart 2006: 258). Her response to Sennacherib is derision tinged with pity, signalled in the tossed head (hiph. of *nw'*; see Pss 22:7[8]; 109:25; Job 16:4; Lam. 2:15; Zeph. 2:15). Her words take up the dual charge of 'reproach' and 'blasphemy' levelled against Assyria (v. 22; cf. 19:4, 6, 16). In addition, Sennacherib has exceeded his station by raising (*rwm*) his voice and lifting (*rwm*) his eyes (v. 22). His folly, enacted in the boasts and claims of his messengers (v. 23; i.e. the Rab-shakeh and the subsequent letter), is not against Hezekiah but a much higher king, the Holy One of Israel.

Sennacherib's bid for the lofty heights of YHWH's station is next expressed in a second voice. Sennacherib boasts of ascending (from *rwm*) lofty heights (from *rwm*; v. 23). His boast is accentuated through the first-person verbs and emphatic pronoun ('I ascended . . . I dug'; vv. 23–24) and reiterates in hyperbolic detail his military successes. With his large army ('many' chariots) he has ascended Lebanon's mountains to Lebanon's 'far reaches'. Of their legendary cedars (1 Kgs 4:33; 2 Kgs 14:9) he has cut the 'tallest' together with the best of their firs. Neither Lebanon's furthest shelter nor their densest forests safeguard against Assyria. Even foreign waters are subject to Assyria. Here the hyperbole is clear, for Sennacherib's campaigns never reach the borders of Egypt – yet he proudly claims sweeping power over their rivers.

The third voice – YHWH's – answers Sennacherib's taunt. YHWH initially affirms Sennacherib's claim that his military success is by YHWH's hand (18:25). It was ordained in primeval times and is now fulfilled against unassailable cities. Sennacherib has taken forty-six fortified Judean cities (*ANET* 288), including Lachish. By YHWH's predetermination they are as susceptible as sun-blasted weeds and rooftop grass, a stark comparison to the flourishing restoration of Israel (vv. 29–31).

YHWH knows the doings of Sennacherib, but also how he has raged in arrogance (vv. 27–28). Overstepping himself, Sennacherib must be tamed as a beast subdued with hooks and bridle – the imagery is that of ANE records (*ANET* 447; *ANET* 300; cf. Ezek. 38:4). Sennacherib will be turned back (*šwb*; cf. v. 33) as Hezekiah originally urged (18:14) and the prophetic word promised (19:7).

29–31. As here, the prophetic word is elsewhere accompanied by a sign (1 Kgs 13:3; Isa. 7:11–12). Utilizing further agrarian imagery (vv. 29–30; cf. v. 26), YHWH promises, despite the lands' severe devastation, that crops will be sown and harvested within three years. In the same way YHWH promises that the seed of the remnant of Judah will be planted and fruitful, with growth enabled by the zealous gardener, YHWH. For the remnant in Babylon who receive this narrative the promise of renewal must elicit hope for their restoration out of captivity.

32–34. Restoration requires the removal of Sennacherib, which this oracle of salvation promises. Four negative particles (*lōʾ*) reveal four things Sennacherib will not do: enter the city, shoot an arrow in it, bring a shield against it and build a siege ramp. He will instead do one thing: return (*šwb*; cf. v. 28; 18:14; 19:7). The divine king and warrior thus wins against Assyria's boastful claims. Any shield (from *gnn*) Sennacherib hopes to raise against Jerusalem (v. 32) will encounter YHWH's defence (from *gnn*; v. 34). By defending Jerusalem YHWH redresses the reproach and blasphemy levelled against him. He likewise honours the ancient promises made to David, whose royal seat and national shrine is in Jerusalem.

35–37. The deliverance occurs immediately ('that night'), although the location of the miracle is ambiguous. If troops remain stationed around Jerusalem, there is a certain satisfaction to the miraculous deliverance in this venue. It is here that Sennacherib voiced his blasphemies. However, if the troops had earlier withdrawn to the battle against Tirhakah (Kitchen 1986: 385–386), the miracle may occur on that field. Assuming a Jerusalem location, the 'they' who arose in the morning (v. 35) are the Jerusalemites. The number of troops is particularly large (by comparison, the allied coalition at Qarqar totalled only fifty thousand (*ANET* 278), and may be hyperbolic, emphasizing YHWH's power to effect an extensive miracle.

The miraculous nature of the event is disputed. Often it is linked to an account in Herodotus' *Histories* (Book 2.141) that describes an attack of the Assyrian army by mice. Speculation considers a deadly mice-borne plague accounts for the wholesale and rapid death. However, the campaign Herodotus mentions is a different campaign in Egypt in a later era; it does not refer to the present event. The biblical account does not describe the mechanics of the miracle; to do so would miss the point. It is YHWH's sovereign power that effects the deliverance – how that is accomplished is utterly irrelevant. If YHWH is sovereign, a miracle is well within his able power.

Admitting defeat, Sennacherib departs home. He may have received a 'report' (v. 7) of the army's devastation, or perhaps other or additional news caused alarm and withdrawal. His return (the root *šwb* appears for the last time in v. 36) home fulfils the prophetic word (vv. 7, 28, 33). After a lapse of several years (telescoped in the narrative phrase 'he dwelt in Nineveh'), he is assassinated in 680 BC. The extant ANE record provides a plausible context for the assassination, although it is not itself recorded. Sennacherib in his life gave preference to his younger son, Esarhaddon. A sibling rivalry apparently existed as Esarhaddon struggled to secure the throne upon his father's death (*ANET* 289–290). The succession conflict suggests a context for the assassination.

Ironically, Sennacherib dies in the house of his god Nisroch. The god is not elsewhere attested and perhaps is Marduk or Nusku (Gray 1970: 694–695). Regardless, the king who scorned the powerlessness of the nations' gods (18:33–34; 19:12–13) is himself undefended by the god of his own nation. None can stand against the God of Israel. The final proof of YHWH's sovereignty appears in the succession formula given for Esarhaddon. It is that used for Israelite kings. YHWH exercises the same sovereignty, overseeing Israelite and Assyrian succession. He truly is God of all the nations.

Explanation

Will Hezekiah trust YHWH? This question produces narrative tension in the king's encounters with Assyria. The Rab-shakeh presents two reasons why Hezekiah and the people should forgo such trust: (1) that YHWH is not willing to deliver, and (2) that YHWH is not able to deliver. The logic of the Rab-shakeh's argument and the evidence of Assyria's power could easily undermine trust.

An explanation of this passage acknowledges Hezekiah's trust but raises a more basic question: Why *should* YHWH be trusted? The narrative provides two reasons. Together they show that trusting YHWH is the only faithful, wise and safe course for YHWH's people. Each of these reasons is witnessed in the biblical canon, and each is a necessary component of YHWH's character.

The narrative affirms that YHWH is to be trusted because he is sovereign. Particularly, that sovereignty is demonstrated over the nations. Assyria can boast of success only because it is planned and enabled by YHWH (19:25). This sovereignty over the affairs of the nations arises long before Assyria's might. YHWH's covenant with Noah binds him to all the peoples of the earth (Gen. 9:9–10, 15) whom he has created. Thus his concern for all humanity predates the call of Israel. Even the beginnings of nations and languages stem from YHWH's dispersal of the peoples (Gen. 11:8). The Table of Nations shows an elementary understanding of peoples and nations (Gen. 10), and Deuteronomy shows YHWH appoints the nations' territories (Deut. 2:4–5, 9, 19; 32:8). The inclusion in Scripture of such events shows an understanding that the nations are within YHWH's purview.

The universality of YHWH's sovereignty is noted in Isa. 14:26 and Dan. 4:35, as he alone plans the nations' affairs. He directs the rise and fall of all nations (Dan. 2:21, 36–45; Dan. 7 – 8; Hab. 1:5–6). He also appoints rulers not only over his own people, Israel (2 Sam. 7:11–16; 1 Kgs 2:46; 11:29–39), but over other nations, often for the purpose of providing discipline, judgment or blessing for Israel (1 Kgs 19:15; 2 Kgs 8:7–15; Isa. 44:28).

Kings has shown several times that YHWH intervenes in Israel's wars (1 Kgs 20, 22; 2 Kgs 3, 13). He brings peace from enemies (1 Kgs 5:4) as well as warfare, defeat and exile (1 Kgs 11:14, 23; 2 Kgs 17:3–7), all as YHWH has promised (Deut. 28:7, 25). A similar sovereign oversight attends to the warfare conducted by the nations. YHWH enables foreign nations to have victory (2 Kgs 5:1) and directs their battles (Isa. 7:18–20; 10:5–6; Dan. 11) – a reality that Sennacherib claims and Hezekiah witnesses.

In the same way YHWH also superintends the final ends of the nations. This is initially hinted at in the many prophetic messages of judgment spoken against the nations. Extensive collections of such prophetic messages are included in the major prophets (Isa. 14:28 – 24:23; Jer. 46 – 51; Ezek. 25 – 32) and are not lacking in the minor prophets (Joel 3; Amos 1 – 3). Some minor prophets are wholly devoted to such future-casting regarding the nations (Obadiah, Nahum). Many of these messages speak to historical judgments against the nations for their stance towards YHWH's people (see e.g. Ezek. 25:2–4, 8–9, 12–13, 15) or for acts of violence and sin (see e.g. Amos 1:3, 6, 9, 11, 13). Included in these prophecies is the eschatological expression of YHWH's sovereign judgment of the nations. Eventually, YHWH's judgment leads to the people's humble submission to YHWH. Walking in repentance, the nations experience the eschatological benefits of YHWH's care. The nations join Israel to worship YHWH, and peaceful international relations arise (Isa. 25:6–12; 2:2–4). These eschatological visions look to the fulfilment of the promises made to Abraham by which YHWH assured blessings to all the nations.

The promise made to Abraham furthers YHWH's purposes originally expressed in the creation of all humanity. Although the original creation was marred by sin and rebellion, YHWH did not abandon it. Through Abraham, and later through his descendant Israel, YHWH worked to rectify all that sin and rebellion had sowed into his creation. He would sovereignly direct the affairs of individuals and nations to this purpose.

On the strength of YHWH's sovereignty over all the affairs of humankind Hezekiah does well to trust him. He alone has inscribed his plans and purposes upon those nations, and can move the nations to accomplish them. Hezekiah has a long history to assure him of this reality. The Rabshakeh's taunts and the desperate situation in which the nation finds itself do not militate against that history.

The second reason the narrative gives for YHWH's trustworthiness is that while he is sovereign over the nations, he also attends to cries of individuals. When Hezekiah is faced with the Assyrian threat, he petitions YHWH through his prophet. YHWH attends to his distress and responds (19:6). Hezekiah also petitions YHWH a second time, addressing the sovereign lord not through his prophet, but directly (19:15–19). Because this righteous king prays towards YHWH, YHWH hears and responds (v. 20), proving the truth of Solomon's dedicatory prayer (1 Kgs 8:28–53).

Hezekiah predicates his petition on the potential damage to YHWH's sovereign reputation should Sennacherib take Jerusalem (19:4, 15–19). But this concern is only partially responsible for YHWH's action (vv. 21–28).

God also acts against Sennacherib for other reasons, each of which shows his personal relationship and attentiveness to his people. First, YHWH moves out of concern for the remnant of Israel (19:4, 30–31). Because of his covenant relationship with his people, he pledges personal intervention on their behalf. He will not abandon his people, even if only a few acknowledge him. Secondly, YHWH moves against Sennacherib 'for the sake of David' (v. 24). This is a reference to the Davidic Covenant (2 Sam. 7), which is YHWH's personal commitment to David and his descendants.

The personal nature of YHWH's attentiveness is not unique to Hezekiah. He has repeatedly attended to, and responded to, the cries of his people (Exod. 2:23–25; Judg. 2:18 *et passim*). He has heard the cries of leaders (Exod. 32:11–14, 31–32; 1 Sam. 12:16), barren women (Gen. 25:22–23; 1 Sam. 1:10–20) and doubters (Ps. 73:16–17). He has sent prophets, food, healing and life itself in answer to these prayers.

Hezekiah should trust YHWH for both his sovereign power and his personal attentiveness to his people. Each of these characteristics is a necessary correlative in YHWH's character. Should he be only sovereign but not attentive, there is a terrible sense of humans as merely cogs in his grand designs – their woes and needs unheeded and unimportant within a larger plan. And should he be personally attentive without being sovereign, his attention would be cloying: always sympathetic and caring but never able to effect change. Or, in an equally distressing scenario, acting in sympathy but without attention to how or when those actions might offset his plans and purposes. In concert YHWH is both attentive and powerful. He is able to order the world rightly and to his purposes while still ministering in compassion to his people towards their best end.

At several points Scripture asserts this dual nature of YHWH and thus affirms the trustworthiness of YHWH's character. Ps. 113 recalls YHWH's exaltation over the nations while he stoops from his lofty throne to raise the poor and needy. This is a similar theme in Hannah's prayer (1 Sam. 2:2–10). In it YHWH's sovereign power is expressed over the nations, over life and death, and over creation. But he still attends to the poor and needy – as witnessed in Hannah's own experience. Jesus' mother, Mary, likewise glorifies God, asserting his sovereign power over the proud, the rulers and the rich without neglecting the humble. Indeed, both Hannah and Mary assert that YHWH's sovereign will works to reverse the hubris of the proud (as he did Sennacherib's). In the display of his power the strong and proud have no refuge, while the weak display God's glory.

Finally, the early church in Acts recognized in the ascended Christ that YHWH's sovereign power was incontestably displayed. They saw the fulfilment of the nations' rage against YHWH (Ps. 2) in the actions of Pilate and Herod against Jesus. This, however, occurred as part of YHWH's sovereign plan (Acts 4:23–31). They understood that they now lived in an age in which no power could stand against YHWH. As they boldly proclaimed God's word, his sovereign power in Christ worked wonders and signs (v. 30). The world envisioned by Hannah and Mary now existed in the reality of Christ.

It is in times of crisis (such as Hezekiah experienced), or at the hinges of the world, when paradigms shift (as for Hannah, Mary and the church), that YHWH shows himself trustworthy: willing and able to listen and act for his plans and his people. But it is also true that when life runs smoothly, when the crisis passes and the hinges of history have moved the world into new paradigms, there too God's people are called to trust YHWH. And for the same reasons: he is a sovereign lord, enthroned above the heavens, able and willing to act. And he is an attentive personal lord, stooping from his lofty throne to hear the prayers of all his people.

Such a message must speak powerfully to an exilic people who now live in a new paradigm. The time to trust YHWH for the preservation of the city or the temple has passed – both are now destroyed. However, trusting YHWH for such deliverance is not the only way to demonstrate trust in his word. For instance, in the era of Zedekiah, the last monarch on Judah's throne (2 Kgs 24:18 – 25:21), trust of YHWH was not synonymous with trusting YHWH to *deliver*. Rather, it was demonstrated in surrendering to Babylon (Jer. 21:1–10; 27:12–22; 38:2, 17–18) and trusting YHWH to *sustain* the people through the horror of exile (Jer. 24:5–7; 27:22; 29:4–14; see also the far-reaching promises given in the Book of Comfort [Jer. 30 – 33] that speak of YHWH's sustaining and restoring power).

Most of the exiles did not voluntarily surrender to Babylon (although some did; see Jer. 38:19) and thus did not demonstrate their trust of YHWH in that obedience. But now, in exile, they can begin to trust YHWH. They are to settle down, build houses and seek the welfare of the Babylonian state. And they are to look ahead to the prophesied time of return (Jer. 25:11; 29:10–14), trusting that YHWH will perform his word. The exiles know the events recounted to them in 1 – 2 Kings have come to pass. Now, they can exhibit the trust of Hezekiah by believing in the promises of national return, and by joyfully aligning their individual lives to the covenant of the faithful God.

2 KINGS 20:1–21

Translation

[1]In those days Hezekiah became mortally ill. Isaiah son of Amoz, the prophet, came to him. He said to him, 'Thus says YHWH, "Set your house in order, for you will die and not recover."' [2]Then he turned his face to the wall and prayed to YHWH, saying, [3]'Ah, YHWH, I pray you remember how I have walked before you in truth and with a whole heart, and how I have done the good in your eyes.' Then Hezekiah wept bitterly.

[4]Now Isaiah had not yet gone out to the middle court when the word of YHWH came to him, saying, [5]"Return and say to Hezekiah the ruler of my people, "Thus says YHWH, the God of David your father, I have heard your prayer; I have seen your tears. Behold, I shall heal you; on the third day you shall go up to the house of YHWH. [6]I will add fifteen years to your life and I will deliver you and this city from the hand of the king of Assyria. I will defend this city for my own sake and for the sake of David my servant."' [7]Then Isaiah said, 'Take a fig cake.' So they took it and laid it on the ulcer, and he recovered.

[8]Hezekiah said to Isaiah, 'What sign is there that YHWH will heal me, and I will go up on the third day to the house of YHWH?' [9]Isaiah said, 'This will be the sign to you from YHWH that YHWH will do that which he has spoken: shall the shadow advance ten steps, or retreat ten steps?[a]' [10]Hezekiah replied, 'It is not difficult for the shadow to lengthen ten steps. No, let the shadow turn back ten steps.' [11]So Isaiah the prophet cried to YHWH and he turned the shadow back ten steps by which it had gone down on the stairway of Ahaz.

[12]At that time Merodach[a]-baladan son of Baladan king of Babylon sent letters and a gift to Hezekiah, for he had heard that Hezekiah had been sick. [13]Hezekiah received them and showed them all his treasure house: the silver and the gold, the spices, the precious oil, his armouries, and everything that was found in his treasuries. There was nothing that Hezekiah did not show them in his house and in all his dominion.

[14]Then Isaiah the prophet came to King Hezekiah and said to him, 'What did these men say, and from where have they come to you?' Hezekiah answered, 'From a far land; they have come from Babylon.' [15]He said, 'What have they seen in your house?' and Hezekiah answered, 'They have seen all that is in my house. There is nothing that I have not shown them in my treasuries. [16]So Isaiah said to Hezekiah, 'Hear the word of YHWH: [17]Behold, days are coming when everything that is in your house and that your fathers stored up until this day will be carried away to Babylon. Nothing shall remain, says YHWH. [18]And some of your sons that shall be borne to you[a] shall be taken and they shall be eunuchs in the palace of the king of Babylon.' [19]And Hezekiah said to Isaiah, 'The word of YHWH that you have spoken is good.' For he thought, 'Why not, if there will be peace and surety in my days?'

[20]And the rest of the acts of Hezekiah and all his might, and how he made the pool and the conduit and brought water to the city, are they not written in the Book of the Chronicles of the Kings of Judah? [21]Then Hezekiah slept with his fathers[a] and Manasseh his son reigned in his place.

Notes on the text

9.a. MT can be read as an indicative followed by an interrogative: 'The shadow has advanced ten steps; shall it retreat?' But reading both as interrogative fits the context better. Montgomery (1951: 512) notes MT inf. abs. *hǎlak* can be read interrogatively. Emending with Tg, LXX, Vg to *hǎyēlēk* is not required.

12.a. MT *bĕrō'dak* is read here with some MSS, LXX, Syr, Tg, Vg and Isa. 39:1 as *mĕrō'dak*.

18.a. MT has repetitious *'ăšer yēṣĕ'û mimmĕkā 'ăšer tôlîd*, 'which will go out from you which you will bear', and *BHS* suggests elision of one or the other relative clause. Montgomery (1951: 513) holds the second as an explanatory gloss. Gray's emendation (1970: 701) of *mimmĕkā* to *mimmē'ekā*, 'from your loins', is counted unnecessary by both Montgomery (1951: 513) and Hobbs (1985: 286).

21.a. Some LXX MSS add 'and was buried'; LXX^L further adds 'with his fathers in the City of David'.

Form and structure

Two addenda round out Hezekiah's story (vv. 1–11, 12–19) before closing with a regnal summary (vv. 20–21). The vignettes provide another ominous reminder – as in the reflection on Israel's exile (2 Kgs 17) – that Judah and Jerusalem are not exempt from judgment. This chapter takes up that threat, connecting it to Babylon rather than Assyria.

Temporal markers ('in those days'; 'at that time') align the events with those of the Assyrian threat. As discussed in the 'Comment' section below, the second vignette is best placed historically before the events of 701 BC; its literary placement highlights the vignettes' shared themes. Both deal with the issue of death – of the king, and of the nation – and a gracious extension of life. In this way Hezekiah's experience foreshadows that of Jerusalem. But while YHWH defends the city 'for his own sake and for the sake of David my servant', and honours the righteous plea of Hezekiah, there is no indication he counters the judgment against the city and people foretold long before (1 Kgs 9:6–9).

The first vignette utilizes but significantly alters the type scene of a dying king (1 Kgs 14; 2 Kgs 1; 8:7–15). In the type an ill king makes enquiry through a prophet and receives a death sentence, often in response to his apostasy. With Hezekiah the oracle forecasting death comes unbidden and is not in response to apostasy. It begins the narrative, providing the complication that is then resolved. A further difference to the type scene is that two oracles are provided. The first, forecasting death, provides the narrative's initial problem; the second resolves the problem by forecasting healing for Hezekiah. The oracle of healing expands to a salvation oracle concerning the city (v. 5–6). The salvation oracle provides a context for the second vignette, which also concerns the city.

The request for a sign that is narrated after Hezekiah's healing, and the variant spelling of Hezekiah's name in vv. 9–11, suggests to many the addition of a separate tradition (Gray 1970: 696; Jones 1984b: 584; B. Long 1991: 236). Such a compositional history is not the only possibility and the NIV proposes a flashback in which 'Hezekiah had asked Isaiah', although the verbal form does not support such a reading. The request is best read consecutively and serves to characterize Hezekiah, who doubts or questions the fullness of the healing experience and seeks an assuring sign (Hobbs 1985: 293; Provan 1995: 264).

The thematic parallels between the two vignettes are highlighted by the repetition of the terms 'hear' (*šmʿ*; vv. 5, 12) and 'see' (*rʾh*; vv. 5, 12–15 [five times]). In the first instance YHWH both hears and sees Hezekiah's petition and graciously responds when Hezekiah (who trusts YHWH, 18:5) prays. In the second, the words take on negative connotations, for Merodach-baladan's visit is precipitated by hearing of Hezekiah's illness. During that visit Hezekiah's trust is displaced from YHWH to the foreign king. It is this action on Hezekiah's part that precipitates YHWH's word of judgment.

Comment

20:1–11

1–7. Hezekiah's near-death experience occurs 'in those days', a time that can be set just prior to or during the Assyrian threat of 701 BC. In that year he is fourteen years into his reign, and the additional fifteen years granted him (v. 6) total his twenty-nine year reign (see 'Comment' at 18:1). The city has not yet been delivered (v. 6).

Isaiah is again introduced by patronym ('son of Amoz') and role ('the prophet') (see 19:2, 20), possibly indicative of the integration of a new tradition. In the present narrative this emphasizes the prophet's central role. His first oracle is succinct, calling the king to arrange his affairs in view of his impending death. It may be at this time that Hezekiah appoints Manasseh as co-regent; if so, the parallels to David's life that appear throughout this section (see 'Comment' below) are echoed here as well. Like Hezekiah, as David's death drew near he appointed a successor as co-regent to avoid a threatening succession battle (1 Kgs 1).

Hezekiah turns his face to the wall, an action that elsewhere demonstrates Ahab's pique (1 Kgs 21:4), but here accompanied by prayer suggests a desire for solitude, reflection or even mourning. Hezekiah has prayed before for the city (19:15); now his prayer is on his own behalf. His positive self-assessment is not hubris but follows the patterns of petition common to psalmnody (Pss 17:1–5; 18:4–6[5–7], 20–24[21–25]; 26:1–11). The pattern includes weeping bitter 'tears' (*dimʿâ*; vv. 3, 5; cf. Pss 6:6[7]; 39:12[13]; 42:3[4]). His phraseology is Deuteronomistic, for he has a 'whole heart' (1 Kgs 8:61; 11:4; 15:3, 14) and 'doing the good in your eyes' is obedience per Deuteronomy (6:18; cf. similarly 2 Kgs 12:2; 14:3; 18:3; 22:2). He also characterizes himself as a second David who 'walked before you in truth' (1 Kgs 2:4; 3:6). For these reasons he asks YHWH's remembrance, implying a petition for healing.

YHWH's answer is immediate, necessitating Isaiah turn back while still in the 'middle court' in the palace-temple precincts (1 Kgs 7:8). In the second oracle YHWH's words allude to David, not only in the reference to 'David your father' and the defence of the city for 'David my servant' (v. 6), but in calling Hezekiah 'the ruler' (*nāgîd*), an older term applied to David (2 Sam. 6:21; 7:8). The allusions align righteous Hezekiah with this favoured king and are a reminder of YHWH's commitment to the Davidic dynasty.

YHWH, having 'heard' and 'seen' Hezekiah's petition, responds with a promise of healing. The ailment involves inflamed skin ulcers or boils (*šĕḥîn*; v. 7) and is the affliction named in Exod. 9:9–11; Lev. 13:18–23; and Job 2:7. The promise of healing assures the restoration of temple attendance 'soon' (the meaning of 'in three days'). YHWH's healing allows for a gracious extension of life. The extension is bound up with continued life for the city, for YHWH promises to 'deliver you and this city'. But, lest any false royal ideology be mounted that ties Jerusalem's survival to Hezekiah's personal righteousness, YHWH reveals his commitment to Jerusalem remains for YHWH's sake and for David's sake (19:34).

In applying a plaster made of fig cake, Isaiah joins Elisha who similarly used common elements to effect uncommon healing (2 Kgs 2:20–22; 4:4; 5:10). The fig plaster utilizes medical practices of the ANE (Harrison, *IDB* 3:331–334). Whether the plaster's antiseptic or astringent value is the means of healing or is only an adjunct to YHWH's direct power, Hezekiah is healed.

8–11. Uncertain or doubting the extent of his healing, Hezekiah requests a sign (see 'Form and structure'). His concern is only personal, but Isaiah's answer has in view all that YHWH has spoken – regarding both Hezekiah and the city. He involves Hezekiah in determining the sign: whether the advancing afternoon shadow should lengthen more rapidly than is normal, or whether it should retreat. Because the sign includes the measurement of time, the 'steps' (*maʿălôt*) are sometimes construed as a sundial (so Montgomery 1951: 508). But the term normally has the sense of 'steps' (Exod. 20:26; 1 Kgs 10:19; 2 Kgs 9:13) and the passage of time by the sun's shadow would be clearly revealed on a stairway. Gray (1970: 699) argues the stairway leads to a rooftop astral shrine, but the text provides no such hint and Hezekiah's reforms militate against it – the stairs are just stairs.

Seeking full assurance that YHWH is able to effect a cure, Hezekiah chooses the more difficult of the possible signs. The western-setting sun will cause the shadow to lengthen anyway; Hezekiah chooses the option that will most clearly reveal YHWH's power. Certainly, YHWH's sovereign power (19:25–30) is not daunted by the task – and he has in the past acted similarly (Josh. 10:12–14).

20:12–19

The second vignette is connected literarily to the time of Hezekiah's illness but it is difficult to place the visit during the crisis of 701 BC (contra Hobbs 1985: 289). Merodach-baladan ruled in Babylon 720–709 BC, was exiled by Assyria, and then ruled again briefly in 703 BC before defeat at Sennacherib's hand. A visit in 701 BC is not impossible, but its purpose is difficult to imagine. More, Hezekiah's treasuries are filled, which is unlikely given the tribute paid to Sennacherib. His visit is better placed before 701 BC, possibly in Merodach-baladan's last, brief reign.

The Babylonian arrives in response to Hezekiah's illness but his visit is much more than bedside politeness. As the most powerful of the western anti-Assyrian allies, Merodach-baladan seeks Hezekiah's goodwill or even an alliance. B. Long (1991: 243) argues on the basis of royal inscriptions from Shalmaneser that inspections of wealth such as conducted by Merodach-baladan signal a 'diplomatic concordat' by which Hezekiah hopes to ensure Jerusalem's safety. This would certainly provide the background to Isaiah's displeasure and YHWH's judgment, for Hezekiah should be looking to YHWH alone for defence of the city.

The display of all Hezekiah's wealth that left nothing undisclosed is reminiscent of the Queen of Sheba's visit to Solomon (1 Kgs 10). But where her visit revealed Solomon's wisdom (1 Kgs 10:4, 6–8), Merodach-baladan's visit reveals Hezekiah's folly. Seeking assurance of Jerusalem's future from a foreign king, he foolishly disregards YHWH's commitment to Jerusalem. Moreover, his display of Jerusalem's wealth can do nothing but make the city tantalizing to the Babylonians.

For these reasons Isaiah brings the chapter's third oracle. In the first vignette YHWH heard and saw Hezekiah's plea and responded favourably. Now Merodach-baladan has heard of Hezekiah's sickness (v. 12) and seen all Hezekiah's wealth (vv. 13–15; see 'Form and structure'), and YHWH responds unfavourably.

The oracle holds no certain word of Jerusalem's fall, nor provides a time line. But the promise is telling: a future is coming in which the accumulated riches Hezekiah trusted in and boasted of will be taken away to Babylon, leaving nothing. Further, the Davidic dynasty will similarly be sacked as Hezekiah's descendants ('sons' may be biological sons or descendants) are likewise deported. As the narrative unfolds, the events of 2 Kgs 24 – 25 fulfil the oracle.

The oracle includes no date for its fulfilment, but there is no uncertainty that the day is coming. The word is YHWH's and Kings has repeatedly demonstrated that word's inviolability. Additionally, the oracle stands in the tradition of warnings previously given Judah and its kings. The 'far land' of captivity (v. 14) was long ago noted by Solomon (1 Kgs 8:46) and exile was part of YHWH's word of judgment upon Solomon's descendants (1 Kgs 9:7). Judah has not mended their ways in response to the warning provided in Israel's exile, and not even Hezekiah's personal righteousness changes YHWH's purposes. The righteous king's folly vis-à-vis Babylon precipitates a word of judgment that will be enacted. YHWH's sovereignty, so aptly demonstrated in the Hezekiah narrative (chs. 18–20), can effect the judgment he has long proclaimed.

The first vignette provided YHWH's judgment against Hezekiah, followed by a reprieve. The same pattern appears in the second vignette. Granted, the reprieve is not what one would hope – no word is given that the judgment will be set aside, and in this one recognizes the extent of Hezekiah's folly and Judah's ongoing sin. But there is a truncated reprieve. Hezekiah acknowledges the veracity of YHWH's word. He notes it is 'good', that is, well said (1 Sam. 9:10; 1 Kgs 2:38) and not to be accomplished in his own day. The king who trusted YHWH, and who characterizes himself as having a 'whole' (*šlm*) heart and 'truth' ('*mt*; v. 3), selfishly rests content that 'peace' (*šlm*) and 'surety' ('*mt*; v. 19) will remain through his days. There is no acknowledgment of his folly in trusting the riches of Jerusalem for deliverance, and there is none of his previous concern for the ongoing welfare of Jerusalem.

By placing this narrative as the last in Hezekiah's account, his portrait ends in a less complementary way than it began. Juxtaposed to positive accounts of the king, it prepares for the final chapters of Kings. Jerusalem's fall is certain, and even a righteous king contributes to its certainty. The only remaining questions are how and when Jerusalem will fall to Babylon.

20:20–21

The regnal summary is unremarkable. It includes the usual citation of sources, notice of death, and successor. The additional material remarks on Hezekiah's work to provide a water source to Jerusalem, secure even during siege. The famous tunnel brings the Gihon waters into the city by way of an extensive underground channel. An engineering feat: two teams tunnelled from either end, meeting in the middle. The completion of the tunnel is commemorated in the contemporaneous Siloam Inscription, now housed in the archaeological museum in Istanbul.

Explanation

The miraculous deliverance of Jerusalem in chs. 18–19 is only a temporary reprieve and the judgment forecast against the southern kingdom, the holy city and its temple remain in place. Hezekiah's personal righteousness is insufficient to offset the judgment against the nation. The encroaching presence of Assyria in the Levant, the fall of the northern kingdom and the clear and present danger to Jerusalem by Sennacherib are all ominous signs of what is to come.

Yet this chapter demonstrates that in the face of judgment YHWH is able to extend life. He gives personal reprieve to Hezekiah on account of his personal righteousness. The extension of life granted the king is a parable of the extension of life granted the city. The Assyrian threat will be overcome for the sake of YHWH's name, and for the promises made to David (v. 6). Though future judgment at Babylon's hand is now introduced, an undisclosed number of years is granted before that experience.

The chapter revisits a theme common to 1 – 2 Kings: YHWH's ability to extend life in the face of impending death. It is most apparent in the Elijah–Elisha narratives (see 'Comment', 1 Kgs 17 – 18; 2 Kgs 4), where the northern kingdom is threatened by Baal worship. The work of YHWH's prophets there show it is YHWH (and not Baal) who is the Lord of life. Through restored rains, resurrection and miraculous provision of food and means YHWH's people are summoned back to covenant faithfulness. Sadly, however, the people turn away again to Baal and this sin accounts in part for the ultimate judgment of the northern kingdom. Yet, by YHWH's gracious intervention, the goodness of covenant life was for a time extended.

Extension of life in the face of death is also apparent in the judgments spoken against dynastic rulers, which are forestalled to later generations. Thus though Solomon's sins place the Davidic dynasty under judgment, it does not fall immediately. Because of the promises given David the dynasty continues for three hundred years, before the southern kingdom falls. Similarly, the judgments against Jeroboam and Ahab are forestalled to later generations.

In these periods of extended life there are many stories of YHWH's faithful people. A remnant does not bow its knee to Baal (1 Kgs 19:18), rich (2 Kgs 4:8–37; 6:32) and poor (2 Kgs 4:1–7, 38–41) turn to YHWH's prophets for needed help, YHWH's power is proclaimed (2 Kgs 5:3), risks are taken to preserve David's royal line (2 Kgs 11:2–16), and righteous kings purify worship (2 Kgs 18:3–4; 23:4–24). There are many who stand in the 'hall of faith' of Heb. 11 who lived during these years of extended national life. Heb. 11 commends their faith as they honoured YHWH and walked in his covenant. Although they did not know the nation's future – be it long or short – they did not turn from serving YHWH.

But, as 2 Kgs 20 also reminds us, those who trusted and served YHWH were not perfect. Hezekiah was lauded for his trust of YHWH in the previous chapters but now his trust is not so unwavering. Faithful people can falter even in the face of YHWH's gracious extension of life. But this depiction of Hezekiah reverberates on another common theme throughout 1 – 2 Kings. That is, that YHWH's plans and purposes no less than his grace do not depend upon his people's faithfulness. Knowing that they would not wholly succeed to live the covenant life (Josh. 24:19–20), he himself yet remains faithful. He extends grace, all the while shepherding history to its determined ends and by his determined timetable – even though that end is one of judgment under the covenant. Hezekiah's failures are real, but are read against the deeper reality of YHWH's sovereign control of history and his gracious provisions to his people.

2 KINGS 21:1–26

Translation

¹Manasseh was twelve years old when he began to reign, and he reigned fifty-five years in Jerusalem. The name of his mother was Hephzibah. ²He did what was evil in the eyes of YHWH according to the abominations of the nations that YHWH dispossessed from before the sons of Israel. ³He rebuilt the high places that Hezekiah his father had destroyed and erected altars to Baal, and made a sacred pole as Ahab king of Israel had done. He bowed down to all the host of heaven and served them. ⁴He built altars in the house of YHWH concerning which YHWH had said, 'In Jerusalem I will set my name,' ⁵and he built altars to all the host of heaven in the two courts of the house of YHWH.

⁶He passed his sonª through the fire and practised soothsaying and divination, and dealt with mediums and spiritists. He did much evil in the eyes of YHWH, provoking himᵇ to anger. ⁷He set the carved image of Asherah that he had made in the house of which YHWH had said to David and Solomon his son, 'In this house and in Jerusalem, which I have chosen from all the tribes of Israel, I will set my name for ever. ⁸And I will not again cause the feet of Israel to wander from the land that I gave to their fathers, if only they will be careful to do according to all that I have commanded them, and all the torah that my servant Moses commanded them.' ⁹But they did not listen and Manasseh misled them to do more evil than the nations that YHWH had destroyed before the sons of Israel.

¹⁰And YHWH spoke by the hand of his servants the prophets, saying, ¹¹"Because Manasseh king of Judah has done these abominations, doing more evil than all the Amorites who were before him, and has made Judah also sin with his idols, ¹²therefore, thus says YHWH the God of Israel, "Behold I am bringing evil upon Jerusalem and Judah, that whoever hears it, his two ears will tingle. ¹³And I will stretch over Jerusalem the line of Samaria and the level of the house of Ahab, and I will wipe Jerusalem as one wipes a dish, wiping it and turning it upside down. ¹⁴I will forsake the remnant of my inheritance, and give them into the hand of their enemies. And they will be for spoil and plunder for all their enemies ¹⁵because they have done evil in my eyes and have been provoking me to anger from the day their fathers came out from Egypt, even until this day."'

¹⁶Also Manasseh shed a very great deal of innocent blood until he filled Jerusalem from one end to the other, besides his sinª, which he made Judah sin, doing what was evil in the eyes of YHWH. ¹⁷And the rest of the acts of Manasseh, and all that he did, and his sin that he sinned, are they not written in the Book of

the Chronicles of the Kings of Judah? [18]So Manasseh slept with his fathers and was buried in the garden of his own house, in the garden of Uzza. And Amon his son reigned in his place.

[19]Amon was twenty-two years old when he began to reign, and he reigned two years in Jerusalem. And his mother's name was Meshullemeth the daughter of Haruz of Jotbah. [20]He did what was evil in the eyes of YHWH just as Manasseh his father had done. [21]He walked in all the way that his father had walked, and served the idols that his father had served, and he bowed down to them. [22]He abandoned YHWH the God of his fathers and did not walk in the way of YHWH. [23]Then the servants of Amon conspired against him and they killed the king in his house. [24]The people of the land struck all who had conspired against King Amon, and the people of the land made Josiah his son king in his place. [25]Now the rest of the acts of Amon that he did, are they not written in the Book of the Chronicles of the Kings of Judah? [26]And they buried him in his grave in the garden of Uzza, and Josiah his son reigned in his place.

Notes on the text

6.a. LXX and 2 Chr. 33:6 pl., 'sons'.

21.6.b. Providing the 3 m. sg. suff. to read, 'provoking *him*' (*lĕhak'îsô*), with MSS and Vrs.

16.a. Vrs pluralize to 'his sins'. Here the sg. is collective or highlights the particular sin of the calves.

Form and structure

The character of Manasseh is compared to that of Ahab and Jeroboam I. As such he is the arch-villain of the southern kingdom and his non-Deuteronomistic behavior incurs YHWH's wrath. This wrath and its concomitant judgment act on the warnings given Judah in 2 Kgs 17, which themselves hearken back to the warning given Solomon (1 Kgs 9:6–9). Although YHWH's judgment was forestalled in accordance with the promise given David (1 Kgs 11:34; 15:4; 2 Kgs 8:19), the gravity of Manasseh's sins apparently make judgment inevitable. Yet one wonders whether YHWH's judgment will once again be forestalled.

The reigns of Manasseh and Amon each are enclosed in typical regnal summaries. Very little is said of Amon beyond his repetition of Manasseh's sins and the mode of his death. Much is said of Manasseh but it comes not as part of a narrative but as part of the regnal summary.

Manasseh's summary divides into three sections: an extended opening summary that details his sins and also indicts the people (vv. 1–9, 16), a prophetic judgment against king and people (vv. 10–15), and the closing summary (vv. 17–18). The prophetic judgment (vv. 10–15) is enclosed by verses focused on Manasseh. V. 16 begins with the resumptive particle *wĕgam* and adds additional details to the earlier catalogue of Manasseh's sins (vv. 2–9).

The resumption can be taken as indicative of redactional layering but need not be, for it provides a narrative chiastic structure (see below) that speaks to the expansion of sin from Manasseh to the people. Further evidence for later redactional layering is claimed in that the exile is presupposed in vv. 8, 10–15 and various theories regarding original and later materials exist (Montgomery 1951: 519; Gray 1970: 708; B. Long 1991: 294).

The passage in its present form is held together by strong connective tissues. First, a chiastic pattern joins Manasseh and the people together in sinfulness:

A   Manasseh does 'what was evil in the eyes of YHWH' (v. 2)
   B   Manasseh did 'much evil in the eyes of YHWH, provoking him to anger (*k's*)' (v. 6)
   B'   The people follow Manasseh into evil and similarly provoke YHWH to anger (*k's*; v. 15)
A'   Manasseh is remembered as doing 'what was evil in the eyes of YHWH' (v. 16; cf. v. 2)

Further unifying the passage, both Manasseh (vv. 2, 11) and the people (v. 9) are indicted for doing the same evil as credited to the nations. For that evil the nations were dispossessed and destroyed before Israel – obviously a clear warning to Judah. Indeed, for the evil (*ra'*) of Manasseh (vv. 2, 6, 11, 16) and Judah (v. 15) YHWH promises a matching judgment: evil (*ra'*) upon Jerusalem and Judah (v. 12).

Comment

21:1–9

Manasseh is the longest-ruling southern monarch. He begins as co-regent with Hezekiah (696–686 BC) before ruling as sole regent (686–642 BC; Thiele 1983: 176–178). The typical regnal summary quickly moves to evaluation (vv. 2–9). Earlier southern monarchs (Rehoboam, Jehoram, Ahaziah, Abijam and Ahaz) have been negatively evaluated, but Manasseh is uniquely compared to notorious northern monarchs. The lengthy evaluation is all Kings recounts of Manasseh's reign before pronouncing judgment (vv. 10–15). The chronicler's narrative account of Manasseh's captivity and resultant repentance (2 Chr. 33:10–19) is absent. No extra-biblical historical verification of the chronicler's account exists and, while it may arise solely from the chronicler's theological agenda, extant accounts of similar punitive action against Neco suggest a plausible historical core to the chronicler's account (*ANET* 296–297; Cogan 1974: 67–70). If such a historical reality was known to the author of Kings, its absence signals an intentional characterization of Manasseh as wholly evil.

The king's wickedness is summed up in the opening phrase 'he did what was evil in the eyes of YHWH' (vv. 2, 16). By these evils he 'provokes YHWH to anger' (v. 6). Even more, the enumeration of his sins begins by citing they are 'according to the abominations of the nations' (v. 2; cf. vv. 9, 11). Not only does this phrase couch Manasseh in terms of Ahaz (2 Kgs 16:3) and the northern kingdom (2 Kgs 17:8), but it reveals he is a truly non-Deuteronomistic king, heedless of Moses (Deut. 18:9). Moses blames these abominations for the nations' dispossession (Deut. 18:12), a correlation Kings also makes clear (v. 2), preparing the reader for the judgment against YHWH's own nation. Manasseh's sins include misleading the people to do 'more evil than the nations' (v. 9) and to do evil in YHWH's eyes, provoking him to anger (v. 15).

Comparisons made to other monarchs also negatively characterize Manasseh. He rebuilds high places Hezekiah had removed (2 Kgs 18:4) and at which Israel had sinned (1 Kgs 14:23; 2 Kgs 17:9). Manasseh is also explicitly compared to Ahab (vv. 3, 13). The two are the first kings in each kingdom to 'erect' (hiph. of *qwm*) altars to Baal (1 Kgs 16:32; 2 Kgs 21:3), and the only kings who made ('*śh*) sacred poles (1 Kgs 16:33; 2 Kgs 21:3, 7). More pointedly, only these two kings are said to have 'acted abominably' or 'committed abominations' (the nominal and verbal root is *t'b*) regarding 'idols' (*gillulîm*) as the 'Amorites' did (1 Kgs 21:26; 2 Kgs 21:11). Even Manasseh's shedding of 'innocent blood' (v. 16) evokes the murder of innocent Naboth. Truly, Manasseh is the southern Ahab.

Implicitly, but no less damning, Manasseh is presented in the guise of Jeroboam, the founder of the northern kingdom whose sins seal the kingdom's fate (1 Kgs 14:14–16). Both kings 'cause Israel to sin' (1 Kgs 14:16; 2 Kgs 21:11; each use hiph. of *ht'*) and for this their respective kingdoms are judged under the covenant (van Keulen 1996a: 146–154).

Manasseh sins according to the 'abomination of the nations'. Yet although Manasseh is an Assyrian vassal, there is no requirement laid upon vassals to adhere to Assyrian worship practices (McKay 1973: 5–12; Cogan 1974: 74–77; see also discussion at 2 Kgs 16). In Deuteronomy and Kings 'abominations' (*tô'ăbôt*) are specifically Canaanite (Deut. 7:25–26; 20:18; 1 Kgs 14:24; 2 Kgs 16:3) and it is these practices – against which Moses warned – that Manasseh institutes. The evaluation first cites the high places, Baal altars, and sacred poles (v. 3). In addition, Manasseh worships the West Semitic 'host of heaven' (Deut. 4:19; 17:3; Cogan and Tadmor 1988: 266).

The evaluation next speaks to autochthonous practices conducted within the temple precincts. Manasseh builds altars in the temple (presumably to Baal [vv. 3–4; cf. 23:4]) and for the host of heaven in the temple courts (v. 5). While only one temple court is specifically mentioned when the temple is built (1 Kgs 6:36), a 'middle' court (2 Kgs 20:4), part of the adjoining palace, is by its proximity considered part of the temple structure.

Perhaps conducted in the same court are the next practices, each of which is specifically outlawed in Deut. 18:10–14 and for which the nations were dispossessed. Like Ahaz before him, Manasseh 'passed his son through the fire', a divinatory rite of immolation (see 'Comment' at 2 Kgs 16:3). He practices soothsaying (*'ônēn*), perhaps by divining cloud (*'ānān*) formations, practices divination (*niḥēš*), perhaps using snakes (*nāḥāš*), consults mediums and spiritists (*'ôb wĕyiddʿōnîm*; cf. at Lev. 19:31; 20:6, 27; 2 Kgs 23:24; Isa. 8:19; 19:3; 28:3, 9) who commune with the nether-world and its spirits (Hoffner 1967; McKay 1973: 118–119; Jones 1984b: 597). Finally, Manasseh sets an image of the goddess Asherah into the temple (cf. 2 Kgs 23:4).

What makes these practices 'evil in the eyes of YHWH, provoking him to anger' (v. 6) is not only that each is prohibited by Moses. It is also that these practices are 'set' (*śym*; v. 7) and performed in the very place that YHWH chose to 'set' (*śym*; vv. 4, 7) his name: the effrontery is appalling. The reference to David, Solomon and the Jerusalem temple recalls the Davidic Covenant as does the promise that Israel would no longer wander (2 Sam. 7:10). The promise of continued abiding in the land was given on condition of obedience to the torah of Moses (v. 8). It is Manasseh's actions and the people's subsequent failure to 'listen' (v. 8) that subvert YHWH's gracious promise. Because king and people do 'more evil than the nations that YHWH destroyed before the sons of Israel' (v. 9) punishment comes upon them. Participating in the sins of the nations in the temple itself, they provoke YHWH and are destroyed.

21:10–16

Evaluation moves immediately into prophetic judgment. No known prophets minister during Manasseh's era, and the ministry of YHWH's 'servants the prophets' reinforces the serious nature of Manasseh's sins, for they require more than one confronting voice. These unknown prophets stand with 'my servant Moses' (v. 8), for they also challenge breaches of covenant commands. As well, their voice aligns with that of Dtr, for they use phrases found in the regnal evaluation (specifically, 'doing evil in my eyes', 'provoking to anger'). Thus the voices of torah, the prophets and Dtr are unified in their concern and they level the same message against the apostate king.

Three charges form the basis of YHWH's judgment. The first indicts Manasseh (v. 11ab) and provides a succinct summary of all of vv. 2–8. The second (v. 11c) recalls v. 9 as it indicts the people and reveals the leader's influence on them. The third (v. 15) turns the focus to the people alone, although Manasseh is not far from view: like him, they have 'done evil in my eyes . . . provoking me to anger' (v. 5; cf. vv. 2, 11, 16). But while Manasseh introduces several new cultic offences, the people are part of a long history of similar action that stretches back to Egypt. It is a sad history that prophets elsewhere recall (Jer. 7:25–26).

For the evil (vv. 2, 6, 9, 11, 15–16) perpetrated by Manasseh and the people YHWH will bring evil (v. 12) upon Jerusalem and Judah. The phrase 'I am bringing evil' occurs only here and in the judgment upon Jeroboam (1 Kgs 14:10) and Ahab (1 Kgs 21:21). Using the same phrase is a reminder that Manasseh's sins are those of the notorious northern kings whose kingdom has fallen. The final instance of the phrase is found in 2 Kgs 22:16 and is the prophetic word of Huldah that finally sets in motion the judgment of YHWH against Judah and by which Judah's fate repeats their northern sister's.

In the light of the promises given David, which YHWH has sustained through long years of increasing Judahite apostasy, the 'evil' that YHWH will bring against his chosen people, city, temple and dynasty elicits shock from those who hear of it. This is signified by their ears 'tingling' (*ṣll*). The same reaction occurs when the dynasty of Eli is overturned (1 Sam. 3:11), and when Jeremiah (using similar indictments as in the evaluation of Manasseh) prophesies the overturn of Judah and Jerusalem (Jer. 19:3). The extreme reaction is an interesting counterpoint to the reaction in the original prophetic word given Solomon regarding exile and destruction (1 Kgs 9:6–9). There, people are appalled and hiss at the destruction of city and temple – but also exhibit an understanding of why the events have occurred. Now the people are shocked but offer no explanation for the destruction. It is either too apparent to comment upon, or the many years of YHWH's patient grace make an explanation more difficult to summon.

The judgment's totality is communicated through several evocative statements. First, Jerusalem is measured by the 'line (*qaw*) of Samaria' and the 'level (*mišqelet*) of Ahab'. The 'line' is an instrument by which buildings are measured (Jer. 31:39; Zech. 1:16), and the 'level' suggests a similar function. The two terms 'line' (*qaw*) and 'level' (*mišqelet*) occur together only here and in Isa. 28:17, where the measurement is one of righteousness that reveals sin so it may be removed. By this reading the metaphor suggests Jerusalem will be measured by the righteous torah – as was the kingdom of Samaria and Ahab – and its sin revealed and removed. Certainly, this occurs in the judgment of YHWH against the city. The metaphor could also suggest the measurement itself is negative, if the modifier (Samaria, Ahab) in each case is subjective (v. 13). That is, the measuring instruments of crooked Ahab and Samaria are held up to Jerusalem and it is shown to be likewise crooked. By either reading an interesting connection is made to Isa. 34:11. There, a 'line (*qaw*) of desolation (*tōhû*)' and a 'plumbline (*'eben*) of emptiness (*bōhû*)' bring to mind

the *tōhû wābōhû* of creation before it is ordered (Gen. 1:2). When disobedient Jerusalem is measured and found wanting, it is precisely this
degree of disorder that is unleashed in coming judgment (van Keulen
1996a: 129–130).

A second indication of the judgment's totality lies in the statement that
Jerusalem is found wanting by the measurement applied to her and is
wiped clean. The image of 'wiping' (*mḥh*) in the qal form is always of
total removal of an object: names (Exod. 32:32; Deut. 9:14; 2 Kgs 14:27),
life (Gen. 6:7), crumbs from one's mouth (Prov. 30:20) or tears (Isa. 25:8).
Here the image suggests the finality of the meal's end: the last crumb has
been consumed, and the overturned dish signals this. The image is a
chilling picture of the complete destruction to come upon Jerusalem: there
will be nothing left for YHWH to 'eat'.

A final indication of the judgment's totality lies in the statement that
destruction occurs because YHWH forsakes his people. This, despite
Solomon's plea for YHWH's abiding presence (1 Kgs 8:57; cf. 1 Sam.
12:22). Earlier, during the hopeful reign of Hezekiah, promises of a
remnant were given (2 Kgs 19:31). Now, in the bleakness of Manasseh's
sinful reign, no such hope is granted. Even the remnant of YHWH's people
(his 'inheritance'; Deut. 4:20; 9:26, 29; 32:9; 1 Kgs 8:51, 53) is given over.
The action is evocative of the period of the judges, as the people are given
over to 'the hand of their enemies' for spoil and plunder (Judg. 2:14; 6:13).
As has always been the case, YHWH once again uses the nations to punish
his people (Deut. 1:27; Josh. 7:7; 2 Kgs 3:10, 13; 13:3; 17:20).

The prophetic voice enumerates the sins of Manasseh and the people
and the punishment to be meted out. In the northern history Jeroboam is
repeatedly the cause of the northern kingdom's downfall. Now, in a similar
move, Manasseh is named again as the cause of the south's fall. In a final
reprise (signalled by the particle *wĕgam* [also] in v. 16) his actions against
the innocent are appended as a final example of his non-covenantal life.
And, as the earlier indictment against Manasseh (vv. 2–11a) segued to the
indictment against the people (v. 11b; cf. v. 9), a similar movement occurs
here. Manasseh spills innocent blood in addition to his other sins (v. 16a)
but he is also held accountable for making Judah sin (v. 16b). Thus, while
the focus remains on Manasseh as the initiating cause of Judah's downfall
(see 2 Kgs 23:26–27), both king and people precipitate the judgment.

21:17–18

Such a heinous king has a remarkably tame concluding regnal summary.
Yet even here the magnitude of his sin intrudes, for he is the only southern
king whose misdeeds are specifically noted in the closing summary ('his
sins which he sinned'). Manasseh is not buried in the 'city of David' but
in the 'garden of Uzza'. Up to the time of Hezekiah all Judahite kings are

buried in the city of David. But from Hezekiah onwards no king (not even righteous Hezekiah and Josiah) is specifically noted as buried in the city of David. Given that not even Hezekiah or Josiah have such a burial notice, the lack of such notice for Manasseh should not be construed as an intentional slight. Nor must the garden of Uzza hold unsavoury connotations (contra Provan 1995: 269, who associates the garden with Uzza, who is struck down for disregarding the sacred ark [2 Sam. 6:1–8]). It may simply be that burial practices changed from Hezekiah's time onwards, perhaps due to changes wrought by his reforms, or lack of space (Cogan and Tadmor 1988: 269; Fritz 2003: 392).

21:19–26

The two-year reign of Amon falls under the shadow of his father's, both in duration and in character. Amon's mother's name is derived from the root *šlm*, as are many Hebrew names, including Solomon, Absalom, Shallum, and others. Her father's name, Haruz, is attested in Arabic but is also a Hebrew word; homonyms can mean 'gold' (Ps. 68:14) or 'industrious' (Prov. 10:4; 12:24, 27). The location of Jotbah is contested, but is best placed in Galilee (Frankel, *ABD* 3:1020). While the mother may not be Judahite, given the Hebraic associations of name and birthplace it is difficult to argue she is a foreigner (so McKay 1973: 24; Jones 1984b: 601). Forwarding her foreign birth would certainly further denigrate Manasseh, but such an association would be better made in Manasseh's own account, and not that of his son's. Further elements of Amon's regnal summaries align with the expected pattern.

Amon is evaluated in the same negative terms as his father, and the paternal influence is specifically noted. Amon did evil 'just as Manasseh his father had done'; he walked in the way 'that his father had walked'; he served idols 'that his father had served' and abandoned YHWH. There is little hope of redemption for Judah under this duplicate Manasseh.

The coup against Amon probably has tangible realpolitik behind it, but here it is juxtaposed to Amon's cultic sins as if in direct response to them. The 'people of the land', that is, the enfranchised citizens of Judah (see 'Comment', 2 Kgs 11:18), avenge Amon's death and install Josiah on the throne.

Explanation

This chapter draws together crucial theological emphases apparent not only in the book of Kings but through the entire history of Israel's life in the land. Israel's propensity to sin, YHWH's judgment against sin, and his grace are bound together in this chapter.

The chapter notes that Israel's sins 'have been provoking [YHWH] to anger from the day their fathers came out from Egypt, even until this day' (v. 15). Moses prepares the people for life in the land by delivering to them covenant laws by which they are to live (Deut. 12 – 26) and Israel is repeatedly charged to obey the law (Deut. 4:1–9; 5:1, 32–33; 6:1–3, 24–25; 7:11–12; 8:1; 10:12–13; 11:1, 8–9, 13, 16, 22, 26–28; 12:1, 32). The necessity for the repeated urging lies not only in Israel's past disobedience at Sinai (Deut. 4:9–24; 9:7–29) and in the wilderness (Deut. 1:26–46; 4:3), but also in the possibility of continued sin once established in the land (Deut. 4:9–40; 6:10–19; 8:10–18).

Despite Moses' admonitions and the reaffirmation of covenant relationship (Deut. 27 – 29), sin remains a constant reality in Israel's life. In Joshua, Achan's sin threatens Israel's military actions (Josh. 6). In Judges a familiar cycle of sin pertains (2:10–19), leading Israel away from obedience of YHWH's righteous law to submission to individual human inclination (Judg. 17:6; 21:25) epitomized in the terrible events recorded in the book's epilogue (chs. 17–18). The ultimate sin of the period of judges occurs when Israel demands that Samuel, the last judge, appoint a king over them. In this they reject YHWH as king to serve other gods, doing as they had done since their deliverance from Egypt (1 Sam. 8:7–8; 12:19).

The monarchic era does not relieve the people of sin. David as an adulterer and murderer acts against the law (2 Sam. 11). Solomon defies the law with amassed riches and foreign wives (1 Kgs 10 – 11), and subsequent southern monarchs are indicted for sin (1 Kgs 14:22; 2 Kgs 18:18, 27; 21:2, 20; 23:32, 37; 24:9, 19). Jeroboam's sins define the northern kingdom (1 Kgs 12:25 – 14:20) and Ahab increases the burden of sinfulness (1 Kgs 16:29–33) so that the people are led into sin (1 Kgs 17:7–23).

Concomitant with the narrative of Israel's sins is the narrative of judgment pronounced upon sin. Moses not only prepares the people for life in the land by urging covenant obedience upon them, but also makes clear that disobedience has and will be judged (Deut. 1:35–40, 42–45; 3:26–27; 4:3, 25–28; 6:13–15; 7:10; 8:19–20; 11:16–17, 28). As Moses looks to Israel's life in the land, judgment against sin is clearly enumerated in covenant curses that eventuate in exile (Deut. 28:15–68).

In Joshua the sin of Achan is judged not only through Israel's failure to take Ai, but in the community's execution of the perpetrator (Josh. 7:10–26). The spiralling cycles of sin in the book of Judges consistently include judgment through foreign oppression and loss of land. Often judgment against sin is pronounced by prophets. Thus the sins of Eli and his sons are judged through an anonymous prophet (1 Sam. 2:27–36), Saul's sins are confronted and judged by the prophet Samuel (1 Sam. 13:10–14; 15:10–35) and David's sins against Bathsheba and Uriah are judged through the prophet Nathan (2 Sam. 12) with disastrous consequences through the remainder of his reign.

The pattern of judgment through the prophetic word continues strongly in Kings (1 Kgs 11:29–39; 14:7–16; 16:1–4; 20:42; 21:17–24; 22:17–23; 2 Kgs 1:15–16; 9:6–10; 20:16–18; 21:10–15). But judgment in Kings is not only communicated through the prophetic word; it arises in the events of history and natural disaster. In all these, instead of the blessings promised under the covenant (Deut. 28:1–14), it is the covenant curses that are experienced in Kings: foreign oppression and military defeat (Deut. 28:25), famine (Deut. 28:17–18) and drought (Deut. 28:24).

These two emphases (Israel's sinfulness and YHWH's judgment against sin) culminate in Manasseh's reign. He is not the first Israelite to sin, nor is the people he rules. But the narrative makes clear that his sins indict him beyond any other monarch. In him all the previous sins of the northern and southern kingdoms are accumulated and find expression; more, he sins as did the nations who were driven from the land. Through him the people participate in sinfulness. Israel can sink no lower in their rejection of covenant life and law and it is for this reason judgment is pronounced. More, as Manasseh's reign brings Israel to the nadir of their sinfulness, ultimate judgment is pronounced: YHWH will abandon his people, delivering them into the hand of foreign enemies and exile (Deut. 28:49–52, 63–68).

A third emphasis appears in tandem with Israel's sin and YHWH's judgment, appearing throughout the history of Israel in the land. It is the reality of YHWH's grace that mitigates or forestalls judgment. On the basis of anticipated grace David petitions YHWH to forestall judgment (2 Sam. 12:13–22). Judgment against the house of Jeroboam is mitigated in respect of his good son (1 Kgs 14:10–13), YHWH graciously forestalls judgment against Ahab (1 Kgs 21:29), and YHWH's mitigation spares Josiah the experience of the coming judgment (2 Kgs 22:20). Even the long continuance of the southern kingdom, before judgment, occurs solely because of YHWH's gracious commitment to the Davidic house (1 Kgs 11:34–36; 15:4–5; 2 Kgs 8:19, 19:34; 20:6).

Of course, the gravity of Manasseh's sin precludes any expression of YHWH's grace towards the monarch. In him the cup of YHWH's patience is drained dry, making judgment inevitable. How, then, to consider the absence of the emphasis of grace that has been apparent throughout Israel's history? The answer lies in understanding the intertwined purposes of grace and judgment in the DH (Boda 2009: 187–188).

First, while judgment is for the purpose of punishing sin (Deut. 28:45–48), it is also for the purpose of disciplining Israel to repentance. Thus the judgment of foreign oppression serves to discipline the people to repentance. They turn back to YHWH and plead for mercy (Judg. 3:9, 15; 4:1; 6:6). The phenomenon is especially apparent in places such as Judg. 10:10 and 1 Sam. 12:9–11, where it is Israel's distress that leads them to acknowledge their sin and their misplaced trust in other gods. Samuel also notes this disciplinary aspect of YHWH's judgment during the Philistine oppression (1 Sam. 7:2–4). In his great dedicatory prayer Solomon repeatedly acknowledges that the judgments experienced by Israel are for the purpose of turning their hearts back to God in prayer (1 Kgs 8:33, 35, 37–38, 44, 46–48).

Secondly, YHWH's gracious mitigation or postponement of judgment also works towards repentance. It demonstrates YHWH's gracious wish of goodness and blessing towards Israel, thus revealing his covenant faithfulness. By this he seeks to woo Israel back to covenant life. As well, YHWH's grace that forestalls or mitigates judgment provides the needed time for amendment of life. Even the motivation for such amendment lies in the knowledge that YHWH acts and responds in grace towards a repentant people.

Even in the place of judgment his grace still summons people to repentance (1 Sam. 7:3; 1 Kgs 8:33, 35, 46–50; 2 Kgs 17:13; von Rad 1962: 346). Thus in the case of Manasseh, in which no grace is extended but unmitigated judgment is pronounced, YHWH's grace is not fully obscured. There remains the hope that Israel – even from the place of judgment – will repent and return. Though judgment expressed towards Manasseh and the people is deserved and complete, it is not the last word. From the place of judgment repentance may spring in response to a gracious God, and covenant life be restored.

This gracious hope was not absent from Moses' words to the people. Poised to enter the land long promised, in which they could experience the fullness of blessed covenant life, he saw the reality of continuing sin. His vision of Israel's future spoke of exile and servitude should such sin continue (Deut. 4:25–28). In Manasseh that bleak future is sealed. But Moses also envisioned the discipline of judgment as the work of a gracious God:

> But from there you will seek YHWH your God and you will find *him*, if you seek for him with all your heart and all your soul. When you are in distress and all these things have happened to you, then in later days you will return to YHWH your God and obey him. Because YHWH your God is a compassionate God, he will not abandon you or destroy you; he will not forget the covenant with your ancestors which he swore to them. (Deut. 4:29–31)

The bleakness of death and judgment is not the last word. Thanks be to God.

2 KINGS 22:1 – 23:30

Translation

[22:1]Josiah was eight years[a] old when he began to reign, and he reigned thirty-one years in Jerusalem. His mother's name was Jedidah daughter of Adaiah of

Bozkath. ²He did what was right in the eyes of YHWH and he walked in all the way of David his father, and did not turn aside to the right or the left.

³In the eighteenth year of King Josiah, the king had sent Shaphan the son of Azaliah the son of Meshullam the scribe to the house of YHWH, saying, ⁴"Go up to Hilkiah the high priestª and have him countᵇ the silver that has been brought into the house of YHWH, which those who keep the threshold have collected from the people. ⁵They shall give it into the hand of the workers appointed over the house of YHWH. Then they shall give it to the workers who are in the house of YHWH to repair the damage to the house: ⁶to the carpenters, the builders and the masons to buy timber and hewn stone to repair the house. ⁷However, no accounting for the silver given into their hand shall be required from them, for they deal faithfully.'

⁸Then Hilkiah the high priest said to Shaphan the scribe, 'I have found the book of the torah in the house of YHWH,' and Hilkiah gave the book to Shaphan, who read it. ⁹Then Shaphan the scribe came to the king and reported to the king. He said, 'Your servants have emptied outª the silver found in the house and they have given it into the hand of the workers appointed over the house of YHWH.' ¹⁰Then Shaphan the scribe reported to the king, saying, 'Hilkiah the priest has given a book to me,' and Shaphan read it in the king's presence.

¹¹Now when the king heard the words of the book of the torah, he tore his clothes. ¹²The king commanded Hilkiah the priest, Ahikam the son of Shaphan, Achbor the son of Micaiah, Shaphan the scribe and Asaiah the king's servant, ¹³"Go, enquire of YHWH for me, the people and all Judah concerning the words of this book that has been found, for great is YHWH's wrath kindled against us, because our fathers have not listened to the words of this book to do according to all that is written concerning us.'

¹⁴So Hilkiah the priest, Ahikam, Achbor, Shaphan and Asaiah went to Huldah the prophetess, the wife of Shallum son of Tikvah the son of Harhas, the keeper of the wardrobe (now she dwelt in Jerusalem in the Second Quarter) and spoke to her. ¹⁵She said to them, 'Thus says YHWH, the God of Israel, "Tell the man who has sent you to me, ¹⁶thus says YHWH, Behold, I am bringing evil toª this place and upon its inhabitants – all the words of the book that the king of Judah has read – ¹⁷because they have abandoned me and burned incense to other gods, so that they might provoke me to anger with all the work of their hands. Therefore my wrath is kindled against this place and shall not be quenched."

¹⁸"But to the king of Judah who has sent you to enquire of YHWH, thus you shall say to him, "Thus says YHWH, the God of Israel, '*Concerning* the words that you have heard, ¹⁹because your heart was tender and you humbled yourself before YHWH when you heard what I had spoken against this place and its inhabitants, that they would be a desolation and a curse, and you have torn your clothes and wept before me, I also have heard *you*,' declares YHWH. ²⁰'Therefore, behold, I will gather you to your fathers and you will be gathered to your graveª in peace. Your eyes will not see all the evil that I am bringing upon this placeᵇ.'"'

So they brought the word back to the king.

^{23:1}Then the king sent, and all the elders of Judah and Jerusalem were gathered[a] to him. ²The king went up to the house of YHWH and with him went all the people of Judah and all the inhabitants of Jerusalem and the priests and the prophets[a] and all the people both small and great. He read in their hearing all the words of the book of the covenant that had been found in the house of YHWH. ³Then the king stood by the pillar and made a covenant before YHWH, to walk after YHWH and to keep his commandments, his testimonies and his statutes with all *his* heart and with all *his* soul, to establish the words of this covenant written in this book. And all the people committed to the covenant.

⁴The king commanded Hilkiah the high priest and the priests of the second order and the keepers of the threshold to bring out from the temple of YHWH all the vessels made for Baal and Asherah and all the host of heaven. He burned them outside Jerusalem in the environs[a] of the Kidron and took their ashes to Bethel. ⁵He removed the idolatrous priests whom the kings of Judah had appointed to burn incense[a] on the high places in the cities of Judah and the environs of Jerusalem, and the ones who burned incense to Baal, to the sun and the moon and to the constellations and to all the host of heaven. ⁶He brought the Asherah out from the house of YHWH to the Kidron Valley outside Jerusalem. He burned it in the Kidron Valley and ground it to dust and threw its dust on the graves of the common people. ⁷He pulled down the houses of the male cult personnel that were in the house of YHWH where the women were weaving coverings[a] for Asherah.

⁸He brought all the priests[a] out from the cities of Judah and defiled the high places where the priests burned incense, from Geba to Beer-sheba. He tore down the high places of the gates that were at the entrance of the Gate of Joshua the city governor; they were on one's left at the city gate. ⁹The priests[a] of the high places, however, did not go up to the altar of YHWH in Jerusalem but ate unleavened bread in the midst of their brothers. ¹⁰He defiled Topheth, which is in the Valley of Ben-hinnom, to prevent anyone passing his son or daughter through the fire to Molech.

¹¹He destroyed the horses which the kings of Judah had dedicated to the sun at the entrance of the house of YHWH, by the chamber that was close by belonging to Nathan-melech the eunuch. Then the chariots of the sun he burned with fire. ¹²The altars that were on the roof of Ahaz's upper chamber, which the kings of Judah had made, and the altars that Manasseh had made in the two courts of the house of YHWH, the king pulled down and smashed[a] them there and threw their dust into the Kidron Valley. ¹³And the high places that were east of Jerusalem, to the south of the Mount of Destruction[a], which Solomon king of Israel had built for Ashtoreth the abomination of the Sidonians, and for Chemosh the abomination of Moab, and for Milcom the abomination of the sons of Ammon, the king defiled. ¹⁴He smashed the pillars and cut down the sacred poles and filled their sites with human bones.

¹⁵Furthermore, the altar that was in Bethel, the high place made by Jeroboam son of Nebat, who caused Israel to sin, that altar and the high place he also tore down. He burned the high place, ground it to dust and burned the sacred pole.

¹⁶When Josiah turned, he saw the graves there on the mount. He sent and took the bones from the graves and burned *them* upon the altar and defiled it, according to the word of YHWH, which the man of God cried out who proclaimed these things. ¹⁷He said, 'What is that gravemarker I see?' The men of the city answered him, 'This is the grave^a of the man of God who came from Judah and proclaimed these things that you have done to the altar at Bethel.' ¹⁸He replied, 'Let him be; no one shall disturb his bones.' So they left his bones undisturbed, with the bones of the prophet who had come from Samaria.

¹⁹And Josiah also removed all the houses of the high places that the kings of Israel had made in the cities of Samaria, provoking YHWH^a to anger; he did to them just as he had done at Bethel. ²⁰He slaughtered all the priests of the high places who were there upon the altars and he burned human bones on them. Then he returned to Jerusalem.

²¹The king commanded all the people, saying, 'Keep the Passover to YHWH your God, as it is written in this book of the covenant.' ²²For such a Passover had not been kept from the days of the judges who judged Israel, throughout all the days of the kings of Israel and the kings of Judah. ²³But in the eighteenth year of King Josiah this Passover was kept to YHWH in Jerusalem. ²⁴Morever, Josiah removed the mediums, spiritists, teraphim, idols, and all the detested things that were seen in the land of Judah and Jerusalem, so as to fulfil the words of the torah written in the book that Hilkiah the priest had found in the house of YHWH.

²⁵Before him there was no king like him, who turned to YHWH with all his heart and with all his soul and with all his strength according to all the torah of Moses, nor did any like him arise after him. ²⁶Yet YHWH did not turn from the heat of his great anger that burned against Judah for all the provocations with which Manasseh provoked him. ²⁷YHWH said, 'I will remove Judah also from my presence, as I removed Israel. And I will reject this city that I have chosen, Jerusalem, and the house of which I said, "My name will be there."'

²⁸And the rest of the acts of Josiah, and all that he did, are they not written in the Book of the Chronicles of the Kings of Judah? ²⁹In his days Pharaoh Neco king of Egypt went up to^a the king of Assyria at the river Euphrates. King Josiah went to meet him and when he saw him at Megiddo, he killed him. ³⁰His servants transported his body by chariot from Megiddo. They brought him to Jerusalem and buried him in his own grave. The people of the land took Jehoahaz son of Josiah and anointed him and made him king in place of his father.

Notes on the text

22:1.a. MT reads with a sg. object, 'eight year' (*šĕmōneh šānâ*), a rare exception to the anticipated pl. object 'eight years' (*šĕmōnîm šānâ*; see GKC §134e, f). Montgomery (1951: 526) posits the pl. object is written in abbreviated form.

4.a. 'high priest' need not be an exilic gloss (so Gray 1970: 723). See 'Comment' at 2 Kgs 12:10[11].

4.b. 'have him count' (*wĕyattĕm*) is a sense not elsewhere attested. LXX^L reads, 'let him melt down', assuming Hebr. *wĕyattĕk*. See discussion at 2 Kgs 12:10[11].

9.a. hiph. *hittîkû*, from *ntk* usually means 'melted down' (see 'Comment' at 2 Kgs 12:10[11]), or here figuratively as 'poured out', that is, 'emptied'.

16.a. Reading *'el* with MT 'I am bringing evil to' and not *'al*, 'upon', as *BHS* suggests. The prep. *'el* aligns the judgment to that given Ahab (1 Kgs 21:21) and Jeroboam (1 Kgs 14:10). See 'Comment'.

20.a. MT reads 'your graves', and Hobbs 1985: 314–315 understands 'family graves' are in view. Montgomery (1951: 528) emends to sg., as do two MSS.

20.b. LXX^L, 2 Chr. 34:28 specifies judgment is upon Jerusalem 'and upon its inhabitants'.

23:1.a. *'sp* is read as ni., 'were gathered' (Montgomery 1951: 538).

2.a. 2 Chr. 34:30 includes 'Levites' rather than 'prophets'. Montgomery holds with prophets, noting their anticipated role in the reformation (1951: 528).

4.a. MT reads 'fields' (*šadmôt*), which does not match the topography of the Kidron Valley; 'open country' is only marginally better (Hobbs 1985: 328, 330). Gray finds support from LXX for the reading *miśrĕpōt*, 'burning places', and suggests 'limekilns' (Gray 1970: 730). Montgomery (1951: 538) suggests the refuse fires of the Kidron align with this reading.

5.a. Reading with LXX^L, Syr, Vg *lĕqaṭṭēr*, 'to burn incense', for MT *wayqaṭṭēr*, 'and he burned incense'.

7.a. MT *bāttîm* ('houses'; here 'coverings') may refer to tentlike shrouds. Montgomery (1951: 539) and Gray (1970: 730) follow G. Driver (1936: 107) and link MT to Arab. *batt*, 'garments'. LXX^L στολάς is also clothing.

8.a. The *kōhănîm* in vv. 8–9 may be Yahwistic, but they 'burn incense', which is elsewhere unorthodox, and (in v. 5) the practice of the idolatrous *kĕmārîm*. As such, the law of Deut. 18:6–8 does not apply to them. They are barred from Jerusalem (the collocation used here of *'lh* with prep. *'el* refers not to going up to an altar to officiate, but going to where the altar is located [Nicholson 2007]). See 'Comment'.

9.a. See n. 8.a above.

12.a. The difficult MT *wayyārāṣ miššām*, 'he ran', emended to *wayyĕraṣṣēm šām*, 'he smashed'. See discussion, Montgomery 1951: 540.

13.a. 'Destruction' (*hammašḥît*) as a deliberate corruption of 'Oil' (*hammišḥâ*), an earlier appellation for the Mount of Olives (Montgomery 1951: 540; Hobbs 1985: 331).

17.a. The definite *haqqeber*, 'the grave', is difficult in the const. phrase and is read with LXX^L as *zeh qeber*, 'this is the grave'.

19.a. 'provoking YHWH' assumes *'et YHWH*, with LXX, Syr, Vg.

29.a. Reading MT *'al* as *'el* (a common variance) and with support of the historical circumstances of the Babylonian Chronicles (Wiseman 1956: 61, 63). Neco supports Assyria against Babylon. See 'Comment'.

Form and structure

Josiah's reign is the pinnacle of the history of the kings. It takes up the specific prophetic word given Jeroboam in 1 Kgs 13, sets right the sins of Jeroboam, and draws together the history's key thematic threads. Despite the reform of righteous Josiah, Judah teeters on the edge of the precipice. With his death the nation begins the final slide to exile.

The two chapters are carefully structured. Following the pattern established for monarchs, regnal formulae open and close the reign (22:1–2; 23:25–30) and laud the king (see 'Comment'). The formulae bracket concentric rings with Josiah's reform – the most important element of his reign – at their centre. It is Josiah's reform that most surely warrants the praise he is given, for in the face of impending doom he chooses to walk in the way of David his father, turning aside neither to right or left:

> Opening regnal summary (22:1–2)
> > Discovery and response to the book of the torah (22:3–20)
> > > Ceremony prompted by the book of the covenant (23:1–3)
> > > > Cultic reforms of King Josiah (23:4–20)
> > > Ceremony prompted by the book of the covenant (23:21–23)
> > Final notation of reform according to the book of the torah (23:24)
> Closing regnal summary (23:25–30)

The narrative's unified structure is also directed by five main actions of which Josiah is the subject. Josiah first sends (*šlḥ*) to secure temple repairs (v. 3). His instructions form a type scene that echoes Jehoash's earlier reform (vv. 3–7; 2 Kgs 12:9[10]–16[17]; see 'Comment'). His command, the subsequent discovery of the book of the torah, and the ensuing consultations (vv. 3–11) are the background of the main narrative. It begins with the second structuring verb as the king commands (*ṣwh*) an enquiry of YHWH (vv. 12–20). The report prompts the third action as the king again sends (*šlḥ*) and then leads the people in covenant (23:1–3). Again the king commands (*ṣwh*) and extensive cultic reform is the result (vv. 4–20), moving in a geographically patterned order from Jerusalem and its environs (vv. 4–14) to Bethel and Samaria (vv. 15–20a), and back to Jerusalem (v. 20b). The fifth structuring action occurs as the king commands (*ṣwh*) a final time and institutes a Passover feast (23:21–23). A final notation concludes the reforming activity (v. 24). The note is not a misplaced addendum to the reforms in vv. 4–20. Its citation of the discovery of the book of the torah (v. 24) consciously returns the narrative to its opening scene (see structural outline above).

While the story's structure is apparent, its compositional history is widely disputed. For instance, it is noted that the enumerative style of the list of reforms (23:4–20) contrasts to the enclosing narrative, and that the prophecy of Josiah's peaceful death stands at odds with the narrative of the event. Various redactional theories attempt to account for such discrepancies and posit pre-exilic and exilic redactions (see Mayes 1983: 106–132; B. Long 1991: 251–256). However, because no agreement exists regarding the extent of the redactional layers or the era to which they belong, it is the final form that once again provides a certain field for commentary. At some point during the exilic period (which is where Kings ends) the book came together in its present form; this is the form with which this commentary interacts.

Compositional history is only one of several critical issues the narrative prompts. The identity and provenance of the book of the torah discovered in the temple have long been discussed (Childs 1979: 201–205; Sweeney 2001: 137–169), together with its relationship to Deuteronomy and its place in the dating of Pentateuchal texts. 'The book of the torah' is an identification used elsewhere of Deuteronomy (Deut. 28:61; 29:21; 30:10; 31:26; Josh. 1:8; 8:30–35; 23:6; 24:26) and its orthodoxy – particularly its concern for centralization of worship and avoidance of Canaanite worship forms (Deut. 12:1–6; 16:1–2, 5–6; 18:9–13) – appears to underpin Josiah's reform (Nicholson 1967). The discovered book is thus often considered some form of an original or *Ur*-Deuteronomy (possibly the legal core of chs. 12–26; Gray 1970: 715; McConville 2002: 34, 40; Sweeney 2007: 444) that guided the people since pre-monarchic days. It was subsequently lost or purposefully hidden during Manasseh's wicked purge of Yahwistic worship. Although the theory is contested, the 'affinity between Josiah's reforms . . . and the most distinctive features of Deuteronomy is palpable' (Cohn 2000: 151).

A critical issue concerning chronological and historical detail deserves note here. In Kings Josiah begins his reform in his eighteenth year after discovery of the book of the torah. Yet in Chronicles the reform begins six years earlier, is more geographically extensive (2 Chr. 34:3–7) and precedes the discovery of the law book (2 Chr. 34:14–28).

A further historical difficulty concerns the death of Josiah. In Kings it occurs in ambiguous circumstances at Megiddo, while in Chronicles (2 Chr. 35:20–24) it unambiguously occurs in battle and although Josiah is wounded at Megiddo, he dies at Jerusalem.

To a certain extent these two problems can be harmonized but they cannot be wholly resolved either historically or chronologically. Josiah either began his reform in his twelfth or eighteenth year; he died either at Megiddo or Jerusalem; both cannot be historically accurate. It may be that each account draws upon variant traditions but this still does not resolve the difficulties (and indeed, introduces others). It may be that one account or the other should be regarded as historically accurate and the other a tendentious reconstruction but no consensus exists in the assignment of historical accuracy.

Perhaps the best solution allows that both accounts are selective in their material, and their different theological emphases drive the variations in chronology and even historical reportage. As it stands, placing the discovery of the law book prior to Josiah's reforms highlights his utter obedience to the deuteronomic law code. It is by this obedience that he is shown to be the king par excellence according to Dtr. Similarly, the silence in Kings on the instrumentality of Josiah's death places the focus only on the death's fulfilment of the prophetic word – a key theme throughout Kings. That the shapers of the canon brought no historical or chronological corrective to the two accounts suggests a way for modern readers to approach each text, allowing each to speak from its own theological concerns.

Comment

22:1–2

Like the reformer Jehoash (2 Kgs 12:7) Josiah comes to the throne at an early age and reigns from 640 to 609 BC. The anticipated details of the summary (age at accession, length and place of reign, mother's name) are provided as well as an evaluation. The evaluation begins with a comparison to David (1 Kgs 15:11; 2 Kgs 18:3) that places Josiah in very favourable company. But it then evaluates Josiah above David by stating the king turns aside (*swr*) 'to neither right nor left'. No other king is lauded with this wholly Deuteronomistic virtue (Deut. 5:32; 17:11, 20; 28:14; Josh. 1:7; 23:6; of David it is only said he 'did not turn aside', 1 Kgs 15:5). Though brief, the evaluation is powerful.

Given the extent of Josiah's reforms, the evaluation is especially brief when compared to the previous reformer, Hezekiah (2 Kgs 18:1–8). Though a reformer, and evaluated in more verses than accorded Josiah, Hezekiah's reign is not without criticism (especially apparent in 2 Kgs 20). One wonders whether Josiah, with a much shorter evaluation, will also fail in some way. The succeeding narrative repudiates this possibility.

22:3–20

3–10. Josiah turns his attention to the 'repair of the house' several years after his accession. This is not to be aligned with the reform of 2 Chr. 34:3–7 (contra Jones 1984a: 609), which occurs before the book is discovered and makes no mention of temple repair.

Josiah's actions are intentionally compared with those of Jehoash, who also begins repair on the temple well into his reign (2 Kgs 12). The comparison uses the same phrasing in each account (see 2 Kgs 12:9[10]–16[17]). In both cases the king is concerned with 'silver brought into the house', which is collected by 'those who keep the threshold' to be given into the 'hand of the workers appointed over the house'. The money is for repair work and is given to virtually the same individuals: 'carpenters, builders, and masons' for the same purchases and of whom 'no accounting is required' because they 'deal faithfully'.

It is, however, the dissimilarities in the type scene that move the Josiah narrative forward. First, it is Josiah who gives the instructions, rather than the third-person narrator as in the Jehoash account. Thus the king's concern for the house is highlighted and adds to the portrait of righteous Josiah. Secondly, the narration in Jehoash's tale is part of the main action: it is the repair to the temple that is prominent. But in Josiah's tale the king's instructions are the background to the main event: the discovery of the law. Thus vv. 3–7 are simply a means to an end, rather than the point of the narrative.

Throughout 2 Kgs 22 – 23 Josiah is the prominent actor. The discovery of the law book is facilitated because he 'sends' (šlḥ) Shaphan. The importance of the task is signalled by the messenger's important rank: he is identified by a double patronym and a role at court. His important message is for none other than Hilkiah the high priest. Throughout vv. 3–10 the roles of Shaphan and Hilkiah, although already known, are repeated to emphasize the discovery's importance.

In the consultations in vv. 8–10 narrative strategies move the focus from temple repair to the discovered book. Hilkiah's report contains no reference to the repairs, although presumably they are underway. Similarly, Shaphan brushes past the repairs (v. 9) to speak of the book (v. 10), which he immediately reads to the king. Further, the Hebrew constructions in both v. 8 and v. 10 awkwardly place 'the book (of the torah)' in the first grammatical slot ('the book of the torah I have found'; 'a book is given'). It is the import of the book that is thus signalled.

The book's discovery causes consternation to priest and scribe and they quickly bring it to the king. Yet no inkling of the book's content is given either in Hilkiah's speech to Shaphan or in Shaphan's private reading of the book. Even when the book is read to the king its content is withheld from view. What, then, does the book say of blessing or curse? No clue is yet given.

11–20. Josiah responds by tearing his robes (v. 11) and weeping (v. 19), classic signs of mourning and penitence (Judg. 11:35; 2 Sam. 13:31; 1 Kgs 21:27; 2 Kgs 6:30; 19:1). Because Josiah has heard (šmʿ) the words of the book of the torah, he knows that the people have not heard (šmʿ) – that is, obeyed – them (v. 13), and for this YHWH's wrath is kindled. Assuming the book contains some version of Deuteronomy (see 'Form and structure' above), it would make the people's failure very apparent. Passages such as Deut. 28 clearly reveal YHWH's wrath against such failure.

Before acting, Josiah commands (ṣwh) a delegation to enquire of YHWH (1 Kgs 14:1–5; 22:5–9; 2 Kgs 3:11–19; 8:8). The delegation comprises important figures close to the king, and each is introduced by patronym or role. Many of them or their relations feature elsewhere as loyal Yahwists, supporting the prophet Jeremiah. Besides Hilkiah and Shaphan, Shaphan's son Ahikam (Jer. 26:24; 36:11–15; he is also Gedaliah's father [2 Kgs 25:22]), Achbor the son of Micaiah (Jer. 26:22; 36:12), and Asaiah the king's servant are sent to Huldah.

Huldah is one of several Israelite prophetesses (Exod. 15:20; Judg. 4:4; Neh. 6:14; Isa. 8:3). She is identified by her husband Shallum, who attends to the wardrobe, perhaps of the palace or even the temple. If he is the Shallum of Jer. 32:7, Huldah is of a priestly family. Her residence in the northern extension of the old Jebusite city (Burrows, *IDB* 2:846) enables rapid consultation.

The enquiry is made on behalf of the king, the people and all Judah (v. 13). Huldah's prophetic word addresses first the people and Judah, and then the king. The dual prophecy uses the messenger formula ('Thus says YHWH') three times in vv. 15–18. Moreover, YHWH affirms (vv. 16, 19) that the words heard in the book of the torah are indeed 'what I had spoken'. There can be no doubt that the prophecy aligns with the book. Although both speak of judgment, they are truly YHWH's words.

Twice YHWH addresses the man who has 'sent' (*šlḥ*) the delegation (vv. 15, 18). Josiah has sent before (v. 3) and will again (23:1); each 'sending' has been in service of YHWH. The prophetic word comes from YHWH's own perspective, signalled by the particle *hinnê* (behold).

The first prophetic word declares YHWH is 'bringing (*mēbî'*) evil (*rā'â*) to ('*el*) this place' (vv. 16–17, 19, 20) – that is, the city, including its temple – and 'upon ('*al*) its inhabitants' (vv. 16, 19). The judgment initially evokes that given Manasseh (*mēbî' rā'â 'al yĕrûšālayim*; 2 Kgs 21:12; see also 1 Kgs 9:9) but, grammatically, the closer parallel is to the judgment given Jeroboam (1 Kgs 14:10) and Ahab (1 Kgs 21:21). Only these three judgments use the hiph. part. plus prep. '*el*. The parallel is intentional and chilling: the word against Jerusalem is as certain of fulfilment as that given Jeroboam and Ahab (Sweeney 2001: 49–50; 2007: 442).

Judgment comes because the people have abandoned YHWH and turned to other gods (see 1 Kgs 9:6–9) and thus provoked YHWH's anger (v. 17). Manasseh was indicted for these sins (2 Kgs 21:6, 15), and for these the southern kingdom falls (2 Kgs 21:6, 15; 23:26–27). Josiah has heard the book rightly: YHWH's wrath is indeed 'kindled' (vv. 13, 17). Now the prophecy adds a final knell: YHWH's wrath will not be quenched. The final hurdle of sin has been broached and there is no hope of reprieve.

The second prophecy concerns Josiah but it too describes the coming judgment. It is 'evil' (*rā'â*) brought by YHWH. The evil makes the people a desolation and a curse (Deut. 28:15, 37; 29:20–21), enacting ancient judgments upon the people (Jer. 25:11; 44:12). Josiah, however, is granted reprieve for his penitence.

Josiah's reprieve is that he will not see the evil visited upon the place and its people. Instead, before Jerusalem's destruction Josiah will be 'gathered to his fathers'. The phrase is similar to that found in Judg. 2:10 and, like the expression 'be gathered to one's people' (Gen. 25:8–9, 17; 35:29; 49:29, 33; Num. 20:24; 27:13; 31:2; Deut. 32:50), refers to death per se, with no reference to the means of death (whether peaceful or violent). Secondly, Josiah will be 'buried in peace', that is, his body will be interred rather than experience dishonourable exposure. The expression 'buried in peace' is related to those found in 2 Sam. 21:13–14; Jer. 8:1–2; 25:33; Ezek. 29:5. In those passages burial (the 'gathering of bones') is not experienced because warfare is underway. By contrast, Josiah will be buried 'in peace', that is, before the holocaust of the coming warfare and destruction (van Keulen 1996b; Provan 1988: 147–149; Mayes 1983: 128–130). Additionally, given the fullness of his reform that returns worship to Deuteronomistic norms, 'peace' may also be construed as the wholeness of life and worship under those norms (Wray Beal 2007: 156–166).

It is important to note the differentiation between the phrases 'gathered to one's fathers' and 'gathered to one's grave in peace'. The two phrases are often misunderstood to refer to one event; the resulting conflation concludes that Josiah will die peacefully, without violence or warfare (e.g. Gray 1970: 727; Cross 1973: 286; Nelson 1981: 76–79). Such a reading is difficult to account for in the light of Josiah's death, which is violent. In an effort to align the known facts of Josiah's violent death to the (misunderstood) reading that Josiah will die peacefully, the veracity of the prophetic word can be undermined as mistaken, or blatantly denied. Yet such a conclusion is not warranted in the summative narrative of a corpus that repeatedly affirms the prophetic word as truly reliable. Nor is such a conclusion necessary in the light of the reading that Josiah will be 'gathered to his fathers' *and* his body will be 'gathered to his grave in peace'.

Josiah 'heard' (*šm'*) YHWH (vv. 11, 18–19) when the people would not (v. 13), and his hearing heart expresses humility, mourning and penitence. In response YHWH 'hears' (*šm'*; v. 19) the righteous king and grants a personal mitigation. An instructive parallel is apparent, for Ahab also 'humbled himself before YHWH' (1 Kgs 21:29) in the face of judgment. In recognition of his humility judgment was similarly forestalled to a future generation. Yet the stakes are much higher in Josiah's case. Ahab repented for only his own sin, and judgment concerned only one dynasty. Josiah repents for the nation's sin, and judgment engulfs the whole nation.

23:1–24

1–3. Although Josiah will be 'gathered' (*'sp*) to his fathers, he is not content to rest in his personal reprieve (as was Hezekiah, 2 Kgs 20:19). Instead,

righteous Josiah sends and 'gathers' (*'sp*) the people. The comprehensiveness of the diverse group is emphasized in the repeated use of 'all' (five
times in vv. 1–3) and mirrors the comprehensiveness of earlier covenant
ceremonies (Deut. 29:1–28; 31:9–13; Josh. 24:1–26).

The book is now named the 'book of the covenant', acknowledging the
ceremony it prompts. 'All' the book is read to the gathering and the king
stands (*'md*) by the pillar to make a covenant before YHWH. In the same
way, Jehoash stood by the pillar during a covenant-making ceremony
(2 Kgs 11:12–14); the pillar may be an important adjunct to such ceremonies. Echoing the king, the people also 'stand' (*'md*). This could refer
to their physical stance but is here understood metaphorically as 'commit'.

Vowing to keep YHWH's 'commandments, testimonies and statutes
. . . with all his heart and soul' (v. 3), Josiah as a paradigmatic Deuteronomistic king follows the central text of Deuteronomy (6:1–5). Solomon
was likewise charged (2 Kgs 2:3; cf. 9:6), but it is Josiah's listening heart
(vv. 11, 18–19) that enables fulfilment where Solomon failed.

4–14. The second response to the book is extensive reform (vv. 4–20).
Whether judgment can be forestalled is uncertain, but Josiah acts regardless because reform is right. He could have rested in the assurance of his
personal reprieve but he does not. His acts evidence singular commitment
to YHWH (22:2; 23:25). The reform's focuses are against all non-Yahwistic
and non-Jerusalemite cultic elements, and this is a sure clue to the book's
contents.

Josiah gives his command (*ṣwh*; see 'Form and structure') and sets in
motion all three orders of Yahwistic officials (v. 4; 2 Kgs 25:18). But
throughout the reform Josiah is virtually the sole actor, emphasizing the
instrumentality of the righteous king. The verbs are intense; the reform is
rapid, brutal and total in its reach. Josiah burns (vv. 4, 6, 11, 15 [twice],
16, 20), grinds to dust (vv. 6, 15), tears down (vv. 7, 8, 12, 15), destroys
(v. 11), smashes (v. 12, *rṣṣ*; v. 14, *šbr*), cuts down (v. 14), removes (v. 5,
šbt; v. 19, *swr*), slaughters (v. 20), throws (vv. 6, 12) and defiles (vv. 8, 10,
13, 16).

The reform first deals with the cults of Baal, Asherah and various
Canaanite astral deities (Deut. 4:19; 17:3), and moves outwards from the
temple to Judah (vv. 4–7). Cult objects are burned in the Kidron, a place
of burial. Contact with dead bodies brings defilement (Num. 19:1–22)
and the objects are disposed of in a defiling place suited to them. The
ashes of these objects are scattered in Bethel when Josiah later destroys
Baal's great high place located there (vv. 15–18). The image of the Asherah
prepared by Manasseh and placed in the temple (2 Kgs 21:7) is also burned
(*śrp*). Additionally, its utter destruction is assured when it is ground to
dust (*dqq*) and thrown (*šlk*) in a defiling place. The verbs used (*śrp*, *dqq*,
šlk) also describe the destruction of Aaron's calf (Exod. 32:20; Deut. 9:21).
The image of Asherah (and later the Baal high place, v. 15) is considered
as heinous and must similarly be destroyed.

Priests (here named *kĕmārîm* rather than the usual *kōhănîm* [v. 8]) are removed and possibly slaughtered (as in v. 20). *Kĕmārîm* officiate before other gods, including Baal and the heavenly host (*HALOT* 2:482; Hos. 10:5; Zeph. 1:4) and were appointed by Judahite kings (such as Solomon [1 Kgs 11:7–8] and Manasseh [2 Kgs 21:3–5]). The male cult personnel are also affected, as their residences are removed. These *qĕdēšîm* are thought by some to function as cultic prostitutes. While ritual sexual practice was a part of Canaanite (and aberrant Israelite) religion, the idea of cultic prostitution has largely been set aside. These functionaries operated in non-sanctioned priestly roles (see 'Comment', 1 Kgs 14:24). The women weaving 'coverings for Asherah' prepare vestments for the deity's image, a practice attested throughout the ANE, including Ugarit (McKay 1973: 31). The atrocity of their actions is heightened as it takes place in YHWH's house.

Mentioned once in vv. 4–7, the 'high places' are more specifically targeted in the following reforms (vv. 8 [twice], 9, 13) as Josiah seeks to centralize all worship in Jerusalem. The local shrines from Geba (near Bethel) south of Beer-sheba are defiled, disqualifying them as worship sites. Officiating at these sites are priests (*kōhănîm*) who burn incense (pi. of *qṭr*). The action is used in Kings of pagan cult practice (1 Kgs 12:33; 13:1–2; 2 Kgs 17:11) and within a Yahwistic context is a common negative assessment (1 Kgs 22:43; 2 Kgs 12:3[4]; 14:4; 15:4, 35; 16:4). The *kōhănîm* may be Yahwistic (versus the priests [*kĕmārîm*] of other gods in v. 5), but offering incense at the high places is unorthodox.

The priests at these shrines are brought out from the cities of Judah. If they were brought up to Jerusalem, it could be argued that Josiah applies the law of Deut. 18:6–8 and allows these priests to share in the benefits of the Jerusalem altar. But it is unlikely that a king who wholly follows YHWH's law would break it by conscripting the removal of the priests to Jerusalem (the law states a voluntary move), and by applying it to unorthodox priests (the law clearly refers to orthodox priests). And why bring unorthodox priests to the purified Jerusalem altar at the risk of violating it? A better solution presents itself: Josiah removes the priests from the high places but does not bring them to Jerusalem (see 'Notes on the text'). They return to their kinship settings where they eat bread in the 'midst of their brothers' (Provan 1995: 275–276; Nicholson 2007).

Removal of high places includes one at the city gate named after the governor. No such gate or high place is elsewhere named and, while naming a city governor suggests Jerusalem is in view (Emerton 1994), the context is of action outside Jerusalem and another city is probably in view. No determination can be made; what is certain is that even important worship sites are systematically removed.

Finally, Josiah turns again towards Jerusalem. The Valley of Ben-hinnom is south-west of Jerusalem and Tophet (which combines the consonants for 'fire hearth' with the vocalization of 'shame' [*bōšet*]) denotes a location at which child sacrifice by fire to the netherworld deity Molech is made (see 'Comment', 2 Kgs 16:3).

Back in Jerusalem vv. 11–14 focus on cultic aberrations introduced by anonymous Judahite kings (vv. 11–12) and the specific contributions of Ahaz, Manasseh and Solomon. As in vv. 4–7 the movement goes from the temple outwards to Jerusalem's environs. Horse figurines pulling chariots dedicated to the sun deity (representing the sun's journey through the heavens) are destroyed at the temple's very doors. The altars atop Ahaz's upper chamber may be associated with the 'stairway of Ahaz' (2 Kgs 20:11) and could be attributed to him, but the reference to anonymous kings allows that several (and prior) kings besides Ahaz could have made them. Manasseh's altars inhabit the two temple courts (20:4; 21:5). All of these altars fall under Jeremiah's condemnation (Jer. 19:13; 32:29) and each is violently reduced to dust and disposed of in the Kidron (see v. 6).

Moving further afield, Solomon's high places erected for his foreign wives (1 Kgs 11:5–7) are defiled. Three altars of the original four gods named are now defiled (Ashtoreth [a bastardization of Astarte vocalized with *bōšet*, 'shame'; see 'Comment', 1 Kgs 11:5, 7], Milcom and Chemosh). Solomon's altar to Molech is not named, as the Tophet site dedicated to Molech (v. 10) replaced it. Defilement by sowing with human bones renders these abominations (1 Kgs 11:5, 7) unusable. As a final flourish, in good Deuteronomistic style, the pillars (*maṣṣēbôt*) and sacred poles (*'ăšērîm*) that often appear together as representative of Baal and Asherah (De Moor, *TDOT* 1:443; Exod. 34:13; Deut. 7:5; 12:3; 1 Kgs 14:23; 2 Kgs 17:10; 18:4) are destroyed.

15–20. Action against the high places (vv. 15 [three times], 19–20) brings the reform to Bethel, the centre of Jeroboam's cult. No mention is made of the golden calf at Bethel, but its destruction with the high place is assumed. It is instead the altar (which is emblematic of Jeroboam's cult; see 'Comment', 1 Kgs 12:32–33; 13:1–3) that is in focus. It is mentioned four times in vv. 15–17, and specifically identified in negative terms as the altar in Bethel, that is, the high place made by Jeroboam who caused Israel to sin (v. 15). Further, the focus on the altar is apparent, as the grammar orders the object (the altar; v. 15) first, rather than the verb subject, as is usual. The altar is singled out because Josiah prophesied its destruction centuries earlier (1 Kgs 13:2–3).

The Bethel high place meets a violent end. It is torn down, burned and ground to dust, as was Aaron's golden calf (Exod. 32:20; Deut. 9:21; cf. v. 6). The sacred pole (*'ăšērâ*) that remained through Jehu's purge (2 Kgs 10:26–27; 13:6) is likewise burned, but the pillar (*māššēbâ*) to Baal that commonly stood with the pole (as in v. 14) was destroyed by Jehu and is not here mentioned.

After the initial rush to destroy the hated altar and high place, the narrative backtracks to preceding events. Human bones are disinterred from the high place precincts and burned upon the altar to fulfil the prophetic word (1 Kgs 13:2). The fulfilment is clearly emphasized: first, Josiah – unnamed since 22:3 – is now named as the episode begins (v. 16), a subtle reminder of Josiah's role in the prophecy. Secondly, the actions are 'according to the word of YHWH', and thirdly, the man of God is remembered as 'proclaiming' (*qrʾ*; vv. 16–17) these things – the exact word used in the original oracle (1 Kgs 13:2).

The word as proclaimed is now fulfilled, although the priests of the high place are not slaughtered as prophesied (1 Kgs 13:2). The lacuna is later filled, as 'just as he had done at Bethel' Josiah slaughters priests of the high places upon the altars (vv. 19–20). The fulfilment affirms the important theme of the inviolable power of the prophetic word. Thus one cannot doubt the prophetic word spoken through Huldah will also be fulfilled: Judah will fall but Josiah will be reprieved.

Despite the rapid, frenzied activity at Bethel, the disinterment is arrested when Josiah's attention is drawn to one particular grave, which he learns belongs to the man of God from Judah. In 1 Kgs 13 the Bethel prophet begs interment with this man in acknowledgment that his prophecy was accurate: Josiah would come and destroy Bethel's altar and priests (vv. 31–31). The narrative pause identifies the two men buried together and the honour Josiah accords the pair. He thus affirms their ministries and acknowledges the inviolability of the prophetic word concerning the altar (see further at 'Comment', 1 Kgs 13:25–32).

The Bethel prophet specified the prophecy was against high places, including those in 'all the cities of Samaria' (1 Kgs 13:32), and it is to this that the narrative turns. No mention is made of all the places of worship instituted since the northern exile (2 Kgs 17:29–32); only those made by the 'kings of Israel'. In this way an effective contrast is made: the 'kings of Israel' made high places, but righteous Josiah destroys them all. Only then does he return to Jerusalem.

21–24. In the same year in which the reform takes place Josiah institutes a Passover according to the 'book of the covenant'. In Deut. 16:1–8 the festival occurs at a central shrine. Since the temple that central shrine is in Jerusalem. This makes Josiah's Passover unique when compared to the local family celebration detailed in Exod. 12:1 – 13:16 and that may have been observed during the monarchic era. The uniqueness of Josiah's festival is also noted in that no such celebration has occurred since the judges (and last mentioned in the DH in Josh. 5:10–12). Although 2 Chr. 30:1–27 reports Hezekiah did hold a Passover festival, this is omitted in the Kings account. This selective recounting emphasizes the uniqueness and completeness of Josiah's reforming actions. The people return to covenant, the cult is purified and the Passover is observed as the book requires.

The final notation turns once again to the narrative's opening: the 'book of the torah' found by Hilkiah in the temple. Its ongoing influence directs the removal of particular divinatory and occultic practices (Deut.

18:10–12). The 'mediums and spiritists' who accessed the world of the dead first appear during Manasseh's apostasy (see 'Comment', 2 Kgs 21:6). Teraphim, used for divination and mentioned only here in Kings, are nonetheless noted throughout Israel's history, always negatively (Gen. 31:19–35; Judg. 17:5; 18:14–20; 1 Sam. 19:13, 16; Hos. 3:4–5). Idols, specifically introduced by Ahab (1 Kgs 21:26) and Manasseh (2 Kgs 21:11) were followed by the people (2 Kgs 17:12). In a final blanket phrase Josiah removes 'all the detested things' (*šiqqûṣ*), which can refer specifically to idols (Deut. 29:16; 1 Kgs 11:5, 7; Jer. 7:30; 32:34) or other similar abominable practices (Jer. 4:1; 16:18).

23:25–30

The evaluation lauds Josiah above all kings and uses the language of Deut. 6:5. He is juxtaposed to Manasseh (v. 26), who, like a southern Jeroboam or Ahab, is an apostate whose sins bring about the south's fall.

Given the certain judgment for Manasseh's sins (2 Kgs 21:10–15; 22:26–27; 23:26), though Josiah 'turned' (*šwb*) to YHWH, YHWH will not 'turn' (*šwb*) from his great anger. Josiah 'did not turn aside' (*swr*; 22:2) from YHWH, but YHWH still will 'remove' (*swr*) Judah as he 'removed' (*swr*) Israel.

The circumstances of Josiah's death are difficult to construe fully. The Babylonian Chronicles confirm that Babylon in 609 BC continued its advance against Assyria. The MT reads that Neco 'went up against' (*'ālâ 'al*) Assyria, and the phrase usually suggests warfare. The historical record, however, shows Egypt and Assyria allied against Babylon and thus the MT is amended to read 'went up to' (*'ālâ 'el*; see 'Notes on the text'). The phrase has no connotation of warfare and better represents the historical alliance. While in the chronicler's account Josiah meets Neco in battle (2 Chr. 35:20), his intentions in Kings are left unstated and thus ambiguous. They are, however, an interference that provokes his death (Provan et al. 2003: 276 with notes). He is killed and buried in his own grave in Jerusalem, in the relative peace before the coming holocaust.

Once again, the enfranchised 'people of the land' act (see 'Comment', 2 Kgs 11:13–14) and the succession passes to Josiah's son when he is anointed.

Explanation

The most striking aspect of Josiah's reforms is that he undertakes them at all. There is no certainty his reforms will forestall YHWH's wrath; rather, what he reads in the book of the law convinces him wrath is inevitable. Additionally, the prophetic word given Manasseh and the word Josiah receives from Huldah offer no consolation. There is no hint that YHWH will once again relieve Jerusalem for the sake of the lamp granted David (1 Kgs 15:4; 2 Kgs 8:19). Yet Josiah undertakes an extensive reforming programme. He could easily have accepted his personal reprieve and left Israel to its deserved fate, but he does not. Something moves him to the effort and expense of reform.

The motivation for Josiah's reform lies in the Deuteronomistic evaluation of the king. He turns to YHWH with all his heart and with all his soul and with all his strength according to all the torah of Moses (23:25). The evaluation clearly alludes to Deut. 6:5, which urges Israel to love YHWH with heart, soul and strength. Out of that wholehearted love comes Israel's obedience to the torah of Moses. It is the torah of Moses – the covenant law – that provides the framework within which Israel express their love for God (Craigie 1976: 170). Josiah is favourably evaluated because he alone of all kings fully expresses the loving invitation of Deut. 6:5.

Other elements within Deut. 6 shed light on Josiah's motivation towards covenant obedience. First, some elements within the chapter make no sense as motivators of Josiah's actions. For instance, several promises follow on Israel's wholehearted devotion to YHWH (v. 5). Life itself – and long life – is promised them (vv. 2, 24). More, they are promised success as they enter the land (vv. 3, 18) so that they will prosper in it (v. 24). But, as noted above, the prophetic word to Manasseh confirmed in Huldah's oracle shows the duration and weight of Israel's sin exceeds YHWH's patience and activates covenantal judgments. The promises noted in Deut. 6 are no longer available to the people. Josiah's wholehearted love comes too late in the history to turn YHWH's wrath from his people and city. Therefore, Josiah's motivation for reform seems unlikely to lie in any hope of securing a reprieve and security along the lines noted in Deut. 6.

Secondly, although these elements of Deut. 6 do not explain Josiah's motivation, there is another element in the chapter that does. Besides enumerating covenantal promises, Deut. 6 also recalls a crucial event from Israel's history. A passing reference (Deut. 6:16) remembers events that transpired after Israel's deliverance from Egypt. At a place Moses named Massah ('test', from *nsh*) and Meribah ('contend', from *rîb*) Israel tests and contends with YHWH (Exod. 17:1–7; Deut. 9:22). In a situation when faith and trust were called for, Israel instead rebelled. For that rebellion YHWH loathed a whole generation, barring their entry into the land of rest (Ps. 95:8–11). The psalmist uses the event as a warning so that those appropriating the psalm would not similarly harden their heart (Ps. 95:7).

As one who loves YHWH with his heart, soul and strength, Josiah demonstrates the softened heart for which the psalmist calls. Having learned the history lesson of Massah, Josiah responds to YHWH's law. He exhibits the faith and trust lacking at Massah, and upon hearing the law immediately submits to its precepts. He mourns as he recognizes the judgment under which the nation stands. He demonstrates the softened heart of covenant love when with no hope of personal or national gain he institutes the law and reforms the cult (see 'Comment', 2 Kgs 23:3). He does what is right for no other reason than that it is right and pleases YHWH. His reform is the action of one who loves with heart, soul and strength and who expresses that love within the framework of covenant law.

Thirdly, Josiah makes a choice to love YHWH after the fashion of Deut. 6. By his Deuteronomistic commitments Josiah faithfully answers another ancient covenant challenge. When Israel enters the land, Joshua renews the covenant with the people. He reminds them in the words of Deut. 6:10–11 that they dwell on land for which they did not toil and in cities they did not build, they eat of vineyards and olive trees they did not plant (Josh. 24:13). Then, lest they fall into the trap of satisfied indifference of which Deuteronomy warns (Deut. 6:11–12), he calls the people to fear YHWH reverently and to serve him faithfully. To evidence this they are to dispose of all false gods and to worship YHWH. And, whether or not the people make the choice for YHWH, Joshua commits himself and his household to worship the God of Israel (Josh. 24:14–15). Standing at the opposite end of Israel's history and faced with a similar choice, Josiah echoes Joshua. He is the monarchic example of Joshua's covenant obedience to the precepts of Deut. 6:10–12.

Josiah did not stand alone in the covenant love he expressed. Prophets such as Jeremiah and Ezekiel show the Deuteronomistic ideal of loving YHWH with heart, soul and strength and expressing that in commitment to the covenant law. They faithfully serve YHWH through terrible times when the choice to abandon YHWH may have tempted them – and do so without the personal reprieve granted Josiah.

For the exilic community the same choice lies open to them. Some of them will not live to see the end of the seventy years in captivity prophesied by Jeremiah (Jer. 25:11; 29:10–14). They will die in the land of Babylon. Others will return – but to less than a shadow of Jerusalem's glory: the temple and city are destroyed; the king is deposed. Exiles who can envision such a future might conclude that choosing for YHWH is of no practical value: life will not change materially. But they, too, are called to emulate Josiah's deuteronomic commitment and live out the Deut. 6 ideals. Not for base pragmatism, but for love of YHWH who delivered them from Egypt and entered into covenant with them, promising to be their God and they his people. The history in Kings has shown them the tragedy of hardened hearts that reject covenant life offered by this God. They can respond to the history and again love YHWH with heart, soul and strength. Then, whatever personal fates await them in the coming years, they will know the joy of the torah, and the blessing of YHWH bestowed through covenant life.

Josiah's faithful stance also serves to foreshadow the faithful stance of Jesus. In Luke 4:1–13 the devil tempts Jesus to turn his service of worship from YHWH. Jesus' response to the challenge is (like Josiah's) couched in the scriptures of Deuteronomy, particularly Deut. 6 (Luke 4:4 and Deut. 6:13; Luke 4:8 and Deut. 8:3; Luke 4:12 and Deut. 6:16). His heart is wholly Deuteronomistic: he loves YHWH with heart, soul and strength and worships him alone. Like Josiah, he has learned the history lesson of Massah and does not put YHWH to the test. Instead, with a heart committed to the Scriptures and sustained by trust in his Father, he rejects God's enemy and all his works. As the living Word he is the Scriptures enfleshed, embodying Deuteronomy's precepts.

God's people who make the choice of serving YHWH in the face of easier or more pragmatic choices experience the reality expressed in the final verse of Deut. 6: 'It will be righteousness for us if we are careful to keep all this commandment before YHWH our God, just as he commanded us.'

The verse is a summative comment on a chapter which argues that those who love YHWH with wholehearted love (Deut. 6:5) do so as a response to what YHWH has first done. In rescuing his people, in covenanting himself to them, in providing many and great promises, he shows it is his own self that is first given in love. It is that saving love that calls forth a total response to YHWH from one's heart, soul and strength. This is the essence of faith by which love for God is evident in daily life: in choices made, in loving obedience, in reverent service. Reverence and obedience are the righteous result of the underlying life of faith (Gen. 15:6). It is this life of faith that enables Josiah and God's people through all time to walk in the ways of the Lord.

2 KINGS 23:31 – 24:17

Translation

[23:31]Jehoahaz was twenty-three years old when he began to reign, and he reigned three months in Jerusalem. His mother's name was Hamutal daughter of Jeremiah of Libnah. [32]He did what was evil in the eyes of YHWH, according to all that his fathers had done. [33]Pharaoh Neco imprisoned him in Riblah in the land of Hamath so he might not reign in Jerusalem. He imposed a fine on the land of 100 talents of silver and 1 talent of gold. [34]Pharaoh Neco made Eliakim son of Josiah king in place of Josiah his father, and changed his name to Jehoiakim. He took Jehoahaz and brought him[a] to Egypt and he died there. [35]Jehoiakim gave the silver and gold to Pharaoh, but taxed the land to give the money at Pharaoh's command. He exacted the silver and the gold from[a] the people of the land, each according to his assessment, in order to pay Pharaoh Neco.

[36]Jehoiakim was twenty-five years old when he began to reign and he reigned eleven years in Jerusalem. His mother's name was Zebudah daughter of Padaiah of Rumah. [37]He did what was evil in the eyes of YHWH according to all that his fathers had done. [24:1]In his days Nebuchadnezzar king of Babylon came up and

Jehoiakim became his vassal for three years. Then he turned and rebelled against him. [2]YHWH[a] sent bands of Chaldeans, Arameans, Moabites and Ammonites against him. He sent them against Judah to destroy it according to the word of YHWH, which he spoke by the hand of his servants the prophets. [3]Surely this happened to Judah because of YHWH's command[a], to remove *them* from his presence for the sins of Manasseh and all he had done, [4]and also for the blood of the innocent that he had shed; for he had filled Jerusalem with innocent blood and YHWH was not willing to pardon. [5]Now the rest of the acts of Jehoiakim and all which he did, are they not written in the Book of the Chronicles of the Kings of Judah? [6]Then Jehoiakim slept with his fathers and Jehoiachin his son reigned in his place. [7]The king of Egypt did not come out of his land again, for the king of Babylon had taken all that belonged to the king of Egypt, from the River of Egypt to the river Euphrates.

[8]Jehoiachin was eighteen years old when he began to reign, and he reigned three months in Jerusalem. His mother's name was Nehushta daughter of Elnathan of Jerusalem. [9]He did what was evil in the eyes of YHWH according to all that his father had done. [10]In that time the servants of Nebuchadnezzar king of Babylon went up to Jerusalem and the city came under seige. [11]Nebuchadnezzar king of Babylon arrived at the city while his servants were besieging it, [12]and Jehoiachin king of Judah surrendered to the king of Babylon; he and his mother, his servants, officers and officials. The king of Babylon took him captive in the eighth year of his reign. [13]He brought out from there all the treasures of YHWH's house and the treasures of the king's house. He cut in pieces all the vessels of gold in the temple of YHWH, which Solomon king of Israel had made, just as YHWH had spoken. [14]He exiled all Jerusalem, all the leaders and the warriors – ten thousand exiles[a] – and all the artisans and smiths; none remained but the poorest people of the land. [15]He exiled Jehoiachin to Babylon, and the king's mother and wives and his officials, and the leading men of the land he carried captive from Jerusalem to Babylon. [16]All the men of valour were seven thousand, and the artisans and smiths were one thousand, all strong and able to fight. The king of Babylon brought them captive to Babylon. [17]Then the king of Babylon made Mattaniah, *Jehoiachin's* uncle[a], king in his place and changed his name to Zedekiah.

Notes on the text

23:34.a. Reading for MT *wayyābō'*, 'he came', *wayyĕbî'ēhû* (hiph. 'he brought him') with LXX, Vg. The 3 m. sg. suff. is added with LXX[L], 2 Chr. 34:4.

35.a. Following LXX, and in agreement with Hobbs (1985: 332), reading *'et* as a prep. 'with the help of, from' in *'et 'am hā'āreṣ*.

24:2.a. LXX* omits 'YHWH' as subject, implying the bands are sent by Nebuchadnezzar. Yet raiders elsewhere are a sign of YHWH's judgment (2 Kgs 5:2; 6:23), and lions are also sent as YHWH's judgment (2 Kgs 17:25).

3.a. A phrase similar to 'because of YHWH's command' (*'ak 'al-pî yhwh*) is found in 24:20 (see next commentary chapter) and reads, 'because of YHWH's anger' (*kî 'al-'ap yhwh*). LXX uses θυμόν in v. 3 ('because of YHWH's will') and v. 20 ('because of YHWH's anger'). Cf. Syr, Tg.

14.a. Part. *gôleh*, 'the one exiled', is read as a collective noun, *gôlâ*, with LXX[L], Syr, Tg, Vg. θυμόν

17.a. MT *dōdô*, lit. 'his beloved', here as 'his uncle' as in Lev. 10:4; 20:20; 1 Sam. 14:50; Jer. 32:7.

Form and structure

The chapter covers approximately twelve of Judah's last years (609–597 BC) and the reigns of two sons and one grandson of Josiah. The rapid succession is due to the tumultuous events of the era and is linked to the power struggle between Egypt and Babylon. Babylon's placement as the new imperial power in the Levant occurs by YHWH's hand, and through Babylon YHWH's judgment against Judah (20:16–18; 21:10–15; 22:16–17; 23:26–27) is effected.

Each reign is structured by the now-familiar regnal summaries. An opening summary includes the king's name, age at accession, length and place of reign, mother's name, and evaluation. The evaluations are virtually identical, as each king 'did what was evil in the eyes of YHWH, according to all that his father[s] had done' (23:32, 37; 24:9; cf. 24:19). The unique similarity, shared by consecutive reigns at the end of the history, has led to various redactional theories (Weippert 1972; Campbell 1986). There may indeed be redactional layers behind the text, but no consensus is forwarded on the provenance, extent or purpose of such layers. What is certain is that if sources lie behind the present text, they now cohere as a narrative whole. Within the narrative's present shape the evaluations signal the monarchy's theological bankruptcy, as the cultic nadir of Manasseh's reign serves as a blueprint for successive wicked monarchs.

Variation occurs in the closing summaries regarding the monarchs' deaths and burials, but the narratives account for these variations. Thus Jehoahaz is brought as a prisoner to Egypt and dies there. From the perspective of the land of Israel's captivity he is truly out of the picture and the details of his burial are deemed insignificant. Neither is a burial notice provided for Jehoiakim (24:6). This may reflect confusion over Jehoiakim's fate in the mêlée of Jerusalem's fall or an intentional denigration of the king. By not recording any burial, the narrative reflects the scorn of Jeremiah's prophecy whereby Jehoiakim is thrown outside the city gates as a donkey's burial (see 'Comment'). Finally, Jehoiachin, too, receives no notice of death or burial because his narrative is taken up again in the final verses of the book. The history ends with Jehoiachin still living.

The lengths of reigns form a patterned structure over chs. 24–25, alternating between three months (Jehoahaz, Jehoiachin) and eleven years (Jehoiakim, Zedekiah). Regardless of regnal years, each reign interacts with the imperial powers active during Judah's demise. Neco's appointment of Jehoahaz and the imposition of tribute mark Egyptian dominance over Judah. During Jehoiakim's reign that dominance transitions as Babylon wrests control (v. 7).

There can be no doubt that Dtr reads Babylon's rise as YHWH's will, for it occurs by YHWH (v. 2), through his word spoken by his prophets (v. 2), at YHWH's command (v. 3) and evidences YHWH's unwillingness to pardon Manasseh's sins (v. 4). Several techniques are used to demonstrate that in Jehoiachin's reign Babylon is dominant. After Jehoiachin's evaluation (vv. 8–9) he acts only once, when he surrenders (v. 12). For every other action (vv. 10–17) Nebuchadnezzar is the subject. Moreover, the capture of Jehoiachin is chronologically related to the reign of Nebuchadnezzar (the phenomenon increases in ch. 25 as Judah falls further under Babylonian dominion). Finally, the chapter ends as it began, with the appointment of Judah's king by the foreign power. Now, however, that power is Babylon and not Egypt.

The chapter provides many narrative details of the events of these eleven years, but there also exists an extant, extra-biblical annalistic account detailing Babylon's several campaigns into the Levant during the same time period. Careful consideration of the Babylonian Chronicles (Wiseman 1956) provides a chronology during the time of the siege of Jerusalem in 597 BC.

Comment

23:31–35

Jehoahaz is the throne name of Shallum (Jer. 22:11), appointed by the 'people of the land' (v. 30) over his elder brothers (v. 8; 1 Chr. 3:15). The unusual succession could not be due to hopes of a continuance of Josiah's reform policies, for the new king's reign is 'evil'. Whatever the religious affiliation of the people of the land, it appears political realities motivate Jehoahaz's appointment. He probably continues the anti-Egyptian policy of his father, as this would account for his rapid removal by Neco.

Neco proceeds to support Assyria against Babylon's advance, and Riblah, on the Orontes River 19 miles (30 km) south of Hamath serves as a military and administrative centre for Assyria (as it later serves Babylon; 25:6). Neco imprisons Jehoahaz in Riblah before transporting him to Egypt with Neco's retinue. The deposed king dies in the land of Israel's captivity and little comment is accorded the event. Neco's motives for the appointment are unclear. He may simply wish to assert overlordship by appointing a different Judean king, or he may remove Jehoahaz because he engaged against Egypt.

Neco appoints Eliakim, Josiah's second son (1 Chr. 3:15). To warrant the appointment, Eliakim must be a supporter of Egypt's authority. The name change is a common demonstration of an overlord's authority, and 'Eliakim' ('God establishes') becomes 'Jehoiakim' ('YHWH establishes'). The change may signal a concession to a pro-Yahwist party, possibly among the same 'people of the land' who elected Josiah's anti-Egyptian son.

Neco imposes a fine that Jehoiakim exacts 'each according to his assessment', which is a standard term for taxation (2 Kgs 12:5; Lev. 5:15, 18, 25). That the tribute is raised from the 'people of the land' implies its imposition punishes their challenge to Egyptian authority by the election of Jehoahaz. The tribute is substantial, but smaller than that imposed under Sennacherib (2 Kgs 18:14).

23:36 – 24:7

Jehoiakim reigns eleven years (609–598 BC) and his rule sees the transition to Babylonian power in the Levant. Like his younger brother he too does 'evil . . . as his fathers had done' and evidence of this appears in Jeremiah (19:3–5; 26:20–23; 36:9–26).

Though initially an Egyptian appointee, he first switches his allegiance to Babylon and then, three years later, rebels against that allegiance. A probable historical chronology can be posited for these actions from the Babylonian Chronicles. After the decisive Babylonian victory at Carchemish (605 BC), Nebuchadnezzar returns to Babylon for his coronation. He mounts another invasion in 604 BC, during which Ashkelon is taken and 'all the kings of the Hatti-land came before him and he received their heavy tribute' (Wiseman 1956: 69). It is during this year that Jehoiakim becomes a Babylonian vassal. Three years later (601 BC) Babylon suffers a defeat at the hands of Egypt, subsequently withdraws and remains in Babylon for a whole year to regroup (Wiseman 1956: 71). The defeat of Babylon and their absence from the Levant for a time provides the probable period for Jehoiakim's rebellion.

Though Jehoiakim may have hoped to gain Judean independence, vv. 2–4 reveal that YHWH had already determined Judah would fall even further under Babylonian control. Raiders (gĕdûdîm; 2 Kgs 6:23; 13:20) from Babylon and from surrounding nations under Babylonian control enter Judah 'to destroy it'. Whatever earthly powers direct the raids, they are clearly depicted as under YHWH's command and in fulfilment of his words by 'his servants the prophets'. The phrase evokes the message given by YHWH's servants the prophets (1 Kgs 21:10) and is a reminder that the prophetic word given to Manasseh is coming to pass.

The motivation for YHWH's command against Judah (v. 3) continues to draw a connection to the sins of Manasseh, including the innocent blood he shed, so that YHWH was unwilling to pardon. The sense of inevitability that accompanied the word to Manasseh (1 Kgs 21:10–15) and that was reinforced in Huldah's prophecy (2 Kgs 22:16–17) now proves true: YHWH will not pardon Jerusalem. Jehoiakim's rebellion is merely the spark to the tinder of YHWH's word accomplished through Nebuchadnezzar. And Babylon is now positioned to accomplish the task: Egypt's subjugation is complete and Babylon holds all their lands (including Judah) from the Euphrates to the wadi el-'Arish. That the description of Babylon's reach is that of Solomon's old empire (1 Kgs 4:21, 24; 8:65) is telling. Former glory is long lost; Assyria is gone; Egypt is gone. There is nothing now to stand between Judah and God's agent Babylon.

Jehoiakim's death includes no mention of burial, and even the textual evidence regarding his fate is ambiguous. 2 Chr. 36:6–7 and Dan. 1:1–7 indicate he lives through Jerusalem's fall. This contradicts Kings, which places Jehoiachin's three-month rule after his father's death and before Jerusalem falls (2 Kgs 24:6, 8). A possible solution is a co-regency during the final three months before Jerusalem's fall. When the city is taken, both monarchs are prepared for exile to Babylon. Before the deportation is effected, Jehoiakim dies (of natural causes, assassination or at Nebuchadnezzar's command). It is of note that the chronicler does not state Jehoiakim is actually deported, and similarly 2 Kgs 24:15 mentions only the deportation of Jehoiachin, his mother and wives, but not his father. Both these passages could support (but do not require) a scenario of co-regency as sketched here.

The non-burial of the king may be a textual omission. Septuagintal texts here and in Chronicles contain a notice of burial in Jerusalem but may supply the lacuna to smooth the difficulty. Jeremiah also places Jehoiakim's death in Jerusalem (22:18–19), but accords him only the 'burial of a donkey', that is, to be thrown outside the city and left unburied. Jeremiah's words, however, may be no more than a rhetorical denigration of a hated king. Although Jehoiakim's burial is not specified in Kings, that he 'slept with his fathers' suggests an interment in Jerusalem (Provan et al. 2003: 381).

24:8–17

Jehoiachin is the throne name of Jeconiah (Jer. 24:1; 28:4; 29:2 [abbreviated to Coniah in Jer. 22:24, 28; 37:1]) and he is Josiah's grandson. That godly heritage does not influence Jehoiachin's conduct and he does the same evil as Jehoiakim, thus continuing the sins of his ancestors.

As noted above, Jehoiachin's father, Jehoiakim, rebels following Babylon's defeat in 601 BC. Reprisals do not immediately follow, for

Babylon advances no campaign into the Levant until 599 BC. The Babylonian Chronicles record no campaign against Judah in that year and it is not until December 598 BC that Jerusalem is besieged by Nebuchadnezzar's army for a brief three months during which time Jehoiachin comes to the throne. In March 597 BC Jehoiachin's rule in Jerusalem ends, as the city is taken (Wiseman 1956: 73; Thiele 1983: 186–187).

Jehoiachin surrenders in Nebuchadnezzar's eighth year (v. 12). Both the Babylonian Chronicles (Wiseman 1956: 73) and Jer. 52:28 place the siege in Nebuchadnezzar's seventh year. The discrepancy is explained by the different systems used in Judah and Babylon for calculating regnal years (see Introduction). Noting the event by the regnal year of the conquering king is unusual, but is an indication of Babylon's authority in Judah at this time. This authority is also implied in that Jehoiachin is the subject of only one verb in vv. 10–17: he surrenders to Nebuchadnezzar. His one action is juxtaposed to Nebuchanezzar's many actions (his servants 'went up', he 'arrived', 'took captive', 'brought out treasures', 'cut in pieces', 'exiled' Jerusalem and 'exiled' Jehoiachin, 'carried captive', 'brought captive', 'made Mattaniah king' and 'changed his name'). The juxtaposition shows Babylon has complete control over Judah and its monarchy.

Two symbols of Jerusalemite freedom and power are depicted as brought under Babylonian control: the ruling family is taken captive (v. 12) and the palace and temple are plundered (v. 13). Although the vessels of gold 'that Solomon king of Israel had made' are cited among the treasures, this is most probably a rhetorical flourish showing the plunder's significance. While it is not impossible that some of these items survived, it is unlikely given the numerous times the temple riches have been taken. This is the next-to-last notice of temple treasuries lost (2 Kgs 25:13–17), and is one of a string of similar events that have all shed negative light upon a king's rule (1 Kgs 14:26; 15:18; 2 Kgs 14:14; 16:8; 18:15–16; see 'Comment', 1 Kgs 15:18). Now the plunder is effected by Nebuchadnezzar and fulfils what 'YHWH had spoken' (v. 13). The reference is to 2 Kgs 20:17, and is part of the disaster forecast against the temple in 1 Kgs 9:8. Nebuchadnezzar will complete the destruction of the temple within eleven years.

Babylonian policy differs from Assyrian policy, as Babylon does not practice two-way deportation. Babylon instead deports the population's elites and skilled people, leaving the 'poorest of the land' (v. 14; 2 Kgs 25:22). Thus the attestation that 'all' Jerusalem is deported (v. 14) is a hyperbolic commentary on the drastic events. Many educated and skilled deportees came to serve in various capacities in the Babylonian regime (Dan. 1 – 6). With so many skilled leaders stripped from positions in Jerusalem, the city's functionality is severely crippled.

The round number of 10,000 deportees (v. 14) includes the royals, leaders, warriors, and skilled artisans and craftsmen. It is difficult to know exactly how the figure of 10,000 deportees relates to the 7,000 'men of valour' and the 1,000 craftsmen (v. 16). Additionally, Jeremiah speaks of deportees numbering 3,023 called simply the 'Judeans' (Jer. 52:28). These 'Judeans' were deported during 597 BC, and may denote a separate deportation rounded up from the countryside and not included in the 10,000 enumerated in v. 14. If so, the 7,000 men of valour, the 1,000 craftsmen (v. 16) and the addition of the royal elites (v. 14) may comprise the rounded number of 10,000 in the Kings text. Alternatively, if the 3,023 'Judeans' enumerated in Jeremiah are some portion of the 10,000 enumerated in Kings, they may represent the ruling elite and leaders. Thus 7,000 men of valour, plus 1,000 craftsmen, plus 3,023 ruling elite still falls within the parameters of 10,000 as a rounded number. However the figures are calculated for the deportation in 597 BC, most of the skilled and ruling classes are included. So great is the deportation that only a few of the skilled population remain; available deportation numbers from the later deportation (586 BC) list only 832 individuals (Jer. 52:28).

Jehoiachin makes the arduous journey to Babylon under the crushing reality of Jerusalem's fall. Another son of Josiah, Mattaniah, is Babylon's appointee to the throne. His name is changed by Nebuchadnezzar (to Zedekiah) as a demonstration of Babylonian authority over him. The Judahite hope in the monarchy, the city and the temple is seriously undermined as the first wave of YHWH's wrath breaks. The final irony is that 'Zedekiah' means 'The Righteousness of YHWH'. The events of this chapter are just the beginnings of the prophesied righteous anger of YHWH (2 Kgs 22:17). Its full expression will come during this king's reign.

Explanation

The narrative pace of the chapter moves rapidly from one reign to another. The pattern is similar to that found in the northern kingdom in its final years (2 Kgs 15). For both kingdoms the narrative pace communicates the inevitability of the nations' progress towards prophesied destruction (see 'Form and structure', 2 Kgs 15). Judgment is pronounced against Judah, and YHWH will not relent (1 Kgs 9:6–9; 2 Kgs 21:10–15; 23:26–27). The changing fortunes of Egypt and Babylon answer to YHWH's sovereign plan and through them he enacts judgment against the apostate nation.

From the vantage point of the exile, the author clearly recognizes that disaster fell upon the nation as a result of the withdrawal of YHWH's favour. By that favour they have experienced covenant blessings; now as that favour is withdrawn nothing prevents the rapid advance of the final covenant curses (Deut. 28). Should he again turn his face towards his people they would be restored (Ps. 80:3, 7, 19).

The truth of YHWH's withdrawn favour is part of his word to Moses. YHWH makes clear that the people will rebel against him, follow other gods, forsake YHWH and break the covenant (Deut. 31:16). This is evidenced throughout Israel's history, but for Judah it becomes particularly apparent in the reign of Manasseh. In response to anticipated rebellion YHWH declares to Moses that he will hide (hiph. of *str*) his face from his people. As a result, they will be made easy prey. Disaster and calamity will come upon them (Deut. 31:17–18; 32:20). The experience of such calamity will prove the connection between the people's past blessings and YHWH's bestowed favour, and their present calamities and YHWH's withdrawn favour. This is precisely the recognition apparent in 2 Kgs 24 as blow after blow falls in rapid succession, all because YHWH has turned his face away (2 Kgs 23:27).

David, in a psalm ascribed to the temple's dedication (Ps. 30, superscription), also knows the connection between disaster and favour and YHWH's stance towards his people. David affirms that when YHWH hid (hiph. of *str*) his face, the king was dismayed (v. 7[8]). The psalm recounts the action of enemies, sickness and near death – all the result of YHWH's hiding his face. David also knows the reality of YHWH's face turned towards him: security for the throne and city (v. 7[8]; see similarly at Ps. 27:5). Sadly for the people in the reigns of Jehoahaz, Jehoiakim and Jehoiachin this reality is long past. Now YHWH's face is hidden and throne, city and even temple are attacked by YHWH's hand.

The connection of disaster or blessing to the disposition of YHWH's favour is not limited to Israel and Judah – nor even to humanity. Ps. 104 praises God's great majesty and sovereign power over all the earth (vv. 1–26). He controls the world and its creatures, providing shelter and food for them. This provision is an expression of his sovereign favour to all creatures, including humans (v. 23). Should he hide his face (v. 29; hiph. of *str*), his creatures immediately feel the withdrawal of sovereign favour that sustains the world, and are dismayed. The psalmist seeks to remind his audience that the smooth workings of the world they experience are not by chance: they are by YHWH's attention, favour and power. For this the psalmist calls for praise.

As the reigns of the final monarchs tick past in rapid succession, the author acknowledges that disaster comes rapidly upon Judah as a result of YHWH's hiding his face. This is clear from the perspective of the exile. They know experientially what life is like when YHWH hides his face. But in the place of punishment for sin, and with the possibility of repentance before them, the exilic people might also dare to believe another truth about YHWH's face. When it is hidden, they know disaster. But should it turn to them again, YHWH's favour is promised. Isaiah speaks of this restoration. In it YHWH forgets Israel's shame of covenant breaking and Israel comes to know YHWH's favour as redeemer:

> 'For a brief moment I abandoned you,
> But with great compassion I will gather you.
> In a flood of wrath I hid (hiph. of *str*) my face from you
> > for a moment,

> But with everlasting kindness
> I will have compassion on you,'
> Says YHWH your Redeemer.
> (Isa. 54:7–8)

This hope, however, lies in the narrative future of 2 Kgs 24. For the moment YHWH has hidden his face and disaster must come. It does come, and quickly, bringing to bear the curses under a covenant from which the people have turned.

Should the people experience the future return of YHWH's favour, they will take up Ps. 30 once more, not to acknowledge YHWH's hidden face, but to acknowledge his face turned towards them in gracious favour:

> For his anger lasts only a moment,
> While his favour lasts a lifetime;
> Weeping may spend the night,
> But in the morning, joy comes.
> (Ps. 30:5[6])

2 KINGS 24:18 – 25:30

Translation

24:18aZedekiah was twenty-one years old when he began to reign, and he reigned eleven years in Jerusalem. His mother's name was Hamutal daughter of Jeremiah of Libnah. 19He did what was evil in the eyes of YHWH according to all that Jehoiakim had done. 20Because of YHWH's anger this happened to Jerusalem and Judah, until he cast them from his presence. Now Zedekiah rebelled against the king of Babylon.

25:1In the ninth yeara of his reign, in the tenth month on the tenth day, Nebuchadnezzar king of Babylon came, he and all his army, against Jerusalem. He camped against itb and built siege worksb around it. 2The city came under siege until the eleventh year of King Zedekiah. 3By the ninth day of the *fourth*a month the famine was severe in the city and there was no food for the people of the land. 4The city was breached and all the men of war *fled*a by night by the way of the gate between the two walls by the king's garden, though the Chaldeans surrounded the city. They wentb by the way of the Arabah. 5The Chaldean army pursued the king and overtook him on the plains of Jericho and all his army was scattered from him. 6They captured the king and brought him to the king of Babylon at Riblah and he passed sentencea on him. 7He slaughtereda Zedekiah's sons before his eyes, then blinded Zedekiah's eyes, bound him with bronze and brought him to Babylon.

8In the fifth month, on the seventh daya, which was the nineteenth year of King Nebuchadnezzar king of Babylon, Nebuzaradan the captain of the guard, servant of the king of Babylon, came to Jerusalem. [9]He burned the house of YHWH and the king's house and all the houses of Jerusalem; every great house he burned with fire. [10]All the Chaldean army with the captain of the guard tore down the walls of Jerusalem all around. [11]The rest of the people who remained in the city and the deserters who had deserted to the king of Babylon and the rest of the multitude, Nebuzaradan captain of the guard carried away captive. [12]But the poorest of the land the captain of the guard left as vinedressers and farmers.

[13a]The Chaldeans broke up the bronze pillars in the house of YHWH, the stands and the bronze sea in the house of YHWH, and carried the bronze to Babylon. [14]They took the pots, the shovels, the snuffers, the bowls and all the bronze vessels used for service, [15]as well as the firepans and basins – the captain of the guard took what was gold for gold, and silver for silver. [16]And the two pillars, the one sea and the stands that Solomon had made for the house of YHWH – the bronze of all these vessels was beyond measure. [17]The one pillar was 18 cubits high, with a bronze capital upon it. The height of the capital was 3 cubits with lattice work and pomegranates surrounding the capital, all of bronze. And the second pillar was the same, with the lattice work.

[18]The captain of the guard took Seraiah the chief priest and Zephaniah the second priest and the three keepers of the threshold. [19]And from the city he took one official appointed over the men of war, and five men who advised the king who were discovered in the city, also the scribe (the captain of the army who mustered the people of the land) and sixty men from the people of the land who were discovered in the city. [20]Nebuzaradan the captain of the guard took them and brought them to the king of Babylon at Riblah. [21]The king of Babylon struck them and put them to death in Riblah in the land of Hamath. Thus Judah was exiled from its land.

[22]He appointed over the people who remained in the land of Judah whom Nebuchadnezzar king of Babylon had left Gedaliah son of Ahikam son of Shaphan. [23]Now when all the captains of the forces, they and the men, heard that the king of Babylon had appointed Gedaliah, they came to Gedaliah at Mizpah – Ishmael son of Nethaniah, Johanan son of Kareah, Seraiah son of Tanhumeth the Netophathite, and Jaazaniah son of the Maacathite – they and their men. [24]Gedaliah swore to them and their men and said to them, 'Do not be afraid of the Chaldean officials. Live in the land and serve the king of Babylon and it will be well with you.' [25]But in the seventh month Ishmael son of Nethaniah son of Elishama of the royal family came with ten men and they struck Gedaliah and he died, along with the Judeans and Chaldeans with him at Mizpah. [26]Then all the people small and great and the captains of the forces fled to Egypt, for they feared the Chaldeans.

[27]In the thirty-seventh year of the exile of Jehoiachin king of Judah, in the twelfth month, on the twenty-seventh day of the month, Evil-merodach king of Babylon in the year he began to reign released Jehoiachin king of Judah from prison. [28]He spoke kindly with him and set his seat above the seat of the kings with him in Babylon. [29]He changed his prison clothes and ate meals regularly in *the king's* presence all the days of his life. [30]His allowance was a regular allowance, given him by the king as a daily portion, all the days of his life.

Notes on the text

24:18.a. – 25:12. Found also at Jer. 52:1–16; 25:1–12; substantially at Jer. 39:1–10.

25:1.a. MT *bišnat* erroneously pointed as a const.; read as abs.

1.b. MT 'camped against' is sg., but 'built siege works' is pl. The Vrs. variously harmonize one to the other.

3.a. The month is specified in Jer. 52:6 and fills the lacuna here (so NRSV, NASB, NIV).

4.a. No verb appears in the MT. With some additions, Jer. 39:4 specifies Zedekiah is included with the 'men of war' who fled.

4.b. MT read sg. 'he went'. Some MSS, LXX-BO56 read pl., 'they went'. Both Jer. 39:4 and 52:7 have the pl. verb 'they went'.

6.a. MT 'they passed sentence' is read as sg. with MSS, Vrs and Jer. 52:9–10.

7.a. MT 'they slaughtered', sg. with MSS, Vrs and Jer. 52:9–10.

8.a. The day varies: LXX-L, Syr reads 'ninth'; Jer. 52:12 reads 'tenth'.

13.a.–21. Also appears at Jer. 52:17–27.

Form and structure

The chapter has a clear structure that plays with ideas of destruction and continuance, exile and hope. The brief opening regnal summary for Zedekiah contains nothing more than the expected elements (see 'Form and structure', 2 Kgs 24). No closing summary is provided, only a narrative account of Zedekiah's capture and deportation to Babylon (25:6–7). A bridge (24:20) follows the opening summary and focuses the narrative upon the crucial end moments of the king's eleven-year reign (597–586 BC).

The remainder of the chapter is easily divided into three sections (25:1–7, 8–26, 27–30), each beginning with a chronological notation. The first is Zedekiah's ninth year (588 BC) and focuses upon the loss of the monarch. Although he escapes when the city is breached, his capture is swift and he is deported to Babylon. No further reference is made to the king appointed by a foreign conqueror and who continually disregarded Jeremiah's urgings that he surrender (Jer. 27). Zedekiah presumably dies in Babylon but the narrative is silent. Rather, Jehoiachin's story is re-engaged, signalling that he remains the rightful king of Judah, even though in captivity.

The second section (vv. 8–26) likewise begins with a chronological notation, unusually aligned to a foreign king's regnal years. The fall of the city and the monarchy prove their ineffectiveness: Nebuchadnezzar is in control of both, and is so acknowledged by the reference to his reign. These verses (vv. 8–26) provide four vignettes of the city's fall. The first (vv. 8–12) narrates the disposition of the city. Various 'houses' are destroyed, beginning with YHWH's house (v. 9). The city walls are destroyed, and the inhabitants carried away captive (v. 11). A final notation of those who 'remain in the land' (v. 12) is taken up again later in the chapter.

The second vignette (vv. 13–17) focuses upon the first of the buildings destroyed – the temple (v. 9). Various items, mostly those of bronze, are prepared for transport to Babylon. A fuller description is found in Jer. 52:17–23, but the summary in Kings is clearly patterned after the account of the items prepared for Solomon's temple (1 Kgs 7:15–45). As those items are now destroyed, YHWH's word given in 1 Kgs 9:8 is fulfilled.

The third vignette (vv. 18–21) expands upon the earlier statement regarding the disposition of the city's inhabitants (v. 11). Now a selected group of leaders from the cultic, military and civic realms is executed. The execution emphasizes the total control of Babylon over the populace.

The final vignette (vv. 22–26) turns to the fate of those left in the land (v. 12). Life continues, but an abortive attempt by a remaining royal leads to disaster. The Judahite remnant ends without hope as they return to the land of captivity: to Egypt.

The chapter's third section opens with the final chronological notation. While the chronology with which the second section opened aligned to the foreign Nebuchadnezzar (v. 8), the chronology of the third section reckons time once again according to Judean concerns (v. 27). This section acts as an appendix, turning from the fate of Jerusalem and its inhabitants to those exiled in Babylon, particularly Jehoiachin. His continuing existence and elevation within the foreign court leave the narrative open to hope. The king lives, so may the Davidic promise yet remain?

Comment

24:18–20

Zedekiah's rule of eleven years closes the history of Israel in the land. He is the third son of Josiah (1 Chr. 3:15) and full brother to Jehoahaz, as they have the same mother (24:18; 23:31). The evaluation of Zedekiah's reign is a variant of that given for Jehoahaz, Jehoiakim and Jehoiachin; the final king in Judah continues in the cultic and moral bankruptcy of his predecessors. The particular comparison to Jehoiakim suggests another connection between these two of the final four kings. Both Jehoiakim and Zedekiah rebel against Babylon (24:1, 20) and thus resist YHWH's will worked through the conqueror.

Little is known of Zedekiah's reign from the Kings account but Jeremiah provides several details and paints the king as a weak leader, vacillating between commitment to Babylon and rebellion against his overlord (Jer. 21, 27, 32 – 34, 37 – 39). The regnal summary closes by citing the rebellion, and it is this that precipitates Babylon's decisive action against the nation (25:1). Zedekiah's rebellion may be the spur to that action in the world of realpolitik, but it is YHWH's righteous anger that ultimately controls the events, until YHWH 'cast [Judah and Jerusalem] from his presence' (24:20).

No date is given for the rebellion, although biblical clues suggest it began early in Zedekiah's reign. At that time Zedekiah consults envoys from surrounding nations, including Egypt, to throw off the Babylonian yoke (Jer. 27 − 28; Ezek. 17:11–21). The consultation may also have been prompted in some measure by the campaign of Pharaoh Psammeticus II in 591 BC against Phoenicia. The campaign destabilized the area and can only have fed Judean hopes of independent rule (Provan et al. 2003: 280). The withholding of vassal tribute was a common expression of rebellion. At some point Zedekiah's non-allegiance is troublesome enough that Babylon marches to quell the rebellion. En route to Jerusalem many of the cities of Judah are destroyed (Jer. 34:6–7; 44:2; Lam. 2:2–5). Jeremiah records that during Zedekiah's fourth year the king appears in Babylon (Jer. 51:59; see also Jer. 29:3) perhaps to answer for his actions and renew his oath of loyalty to his overlord.

25:1–7

Zedekiah's ninth year is 588 BC and the siege begins in January. The Babylonian Chronicles extend only to Nebuchadnezzar's tenth year (595 BC) and not to the fall of Jerusalem in his nineteenth year (v. 8). No other extant records record Jerusalem's siege. However, the biblical account of the siege can be set in relation to the reigns of Jehoiakim and Jehoiachin, whose reigns can be chronologically verified by the Babylonian Chronicles. Ezekiel 40:1 is also useful in dating Jerusalem's fall. Ezekiel looks back twenty-five years to the exile (597 BC) and fourteen years to the fall of Jerusalem; the difference of eleven years is the time between the exile (597 BC) and the city's fall (586 BC; see Thiele 1983: 190–191 for dates throughout).

The siege continues until July 586 BC and its eighteen-month duration provokes severe famine (see 2 Kgs 6:24–30 for a window into the desperate situation of besieged cities). Despite Jeremiah's repeatedly urging surrender, Zedekiah dithers. Only when the city is breached and its doom is at hand does he act decisively, fleeing under cover of darkness with the men of war. The escape is made through a gate at the south-eastern city corner. This is near the king's gardens and is possibly the Gate of the Spring named in Neh. 3:15. The point of egress places them at the furthest remove from the north-west corner of the city where the besieging troops were concentrated.

Certainly at the height of the siege, watch would be kept for escapees. The king's departure is discovered and the escape short-lived. Overtaken on the plains east of Jericho, the men of war scatter in flight and Zedekiah is captured. Nebuchadnezzar, although present when the siege was first engaged (v. 1), is now at Riblah, a military and administrative centre previously used by Assyria (2 Kgs 23:33). The judgment against the recalcitrant vassal is not uncommon: his sons are killed to forestall any attempt at re-establishing rule and, with the death of his sons before his eyes, the king is blinded. The humiliation continues as the king is shackled in bronze and shipped to Babylon. The narrative completes the humiliation by citing no further details of his life there.

25:8–26

One month after the city is breached Nebuchadnezzar's troops destroy the prominent buildings and city walls. The resultant loss of civic prestige further debilitates both those left in the land and the exiles (as witnessed by the profound mourning in the book of Lamentations). The destruction also further asserts the conqueror's control and, together with the deportations, effectively reduces the possibility of future resistance. The conqueror's control is also attested in that the event is reckoned per Babylonian chronology. The city's destruction in the nineteenth year of Nebuchadnezzar further effaces the still-living Judean kings Jehoiachin and Zedekiah.

The demolition occurs under the direction of the king's servant Nebuzaradan. The term 'captain of the guard' (*rab ṭabbāḥîm*) derives from the root *ṭbḥ*. In verbal forms the root carries the idea of slaughtering animals for sacrifice (Gen. 43:16). More frequently, the idea is applied metaphorically to humans (Jer. 25:34; Lam. 2:21). The singular nominal form denotes a butcher or cook and is present only in 1 Sam. 9:23–24. The more frequent plural form is used of Nebuzaradan. An alternative plural form (*śar ṭabbāḥîm* or *śārîs ṭabbāḥîm*) is applied to the chief Egyptian officials Potiphar and the prison warden in Gen. 37 – 41. The plural form includes the basic idea of slaughterer or executioner now held by one whose position enables the official initiation of such activity. And (if one pardons the pun), Nebuzaradan is certainly Babylon's 'hatchet man' in Jerusalem.

Burning the temple and palace and the houses of the powerful removes the primary visual evidences of governmental power and the deity's patronage. The people had erroneously trusted in the temple as evidence YHWH would always protect his city, and disregarded warnings that he would abandon both temple and city should the people sin against him (1 Kgs 9:6–9; Jer. 7). Destroying the city also includes removing its people. The parallel account in Jeremiah cites 832 deportees at this time (Jer. 52:28–29; the verses also cite the 3,023 deported in 597 BC, and a later deportation of 745 persons). Those remaining elites, skilled workmen, various others of the city population, and the deserters who had heeded

Jeremiah (Jer. 38:17–22) are exiled, leaving only the poorest Judahites per Babylon's policy (2 Kgs 24:14).

Babylon had earlier transported the contents of the temple and palace treasuries (2 Kgs 24:13). Now bronze items and furnishings for temple service, the massive pillars fashioned by Solomon, and a few items of silver and gold are transported. The list of items reflects the account of their preparation (1 Kgs 7:15–45). The mirroring of the two passages emphasizes the loss of hopefulness with which the temple project began. Now the great edifice, built for the worship of YHWH, is taken apart piecemeal to be melted down.

It is initially unclear what Nebuzaradan intends for the representative group he assembles (vv. 18–20). Each of the three orders of priest (v. 18; 2 Kgs 23:4) is represented (the chief priest [kōhēn hārō'š] is the 'high priest' [hakkōhēn haggādôl] of 22:4; 23:4). With them are select city officials involved in military and advisory capacities, a scribe whose role in wartime has expanded to include the mustering of troops, and a representative selection of sixty enfranchised Judahites. The worst is realized as they are presented to Nebuchadnezzar in Riblah, and summarily slaughtered. Those left in the land are thus warned of Babylon's power against any who rebel.

With these executions Judah is 'exiled from its land' (wayyigel mē'al 'admātô). The identical phrase marks the end of Judah's northern sister (2 Kgs 17:23). Both nations sinned against YHWH, disregarding his repeated warnings. Now both suffer the same fate as YHWH draws down upon each the ultimate punishment under the deuteronomic covenant (Deut. 28). The magnitude of the tragedy is overwhelming.

A final vignette closes the chapter on the fall of Jerusalem (vv. 22–26). The events are narrated in greater detail in Jer. 40:7 – 41:18. Those who remain in the land are left under the administration of Gedaliah, a nobleman whose father served Josiah (2 Kgs 22:12; Jer. 26:24) and whose grandfather was Josiah's scribe (2 Kgs 22:8). Jeremiah's loyalty to Gedaliah (Jer. 40:1–6) suggests the two similarly supported the Babylonian incursion as YHWH's will and that both urged surrender. Such an individual would be a logical appointee within Babylon's new Judean regime.

Mizpah, undestroyed by Babylonian troops, becomes the new administrative centre. Judeans who had fled Babylonian forces, and scattered Judahite troops, gather to Mizpah when Gedaliah's appointment becomes known. Despite the general amnesty Gedaliah promises the troops, a coalition led by an otherwise-unknown member of the royal family murders him and his Judean and Babylonian supporters. Assuming such resistance against Babylonian power will result in reprisal and despite Jeremiah's assurance of continued leniency, the coalition flees to Egypt. Many of those who had gathered to Gedaliah also flee in fear. Taken against his will is Jeremiah (Jer. 42 – 43). In Egypt he continues to speak against their cultic sins and warns of coming judgment for their actions

(Jer. 43 – 44). The Kings account, however, relates none of these events in Egypt. The exodus is the great demonstration of YHWH's saving covenantal mercy (1 Kgs 6:1; 8:9, 16, 21, 51, 53; 9:9; 2 Kgs 17:7, 36; 21:15). By voluntarily returning to the land of slavery, the people reject that covenant and the Deuteronomist says no more of them.

25:27–30

After the removal of the monarchy, the destruction of the city and temple (vv. 8–17), the conclusion that Judah 'was exiled from its land' (v. 21) and the voluntary exile back to Egypt (v. 26) the notation regarding Jehoiachin comes as a surprising appendix.

Earlier the destruction of the city was recorded per Babylonian chronology (v. 8). Now events are measured by Judean chronology (v. 27), signalling the refocus on Judean concerns. The Babylonian king comes to the throne in 561 BC, Jehoiachin's thirty-seventh year of captivity. The amnesty given the captive king is a not-uncommon pardon granted by a Babylonian monarch as his reign commences (Jones 1984b: 649).

Throughout, the narrative places Jehoiachin in a positive light. Besides the Judean-based chronology, Jehoiachin is still referred to as the 'king of Judah' – despite his captivity, the narrative still places him in the royal role. Released from prison, Jehoiachin holds a position above that of all other captive kings at the Babylonian court. His needs are met by way of food, lodging and clothing. Though he is still a captive, the king's life improves (2 Chr. 3:17–18 notes seven sons are born to him in exile). Finally, the narrative remains open to the future: while Jehoiachin dies in captivity, no regnal formula closes his reign. One is invited to ponder the future of the Judean monarchy.

Explanation

Comparing the chapters in which the two kingdoms fall (2 Kgs 17, 25), one is struck by the absence in 2 Kgs 25 of any peroration on the southern kingdom's fate. The northern kingdom falls and a lengthy peroration gives detailed reasons for the nation's demise (2 Kgs 17). But for the southern kingdom no such peroration exists. The destruction of city and temple, the deportation of the remaining populace, and the sorry account of those who remain in the land is related baldly. No explanation justifies YHWH's actions; only a brief comment that the events occur because of YHWH's anger (24:20).

One might account for the narrative reticence by positing that the deep pain of the events (as witnessed by Lamentations) prevents reflection – the event remains too raw for such introspection. But this actually neglects the narrative; it provides such introspection although not in the extended style of the peroration of 2 Kgs 17. In v. 21 the narrative notes that 'Thus Judah was exiled from its land.' The phrase is identical to that found in 2 Kgs 17:23 and functions as a cross-reference. A careful reader is asked to refer back to the narrative of Israel's fall and the reasons for it. These same reasons stand behind Judah's fall and are encapsulated in this phrase. The narrative does, by this rhetorical technique, provide a full accounting for Judah's fall.

Besides this cross-referencing technique, these reasons are otherwise available to the reader. The reality is that the reasons for the fall of Judah and Jerusalem are found throughout the monarchic narrative, and even further back to the deuteronomic covenant. Given the history of God's people in the land and the certain conditions of the covenant by which obedience and disobedience have consequences (Deut. 27 – 28), the final end for the southern kingdom is not unexpected. More, in the light of the judgment experienced by the northern kingdom and the warnings directed towards Judah in the narration of the north's fall (2 Kgs 17; see comments there), the final end of the southern kingdom is anticipated. Finally, given the repeated calls for kings to lead the people in covenant obedience, and the prophetic words of judgment repeatedly levelled against disobedience (1 Kgs 9:6–9; 2 Kgs 21:10–15; cf. 23:26–27), the final end for the southern kingdom is certain.

These reasons are transparent to one who has read the whole narrative rightly – that is, with a listening heart. The message *is* there: YHWH enacts a covenant and calls kings and people to walk in it. This safeguards the precious relationship of a chosen people to a redeeming God. Now in exile, YHWH's repentant people ponder and retell their own history. They now see clearly the tragedy of broken covenant and disobedient king and people, and these realities colour the whole narrative. In these realities, related throughout the narrative, is the peroration on Judah's fall. The final chapter does not need, then, to belabour the reasons for the fall. Instead, it simply narrates the tragedy as the only outcome possible given the history's parameters.

However, though the narrative presents the terrible consequences of the nation's history without blinking, it does not rest only on the realities of punishment and despair. That is because the narrative has not only come to grips with the terms of the covenant and the punishments under the covenant, but it has come to grips with the God of the covenant. YHWH is a God who punishes sin and holds his people to covenant consequences. But he is also a God who has spoken promises of eternal covenants and thrones, and restoration for a repentant people.

Rather than bleak despair, it is these possibilities that the final verses of the narrative raise. In the change of Jehoiachin's fortunes, might the promise of an eternal dynasty granted David remain (2 Sam. 7:15–16; 1 Kgs 8:25–26)? Will the punishment levelled against the Davidic house truly not last for ever (1 Kgs 11:39)? Will the Davidic lamp (1 Kgs 11:36; 15:4; 2 Kgs 8:19) burn once again in Jerusalem? The openness of Jehoiachin's story to the future keeps these possibilities alive (Joo 2012).

The openness of the king's story leads to still greater possibilities. The prophetic word of complete destruction for Judah and Jerusalem came on account of the cultic sins of king and people (2 Kgs 21:14; 23:27). But if one should still hope for monarchic restoration, should not one also hope that destruction of city and nation is also not the last word? That is, could it be that the covenant given Abraham, Isaac and Jacob, YHWH's commitment to his people, and prophetic words of restoration are stronger than judgment, and restoring mercy stronger than punishment?

If the narrative has shown the prophetic word of judgment to be sure, then the prophetic word of restoration and hope must equally be sure. The openness of the final verses of 1 – 2 Kings invites those in exile, and every reader afterwards, to dare to believe in such words, and in the audacious grace of the God of such words.

BIBLIOGRAPHY

COMMENTARIES ON 1–2 KINGS

Burney, C. (1903), *Notes on the Hebrew Text of the Books of Kings*, Oxford: Clarendon.

Cogan, M. (2001), *I Kings*, AB 10, New York: Doubleday.

Cogan, M., and H. Tadmor (1988), *II Kings*, AB 11, New York: Doubleday.

Cohn, R. (2000), *2 Kings*, Berit Olam, Collegeville: Liturgical.

DeVries, S. (2003), *1 Kings*, 2nd ed., WBC, Nashville: Thomas Nelson.

Fritz, V. (2003), *1 & 2 Kings*, trans. A. Hagedorn, Minneapolis: Fortress (German original 1996, 1998).

Gray, J. (1970), *I & II Kings*, 2nd ed., Philadelphia: Westminster.

Hobbs, T. (1985), *2 Kings*, WBC, Waco: Word.

House, P. (1995), *1, 2 Kings*, NAC, Nashville: Broadman & Holman.

Jones, G. (1984a), *1 and 2 Kings*, vol. 1, NCBC, Basingstoke: Marshall, Morgan & Scott; Grand Rapids: Eerdmans.

—— (1984b), *1 and 2 Kings*, vol. 2, NCBC, Basingstoke: Marshall, Morgan & Scott; Grand Rapids: Eerdmans.

Keil, C. (1988), *I & II Kings, I & II Chronicles, Ezra, Nehemiah, Esther*, Grand Rapids: Eerdmans.

Konkel, A. (2006), *1 & 2 Kings*, NIVAC, Grand Rapids: Zondervan.

Leithart, P. (2006), *1 & 2 Kings*, Grand Rapids: Brazos.

Long, B. (1984), *1 Kings with an Introduction to Historical Literature*, FOTL, Grand Rapids: Eerdmans.

—— (1991), *2 Kings*, FOTL, Grand Rapids: Eerdmans.

Montgomery, J. (1951), *A Critical and Exegetical Commentary on the Books of Kings*, ed. H. S. Gehman, Edinburgh: T. & T. Clark.

Nelson, R. (1987), *First and Second Kings*, Interpretation, Louisville: John Knox.

Noth, M. (1968), *Könige*, BKAT 9.1, Neukirchen-Vluyn: Neukirchener Verlag.

Provan, I. (1995), *1 and 2 Kings*, NIBC, Peabody: Hendrickson.

Seow, C. (1999), 'The First and Second Books of Kings', *NIB* 3:3–295.

Stade, B., and F. Schwally (1904), *The Books of Kings*, trans. R. E. Brünnow, Baltimore: Johns Hopkins University Press.

Sweeney, M. (2007), *I & II Kings*, OTL, Louisville: Westminster John Knox.

Walsh, J. (1996), *1 Kings*, Berit Olam, Collegeville: Liturgical.

Würthwein, E. (1977), *Das erste Buch der Könige: Kapitel 1–16*, Göttingen: Vandenhoeck & Ruprecht.

—— (1984), *Die Bücher der Könige*. Vol. 1: *Kön. 17–2. Kön. 25*, Göttingen: Vandenhoeck & Ruprecht.

OTHER WORKS

Abbott, N. (1941), 'Pre-Islamic Arab Queens', *AJSL* 58:1–22.

Aberbach, M., and L. Smolar (1967), 'Aaron, Jeroboam, and the Golden Calves', *JBL* 86:129–140.

——— (1969), 'Jeroboam's Rise to Power', *JBL* 88:69–72.

Ackerman, S. (1992), *Under Every Green Tree: Popular Religion in Sixth-Century Judah*, Atlanta: Scholars Press.

——— (1993), 'The Queen Mother and the Cult in Ancient Israel', *JBL* 112:385–401.

Ackroyd, P. (1984), 'The Biblical Interpretation of the Reigns of Ahaz and Hezekiah', in W. Barrick (ed.), *In the Shelter of Elyon: Essays on Ancient Palestinian Life and Literature in Honor of G. W. Ahlström*, JSOTSup 31, Sheffield: JSOT Press, 247–259.

Aharoni, Y. (1963), 'Tamar and the Roads to Elath', *IEJ* 13:30–42.

——— (1967), 'Forerunners of the Limes: Iron Age Fortresses in the Negev', *IEJ* 17:1–17.

——— (1979), *The Land of the Bible: A Historical Geography*, trans. A. F. Rainey, 2nd ed., Philadelphia: Westminster.

Ahlström, G. (1961), 'Der Prophet Nathan und der Tempelbau', *VT* 11:113–127.

——— (1993), *The History of Ancient Palestine*, Minneapolis: Fortress.

Albert Nakhai, B. (1994), 'What's a Bamah? How Sacred Space Functioned in Ancient Israel', *BAR* 20.3:19–29, 77–78.

Albright, W. (1952), 'Review of *A Critical Commentary on the Books of Kings* "The International Critical Commentary", by James A. Montgomery. New York: Scribner's, 1952. Pp. xlvii+575', *JBL* 71:245–253.

——— (1968), *Yahweh and the Gods of Canaan: An Historical Analysis of Two Contrasting Faiths*, Garden City: Doubleday.

Alfrink, B. (1943), 'L'Expression נֶאֱסַף אֶל־עַמָּיו', *OtSt* 5:118–131.

Alt, A. (1953a), 'Israels Gaue unter Salomo', in *Kleine Schriften zur Geschichte des Volkes Israel*, vol. 2, Munich: C. H. Beck'sche, 76–89.

——— (1953b), 'Die Weisheit Salomos', in *Kleine Schriften zur Geschichte des Volkes Israel*, vol. 2, Munich: C. H. Beck'sche, 90–99.

——— (1959), 'Menschen ohne Namen', in *Kleine Schriften zur Geschichte des Volkes Israel*, vol. 3, Munich: C. H. Beck'sche, 198–213.

——— (1966), 'The Monarchy in the Kingdoms of Israel and Judah', in *Essays on Old Testament History and Religion*, trans. R. A. Wilson, Oxford: Basil Blackwell, 239–259.

Alter, R. (1981), *The Art of Biblical Narrative*, New York: Basic.

Amit, Y. (2001a), *Reading Biblical Narratives*, Minneapolis: Fortress.

——— (2001b) 'The Shunammite, the Shulamite and the Professor Between Midrash and Midrash', *JSOT* 93:77–91.

——— (2003), 'A Prophet Tested: Elisha, the Great Woman of Shunem, and the Story's Double Message', *BI* 11:279–294.

Andersen, F. (1966), 'The Socio-Juridical Background of the Naboth Incident', *JBL* 85:46–57.

Anderson, J. (2012), 'A Narrative Reading of Solomon's Execution of Joab in 1 Kings 1–2: Letting Story Interpret Story', *JESOT* 1:43–62.

Andreasen, N. (1983), 'The Role of the Queen Mother in Israelite Society', *CBQ* 45:179–194.

Angel, H. (2005), 'When God's Will Can and Cannot Be Altered: The Relationship Between the Balaam Narrative and I Kings 13', *JBQ* 33:31–39.

—— (2007), 'Hopping Between Two Opinions: Understanding the Biblical Portrait of Ahab', *JBQ* 35:3–10.

Ap-Thomas, D. (1960), 'Elijah on Mount Carmel', *PEQ* 92:146–155.

—— (1970), 'All the King's Horses?', in J. Durham (ed.), *Proclamation and Presence: Old Testament Essays in Honour of Gwynne Henton Davies*, London: SCM, 135–151.

Arnold, P. (1992a), 'Geba', *ABD* 2:921–922.

—— (1992b), 'Mizpah', *ABD* 4:879–881.

—— (1992c), 'Ramah', *ABD* 5:613–614.

—— (1992d), 'Ramoth-gilead (Place)', *ABD* 5:620–621.

Ash, P. (1995), 'Solomon's? District? List?', *JSOT* 67:67–86.

—— (1998), 'Jeroboam I and the Deuteronomistic Historian's Ideology of the Founder', *CBQ* 60:16–24.

Aster, S. (2008), '"They Feared God" / "They Did Not Fear God": On the Use of *yĕrē' YHWH* and *yārē' 'et YHWH* in 2 Kings 17:24–41', in C. Cohen et al. (eds.), *Birkat Shalom: Studies in the Bible, Ancient Near Eastern Literature, and Postbiblical Judaism Presented to Shalom M. Paul on the Occasion of His Seventieth Birthday*, vol. 1, Winona Lake: Eisenbrauns, 135–141.

Astour, M. (1962), 'Hittites', *IDBSup* 411–413.

Asurmendi, J. (2005), 'Elisée et la Guerre. 2 R 3:4–27', *BI* 13:1–12.

Aucker, W. (2007), 'A Prophet in King's Clothes: Kingly and Divine Re-Presentation in 2 Kings 4 and 5', in R. Rezetko (ed.), *Reflection and Refraction: Studies in Biblical Historiography*, VTSup 113, Leiden: Brill, 1–25.

Auld, G. (2000), 'Prophets Shared – but Recycled', in T. Römer (ed.), *The Future of the Deuteronomistic History*, Louven: Peeters, 19–28.

Avalos, H. (1992a), 'Arpad (Place)', *ABD* 1:401.

—— (1992b), 'Ivvah (Place)', *ABD* 3:587–588.

—— (1992c), 'Sepharvaim (Place)', *ABD* 5:1090.

Avigad, N. (1993), 'Samaria (City)', *NEAEHL* 4:1300–1310.

Axskjöld, C. (1998), *Aram as the Enemy Friend: The Ideological Role of Aram in the Composition of Genesis–2 Kings*, ConBOT 45, Stockholm: Almqvist & Wiksell International.

Baker, D. (1992a), 'Ophir', *ABD* 5:26–27.

—— (1992b), 'Tarshish (Place)', *ABD* 6:331–333.

Balentine, S. (1999), *The Torah's Vision of Worship*, Minneapolis: Fortress.

Ball, E. (1977a), 'The Co-Regency of David and Solomon (1 Kings 1)', *VT* 27:268–279.

—— (1977b), 'A Note on I Kings XXII. 28', *JTS* 28:90–94.

Barclay Burns, J. (1991), 'Solomon's Egyptian Horses and Exotic Wives', *Forum* 7:29–44.

Barnett, R. (1935), 'The Nimrud Ivories and the Art of the Phoenicians', *Iraq* 2:179–210.

Barré, L. (1988), *The Rhetoric of Political Persuasion: The Narrative Artistry and Political Intentions of 2 Kings 9–11*, Washington, D.C.: Catholic Biblical Association of America.

Barré, M. (1992), 'Treaties in the ANE', *ABD* 6:653–656.

Barrick, W. (1985), 'Elisha and the Magic Bow: A Note on 2 Kings XIII:15–17', *VT* 35:355–363.

—— (2000), 'Dynastic Politics, Priestly Succession, and Josiah's Eighth Year', *ZAW* 112:564–582.

—— (2001), 'Another Shaking of Jehoshaphat's Family Tree: Jehoram and Ahaziah Once Again', *VT* 51:9–25.

Barth, K. (1957), *Church Dogmatics* II/2, trans. and ed. G. Bromiley, T. & T. Clark: Edinburgh; trans. of *Die kirchliche Dogmatik* II/2, Zurich: Evangelischer Verlag, 1946.

Bartlett, J. (1983), 'The "United" Campaign Against Moab in 2 Kings 3:4–27', in J. Sawyer (ed.), *Midian, Moab and Edom: The History and Archaeology of Late Bronze and Iron Age Jordan and North-West Arabia*, JSOTSup 24, Sheffield: JSOT Press, 135–146.

Battenfield, J. (1988), 'YHWH's Refutation of the Baal Myth Through the Actions of Elijah and Elisha', in A. Gileadi (ed.), *Israel's Apostasy and Restoration: Essays in Honor of Roland K. Harrison*, Grand Rapids: Baker, 19–37.

Beck, J. (2003), 'Geography as Irony: The Narrative-Geographical Shaping of Elijah's Duel with the Prophets of Baal (1 Kings 18)', *SJOT* 17:291–302.

Becking, B. (1997), 'From Apostasy to Destruction: A Josianic View on the Fall of Samaria (2 Kings 17, 21–23)', in M. Vervenne (ed.), *Deuteronomy and Deuteronomic Literature: Festschrift C. H. W. Brekelmans*, Leuven: Leuven University Press; Peeters, 279–297.

—— (2000), 'From Exodus to Exile: 2 Kgs 17, 7–20 in the Context of Its Co-Text', in G. Galil (ed.), *Studies in Historical Geography and Biblical Historiography*, Leiden: Brill, 215–231.

—— (2007), *From David to Gedaliah: The Book of Kings as Story and History*, OBO 228, Fribourg: Academic; Göttingen: Vandenhoeck & Ruprecht.

Beek, G. van (1962), 'Ophir', *IDB* 3:605–606.

Begg, C. (1985), 'Unifying Factors in 2 Kings 1:2–17a', *JSOT* 32:75–86.

—— (1989), '"This Thing I Cannot Do" (1 Kgs 20,9)', *SJOT* 2:23–27.

Beitzel, B. (1985), *The Moody Atlas of Bible Lands*, Chicago: Moody.

Ben-Barak, Z. (1991), 'The Status and Right of the Gᵉbîrâ', *JBL* 110:23–34.

Benjamin, D. (1991), 'The Elijah Stories', in Paul Chandler (ed.), *The Land of Carmel: Essays in Honor of Joachim Smet, O. Carm.*, Rome: Institutum Carmelitanum, 27–41.

Bennett, B. (1972), 'The Search for Israelite Gilgal', *PEQ* 104:111–122.

Ben Zvi, E. (1991a), 'The Account of the Reign of Manasseh in II Reg 21,1–18 and the Redactional History of the Book of Kings', *ZAW* 103:355–374.

—— (1991b), 'Once the Lamp Has Been Kindled . . . A Reconsideration of the Meaning of the MT *Nîr* in 1 Kgs 11:36; 15:4; 2 Kgs 8:19 and 2 Chr 21:7', *ABR* 39:19–30.

—— (2008), 'Imagining Josiah's Book and the Implications of Imagining it in early Persian Yehud', in I. Kottsieper (ed.), *Berührungspunkte: Studien zur Sozial- und Religionsgeschichte Israels und seiner Umwelt: Festschrift für Rainer Albertz zu seinem 65. Geburtstag*, Münster: Ugarit-Verlag, 193–212.

Bergen, W. (1992), 'The Prophetic Alternative: Elisha and the Israelite Monarchy', in R. Coote (ed.), *Elijah and Elisha in Socioliterary Perspective*, Atlanta: Scholars Press, 127–137.

Berlejung, A. (2009), 'Twisting Traditions: Programmatic Absence-Theology for the Northern Kingdom in 1 Kgs 12:26–33 (The "Sin of Jeroboam")', *JNSL* 35:1–42.

Berlin, A. (1982), 'Characterization in Biblical Narrative: David's Wives', *JSOT* 23:69–85.

Berlyn, P. (2002), 'The Wrath of Moab', *JBQ* 30:216–26.

—— (2005), 'The Rise of the House of Omri', *JBQ* 33:223–230.

Betylon, J. (1992) 'Coinage', *ABD* 1:1076–1089.

Beuken, W. (1989), 'No Wise King Without a Wise Woman (I Kings iii 16–28)', in *New Avenues in the Study of the Old Testament: A Collection of Old Testament Studies Published on the Occasion of the Fiftieth Anniversary of the Oudtestamentisch Werkgezelschap and the Retirement of Prof. Dr. M. J. Mulder*, Leiden: Brill, 1–10.

Biram, A. (1992), 'Dan', *ABD* 2:12–17.

Bird, P. (1974), 'Images of Women in the Old Testament', in R. R. Ruether (ed.), *Religion and Sexism: Images of Woman in the Jewish and Christian Traditions*, New York: Simon & Schuster, 41–88.

—— (1995), 'The End of the Male Cult Prostitute: A Literary-Historical and Sociological Analysis of Hebrew *Qādēš–Qĕdēšîm*', in J. Emerton (ed.), *Congress Volume*, Leiden: Brill, 37–80.

Blake, I. (1967), 'Jericho (Ain es-Sultan): Joshua's Curse and Elisha's Miracle – One Possible Explanation', *PEQ* 99:86–97.

Blank, S. (1950–51), 'The Curse, Blasphemy, The Spell, and The Oath', *HUCA* 23:73–95.

Bloch-Smith, E. (1994), '"Who Is the King of Glory?" Solomon's Temple and Its Symbolism', in M. Coogan (ed.), *Scripture and Other Artifacts: Essays on the Bible and Archaeology in Honor of Philip J. King*, Louisville: Westminster John Knox, 18–31.

Block, D. (2001), Review of 'Jeremiah's and Ezekiel's Sign-Acts' by Kelvin Friebel, in *JETS* 44:729–731.

—— (2005), 'What Has Delphi to Do with Samaria? Ambiguity and Delusion in Israelite Prophecy', in P. Bienkowski (ed.), *Writing and Ancient Near Eastern Society: Papers in Honour of Alan R. Millard*, New York: T. & T. Clark, 189–216.

Boda, M. (2009), *A Severe Mercy: Sin and Its Remedy in the Old Testament*, Winona Lake: Eisenbrauns.

Bodner, K. (2003), 'The Locutions of 1 Kings 22:28: A New Proposal', *JBL* 122:533–546.

Boling, R., and E. Campbell (1987), 'Jeroboam and Rehoboam at Shechem', in *Archaeology and Biblical Interpretation*, Atlanta: John Knox, 259–272.

Boogaart, T. (1999–2000), 'Elisha's Prayer: O Lord, Open Their Eyes', *RefR* 53:128–143.

Borowski, O. (1995), 'Hezekiah's Reforms and the Revolt Against Assyria', *BA* 58:148–155.

Bosworth, D. (2002), 'Revisiting Karl Barth's Exegesis of 1 Kings 13', *BI* 10:360–383.

Bowen, N. (2001), 'The Quest for the Historical *Gêbîrâ*', *CBQ* 64:597–618.

Bowman, R. (1962), 'Ben-hadad', *IDB* 1:381–382.

Brandfon, F., and D. Manor (1992), 'Beth-shemesh', *ABD* 1:696–698.

Brettler, M. (1989), 'Ideology, History and Theology in 2 Kings XVII 7–23', *VT* 39:268–282.

—— (1991), 'The Structure of 1 Kings 1–11', *JSOT* 49:87–97.

Briend, J. (1995), 'Du Message au Messager. Remarques sur 1 Rois xiii', in J. Emerton (ed.), *Congress Volume Paris 1992*, VTSup 61, Leiden: Brill, 13–24.

Bright, J. (2000), *A History of Israel*, 4th ed., Louisville: Westminster John Knox.

Brodsky, H. (1992), 'Bethel', *ABD* 1:710–712.

Bronner, L. (1968), *The Stories of Elijah and Elisha as Polemics Against Baal Worship*, Leiden: Brill.

Brooks, B. (1941), 'Fertility Cult Functionaries in the Old Testament', *JBL* 60:227–253.

Brueggemann, W. (1972), 'From Dust to Kingship', *ZAW* 84:1–18.

—— (1987), 'The Embarrassing Footnote', *ThTo* 44:5–14.

—— (2001), 'A Brief Moment for a One-Person Remnant (2 Kings 5:2–3)', *BTB* 31:53–59.

—— (2005), *Solomon: Israel's Ironic Icon of Human Achievement*, Columbia, S.C.: University of South Carolina.

—— (2006), 'A Culture of Life and the Politics of Death', *Journal for Preachers* 29:16–21.

Buccellati, G. (1967), *Cities and Nations of Ancient Syria: An Essay on Political Institutions with Special Reference to the Israelite Kingdoms*, Rome: University of Rome.

Buhl, M. (1992), 'Hamath (Place)', *ABD* 3:33–36.

Burnett, J. (2006), 'Forty-Two Songs for Elohim: An Ancient Near Eastern Organizing Principle in the Shaping of the Elohistic Psalter', *JSOT* 31:81–101.

—— (2010), '"Going Down" to Bethel: Elijah and Elisha in the Theological Geography of the Deuteronomistic History', *JBL* 129:281–297.

Burns, J. (1990), 'Why Did the Besieging Army Withdraw? (II Reg 3,27)', *ZAW* 102:187–194.

Burnside, J. (2010), 'Flight of the Fugitives: Rethinking the Relationship Between Biblical Law (Exodus 21:12–14) and the Davidic Succession Narrative (1 Kings 1–2)', *JBL* 129:418–431.

Burrows, M. (1962), 'Jerusalem', *IDB* 2:843–866.

Butler, S. (1998), *Mesopotamian Conceptions of Dreams and Dream Rituals*, Münster: Ugarit-Verlag.

Camp, C. (2000), *Wise, Strange and Holy: The Strange Woman and the Making of the Bible*, JSOTSup 320, Sheffield: Sheffield Academic Press.

Campbell, A. (1986), *Of Prophets and Kings: A Late Ninth-Century Document '1 Samuel 1–2 Kings 10'*, CBQMS 17, Washington, D.C.: Catholic Biblical Association of America.

Carasik, M. (2000), 'The Limits of Omniscience', *JBL* 119:221–232.

Carroll, R. (1969), 'The Elijah–Elisha Sagas: Some Remarks on Prophetic Succession in Ancient Israel', *VT* 19:400–415.

Case, R. (1988), 'Rehoboam: A Study in Failed Leadership', *Presb* 14:55–77.

Chapman, R. (2009), 'Putting Sheshonq I in His Place', *PEQ* 141:4–17.

Childs, B. (1963), 'A Study of the Formula "Until This Day"', *JBL* 82:279–292.

—— (1967), *Isaiah and the Assyrian Crisis*, SBT 2.3, London: SCM.

—— (1974), *The Book of Exodus*, OTL, Louisville: Westminster.

—— (1979), *The Introduction to the Old Testament as Scripture*, Philadelphia: Fortress.

—— (1980), 'On Reading the Elijah Narratives', *Int* 34:128–137.

Chisholm, R. (1998), 'Does God Deceive?', *BSac* 155:11–28.

—— (2010), 'When Prophecy Appears to Fail, Check Your Hermeneutic', *JETS* 53:561–577.

Christiansen, D. (1989), 'The Identity of "King So" in Egypt (2 Kings XVII 4)', *VT* 39:140–153.

Christidès, V. (1970), 'L'Énigme d'Ophir', *RB* 77:240–247.

Chun, S. (2006), 'Whose Cloak Did Ahijah Seize and Tear? A Note on 1 Kings xi 29–30', *VT* 56:268–274.

Clements, R. (1988), 'Solomon and the Origins of Wisdom in Israel', *PRSt* 15:23–35.

—— (2004), 'קטר', *TDOT* 13:9–16.

Cochell, T. (2005), 'The Religious Establishments of Jeroboam I', *Stone-Campbell Journal* 8:85–97.

Cody, A. (1970), 'A New Inscription from Tell āl-Rimah and King Jehoash of Israel', *CBQ* 32:325–340.

Cogan, M. (1973), 'Tyre and Tiglath-Pileser III: Chronological Note', *JCS* 25:96–99.
—— (1974), *Imperialism and Religion: Assyria, Judah and Israel in the Eighth and Seventh Centuries B. C. E.*, Missoula: Scholars Press.
—— (1978), 'Israel in Exile – The View of a Josianic Historian', *JBL* 97:40–44.
—— (1983), '"Ripping Open Pregnant Women" in Light of an Assyrian Analogue', *JAOS* 103:755–757.
—— (1988), 'For We, Like You, Worship Your God: Three Biblical Portrayals of Samaritan Origins', *VT* 38:286–292.
—— (1992), 'Chronology', *ABD* 1:1002–1011.
Coggin, R. (1991), 'On Kings and Disguises', *JSOT* 50:55–62.
Cohen, G. (1980), '*śiaḥ*', *TWOT* 2:876.
Cohen, R. (1979), 'The Iron Age Fortresses in the Central Negev', *BASOR* 236:61–79.
Cohn, R. (1982), 'The Literary Logic of 1 Kings 17–19', *JBL* 101:333–350.
—— (1985a), 'Convention and Creativity in the Book of Kings: The Case of the Dying Monarch', *CBQ* 47:603–616.
—— (1985b), 'Literary Technique in the Jeroboam Narrative', *ZAW* 97:23–35.
—— (1989), 'Reading in Three Dimensions: The Imperative of Biblical Narrative', *Religion and Intellectual Life* 6:161–172.
Conroy, C. (1996), 'Hiel Between Ahab and Elijah–Elisha: 1 Kgs 16,34 in Its Immediate Literary Context', *Bib* 77:210–218.
Coomber, M. (2007), 'Exegetical Notes on 1 Kings 17:8–16: The Widow of Zarephath', *ExpTim* 118:389–390.
Corney, R. (1962), 'Libnah', *IDB* 3:123.
Craigie, P. (1976), *The Book of Deuteronomy*, NICOT, Grand Rapids: Eerdmans.
Crenshaw, J. (1971), *Prophetic Conflict: Its Effect upon Israelite Religion*, Berlin: de Gruyter.
Cross, F. M. (1972), 'The Stele Dedicated to Melcarth by Ben-Hadad of Damascus', *BASOR* 205:36–42.
—— (1973), *Canaanite Myth and Hebrew Epic: Essays in the History of the Religion of Israel*, Cambridge, Mass.: Harvard University Press.
Cross, F. M., and G. Wright (1956), 'The Boundary and Province Lists of the Kingdom of Judah', *JBL* 75:202–226.
Crown, A. (1974–5), 'Once Again 1 Kings 10:26–29', *AbrN* 15:35–38.
Curtis, A. (1990), 'Some Observations on "Bull" Terminology in the Ugaritic Texts and the Old Testament', in A. van der Woude (ed.), *In Quest of the Past: Studies on Israelite Religion, Literature and Prophetism*, Leiden: Brill, 17–31.
Cushman, B. (2006), 'The Politics of the Royal Harem and the Case of Bat-Sheba', *JSOT* 30:327–343.
Dafni, E. (2000), 'רוח שקר und falsche Prophetie in I Reg 22', *ZAW* 112:365–385.

Dalley, S. (2004), 'Recent Evidence from Assyrian Sources for Judaean History from Uzziah to Manasseh', *JSOT* 28:387–401.

Davies, G. (1974), 'The Wilderness Itineraries: A Comparative Study', *TynB* 25:46–81.

Day, J. (1989), *Molech: A God of Human Sacrifice in the Old Testament*, Cambridge: Cambridge University Press.

—— (1992a), 'Asherah (Deity)', *ABD* 1:483–487.

—— (1992b), 'Baal (Deity)', *ABD* 1:545–549.

—— (1992c), 'The Problem of "So, King of Egypt" in 2 Kings XVII 4', *VT* 42:289–301.

Day, J. (ed.) (1998), *King and Messiah in Israel and the Ancient Near East: Proceedings of the Oxford Old Testament Seminar*, JSOTSup 270, Sheffield: Sheffield Academic Press.

Dearman, J. A. (1983), 'The Melqart Stele and the Ben Hadads of Damascus: Two Studies', *PEQ* 115:95–101.

—— (1992), 'Mesha Stele', *ABD* 4:708–709.

Dearman, J. A., and M. P. Graham (eds.) (2001), *The Land That I Will Show You: Essays on the History and Archaeology of the Ancient Near East in Honour of J. Maxwell Miller*, JSOTSup 343, Sheffield: Sheffield Academic Press.

Deboys, D. (1991), '1 Kings XIII – A "New Criterion" Reconsidered', *VT* 41:210–212.

deClaissé-Walford, N. (1997), *Reading from the Beginning: The Shaping of the Hebrew Psalter*, Macon, Ga.: Mercer University Press.

Delamarter, S. (2004), 'The Death of Josiah in Scripture and Tradition: Wrestling with the Problem of Evil?', *VT* 54:29–60.

Delcor, M. (1962), 'Le Trésor de la Maison de Yahweh des Origines a l'Exil', *VT* 12:353–377.

Deurloo, K. (1989), 'The King's Wisdom in Judgement. Narration as Example (I Kings iii)', in *New Avenues in the Study of the Old Testament: A Collection of Old Testament Studies Published on the Occasion of the Fiftieth Anniversary of the Oudtestamentisch Werkgezelschap and the Retirement of Prof. Dr. M. J. Mulder*, Leiden: Brill, 11–21.

Dever, W. (1992), 'Dothan (Place)', *ABD* 2:226–227.

DeVries, S. (1962a), 'Calendar', *IDB* 1:483–488.

—— (1962b), 'Chronology of the OT', *IDB* 1:580–599.

—— (1962c), 'Chronology, OT', *IDBSup* 160–166.

—— (1975), *Yesterday, Today and Tomorrow: Time and History in the Old Testament*, Grand Rapids: Eerdmans.

—— (1978), *Prophet Against Prophet: The Role of the Micaiah Narrative 'I Kings 22' in the Development of Early Prophetic Tradition*, Grand Rapids: Eerdmans.

—— (1979), 'A Reply to G. Gerleman on *malkê ḥesed* in 1 Kings XX 31', *VT* 29:359–362.

—— (1989), 'The Three Comparisons in 1 Kings XXII 4B and Its Parallel and 2 Kings III 7B', *VT* 39:283–306.

Dietrich, W. (1972), *Prophetie und Geschichte; eine redaktionsgeschichtliche Untersuchung zum deuteronomistischen Geschichtswerk*, Göttingen: Vandenhoeck & Ruprecht.

Dijk-Hemmes, F. van (1994), 'The Great Woman of Shunem and The Man of God: A Dual Interpretation of 2 Kings 4:8–37', in A. Brenner (ed.), *A Feminist Companion to Samuel and Kings*, Sheffield: Sheffield Academic Press, 218–230.

Dion, P. (1999), 'The Horned Prophet (1 Kings XXII 11)', *VT* 49:259–261.

Domeris, W. (1984), 'The City of David: A Test Case for Biblical Archaeology', *JTSA* 48:21–29.

Donner, H. (1977a), 'The Separate States of Israel and Judah', in J. Hayes and J. Miller (eds.), *Israelite and Judaean History*, OTL, Philadelphia: Westminster, 381–434.

—— (1977b), 'The Syro-Ephraimite War and the End of the Kingdom of Israel', in J. Hayes and J. Miller (eds.), *Israelite and Judaean History*, OTL, Philadelphia: Westminster, 421–434.

Dorn, C. (2009), 'The Way of God in the World: The Drama of 2 Kings 6:8–23', in J. Ellens (ed.), *Probing the Frontiers of Biblical Studies*, Eugene: Pickwick, 9–20.

Dozeman, T. (1982), 'The Way of the Man of God from Judah: True and False Prophecy in the Pre-Deuteronomic Legend of 1 Kings 13', *CBQ* 44:379–393.

Driver, G. (1925), 'The Modern Study of the Hebrew Language', in A. Peake (ed.), *The People and the Book*, Oxford: Clarendon, 73–120.

—— (1936), 'Supposed Arabisms in the Old Testament', *JBL* 55:101–120.

—— (1937), 'Linguistic and Textual Problems: Isaiah 1–39', *JTS* 38:36–50.

—— (1966), 'Forgotten Hebrew Idioms', *ZAW* 78:1–7.

Driver, S. (1892), *A Treatise on the Use of the Tenses in Hebrew and Some Other Syntactical Questions*, Oxford: Clarendon.

Dubovský, P. (2006), 'Tiglath-pileser III's Campaigns in 734–732 B. C.: Historical Background of Isa 7; 2 Kgs 15–16 and 2 Chr 27–28', *Bib* 87:153–170.

Durham, J. (1983), 'שָׁלוֹם and the Presence of God', in J. Durham and R. Porter (eds.), *Proclamation and Presence: Old Testament Essays in Honour of Gwynne Henton Davies*, Macon: Mercer University Press, 272–293.

Dutcher-Walls, P. (1996), *Narrative Art, Political Rhetoric: The Case of Athaliah and Joash*, JSOTSup 209, Sheffield: Sheffield Academic Press.

—— (2002), 'The Circumscription of the King: Deuteronomy 17:16–17 in Its Ancient Social Context', *JBL* 121:601–616.

—— (2004), *Jezebel: Portraits of a Queen*, Interfaces, Collegeville: Liturgical.

Dyck, E. (1992), 'Shalishah (Place)', *ABD* 5:1153.

Eaton, M. (1994), 'Some Instances of Flyting in the Hebrew Bible', *JSOT* 61:3–14.

Edelman, D. (1985), 'The Meaning of *Qiṭṭēr*', *VT* 35:395–404.

–––––– (1992), 'Abel-meholah', *ABD* 1:11–12.

–––––– (1995), 'Solomon's Adversaries Hadad, Rezon and Jeroboam: A Trio of "Bad Guy" Characters Illustrating the Theology of Immediate Retribution', in S. Holloway and L. Handy (eds.), *The Pitcher Is Broken: Memorial Essays for Gösta W. Ahlström*, JSOTSup 190, Sheffield: Sheffield Academic Press, 166–191.

–––––– (2008), 'Hezekiah's Alleged Cultic Centralization', *JSOT* 32:395–434.

Ehrlich, C. (1992), 'Carites', *ABD* 1:872.

Eissfeldt, O. (1965), *The Old Testament: An Introduction*, trans. Peter R. Ackroyd, Oxford: Basil Blackwell.

Emerton, J. (1994), '"The High Places of the Gates" in 2 Kings XXIII 8', *VT* 44:455–467.

–––––– (1997), 'The House of Baal in 1 Kings XVI 32', *VT* 47:293–300.

Emery, A. (2003a), '*ḤĒREM*', *DOTP* 1:383–387.

–––––– (2003b) 'Warfare', *DOTP* 1:877–881.

Epp-Tiessen, D. (2006), '1 Kings 19: The Renewal of Elijah', *Direction* 35:33–43.

Eslinger, L. (1989), *Into the Hands of the Living God*, Sheffield: Almond.

Etz, D. (1996), 'The Genealogical Relationships of Jehoram and Ahaziah, and of Ahaz and Hezekiah, Kings of Judah', *JSOT* 71:39–53.

Evans, C. (1983), 'Naram-Sin and Jeroboam: The Archetypal *Unheilsherrscher* in Mesopotamian and Biblical Historiography', in W. Hallo (ed.), *Scripture in Context II: More Essays on the Comparative Method*, Winona Lake: Eisenbrauns, 97–125.

–––––– (1995), 'Cult Images, Royal Policies and the Origins of Aniconism', in S. Holloway and L. Handy (eds.), *The Pitcher Is Broken: Memorial Essays for Gösta W. Ahlström*, JSOTSup 190, Sheffield: Sheffield Academic Press, 192–212.

–––––– (2009), 'The Hezekiah–Sennacherib Narrative as Polyphonic Text', *JSOT* 33:335–358.

Evans, D. (1966), 'Rehoboam's Advisers at Shechem, and Political Institutions in Israel and Sumer', *JNES* 25:273–279.

Fensham, F. (1967), 'A Possible Explanation of the Name Baal-Zebub of Ekron', *ZAW* 79:361–364.

–––––– (1980), 'A Few Observations on the Polarisation Between Yahweh and Baal in I Kings 17–19', *ZAW* 92:227–236.

Ferris, P. (1992), 'Sorek, Valley of', *ABD* 6:159–160.

Fewell, D. (1986), 'Sennacherib's Defeat: Words at War in 2 Kings 18:18–19:37', *JSOT* 34:79–90.

Fewell, D., and D. Gunn (1993), *Gender, Power, and Promise: The Subject of the Bible's First Story*, Nashville: Abingdon.

Finkelstein, I., and N. Silberman (2006), 'Temple and Dynasty: Hezekiah, the Remaking of Judah and the Rise of the Pan-Israelite Ideology', *JSOT* 30:259–285.

Fisher, E. (1976), 'Cultic Prostitution in the Ancient Near East? A Reassessment', *BTB* 6:225–236.

Fokkelman, J. (1981), *Narrative Art and Poetry in the Books of Samuel*. Vol. 1: *King David*, Assen: Van Gorcum.

Fontaine, C. (1986), 'The Bearing of Wisdom on the Shape of 2 Samuel 11–12 and 1 Kings 3', *JSOT* 34:61–77.

Fowler, M. (1981), 'Cultic Continuity at Tirzah? A Re-examination of the Archaeological Evidence', *PEQ* 113:27–31.

——— (1982), 'The Israelite *bāmâ*: A Question of Interpretation', *ZAW* 94:203–213.

Fox, E. (2002), 'The Translation of Elijah: Issues and Challenges', in A. Brenner (ed.), *Bible Translation on the Threshold of the Twenty-First Century: Authority, Reception, Culture and Religion*, JSOTSup 353, London: Sheffield, 156–169.

Fox, M. (1995), 'The Uses of Indeterminacy', in *Textual Determinacy, Part II*, Semeia 71, Atlanta: Scholars Press, 173–192.

Fox, N. (1996), 'Royal Officials and Court Families: A New Look at the ילדים (*yĕlādîm*) in 1 Kings 12', *BA* 59:225–232.

Frankel, R. (1992a), 'Aphek', *ABD* 1:275–277.

——— (1992b), 'Jotbah', *ABD* 3:1020.

Franklin, N. (2004), 'Samaria: from the Bedrock to the Omride Palace', *Levant* 36:189–202.

Freedman, D. (1964), 'Divine Commitment and Human Obligation', *Int* 18:419–431.

Fretheim, T. E. (1999), *First and Second Kings*, Louisville: Westminster John Knox.

Frick, F. (1971), 'The Rechabites Reconsidered', *JBL* 90:279–287.

——— (1976), 'Rechabites', *IDBSup* 726–728.

Friebel, K. (2001), 'A Hermeneutical Paradigm for Interpreting Prophetic Sign-Actions', *Did* 12:25–45.

Fried, L. (2002), 'The High Places (*bāmôt*) and the Reforms of Hezekiah and Josiah: An Archaeological Investigation', *JAOS* 122:437–465.

Frisch, A. (1988), 'Shemaiah the Prophet Versus King Rehoboam: Two Opposed Interpretations of the Schism (1 Kings XII 24–4)', *VT* 38:466–468.

——— (1991), 'ועניתם (I Reg 12,7): An Ambiguity and Its Function in the Context', *ZAW* 103:415–418.

——— (2000), 'Jeroboam and the Division of the Kingdom: Mapping Contrasting Biblical Accounts', *JANES* 27:15–29.

——— (2003), 'Three Syntactical Discontinuities in I Regum 9–11', *ZAW* 115:88–93.

Gal, Z. (1990), 'Khirbet Roš Zayit – Biblical Cabul: A Historical-Geographical Case', *BA* 53:88–97.

Galil, G. (2009), 'Israelite Exiles in Media: A New Look at ND 2443+', *VT* 59:71–79.

Galpaz, P. (1991), 'The Reign of Jeroboam and the Extent of Egyptian Influence', *BN* 60:13–19.

Gamberoni, J. (1997), 'מצבה', *TDOT* 8:483–494.

García-Treto, F. (1990), 'The Fall of the House: A Carnivalesque Reading of 2 Kings 9 and 10', *JSOT* 46:47–65.

Garsiel, M. (1991), 'Puns upon Names as a Literary Device in 1 Kings 1–2', *Bib* 72:378–386.

—— (2002), 'Revealing and Concealing as a Narrative Strategy in Solomon's Judgment (1 Kings 3:16–28)', *CBQ* 64:229–247.

Gass, E. (2012), 'New Moabite Inscriptions and Their Historical Relevance', *JNSL* 38:45–78.

Gaster, T. (1962), 'Sacrifices and Offerings, OT', *IDB* 4:147–159.

Gelb, I. (1962), 'Hittites', *IDB* 2:612–615.

Geller, M. (1976), 'A New Translation for 2 Kings XV 25', *VT* 26:374–377.

Geradon, B. de (1958), 'L'homme à l'image de Dieu: Approche nouvelle à la lumière de l'anthropologie du sens commun', *NRTh* 11:681–695.

Geraty, L. (1987), 'Archaeology and the Bible at Hezekiah's Lachish', *AUSS* 25:27–37.

Gibson, J. (1975), *Textbook of Syrian Semitic Inscriptions*. Vol. 2: *Aramaic Inscriptions*, Oxford: Clarendon.

Gileadi, A. (1988), 'The Davidic Covenant: A Theological Basis for Corporate Protection', in A. Gileadi (ed.), *Israel's Apostasy and Restoration: Essays in Honor of Roland K. Harrison*, Grand Rapids: Baker, 157–163.

Gillmayr-Bucher, S. (2007), '"She Came to Test Him with Hard Questions": Foreign Women and Their View on Israel', *BibInt* 15:135–150.

Glatt-Gilad, D. (1997), 'The Deuteronomistic Critique of Solomon: A Response to Marvin A. Sweeney', *JBL* 116:700–703.

Glueck, N. (1965), 'Ezion-geber', *BA* 28:70–87.

Glueck, N., and G. Pratico (1993), 'Kheleifeh, Tell El', *NEAEHL* 3:867–870.

Goldberg, J. (1999), 'Two Assyrian Campaigns Against Hezekiah and Later Eighth Century Biblical Chronology', *Bib* 80:360–390.

Goldenberg, R. (1982), 'The Problem of False Prophecy: Talmudic Interpretations of Jeremiah 28 and 1 Kings 22', in R. Polzin (ed.), *The Biblical Mosaic: Changing Perspectives*, Philadelphia: Fortress; Chico: Scholars Press, 87–103.

Good, E. (1962), 'Peace in the OT', *IDB* 3:704–706.

Gooding, D. (1965), 'The Septuagint's Version of Solomon's Misconduct', *VT* 15:325–335.

—— (1967), 'The Septuagint's Rival Versions of Jeroboam's Rise to Power', *VT* 17:173–189.

—— (1972), 'Jeroboam's Rise to Power: A Rejoinder', *JBL* 91:529–533.

Gordon, R. (1976), 'The Second Septuagint Account of Jeroboam: History or Midrash?', *VT* 25:368–393.

Görg, M. (1975), *Gott-König-Reden in Israel und Ägypten*, BWANT 105, Stuttgart: Kohlhammer.

Gowan, D. (1971), 'The Use of *ya'an* in Biblical Hebrew', *VT* 21:168–185.

Greenberg, M. (1959), 'The Biblical Concept of Asylum', *JBL* 78:125–132.

—— (1962), 'Avenger of Blood', *IDB* 1:321.

Greenfield, J. (1976), 'The Aramean God Rammān/Rimmōn', *IEJ* 26:195–198.

—— (1999), 'Hadad', *DDD* 377–382.

Gregory, R. (1990), 'Irony and the Unmasking of Elijah', in A. Hauser (ed.),
    From Carmel to Horeb: Elijah in Crisis, JSOTSup 85, Sheffield:
    Almond, 91–169.

Gressmann, H. (1907), 'Das salomonische Urteil', *Deutsche Rundschau*
    130:212–228.

Grisanti, M. (1999), 'The Davidic Covenant', *TMSJ* 10.2:233–250.

Groningen, G. van (1980), ''*am*. People, Nation', *TWOT* 2:676.

Gross, W. (1979), 'Lying Prophet and Disobedient Man of God in 1 Kings 13:
    Role Analysis as an Instrument of Theological Interpretation of an OT
    Narrative Text', *Semeia* 15:97–135.

Gunkel, H. (1987), *The Folktale in the Old Testament*, trans. M. Rutter,
    Sheffield: Almond.

Gunn, D. (1976), 'Traditional Composition in the "Succession Narrative"',
    VT 26:214–229.

—— (1978), *The Story of King David: Genre and Interpretation*, JSOTSup 6,
    Sheffield: JSOT.

Gunneweg, A. (1983), 'עם הארץ – A Semantic Revolution', *ZAW* 95:437–440.

Hafpórsson, S. (2006), *A Passing Power: An Examination of the Sources for the
    History of Aram-Damascus in the Second Half of the Ninth Century
    B. C.*, ConBOT 54, Stockholm: Almqvist & Wiksell.

Haldar, A. (1962), 'Hamath', *IDB* 2:516.

Hall, A. (2003), 'Prophetic Vulnerability and the Strange Goodness of God:
    A Reading of Numbers 22 and 1 Kings 17', *STRev* 46:340–348.

Hallo, W. (1960), 'From Qarqar to Carchemish: Assyria and Israel in the Light
    of New Discoveries', *BA* 23:34–61.

Halpern, B. (1976), 'Levitic Participation in the Reform Cult of Jeroboam I',
    JBL 95:31–42.

—— (1981), *The Constitution of the Monarchy in Israel*, Chico: Scholars Press.

—— (1994), 'The Stela from Dan: Epigraphic and Historical Considerations',
    BASOR 296:63–80.

—— (1998), 'Why Manasseh Is Blamed for the Babylonian Exile: The
    Evolution of a Biblical Tradition', *VT* 48:473–514.

—— (2001), *David's Secret Demons: Messiah, Murderer, Traitor, King*,
    Grand Rapids: Eerdmans.

Hamilton, J. (1994), 'Caught in the Nets of Prophecy? The Death of King
    Ahab and the Character of God', *CBQ* 56:649–663.

Handy, L. (1988), 'Hezekiah's Unlikely Reform', *ZAW* 100:111–115.

—— (1997), 'On the Dating and Dates of Solomon's Reign', in L. Handy
    (ed.), *The Age of Solomon: Scholarship at the Turn of the Millennium*,
    Leiden: Brill, 95–105.

Haran, M. (1967), 'The Rise and Decline of the Empire of Jeroboam ben Joash', *VT* 17:266–297.

———(1978), *Temples and Temple Service in Ancient Israel: An Inquiry into the Character of Cult Phenomena and the Historical Setting of the Priestly School*, Oxford: Clarendon.

———(1999), 'The Books of the Chronicles "Of the Kings of Judah" and "Of the Kings of Israel": What Sort of Books Were They?', *VT* 49:156–162.

Harris, G. (2005), 'Does God Deceive? The "Deluding Influence" of Second Thessalonians 2:11', *TMSJ* 16:73–93.

Harrison, R. (1962a), 'Leprosy', *IDB* 3:111–113.

———(1962b), 'Medicine', *IDB* 3:331–334.

Hart, S. (1986), 'Selaʿ: The Rock of Edom?', *PEQ* 118:91–95.

Harvey, D. (1962), 'Sheba, Queen of', *IDB* 4:311–312.

Hasel, M. (2002), 'The Destruction of Trees in the Moabite Campaign of 2 Kings 3:4–27: A Study in the Laws of Warfare', *AUSS* 40:197–206.

Hauer, Christian E. (1963), 'Who Was Zadok?', *JBL* 82:89–94.

Hauser, A. (1990), 'Yahweh Versus Death – the Real Struggle in 1 Kings 17–19', in A. Hauser (ed.), *From Carmel to Horeb: Elijah in Crisis*, JSOTSup 85, Sheffield: Almond, 9–89.

Hayes, J. (1987), 'Historical Reconstruction, Textual Emendation, and Biblical Translation: Some Examples from the RSV', *PRSt* 14:5–9.

Hayes, J., and J. Kuan (1991), 'The Final Years of Samaria (730–720 B. C.)', *Bib* 72:153–181.

Hays, J. (2003), 'Has the Narrator Come to Praise Solomon or to Bury Him? Narrative Subtlety in 1 Kings 1–11', *JSOT* 28:149–174.

Healey, J. (1992), 'Am Ha'arez', *ABD* 1:168–169.

Heaton, E. (1974), *Solomon's New Men: The Emergence of Ancient Israel as a National State*, London: Thames & Hudson.

Heider, G. (1992), 'Molech', *ABD* 4:895–898.

———(1999), 'Molech', *DDD* 581–585.

Heins, B. (1988), 'From Leprosy to Shalom and Back Again: A Discourse Analysis of 2 Kings 5', *Occasional Papers in Translation and Textlinguistics* 2:20–33.

Henige, D. (2007), 'Found but Not Lost: A Skeptical Note on the Document Discovered in the Temple Under Josiah', *JHS* 7:2–17.

Hens-Piazza, G. (1998), 'Forms of Violence and the Violence of Forms: Two Cannibal Mothers Before a King (2 Kings 6:24–33)', *JFSR* 14:91–104.

Henton Davies, G. (1962), 'High Place, Sanctuary', *IDB* 2:602–604.

Herrmann, S. (1953–4), 'Die Königsnovelle in Ägypten und Israel', *Wissenschaftliche Zeitschrift der Karl-Marx-Universität Leipzig* 3:51–62.

Herrmann, W. (1999), 'Baal', *DDD* 132–139.

Herzog, C., and M. Gichon (1997), *Battles of the Bible: A Military History of Ancient Israel*, London: Greenhill.

Hess, R. (1997), 'The Form and Structure of the Solomonic District List in
 1 Kings 4:7–19', in G. Young (ed.), *Crossing Boundaries and Linking
 Horizons: Studies in Honor of Michael C. Astour*, Bethesda: CDL,
 279–292.

—— (1999), 'Hezekiah and Sennacherib in 2 Kings 18–20', in R. Hess (ed.),
 Zion City of Our God, Grand Rapids: Eerdmans, 23–41.

—— (2005), *Song of Songs*, BCOT, Grand Rapids: Baker Academic.

Hillers, D. (1964), *Treaty-Curses and the Old Testament Prophets*, Rome:
 Pontifical Biblical Institute.

—— (1985), 'Analyzing the Abominable: Our Understanding of Canaanite
 Religion', *JQR* 75:253–269.

Hirth, V. (1989), '"Der Geist" in I Reg 22', *ZAW* 101:113–114.

Hobbs, T. (1984), '2 Kings 1 and 2: Their Unity and Purpose', *SR* 13:327–334.

—— (1993), 'Man, Woman, and Hospitality – 2 Kings 4:8–36', *BTB*
 23:91–100.

—— (2001), 'Hospitality in the First Testament and the "Teleological
 Fallacy"', *JSOT* 95:3–30.

Hoffner, H. (1967), 'Second Millennium Antecedents to the Hebrew *'ôb*', *JBL*
 86:385–401.

Høgenhaven, J. (1990), 'The Prophet Isaiah and Judaean Foreign Policy Under
 Ahaz and Hezekiah', *JNES* 49:351–354.

Holder, J. (1988), 'The Presuppositions, Accusations, and Threats of 1 Kings
 14:1–18', *JBL* 107:27–38.

Holladay, W. (1961), '"On Every High Hill and Under Every Green Tree"',
 VT 11:170–176.

Holmes, C. (2012), *Ethics in the Presence of Christ*, London: T. & T. Clark.

Hoop, R. de (1995), 'The Testament of David: A Response to W. T. Koopmans',
 VT 45:270–279.

Horn, S. (1967), 'Who Was Solomon's Egyptian Father-in-Law?', *BR*
 12:3–17.

—— (1986), 'Why the Moabite Stone Was Blown to Pieces', *BAR* 12:50–61.

House, P. (2005), 'Examining the Narratives of Old Testament Narrative: An
 Exploration in Biblical Theology', *WTJ* 67:229–245.

Houtman, C. (1996), 'Der Altar als Asylstätte im Alten Testament:
 Rechtsbestimmung (Ex. 21,12–14) und Praxis (I Reg. 1–2)', *RB*
 103:343–366.

Houwink ten Cate, P. (1992), 'Hittite History', *ABD* 3:219–225.

Huffmon, H. (2009), 'Rechab, Rechabites', *NIDB* 4:744–745.

Hunt, M. (1992a), 'Beth-eked (Place)', *ABD* 1:685.

—— (1992b), 'Jezreel (Place)', *ABD* 3:850.

Hurowitz, V. (1986), 'Another Fiscal Practice in the Ancient Near East: 2 Kings
 12:5–17 and a Letter to Esarhaddon (*LAS* 277)', *JNES* 45:289–294.

—— (1992), *I Have Built You an Exalted House: Temple Building in the Bible
 in Light of Mesopotamian and Northwest Semitic Writings*, JSOTSup
 115, Sheffield: JSOT Press.

——— (2004–5), Review of S. Richter, *The Deuteronomistic History and the Name Theology*, *JHS* 5:n.p.

Husser, J. (1999), *Dreams and Dream Narratives in the Biblical World*, trans. J. M. Munro, Sheffield: Sheffield Academic Press.

Huwiler, E. (1992), 'Shunem (Place)', *ABD* 5:1228–1229.

Ikeda, Y. (1982), 'Solomon's Trade in Horses and Chariots in Its International Setting', in T. Ishida (ed.), *Studies in the Period of David and Solomon and Other Essays. International Symposium for Biblical Studies, Tokyo, 1979*, Winona Lake: Eisenbrauns, 215–238.

Irvine, S. (2001), 'The Rise of the House of Jehu', in M. P. Graham (ed.), *The Land That I Will Show You: Essays in Honour of J. Maxwell Miller*, JSOTSup 343, Sheffield: Sheffield Academic Press, 105–119.

——— (2005), 'The Last Battle of Hadadezer', *JBL* 124:341–347.

Irwin, B. (2003), 'Yahweh's Suspension of Free Will in the Old Testament: Divine Immorality or Sign-Act?', *TynB* 54:55–62.

Ishida, T. (1977), *The Royal Dynasties in Ancient Israel: A Study on the Formation and Development of Royal-Dynastic Ideology*, Berlin: de Gruyter.

Jacobsen, T. (1962), 'Cuth, Cuthah', *IDB* 1:752.

Jenkins, A. (1976), 'Hezekiah's Fourteenth Year: A New Interpretation of 2 Kings xviii 13–xix 37', *VT* 26:284–298.

Jobling, D. (1992), '"Forced Labor": Solomon's Golden Age and the Question of Literary Representation', in *Poststructuralism as Exegesis*, Semeia 54, Atlanta: Scholars Press, 57–76.

——— (2003), 'The Syrians in *The Book of the Divided Kingdoms*: A Literary/ Theological Approach', *BI* 11:531–542.

Joines, K. (1968), 'The Bronze Serpent in the Israelite Cult', *JBL* 87:245–256.

Jones, G. (1994), 'From Abijam to Abijah', *ZAW* 106:420–434.

Joo, S. (2012), 'A Fine Balance Between Hope and Despair: The Epilogue to 2 Kings (25:27–30)', *BI* 20:226–243.

Judge, H. (1956), 'Aaron, Zadok, and Abiathar', *JTS* 7:70–74.

Kalluveettil, P. (1982), *Declaration and Covenant: A Comprehensive Review of Covenant Formulae from the Old Testament and the Ancient Near East*, Rome: Pontifical Biblical Institute.

Kaltner, J. (2004), 'What Did Elijah Do to His Mantle? The Hebrew Root *GLM*', in J. Kaltner (ed.), *Inspired Speech: Prophecy in the Ancient Near East. Essays in Honor of Herbert B. Huffmon*, JSOTSup 372, London: T. & T. Clark, 225–230.

Kang, S. (2010), 'A Philological Approach to the Problem of King So (2 Kgs 17:4)', *VT* 60:241–248.

Kapelrud, A. (1962), 'Sepharvaim', *IDB* 4:273.

Katzenstein, H. (1955), 'Who Were the Parents of Athaliah?', *IEJ* 5:194–197.

——— (1973), *The History of Tyre from the Beginning of the Second Millennium B. C. E. until the Fall of the Neo-Babylonian Empire in 538 B. C. E.*, Jerusalem: Schocken Institute.

Kaufman, I. (1992), 'Samaria the City', *ABD* 5:914–926.

Keber, J. (1996), 'Shalom in the Hebrew Bible', *LJRC* 31:7–23.

Kee, M. (2007), 'The Heavenly Council and Its Type-Scene', *JSOT* 31:259–273.

Keel, O. (1978), *The Symbolism of the Biblical World: Ancient Near Eastern Iconography and the Book of Psalms*, trans. T. J. Hallett, New York: Seabury.

Kelle, B. (2005), *Hosea 2: Metaphor and Rhetoric in Historical Perspective*, Atlanta: SBL.

Kelly, B. (2002), 'Manasseh in the Books of Kings and Chronicles (2 Kings 21:1–18; 2 Chron 33:1–20)', in V. Long (ed.), *Windows into Old Testament History: Evidence, Argument, and the Crisis of 'Biblical Israel'*, Grand Rapids: Eerdmans, 131–146.

Kent, G. (1990), 'The Rechabites: What Do We Know?', *SwJT* 32:40–45.

Keulen, P. van (1996a), *Manasseh Through the Eyes of the Deuteronomists: The Manasseh Account '2 Kings 21:1–18' and the Final Chapters of the Deuteronomistic History*, Leiden: Brill.

——— (1996b), 'The Meaning of the Phrase *wn'spt 'l-qbrtyk bšlwm* in 2 Kings XXII 20', *VT* 46:256–260.

Kim, J. (2005), 'Reading and Retelling Naaman's Story (2 Kings 5)', *JSOT* 30:49–61.

King, P., and L. Stager (2001), *Life in Biblical Israel*, Louisville: Westminster John Knox.

Kitchen, K. (1986), *The Third Intermediate Period in Egypt '1100–650 B. C.'*, 2nd ed., Warminster: Aris & Phillips.

——— (1997a), 'Egypt and East Africa', in L. Handy (ed.), *The Age of Solomon: Scholarship at the Turn of the Millennium*, Leiden: Brill, 107–125.

——— (1997b), 'Sheba and Arabia', in L. Handy (ed.), *The Age of Solomon: Scholarship at the Turn of the Millennium*, Leiden: Brill, 127–153.

Kiuchi, N. (1994), 'Elijah's Self-Offering: 1 Kings 17,21', *Bib* 75:74–79.

Klein, R. (1970), 'Jeroboam's Rise to Power', *JBL* 89:217–218.

——— (1973), 'Once More: Jeroboam's Rise to Power', *JBL* 92:582–584.

Klopfenstein, M. (1966), '1. Könige 13', in E. Busch (ed.), *Parrhesia*, Festschrift for Karl Barth, Zurich: EVZ-Verlag, 639–672.

Knauf, E. (1998), 'Kinneret and Naftali', in A. Lemaire (ed.), *Congress Volume*, Leiden: Brill, 219–233.

——— (2003), 'Jehoash's Improbable Inscription', *BN* 117:22–26.

Knights, C. (1993), 'Kenites = Rechabites? 1 Chronicles II 55 Reconsidered', *VT* 43:10–18.

Knoppers, G. (1993), *Two Nations Under God: The Deuteronomistic History of Solomon and the Dual Monarchies*. Vol. 1: *The Reign of Solomon and the Rise of Jeroboam*, Atlanta: Scholars Press.

——— (1994), *Two Nations Under God: The Deuteronomistic History of Solomon and the Dual Monarchies*. Vol. 2: *The Reign of Jeroboam, the Fall of Israel, and the Reign of Josiah*, Atlanta: Scholars Press.

—— (1995), 'Aaron's Calf and Jeroboam's Calves', in A. Beck (ed.), *Fortunate the Eyes That See: Essays in Honor of David Noel Freedman in Celebration of His Seventieth Birthday*, Grand Rapids: Eerdmans, 92–104.

—— (1996), 'Ancient Near Eastern Royal Grants and the Davidic Covenant: A Parallel?', *JAOS* 116:670–697.

—— (1997), 'Solomon's Fall and Deuteronomy', in L. Handy (ed.), *The Age of Solomon: Scholarship at the Turn of the Millennium*, Leiden: Brill, 392–410.

—— (1998), 'David's Relation to Moses: The Contexts, Content and Conditions of the Davidic Promises', in J. Day (ed.), *King and Messiah in Israel and the Ancient Near East: Proceedings of the Oxford Old Testament Seminar*, JSOTSup 270, Sheffield: Sheffield Academic Press, 91–118.

—— (2007), 'Cutheans or Children of Jacob? The Issue of Samaritan Origins in 2 Kings 17', in R. Rezetko (ed.), *Reflection and Refraction: Studies in Biblical Historiography in Honour of A. Graeme Auld*, Leiden: Brill, 223–239.

Konkel, A. (1993), 'The Sources of the Story of Hezekiah in the Book of Isaiah', *VT* 43:462–482.

—— (1997a), 'צפה', *NIDOTTE* 3:832–833.

—— (1997b), 'חפשׁ', *NIDOTTE* 6:326–327.

Kooij, A. van der (2000), 'The Story of Hezekiah and Sennacherib (2 Kings 18–19)', in J. de Moor (ed.), *Past, Present, Future: The Deuteronomistic History and the Prophets*, Leiden: Brill, 107–119.

Koopmans, W. (1991), 'The Testament of David in 1 Kings II 1–10', *VT* 41:429–449.

Kotter, W. (1992), 'Gilgal (Place)', *ABD* 2:1022–1024.

Kratz, R. (2008), 'Chemosh's Wrath and Yahweh's No', in R. Kratz and H. Spieckermann (eds.), *Divine Wrath and Divine Mercy in the World of Antiquity*, Tübingen: Mohr Siebeck, 92–121.

Kutsch, E. (1952), '*Die Wurzel* עצר *im Hebräischen*', *VT* 2:57–69.

Kuyt, A., and J. Wesselius (1985), 'A Ugaritic Parallel for the Feast for Ba'al in 2 Kings X 8–25', *VT* 35:109–111.

Laato, A. (1997), 'Second Samuel 7 and Ancient Near Eastern Royal Ideology', *CBQ* 59:244–269.

Labuschagne, C. (1965), 'Did Elisha Deliberately Lie? – A Note on II Kings 8 10', *ZAW* 77:327–328.

Laffey, A. (1988), *Wives, Harlots and Concubines*, Philadelphia: Fortress.

Lamb, D. (2007), *Righteous Jehu and His Evil Heirs: The Deuteronomist's Negative Perspective on Dynastic Succession*, Oxford Theological Monographs, Oxford: Oxford University Press.

Lanner, L. (1999), 'Cannibal Mothers and Me: A Mother's Reading of 2 Kings 6.24–7.20', *JSOT* 85:107–116.

Lasine, S. (1989), 'The Riddle of Solomon's Judgment and the Riddle of Human Nature in the Hebrew Bible', *JSOT* 45:61–86.

—— (1991), 'Jehoram and the Cannibal Mothers (2 Kings 6.24–33): Solomon's Judgment in an Inverted World', *JSOT* 50:27–53.

—— (1992), 'Reading Jeroboam's Intentions: Intertextuality, Rhetoric, and History in 1 Kings 12', in D. Fewell (ed.), *Reading Between Texts: Intertextuality and the Hebrew Bible*, Louisville: John Knox, 133–152.

—— (1993), 'Manasseh as Villain and Scapegoat', in J. Exum (ed.), *The New Literary Criticism and the Hebrew Bible*, Valley Forge: Trinity, 163–183.

—— (1995), 'The King of Desire: Indeterminacy, Audience, and the Solomon Narrative', *Semeia* 71:85–118.

—— (2001), *Knowing Kings: Knowledge, Power, and Narcissism in the Hebrew Bible*, ed. D. Fewell, SBL Semeia Series 40, Atlanta: SBL.

—— (2004), 'Matters of Life and Death: The Story of Elijah and the Widow's Son in Comparative Perspective', *BibInt* 12:117–144.

Lawrence, P. (1993), 'Peacocks or Baboons? (1 Kgs 10.22; 2 Chr 9.21)', *BT* 44:348–349.

Lawrie, D. (1997), 'Telling Of(f) Prophets: Narrative Strategy in 1 Kings 18:1–19:18', *JNSL* 23:163–180.

Leithart, P. (2001), 'Nabal and His Wine', *JBL* 120:525–527.

Lemaire, A. (2002), 'La Reine de Saba à Jérusalem: la tradition ancienne reconsidérée', in E. Knauf (ed.), *Kein Land für sich allein: Studien zum Kulturkontakt in Kanaan, Israel/Palästina und Ebirnari für Manfred Weippert zum 65 Geburtstag*, OBO 186, Fribourg: Universitätsverlag, 43–55.

Lemaire, A., and B. Halpern (eds.) (2010), *The Books of Kings: Sources, Composition, Historiography and Reception*, Leiden: Brill.

Lemke, W. (1976), 'The Way of Obedience: I Kings 13 and the Structure of the Deuteronomistic History', in F. Cross (ed.), *Magnalia Dei: The Mighty Acts of God*, Garden City: Doubleday, 301–326.

Leuchter, M. (2006), 'Jeroboam the Ephratite', *JBL* 125:51–72.

Levenson, J. (1979), 'The Davidic Covenant and Its Modern Interpreters', *CBQ* 41:205–219.

—— (1984), 'The Last Four Verses in Kings', *JBL* 103:353–361.

Levin, S. (1983), 'The Judgment of Solomon: Legal and Medical', *Judaism* 32:463–465.

Levine, L. (1972), 'Menahem and Tiglath-Pileser: A New Synchronism', *BASOR* 206:40–42.

Levine, N. (1999), 'Twice as Much of Your Spirit: Pattern, Parallel and Paronomasia in the Miracles of Elijah and Elisha', *JSOT* 85:25–46.

Lind, M. (1980), *Yahweh Is A Warrior: The Theology of Warfare in Ancient Israel*, Scottdale, Pa.: Herald.

Lingen, A. van der (1992), 'BW'-YṢ' ("To Go Out and To Come In") as a Military Term', *VT* 42:59–66.

Lipinski, E. (1971), 'An Israelite King of Hamat?', *VT* 21:371–373.

Lipschits, O. (2006), 'On Cash-Boxes and Finding or Not Finding Books: Jehoash's and Josiah's Decision to Repair the Temple', in Y. Amit (ed.),

Essays on Ancient Israel in Its Near Eastern Context: A Tribute to Nadav Na'aman, Winona Lake: Eisenbrauns, 239–254.

Liver, J. (1967a), 'The Book of the Acts of Solomon', *Bib* 48:75–101.

—— (1967b), 'The Wars of Mesha, King of Moab', *PEQ* 99:14–31.

Liwak, R. (1992), 'Zair (Place)', *ABD* 6:1038–1039.

Long, B. (1973), '2 Kings III and Genres of Prophetic Narrative', *VT* 23:337–348.

—— (1985), 'Historical Narrative and the Fictionalizing Imagination', *VT* 35:405–416.

—— (1987), 'Framing Repetitions in Biblical Historiography', *JBL* 106:385–399.

—— (1995), 'Sacred Geography as Narrative Structure in 2 Kings 11', in D. Wright (ed.), *Pomegranates and Golden Bells: Studies in Biblical, Jewish, and Near Eastern Ritual, Law, and Literature in Honor of Jacob Milgrom*, Winona Lake: Eisenbrauns, 231–238.

Long, J. (2004), 'Unfulfilled Prophecy or Divine Deception? A Literary Reading of 2 Kings 3', *Stone-Campbell Journal* 7:101–117.

—— (2007), 'Elisha's Deceptive Prophecy in 2 Kings 3: A Response to Raymond Westbrook', *JBL* 126:168–171.

Long, J., and M. Sneed (2004), '"Yahweh Has Given These Three Kings into the Hand of Moab": A Socio-Literary Reading of 2 Kings 3', in J. Kaltner (ed.), *Inspired Speech: Prophecy in the Ancient Near East. Essays in Honor of Herbert B. Huffmon*, JSOTSup 372, London: T. & T. Clark, 253–275.

Long, V. (1994), *The Art of Biblical History*, Grand Rapids: Zondervan.

Long, V. (ed.) (2002), *Windows into Old Testament History: Evidence, Argument, and the Crisis of 'Biblical Israel'*, Grand Rapids: Eerdmans.

Longman, T. (2006), *Proverbs*, BCOT, Grand Rapids: Baker Academic.

Longman, T., and D. Reid (1995), *God Is a Warrior*, Grand Rapids: Zondervan.

Lubetski, M. (1992), 'Ezion-geber', *ABD* 2:723–726.

Luckenbill, D. (ed.) (1926–7), *Ancient Records of Assyria and Babylonia*, 2 vols., Chicago: University of Chicago Press.

Lundbom, J. (1976), 'The Lawbook of the Josianic Reform', *CBQ* 38:293–302.

Lust, J. (1975), 'A Gentle Breeze or a Roaring Thunderous Sound?', *VT* 25:110–115.

McCann, J. (1993), *A Theological Introduction to the Book of Psalms*, Nashville: Abingdon.

McCarthy, D. (1965), 'Notes on the Love of God in Deuteronomy and the Father–Son Relationship Between Yahweh and Israel', *CBQ* 27:144–147.

—— (1973), '2 Kings 13,4–6', *Bib* 54:409–410.

—— (1978a), 'Exod 3:14: History, Philology and Theology', *CBQ* 40:311–322.

—— (1978b), *Treaty and Covenant: A Study in Form in the Ancient Oriental Documents and in the Old Testament*, Rome: Pontifical Biblical Institute.

McConville, J. (1992), '1 Kings viii 46–53 and the Deuteronomic Hope', *VT* 42:67–79.

—— (1998), 'King and Messiah in Deuteronomy and the Deuteronomistic History', in John Day (ed.), *King and Messiah in Israel and the Ancient Near East: Proceedings of the Oxford Old Testament Seminar*, JSOTSup 270, Sheffield: Sheffield Academic Press, 271–295.

—— (2002), *Deuteronomy*, Leicester: Apollos; Downers Grove: InterVarsity Press.

McCurley, F. (1974), '"And After Six Days" (Mark 9:2): A Semitic Literary Device', *JBL* 93:67–81.

Macdonald, J. (1969), 'The Structure of II Kings xvii', *TGUOS* 23:29–41.

McFall, L. (1989), 'Did Theile Overlook Hezekiah's Coregency?', *BSac* 146:393–404.

—— (1991), 'A Translation Guide to the Chronological Data in Kings and Chronicles', *BSac* 148:3–45.

—— (1992), 'Some Missing Coregencies in Thiele's Chronology', *AUSS* 30:35–58.

McGee, P. (2003–4), 'Divine Divas', *JITC* 31.1–2:207–214.

Machinist, P. (1995), 'The Transfer of Kingship: A Divine Turn', in A. Beck (ed.), *Fortunate the Eyes That See: Essays in Honor of David Noel Freedman in Celebration of His Seventieth Birthday*, Grand Rapids: Eerdmans, 105–120.

McHugh, J. (1964), 'The Date of Hezekiah's Birth', *VT* 14:446–453.

McKane, W. (1959), 'A Note on 2 Kings 12^{10} (Evv 12^9)', *ZAW* 71:260–265.

McKay, J. (1973), *Religion in Judah Under the Assyrians 732–609 BC*, London: SCM.

McKenzie, S. (1987), 'The Source for Jeroboam's Role at Shechem (1 Kgs 11:43–12:3, 12, 20)', *JBL* 106:297–304.

—— (1991), *The Trouble with Kings: The Composition of the Book of Kings in the Deuteronomistic History*, VTSup 42, Leiden: Brill.

—— (2001), 'The Typology of the Davidic Covenant', in J. Dearman (ed.), *The Land That I Will Show You: Essays on the History and Archaeology of the Ancient Near East in Honour of J. Maxwell Miller*, JSOTSup 343, Sheffield: Sheffield Academic Press, 152–178.

McMahon, G. (1992), 'Hittites in the OT', *ABD* 3:231–233.

Magen, I. (1993), 'Shechem', *NEAEHL* 4:1345–1359.

Maisler, B. (1951), 'Two Hebrew Ostraca from Tell Qasile', *JNES* 10:265–267.

Malamat, A. (1963a), 'Aspects of the Foreign Policies of David and Solomon', *JNES* 22:1–17.

—— (1963b), 'Kingship and Council in Israel and Sumer: A Parallel', *JNES* 22:247–253.

—— (1965), 'Organs of Statecraft in the Israelite Monarchy', *BA* 28:34–65.

—— (1982), 'A Political Look at the Kingdom of David and Solomon and Its Relations with Egypt', in T. Ishida (ed.), *Studies in the Period of David and Solomon and Other Essays*, Winona Lake: Eisenbrauns, 189–204.

Malamat, A., and I. Eph'al (eds.) (1979), *The World History of the Jewish People*, Jerusalem: Massada.

Manor, D. (1992), 'Tirzah', *ABD* 6:573–577.

Margalit, B. (1986), 'Why King Mesha of Moab Sacrificed His Oldest Son', *BAR* 12:62–63.

Margalith, O. (1984), 'The $k^e l\bar{a}b\bar{i}m$ of Ahab', *VT* 34:228–232.

Marx, A. (1999), 'De Shîshaq à Shéshak. A Propos de 1 Rois XIV 25–26', *VT* 49:186–190.

Mastin, B. (1984), '*Wāw Explicativum* in 2 Kings VIII 9', *VT* 34:853–855.

Matheney, M. (1968), 'Interpretation of Hebrew Prophetic Symbolic Act', *Encounter* 293:256–267.

Matthews, V. (1988), 'Kings of Israel: A Question of Crime and Punishment', in D. Lull (ed.), *SBL 1988 Seminar Papers*, Atlanta: Scholars Press, 517–526.

Mattingly, G. (1992a), 'Kir-hareseth (Place)', *ABD* 4:84.

———— (1992b) 'Mesha (Person)', *ABD* 4:707.

Mayes, A. (1983), *The Story of Israel Between Settlement and Exile: A Redactional Study of the Deuteronomistic History*, London: SCM.

Mayhue, R. (1993), 'False Prophets and the Deceiving Spirit', *TMSJ* 4:135–163.

Mays, J. (1994), *The Lord Reigns: A Theological Handbook to the Psalms*, Louisville: Westminster John Knox.

Mazar, B. (1957), 'The Campaign of Pharaoh Shishak to Palestine', in *Congress Volume*, VTSup 4, Leiden: Brill, 57–66.

———— (1960), 'The Cities of the Priests and the Levites', in *Congress Volume Oxford 1959*, VTSup 7, Leiden: Brill, 193–205.

———— (1986), 'The Aramean Empire and Its Relations with Israel', in S. Aḥituv (ed.), *The Early Biblical Period: Historical Studies*, Jerusalem: Israel Exploration Society, 151–172.

Mead, J. (1999), 'Kings and Prophets, Donkeys and Lions: Dramatic Shape and Deuteronomistic Rhetoric in 1 Kings XIII', *VT* 49:191–205.

Meek, T. (1959), 'I Kings 20:1–20', *JBL* 78:73–75.

Mendelsohn, I. (1962), 'On Corvée Labor in Ancient Canaan and Israel', *BASOR* 167:31–35.

Mendenhall, G. (1974), 'The Shady Side of Wisdom: The Date and Purpose of Genesis 3', in *A Light unto My Path: Old Testament Studies in Honor of Jacob M. Myers*, Philadelphia: Temple University Press, 319–334.

Mercer, M. (2002), 'Elisha's Unbearable Curse: A Study of 2 Kings 2:23–25', *AJET* 21:165–198.

Mettinger, T. (1971), *Solomonic State Officials: A Study of the Civil Government Officials of the Israelite Monarchy*, ConBOT 5, Lund: CWK Gleerup.

———— (1976), *King and Messiah: The Civil and Sacral Legitimation of the Israelite King*, Lund: CWK Gleerup.

———— (1982), *The Dethronement of Sabaoth: Studies in the Shem and Kabod Theologies*, ConBOT 18, Lund: CWK Gleerup.

——— (2003), Review of S. Richter, *The Deuteronomistic History and the Name Theology, JBL* 122:753–755.

Meyers, C. (1983), 'Jachin and Boaz in Religious and Political Perspective', *CBQ* 45:167–178.

——— (1992), 'Temple, Jerusalem', *ABD* 6:350–369.

Mihelic, J. (1962a), 'Paran', *IDB* 3:657.

——— (1962b), 'Red Sea', *IDB* 4:19–21.

Milgrom, J. (1962), 'Sacrifices and Offerings, OT', *IDBSup* 763–771.

Millar, A., and H. Tadmor (1973), 'Adad-Nirari III in Syria: Another Stele Fragment and the Dates of his Campaign', *Iraq* 35:57–64.

Millard, A. (1985), 'Sennacherib's Attack on Hezekiah', *TynB* 36:61–77.

——— (1989), 'Does the Bible Exaggerate King Solomon's Golden Wealth?', *BAR* 15:20–34.

——— (1994), 'King Solomon's Shields', in M. Coogan (ed.), *Scripture and Other Artifacts: Essays on the Bible and Archaeology in Honor of Philip J. King*, Louisville: Westminster John Knox, 286–295.

——— (1997), 'King Solomon in His Ancient Context', in L. Handy (ed.), *The Age of Solomon: Scholarship at the Turn of the Millennium*, Leiden: Brill, 30–53.

Miller, J. (1966), 'The Elisha Cycle and the Accounts of the Omride Wars', *JBL* 85:441–454.

——— (1967a), 'Another Look at the Chronology of the Early Divided Monarchy', *JBL* 86:276–288.

——— (1967b), 'The Fall of the House of Ahab', *VT* 17:307–324.

——— (1968a), 'The Rest of the Acts of Jehoahaz', *ZAW* 80:337–342.

——— (1968b), 'So Tibni Died (1 Kings xvi 22)', *VT* 18:392–394.

——— (1992), 'Moab (Place)', *ABD* 4:882–893.

Miller, J., and J. Hayes (1986), *A History of Ancient Israel and Judah*, Philadelphia: Westminster, 1986.

Miller, P. (1973), *The Divine Warrior in Early Israel*, Cambridge: Harvard University Press.

——— (1986), 'The Prophetic Critique of Kings', *ExAud* 2:82–95.

Miscall, P. (1989), 'Elijah, Ahab and Jehu: A Prophecy Fulfilled', *Prooftexts* 9:73–83.

Mitchell, C. (2005), 'Heart and Mind in the Hebrew Scriptures', *Touchstone* 23:5–13.

Moberly, R. (1992), *The Old Testament of the Old Testament: Patriarchal Narratives and Mosaic Yahwism*, Minneapolis: Fortress.

——— (2003), 'Does God Lie to His Prophets? The Story of Micaiah ben Imlah', *HTR* 96:1–23.

Monson, J. (2000), 'The New 'Ain Dara Temple: Closest Solomonic Parallel', *BAR* 26:20–35, 67.

Moor, J. de (1977), 'אֲשֵׁרָה', *TDOT* 1:438–444.

Moore, M. (1990), 'Jeroboam's Calves: Idols or Imitations?', *BT* 41:421–424.

Moran, W. (1963), 'The Ancient Near Eastern Background of the Love of God in Deuteronomy', *CBQ* 25:77–87.

Moran, W. (ed. and trans.) (1992), *The Amarna Letters*, Baltimore: Johns Hopkins University Press.

Morgenstern, J. (1964), 'The Festival of *Jeroboam* I', *JBL* 83:109–118.

Morschauser, S. (2010), 'A "Diagnostic" Note on the "Great Wrath upon Israel"', *JBL* 129:299–302.

Mowinckel, S. (1962), 'Drive and/or Ride in O. T.', *VT* 19:278–299.

——— (2005), *He That Cometh: The Messiah Concept in the Old Testament and Later Judaism*, trans. G. W. Anderson, Grand Rapids: Eerdmans.

Mullen, E. (1983), 'The Divine Witness and the Davidic Royal Grant: PS 89:37–38', *JBL* 102.2:207–218.

——— (1987), 'The Sins of Jeroboam: A Redactional Assessment', *CBQ* 49:212–232.

——— (1988), 'The Royal Dynastic Grant to Jehu and the Structure of the Book of Kings', *JBL* 107:193–206.

——— (1992), 'Crime and Punishment: The Sins of the King and the Despoliation of the Treasuries', *CBQ* 54:231–248.

Müller, H.-P. (1999), 'Chemosh', *DDD* 186–189.

Murray, D. (2001), 'Of All the Years the Hopes – or Fears? Jehoiachin in Babylon', *JBL* 120:245–265.

Myers, J. (1962), 'David', *IDB* 2:776–778.

Na'aman, N. (1979), 'Sennacherib's Campaign to Judah and the Date of the *lmlk* Stamps', *VT* 29:61–86.

——— (1986), 'Historical and Chronological Notes on the Kingdoms of Israel and Judah in the Eighth Century B. C.', *VT* 36:71–92.

——— (1990), 'The Historical Background to the Conquest of Samaria (720 BC)', *Bib* 71:206–225.

——— (1991), 'Forced Participation in Alliances in the Course of the Assyrian Campaigns to the West', in M. Cogan (ed.), *Ah, Assyria . . . Studies in Assyrian History and Ancient Near Eastern Historiography Presented to Hayim Tadmor*, Jerusalem: Magnes, 80–98.

——— (1993), 'Azariah of Judah and Jeroboam II of Israel', *VT* 43:227–234.

——— (1995a), 'The Debated Historicity of Hezekiah's Reform in the Light of Historical and Archaeological Research', *ZAW* 107:179–195.

——— (1995b), 'The Deuteronomist and Voluntary Servitude to Foreign Powers', *JSOT* 65:37–53.

——— (1997), 'Prophetic Stories as Sources for the Histories of Jehoshaphat and the Omrides', *Bib* 78:153–173.

——— (1998a), 'Jehu Son of Omri: Legitimizing a Loyal Vassal by His Overlord', *IEJ* 48:236–238.

——— (1998b), 'Royal Inscriptions and the Histories of Joash and Ahaz, Kings of Judah', *VT* 48:333–349.

——— (2000a), 'New Light on Hezekiah's Second Prophetic Story (2 Kgs 19, 9b–35)', *Bib* 81:393–402.

—— (2000b), 'Three Notes on the Aramaic Inscription from Tel Dan', *IEJ* 50:92–104.

—— (2003), 'The Distribution of Messages in the Kingdom of Judah in Light of the Lachish Ostraca', *VT* 53:169–180.

—— (2005a), 'Forced Participation in Alliances in the Course of the Assyrian Campaigns to the West', in *Ancient Israel and its Neighbors: Interaction and Counteraction*, Collected Essays vol. 1, Winona Lake, Eisenbrauns, 16–39.

—— (2005b), 'Was Ahab Killed by an Assyrian Arrow in the Battle of Qarqar?', *UF* 37:461–474.

—— (2007), 'The Northern Kingdom in the Late Tenth–Ninth Centuries BCE', in H. G. M. Williamson (ed.), *Understanding the History of Ancient Israel*, Oxford: Oxford University Press, 399–418.

—— (2008), 'Naboth's Vineyard and the Foundation of Jezreel', *JSOT* 33:197–218.

Napier, B. (1959), 'The Omrides of Jezreel', *VT* 9:366–378.

Nardoni, E. (2004), *Rise up, O Judge: A Study of Justice in the Biblical World*, trans. S. Martin, Peabody: Hendrickson.

Naveh, J. (1990), 'Nameless People', *IEJ* 40:108–123.

Nelson, R. (1981), *The Double Redaction of the Deuteronomistic History*, Sheffield: JSOT Press.

—— (1983), '*Realpolitik* in Judah (687–609 B. C. E.)', in W. Hallo (ed.), *Scripture in Context II: More Essays on the Comparative Method*, Winona Lake: Eisenbrauns, 177–189.

—— (1989), 'God and the Heroic Prophet: Preaching the Stories of Elijah and Elisha', *QR* 9:93–105.

—— (1992), 'Hezion (Person)', *ABD* 3:193.

—— (2002), *Deuteronomy*, OTL, Louisville: Westminster John Knox.

Ngan, L. (1997), '2 Kings 5', *RevExp* 94:589–597.

Nicholson, E. (1965), 'The Meaning of the Expression עם הארץ in the Old Testament', *JSS* 10:59–66.

—— (1967), *Deuteronomy and Tradition*, Oxford: Blackwell.

—— (2007), 'Josiah and the Priests of the High Places (II Reg 23, 8a.9)', *ZAW* 119:499–513.

Nicolsky, N. (1930), 'Das Asylrecht in Israel', *ZAW* 48:146–175.

Noth, M. (1991), *The Deuteronomistic History*, 2nd ed., JSOTSup 15, Sheffield: JSOT Press. Originally published as *Überlieferungsgeschichtliche Studien*, Tübingen: Max Niemeyer Verlag, 1943.

Obbink, H. (1937), 'The Horns of the Altar in the Semitic World, Especially in Jahwism', *JBL* 56:43–49.

O'Brien, D. (1996), '"Is This the Time to Accept . . . ?" (2 Kings V 26B): Simply Moralizing (LXX) or an Ominous Foreboding of Yahweh's Rejection of Israel (MT)?', *VT* 46:448–457.

O'Brien, M. (1998), 'The Portrayal of Prophets in 2 Kings 2', *ABR* 46:1–16.

Oded, B. (1972), 'The Historical Background of the Syro-Ephraimite War Reconsidered', *CBQ* 34:153–165.

—— (1977), 'Judah and the Exile', in J. Hayes and J. Miller (ed.), *Israelite and Judaean History*, OTL, Philadelphia: Westminster, 435–488.

—— (1979), *Mass Deportations and Deportees in the Neo-Assyrian Empire*, Wiesbaden: Reichert.

Oden, R. (1987), 'Religious Identity and the Sacred Prostitution Accusation', in *The Bible Without Theology: The Theological Tradition and Alternatives to It*, San Francisco: Harper & Row, 131–153.

Oeste, G. (2013), 'The Shaping of a Prophet: Joshua in the Deuteronomistic History', in Mark Boda and L. M. Wray Beal (eds.), *Prophets, Prophecy, and Ancient Israelite Historiography*, Winona Lake: Eisenbrauns, 23–42.

Ohm, A. (2010), 'Manasseh and the Punishment Narrative', *TynB* 61:237–254.

Olley, J. (1998), 'YHWH and His Zealous Prophet: The Presentation of Elijah in 1 and 2 Kings', *JSOT* 80:25–51.

—— (1999), '"Trust in the LORD": Hezekiah, Kings and Isaiah', *TynB* 50:59–77.

—— (2003), 'Pharaoh's Daughter, Solomon's Palace, and the Temple: Another Look at the Structure of 1 Kings 1–11', *JSOT* 27:355–369.

Olyan, S. (1982), 'Zadok's Origins and the Tribal Politics of David', *JBL* 101:177–193.

—— (1984), '*Hăšālôm*: Some Literary Considerations of 2 Kings 9', *CBQ* 46:652–668.

—— (1988), *Ashera and the Cult of Yahweh in Israel*, Atlanta: Scholars Press.

Oppenheim, A. (1947), 'A Fiscal Practice of the Ancient Near East', *JNES* 6:116–120.

Otto, S. (2003), 'The Composition of the Elijah–Elisha Stories and the Deuteronomistic History', *JSOT* 27:487–508.

Ottosson, M. (1984), 'The Prophet Elijah's Visit to Zarephath', in W. Barrick (ed.), *In the Shelter of Elyon: Essays on Ancient Palestinian Life and Literature in Honor of G. W. Ahlström*, JSOTSup 31, Sheffield: JSOT Press, 185–198.

Overholt, T. (1996), 'Elijah and Elisha in the Context of Israelite Religion', in S. Reid (ed.), *Prophets and Paradigms: Essays in Honor of Gene M. Tucker*, Sheffield: Sheffield Academic Press, 94–111.

Page, S. (1968), 'A Stela of Adad-Nirari III and Nergal-Ereš from Tell Al Rimah', *Iraq* 30:139–153.

Pakkala, J. (2002), 'Jeroboam's Sin and Bethel in 1 Kgs 12:25–33', *BN* 112:86–94.

—— (2008), 'Jeroboam Without Bulls', *ZAW* 120:501–525.

Pardee, D. (1982), *Handbook of Ancient Hebrew Letters*, Chico: Scholars Press.

Park, S. (2012), 'A New Historical Reconstruction of the Fall of Samaria', *Bib* 93:98–106.

Parker, S. (1978), 'Possession, Trance and Prophecy in Pre-exilic Israel', *VT* 28:271–285.

—— (1978–9), 'Jezebel's Reception of Jehu', *Maarav* 1:67–78.

—— (1996), 'Appeals for Military Intervention: Stories from Zinjirli and the Bible', *BA* 59:213–224.

Parzen, H. (1940), 'The Prophets and the Omri Dynasty', *HTR* 33:69–96.

Paul, John II (1995), *Evangelium Vitae . . . on the Value and Inviolability of Human Life*. Papal Encyclical delivered 25 March. Available online at http://www.vatican.va/holy_father/john_paul_ii/encyclicals/documents/hf_jp-ii_enc_25031995_evangelium-vitae_en.html, accessed 22 Aug. 2012.

Paul, S. (1969), 'Sargon's Administrative Diction in II Kings 17 27', *JBL* 88:73–74.

Peterson, J. (1992a), 'Gibbethon', *ABD* 2:1006–1007.

—— (1992b), 'Libnah (Place)', *ABD* 4:322–323.

Pitard, W. (1988), 'The Identity of the Bir-Hadad of the Melqart Stela', *BASOR* 272:3–19.

—— (1992a), 'Aram', *ABD* 1:338–341.

—— (1992b), 'Ben hadad', *ABD* 1:663–665.

—— (1992c), 'Damascus', *ABD* 2:5–7.

—— (1992d), 'Hazael', *ABD* 3:83–84.

Pope, M. (1962), 'Rechab', *IDB* 4:14–16.

Porten, B. (1967), 'The Structure and Theme of the Solomon Narrative (1 Kings 3 – 11)', *HUCA* 38:93–128.

Porter, J. (1981), 'בני הנביאים', *JTS* 32:423–429.

Power, B. (2006), '"All the King's Horses . . ." Narrative Subversion in the Story of Solomon's Golden Age', in J. Wood (ed.), *From Babel to Babylon: Essays on Biblical History and Literature in Honour of Brian Peckham*, New York: T. & T. Clark, 111–123.

Priest, J. (1980), 'Huldah's Oracle', *VT* 30:366–368.

Provan, I. (1988), *Hezekiah and the Books of Kings*, Berlin: de Gruyter.

—— (1995), 'Why Barzillai of Gilead (1 Kings 2:7)? Narrative Art and the Hermeneutic of Suspicion in 1 Kings 1–2', *TynB* 46:103–116.

Provan, I., V. P. Long and T. Longman III (2003), *A Biblical History of Israel*, Louisville: Westminster John Knox.

Puech, E. (1999), 'Milcom', *DDD* 575–576.

Purvis, J. (1968), *The Samaritan Pentateuch and the Origin of the Samaritan Sect*, Cambridge, Mass.: Harvard University Press.

Pyper, H. (1993), 'Judging the Wisdom of Solomon: The Two-Way Effect of Intertextuality', *JSOT* 59:25–36.

Rabinowitz, I. (1984), '"az Followed by Imperfect Verb-Form in Preterite Contexts: A Redactional Device in Biblical Hebrew', *VT* 34:53–62.

Rad, G. von (1953), *Studies in Deuteronomy*, trans. D. Stalker, London: SCM.

—— (1958), *Holy War in Ancient Israel*, trans. M. Dawn, Grand Rapids: Eerdmans.

—— (1962), *Old Testament Theology*, vol. 1, New York: Harper & Row.

—— (1964), 'שָׁלוֹם in the Old Testament', *TDNT* 2:402–406.

—— (1966), *The Problem of the Hexateuch and Other Essays*, trans. E. W. Trueman Dicken, Edinburgh: Oliver & Boyd.

Rainey, A. (1963), 'Business Agents at Ugarit', *IEJ* 13:313–321.

—— (1976), 'Sela (of Edom)', *IDBSup* 800.

Redford, D. (1972), 'Studies in Relations Between Palestine and Egypt During the First Millennium B. C.', in J. Wevers and D. Redford (eds.), *Studies on the Ancient Palestinian World*, Toronto: University of Toronto Press, 141–156.

—— (1992a), *Egypt, Canaan, and Israel in Ancient Times*, Princeton: Princeton University Press.

—— (1992b), 'Shishak', *ABD* 5:1221–1222.

Reinhartz, A. (1994), 'Anonymous Women and the Collapse of the Monarchy: A Study in Narrative Technique', in A. Brenner (ed.), *A Feminist Companion to Samuel and Kings*, Sheffield: Sheffield Academic Press, 43–65.

Reis, P. Tamarkin (1994), 'Vindicating God: Another Look at 1 Kings XIII', *VT* 44:376–386.

Rendsburg, G. A. (1988), 'The Mock of Baal in 1 Kings 18:27', *CBQ* 50:414–417.

—— (1998), 'The Guilty Party in 1 Kings III 16–28', *VT* 48:534–541.

—— (2002), 'Hebrew Philological Notes (III)', *HS* 43:21–30.

Reno, R. (2010), *Genesis*, Grand Rapids: Brazos.

Richter, S. (2002), *The Deuteronomistic History and the Name Theology: lᵉšakkēn šᵉmô šām in the Bible and the Ancient Near East*, BZAW 318, Berlin: de Gruyter.

Roberts, J. (1970), 'A New Parallel to I Kings 18 28–29', *JBL* 89:76–77.

—— (1982), 'Zion in the Theology of the Davidic-Solomonic Empire', in T. Ishida (ed.), *Studies in the Period of David and Solomon and Other Essays: International Symposium for Biblical Studies, Tokyo, 1979*, Winona Lake: Eisenbrauns, 93–108.

Roberts, K. (2000), 'God, Prophet, and King: Eating and Drinking on the Mountain in First Kings 18:41', *CBQ* 62:632–644.

Robertson, D. (1982), 'Micaiah ben Imlah: A Literary View', in R. Polzin (ed.), *The Biblical Mosaic: Changing Perspectives*, Philadelphia: Fortress; Chico: Scholars Press, 139–146.

Robinson, B. (1991), 'Elijah at Horeb, 1 Kings 19:1–18: a Coherent Narrative?', *RB* 98:513–536.

Robinson, G. (1977), 'Is 2 Kings XI 6 a Gloss?', *VT* 27:56–61.

Rofé, A. (1988), 'The Vineyard of Naboth: The Origin and Message of the Story', *VT* 38:89–104.

—— (1989), 'The Classification of the Prophetical Stories', *JBL* 89:427–440.

—— (1999), 'Elisha at Dothan (2 Kings 6:8–23): Historico-Literary Criticism Sustained by the Midrash', in R. Chazan (ed.), *Ki Baruch hu: Ancient Near Eastern, Biblical, and Judaic Studies in Honor of Baruch A. Levine*, Winona Lake: Eisenbrauns, 345–353.

Rogland, M. (2001), 'Pro or Contra? 2 Kings 6:11', *Presb* 27:56–58.

Roncace, M. (2000), 'Elisha and the Woman of Shunem: 2 Kings 4.8–37 and 8.1–6 Read in Conjunction', *JSOT* 91:109–127.

Rose, M. (1977), 'Bemerkungen zum historischen Fundament des Josia-Bildes in II Reg 22f.', *ZAW* 89:55–62.

Rosenbaum, J. (1979), 'Hezekiah's Reform and the Deuteronomistic Tradition', *HTR* 72:23–43.

Rost, L. (1982), *The Succession to the Throne of David*, trans. M. D. Rutter and D. M. Gunn, Sheffield: Almond.

Roth, R. (1992), 'Abana (Place)', *ABD* 1:6.

Roth, W. (1982), 'The Story of the Prophet Micaiah (1 Kings 22) in Historical-Critical Interpretation 1876–1976', in R. Polzin (ed.), *The Biblical Mosaic: Changing Perspectives*, Philadelphia: Fortress; Chico: Scholars Press, 105–137.

Routledge, R. (2008), *Old Testament Theology: A Thematic Approach*, Leicester: Apollos; Downers Grove: InterVarsity Press.

Rowley, H. H. (1939), 'Zadok and Nehushtan', *JBL* 58:113–141.

—— (1963), 'Hezekiah's Reform and Rebellion', in *Men of God: Studies in Old Testament History and Prophecy*, London: Thomas Nelson & Sons, 98–132.

Rudman, D. (2000), 'A Note on the Personal Name Amon (2 Kings 21,19–26 // 2 Chr 33,21–25', *Bib* 81:403–405.

Rusak, T. (2008), 'The Clash of Cults on Mount Carmel: Do Archeological Records and Historical Documents Support the Biblical Episode of Elijah and the Ba'al Priests?', *SJOT* 22:29–46.

Sailhamer, J. (1992), *The Pentateuch as Narrative: A Biblical-Theological Commentary*, Grand Rapids: Zondervan.

Sarna, N. (1997), 'Naboth's Vineyard Revisited (1 Kings 21)', in M. Cogan (ed.), *Tehillah le-Moshe: Biblical and Judaic Studies in Honor of Moshe Greenberg*, Winona Lake: Eisenbrauns, 119–126.

Sasson, J. (1968), 'Bovine Symbolism in the Exodus Narrative', *VT* 18:384–387.

Satterthwaite, P. (1998), 'The Elisha Narratives and the Coherence of 2 Kings 2–8', *TynB* 49:1–28.

Saydon, P. (1952), 'The Meaning of the Expression עָצוּר וְעָזוּב', *VT* 2:371–374.

Scharbert, J. (1975), 'בָּרַךְ; בְּרָכָה', *TDOT* 2:279–308.

Schearing, L. (1997), 'A Wealth of Women: Looking Behind, Within, and Beyond Solomon's Story', in L. Handy (ed.), *The Age of Solomon: Scholarship at the Turn of the Millennium*, Leiden: Brill, 428–456.

Schenker, A. (2000), 'Jeroboam and the Division of the Kingdom in the Ancient Septuagint: LXX 3 Kings 12.24 A–Z, MT 1 Kings 11–12; 14 and the Deuteronomistic History', in A. de Pury (ed.), *Israel Constructs Its History: Deuteronomistic Historiography in Recent Research*, JSOTSup 306, Sheffield: Sheffield Academic Press, 214–257.

Schipper, J. (2009), 'From Petition to Parable: The Prophet's Use of Genre in 1 Kings 20:38–42', *CBQ* 71:264–274.

Schley, D. (1987), '1 Kings 10:26–29: A Reconsideration', *JBL* 106.4:595–601.

Schneider, T. (1996), 'Rethinking Jehu', *Bib* 77:100–107.

Schniedewind, W. (1993), 'History and Interpretation: The Religion of Ahab and Manasseh in the Book of Kings', *CBQ* 55:649–661.

Schulte, H. (1994), 'The End of the Omride Dynasty: Social-Ethical Observations on the Subject of Power and Violence', *Semeia* 66:133–148.

Scott, R. (1955), 'Solomon and the Beginnings of Wisdom in Israel', *VTSup* 3:262–279.

Seebass, H. (1967), 'Zur Königserhebung Jerobeams I', *VT* 17:325–333.

—— (1975), 'Tradition und Interpretation bei Jehu ben Chanani und Ahia von Silo', *VT* 25:175–190.

Seeman, D. (2004), 'The Watcher at the Window: Cultural Poetics of a Biblical Motif', *Prooftexts* 24:1–50.

Seger, J. (1992), 'Gath (Place)', *ABD* 2:908–909.

Seibert, E. (2006), *Subversive Scribes and the Solomonic Narrative: A Rereading of 1 Kings 1–11*, LHBOTS 436, New York: T. & T. Clark.

Sellers, O. (1962), 'Weights and Measures', *IDB* 4:828–839.

Seow, C. (1984), 'The Syro-Palestinian Context of Solomon's Dream', *HTR* 77:141–152.

Shanks, H. (1985), 'Ancient Ivory: The Story of Wealth, Decadence and Beauty', *BAR* 11:40–53.

—— (2003), 'Is It or Isn't It? King Jehoash Inscription Captivates Archaeological World', *BAR* 29.2:22–23, 69.

Shemesh, Y. (2008a), 'Elisha and the Miraculous Jug of Oil (2 Kgs 4:1–7)', *JHS* 8:2–18.

—— (2008b), 'The Elisha Stories as Saints' Legends', *JHS* 8:2–41.

Shields, M. (1993), 'Subverting a Man of God, Elevating a Woman: Role and Power Reversals in 2 Kings 4', *JSOT* 58:59–69.

Shiloh, Y., and H. Geva (1993), 'Jerusalem', *NEAEHL* 2:698–716.

Shiloh, Y., and A. Horowitz (1975), 'Ashlar Quarries of the Iron Age in the Hill Country of Israel', *BASOR* 217:37–48.

Siddall, L. (2009), 'Tiglath-pileser III's Aid to Ahaz: A New Look at the Problems of the Biblical Accounts in Light of the Assyrian Sources', *ANES* 46:93–106.

Siebert-Hommes, J. (1996), 'The Widow of Zarephath and the Great Woman of Shunem: A Comparative Analysis of Two Stories', in B. Becking (ed.), *On Reading Prophetic Texts: Gender-Specific and Related Studies in Memory of Fokkelien van Dijk-Hemmes*, Leiden: Brill, 231–250.

Simon, U. (1976), 'I Kings 13: A Prophetic Sign – Denial and Persistence', *HUCA* 47:81–117.

—— (1997), *Reading Prophetic Narratives*, trans. L. J. Schramm, Bloomington: Indiana University Press.

Slayton, J. (1992), 'Penuel (Place)', *ABD* 5:223.

Smelik, K. (1990), 'The Literary Function of 1 Kings 17,8–24', in C. Brekelmans (ed.), *Pentateuchal and Deuteronomistic Studies: Papers Read at the XIIIth IOSOT Congress, Leuven 1989*, Leuven: Leuven University Press, 239–243.

—— (1995), 'Moloch, Molech or Molk-Sacrifice? A Reassessment of the Evidence Concerning the Hebrew Term Molekh', *SJOT* 9:133–142.

—— (1997), 'The New Altar of King Ahaz (2 Kings 16): Deuteronomistic Re-Interpretation of a Cult Reform', in M. Vervenne (ed.), *Deuteronomy and Deuteronomic Literature: Festschrift C. H. W. Brekelmans*, Leuven: Leuven University Press; Peeters, 263–278.

Smend, R. (1971), 'Das Gesetz und die Völker: Ein Beitrag zur deuteronomistischen Redaktionsgeschichte', in H. Wolff (ed.), *Probleme biblischer Theologie*, Munich: Kaiser, 494–509.

Smith, C. (1998), '"Queenship" in Israel? The Cases of Bathsheba, Jezebel and Athaliah', in J. Day (ed.), *King and Messiah in Israel and the Ancient Near East: Proceedings of the Oxford Old Testament Seminar*, JSOTSup 270, Sheffield: Sheffield Academic Press, 142–162.

Smith, M. (1990), 'The Near Eastern Background of Solar Language for Yahweh', *JBL* 109:29–39.

Soggin, J. A. (1966), 'Der offiziel geförderte Synkretismus in Israel während des Jahrhunderts', *ZAW* 75:179–204.

—— (1982), 'Compulsory Labor under David and Solomon', in T. Ishida (ed.), *Studies in the Period of David and Solomon and Other Essays*, Winona Lake: Eisenbrauns, 259–267.

Spanier, K. (1994), 'The Queen Mother in the Judaean Royal Court: Maacah – A Case Study', in A. Brenner (ed.), *A Feminist Companion to Samuel and Kings*, Sheffield: Sheffield Academic Press, 186–195.

Sprinkle, J. (1999), '2 Kings 3: History or Historical Fiction?', *BBR* 9:247–270.

Stacey, W. (1990), *Prophetic Drama in the Old Testament*, London: Epworth.

Stackert, J. (2006), 'Why Does Deuteronomy Legislate Cities of Refuge? Asylum in the Covenant Collection (Exodus 21:12–14) and Deuteronomy (19:1–13)', *JBL* 125:23–49.

Stade, B. (1886), 'Anmerkungen zu 2 Kö. 15–21', *ZAW* 6:156–189.

Stager, L. (1990), 'Shemer's Estate', *BASOR* 277–278:93–107.

Steinmann, A. (1987), 'The Chronology of 2 Kings 15–18', *JETS* 30:391–397.

Stern, P. (1990), 'The ḥerem in 1 Kgs 20,42 as an Exegetical Problem', *Bib* 71:43–47.

Steussy, M. (1999), *David: Biblical Portraits of Power*, Columbia: University of South Carolina.

Stinespring, W. (1962), 'Temple, Jerusalem', *IDB* 4:534–560.

Stohlmann, S. (1983), 'The Judaean Exile After 701 B. C. E.', in W. Hallo (ed.), *Scripture in Context II: More Essays on the Comparative Method*, Winona Lake: Eisenbrauns, 147–175.

Stone, K. (1994), 'Sexual Power and Political Prestige: The Case of the Disputed Concubines', *BR* 10:28–31, 52–53.

Strand, K. (1996), 'Thiele's Biblical Chronology as a Corrective for Extrabiblical Dates', *AUSS* 34:295–317.

Sukenik, E. (1931), 'Funerary Tablet of Uzziah, King of Judah', *PEQ* 63:217–221.

Swanson, K. (2002), 'A Reassessment of Hezekiah's Reform in Light of Jar Handles and Iconographic Evidence', *CBQ* 64:460–469.

Sweeney, M. (1989), 'The Wilderness Traditions of the Pentateuch: A Reassessment of Their Function and Intent in Relation to Exodus 32–34', in D. Lull (ed.), *SBL 1989 Seminar Papers*, Atlanta: Scholars Press, 291–299.

—— (1995), 'The Critique of Solomon in the Josianic Edition of the Deuteronomistic History', *JBL* 114:607–622.

—— (2001), *King Josiah of Judah: The Lost Messiah of Israel*, Oxford: Oxford University Press.

—— (2004), 'On the Literary Function of the Notice Concerning Hiel's Re-Establishment of Jericho in 1 Kings 16.34', in M. O'Brien et al. (eds.), *Seeing Signals, Reading Signs: The Art of Exegesis*, JSOTSup 415, London: T. & T. Clark, 104–115.

Tadmor, H. (1958), 'The Campaigns of Sargon II of Assur: A Chronological–Historical Study', *JCS* 12:22–40, 77–100.

—— (1961), 'Que and Muṣri', *IEJ* 11:143–150.

—— (1966), 'Philistia Under Assyrian Rule', *BA* 29:86–102.

—— (1983), 'Rab-saris and Rab-shakeh in 2 Kings 18', in C. Meyers (ed.), *The Word of the Lord Shall Go Forth: Essays in Honor of David Noel Freedman in Celebration of His Sixtieth Birthday*, Winona Lake: Eisenbrauns, 279–285.

—— (1994), *The Inscriptions of Tiglath-Pileser III King of Assyria*, Jerusalem: Israel Academy of Sciences and Humanities.

Tadmor, H., and M. Cogan (1979), 'Ahaz and Tiglath-Pileser in the Book of Kings: Historiographic Considerations', *Bib* 60:491–508.

Talbert, R. (1962), 'Ben-hadad', *IDBSup* 95.

Talmon, S. (1958), 'Divergences in Calendar-Reckoning in Ephraim and Judah', *VT* 8:48–74.

—— (1979), 'Kingship and Ideology of the State', in A. Malamat and I. Eph(al (eds.), *The World History of the Jewish People*, Jerusalem: Massada, 3–26.

—— (1981), 'Polemics and Apology in Biblical Historiography: 2 Kings 17:24–41', in R. Friedman (ed.), *The Creation of Sacred Literature: Composition and Redaction of the Biblical Text*, Berkeley: University of California Press, 57–68.

Talmon, S., and W. Fields (1989), 'The Collocation משתין בקיר ועצור ועזוב and Its Meaning', *ZAW* 101:85–109.

Talshir, Z. (2000), 'The Reign of Solomon in the Making: Pseudo-Connections Between 3 Kingdoms and Chronicles', *VT* 50:233–249.

Tångberg, A. (1992), 'A Note on Baʻal Zĕbūb in 2 Kgs 1, 2.3.6.16', *SJOT* 6:293–296.

Tarlin, J. (1994), 'Toward a "Female" Reading of the Elijah Cycle: Ideology and
Gender in the Interpretation of 1 Kings 17–19, 21 and 2 Kings 1–2.18',
in A. Brenner (ed.), *A Feminist Companion to Samuel and Kings*,
Sheffield: Sheffield Academic Press, 208–217.

Terrien, S. (1970), 'The Omphalos Myth and Hebrew Religion', *VT*
20:315–338.

Tetley, C. (2005), *The Reconstructed Chronology of the Divided Kingdom*,
Winona Lake: Eisenbrauns.

Thiele, E. (1954), 'A Comparison of the Chronological Data of Israel and
Judah', *VT* 4:185–195.

—— (1966), 'Pekah to Hezekiah', *VT* 16:83–107.

—— (1974), 'Coregencies and Overlapping Reigns Among the Hebrew
Kings', *JBL* 93:174–200.

—— (1983), *The Mysterious Numbers of the Hebrew Kings*, rev. ed., Grand
Rapids: Zondervan.

Thompson, H. (1992a), 'Hena (Place)', *ABD* 3:137–138.

—— (1992b), 'Pharpar (Place)', *ABD* 5:303–304.

—— (1992c), 'Zeredah', *ABD* 6:1082.

Thompson, J. (1980), *The Book of Jeremiah*, NICOT, Grand Rapids:
Eerdmans.

Thornton, T. (1962–3), 'Charismatic Kingship in Israel and Judah', *JTS*
13.14:1–11.

Tiemeyer, L. (2005), 'Prophecy as a Way of Cancelling Prophecy – the Strategic
Uses of Foreknowledge', *ZAW* 117:329–350.

Todd, J. (1992), 'The Pre-Deuteronomistic Elijah Cycle', in R. Coote (ed.),
Elijah and Elisha in Socioliterary Perspective, Atlanta: Scholars Press,
1–35.

Tonstad, S. (2005), 'The Limits of Power: Revisiting Elijah at Horeb', *SJOT*
19:253–266.

Toombs, L. (1992), 'Shechem (Place)', *ABD* 5:1174–1186.

Toorn, K. van der (1992), 'Prostitution – Cultic Prostitution', *ABD* 5:510–513.

Torrey, C. (1936), 'The Foundry of the Second Temple at Jerusalem', *JBL*
55:247–260.

Trevor, J. (1962), 'Pine, Pine Tree', *IDB* 3:818.

Tsevat, M. (1952–3), 'Some Biblical Notes', *HUCA* 24:107–114.

—— (1958), 'Marriage and Monarchical Legitimacy in Ugarit and Israel',
JSS 3:237–243.

Ullendorff, E. (1962–3), 'The Queen of Sheba', *BJRL* 45:486–504.

Ussishkin, D. (1973), 'King Solomon's Palaces', *BA* 36:78–105.

—— (1979), 'The "Camp of the Assyrians" in Jerusalem', *IEJ* 29:137–142.

—— (1993), 'Lachish', *NEAEHL* 3:897–911.

—— (1997), 'Jezreel, Samaria and Megiddo: Royal Centres of Omri and
Ahab', in J. Emerton (ed.), *Congress Volume: Cambridge 1995*, Leiden:
Brill, 351–364.

—— (2008), 'Jezreel (Yizre'el), Tel', *NEAEHLSup* 1837–1839.

Van Seters, J. (1983), *In Search of History: Historiography in the Ancient World and the Origins of Biblical History*, New Haven: Yale University Press.

———— (1999), 'On Reading the Story of the Man of God From Judah in 1 Kings 13', in F. Black (ed.), *The Labour of Reading: Desire, Alienation and Biblical Interpretation*, Atlanta: Scholars Press, 225–234.

Van Winkle, D. (1989), '1 Kings XIII: True and False Prophecy', *VT* 29:31–43.

———— (1996), '1 Kings XII 25–XIII 34: Jeroboam's Cultic Innovations and the Man of God from Judah', *VT* 46:101–114.

Vater Solomon, A. (1985), 'Jehoash's Fable of the Thistle and the Cedar', in *Saga Legend Tale Novella Fable: Narrative Forms in Old Testament Literature*, JSOTSup 35, Sheffield: JSOT Press, 126–132.

Vaughn, A. (1999), *Theology, History, and Archaeology in the Chronicler's Account of Hezekiah*, Atlanta: Scholars Press.

Vaux, R. de (1964), *Studies in Old Testament Sacrifice*, Cardiff: University of Wales Press.

———— (1967), 'Le lieu que Yahvé a choisi pour y établir son nom', in F. Mass (ed.), *Das ferne und nahe Wort*, Berlin: Töpelmann, 219–228.

———— (1993), 'Far'ah Tell El- (North)', *NEAEHL* 2:433.

Veijola, T. (1975), *Die ewige Dynastie: David und die Entstehung seiner Dynastie nach der deuteronomistischen Darstellung*, Helsinki: Suomalainen Tiedeakatemia.

———— (1977), *Das Königtum in der Beurteilung der deuteronomistischen Historiographie: eine redaktionsgeschichtliche Untersuchung*, Helsinki: Suomalainen Tiedeakatemia.

Viviano, P. (1987), '2 Kings 17: A Rhetorical and Form-Critical Analysis', *CBQ* 49:548–559.

———— (1992a), 'Ethbaal (Person)', *ABD* 2:645.

———— (1992b), 'Tabrimmon (Person)', *ABD* 6:305.

———— (1997), 'Glory Lost: The Reign of Solomon in the Deuteronomistic History', in L. Handy (ed.), *The Age of Solomon: Scholarship at the Turn of the Millennium*, Leiden: Brill, 336–347.

Vogels, W. (1979), 'Les prophètes et la division du royaume', *SR* 8:15–26.

Wagenaar, J. (2007), '"Someone Came from Baal-Shalisha . . .": The Significance of the Topography in 2Kgs 4.42–44', *BN* 135:35–42.

Wagner, S. (1978) 'דָּרַשׁ; מִדְרָשׁ', *TDOT* 3:293–307.

Wallace, H. (1986), 'The Oracles Against the Israelite Dynasties in 1 and 2 Kings', *Bib* 67:21–40.

Walsh, J. (1989), 'The Contexts of 1 Kings XIII', *VT* 39:355–370.

———— (1992a), 'Methods and Meanings: Multiple Studies of 1 Kings 21', *JBL* 111:193–211.

———— (1992b), 'Tishbe', *ABD* 6:577–578.

———— (1995), 'The Characterization of Solomon in First Kings 1–5', *CBQ* 57:471–493.

—— (2000), '2 Kings 17: The Deuteronomist and the Samaritans', in J. de Moor (ed.), *Past, Present, Future: The Deuteronomistic History and the Prophets*, Leiden: Brill, 315–323.

—— (2006), *Ahab: The Construction of a King*, Collegeville: Liturgical.

—— (2010a), *Old Testament Narrative: A Guide to Interpretation*, Westminster John Knox.

—— (2010b), 'The Organization of 2 Kings 3–11', *CBQ* 72:238–254.

—— (2011), 'The Rab Šākēh Between Rhetoric and Redaction', *JBL* 130:263–279.

Waltke, B. (1980) 'נֶפֶשׁ (*nepesh*)', *TWOT* 2:587–591.

—— (1988), 'The Phenomenon of Conditionality Within Unconditional Covenants', in A. Gileadi (ed.), *Israel's Apostasy and Restoration: Essays in Honor of Roland K. Harrison*, Grand Rapids: Baker, 123–139.

—— (2007), *An Old Testament Theology: An Exegetical, Canonical, and Thematic Approach*, Grand Rapids: Zondervan.

Waltke, B., and M. O'Connor (1990), *An Introduction to Biblical Hebrew Syntax*, Winona Lake: Eisenbrauns.

Watson, P. (1965), 'A Note on the "Double Portion" of Deuteronomy 21:17 and II Kings 2:9', *ResQ* 8:70–75.

Weinfeld, M. (1970), 'The Covenant of Grant in the Old Testament and in the Ancient Near East', *JAOS* 90:184–203.

—— (1972), *Deuteronomy and the Deuteronomic School*, Oxford: Clarendon.

—— (1982), 'The Counsel of the "Elders" to Rehoboam and Its Implications', *Maarav* 3:27–53.

—— (1983), 'Zion and Jerusalem as Religious and Political Capital: Ideology and Utopia', in R. Friedman (ed.), *The Poet and the Historian: Essays in Literary and Historical Biblical Criticism*, Chico: Scholars Press, 75–115.

Weippert, H. (1972), 'Die "deuteronomistischen" Beurteilungen der Könige von Israel und Juda und das Problem der Redaktion der Königsbücher', *Bib* 53:301–339.

Wellhausen, J. (1883), *Prolegomena zur Geschichte Israels*, 2nd ed., Berlin: Reimer. Translated as *Prolegomena to the History of Israel* by A. Menzies and J. Sutherland Black, Edinburgh: Adam & Charles Black, 1885, and reproduced as *Prolegomena to the History of Ancient Israel*, Gloucester: Peter Smith, 1973.

—— (1889), *Die Composition des Hexateuchs und der historischen Bücher des Alten Testaments*, Berlin: Reimer.

Wenham, G. (1971), 'Deuteronomy and the Central Sanctuary', *TynB* 22:103–118.

—— (1972), 'Bᵉtûlah "A Girl of Marriageable Age"', *VT* 22:326–348.

Westbrook, R. (2005), 'Elisha's True Prophecy in 2 Kings 3', *JBL* 124: 530–532.

Wesselius, J. (1990), 'Joab's Death and the Central Theme of the Succession Narrative (2 Samuel IX – 1 Kings II)', *VT* 40:336–351.

Westenholz, J. (1989), 'Tamar, *Qĕdēšā, Qadištu*, and Sacred Prostitution in Mesopotamia', *HTR* 82:245–265.

Westermann, C. (1967), *Basic Forms of Prophetic Speech*, trans. H. White, Philadelphia: Westminster.

White, M. (1994), 'Naboth's Vineyard and Jehu's Coup: The Legitimation of a Dynastic Extermination', *VT* 44:66–76.

—— (1997), *The Elijah Legends and Jehu's Coup*, Atlanta: Scholars Press.

Whitley, C. (1952), 'The Deuteronomic Presentation of the House of Omri', *VT* 2:137–152.

Widengren, G. (1957), 'King and Covenant', *JSS* 2:1–32.

Williams, D. (1999), 'Once Again: The Structure of the Narrative of Solomon's Reign', *JSOT* 86:49–66.

Williams, J. (1966), 'The Prophetic "Father": A Brief Explanation of the Term "Sons of the Prophets"', *JBL* 85:344–349.

Williams, P. (2002), 'Lying Spirits Sent by God? The Case of Micaiah's Prophecy', in P. Helm (ed.), *The Trustworthiness of God: Perspectives on the Nature of Scripture*, Grand Rapids: Eerdmans, 58–66.

Williamson, H. G. M. (1982), *1 and 2 Chronicles*, Grand Rapids: Eerdmans; London: Marshall, Morgan & Scott.

Willis, T. (1991), 'The Text of 1 Kings 11:43–12:3', *CBQ* 53:37–44.

Wilson, G. (1985), *The Editing of the Hebrew Psalter*, Chico: Scholars Press.

Wilson, R. (1980), *Prophecy and Society in Ancient Israel*, Philadelphia: Fortress.

Wiseman, D. (1956), *Chronicles of Chaldaean Kings 626–556 B. C. in the British Museum*, London: British Museum.

—— (1973), 'Law and Order in Old Testament Times', *VoxEv* 8:5–21.

—— (1980), 'Ophir', *IBD* 2:1119–1120.

Wolde, E. van (1995), 'Who Guides Whom? Embeddedness and Perspective in Biblical Hebrew and in 1 Kings 3:16–28', *JBL* 114:623–642.

Woods, F. (1994), *Water and Storm Polemics Against Baalism in the Deuteronomistic History*, New York: Peter Lang.

Woude, A. van der (1964), 'I REG 20$_{34}$', *ZAW* 76:188–191.

Wozniuk, V. (1997), 'The Wisdom of Solomon as Political Theology', *Journal of Church and State* 39:657–680.

Wray Beal, L. M. (2007), *The Deuteronomist's Prophet: Narrative Control of Approval and Disapproval in the Story of Jehu '2 Kings 9 and 10'*, LHBOTS 478, New York: T. & T. Clark.

—— (2012), 'Jeroboam and the Prophets in 1 Kings 11–14: Prophetic Word for Two Kingdoms', in M. Boda and L. M. Wray Beal (eds.), *Prophets, Prophecy, and Ancient Near Eastern Historiography*, Winona Lake: Eisenbrauns, 105–124.

Wright, D., and R. Jones (1992), 'Leprosy', *ABD* 4:277–282.

Wright, G. (1967), 'The Provinces of Solomon (1 Kings 4:7–19)', *EI* 8:58–68.

Wright, J. E. (2004), 'Whither Elijah? The Ascension of Elijah in Biblical and Extrabiblical Traditions', in E. Chazon (ed.), *Things Revealed: Studies in Early Jewish and Christian Literature in Honor of Michael E. Stone*, Leiden: Brill, 123–138.

Wright, L. S. (1989), '*MKR* in 2 Kings XII 5–17 and Deuteronomy XVIII 8', *VT* 39:438–448.

Würthwein, E. (1936), *Der 'amm ha'aretz im Alten Testament*, BWANT 17, Stuttgart.

—— (1970), 'Elijah at Horeb: Reflections on I Kings 19.9–18', in J. Durham (ed.), *Proclamation and Presence: Old Testament Essays in Honour of Gwynne Henton Davies*, London: SCM, 152–166.

—— (1973), 'Die Erzählung vom Gottesmann aus Juda in Bethel zur Komposition von 1 Kön 13', in H. Gese (ed.), *Wort und Geschichte*, Neukirchen-Vluyn: Neukirchener Verlag, 181–189.

Wyatt, N. (1985), '"Araunah the Jebusite" and the Throne of David', *ST* 39:39–53.

—— (1992), 'Of Calves and Kings: The Canaanite Dimension in the Religion of Israel', *SJOT* 6:68–91.

—— (1999a), 'Asherah', *DDD* 99–105.

—— (1999b), 'Astarte', *DDD* 109–114.

Yadin, Y. (1955), 'Some Aspects of the Strategy of Ahab and David (I Kings 20; II Sam. 11)', *Bib* 36:332–351.

—— (1963), *The Art of Warfare in Biblical Lands in the Light of Archaeological Study*, 2 vols., New York: McGraw Hill.

—— (1978), 'The "House of Ba'al" of Ahab and Jezebel in Samaria, and That of Athaliah in Judah', in P. R. S. Moorey and P. Parr (eds.), *Archaeology in the Levant: Essays for Kathleen Kenyon*, Warminster: Aris & Phillips, 127–135.

Yamauchi, E. (1973), 'Cultic Prostitution: A Case Study in Cultural Diffusion', in H. Hoffner (ed.), *Orient and Occident: Essays Presented to Cyrus H. Gordon on the Occasion of his Sixty-fifth Birthday*, Kevelaer: Butzon & Bercker; Neukirchen-Vluyn: Neukirchener Verlag, 213–222.

Yee, G. (1992), 'Jezebel', *ABD* 3:848–849.

Yeivin, S. (1959–60), 'Did the Kingdoms of Israel Have a Maritime Policy?', *JQR* 50:193–228.

—— (1974), '"*Edūth*', *IEJ* 24:17–20.

Young, R. (2003), 'When Did Solomon Die?', *JETS* 46:589–603.

Younger, K. (1990), 'The Figurative Aspect and the Contextual Method in the Evaluation of the Solomonic Empire (1 Kings 1–11)', in D. J. A. Clines (ed.), *The Bible in Three Dimensions: Essays in Celebration of Forty Years of Biblical Studies in the University of Sheffield*, JSOTSup 87, Sheffield: Sheffield University Press, 157–175.

—— (1998), 'The Deportations of the Israelites', *JBL* 117:201–227.

—— (1999), 'The Fall of Samaria in Light of Recent Research', *CBQ* 6:461–682.

Younker, R. (1992a), 'Cherith, Brook of', *ABD* 1:899.

——— (1992b), 'Valley of Salt', *ABD* 5:907.

Zannoni, A. (1984), 'Elijah: The Contest on Mount Carmel and Naboth's Vineyard', *SLJT* 27:265–277.

Zertal, A. (1992), 'Beth-haggan (Place)', *ABD* 1:687.

Zevit, Z. (1985), 'Deuteronomistic Historiography in 1 Kings 12–2 Kings 17 and the Reinvestiture of the Israelian Cult', *JSOT* 32:57–73.

——— (2001), *The Religions of Ancient Israel: A Synthesis of Parallactic Approaches*, New York: Continuum.

Ziegler, Y. (2008), '"As the Lord Lives and as Your Soul Lives": An Oath of Conscious Deference', *VT* 58:117–130.

Zohary, M. (1982), *Plants of the Bible*, Cambridge: Cambridge University Press.

Zorn, J. (1992), 'Elath', *ABD* 2:429–430.

INDEX OF SCRIPTURE REFERENCES

INDEX OF AUTHORS

Walsh, J.,   40, 72, 94, 109, 116, 173, 175,
   196, 223, 231, 240, 272, 276, 283, 286
Waltke, B.,   175, 234
Watson, P.,   304
Weinfeld, M.,   32–33, 94, 97
Weippert, H.,   515
Wellhausen, J.,   34, 396
Wenham, G.,   69
Wesselius, J.,   76
Westenholz, J.,   204
Westermann, C.,   171, 296
White, M.,   231, 240
Widengren, G.,   388, 391
Williams, J.,   304, 410
Williamson, H. G. M.,   26
Wilson, G.,   100
Wiseman, D.,   84, 160, 499, 516–517, 519

Wolde, E. van,   88
Wray Beal, L. M.,   76–77, 203, 378, 382,
   505
Wright, D., and R. Jones,   332
Wright, G.,   96
Würthwein, E.,   250, 391
Wyatt, N.,   171, 203
Yadin, Y.,   264–265, 391
Yee, G.,   225
Younger, K.,   430, 449
Younker, R.,   232, 418
Zertal, A.,   376
Zevit, Z.,   85
Ziegler, Y.,   303
Zohary, M.,   106, 161
Zorn, J.,   159

INDEX OF SUBJECTS

Christ (*see also* Jesus), 25, 27, 48–49,
    52–53, 55, 57–58, 81, 91, 110, 128,
    143, 176, 207, 217, 227, 237, 257,
    269, 278–279, 299, 308, 328, 338,
    355–356, 365–366, 394, 414,
    455–456, 476–477
chronology, 24–25, 29, 39, 41–43, 114,
    199, 297, 312, 377, 425–426,
    430–431, 464, 502, 516–517, 525,
    527, 529
City of David, 76, 81, 128, 150–151,
    358, 395, 402, 415, 434, 479
clean, 329, 371, 491
clothing, 155, 162, 295, 329, 333, 336,
    469, 499, 529
conspiracy, 214–215, 218, 221–222, 345,
    379, 390, 415, 424
corvée, 23, 106, 108, 144–146, 150–151,
    153, 181
cosmic mountain, 41, 126–128
counsel, 177–178, 180–182, 184, 186,
    265–266, 288, 334, 338, 360, 457,
    467
counsellor, 95
covenant, 22–26, 31–32, 36–37, 39,
    46–58, 71, 75, 79–80, 82–83, 85–86,
    90, 97, 100–104, 109, 111, 118, 120,
    125–129, 133–143, 148–150,
    152–154, 159, 163, 166–167, 171,
    173–176, 181–182, 184, 187,
    206–207, 216–217, 225–227, 230,
    232, 235–236, 240–249, 251,
    253–254, 256–257, 259, 262–263,
    266, 268–269, 273–274, 277–279,
    288, 290, 298, 301, 303, 306,
    317–318, 325, 327, 337, 346,
    351–352, 363, 365, 374, 378, 380,
    385–386, 389–392, 405, 411–412,
    414, 421, 431–433, 436, 438,
    442–445, 447, 449–451, 453–457,
    465, 474, 476–477, 484–485,
    488–489, 493–495, 497–498, 500,
    506, 509, 511–512, 520–522,
    528–531
cult personnel, 204, 208, 211, 281, 497,
    507
curse, 36, 64, 75, 149, 192, 225, 232,
    306–307, 325, 374, 377, 496,
    503–504

Damascus, 166, 172, 208, 249, 253, 255,
    259, 317, 329, 334, 357, 361, 364,
    412, 415, 420, 429–430, 434,
    439–440
Dan, 92, 97, 140–141, 163, 178, 184,
    208, 213, 244, 268, 289, 305, 332,
    369, 474–475, 518–519
dance, 243
daughter, 57, 67, 81, 84–85, 92, 112,
    116–117, 144–147, 151, 153, 165,
    169–170, 207–208, 210, 219, 281,
    283, 287, 357, 359, 363, 367, 384,
    388, 415, 425, 456, 459, 472, 486,
    495, 497, 513–514, 522
David, 21–22, 26–27, 29, 31–32, 35, 44,
    46, 48–50, 54, 56, 58, 61–82, 85–87,
    94–95, 97, 99, 101–106, 108–109,
    111, 114, 116, 119, 125, 128–129,
    131–133, 136–137, 140–141,
    143–144, 147–148, 150–151,
    165–167, 169–178, 181–184,
    186–187, 196–198, 200, 202,
    207–208, 210–212, 216, 224, 281,
    289–290, 312, 317, 337, 357–358,
    363, 365, 367, 382–383, 385, 387,
    389, 391, 395, 398, 402, 414–415,
    417–418, 420, 424–425, 427,
    433–434, 440–443, 445, 451, 456,
    460, 464–465, 471, 473, 476,
    478–481, 484–486, 489–494, 496,
    500, 502, 511, 521, 530
Davidic Covenant, 31–32, 36, 48–50, 54,
    101, 133, 136–137, 141, 175–176,
    337, 365, 390, 476, 489
Dead Sea, 150, 172, 313, 363, 418
deuteronomic, 22, 26, 31–35, 46–48, 50,
    55, 57–58, 87, 89–90, 97–98, 151,
    163, 170, 195, 204, 211, 263, 268,
    278, 383, 414, 417–418, 431, 450,
    502, 512, 528, 530
Deuteronomist, 35, 134, 213, 529
Deuteronomistic, 21–22, 31, 34–35, 39,
    56, 58, 68, 74, 81, 87, 103, 105, 134,
    147, 149, 159, 170, 179, 202, 210,
    267, 272, 287, 337, 365–366, 373,
    381–384, 402–404, 422, 426, 439,
    442, 449, 465, 480, 486, 488, 502,
    505–506, 508, 511–513
Deuteronomistic History, 34–35